T0194303

FEAR

Other Books by Joanna Bourke

An Intimate History of Killing
Dismembering the Male: Men's Bodies, Britain and the Great War
Working-Class Cultures in Britain

F E A R

A Cultural History

Joanna Bourke

COUNTERPOINT
Berkeley, California

ISBN 978-1-59376-154-7

Cover art © Corbis
Cover design by Gerilyn Attebery

COUNTERPOINT
2560 Ninth Street, Suite 318
Berkeley, CA 94710

www.counterpointpress.com

Printed in the United States of America

For Costas

Contents

Preface

A few years ago, with fear and trembling, I set out to confront the most pervasive emotion of modern society: fear. Politically, the world was a different place then. It was before 9/11, when aeroplanes hijacked by terrorists crashed into the World Trade Center and the Pentagon. But personally, too, that was a more innocent time, before I was diagnosed with a life-threatening illness and reminded of my own mortality. The past seemed safer. Within the austere shelter of dozens of libraries and archives, I spilled the contents of *other* people's lives on to my desk, and voyeuristically eavesdropped as they confessed to feeling scared. Self-proclaimed specialists in emotional management could be heard counselling these timid individuals. Often, however, those writers who preached secular gospels of 'fear not' were found to wallow in scaremongering. People everywhere seemed very apprehensive. Despite the distance in time and place, their frightened stammerings were sometimes deafening; at other times they admitted to their anxieties in faint, hesitant whisperings.

Death and disaster; nightmares and phobias; new killing techniques and dangerous technologies; treacherous bodies – a seemingly endless range of terrifying trials and tribulations seemed to face people in the twentieth century. Worse: there were times when all of history seemed to be reciting a traumatic script, devoid of answers or 'sense'. On these occasions people's terror was so overwhelming that their most fundamental identities were in danger of being engulfed. It took some time to notice the astounding creativity with which these scared men, women and children made sense of their predicament and remade their world in the wake of the crippling energy of fear. Looking at our society's fears, in both their past and present manifestations, enables us to meditate on the future. It is a future of our choosing.

Nevertheless, since I completed this book some threats that sparked great trepidation in the past have grown exponentially. The spectre of 'the Terrorist' has taken on a god-like power, equivalent to the plague of earlier times or the Satan of religion. The proliferation of surveillance systems, the persecution of immigrants, the giddy boasting about the need for 'pre-emptive strikes' are some of the results of this panic. We now use terror-speak to justify terrorising others. As a result, the science and practice of destruction has made rapid and alarming strides in the past few years. In the twenty-first century we must consider the possibility that the most frightening peril is the one we are in the process of forging. Wars in Afghanistan and Iraq have reminded us that we are perpetrators of violence against others, as well as being the victims of terrorist brutality. Torture is now routinely justified, not only in scruffy tabloids but also in supposedly reputable legal circles. The revulsion generated by the pornographic torture snapshots taken by American personnel in the Abu Ghraib prison in 2004 rapidly subsided: only a few people observed the relative indifference expressed in the press when equally shocking photographs of bound and hooded prisoners languishing in a legal no man's land in Guantánamo Bay were published. The routine portrayal of violent death in the mass media has blunted sensibilities: when hearing about real-life viciousness we may feel pity or distaste, but when we identify the emotion of fear it is our fear that concerns us. It is the fear *of* something that may befall us, rather than fear *for* others, those people on whom we inflict suffering. Authoritarian, indiscriminate and disproportionate responses have become the norm. Public policy and private lives have become fear-bound; fear has become the emotion through which public life is administered. It is time we returned to a politics which feared *for* the lives of others, near and far. Although fear is humanity's inheritance, trembling is our testament. And we must always tremble in the face of the stranger glimpsed beneath the rubble of history.

Some of these strangers — albeit British and American ones — are encountered in this book. It would have been impossible to study every type of fear experienced in the past one and a half centuries. Every time I opened a book or even talked to a friend over dinner, a new fear emerged. For example, I became obsessed with the history of scruples, or the excessive fear of God, and would quite happily have penned an entire chapter — nay, an entire book — on the topic. But in the end I had to admit that, in modernity, this was a decidedly minority anxiety. Some friends wanted a lengthy discussion of their fear of flying; others urged me to address existential anxieties relating to the loss of social status; still others wanted more discussion of gothic fiction and horror films. There was also much that could have been said about the appeal of roller-coasters and extreme sports. I resisted such temptations.

Instead, this book moves in broad chronological order through some of the prevailing fears and anxieties expressed by British and American individuals in the past. The fear of death and dying is a constant presence in history (for some commentators it is at the core of every fear), so it is appropriate that we begin with some of the peculiar characteristics of the fear of death in the nineteenth century. Near the end of the book we return to this theme in the context of contemporary death and the ways dying people today deal with their sense of dread. The sudden apprehension of life-threatening events is also addressed: how have individuals and groups come to terms with the senseless, unfair even, nature of disasters? What difference does it make when the calamity is man-made?

The second part of the book focuses much more on individual responses: the defenceless child, the nightmare sufferer and the phobic individual have all been central to psychological and psychiatric understandings of emotions, particularly in the early decades of the twentieth century. In the interwar years, as we shall see in the third part of the book, the mass media take a prominent role in inciting panic. In contrast, by the middle of the twentieth century military might indisputably trumped all other fear stimulants: arguably, modernity's most terrifying creations are shrapnel and nuclear bombs. Nowhere is the ability to inspire terror more persuasive than in this bruising encounter between technology and corporeality. In the fourth part, therefore, we look at three zones of confrontation: the battlefield, the city under bombardment and the borderless nuclear target. Humanity's entire wrath focuses upon puny skeletons.

In the fifth part we finally turn to those contemporary anxieties related to crime, disease, pain and the 'rape' of the environment. The book concludes with a meditation on terrorism and the globalisation of risk. Throughout, fear is portrayed as a powerful driving force in the history of humanity. Its spectre cannot be ignored.

I have many people to thank. The people at Virago made this book possible. Particular thanks must go to Tim Whiting, Elise Dillsworth, Richard Dawes and Kirsteen Brace. I am grateful to my agent, Andrew Wylie, and to the patient labours of Michal Shavit. As always, my family are never stinting in their encouragement, even while disagreeing with many conclusions. Thanks to my parents, siblings and precocious nieces and nephews. Many people contributed to this book by asking pertinent questions in seminars and conferences, as well as over drinks afterwards: I wish I could thank each one of you by name. But special gratitude must go to a number of my comrades in fear and anxiety, particularly Effi Avdela, Alexandra Bakalaki, Sean Brady, Vincent Brome, Nicholas Brown, Charles and Caroline Charlton, Roger Cooter, Marianne Elliott, Richard Evans, David Feldman, Alan Forth, Aubrey Greenwood, Marybeth Hamilton, Vanessa Harding, John Harwood, Robin Haines, Eric Hobsbawm, Michael Hunter, Matthew Innes, Maria Komninos, Eric Leed, Mary-Lou Legg, Christos Lyrintzis, Shaun McVeigh, George Mosse, Avner Offer, Akis Papataxiarchis, 'Teddy' Paradellis, Maria Paschalidi, Dorothy Porter, Robin and Heather Prior, Sue Rickard, Peter Robinson, Hilary Sapire, Naoko Shimazu, F. B. Smith, Frank Trentmann, Kosmas Tsokhas, Gregory Tychopoulos, Julie Wheelwright and Jay Winter. Aglaia Komninos and Phaedra Douzina-Balalaki not only lent a hand compiling the bibliography, but also helped me to laugh at a great many of my worries. But it is to Costas Douzinas that I dedicate this book.

Introduction: Fear

What fear of freedom then
Causes our clasping hands
To make in miniature
That earth anew . . .

AUDEN, 'THE AGE OF
ANXIETY'

A spectre is haunting humanity: the spectre of fear. Death stares unblinkingly at us. Danger dallies in everyday environs. Sometimes a scary person or menacing object can be identified: the flames searing patterns on the ceiling, the hydrogen bomb, the terrorist. More often, anxiety overwhelms us from some source 'within': there is an irrational panic about venturing outside, a dread of failure, a premonition of doom. There often seems no limit to the threats. In this book we will be encountering the fears and anxieties of hundreds of British and American men, women and children who lived in the twentieth century. We hear how Arthur Hubbard's battle experiences made his 'head jump', Vincent's agoraphobia rendered him 'a nervous wreck, weak, worthless' and Edna Kaehele's diagnosis of cancer was 'horror beyond reason'. Sometimes, these people resemble us. We are constantly reminded of the child's vulnerability — infants like eleven-month-old Albert B., whom two psychologists deliberately taught to panic in the presence of furry animals. In sleep, not only children but adults too are at risk: for many of us, Raymond Bellamy's nightmare in which he frantically sought to rescue his loved one from danger but seemed frozen in dream-space will seem familiar. Warfare, too, elicits recognisable fear reactions. Given the degree of terror engendered by military strife throughout much of the twentieth century, it is no coincidence that three out of the eleven chapters in this book confront war's horror. And the 'prayers, curses and meaningless shrieks of terror' of people sealed in the fiery inferno of the Iroquois Theatre in Chicago on 30 December 1903 were echoed by people trapped in the Twin Towers on 11 September 2001.

More frequently, their stories remind us that the past is a foreign country. Often incitements to fear in the past seem bizarre in retrospect. In Chapter Six, for example, we will be examining in greater detail a panic that broke out in Britain in 1926 after a seemingly innocuous radio broadcast. This panic is barely remembered today (unlike a similar one that occurred a dozen years later in America, after Orson Welles's *The War of the Worlds* broadcast), but it tells us a great deal about the emotional vulnerability of interwar Britons.

But even the most commonplace of anxieties may appear different when we look back into history. Take shyness, or the mild apprehension of other people, for instance: early-twentieth-century commentators frequently lamented the fact that humanity was plagued by the fear of others. Shyness was regarded as particularly problematic in class-ridden Britain, where even the most innocuous characteristic, such as accent, could expose a person to ridicule. As 'A Former Sufferer' of stage fright explained in 1921, a person's 'tone of voice' provided irrefutable evidence of their breeding: 'How many people pass muster as "ladies" and "gentlemen" until they open their mouths — then their status in life discloses itself,' he anxiously observed.[1] Uncertainty abounded to such a degree that people were even becoming afraid of their own servants. A book entitled *Casting Out Fear* (1918) bemoaned the fact that the middle classes were becoming 'afraid the servants will not be sufficiently impressed with their superiority and power; afraid they will realise how dependent their employers are on them; they are even afraid of getting fond of them. It would be so undignified.'[2] Class tensions, democratisation and uncertainty about what constituted 'good manners' were swelling the population of nervous citizens.

Strangely to the modern ear, it was men rather than women who were regarded as particularly prone to bouts of timidity.[3] The 'cool self-possession' of modern womanhood was responsible for the epidemic of nervous men.[4] When a socially timid woman was encountered, turn-of-the-century commentators explained their fear as an effect of high-heeled shoes and — even more importantly for commentators in this period — tight lacing. As the author of *Bashfulness* (1906) explained, tight lacing caused an 'undue quantity of blood' to 'stagnate' below the waist, a condition that always resulted in bashfulness, 'particularly when the woman is brought suddenly into the presence of men, or when men come near them'.[5] According to this view, female dress reform was part of the emotional management of society.

If turn-of-the-century assumptions about which gender was more timid seem very different to what we might expect, it is not surprising that even 'basic fears', such as the horror of death, might also turn out to have a surprising history. As we shall see throughout this book, the fear of death was not universal. After all, many people faced death without shrinking, animated by a higher sense of purpose or by a belief in an exalted afterlife. Firemen, lifeguards and air-raid wardens, for instance, routinely risked their own lives to help others. As one physician noted in 1910, the fear of death 'is and always has been very easily dominated by strong emotions. Military valour, religious zeal, the exalted tension of pride or duty or affection, easily lead men of the soundest disposition to wholly disregard death and everything pertaining to it.' At the same time, baser feelings, such as 'jealousy, pique, anger, disappointment, sorrow, sickness, distress of any sort, pecuniary loss, disgrace, and a thousand others that lead to suicide' provided evidence of 'what contempt the act of death may be thrown by other even trivial emotions'.[6] Equally, in battle, when mutilation or death seemed imminent, many people claimed that they were not afraid. During the First World War a Medical Officer observed in his memoir *The Adventure of Death* (1916) that the fear of death

is not a deep-rooted instinct, or it would not be so readily overcome. It is the least of fears. It gives way before many sudden emotions or impulses such as love, the excitement of battle, the call of duty, religious devotion, and the maternal instinct.[7]

Fear could ascend for irrational reasons; it could subside just as impulsively.

In addition, as we will see throughout this book, the nature of the fear of death changed through the century. One hint of these shifts is illustrated by a sermon preached by John Jefferson in the 1830s, in which he argued that life was full of fear caused by uncertainty. He noted that

> Difficulties the most unanticipated, and trials the most unexpected, continually arise. Health cannot be calculated upon for a moment; friends may be suddenly snatched from our embrace; riches 'make themselves wings, and fly away'; the deepest reverses, and the greatest elevations, are occurring in the daily history of men; and 'in the midst of life we are in death'.[8]

Nothing could be further removed from post-Cold War fears, where people are no longer consumed by the terror of sudden, natural death. Indeed, for many this is the preferred death. People are more worried about the excessive prolongation of life after all pleasure has been removed than about sudden death. Organ transplants, life-support systems, intravenous nutrition, dialysis and resuscitation techniques prolong the process of dying. Although people still fear the transition from life to death, it is hard to imagine anyone today responding, as a distinguished literary woman did at the end of the nineteenth century, by acknowledging that fear of 'premature burial' meant that she 'never made a will without inserting a clause requiring my throat to be cut before I am put underground'.[9]

Old terrors about being wrongly declared dead (resulting in live burial) became less meaningful than more recent anxieties about being wrongly obliged to stay alive and so denied the opportunity to 'die with dignity'. Medical personnel, rather than clerics, increasingly presided over death's terrors. Finally, Jefferson's anxiety about sinking swiftly into poverty diminished, but not because increased public provision has eradicated the fear of poverty. The nature of this fear changed from the pain attendant upon not having sufficient food to eat or shelter, to that of deterioration in social status. In the West, people do not fear starvation but are anxious about relative impoverishment, such as being forced to sell their home or car. The 'deepest reverses' spoken about by Jefferson are seen today as internal states, such as the fear of loss of others' respect and of self-esteem, rather than of riches flying away.

In fact, sermons like Jefferson's were part and parcel of a fear-provoking enterprise. Theologians, physicians, psychologists, film-makers and other cultural commentators counselled people to 'fear not' while simultaneously inciting anxiety and terror. As we shall see in Chapter One, religious chronicles aroused fear by threatening sinners with everlasting punishment in the hereafter. Yet scientific discourses have been no less vexatious. In the words of Archdeacon R. H. Charles in 1931, science may have 'exposed many superstitions of the dark ages and laid bare the falsity of the religious and secular magic of the past and present, yet in their stead it has introduced legions of new alarms that beset our lives from the cradle to the grave. In fact, it has changed the character of the fears that encompass human life, but multiplied their number beyond count'.[10] Unseen, yet harmful, microbes and bacteria were equal to the task previously carried out by evil spirits. Scientists replaced sorcerers in threatening to destroy the world. The rise of science provided modern individuals with threats just as chilling as the plague. Indeed, the three most terror-inspiring creations of the past two centuries were born in laboratories. Shrapnel, nuclear bombs and biological weapons were modernity's gift.

It is not unusual to find texts with titles like *Nothing to Fear* (1952) reminding readers that they have a *great deal* to fear: the invention of hand grenades and the atomic bomb, for instance, had placed humanity at greater threat than ever before.[11] Nor is it rare for peddlers of 'life assurance' to use fear to sell 'peace of mind' or for feminist tracts promoting the empowerment of women to warn them that they are *right* to fear all men. Theologians argued that penitents suffering from extreme anxiety about sinning should be frightened further into giving up their fears: a scrupulous man or woman 'teases God, irritates his neighbour, torments himself and oppresses his [spiritual] director — it is useless to argue with men in this disposition, our temptation is to strike them,' fumed one influential moral theologian.[12] Psychologists advising parents on how to raise their children concurred, suggesting that 'should it become a matter of decision between the rod and direful threats in an effort to correct the child, the former ought to be preferred'.[13] Fear was frequently used to drive out fear.

How can we understand the way people in the past experienced emotions such as fear? Although fear, hate, joy and love have always been at the very heart of human experience, in historical scholarship they still tend to be regarded as by-products. In a number of Afterwords to the sections of this book, we will be examining some exceptions.

More generally, however, the reluctance of many historians to analyse emotions stems from problems of nomenclature. Was what people in the 1970s called 'fear' the same thing as it was in the 1870s? Probably not. Or, more accurately, many historians feel that they have no way of knowing. Looked at historically, subjective feelings are invisible. We can identify publicly choreographed panic reactions (during theatre fires or when attacked in the street at night, people might be assumed to be scared), but how do we know what individuals 'really felt'? They might have been angry rather than terrified. To put it another way, how can historians recognise everyday manifestations of fright in the past? Facial expressions as captured in photographs or paintings, for instance, are useless. We know that people frequently confuse the facial expressions of fear with those of anger, amazement and suspicion.[14] Indeed, individuals with damage to the part of the brain known as the amygdala (an almond-shaped neurostructure located in the brain's medial temporal lobe) almost unanimously fail to recognise the fearful face.[15] Does this imply that fear is primarily a physiological perception or does a cognitive (or conscious thought) element predominate? Even if fear is located within the corporeal self, it is clear that the body refuses to surrender unambiguous signs of the emotion. Glandular secretions and the range of arousal experienced by the heart and skeletal muscles can be identical for angry and frightened people.[16] Also, different fears elicit very different visceral responses: adrenalin often overwhelms individuals afraid of being attacked, while individuals terrified of contracting tuberculosis experience no such physiological response.

The only access we have to fearful people from the past is through the things they left behind. Fear acquires meaning through cultural language and rites. Analysis of these 'texts' allows historians to pursue fluctuations in the nature of 'fear' as the emotion is rendered visible in language and symbols. Emotions enter the historical archive only to the extent to which they transcend the insularity of individual psychological experience and present the self in the public realm. As the anthropologist Clifford Geertz famously stated in *The Interpretation of Cultures* (1973), 'not only ideas, but emotions too, are cultural artefacts in man'.[17]

This is not to ignore fear's body altogether. Although there are no *consistent* visceral responses to fear, we all remember the 'feeling' of being afraid. The emotional body rapidly gives forth a multitude of signs: the heart pounds faster or seems to freeze, breathing quickens or stops, blood pressure soars or falls and sometimes adrenalin pours into the bloodstream. Irrespective of any conscious desire to 'carry through', frightened people cannot escape physiological signs of terror. Frightened people possess a body — witness the trembling limbs and hysterical gait of the survivors of earthquakes or tornadoes. It is not enough merely to repress the subjective awareness of fear: the body will betray itself through its respiration, circulation, digestion and excretion. As we shall see later, in wartime combatants suffered from a range of uncontrollable physical disorders. Diarrhoea, stomach upsets and incapacitating illnesses were common. Frightened soldiers experienced epidemics of diarrhoea (as did American troops immediately before landing on Iwo Jima), suffered chronic gastrointestinal problems or escaped into dyspeptic invalidism.[18] Or, as one person tormented by scrupulosity (that is, the fear of having sinned or offended God in some way) described his attacks in the 1950s:

> Suddenly my stomach tightens up, there's a choking in my throat, and my torture begins. The bad thoughts come . . . I want to drive them out, but they keep coming back . . . It is terrible to be in a struggle like this! To have a head that goes around and around

without my being able to stop it; to be a madman and still quite
rational, for all that.[19]

The emotion of fear is fundamentally about the body — its fleshi-
ness and its precariousness. Fear is *felt*, and although the emotion of
fear cannot be *reduced to* the sensation of fear, it is not present *without* sensation. The body is not simply the shell through which
emotions are expressed. Discourse shapes bodies. However, bodies
also shape discourse: people are 'weak or pale with fright', 'paralysed by fear' and 'chilled by terror'.[20] The feeling of fear may be
independent of social *construction* (after all, people in different times
and places may have experienced identical physiological responses to
threats). Nevertheless, emotions are fundamentally *constituted*. In
other words, agents are involved in creating the self in a dynamic
process that, at the same time, is a 'coming into being'. In this way
the body plays a role in social agency. The sensation of fear is not
merely the ornament of the emotion: fear is 'what hurts' — the
most irreducible 'real' of an individual's history.[21]

As these introductory comments imply, all human interactions are
based on emotional expression. The boundaries between fear and
other emotions are not clear-cut. How does fear differ from dread,
consternation or surprise? Anger, disgust, hatred and horror all contain elements of fear. Jealousy may be understood as fear of losing
one's partner; guilt may be fear of God's punishment; shame may be
fear of humiliation. A history of fear would be rendered meaningless
if all negative emotional states were classified as 'really' being fear
states. This makes nonsense of any claim to comprehensiveness in
writing a history of even one emotion. Although fear has a strong
claim to be one of the most dominant emotions, its status depends
upon a distinction between the 'simple' emotions (such as fear) and
the 'complex' ones (such as horror, disgust, awe and jealousy), all of
which contain elements of fear.

It is tempting to allow fear to invade every part of human emotional life. Rather, this book seeks to examine a selection of
representative fears plaguing individuals within British and American
societies in the 'long twentieth century'. Some chapters focus on
areas that are particularly petrifying — external traumas such as

disasters, terrorism and wars, as well as internal ones such as phobias and nightmares. Other chapters focus on frightening themes in the history of all individuals — vulnerability, the decaying body and death. In all cases the bruising encounter between individual subjectivity and social norms defined what it meant for modern Britons and Americans to be fearful.

Afterword to the Introduction:

The Face of Fear

Above, I argued that we cannot ignore emotion's body. Fear, one of the major emotions, has a physiology, albeit a contested one. Throughout history the meaning given to the frightened body has been disputed. A central question is: does the face provide a window into the emotional soul of an individual? Two of the most influential scientists of the nineteenth century believed it did, but for diametrically opposite reasons. For Duchenne de Boulogne, writing in the 1860s, facial signs of the emotions were expressions of the Creator's will. In contrast, for Charles Darwin, writing in the 1870s, they were part of humanity's biological legacy. The questions these two scientists raised — about the relative importance of 'nature' and 'nurture' and the universality of the emotions, for instance — continue to animate debate in the twenty-first century.

Guillaume Benjamin Amand Duchenne de Boulogne believed in the power of human facial expressions. In a series of experiments he used the adept application of electric currents to cause an old man's facial muscles to contract in ways that would accurately mirror human emotional expression. In contrast to Duchenne's abundance of names, the man whose face was made to 'speak the language of fear' was never named. He was only ever referred to as 'An Old Man': toothless, thin and said to possess 'trivial features'. But, as a result of his mortification, he became the iconic face of the emotions in the nineteenth century.

Duchenne's technique was disarmingly simple. An Old Man was taught how to adopt a neutral, calm expression while this eccentric physician applied electrodes to the tender regions of his face and then administered electrical shocks designed to contort the subject's facial muscles in such a way as to resemble an emotion. To create the emotion of fear, Duchenne needed to electrically stimulate a number of facial muscles. He first animated 'a muscle which drags the whole lower part of the face downwards and outwards, and causes the front of the neck to swell'. On its own, the contraction of this muscle 'merely deforms the features', but when Duchenne excited another muscle at the same time 'there comes over the face a strikingly truthful picture of the most violent passions — dread, scare, fright, torture, etc.'. In other words, he showed that by stimulating *m. platysma*, or the neck muscle (he called it the 'muscle of fear'), along with *m. frontalis* (the 'muscle of attention or surprise') of the forehead, An Old Man's face displayed all the signs of unadulterated fear. As a result of these electric shocks, his face became

> tonically contracted by fear . . . This man is frozen and stupefied by terror; his face shows a dreadful mixture of horror and fear, at the news of a danger that puts this life in peril or of inevitable torture. Before the introduction of chloroform, the anticipation of surgical operations induced this expression of terror and horror.

By further contracting *m. corrugator supercilii* (the 'muscle of pain', over the eyes), Duchenne combined the expression of terror with that of extreme pain. This expression 'must be that of the damned', he concluded.

Duchenne was proud of his achievement. For him, the individual's 'spirit' was 'the source of expression. It activates the muscles that portray our emotions on the face with characteristic patterns'. Duchenne applied electrodes to An Old Man's face in order to 'make the facial muscles contract to *speak* the language of the emotions'. He was using electricity 'like nature itself' to 'paint the expressive lines of the emotions of the soul on the face of man'. Duchenne believed that this method of contracting muscles ('living anatomy') was more accurate than the anatomist's scalpel. With the help of electrodes, he claimed, he was able to 'mark the lines of the highest sentiments' as well as the lowest terrors 'on the mundane surface of this dull forehead'. An Old Man was said to be an 'inoffensive character' with 'restricted intelligence', but Duchenne 'preferred this coarse face to one of noble, beautiful features, not because in order to be true to nature one must show her imperfections; I simply wanted to prove that, despite defects of shape and lack of plastic beauty, every human face can become spiritually beautiful through the accurate rendering of emotions.' There was another advantage in choosing An Old Man for the experiments: he had a relatively insensitive face, which allowed him to undergo painful electrical shocks with less distress than most people. Duchenne explained that An Old Man's partially anaesthetised face enabled him to 'experiment on his face without causing him pain, to the extent that I could stimulate his individual muscles with as much precision and accuracy as if I were working with a still irritable corpse'. He admitted that:

> instead of this man I could have used a corpse, which I often did in our hospitals . . . I could animate the face [of a corpse] by localising electrical stimulation to each one of the muscles, and the emotions rendered on the corpse were as genuine as those of the living person. But there is no more hideous or revolting spectacle!

Consequently, the photographs of An Old Man, rather than of a corpse, accompanied Duchenne's book *The Mechanism of Human Facial Expression* when it was published in 1862.

Duchenne's experiments were slow to gain scientific adulation. His pronounced provincial accent and frenzied movements were widely commented upon, and even supporters drew attention to the fact that he was 'slow of speech' and 'not eloquent'.[1] One of his English translators dared to report that while Duchenne was at medical school he 'did not exhibit any particular interests or abilities'.[2] Nevertheless, *The Mechanism of Human Facial Expression* was profoundly original. In part this was because of the fact that the book was accompanied by 100 photographic prints — the first series of published physiological experiments to be illustrated in this way. Indeed, photography was crucial to Duchenne's pioneering work. Not only were emotions too fleeting to be accurately captured by a painter but, he believed, photography was 'as true as a mirror'. For Duchenne, the surface was the story: technological manipulation of the face revealed all there was to know about the emotions.

Perhaps less novel, Duchenne's experiments also had a fierce religious purpose. For him, there was Divine purpose behind every muscle in the body. On the rare occasions when he failed to find such a purpose, Duchenne expressed 'genuine chagrin', although he claimed never to have doubted his initial premise.[3] In his own words:

> In the face, our Creator was not concerned with mechanical necessity. He was able, in his wisdom, or — please pardon this manner of speaking — in pursing a divine fantasy, to put any particular muscle into action, one alone or several muscles together, when he wished the characteristic signs of the emotions, even the most fleeting, to be written briefly on man's face. Once this language of facial expressions was created, it sufficed him to give all human beings the instinctive faculty of always expressing their sentiments by contracting the same muscles. This rendered the language universal and immutable.

In the interests of 'harmonious presentation', the Creator sacrificed doubling the number of expressions by creating bilateral muscles on either side of the face.

For Duchenne, muscular movements were both instinctive and inalterable. 'Education and civilisation' might develop or moderate the expressions, but could never alter them. This was also part of the Creator's purpose. After all, if emotional expressions were not identical and universal, 'the language of the face would have shared the fate of speech; each country, each province would have painted the passions in the face after its own way'. By making the emotions dependent on instinctive or reflex movements, the Creator invented a language shared by 'all people, savages and civilised'. Duchenne proposed that the emotional life of infants supported his arguments. For him the new-born child did not possess a facial expression, since its mind was 'barren of emotions'. It was only when the infant began feeling things that its facial muscles began to 'paint' emotions on its face. The strongest or most often repeated emotions would permanently alter the face. In this way the face was 'a reflection of our habitual thoughts, a portrait of our passions'. For this reason Duchenne disputed the notion that it was possible for a good person to have an evil face, or vice versa: 'It is time alone which develops individual expression, good or wicked, as good or wicked passions have the mastery.' To those scientists who believed that 'a good man may be born with a wicked face', Duchenne contended that 'the workings of a noble mind would soon blot out this monstrosity'. The muscles were God's guarantee of a universal code revealing good and evil.[4]

Ten years after this work on facial expressions, the most influential scientist in the modern period overturned Duchenne's conclusions. Charles Darwin published *The Expression of the Emotions in Man and Animals* in 1872, an offshoot from his classic *The Descent of Man* (1871) in which he argued that humans, like other animals, were products of evolution through natural selection. While Duchenne's book quickly became obscure, Darwin's was a publishing success. At a period when the average print-run for a non-fiction book was less than a thousand copies, Darwin's *The Expression of the Emotions* sold over five thousand copies on its first day of publication. The book was a direct attack on the accounts of creationists, for Darwin was fundamentally opposed to Duchenne's framework: in his copy of Duchenne's *The Mechanism of Human Facial Expression* he pencilled an exclamation mark next to the section where Duchenne mused about the Creator's purpose in making facial expressions universal and unalterable.[5] Nevertheless, the debate was conducted gallantly. Although *The Expression of the Emotions* was based primarily on observations of Darwin's own children and animals in zoos, as well as questionnaires sent to people throughout the world, he made great use of Duchenne's book and even reproduced some of his photographs of An Old Man. In turn, Duchenne refused to accept payment for the use of his photographs, claiming that 'questions of money should not arise between men of science'.[6] In this way, An Old Man's expression of fear remained pivotal to debates throughout the century.

What were the physical manifestations of fear, according to Darwin? He agreed with Duchenne that the m. *platysma* often contracted in frightening situations, although he argued that the muscle could be violently contracted in other emotional situations as well, such as in hydrophobia or disgust. When this movement was accompanied by widely open mouth and eyes, fear was widely recognised. So, when Darwin showed twenty-four educated people the photograph of An Old Man having his facial muscles stimulated to show intense fear, twenty instantly identified the emotion as 'intense fright' or 'horror'; three saw the expression as 'pain'; and one said 'extreme discomfort'.

However, unlike Duchenne and Sir Charles Bell, the second of whose *The Anatomy and Philosophy of Expression as Connected with the Fine Arts* (1806) had proved so influential throughout the century, Darwin was opposed to any notion that God had given humans facial muscles to allow them to reveal their feelings to others. According to Duchenne and Bell, humans were created superior to the other animals. But the 'simple fact that the anthropoid apes possess the same facial muscles as we do', Darwin lectured,

> renders it very improbable that these muscles in our case serve exclusively for expression; for no-one, I presume, would be inclined to admit that monkeys have been endowed with special muscles solely for exhibiting their grimaces. Distinct uses, independent of expression, can indeed be assigned with much probability for almost all the facial muscles.

So, facial expressions were not there for the purpose of communication. Rather, they served the purely biological functions of mastication, dilatation of the nostrils and shading the eyes. There was no transcendental purpose to emotional expressions. According to Darwin, the species which 'feared rightly' increased its chances of survival:

> Men, during numberless generations, have endeavoured to escape from their enemies or danger by headlong flight . . . And such great

exertions will have caused the heart to beat rapidly, the breathing to be hurried, the chest to heave, and the nostrils to be dilated. As these exertions have often been prolonged to the last extremity, the final result will have been utter prostration, pallor, perspiration, trembling of all the muscles, or their complete relaxation. And now, whenever the emotion of fear is strongly felt, though it may not lead to any exertion, the same results tend to reappear, through the force of inheritance and association.

He argued that 'the same involuntary and voluntary actions are performed by animals nearly related to man': this was seen as proof that 'man has retained through inheritance a relic of them, now become useless'.

Darwin developed what he called the 'principles of expression'. The first of these principles was that movements that performed some service to the organism would become habitual. If some expression helped to gratify some desire or relieve some sensation, the movement would continue even in situations where the same desire or sensation was extremely weak and thus the movement was no longer serviceable. In fear and horror, for instance, the eyes open widely, and the eyebrows are raised, enabling the organism to 'see as quickly as possible all around us'. The involuntary bristling of the hair of frightened people made them look larger and more threatening, and would be repeated even when such a response was no longer efficacious.

The second principle was that of antithesis. In Darwin's words: 'When a directly opposite state of mind is induced to those serviceable movements, there is a strong and involuntary tendency to the performance of movements of a directly opposite nature, though these are of no use, and such movements are in some cases highly expressive.' Thus, in anger, an individual's body would raise itself and move upwards and towards the antagonist, while in fear it cowered downwards and became immobile.

The third principle concerned the nervous system: certain physiological actions were largely independent of will and habit. In Darwin's words:

> When the sensorium is strongly excited, nerve-force is generated in excess, and is transmitted in certain directions, dependent on the connection of the nerve-cells, and, as far as the muscular system is concerned, on the nature of the movements which have been habitually practised.

When frightened, people often began trembling — an action that was of no service (and could be of disservice) to the organism. These reflexes were exceptionally powerful. Darwin described visiting the Zoological Gardens in London and putting his face close to the thick plate glass in front of a puff adder 'with the firm determination of not starting back if the snake struck at me'. However, 'as soon as the blow was struck, my resolution went for nothing, and I jumped a yard or two backwards with astonishing rapidity. My will and reason were powerless against the imagination of a danger which had never been experienced.'

At the heart of Darwin's theory about emotional expressions was that they were universal. He actively sought out the views of travellers, missionaries and traders from all over the world, asking them to complete a survey. This included questions such as: 'Is astonishment expressed by the eyes and mouth being opened wide, and by the eyebrows being raised? . . . Is extreme fear expressed in the same general manner as with Europeans?' His conclusion was that 'the same state of mind is expressed throughout the world with remarkable uniformity', and this provided further proof of the 'close similarity in bodily structure and mental disposition of all the races of mankind.' Darwin's theory of emotional expression was strictly materialist, and represented a dramatic overturning of the views of scientists like Duchenne.[7]

These debates still have resonance today. Duchenne's *Mechanism* and Darwin's *The Expression of the Emotions* have excited generations of scientists fascinated with questions concerning the universality of human facial expression. As one of the 'primary emotions', fear was pivotal to these debates. The literature is too large to summarise, but two examples of diverse approaches may be mentioned. In the 1920s psychologists such as Carney Landis duplicated Duchenne's use of photography to identify emotional expressions. Instead of using electrical shocks to the face, however, Landis photographed people in 'real-life' emotional situations — even going so far as to deliberately terrorise his subjects in order to capture their 'unadulterated fear' on film. By the end of his experiments, many of his subjects were crying and begging him to stop. Landis drily observed that 'there was no doubt as to the fact that this experiment did produce real emotional disturbance', but he concluded that there was no expression or group of expressions which uniformly accompanied any emotional situation.[8]

The opposite conclusion was reached by Paul Ekman, the psychologist who published a commentary on Duchenne's book and edited an edition of Darwin's. In a prodigious series of books and articles, Ekman and his collaborators photographed and analysed emotional expressions from all over the world. Ekman's revised version of Duchenne's study was eventually used to develop the Facial Action Coding System (FACS), which is still used by scientists worldwide. According to Ekman, facial expressions were universal, although there were huge variations as a result of the cultural diversity of display rules and some emotions were more universally recognised than others. In one series of experiments all respondents correctly identified photographs of people with happy, sad and angry facial expressions while only 43 per cent recognised frightened faces.[9] In other words, the jury is 'out' as to whether the face is a window to the emotional soul of an individual.

But even if there were agreement, what would it mean? In the view of the historian Peter N. Stearns, the problem with research on facial expressions is that it 'explains so little of real emotional life. Knowing what face shows [fear] does not greatly advance an understanding of what [fear] is or what results it may bring.'[10]

PART ONE

Worlds of Doom

Introduction

'Spike' Mays was only three years of age when he realised that he might starve to death in the idyllic fields of rural Essex; Miss Eleanor Markham was 'a young woman of respectability' when she was buried alive in a village just outside New York; the 600 men, women and children who were burned to death in the Iroquois Theatre in Chicago in 1903 were victims of panic as much as of smoke inhalation. These are some of the people whose fears appear in the following chapters. Their encounters with death in the early decades of the twentieth century contain both familiar and unfamiliar elements.

In the twenty-first century the fear of starvation has been muted (although not eradicated) by public and private welfare provisions: indeed, rather than worrying about becoming skinny, Americans and Britons are much more likely to be scared by fatty bodies signalling excessive consumption. Rather than premature burial, we are threatened by precocious animation as a result of the use of sophisticated medical techniques. Crowds still panic when trapped in burning buildings, but fire regulations, building ordinances and threats of litigation in the event of a tragedy have fundamentally altered the meaning of being crushed to death in a stampede for the doors.

More precisely, the way people attempt to come to terms with fears of death underwent dramatic shifts in the late nineteenth and early twentieth centuries. While religious language became increasingly sidelined, a humanistic and scientific rhetoric emerged. In these pages the divine confronts the profane in a brutal competition for authority over some of the most profound fears of humanity. Never is the fear of death more breathtaking than in disasters. Terrified people fling aside their faith in God and their ties to neighbours in their haste to forestall their own outrageously public dying. In the individual's confrontation with death, mass panic ensues.

The problem for twenty-first-century authorities is how to prevent individuals from realising the full extent of their fear in disastrous situations. When flames lick the theatre ceiling, when trains tumble off bridges and when the store of explosives detonates, how are terrified people supposed to harness their terror? Both theologians and secular commentators fail to provide an adequate answer to this question: neither preparing for disaster in this world or in the next will make us ready for our own personal encounter with death. We are all sorely afraid.

CHAPTER ONE

Death

Ye little larvae, lords of the household,
Potty, P-P, Peppermill, Lampshade,
Funnybone, Faucet, Face-in-the-wall,
Head-over-heels and Upsy-daisy
And Collywobbles and Cupboard-Love,
Be good, little gods, and guard these lives . . .
That no paranoic notion obsess
Nor dazing dump bedevil their minds
With faceless fears . . .

AUDEN, 'THE AGE OF ANXIETY'

In the first decade of the twentieth century 'Spike' Mays was born into the impoverished family of a postman who delivered mail to the villagers of north-west Essex. Although he was raised in the midst of the idyllic farmland and hedgerows depicted by John Constable and his many painterly imitators, Mays's earliest memories revolved around the two terrifying threats facing people of his class and generation: the danger of suffering a swift descent into poverty, followed by an ignoble death. By the age of three his dread of destitution was already pronounced. One day, when he was playing at his family's allotment, he heard his father insisting on the need to pull out every stray weed because 'if we don't keep a short lookout an' pull 'em up the minute we see 'em, we shall starve'. Startled by the vehemence with which his father uttered the word

'starve', Mays returned to the allotment alone while his father was
singing at the Harvest Festival, and began to energetically weed the
plot. Hours later his furious mother dragged him home for a severe
beating, having observed that her son had just destroyed the family's
crop of carrots and onions. The infant Mays had no words with
which to express his 'fear of starvation', his dread that 'because my
father was thanking God at the top of his voice for all things safely
gathered in, instead of being at his plot fighting the weeds, starvation
was imminent'.

His fear of impoverishment persisted, and indeed was com-
pounded only three years later when he observed how his mother
turned pale with fright after a black-bordered envelope was delivered to their doorstep. Aunt Harriet had died. With empty
stomachs, the Mays family walked nine miles in a thunderstorm to
attend the funeral. The six-year-old boy was taken into his aunt's
room so that he could pay his last respects to her already putrefying
corpse. Initially he was not afraid:

> Her face was white and waxy as the lily petals. She was smiling and
> looked beautiful. But the smile looked a long way off, almost as
> though it was not on her face at all . . . I had to touch her. To feel if
> she was real, but I was scared of her stillness because I had seen her
> before, full of fun and smiles and jokes.
>
> 'Don't be afraid,' said my mother. 'She's a-goin' on a long, long
> journey. Say goodbye!'
>
> And then I did it. I pressed her cheek with my finger. She felt
> cold. It was like putting a finger on the ice in the water-butt, but on
> soft ice. There was another difference. Where I had pressed there
> was a little dint which did not fill up again. That scared me. I had
> spoiled the face of my pretty Aunt Harriet and I thought that because
> of my finger-puggling God might not let her into Heaven.

Thereafter, the boy's nights were plagued with nightmares in which
his favourite friends and family members died, leaving him to struggle alone in a pitiless world. His dead companions 'floated in the
sky in boxes, rejected equally by both heaven and hell' because of
the holes he had bored in their faces with his finger. These

nightmares continued for many months, until his mother once again meted out punishment. Impatient with hearing him crying out in his sleep, she cuffed him across the face and served him a mug of senna-pod tea laced with castor oil. This particular nightmare ceased, but a free-floating anxiety about the inevitable degradations of dying and the uncertainties of 'death itself' vexed his entire childhood.[1]

Many people shared Mays's fear of destitution and an ugly death. Poverty — 'the hell that Englishmen fear most', as the essayist Thomas Carlyle put it[2] — seared the emotional lives of Britons and Americans in the nineteenth and early twentieth centuries. This fear of destitution was a visceral emotion, expressing itself in the roaring protest of the stomach or goosebumps on the skin. As Mays was to discover, increased state provision of welfare instigated by the Liberals in the 1890s did not eradicate the fear of poverty: it merely diluted its intensity. Dread of hunger or the cold might have diminished but fears associated with social status grew. Rather than trembling about the effects of absolute privation, people shuddered to think about the consequences of *relative* impoverishment, such as being rehoused in a rougher area or forced to sell a prized possession. The providers of public assistance were determined to retain (indeed, even boost) this element of fear. After all, they reasoned, public assistance should not be made *too* easy in case people jettisoned all economic anxieties, thus damaging the economy. As a consequence, moral panics arose around unscrupulous individuals and groups who did not feel sufficiently apprehensive of the stigma attached to the receipt of poor relief.

Death's fears were more trenchant. In the late nineteenth century fear seemed to loiter at the very boundary between life and death, occasionally edging over the perimeter to arouse a generalised anxiety about the status of body and soul after the performance of the last rites. Hesitancy replaced certitude. Both in Mays's decaying rural world and in the troubling flux of the urban sphere, traditional forms of ritualistic succour were losing authority, exacerbating misgivings about the integrity of the modern Self and intensifying the terrors of the deathbed. The manner of dying no longer provided any clue about the individual's fate in the afterlife. Fears associated with the act of dying were severed from anxieties relating to death itself. Analgesics attempted to numb physical terrors while secularism sought to deaden those of the soul, but both failed to ease the dying individual's confrontation with extinction. This was a democratic fear: rich and poor alike trembled in the face of that eternal unknown.

Pauperisation, a most undemocratic source of fear, was a disgraceful state in which to die. In the late nineteenth century the fear of destitution was not primarily associated with dismay about being unable to 'leave behind' inheritable wealth: dying without passing on assets to one's family might have been thoughtless, but it was not terrifying. Rather, the dread of poverty was a fear of 'spending one's last days in the poor house' and therefore 'being buried at public expense and taking one's eternal rest in the potter's field', a fate that troubled many paupers at the end of that century.[3] The individual who died in abject poverty could be relegated to a final bedding-down on top of strangers in a mass grave and covered in a sheet of quicklime to hasten decay. No plaque would be mounted to commemorate a life, thus symbolically attesting that the pauper's passing would not be remembered, let alone mourned. Merely the *fear* of meeting with such a fate could be lethal, as it was for sixty-eight-year-old Susan Starr of St Pancras, London, in 1871. Starr had been dependent upon financial handouts from the parish but had been informed that unless she 'kept herself and room cleaner, the relief would be stopped'. On 21 April 1871 *The Times* reported that Starr had 'refused to enter the workhouse, and last Monday died from syncope, from heart disease, caused by the shock from apprehension that she would lose her relief'.[4] Her surviving sister might also have been discomforted by her death: after all, it was widely believed that the disrespect shown to the corpse during a pauper burial could infuriate the spirit of the departed. There were no rites capable of placating the lingering ghost of a pauper.

The possibility of a humiliating burial was only one threat facing infirm paupers. While sentimental lore portrayed indigents taking comfort in death as an angel coming to provide release from a life of hardship, sensational tales increasingly depicted death as the grim reaper, stalking the anonymous corridors of workhouses in order to glean bodies for the ultimate desecration: dissection. The dissection table was an intermediate resting-place for only a tiny number of economically precarious Britons and Americans. Nevertheless, alarm about the possibility of being dissected after death was disproportionately large and growing, especially as demand for corpses to teach anatomy to physicians and surgeons increased.

In Britain the 1830s proved to be a turning point. From the mid-eighteenth century to 1832 the only legal source of corpses for anatomical teaching in medical schools came from the gallows but, because supplies were woefully inadequate, criminals were known to snatch bodies from their graves in the dead of night for sale to hospitals. Wealthy families took protective measures: they encased the corpses of their loved ones in iron coffins with locks, covered tombs with heavy stones, posted grave-watchers and employed the increasingly privatised services of funeral professionals. In contrast, the shoddy mass burial grounds of the poor provided few safeguards against body thieves. For these people the threat of grave-robbers ended in 1832 with the passing of the Anatomy Act — but, ironically, the probability of being dissected in an anatomy school actually increased: the Act authorised anatomists to collect corpses from Poor Law institutions. Henceforth all Britons who died as paupers and whose bodies remained unclaimed forty-eight hours after death risked dissection. In the century after the Act, around fifty-seven thousand bodies of the poor were dissected in London's anatomy schools alone.[5] Even as late as the mid-1930s, less than 4 per cent of corpses dissected in medical schools in Britain were the result of bequests.[6] Although progressively fewer paupers were at risk of meeting with such an ignominious end as the number of unclaimed bodies from patients dying in Poor Law institutions dwindled, this regularisation of the economy in corpses ensured that the fear of desecration remained a potent one for the poorest Britons. After death, poverty licensed desecration.[7]

The terror of being cleaved and quartered after death was stirred up by the popular press, which delighted in reporting gruesome scenes of carnage on the dissection table. For instance, on 19 January 1888 a headline in the *Pall Mall Gazette* trumpeted: 'Horrors of the Dissecting Room'. Readers were treated to an 'everyday' scene in an anatomy school, in which a corpse was removed from 'the pickle' and distributed among the medical students:

> One wants a forearm, another a foot, hand, etc. The parts of the body are sold in this way . . . During the cutting up of the body and subsequent dissection of its parts a good many pieces are thrown upon the floor of the room. A porter is employed who goes around at intervals with a brush and pan collecting these morsels, which are removed to a cellar. In due time follow all the other pieces of flesh, bones, etc. These are all thrown into one heap in the cellar. It must be understood that perhaps half a dozen bodies are 'going' at one time in the dissecting room, and this heap is composed of fragments of all. In the cellar is a pair of scales and some ordinary workhouse 'shell' coffins. When not occupied in sweeping up the bits, the porter is engaged in weighing up these unsavoury morsels into a certain quantity which is supposed to equal the body. With this mass the coffin is fitted and screwed down.[8]

The horror of this scene resided in more than merely the way the students disregarded the integrity of the deceased: in the hereafter the dilemma was even more acute. As a Poor Law Guardian in Kensington lamented, medics could not guarantee that the bodies would be 'pieced together' accurately: what was the risk of someone being buried with 'a Protestant head and a Catholic body'? he asked. And how would such confusion be rectified in the afterlife?[9] Anxiety about the risk of dissection added to pre-existing consternation about the commodified body of the poor — but it was all the more terrifying because the desecration was perceived to be absolute and final. Neither in this life nor in the next could the profaned body be 'made whole' again.

Death's sting was becoming more agonising for other reasons as well. During the course of the nineteenth century dying attracted the employment of an ever-increasing range of expert 'assistants'. A link between fear and corporate profit was forged, with the increase in the sale of Industrial Assurance (life insurance for workers in industry) to provide for a 'decent funeral' and to give financial assistance for relatives after the death of the breadwinner. According to one estimate, around 10 per cent of the income of women in London's working-class district of Lambeth was used to pay for Industrial Assurance.[10] Fear of desecration and the consequences of such defilement on the family's status within poor communities encouraged this commercialisation of death. Predictably, the same organisations dedicated to relieving anxieties devoted energy to inciting fear. As one report into the business admitted, 'agents play on the fears of those whom they approach: they arouse apprehension and even fright, indulging in overstatements and exaggerations which may prejudice a really free and independent decision'.[11]

The privatisation of dying accompanied its commercialisation. By the early years of the twentieth century death was no longer a public event: as dying retreated into private spaces, its script became more mysterious and frightening. Denied access to the deathbed, people turned to physicians and other professional observers to depict and decipher acts of dying. Part of the duty of these observers was to curtail people's fears by reassuring them that the individual in death's embrace felt little, if any, fear.[12] In fact, as one American authority at the end of the nineteenth century hastened to record, three-quarters of very elderly people positively craved to meet their destiny.[13] In contradiction (although equally comfortingly), another study insisted that four-fifths of people on their deathbeds were emotionless: 'like their birth, their death was a sleep and a forgetting'.[14]

Even when these physicians admitted that some patients exhibited behaviours that would 'normally' be interpreted as indicating some degree of distress, the significance of these manifestations was disputed. For instance, in 1863, William S. Savory, lecturer in Anatomy and Physiology at St Bartholomew's Hospital, London, adhered to the prevailing medical view that dying patients experienced no physical or emotional distress as they passed out of this world and into the next. Any 'signs of intense suffering' were deceptive, he argued:

> The cold dew upon the face and surface generally, the collapsed and perhaps distorted features, the heaving, gasping or gurgling respiration, or it may be the convulsive agitation, are by no means

necessarily the signs of pain and distress. Therefore, whatever may
have been the amount of previous suffering, we may fairly assume
that, except in extreme cases, the actual process of dying is not one
of intense agony, or indeed, for the most part, even of pain.[15]

Oswald Browne's *On the Care of the Dying. A Lecture to Nurses*
(1894) made a similar point. As a physician at the Royal Hospital for
Diseases to the Chest, Browne admitted that nurses might witness
dying patients engaged in 'an agony or struggle'. However, they
should be reassured: this activity was 'purely physical, the expression of the last labouring efforts of the respiratory muscles to
perform their work'. It might be distressing to nurses, but it was
unlikely that the patient was encountering 'bodily or mental suffering', he confidently insisted.[16] In other words, death's passion was
mercifully independent of consciousness and therefore unencum-
bered by anxiety.

This medicalised view of the deathbed saw human subjectivity as
residing primarily in the body: death was a decisive event of the
flesh, as opposed to a process involving interaction between body
and soul. Once the corporeal self waned, the spirit had already
departed. Consciousness relied upon adequate quantities of healthy
blood reaching the nerve centres, and because the brain was the first
organ to be deprived of blood, seriously ill individuals rapidly lost all
apprehension of fearful stimuli. As a consequence, medical personnel insisted that dying patients were simply *incapable* of feeling
fearful. Consciousness was no longer a matter of the spirit or soul,
but a physiological process.

Even from their graves, corpses generated fears in the living. In
the nineteenth century the fusty odours emanating from overcrowded burial grounds situated in close proximity to high-density
residential housing were believed to be responsible not only for
catatonic states that made people vulnerable to premature burial but
also for a large proportion of physical ailments. The problem was
smell. Mid-nineteenth-century theories of contagion postulated that
disease was spread through 'miasma' or noxious odours. In the
words of the public-health promoter William Eassie, writing in
1875, the 'foetid air exhaled from the dead is fatal if breathed in a

concentrated state'. Even when 'dissipated by the wind, it lowers the vital powers of the community'. The 'miasma which escapes from coffins' was posited as the reason for the 'cadaverous appearance' of gravediggers.[17] Although in 1849 William Budd and John Snow had proposed a theory of disease based on bacteria, their views were not generally accepted. Even Louis Pasteur's *Germ Theory and Its Applications to Medicine* (1861), arguing that disease was caused by organisms invisible to the naked eye, took a long time to be accepted. Indeed, in late-nineteenth-century popular literature, many commentators retained a belief in *both* miasma and germs. One influential tract on burial customs, written in 1881, paid homage to Pasteur's germ theory, noting that tiny scales from the skin of a scarlet-fever patient infected any healthy tissue they came into contact with. Yet the author still found it necessary to warn his readers that corpses gave off 'irrespirable' gases that were fatal if breathed in concentrated form. The tract informed its readers that, even if extremely faint, the nauseating odour of a decomposing corpse could lead to a 'constant depreciation of the final functions', chronic indigestion and any number of other debilitating illnesses.[18] With the gradual recognition of germ theory, fear of contagion emanating from the smelly corpse was transformed into a more invidious fear of invisible germs that could reside anywhere and could not be detected.

Gradually, however, fears of burial were tamed. The removal of burial sites from heavily populated areas and the 'new style' cemeteries (the word had begun to replace 'graveyard' and 'burial ground' from the 1820s and was popular by the second half of the century) did attempt to forge a new way of reducing death anxiety by sweetening the appearance of death. Classical forms replaced the skull and crossbones; urns and broken columns romanticised death. Cemeteries were transformed into gardens which people could stroll about in and enjoy as sites of leisure rather than burial. In the rural elegiac, all attempts were made to disguise the fact that the graveyard was a place of violence where human flesh was devoured.

There still remained the problem that many people lacked confidence in the ability of physicians to accurately diagnose physical death. In the last decades of the nineteenth century many dying individuals and those contemplating death became transfixed by a terror of being prematurely laid in the tomb. In the 1890s an influential sociologist was surprised to find that the dread of being buried alive was spontaneously mentioned by people when they were asked to describe their major fears.[19] On the deathbed, faith in medical expertise languished. Indeed, the dignified voice of scientific reassurance was no match for the roar of moral panic. Terrifying rumours spread. Campaigners against premature burial claimed to have collected over a hundred sworn testimonies from men and women who had survived this ordeal.[20]

Others focused on the evidence of exhumed graves. Of 1200 corpses exhumed from their resting-places in New York during the 1860s and 1870s, six were believed to have shown signs of live burial.[21] Estimates of the proportion of burials that were premature varied from two in every thousand (1908)[22] to one in every one hundred thousand persons or eight hundred people per annum (1911).[23] Since most examples of premature burial were uncovered by accident, it was argued that, in all probability, many more poor wretches had been damned to this end.[24] But even if it was rare, campaigners argued that premature burial was sufficiently terrorising to justify the introduction of procedures designed to restore confidence.[25]

Much was made of freakish occasions when the cadaver actually drew breath on the embalmer's slab or within the coffin. Miss Eleanor Markham ('a young woman of respectability') was one person for whom the fantastical terror of live burial became a reality. Markham lived in Sprakers, a village seventy-five miles from Syracuse, New York State. She had complained of heart trouble and, on 8 July 1894, died. Her relatives and friends bid their tearful farewells and the undertakers screwed down the coffin lid. As the undertakers and a physician carried Markham's body to the hearse, something stirred inside the coffin. Upon opening the lid, they saw 'poor Eleanor Markham lying on her back, her face white and contorted, and her eyes distended'. 'My God!' she cried in broken accents. 'You are burying me alive!' Her doctor responded by saying, 'Hush! Child. You are all right. It is a mistake easily rectified.' In Markham's words:

I was conscious all the time you were making preparations to bury
me . . . The horror of my situation is altogether beyond description.
I could hear everything that was going on, even a whisper outside the
door, and although I exerted all my will power, and made a supreme
physical effort to cry out, I was powerless.

She was removed from her coffin and — having learned her
lesson — never complained of 'flutterings of the heart' again.[26]

As in this tale, the victim was most frequently depicted as a beautiful, young woman shamefully buried 'in the usual hurry'. Miss
Markham was lucky: evidence of premature burial was usually only
elicited months later when the body was exhumed, bearing signs of
a frightful struggle. In one such exhumation the female corpse's
face was described as 'gashed, her hands and arms frightfully torn,
her feet drawn up in a wild endeavour to extricate herself from the
horrible prison, her breasts furrowed and lacerated by finger-
nails'.[27] Other supposed corpses were found 'inside the doors of
vaults, with coffins broken open, and every indication of desperate
struggles for — escape'.[28] Edgar Allan Poe's masterpiece 'The
Premature Burial' (1850) is an early example of this terrorising literature.[29] As he explained it:

no event is so terribly well adapted to inspire the supremeness of
bodily and mental distress, as is burial before death. The unen-
durable oppression of the lungs — the stifling fumes of the damp
earth — the clinging to the death garments — the rigid embrace of
the narrow house — the blackness of the absolute Night — the
silence like a sea that overwhelms — the unseen but palpable presence of the Conqueror Worm . . . these considerations, I say, carry
into the heart, which still palpitates, a degree of appalling and
intolerable horror from which the most daring imagination must
recoil. We know of nothing so agonising upon earth — we can
dream of nothing half so hideous in the realms of the nethermost
Hell.[30]

Nearly half a century later the *Spectator* decreed that 'burning,
drowning, even the most hideous mutilation under a railway train'

was 'as nothing compared with burying alive'.[31] In the newly evolving democratic state, this was a most undemocratic fear, sentencing a person to 'perpetual silence', beyond appeal or escape.[32]

Risk was not distributed evenly: this moral panic identified particular groups as being in greater peril of live burial. The *Jewish World*, for instance, expressed concern that Jewish law decreeing that the dead be interred within a few hours after death dramatically increased their community's vulnerability to this 'horrible catastrophe'.[33] Early interment of corpses in Ireland and the fact that physicians in that country were not required to certify death (in 1909 a quarter of burials in Ireland went uncertified),[34] were also identified as suspect practices. An anti-papist agenda might have been behind the warning that the Roman Catholic rite of extreme unction raised 'a serious impediment to the use of means for restoring animation'.[35]

Gender and class were additional factors increasing danger. Women of a hysterical temperament, together with men exhibiting a 'feminine nervous organization', were in jeopardy.[36] According to one of the leading textbooks on premature burial, published in 1905, women who 'take but little nourishment, and who allow their imaginations to run riot upon every gloomy subject which arrests them' should be watched attentively lest their 'nervous system becomes prostrate, and they fall into a state of lethargy' that could be mistaken for death.[37] According to a professor of physiology and psychological science at the United States College in New York, both men and women needed to guard against 'any strong emotion, any unusual or protracted intellectual exertion, great physical exhaustion, unsatisfied sexual desire, or excessive indulgence' that could debilitate the body and lead to a cataleptic attack. He noted that men should be wary of disorders of the digestive system, while women should watch for diseases of the womb. Everyone had to be careful lest they indulge excessively in tobacco, cannabis and morphine. Other dangerous activities included 'overtaxing the brain, excessive bathing, mental excitement, sexual aberrations, . . . [and] unwholesome postures in bed'.[38]

Finally, in death, as in life, paupers were endangered: overexertion, hunger, economic stress and foul air increased their likelihood of suffering this fate,[39] and reduced their ability to purchase the 'care and attention given to people in a superior station' who feared premature burial.[40] As an article in the *Embalmers' Monthly* in 1908 reasoned:

> the persons most subject to one or more of the various forms of death counterfeit are to be found chiefly among those whose daily avocation necessarily exhausts the nervous force faster than the natural powers are able to recuperate it, and who have frequent recourse to stimulants or to narcotics in the hope of counteracting the feeling of depression that usually follows.[41]

The body was a crafty operator, counterfeiting death as punishment for abuse sustained in life. And, as usual, the poor suffered more than most.

Nevertheless, the panic about premature burial subsided as quickly as it had begun. By the time war was declared in 1914, it was over.[42] Ironically, this occurred at precisely the time when live burial became prevalent. In the trenches of Flanders, thousands of healthy young men were buried alive. In a typical account committed to his diary on 15 September 1916, Captain Ralph Smith described the effect of being buried alive upon one man:

> The poor fellow was hysterical all the time, and kept telling us over and over again, that it was his first time in the trenches, that his pal was lying underneath him dead, and that it was the second time that he had been buried. The first time he had just been dug out when another shell landed and buried him again whereupon the others ran away and left him.[43]

Burial alive represented the most heinous desertion.

Even during the Second World War, live burial was a rare, but well-known, experience of bombardment, not only in the combat zones but also on the 'home front'. For instance, in 1941 a factory inspector complained of tremor, nightly bedwetting and attacks of intense, cramp-like pains in his limbs. It was discovered that he had been buried alive for five hours when a club where he was having a drink was bombed. When asked to describe being buried alive, he became severely frightened and spluttered out the following words:

> If only my watch had been luminous it would have been better. I was dying to see something. I was wanting to pass water the whole time but I did not want to wet myself. And the cramp was horrible, I could not move my legs. They were pinned down.

He then confessed that he had micturated and this 'gave him as much displeasure as anything'. Thereafter, each night he re-lived these symptoms of terror.[44]

Nevertheless, in peacetime the fear of premature burial was no longer as trenchant. Why did the scare flare up in the late nineteenth century and then speedily fizzle out a couple of decades later? This was not the first time there had been alarm about premature burial. In the fourteenth century, for instance, recurrent epidemics produced comparable panics. Similarly, in the eighteenth century, a panicky alertness to new resuscitation techniques led to the establishment of Humane Societies, dedicated to developing more accurate means of diagnosing 'final' death. However, by the late nineteenth century fear of too-speedy burial and uncertainty about resuscitation possibilities combined with a more generalised distrust of physicians and civil authorities to heighten panic. A distinguished literary woman wrote a letter to the authors of one of the popular books on premature burial explaining how it had changed her life: 'It is a terrible subject,' she began,

> and one which has haunted me all my life insomuch as I have never made a will without inserting a clause requiring my throat to be cut before I am put underground. Of course one can have no reliance on doctors whatever, and I have myself known a case in which a very eminent [physician] insisted on a coffin being screwed down because the corpse looked so life-like and full of colour that the friends could not help indulging in hopes.[45]

There were other complaints, including claims that, when the kin of (suspected) deceased people sought to 'hold back the interment for many days', local authorities 'compelled' them to bury their loved ones hastily.[46] In response, in 1895 the *Manchester Courier* pleaded that neither inconvenience nor sanitary considerations should be regarded as more important than the need to ensure that the corpse was indeed a corpse.[47] Of course, the real problem was that no one claimed to be absolutely certain about when that border between life and death was crossed. As Edgar Allan Poe perceptively remarked, this border was 'shadowy and vague'.[48] The unreliability of 'signs of death' threatened medical attempts to transform death into an orderly, recognisable event.

Uncertainty was exacerbated by disagreements within the death professions. Physicians, undertakers and embalmers aggressively attacked one another's preferred 'sign' of mortality. Physicians emphasised their profession's long apprenticeship with death and the superiority of their diagnostic instruments. They insisted that death was a physiological event that could be determined objectively. Substituting a properly trained physician for the layperson near the deathbed and utilising a stethoscope should restore confidence in the ability of physicians to diagnose death accurately.[49] As we shall see in Chapter Ten, physicians may have won the battle for the hopes and fears of dying people and their relatives at the beginning of the twentieth century, but their confidence was eventually deflated by the rapidly advancing technologies at the end of the twentieth century.

Undertakers and embalmers scoffed at the arrogance of turn-of-the-century physicians. In a typical rebuttal the *American Undertaker* in 1904 castigated 'ignorant' doctors for their 'absurd' faith in the value of the stethoscopes and other contraptions in ascertaining whether there was still breath left in the body. The author claimed that cutting the artery was the definitive way of determining death: 'when properly described' to grieving relatives, it reported, the 'practical tests' employed by undertakers 'show the family that the undertaker is in position to determine more positively [when death had occurred] than any tests which the physician could use'. Undertakers promised to ensure that 'no doubt could possibly remain in the minds of the most prejudiced that there was any possibility of life remaining'.[50] Embalmers also staked their reputation on their skill in deciding death, arguing that embalming not only reduced the fear of death by making the cadaver look as if it was simply taking a nap, but also guaranteed that foolproof methods were used to ascertain death. For instance, embalmers recommended injecting solutions of fluorscine deep into the tissues: if blood was still circulating, skin and mucous membranes would be stained yellow and eyes would glow an uncanny emerald green.[51]

Nevertheless, promoters of 'safe burial' did not help their case by recommending procedures that would kill any body that was not already beyond breath. Decapitation prior to burial was an effective way of ensuring that no man, woman or child need fear being prematurely buried. Cutting arteries and putting a steel needle through the heart were also widely promoted, 'even at the risk of killing a few entranced subjects', observed an article about premature burial in the *Spectator* in 1895.[52] Injecting strychnine into the 'supposed corpse' would also ensure that death took place before burial, according to the *Morning Post*.[53]

Cremation — the most popular procedure of all for burial reformers — also fell into the category of deadly procedures. For people terrified by the thought of being interred under six feet of earth, the alternative of being subjected to fire held many advantages. In the words of a proponent of cremation in 1894, burial was 'defilement', 'dreadful', the ultimate 'degradation of the body'. Cremation was 'purification' and 'sublimation':

> A few moments of pure and blessed searching; and then all is beautiful. For what is more beautiful than that the poor dead body, purified, should be dismissed into sunshine? . . . should be sent, not into the defiling grave, but into the bright summer air, to the blue sky and the birds; itself presently, as uncontaminated as they.[54]

Cremation promised to bypass fears of defilement. Decomposing flesh 'offends our senses, shocks our memory, daunts our courage', noted one proponent of cremation, whereas it was so easy 'to avoid the hateful test'.[55] In 1892 the vice-president of the New York Cremation Society pointed out that there was no more 'revolting' way of treating the body of a loved one than burial. Purposely thrusting sentimentality aside, he testified that when some graves were opened they revealed dens of black snakes 'gorged with the content of the empty coffins'. These 'ugly facts' of earth-burial were responsible for people's terror of death: cremation would remove this dread by substituting a clear, purifying end to life.[56] The bereaved would be spared tormented nightmares of 'putrefactive horrors': the dead would be granted 'everlasting peace'.[57] But the other benefit of cremation was that it promised an instantaneous death.[58] Cremation ensured that people would not find themselves 'buried and then living a few hours more in the grave, only to die there the most horrible of deaths known to man'.[59] There was no chance of 'suffering any agony whatever'.[60] In particular, promoters of cremation admitted that 'to cremate a man alive is a rather serious responsibility', but insisted that it was the best of all the options.[61]

Such logic impressed Molly Weir, a Glaswegian slum child in the early decades of the twentieth century. Her friends were tormented with the fear of live burial. She recalled listening 'trembling, to stories of coffins having been dug up and the corpses turned over on their faces, or eyes staring with terror, and clawed marks in the coffin lid where they had scrabbled to get out'. These 'stories of people being buried alive so tormented me that I made everybody promise . . . that when I died they would see to it, "cross their hearts and hope to die", that I was well and truly cremated'.[62]

But, for others, the idea of having to choose between premature burial and being burned to death was terrifying in itself. Mistrustful of claims made by physicians, undertakers, embalmers and cremators, some people took their own precautions against premature burial. As we have already seen, some directed physicians to sever their heads before burial.[63] For people with an engineering frame of mind, mechanical assurances were popular. These included devices for observing corpses through glass walls and fitting coffins with pipes running to the surface (enabling reviving 'corpses' to breathe), as well as providing coffins with mechanical and electrical methods of summoning help. For instance, in 1868 Franz Vester of Newark, New Jersey, was granted a patent for his design of a coffin complete with a tube which contained a bell and a ladder, enabling the entombed individual to climb to safety or summon help. In 1871 Dr Theodore A. Schroeder and Hermann Wuest of Hoboken, New Jersey, used a battery to create a circuit within the coffin. If the 'corpse' moved, the circuit would break, causing a bell to ring and releasing fresh air into the tomb.

Eleven years later an Indianapolis man — suitably named Albert Fearnaught — proposed placing a spring in the hand of the 'corpse'. Any movement would cause a pin to be released, forcing a signal out of a tube which led to the surface. However, as one commentator who studied these patents in 1948 concluded, the mechanisms were so complicated that there was a strong possibility of failure. Patented signals would be of little use in the large, 'modern' cemeteries, with much landscaping, uneven terrain and only the occasional patrol. Most patented coffins would be effective only in vault entombment, an infrequent method of burial.[64] Wealthier members of the community were more liable to be shielded from the fear of live burial.

There was another particularly middle-class response to the fear of premature burial: organisation. Some frightened people sought safety in numbers, and joined the (British) Association for Prevention of Premature Burial, established in 1899. As well as ensuring that independent physicians would verify their deaths, members carried out experiments into suspended animation (bodily states that feign death). Appalled by the lack of legal safeguards to prevent premature burial (even the House of Commons Committee on Death Certification admitted that death certificates were gener-ally 'misleading and untrustworthy'),[65] the Association lobbied politicians to pass legislation requiring that trained physicians exam-ine every body before medical certification of death.[66] Since the only failsafe way of ascertaining death was putrefaction, the Association recommended the establishment of 'waiting mortuaries' in every sanitary district in the country. These mortuaries would be 'furnished with every appliance of resuscitation, watched by quali-fied attendants, and in telephone communication with a medical superintendent, who shall be authorised to grant removal of the body to the cemetery only when the fact of death has been unequiv-ocally established by the sign of decomposition.'[67]

The American Society for the Prevention of Premature Burial was established a year after its British equivalent. It insisted that medical schools introduce formal instruction about how to ascertain death.[68] The Society also called for legislation to ensure that physicians certifying death examined the body and applied tests to ascertain whether there was any life left in it. These tests included making two or more incisions in an artery, exposing the palm of the hand to the flame of a candle, holding a crystal mirror to the lips and testing to see if a hot iron or steel placed against the skin caused blistering. The American Society urged the building of mortuary chapels where bodies could rest for some hours before burial.[69] Concerned that burials were often carried out too hastily (especially during epidemics), it was as keen as its British counterpart to provide legal safeguards against premature burial.[70] Improvements in certification were high on its agenda — it was no longer acceptable for physicians to accept the statements of 'quacks' or 'ignorant old women' that death had taken place.[71] The signing of death certificates needed to be taken more seriously.[72] The professionalisation of dying was imperative to allay fears of premature burial. In the increasingly secular society of late-nineteenth and early-twentieth-century Britain and America, premature burial provided an authentic hell on earth.

If the process of dying and being buried periodically led to twitches of terror, the emotion associated with death itself inspired something more akin to endemic anxiety. Speculation about the existence of the hereafter, coupled with a more democratic emphasis upon individualism, materiality and the pleasures of the senses, created a new range of worries about death. Attempts to diminish this fear of death met with religious hostility. After all, theologically it was 'right and proper' to fear death. In the words of William Booth, revivalist preacher and founder of the Salvation Army:

> Nothing moves people like the terrific. They must have hell-fire flashed before their faces, or they will not *move*. Last night I preached a sermon on Christ weeping over sinners, and only one came forward [for conversion] . . . When I preached about the harvest [of

souls at the end of time] and the wicked being turned away [from
heaven], numbers came. We must have that kind of truth which
will move sinners.[73]

Fear was the rock upon which Christ built His Church. No other
Western institution claimed with as much authority as the Christian
Church to know what happened after death. Although the various
branches of Christianity often disagreed over the timing of the individual's confrontation with God and the precise character of hell's
torment, all accepted that humans were right to be sorely afraid.
Even though Christianity's foundations were crumbling (some
would say that, by the late nineteenth century, they had already
been scattered like dust), anxiety about what happened after death
haunted late-nineteenth-century consciences.

For clergy of all denominations, it could do only good to remind
people of death's imminence and the prospect of an afterlife. As a
chaplain at St Agnes's hospital in London put it in 1879: 'If you
have tried to prepare for death, and you seem not to have any fear of
it, it is better not to say so. If you believe death passes your soul into
the presence of its Maker, . . . you must, and you ought to have ——
fear.'[74] Since these comments were made as part of his 'practical
advice to those in charge of the dying', the implication was that
deathbed witnesses had a duty to incite fear of death.

His views were widely shared. In 1878, for instance, the
Reverend Walter James Wyon (a member of the Society of St John
the Evangelist in Cowley, Oxford) spoke about 'The Christian Man's
Fear'. According to him, fear was a central emotion in this 'world of
probation'. Those who might reply that it was 'not good of God thus
to expose us to trial' he enjoined to remember that 'if God has put
us here to try us, it is because we cannot enjoy Him without the
trial'. Fear of the deity was a consequence of free will: individuals
had been given the option of rejecting God. The final reckoning
would be decided at that Last Judgement:

Yes; the soul which has died in grace will wake up on the last terrible
day. It has been in paradise enjoying the vision of Jesus; it has been
calmly expectant, in a state of joy, and felicity, but it comes to take

up its body on the last terrible day, and it sees it all stained with sin as God restored it to consciousness, with all the scars of its old infirmities and bad habits upon it, and the soul shudders as it sees this terrible thing which it used to inhabit; and then that body must by fire on that last terrible day, perhaps in a moment, be purged, be made fit to be taken into the Body of Christ. Oh! what a terrible awakening that will be to see the body thus; the fire will have to consume all that is not Christ. Yes, then indeed we may well fear.[75]

As this sermon implied, what incensed clergy most of all was 'backsliders' and 'doubting Thomases'. As one minister of the Free Church of Scotland lamented in the 1860s, many people attending church 'hear all our doctrine, sit at our feasts, and in outward life are blameless', but 'know nothing of the fear of God, or of the love of Christ'. There was little point in seeking to 'melt them by the tale of a Redeemer's love' or attempting to 'charm them into His alliance with descriptions of His beauty'. This would be like throwing pearls before swine. 'We have need rather to mediate terror,' he ruled, causing 'these sinners in Zion to be afraid.'[76] In an age where the germ of secularism was penetrating even religious circles, people needed to be prompted to fear the afterlife, to be reminded of the fires of hell.

Graphic visions of anguish were a staple in such literature. Hell's flames would burn, but not consume.[77] There could be no remission, no retreat. 'I may . . . justly fear,' pontificated Christopher Newman Hall in his meditations on the Prophet Isaiah, published as *The Antidote to Fear* (1866), because all of Nature provided evidence of the Creator's 'ability to punish. There is no refuge to which I may escape from His Omnipresence; no darkness where I may hide from His Omnipresence. I cannot evade the scrutiny of His all piercing eye. There is never a moment when I am not within reach of His irresistible hand.' No one was exempt. Even true believers had to be terrorised by death. After all, Christians also embarked on their final death throes consumed with anxiety lest 'the struggle be too terrible': 'May we not through "pains of death, lose confidence" in God?' fretted distraught believers on their deathbeds.[78]

From the 1870s, however, recoil from this malevolent deity

became widespread. 'Science' faced up to 'theology' in a series of bruising battles. In one sensational instance in March 1878, the editors of the *Popular Science Monthly* published an article entitled 'Concerning the Belief in Hell' in which they curtly announced that Hades had become obsolete. Going further, they claimed that the idea of hell had originated 'in ages of savagery and low barbarism' and developed 'in periods of fierce intolerance, sanguinary persecutions, cruel civil codes, and vindictive punishments'. As such it 'harmonized with the severities and violence of society, and undoubtedly had use as a means of the harsh discipline of men when they were moved only by the lowest motives'. These vengeful times were over. 'With the advance of knowledge, and the cultivation of the humaner sentiments,' they preached, the doctrine of hell 'has become anomalous and out of harmony with the advance of human nature'.[79]

This coupling of theological tenets concerning the afterlife with pre-modern savagery incited uproar. Perhaps none was more strident than an article titled 'Hell and Science', published in the *Catholic World* three months later. This article began by reminding believers that the doctrine of hell was not theological opinion but revealed dogma. It went on to launch a scathing attack on Protestant insolence and scientific arrogance for setting in place mechanisms for unbelief. According to the authors, theology was 'based on authority' and therefore could not exist in the Protestant tradition (which insisted upon private interpretation and was, they claimed, contemptuous of authority). Equally, science was not qualified to comment on theological matters. Scientific certitude stemmed only from observation and experiment, while 'the torments of hell' could be neither scrutinised nor investigated, at least not 'during the present life'. Science possessed only a limited range of knowledge: it knew nothing about right or wrong, virtue or vice. They berated scientists for being insolent enough to refuse to acknowledge the need for a creator. Admittedly, if humanity had evolved from apes, then scientists were right to reject hell since 'apes do not go to hell'. But human beings needed to be afraid of the afterlife precisely because they were not the product of evolution but were created in the image of God. The *Catholic World* warned scientists

that, more than any other group within society, they were destined
to an eternity in Hades.[80]

By the turn of the century the debate about the afterlife was
increasingly confined to religious circles, where devout believers
professed competing religious views on the nature of hell. This
debate was played out in a book called *That Unknown Country, Or
What Living Men Believe Concerning Punishment After Death* (1889), in
which men such as Bishop Fowler of the Methodist Episcopal Church
and Dr A. A. Miner of the Universalists pondered the issue with min-
isters such as the Presbyterian Mr Talmage. Fowler and Miner
represented a shift in the conception of hell. For Fowler, hell had to
be 'freed from the physical flames', while Miner went further, assert-
ing that 'punishment after death for the sins of this life is not taught
in the word of God'. Such revisionism was heresy for Christians like
Talmage. He made the fundamentalist (or 'literalist') case brusquely:

> What is the use of explaining away a furnace of fire, when God says
> there is one? . . . I am not opposed to saying it may be figurative; but
> I know very well that if it is not fire it is something as severe as
> fire . . . God says it is fire, and a furnace of fire. Besides that, I do
> not know that it is figurative. It may be literal. The Bible sixteen
> times says it is fire.[81]

The debate raged. In 1900 the Reverend George Wolfe Shinn, of
the Church of England, came out on the side of the literalists. 'What
has become of hell?' he asked. Although the word was still used in
the Apostles' Creed, Shinn lamented the fact that clergymen were
wont to explain that hell was not 'the place of punishment, but
simply the place of departed spirits; that it has no reference to their
condition as happy or unhappy, but simply refers to the separation of
soul and body, and to the residence of the soul in an intermediate
state or place until resurrection day'. Shinn blamed anti-Calvinist
Universalists for the situation in which many Protestants scorned the
idea of an everlasting hell for sinners. By introducing the notion of
a 'second probation' (whereby unsaved souls loitered in a kind of
limbo away from God until resurrection day), these Christians had
dangerously reduced the fear of death.

Shinn was also appalled by the tendency of many theologians to transform hell's fire into merely a symbol of grief ensuing from spiritual separation from God. Their figurative rhetoric was hazardous: after all, Shinn reasoned, if there was no lake of liquid fire, how could there be a heavenly city whose streets were paved with gold? He called for a return to a doctrine of hell. Hell was not only a scriptural promise, it was also consistent with what he called the 'law of retribution'. As Shinn explained it:

The appeals to fear [within the Church] have well nigh ceased, and yet there is no fact which we are so compelled to see as the fact of retribution. The law of retribution works in our present life. We have become aware of it in our earliest infancy, and we never become developed in character until we have learned to fear that which is evil and to shun the consequences of sin. There is a great sense of righteousness in all men, and all men know that unrighteousness brings punishment. It is fair to assume that what holds good in the present life . . . will continue hereafter.

In other words, people were free to jettison the idea of a material hell, but they were unable to escape an inbred fear of retribution for wrongdoing. Appealing to fear was not only legitimate but was 'in accordance with the structure of man's nature'. Inciting the fear of hell might be 'distasteful' but it was a duty for all preachers: 'incorrigible souls' needed the terror of hell in order to repent of their evil ways. In fact, Shinn believed, it was misguided to assume that people's consciences were receptive to appeals to their better nature: 'the fact has been overlooked that the better nature is often hidden from sight by the encrustation of worldliness and sin', he grimly insisted. The pulpit 'was losing some of its power because it so seldom appealed to healthy fear'.[82]

Shinn's summons to a 'healthy fear' of a netherworld proffering eternal physical suffering failed to engage the modern conscience. Graveside rites progressively renounced the rhetoric of fear and judgement, highlighting instead the love of God and hope for the fulfilment of His covenant with humanity. As early as 1884, the burial service for Methodists added a prayer describing the afterlife as characterised by 'joy and felicity' and asking for 'perfect consummation and bliss, both in body and soul, in thy eternal and everlasting glory'. Even more decisively, in 1916 they altered their 'Order for the Burial of the Dead', excising mention of worms and God's wrath and introducing words of comfort to the bereaved.[83] This latter shift was partly a response to the death-fest of the First World War, which hurled more cold water into the chasm of hell. The unprecedented number of young men of all classes and religious backgrounds who were slaughtered during that conflict reduced the propensity of clergymen to thunder about hellfire.

Dying, burial and the nature of any afterlife were potent themes in moral education. But there was increasing uncertainty about the exact message. The mumbled prayers of clergy and the clumsy ministrations of the newly professionalised medical trade failed to provide individuals with that sense of transcendence desired by the dying. The efficacy of exhortations to fear God's omnipresence and omnipotence waned, along with the terror of hellfire, but what replaced it was no less terrifying. A fear of 'nothingness' replaced the fear of God's judgement. Death came to be feared merely as the existential void of non-identity. Or even worse. In 1944 an article in the *American Journal of Sociology* fretted over the fear of the 'nothingness' of death, lamenting that

> this nothing is still something . . . It fits no scheme; it is beyond our reach. It deprives us of our trust in any order. It is not absolute nothingness but absolute 'otherness'. It would not be frightening if it were 'nothing'. It is frightening because it is still 'something' — though not to be known.[84]

In other words, the secular vision of 'nothingness' was only temporarily comforting: it was the fear of the unknown that made death so frightening.[85]

Nevertheless, secularism had left its mark. Fewer and fewer people felt the need to appeal to a deity in attempts to calm fears and anxieties. More were willing to consign their bodies to the flames in *this* life: by 1967 cremations in England outnumbered burials.[86] The dead no longer had anything to fear from the inferno. More to the point, perhaps, many people began to turn to extra-religious sources for information on the afterlife. People who claimed 'after-death experiences' attracted curious crowds.[87] The thunderous rhetoric of theologians in the late nineteenth and early twentieth centuries was exchanged for a domesticated and sentimental vision of 'out of body survival'. Death's border was disrupted once again, but the active agents were all too obviously non-metaphysical. Death was neither transcendent nor transgressive, but subjected to banal clichés or, at best, a new range of scientific and psychological codes.

Fears of the weakening body and hapless soul continue to prick the modern conscience. As we shall see later in this book, the border between life and death remains unfixed. In recent times fears about being 'wrongly obliged to stay alive' have been substituted for the fear of being 'wrongly buried'. However, although many people still suffer the indignity of a burial in an unmarked, communal grave (today, for instance, around three thousand people a year are given a 'city burial' in Potter's Field, Hart Island, the Bronx),[88] it did not develop into a panic. The late twentieth century may have seen a hushing of talk about what the individual might encounter after death, but popular conviction that there simply 'must be something' continued to be accepted. In the 1980s around 70 per cent of Americans still believed in life after death.[89] In many religious circles this fear of death continued to be viewed as part of God's inheritance to humanity. In other words, death anxiety was the language that separated humans from animals. As an Episcopalian sermon in 1960 put it, the fear of death was evidence of 'man's primal hunger for a life that runs beyond death. If our very nature told us that death is the end of our being, we should accept it as casually as the dog accepts it. But our nature seems to tell us something — hence our anxiety.' God would not have given humans 'a hunger that is all for nothing'.[90] To be human was to be anxious.

CHAPTER TWO

Disasters

All that exists
Matters to man; he minds what happens
And feels he is at fault, a fallen soul
With power to place, to explain every
What in his world but why he is neither
God nor good

AUDEN, 'THE AGE OF ANXIETY'

On the morning of Wednesday 30 December, 1903, the Iroquois Theatre in Chicago could still be described as a 'beautiful temple of drama', its imposing façade a splendid monument to modernism in that most modernist of cities.[1] By that evening its grandeur had been stained with the ashes of six hundred men, women and children incinerated within its walls. A further thousand people survived, albeit with severe physical and emotional scars. The 'most perfect theatre in America', which had opened to great fanfare only one month previously, had fallen victim to fire, poor safety facilities and, most ominously, mass panic among its terrified audience.

The fire started during a matinee performance of the 'glorious scenic extravaganza' of *Mr Blue Beard*, starring the vaudeville comedian Eddie Foy (dressed in drag) and Annabelle Whitford (famous for her Butterfly Dance). At 3.15 the stage had just been darkened for the popular tune 'Let Us Swear by the Pale Moonlight', when a

floodlight ignited the drapery. Sheets of flame shot into the audience, scorching everyone in their path. Ushers and other theatre
personnel had no idea what to do. The fireman on duty was
equipped with nothing more than a couple of tubes of a patent
powder called Kilfyres, which made no impression on the flames.
The fire curtain was probably not fireproof, and anyway it got stuck.

In terror, some people jumped to their death from the balcony
and gallery, but the majority of those who died were crushed in the
scramble for the exits. The carnage was made worse by the fact
that all the lights had been turned off for the song and, in the panic,
no one thought to turn them on again. People stumbled on the
steps and fell; crowds behind trampled on their bodies. The exits
were obscured. Indeed, some of the emergency exits were not even
open. The doors jammed.

Of the 1900 people in the audience, six hundred were killed. At
the time it was the worst theatre fire in the history of America, and
gleaned a higher number of charred corpses than the Great Chicago
Fire of 1871. Despite overwhelming evidence of flagrant abuse of
fire regulations, the only person eventually imprisoned was a tavern
keeper whose saloon had been used as a temporary morgue. He had
plundered the dead.

Tragedies such as this forced individuals and communities to confront a corporeal, material and moral threat. An inquiry into what
happened at the Iroquois Theatre described the panic in apocalyptic
tones, typical of disaster reportage at the fin de siècle. The 'frenzied
mass of humanity' ended up 'fighting like demons incarnate':

Purses, wraps, costly furs were cast aside in that mad rush. Mothers
were torn from their children, husbands from their wives. No hold,
however strong, could last against the awful, indescribable crush!
Strong men who sought to the last to sustain their feminine companions were swept away like straws, thrown to the floor and
trampled into unconsciousness in the twinkling of an eye. Women to
whom the safety of their children was more than their own lives had
their little ones torn from them and buried under the mighty sweep
of humanity, moving onward by intuition rather than through exercise of thought to the various exits. They in turn were swept in

before their wails died on their lips — some to safety, others to an unspeakably horrible death . . . With prayers, curses and meaningless shrieks of terror all faced their fate like rats in a trap.[2]

No one could buy themselves out of the disaster. Expensive clothes were no protection against insurmountable danger. Gender roles were rendered insignificant: no chivalrous determination could protect delicate womanhood; no maternal passion could safeguard the young. The crowd was inhuman, death inevitable.

Ultimately such disasters struck individuals as bewildering events: unexpected, undeserved and incomprehensible. 'Why me?' was the frightened refrain. Yet nothing was more certain than threat. Danger lurked everywhere: it waited in the centre of the thunderstorm or at the base of the earthquake, it was woven into the fabric of domestic cushions and theatre curtains, it was even present in the new symbol of modernity, the motor car, rust piercing a single bolt in the brakes. It was the seemingly random nature of disaster that scared people most of all. Coping with swift terror depended upon a range of factors, including the precise nature of the threat, the amount of warning given, the extent to which preparations could be made to limit devastation, familial and institutional supports, and the immensity of destruction visited upon the survivors. At its worst, the 'often primitive, ambiguous or inchoate' nature of sudden disasters stripped people of language and the ability to construct meaning from events.[3] A poem, written in the same year as the Iroquois Theatre disaster, epitomised the hysterical pornography of such 'panic-speak':

> Hush! Hear the despair of humans,
> The wail of mother and wife,
> The shrieks of girls and children
> As they rush in frantic strife.
> See Mothers clasping offsprings,
> Then reeling to the floors,
> 'Mid fumes of smoke and burning,
> All trying to make for the doors.
> The Children young and weaklings,

    Are trampled under foot,
    As the howling mob now charges
    On doors that are surely shut.
    The Cries, the prayers, entreaties,
    Are hushed as with a pall,
    For there five hundred bodies,
    Lie piled in the fiery hall![4]

As a consequence, the great bogey of disasters was panic — not individual hysteria, but the more sickening madness of the mob.

In the late nineteenth and early twentieth centuries, people were more obsessed by fears about the crowd than at any time since the French Revolution. The troubling propensity of people within groups to panic at the slightest hint of danger was partly a response to an important shift in the meaning given to social scourges: the spectre of disaster had almost imperceptibly slipped away from its religious moorings and gradually metamorphosed into something profane and humanistic. Rather than signalling a rupture between humanity and the Deity, disaster now manifested the frailty of scientific knowledge and practices.

The older interpretation of disaster may be illustrated by a penny pamphlet titled *Disasters on Sea and Land* (1881). The anonymous author's main contention was that calamities were always 'permitted by an All Wise Providence' as moral instruction and 'awful warnings to us of the uncertainty of this transitory life'. He illustrated his argument about the didactic function of disasters by referring to recent tragedies at the Tay Bridge (near Dundee) and at the opera house in Nice. According to this author, the collapse of the Tay Bridge two days after Christmas in 1879 was God's retort to a blasphemous nation. At 7.13 in the evening on this Sabbath, one of the most famous bridge disasters occurred. At the time, the bridge was the longest in the world; designed by Thomas Bouch (who was knighted for his efforts), it was an engineering triumph. The two-mile-long bridge had been opened only nineteen months earlier. On the evening of the tragedy, gale force winds caused the central navigation spans to collapse just as the six-carriage train from Edinburgh was crossing. All seventy-five passengers, locked into their carriages, drowned in the Firth of Tay.

The author of *Disasters on Sea and Land* drew attention to what he regarded as the 'true' import of the calamity. The author observed that:

> The *strongest part* of a structure that was looked upon as one of the wonders of the world — one of the triumphs of man's skill and art, and supposed to be equal to all its requirements, and to be strong enough to resist the strain of wind and tide, and to bear the wear and tear of years — was destroyed in a moment, as it were, and with it a train and its human freight.

Evidently God intended a lesson to be learned. The disaster was a momentous reminder of the fragility of the human physique and technical skill, but it was also a summons to the Cross. After all, the author insisted, it was no coincidence that the violent events occurred on a Sunday. The victims on the train were violating the Fourth Commandment. In the author's words, the disaster

> might not have happened — humanly speaking — if the trains had not been running on a Sabbath; because, although it blew a most unusual gale that evening, still the structure might have remained firm . . . had not the vibrations of the train taken place; and GOD, in whose Hands are the 'Wind and the sea and they obey Him', knew also all that would happen, and might not have allowed it, had His Day been duly observed.

As 1 Samuel 2:30 decreed: 'Them that honour me, I will honour, and they that despise Me shall be lightly esteemed.'

In case his readers needed further proof of God's omnipresence, the author of *Disasters on Sea and Land* was even less restrained when describing the terrible panic and agonising deaths of patrons of the opera house in Nice when it burned down on 23 March 1881, killing forty-six patrons. 'What an awful scene that must have been,' he wrote,

> What if such a thing happened to any of us? HOW WOULD YOU LIKE TO DIE IN AN OPERA HOUSE? Even supposing that you

were what the world calls religious, would you be in a fit state to
enter upon the unseen state? That future state of either everlasting
joy or (!) unutterable woe and anguish and gnashing of teeth *'where
the worm dieth not and the fire is not quenched'* (St. Mark ix.44) . . . *I
put it to the conscience of everyone that reads this* whether [an opera
house] is a place where you can go, and ask God's blessing upon, and
if it is acting consistently to go there, after praying 'lead us *not* into
temptation but *deliver us from evil!*' but rather the reverse.

According to this author, no Christian could righteously exchange
'everlasting joy' for the 'fleeting pleasures of sin'. The miserable
men and women trapped in the fiery inferno at Nice were God's sacrifice, warning all good Christians of the need to follow Him in all
dreams and deeds.[5]

The author of *Disasters on Sea and Land* was speaking a language of
calamity that was discredited by a rising generation of disaster
experts who adopted a self-consciously scientific language of experimentation and probabilities to talk about disaster. Indeed, even the
examples the anonymous author in 1881 chose to illustrate his argument had already been at the forefront of the energies of these
experts. After all, the Tay Bridge disaster shook Britain's engineering elite and eventually led to a greater codification of building
regulations and improvements in devices to measure winds.
Scientific speech and the rhetoric of risk had already supplanted the
didactic language of the pulpit. Instead of waiting for bridges to
collapse or people to be burned alive in opera houses, structural
engineers and social psychologists were employed to *predict* the
effectiveness of design and the psychology of crowds in danger.
Experimental procedures in laboratories meant that designs could be
tested well before they were built; psychological observation offered
ways of forecasting and preventing panics. Anxiety about the rend-
ing of ties between humanity and God was replaced by trepidation
about the place of humanity in *this* world, particularly that of groups
massing in dangerous urban spaces.

The insurance business, fire services and engineering industry
were central to this shift. These professionals were not only crucial
to urban growth but were also mindful of fears spawned by hasty

urban sprawl. For instance, in America in 1880 around fourteen million people lived in cities. By 1920 city dwellers totalled more than
fifty-four million, or more than half of America's population. City
boundaries also increased dramatically. In 1899 the city area of
Chicago increased from 36 to 170 square miles. The implication of
such growth for the management of crowds was obvious to these
new professional groups.

They regarded panic as inevitable (and therefore impossible to
prevent) when people confronted danger, but were convinced that
it was feasible to reduce the catastrophic effects of a mass panic.
Despite major differences between these groups, they shared a tendency to regard panic as a structural problem. For them, 'structure
dictated psychology'. Although their work was carried out on an ad
hoc basis, as responses to individual tragedies rather than reflecting
an encompassing theory of panic-abatement (which did not occur
until the threat of nuclear holocaust during the Cold War made it
imperative, as we shall see in Chapter Nine), their efforts were
gradually incorporated into a coherent body of legislation.

A typical example of the response of these professional groups to
disaster can be seen by examining the tragedy at the Victoria Hall in
Sunderland, England. On Saturday 16 June, 1883, Mr A. Foy and his
wife stepped on to the stage to entertain 1200 local children with a
bewitching pageant involving conjuring, marionettes and prancing
wax figures. Within minutes the children, aged between three and
fourteen, were open-mouthed with wonder. They were also nervous with anticipation, each having been promised an individual prize
at the end of the performance (according to the ticket, it was to be
'The Greatest Treat for Children Ever Given'). It was as a consequence of their heightened emotions that, as the show concluded,
things suddenly went terribly wrong. One of the conjurer's assistants
had just gathered up the prizes and was proceeding to the gallery,
where most of the children were sitting. Not seeing him, hundreds
of children from the gallery jumped off their seats and began stream-
ing down the stairs determined to grab their prizes directly from the
stage. What no one realised was that half-way down the landing
there was a wooden swing door that had become locked with a
heavy iron bolt. Some of the children tripped and fell against this

door. Those behind, panicking that they were going to be denied a prize, pushed forward. Within minutes 183 children had been crushed to death. Corpses of infants and children were piled twenty deep.[6] One of the prizes being fought over was found later — a little wounded horse with two missing legs.[7] Devastated parents listened while Queen Victoria's letter of condolence was read out at funeral services. The Queen enjoined parents to recall the biblical text: 'Suffer little children to come unto me, for such is the Kingdom of God'.[8]

Such a deity would not thwart further disasters. How could it be prevented from happening again? Against the wails of mothers, fathers and siblings, the cool logic of the engineers was heard. The panic of children was accepted as inevitable: instead, inappropriate structural safeguards were blamed. In the case of the Victoria Hall in Sunderland, the swing door with its bolt (which could have been either deliberately or accidentally locked) transformed a simple mis-understanding into a death-dealing panic. In the case of the Iroquois Theatre in Chicago, the role of engineers in improving safety pro-cedures was even more direct: hardware salesman Carl Prinzler had a ticket for the fateful performance but was unable to attend at the last moment. After the tragedy, Prinzler and two colleagues devised the first 'panic-release bar' for doors 'in response to a need for pro-tecting life safety while providing security'.[9] Structural engineers and salesmen had a central role to play in managing urban panics.

These experts had a large stake in dangers such as mass panics and public blazes. It was no coincidence that the British Fire Prevention Committee, a body of architects, surveyors and engineers dedi-cated to fire prevention, was founded in 1896. William Paul Gerhard was a typical example of a disaster specialist at the turn of the century. He was a consultant engineer and a member of both the American Institute of Architects and the British Fire Prevention Committee. In 1899 he published *The Safety of Theatre Audiences and the Stage Personnel Against Danger from Fire and Panic*, which focused on eliminating, or at the very least reducing, the death toll resulting from theatre fires. According to Gerhard, in the nineteenth century nearly ten thousand people in Britain had been killed as a result of these.

Speed of evacuation was at the heart of preventing carnage. Because it took only five minutes from the start of a blaze in a crowded theatre for people to start dying, audiences had to be able to flee the building within three to four minutes if they were to survive. Although a sufficient number of exits was crucial, attention also had to be paid to the size of the seats and their arrangement, the width and number of aisles, the location of foyers, lighting, the dimensions and construction of staircases, the direction in which doors opened and the location of fire escapes. Fire drills and other ways of familiarising staff and audiences with what to do in an emergency were also essential.

Nevertheless, Gerhard admitted that such physical safeguards would not prevent panics from *ever* occurring. Indeed, he was convinced that they were inevitable, in part because it was 'well known to many theatre visitors' that 'it requires but a few minutes in a burning building for the smoke and fire gases to suffocate people'. In his words, knowledge about the danger of theatre fires 'explains the terror, the wild fright, the haste and confusion, the loss of both courage and presence of mind, the dangerous stampedes, the mad struggles at the exit doors, the trampling to death, and the jam following a panic'. The 'instinct of self-preservation often drives people even to kill one another'. However, if audiences could be made aware of the planning that had gone into ensuring their safety in case of fire, they might react more sensibly, even if this 'feeling of security' could never compensate for sloppy architectural design.[10]

But engineers and lobbyists did not easily persuade theatre owners. After all, disaster experts already recognised that the fire at the Iroquois Theatre would not have occurred if its managers had not bribed fire inspectors with free tickets to ignore safety infringements. Concerns over panic in public spaces were increasingly regarded as too important to be left to the good intentions and shallow pockets of entertainment capitalists. Increasingly, this generation of disaster experts demanded greater centralised regulation of public space, and this regulation was explicitly modelled on factory legislation. One of the most vocal proponents of regulation was John Ripley Freeman, President of the American Society of Mechanical Engineers and President of the Manufacturers' Rhode

Island and Mechanics Mutual Fire Insurance Companies of Providence. In 1906, at the annual meeting of the Society in New York City, Freeman made the point that theatres should be regulated in much the same way as factories. He was appalled by the low standards of safety within theatres and auditoriums, insisting that such conditions 'would not be tolerated by the managers of our best industrial works'. He reminded his listeners that it was still legal in Boston to install sprinkler pipes that had to be opened by hand during a fire. Indeed, a few months after the Iroquois Theatre tragedy, aldermen had actually rescinded the rule calling for automatic sprinklers in theatres because managers believed that they 'wouldn't do any good' and 'might start a panic should one happen to open prematurely'. In Freeman's words:

> Most dangerous of all, I have found behind the scenes and in the mechanics' rooms a lack of the scrupulous neatness and order that characterizes a modern, well-organized factory; have found a multitude of dark, concealed spaces used as catch-alls, and an apparent lack of appreciation by owners and architect that a *flood of daylight in storerooms, workrooms and dressing-rooms is the best of all safeguards*, by making dirt, disorder and dangerous rubbish conspicuous. While there are notable exceptions, the atmosphere of the theatre is largely of show and tinsel, and this contributes to the less thorough-going standards of neatness and completeness than in the factory.

He insisted that the ethos of order, cleanliness and efficiency had to be applied to the entertainment business, as it was to manufacturing. It was not enough for the law to prescribe the width of stairways (at the Iroquois Theatre, the gallery's exits were 100 per cent wider than the law required, yet nearly three-quarters of the audience in the gallery were killed in the fire).[11] Instead, full-scale legislative intervention in all aspects of the entertainment business was necessary to 'tame' the masses in the case of catastrophe.

Crowds of mobile people only became a 'terrorised mob' if architecture made them so by providing insufficient escape routes. This was a theme dominating 'panic-speak' at the turn of the century. It was regarded as especially important in cinemas, theatres and sports

stadiums because these were the places where the emotions were
stirred. Here human emotions were deliberately manipulated and,
critically, these sites attracted a disproportionate number of people
from the lower orders — that is, people regarded as emotionally less
developed by these experts. If the emotions were to be subdued, the
physical structures around people had to be designed in a way that
would reduce the risk of disaster and ensure that, if disaster struck,
the movements of the victims would fall naturally into a pre-
ordained pattern. By the end of the nineteenth century there were
greater calls for state intervention in the emotional management of
crowds, through spatial reorganisation. The inevitability of disaster — and thus the certainty of severe fear reactions — encouraged
disaster experts to experiment with a different construction of
power: physical architecture. In contrast to the Freudians, who
believed that fear was lodged behind the superficial veneer of the
conscious mind, these disaster experts insisted that the emotions
themselves possessed an architecture. According to this view, it was
not necessary to root out subconscious fears, since individuals lacking internal constraints in dangerous situations could be controlled
through the imposition of external restraints.

In contrast to the calculations and measurements of engineers, architects and insurance brokers, the burgeoning profession of social
psychology was predicated on the belief that only by understanding
the unique psychology of individuals could science predict how
people would behave in disasters and actually prevent panic erupt-
ing in the first instance. Part of this project involved categorising
people according to their propensity to panic. As we have already
seen, children were regarded as particularly susceptible to panic.
This was brought out in the report of a fire at a cinema in Paisley,
Scotland, in 1929 where seventy children between the ages of two
and sixteen were killed in a stampede. An editorial in *The Times* was
not surprised that the children failed to act 'appropriately'. 'It was
not to be expected that 700 young children, with hardly an adult to
control them, could keep calm in face of such a sudden and terrifying alarm,' the piece observed, continuing:

Naturally they all struggled for the doors farthest from the appearance of the smoke. The manager strove desperately to get some of
them to come back and go out by the other doors which had been
flung open; but that would have meant passing through the smoke,
and in their frenzy the poor little creatures could pay no heed. They
crowded blindly and pitifully to their deaths . . . A few cool and res-
olute persons can prevent [panic] in the case of a fire in a theatre
filled with adults; but when children — to whom the mere word
fire is particularly terrifying — are assembled in hundreds in a confined space, they will not always be amenable to the calming voice if
once they see smoke bursting out.[12]

Gender too played a large role in explaining panics. According to
commentators influenced by 'crowd theory' (of which more later),
the 'mass' was feminine and thus liable to hysteria and panic.[13] In the
nineteenth century attention focused upon innate physiological
weaknesses. In 1871 Dr M. Roth produced a long list of the type of
person predisposed to extreme states of fear, and included 'women
during periods of catamenia, pregnancy, confinement, of secretion
of milk and excretion of lochia', people whose 'mental education
has been conducted on false principles', alcoholics, masturbators
and those suffering sexual excesses. In some cases, he observed, it
was a hereditary condition.[14] By the twentieth century it was admitted that cultural norms meant that women were permitted to show
fear, unlike men.[15] Men who expressed fear reactions in disasters
were much more liable to be stigmatised by it in later times. In a
report on reactions to an earthquake, W. G. Slade admitted that
women's innate weakness made them more liable to express fear or
panic reactions, but he noted that men were not wholly innocent of
similar reactions. However, men who behaved in an hysterical and
panic-stricken manner were 'held up to ridicule' and the other
earthquake victims 'stigmatized them with contempt'. Men were
also less likely to admit to feeling frightened in interviews after the
disaster — it was only in private and intimate conversations that
they felt able to admit that they had been seriously unnerved.[16]

Class and ethnicity became crucial signifiers of proneness to panic
in nearly all disaster reportage. For instance, when the steamship *San*

Francisco sank in 1854, the *New York Times* distinguished between 'ladies' and 'camp women', or working-class women following soldiers ('camp followers'). According to this report, some of the passengers

> were praying. The children were screaming lustily, but the ladies were almost universally calm. The camp women, however, were shrieking a great deal, but the ladies were clinging to each other and the little ones, and were calm and speechless.[17]

Similarly, popular accounts of the sinking of the *Titanic* in 1912 accused certain 'foreign' male passengers of attempting to storm the boats. Interestingly, it was the 'emotional' and 'excitable' Italians who were singled out for criticism whereas an 'inscrutable' Japanese passenger, rescued from the ocean, was described as acting 'like a hero' and his rowing exploits caused other survivors to watch 'in open-mouthed surprise'.[18] Working-class occupants of steerage accommodation were also accused of acting in a 'disorderly' fashion as the ship sank. Unlike wealthier passengers, who were said to have acted with self-restraint and chivalry, men from the steerage class were described by the *New York Times* as 'determined to save their own precious lives in spite of the orders to let the women and children go first'.[19] No account was taken of resource allocations that exacerbated the plight of steerage passengers, who were disadvantaged in terms of escape routes, the number of crew members guiding them to safety and basic information about what was happening. Rather than ascribing the panic of steerage passengers to their greater cynicism about how much their so-called superiors valued their lives, the report regarded the perceived lack of self-control of these passengers as inherent to their ethnic and class-based place in society.

A long tradition in the social sciences provided theoretical bases for such generalisations based on ethnicity and class. Evolutionary classifications enabled some commentators to ascribe different levels of emotional 'control' according to the 'primitiveness' of a group of people. From the quantity, quality and variety of their fears one could ascertain a group's position within evolutionary stages of development. For instance, according to Josiah Morse in *The Psychology and Neurology of Fear* (1907), 'the snail fears more than the amoeba, the chick fears more than the snail, the ape more than the chick, and primitive man most of all; but with civilized man the fear curve begins to drop rapidly, or rather physical, animal fear gives place to the higher spiritual and human fears'.[20] In even more blunt terms, William Charles Loosmore of Glasgow University argued in *Ourselves and Our Emotions* (1928) that primitive races expressed more fear than civilised ones. He hastened to add that this was not because primitive man *felt* 'more deeply' but because 'he has not acquired the art of self-control as we have'.[21] In the words of another psychologist, writing in the 1940s, 'primitive defense-reactions' were 'encountered mostly among people on the lowest rung of training and civilization' or among children and the mentally 'degenerated'.[22]

For some commentators the increased propensity of certain races to panic was actually inscribed on their body. In the Afterword to the Introduction to this book, we looked at the belief of some scientists that emotional expressions were encoded in the facial muscles — either because the Great Creator 'willed it' (as Duchenne believed) or through evolutionary processes (as Charles Darwin insisted). This view was taken up by men like Ernst Huber, Associate Professor of Anatomy at Johns Hopkins University and author of *Evolution of Facial Musculature and Facial Expression* (1931), to explain the propensity of African Americans to panic, and their lack of the 'nobler' emotions. According to his inspection of cadavers in dissecting rooms around America, the facial muscles of African Americans were 'much coarser' than those of white Americans. These muscular differences had a profound effect on emotional expression. While white Americans had 'responsive faces' which were capable of serving as 'an admirable index of character or mental state', African American faces lacked this capability. Their 'thick skin', thickly graded nerve impulses and 'less differentiated, coarsely bundled mimetic musculature' rendered them incapable of expressing sensitive or 'civilised' emotions.

According to Huber, this inability of African Americans to *express* emotions also meant that they were incapable of *possessing* these emotions. He believed that 'the elaboration of facial expression during the phylogeny of man closely followed the evolution of emotional life'. The 'primitive' facial muscles of African Americans were simply a reflection of their primitive emotions. Noble facial expression was absent, while the neck muscle (the one which Duchenne identified as the 'fear muscle') was particularly well developed in the African American face, providing further evidence for Huber's assumption that African Americans were at a lower stage of evolution compared with white Americans and were susceptible to fright.[23] Discussions about the racial nature of fear provided a way to identify a threatening 'other' within society during any particular period.

But there were other theorists who insisted that everyone was liable to panic in the presence of calamity. These commentators were influenced by crowd theorists such as the French psychologist Gustave Le Bon in *La Psychologie des foules* (1895) (translated into English as *The Crowd*, 1896). This book was one of the most influential in social psychology at the time and had a major influence on psychiatrists such as Sigmund Freud (most notably in his *Group Psychology and the Analysis of the Ego*) and historians such as George Rudé (especially in his *The Crowd and the French Revolution*).[24] In response to crowd violence in France in 1789, 1830, 1848 and during the Third Republic, Le Bon developed the theme that individuals reacted differently when they were in a crowd than they did when alone. In a crowd the 'group mind' took over, bestowing individuals with a sense of power and irresponsibility. Group solidarity led to a return to primitive forms of behaviour, and emotions swung deep and wide through a process of emotional contagion. The crowd was easily frightened and always violent: unless controlled by a powerful leader, it would wreak political, social and economic havoc. In the words of Wilfred Trotter, Britain's most eminent crowd theorist, the individual was 'subjected to the passions of the pack in his mob violence and the passions of the herd in his panics'.[25]

In Britain and America these ideas were popularised by the father of functional psychology, William McDougall. According to McDougall, in acute attacks of fear people lost 'all human attributes' and sank 'to the level of pure animal behaviour'.[26] In one of his

influential books, *The Group Mind* (1921), he argued that during disasters everyone's 'instinct of fear'

> is intensely excited; he experiences that horrid emotion in full force
> and is irresistibly impelled to save himself by flight. The terrible
> driving power of this impulse, excited to its highest pitch under the
> favouring conditions, suppresses all other impulses and tendencies,
> all habits of self-restraint, of courtesy and consideration for others,
> and we see men, whom we might have supposed incapable of cruel
> or cowardly behaviour, trampling upon women and children, in
> their wild efforts to escape the burning theatre, the sinking ship, or
> other place of danger.[27]

In the presence of danger, a mass of frightened individuals very
easily transformed themselves into a mob, united by the evocation of
one emotion: fear.

McDougall then reiterated the central observation that individual
psychology was very different from group psychology. In a crowd
emotions were 'stirred to a pitch' that was rarely achieved in other
ways. He elaborated, arguing that crowds were incapable of respect-
ing other people: self-consciousness, restraint, morality and
refinement simply evaporated. Panic was a natural consequence. It
was 'the crudest and simplest example of collective mental life'. In
a crowd emotions such as terror and hatred were literally contagious. McDougall called this the 'principle of primitive sympathy':

> The principle is that, in man and in the gregarious animals generally,
> each instinct, with its characteristic primary emotion and specific
> impulse, is capable of being excited in one individual by the expres-
> sions of the same emotion in another, in virtue of a special congenital
> adaptation of the instinct on its cognitive or perceptual side. In the
> crowd, then, the expressions of fear of each individual are perceived
> by his neighbours; and this perception intensifies the fear directly
> excited in them by the threatening danger. Each man perceives on
> every hand the symptoms of fear, the blanched distorted faces, the
> dilated pupils, the high-pitched trembling voices, and the screams of
> terror of his fellows; and with each such perception his own impulse

and his own emotion rise to a higher pitch of intensity and their expressions become correspondingly accentuated and more difficult to control.

The mob was extraordinarily suggestible.[28]

McDougall's account of the nature of the crowd in disasters was highly influential. It was taken up by a new breed of sociologists who turned their attention to the drama of 'real-life' disasters in order to observe the ways panic-stricken people seemed to revert to a lower state of civilisation by acting in ways that exposed the superficiality of modern emotional management. One of the most astute of these commentators in the early twentieth century was Samuel Prince, a sociologist from King's College London, who studied reactions to a catastrophic shipping disaster in Halifax, Nova Scotia. Halifax was the most important Canadian port on the Atlantic seaboard when, on 6 December 1917, there was a huge explosion. A French munitioner, SS *Mont Blanc*, laden with 2300 tons of wet and dry picric acid (used for making lyddite for artillery shells), two hundred tons of the powerful explosive trinitrotoluene (TNT) and ten tons of gun cotton, along with drums of benzol (high-octane fuel) stacked on the decks, arrived in Halifax from New York. As it was steaming up the harbour, the munitioner collided with SS *Imo*, an empty Norwegian relief ship. The benzol drums broke open and the ship burst into flames. Because of the severity of the fires, the captain ordered all crew to abandon ship, leaving the burning vessel to drift towards Halifax, where it rested against Pier 6. Twenty minutes later, at 9.05, there was a terrifying explosion, which produced a colossal mushroom cloud and caused three thousand tons of sizzling metal to rain down on the city's inhabitants. The blast was followed by raging fires and a man-made tsunami that swept away hundreds of residents, including an entire encampment of Micmac, a native American tribe. At the north end of Halifax and part of Dartmouth, nearly two thousand men, women and children were rent asunder, burned to cinders or drowned. Another nine thousand people were injured. Thirty-five million dollars' worth of property was destroyed; 130 hectares were set afire; twenty-five thousand people were left without adequate housing (their misery made worse by the fact that there was a blizzard that evening). It was the largest man-made explosion until the dropping of the bomb at Hiroshima in 1945.

A man near the disaster zone recalled the devastating shock of the calamity:

> It was all of a sudden — a single devastating blast; then the sound as of a thousand chandeliers. Men and women cowered under the shower of debris and glass. There was one awful moment when hearts sank, and breaths were held. Then women cried aloud, and men looked dumbly into each other's eyes, and awaited the crack of doom. To some death was quick and merciful in its coming. Others were blinded, and staggered to an [sic] fro before they dropped. Still others with shattered limbs dragged themselves forth into the light — naked, blackened, unrecognizable human shapes. They lay prone upon the streetside, under the great death-cloud which still dropped soot and oil and water. It was truly a sight to make the angels weep. Men who had been at the front said they had seen nothing so bad at Flanders.[29]

In the town a sense of 'utter helplessness' enveloped many people. 'We died a thousand horrible deaths,' recalled one survivor. 'The nervous shock and terror were as hard to bear as were the wounds.' Many of the survivors seemed dazed: 'they have almost ceased to exercise the sensation of pain', noted one observer. Physiologically, fear made a major impression. As Prince reminded his readers:

> A physiological accompaniment of shock and distraction is the abnormal action of the glands. The disturbance of the sympathetic nervous system produced by the emotional stress and strain of a great excitement or a great disappointment is reflected in the stimulation or inhibition of glandular activity.[30]

He reflected positively on the observations of an eminent physiologist of the emotions, Walter B. Cannon. For Cannon, fear was accompanied by a rush of adrenalin into the blood and the release of glycogen in the liver. These reactions were reflexes rather than 'willed', and they had a purpose — the welfare of the organism. The mobilisation of sugar in the blood energised the muscles for flight and diverted energy from less important activities. Under command of the fear instinct, the activities of the alimentary canal ceased and blood was shifted from the abdominal viscera to the lungs, heart, central nervous system and skeletal muscles. Fear and rage were 'organic preparations'.[31]

In other words, the organic expression of fear was a consequence of humanity's instinctual inheritance. People retreated to more primitive life, Prince insisted. The instinctive tendencies might have been 'buried beneath barriers of civilization' but they were buried alive, 'covered not crushed'. Only in the presence of 'extraordinary catastrophe' would civilisation be revealed for what it was — 'a very thin veneer over the primitive tendencies which have held sway for ages'. Conventionality, custom and law provided very flimsy safeguards. Prince contended that if 'the period of man's residence on earth considered as having covered one hundred thousand years, that of civilization would be represented by the last ten minutes'.[32]

The positive side to the eruption to the surface of primitive instincts was the flourishing of the gregarious instinct. People sought out their families and friends and huddled together for protection and succour. Nevertheless, Prince provided more examples of the negative instinct of 'flight for self-preservation'. Instead of rushing to the rescue of their neighbours and fellow citizens, people let their communal relationships be torn apart by fear. This was seen, for instance, in the behaviour of the ship's crew who leapt into lifeboats and rowed to the shore opposite Halifax, failing to warn people of the approaching danger. In many other ways, Prince noted, the disaster resulted in total collapse of social and community structures: 'the city ceased to be a city, its citizens a mass of unorganized units — struggling for safety, shelter, covering and bread.'[33] People observed the sudden appearance of thieves, looters and ghouls: corpses were desecrated as people scrambled around searching for beer in the shattered breweries; empty homes and shops were plundered; prowlers rifled the pockets of the dead and dying; profiteering soared.

Survivors proved incapable of understanding what was happening. Many hallucinated, their eyes tricking them into seeing German Zeppelins attacking them from the air. A man on the outskirts of the town claimed to have heard a German shell whistling past him. Such visions had been stimulated over the preceding months by rumours of the possibility of a German attack. Residents with German-sounding names were set upon. Some survivors still believed that the Germans had something to do with the disaster. Religious dogma inspired the second kind of hallucination: people were certain that the world had come to an end. They fell to their knees in prayer as Christ's face was observed peering through the clouds.[34] One woman was found reciting the general confession of the Church in her yard. Many of these emotional responses to disaster lasted months or longer. People suffered from 'inexplicable breakdown', which resembled the types of neuroses that had occurred among men in the front lines of battle. Everyone took a long time to settle back to post-disaster life, living 'on the edge' for months. People were highly suggestible and easily scared afresh (on two occasions the schools were emptied when a rumour of danger led parents and children to scatter in 'pell-mell flight'). Prince described the minds of the survivors as being 'blown about by every gust of passion or sentiment'.

Prince's new psychology of disaster stressed the ways in which emotional succour could only be achieved through the reinvention of humanistic myths, particularly those of family and community. This process was frequently not a benign one: an evil 'other' was central to coping with disaster. Hatred dispelled terror. For this reason the reactions of people in disaster were seen by sociologists like Prince as crucial not only for individual survival, but also for the stability of civic society. The psychology of individuals in disasters was a powerful anti-social force. While moderate fear encouraged people to unite, excessive fear or panic had the opposite effect. As one American commentator lamented in 1914, fear was capable of turning people into 'maddened beasts each of whom seeks only his own safety'. Panic 'de-socialised' people.[35] Fear was accused of 'driving the world almost mad, and unless man can recover his sanity and live by his high purpose, civilisation will rush down the slope of fear —

like the Gadarene swine — and destroy itself'.[36] That was why, in
the early years of the twentieth century, these 'disaster experts' set
out to ensure that everything possible was done to promote emotional mastery. Fear must not be allowed to overwhelm people.
Self-control was the mantra of early-twentieth-century emotional
management.

In the early years of the century fear of the panicking urban crowd
threatened society's most cherished attributes: efficiency and
progress. The behaviour of people in times of calamity was the most
powerful evidence for the inextricable link between emotional comportment and morality. Whether it was a small but deadly theatre
fire or, as in Halifax, the biggest man-made explosion before the
nuclear age, groups assumed to be at greatest risk of panic reactions
had to be identified and controlled. Their emotional stability
depended upon the development of new forms of environmental
and architectural shields. These modes of control were applied more
broadly: within democratic states, their techniques in moulding
behaviour were highly efficacious. The dangerous crowd — whether
a theatre throng or a gathering of protesters — could not be effectively repressed, but it could be manipulated and its social or
political 'impulses' subverted. In a world of infinite risks, scientific
tomes written by insurance agents, engineers and social psychologists were forging a balance between profit and safety. Their
calculations seemed convincing — that is, until the unprecedented
threat posed by the prospect of nuclear conflict collapsed the notion
of a 'risk society' in which danger could be calculated and a price tag
fixed. As we will see in a later chapter, the post-modern condition
of fear was much more free-floating than earlier disaster experts had
contemplated.

Afterword to Part One: Emotionology

How can historians study emotional responses to death and disaster? After all, looked at historically, the subjective experience of fear is invisible. How can historians 'know' when people are 'scared' rather than 'angry'? This question has dogged the efforts of people writing about emotional experiences, both in the present and in the past. One interesting response was provided by the psychologist Knight Dunlap of Johns Hopkins University in an article in the *American Journal of Psychology* in 1932. For Dunlap, emotions were nothing more than teleological constructs. According to him, although people spoke about emotions such as fear and anger, they were not psychological entities and possessed no unique affective processes. Searching for 'primary emotions' made as much sense to him as searching for the soul ('and it is a search of the same sort,' he caustically noted).

Dunlap took as one of his examples the emotion 'fear'. He noted that fear involved a wide range of responses, including contradictory ones such as flight and immobility. These responses were not unique to 'fear' but were shared by people experiencing other emotions, including anger and love. Equally, there were no *inner* responses to 'fear' which were not shared by other emotions. Even if the introspective views of the frightened person were accepted as sufficient to label the emotion 'fear' rather than some other emotion, it was obvious that different 'fears' felt very different.

So, Dunlap asked, what do the names of 'the emotions' signify? His answer was ingenious: emotion-words (like 'fear') are nothing more than the situations in which we are emotional. In one circumstance, there is a threat of danger . . . and the emotion I feel in this situation I call 'fear', although the actual emotion may vary. But, hold, wait a bit: I do not always call it 'fear'. Sometimes I call it 'anger'. Yes: but then certain features in my environment are emphasized, which are less conspicuous in the situation in which I call my emotion 'fear'. If a person threatens me, and I emphasize his part in the portended happening I may still 'fear' him, if I admit his greater power. Or I may be 'angry' at him. It all depends on the way I think about the situation, not on the actual state of feeling.

In other words, what made different 'fears' resemble each other more than they resembled various 'angers' was the 'likeliness of the situations in which these states arise, or rather, in the perceptual and ideational apprehension of these situation'. Further, the 'perceptual and ideational apprehension of these situations' varied according to the standpoint of the commentator. A person might evaluate his own feeling when faced with a danger as 'fear', while an outsider might interpret the emotion as 'anger'. And both were correct.[1]

Dunlap was writing as a psychologist, but (independently) some historians have agreed that the answer to the question 'What is fear?' depends as much upon the situation in which the emotion appears as it does on the psychological and philosophical theory of the commentator. In recent years the most useful historical work on the emotions has been done by 'emotionologists'. American scholars such as Peter N. Stearns, Carol Z. Stearns and Jan Lewis have reminded historians of the need to distinguish between the 'collective emotional standards of a society' and subjective feelings.[2] As the Stearns put it in their decisive contribution to the history of the emotions, 'Emotionology: Clarifying the History of Emotions and Emotional Standards' (1985): 'The concept of emotionology is necessary, quite simply, to distinguish between professed values and emotional experience.'[3]

Emotionology aims to show how emotions were classified and recognised within particular cultures. The important questions were 'How is the word "fear" used in cultural contexts?' and 'What are the social norms in the expression of fear?' In their history of anger, Carol and Peter Stearns correctly observed that 'a tantrum in a society that has no word for the phenomenon is a different experience for both parent and child than is a tantrum that is labeled, and labeled with a judgmental connotation'.[4] As the words changed, so too did the meaning of the emotion within a particular culture. According to Ludwig Wittgenstein, 'mental language is rendered significant not by virtue of its capacity to reveal, mark, or describe mental states, but by its function in social interaction'.[5]

For instance, parts of Chapter One adopted an emotionological perspective by interrogating the transformation in the fear of dying by mapping out shifts in the literature of death. In that chapter we saw how, in the nineteenth century, consciousness during the process of dying tended to be regarded as having definite benefits. The terror of dying was God-given, providing the penitent with time to ensure that 'in the day of his decease he shall be blessed'.[6] In contrast, as we will see in Chapter Ten, by the mid-twentieth century fear of pain loomed larger than the fear of the hereafter. Even in the final throes of corporeal existence, 'quality of life' was more important than any advantages that might be achieved by purging the soul.

Emotionologists were careful not to say whether individuals 'really' felt more fear in the process of dying as the century progressed. They simply asked about the rules for displaying the fear of death (was it acceptable or not?), the meaning ascribed to the fear of dying (piety or 'civilised' pain avoidance) and the effect of these rules (levels of sedation and institutional inventions such as the post-1967 hospice movement). They do, however, adopt a social constructivist position, in that language and cultural norms 'constructed' the emotion. Thus the Stearns admitted that 'in the long run, emotionology, by shaping articulate experience, does influence actual emotional experience'.[7] After all, a *belief in* the desirability of experiencing pain in dying profoundly influenced an individual's feelings about pain. But the central focus is in the cultural rules determining the display of fear.

A stronger version of social constructivism posited that emotional norms were both produced and sustained by dominant institutional arrangements. There was no such thing as a 'natural' fear response, only socially assembled ones. This approach received much support from anthropological work that demonstrated that no universal emotional reactions existed. The words used to describe feelings similar to those expressed by the English word 'fear' varied culturally, and this variation profoundly changed that culture's emotional world.[8] For instance, we could rephrase in social constructivist terms the argument in Chapter Two to argue that emotional responses to calamity were 'constructed discursively by particular interpretive communities'. All emotional experiences were filtered by the prevailing emotionology. That chapter examined the shift from regarding calamities as moral instruction and as 'awful warnings to us of the uncertainty of this transitory life' towards its discussion in scientific discourses. To say 'I am afraid of God's wrath' or 'I am afraid of low safety standards' was to experience fundamentally different feelings. The emotion 'fear' was fundamentally different for these groups of people because it was constructed in distinct ways. Humanity could only fear within the context of the discourse of fear, even if, without the emotion-label, there was no emotion.

PART TWO

Spheres of Uncertainty

Introduction

Anyone who has attempted to reassure a scared child, endured a nightmare or suffered a phobic attack knows the difficulties involved in understanding *why* we become frightened for 'no good reason' and why it is such a painful emotion. The next three chapters examine some of the competing scientific explanations for emotional responses such as fear. In particular, evolutionary psychology, psychoanalysis, behaviourism and neurology provide bold, yet conflicting formulas for interpreting people's fears. They do agree on one thing, however: religious constructions of fear (as discussed in the previous two chapters) are resoundingly ousted. Nightmares, for instance, are not caused by devils pressing upon the sleeper's chest, but can be explained in terms of human physiology, racial memories, unconscious conflicts or the random undulations of brain waves. Whatever approach is taken, the scientific mind seeks objective evidence of fear, even if this entails deliberately fostering it.

In Chapter Three an eleven-month-old child called 'Albert B' becomes the subject of a scientific attempt to purposefully create a phobia in an otherwise normal child. At other times a pre-existing dread (such as the fear in some children of going to school) is simply redefined, effectively inventing a new affliction (such as school phobia) that can be cured by a burgeoning population of school psychologists and child guidance professionals. Cure was crucial and the treatments could be remarkably radical. Freud believed that five-year-old 'Little Hans' could be gently talked out of his phobic fears of horses and the street; but a young mother, 'Marsha', was cured of her violent anxieties by being made to relive her fears in terrifying detail and fourteen-year-old 'O.T.' had part of her brain cut away to make her less timorous. More usually, scientific attempts to understand and manipulate people's fears tell us a great deal about emotional management more generally within society: authoritarian versus egalitarian responses to scared individuals reflect contrasting meditations on the future. Indisputably, though, uncontested 'truth' about fear is always elusive.

CHAPTER THREE

The Child

Behold the infant, helpless in cradle and
Righteous still, yet already there is
Dread in his dreams at the deed of which
He knows nothing but knows he can do,
The gulf before him with guilt beyond.

AUDEN, 'THE AGE OF ANXIETY'

The infant has no verbal language as a conduit for emotional
expression. Nevertheless, physical signs of terror were utilised
by one of the most famous infants in the modern history of psychology. Eleven-month-old 'Albert B' was the son of one of the
wetnurses at the Harriet Lane Hospital in Baltimore and had lived
his entire life within its walls.[1] He was described as a 'good baby'
who never cried — at least not until eminent psychologist John B.
Watson began experimenting on him.

In 1920 Watson and Rosalie Rayner systematically set out to teach
Albert to be deeply afraid of furry animals and objects. In the weeks
before their experiments Albert had been presented with a white
rat. Each day the rat would be taken from a basket and given to
Albert, who would spend long periods playing with it. This routine
was abruptly changed when Albert was eleven months and three
days old. Henceforth, whenever Albert reached out to grab his
playmate, Watson would energetically strike a steel bar with a

carpenter's hammer immediately behind Albert's head. The first time he did this Albert 'jumped violently and fell forward, burying his face in the mattress'. On the second occasion he began to whimper. Albert was so 'disturbed' that the researchers desisted from further tests for a week.

It was only a brief respite. When Albert was eleven months and ten days old, the rat was once again presented to him but he refused to touch it. When Albert was given the rat for a second time, Watson once again struck the steel bar immediately behind his head. Albert was 'startled, then fell over immediately to right side'. The third and fourth time Albert 'fell to right side and rested on hands with head turned from rat'. On the fifth occasion Watson presented Albert with the rat without sounding the steel bar, but Albert made a 'puckered face, whimpered and withdrew body sharply to the left'. Again and again Watson tested the infant, sometimes with the noise and other times with the rat alone. On the eighth occasion Albert began to wail the moment he spied the rat and 'almost instantly he turned sharply to the left, fell over, raised himself on all fours and began to crawl away so rapidly that he was caught with difficulty before he reached the edge of the mattress'.

Watson's delight at Albert's terror was augmented when he discovered that Albert had developed a fear of a *range* of furry animals and objects. A rabbit that Albert used to cherish was now greeted with whimpering, tears and avoidance behaviours. A familiar dog made him shrink away. The sight of a fur coat had Albert once again attempting to crawl away as quickly as possible. Watson and Rayner had succeeded in conditioning an 'undifferentiated emotional state' (in this case, of fear) in the one-year-old. According to them, undifferentiated emotional states were typical of infancy and early youth, but Watson insisted that 'many adults, especially women, remain in it. All primitive peoples remain in it (superstitions etc.). But educated adults by the long training they get in manipulating objects, handling animals, working with electricity, etc., reach the second or differentiated state of the conditioned emotional reaction.'

Watson believed that, with more time, he could have conditioned Albert to fear white rats alone, as opposed to furry animals and objects more generally. Nevertheless, he was pleased by the ease with which the previously fearless Albert could be reduced to a whimpering coward within a few weeks. As a result of Watson's success in concocting fear in young Albert, 'conditioning' became the foundation stone of behaviourism. It was Watson's 'prolific goose for laying golden eggs' because it yielded 'an explanatory principle that will account for the enormous complexity in the emotional behavior of adults'. In accounting for such behaviour, 'we no longer . . . have to fall back on heredity'. Behaviourism was an ideology that was in harmony with the democratic *Zeitgeist* of the time: discriminatory environments corrupted the basic equality of all individuals. Poor Albert's emotional fragility was a result of his environment, not his heredity.[2]

Albert's mother left the hospital shortly after these experiments, so Watson and Rayner were unable to continue their experiments on the infant. Nevertheless, their tests demonstrated the fact that the most vulnerable of humanity were infants. Before birth, their fate may already be sealed. Throughout the centuries pregnancy remained a period of vague trepidation for many women precisely because of the burden of their unique biological inheritance. The proliferation of theories about the impact of a woman's physiology and emotions during pregnancy meant that it was a period of her life most likely to be beset by fears. Even after the safe birth of the infant, fears and anxieties abounded. Frightened children could not be ignored. Their fears were legion. Will swallowing pips cause a tree to grow out of my mouth? Will I wet my bed? Will the man in the moon come down and take me, or my mother, away? Will my parents love my little brother more than me? Will my home disappear while I am at school? What lurks in the dark? Will lightning kill me? What happens when I die? Their cries were distressingly audible and the degree to which they could disrupt adult interaction boundless.

In contrast, the responses of parents and other people responsible for caring for children were more limited. Children had to either face their fears or be shielded from them; they had to become confident of their own courage or made to feel secure. Over the centuries a range of patronising, cajoling or imperturbable experts claimed to be able to decode those fears expressed in the howls and lisping tongues of the young. In their efforts, what became most audible, however, was not the fears of children, but those of their parents.

Even before birth, the foetus was threatened by its mother's emotions. The belief that a pregnant woman's fears would be imprinted upon her foetus was widespread. Thus a pregnant woman scared by a snake would bear a child with a snake-like deformity, while a pregnant woman beset with general anxieties would be delivered of an infant already stained with that neurotic taint. The exact science behind the theory of 'maternal impressions' was uncertain, but its popularity incontestable. Was it due to pangenesis (an early idea that acquired characteristics of parents could be transmitted to their offspring), as Charles Darwin believed, or a result of telepathy, as others contended?

Henry C. Wright set out the basic tenets of maternal impressions in his magisterial *The Empire of the Mother Over the Character and Destiny of the Race* (1863). In this book he announced that while the empire of civil government ruled the external world, the 'Empire of the Mother [was] Internal'. Crucially, it was woman's 'internal empire' which had the greatest impact upon civilisation, because it was in the pre-natal state that each individual's 'organic tendencies' were 'formed and fixed'. In other words, 'What is *organized* into us in our pre-natal state, is of more consequence to us . . . than what is *educated* into us, after we are born.' The mechanism for this transmission was through the mother's blood. Her blood governed the temperature of the infant's soul. According to Wright:

> The conditions of the blood are, to a great extent, controlled by the action of the soul. Certain actions of the mind produce corresponding actions of the blood. The temperature and motions of the blood are heightened and accelerated by the operations of the soul. The character of the thoughts and feelings characterize the action of the blood.[3]

Others concurred, although placing more emphasis on the effects of the nervous system. Dr M. Roth, the author of *A Few Notes on Fear and Fright, and the Diseases They Cause and Cure* (1871) argued that 'fearful, dreadful, frightful, horrible, and terrible impressions' were conveyed to the brain or spinal cord through the senses, which were 'connected by the nerves with the various organs'. This explained why 'fear and terror causes shortness of breath, irregularity of pulsation, palpitation of the heart, derangement of the circulation, and thus indirectly arrest the development of the foetus, or change its form.'[4] Others, such as the teacher Georgiana B. Kirby, recognised the import of such ideas for improving women's lives. Kirby's *Transmission; or, Variation of Character Through the Mother* (1877) insisted that 'all variation of character, physical and mental, takes place in foetal life'. Education might modify but 'never overrule' inherited defects. She drew two lessons from these axioms. The first was that it was crucial that conception should never be attempted if *either* party was ill, exhausted or depressed. It was even ill-advised to engage in sexual intercourse if the wife was not 'in full sympathy' with her husband. Before conception, Kirby argued, the father-to-be had an important function in fashioning the infant-to-be. After all

> the material supplied by the father for the vitalizing of the ovum, represents his THEN state of being, and will continue to represent it in the life it has helped to organize. If, therefore, this communicated principle be wanting in vitality or diseased, physical perfection in the child is not to be expected. This finest secretion of the man's whole being — this subtle essence of his nature, which is both spiritual and physical — should express his best possible condition.

Nevertheless, after conception the father was restricted to an indirect role, that is, 'through his influence on the mother's mind'.

The second lesson was that women had to be tenderly nurtured throughout their pregnancy. Kirby reminded her readers that birthmarks, club feet and strabismus (or crossed eyes), for instance, were not caused by a 'first impression' of ugliness, but by the mother's 'subsequent and frequent reproduction of the image'. This explained why people in the lower orders of society were more liable to give birth to deformed children. She alleged that the 'unfurnished mind of the illiterate woman seizes on and retains the ugly or grotesque picture', which a woman who was 'rich in thought and experience would have dismissed at once'. It was crucial, therefore, that the mother who wished to protect her foetus should exercise will power to focus only upon agreeable things.[5] The implication was that there was a positive aspect to the theory of maternal impressions: virtuous as well as pitiful traits could be transmitted. Readers of *A View at the Foundations: Or, First Causes of Character As Operative Before Birth, From Hereditary and Spiritual Sources* (1865) were treated to a story of a pregnant woman who sought an abortion on the grounds that she had suffered a fright from a 'disagreeable animal' and was convinced that her child would be born with some grotesque disfigurement. Her physician advised her to spend the rest of her pregnancy focusing upon a 'higher pattern'. The woman fervently obeyed, fixing her mind upon 'a certain individual of high and commanding reputation in the nation' (could it have been William Ewart Gladstone?) and, in good time, gave birth to a flawless child who resembled her hero. In endorsing this approach, the author warned only that pregnant women should be careful that they did not become '*too* anxious to secure results', lest this new anxiety spawn its own 'enormities' in the infant.[6]

The belief that fear could seep into the sanctum of the womb and poison the foetus lasted throughout the twentieth century.[7] There were to be many modifications of the theory of maternal impressions, including the view that the fright experienced by the pregnant woman did not directly *cause* fear in infants, but merely *predisposed* them to such fears. 'The children of such pregnancies are always sensitive and nervy,' declared one medical psychologist in 1939.[8] Or, in the words of the author of *The Emotional Care of Your Child* (1969), the emotions of pregnant women 'constitute an environment which molds the behavior pattern of a coming child'.[9] Psychoanalysis took the hypothesis in a different direction, claiming that the panic that a foetus experienced while its parents had sexual intercourse could have fearful effects in adult life. From such a perspective, the fear of the mother was imprinted on the foetus's unconscious, rather than its physique. In the words of one psychoanalyst, fears in infancy and in adult life were due to 'an actual happening in pre-natal life'.[10] Either way the foetus had no option but to submit to the fate bestowed upon it, not by the gods but by 'foolish' mothers and 'sexually incorrigible' fathers.[11]

Once the infant was born, fear was a constant companion.[12] Despite an alarming range of interpretations, all adult commentators agreed on one thing: if a child remained tearful, blame had to be apportioned. Most reprehensible were adults who used fear to procure obedience from their young charges. A central contention of childcare manuals in the late nineteenth and early twentieth centuries was that it was servants who were needlessly terrifying children with vivid stories about bogeymen, ghosts and policemen.[13] As the *physical* chastisement of children by servants was becoming unacceptable, there were concerns that servants were increasingly using verbal threats to discipline their charges.[14] Consequently it was common for mothers of frightened children to be reproached for their poor choice of employee. For instance, mothers were exhorted not to employ nursery nurses from 'certain [unnamed] nationalities in Europe', on the grounds that foreigners regarded it as legitimate to 'tell falsehoods . . . to accomplish a charitable and useful end', such as obedience.[15]

At other times the threat was more general. The author of one advice manual, *Hints for the Nursery* (1866), recalled overhearing a nursery nurse warning her young charge against going upstairs lest he be eaten ('Don't go upstairs, Willie! Old Man lives up stairs! Old Man lives up in a great dark hole! Old Man will catch Willie and eat him!'). The author castigated mothers who allowed servants to recite such stories to their children, cautioning them that the consequences of inciting fears could be grave. Insanity lurked at the child's bedside.[16]

Fear-wielding servants might produce docile children, but 'obedience purchased at this price is an evil and worthless thing'.[17] The author of 'How to Keep Your Child From Fear' (1908) was troubled by the fact that even kind nurses who acted 'conscientious concerning the little one's physical welfare', at the same time were prepared to rob the child of its emotional 'rights' in order to save time and trouble. For the nurse, the 'mysterious and unseen bogie man, and the obvious and substantial policeman' were 'her allies in enforcing a paralyzed obedience; and all her discipline revolves around some form of dread: some fear held before the charge whom she often loves devotedly.'[18] Fear 'dulls' and 'restrains' the child's spirits and movements, without establishing any positive moral influence.[19] As late as 1929 one influential book added a particularly modern note by arguing that allowing nurses or maids to frighten children was not only 'stupid', but was a sure way to turn the child into a neurotic adult.[20]

To avoid condemning their children to such a fate, responsible mothers were advised to take immediate action if they caught their nursery maids inciting emotional distress. In 1915 *The Child's Welfare Manual* sanctioned a comprehensive programme of humiliation for the hapless nurse. Furthermore, the disgraced nurse had to be humbled in front of the child. The authors favoured the following scenario:

> 'Robert', [his mother] said, 'Nurse Mary is going to tell you that there are no black men who creep into little boys' rooms in the dark and carry them off when they are naughty . . . I want you to listen while Nurse Mary tells you this, for she is going away to-day, and you will probably never see her again.'
>
> The nurse was crying, but she obeyed the mother's order. The little boy stood within the shelter of his mother's arms and listened gravely while the nurse went back over all of the tales that she had told him, saying with each one, 'It is not true.' At the close the little man held out his hand. 'Thank you, nurse,' he said, 'I ought not to have been afraid, but I believed you, you know.' Then, looking at his mother's unsmiling face, he said, 'I shall not be afraid, now, mother.'[21]

By the 1920s, however, a decisive shift had taken place. Working-class women were reluctant to apply for jobs as menial domestic labourers. Domestic service had been shrinking before the First World War, but the burgeoning of less fettered and more lucrative forms of female employment from 1914 onwards dealt it a death-blow. As servants and nursery maids relinquished command of the nursery, the labour of parents in the emotional management of their children increasingly came under scrutiny. All a child's irrational fears could be traced directly to its 'unwise upbringing', pontificated one neurologist in 1923.[22] Parents were scolded if their children expressed any fear. 'No children should be brought up to fear their parents or anything else,' argued the President of the Royal Medico-Psychological Society in 1929.[23] Maladjusted adults were the 'victims of parental mismanagement'.[24]

Although the word 'parent' was used in these manuals, it was the mother, rather than the father, who was ultimately responsible for the child's fears. If mentioned at all, the father was in charge of the child's financial as opposed to emotional management.[25] When fathers were given an emotional role, it was sometimes to provide their young children with authoritative explanations for frightening things. More commonly, they were depicted deriding childish fears, especially those of sons. Indeed, fathers were frequently depicted as the *cause* of fear. In the battle for the heart and soul of the child, mothers were accused of stimulating fear of the father by giving him the job of meting out punishment.[26] The book *In Defense of Children* (1941) even claimed that when children were asked to identify the threatening presence in their nightmares, they frequently said that their antagonist resembled their father. The author (a paediatrician) asked his readers, especially fathers, to reconsider their attempts to rear their children 'by force or fear'. The father's strength should be 'a source of security just as easily as a source of fear', he feebly advised.[27]

Nevertheless, in the vast majority of cases, from the 1920s onwards it was the mother, as opposed to maid or father, who was rebuked for the child's anxieties. In *Faith or Fear in Child Training* (1934) the scenario played out two decades earlier in *The Child's Welfare Manual* was turned upon the mother. With relish, the author recounted a story about a mother who frightened her child by threatening him with the figure of a postman. She was publicly scolded for her misplaced maternal indoctrination. 'I hope you will never make Bobby afraid of me again,' the postman loudly rebuked her. 'I think you, not he, ought to be punished, for you told him an untruth.'[28] The chastised mother had taken the place of the down-trodden servant.

There were some 'big occasions' that generated anxious debate in childcare manuals throughout the century — none more potent than the question of whether or not parents should expose children to death. In middle-class circles, subjecting the delicate sensibilities of children to death and corpses had long been regarded as abhorrent. A book entitled *How to Educate the Feelings or Affections, and Bring the Dispositions, Aspirations, and Passions into Harmony with Sound Intelligence and Mortality* (1880) bluntly informed parents that to allow children to view death was 'hideous and revolting'. Parents who allowed maids to frighten children with images of death were actually committing a sin, because such children would 'never feel the charm which there is in the thought of that gentle sleep which dissolves our mortal body, and perhaps reposes the spirit, intervening between its earthly and heavenly career'.[29] By the 1920s such views had spread to all classes. The advice book *Parents and Children* (1928) insisted that parents guard against a child being in the house when a death occurred. No matter how close he or she was to the dead person, the child should not attend the funeral. Any parent who ignored this advice, they insisted, was doing 'lasting harm'.[30]

It was not always possible, however, to shield children from death. After all, working-class children witnessed dying playmates and relatives well into the twentieth century. Before improvements in water and milk supplies, advances in the understanding of infections and the professionalisation of medicine, death rates in poor areas were high. As late as 1900 in Britain, 18 per cent of children died before the age of five years.[31] Furthermore, the majority died in their own homes rather than in institutions. It was highly probable that before a child reached the age of ten, he or she would have experienced the death of at least one member of the family.[32]

Being accustomed to death did not diminish its terror. Even nightly prayers about death could be scary. For instance, Mary Wade, who grew up in a mining village in the north of England, said this prayer each night:

Gentle Jesus, meek and mild,
Look upon a little child,
Pity my simplicity,
Suffer me to come to Thee.

She recalled being 'a bit doubtful' about the last line, 'so always spoke it in a quiet voice, because I did know it was a one-way journey'.[33] Others harboured more prosaic anxieties about death. In Chapter One we discussed some of the perils of pauper burial. The fear of such a fate was not only due to anxiety about dissections or being dumped in a common grave. For instance, one working-class girl from a small east Lancashire community recalled being very worried when told that when poor people died they were only given shrouds that covered their fronts. 'What were they going to do at the Resurrection?' she anxiously enquired.[34] When face to face with a corpse, the effect could be chilling. Molly Weir, who lived in a Glasgow tenement in the early years of the twentieth century, recalled her intense fear when faced with a corpse. Like 'Spike' Mays in Chapter One, she recalled how:

> Adults lifted us children up to place a hand on the brow of the corpse, because this was said to prevent nightmares afterwards, but in my case it induced them, and I used to shudder with fear at actually making physical contact with those waxen faces. 'No, no,' I would whimper, 'I don't want to touch wee Jimmy's forehead. No, I don't care if I get nightmares. No, no, no.' If I were forced to lay a hand on a clammy brow I felt haunted for weeks afterwards.[35]

Similarly, in working-class Preston, Lancashire, Kathlyn Davenport was taken to say farewell to a girl whose body was lying at the back of a sweet shop. She described it thus:

> we were allowed into the kitchen and behind the hanging curtain covering the doorway. I couldn't see anyone. In the dimness at the back of the room was a long sideboard. The girls went over to it and then lifted me up so that I could see Agnes. She was lying in a coffin, all dressed in white, with a lily across her chest. She was like a great doll, waxen and with long hair. I was petrified! It took me a very long time to get over that little visit.[36]

Increasingly, child guidance manuals warned that inspiring children to fear death and the afterlife ruined young lives. The

anonymous author of *The Fears of a Child* (1906) confessed to his fears
of hell as a child, while admitting at the same time that such a fear
did not make him a better child but merely left him feeling miserable
after each minor transgression. Fear of hell barred him from reaping
the joys that were every child's due. He warned his readers to
beware of such threats of eternal punishment after death — they
come from 'diseased brains' and those who spread them should be
pitied and ignored.[37] Other books advised parents against appealing
to fear of God when teaching children. Frightening children with the
'awful mysteries and punishments of religion' would serve only to
terrify them.[38] Even the charismatic Chicago-based preacher
Preston Bradley, recalling his childhood in the 1890s, spoke out
vigorously against the use of fear in revival meetings: as a child he
had endured hours of terror after an ebullient evangelist persuaded
him that he would die and burn in hell if he remained a sinner.[39]

Advice books in the 1920s reminded parents that children who
had been taught religion through fear often harboured long-term
hostility towards religion and were incapable of making a 'harmonious commitment' to religion as adults.[40] Parents were admonished
for inciting such fears. The harm that talk of hell could do to a child
was immense. *Your Growing Child. A Book of Talks to Parents on Life's
Needs* (1927) specifically addressed this question of religious instruction of children. After relating a story of a young man tormented
with the fear that he had committed the unforgivable sin and having
traced (through hypnosis) this story back to an instance in his childhood when an elderly woman had threatened him with hell's
tortures if he was not a good boy, the author advised parents:

> Of course, a case such as this should not be interpreted as a warning
> against giving children religious instruction. Such an interpretation
> would be absurd. All children need religious instruction. But . . .
> when in the course of instruction the parent or Sunday-school
> teacher says too much about such things as hell, the devil, and the
> punishment of sin, much harm may be done.[41]

Death and hellfire were increasingly regarded as too terrifying for
youthful sensibilities.

Increasing sensitivity to the child's apprehensions about death and the afterlife were not only reflections of improvements in living standards and the secularisation of society. With the middle-class mother taking over the primary care of her offspring, a new sympathy to children's emotions developed. In the early interwar years it was almost axiomatic in childcare manuals that children should be protected from frightening things, rather than encouraged to 'face' them. Popular literature and film were vilified for frightening the nation's most tender subjects. Indeed, one study in the 1930s claimed that, at some stage, as many as 93 per cent of schoolchildren had been frightened when watching a motion picture.[42] Parents needed to devise a 'rigid regimen' regarding the films their children watched: horror films inflicted a 'serious wound' upon the child's consciousness and could give the child a shock 'virtually the same as shell-shock', lectured the author of *Our Movies Made Children* (1935).[43]

As the above example implies, fear endangered both the child's body and soul. It could inhibit nervous functions, render children 'permanently neurotic', provoke that 'dread malady' of epilepsy or encourage a huge array of ominous ailments.[44] Adopting the physiologist Walter Cannon's approach to the emotions, many childcare advisers warned that because fear stopped the secretion of gastric juices, increased blood pressure and led to excessive secretion of sugar in the blood, the physical development of scared children would be inhibited.[45]

The fact that these manuals continued to warn parents against forcing their children to face fearful stimuli suggests that some parents were not heeding their advice. Books such as Henry Addington Bruce's *Your Growing Child* (1927) were explicitly addressed to those parents who still did not appreciate 'fear's dire possibilities' but continued to 'treat their children as almost inevitably to make them victims of fear'.[46] Time and again manuals reminded parents that processes of 'hardening' never worked: the best a parent could do was try to allay the child's fears.[47]

Nevertheless, a minority of commentators was already warning parents that their desire to protect children from fear had gone too far. Some childcare literature expressed concern that parents were 'mollycoddling' their children and, as a consequence, actually retarding emotional development. For instance, the authors of *The Manual for Character Training. A Guide-Book for Teachers and Parents Based on the Young Folks Treasury* (1925) insisted that three-year-old children had to overcome their fears through self-control. The authors admitted that children so young were not strong enough to confront all their fears at once, but advised parents to encourage them to brave their milder fears first, gradually working up to the more extreme 'bugbears' in life. Courage must be learned, they argued. Precisely because fear was the 'most weakening of emotions', the child who lacked courage would prove unable to 'get through this difficult and dangerous world at all'. Lily-livered mothers who discouraged their boys from fighting were reminded that 'gentleness may, under bad management, degenerate into weakness and cowardice and cowardice is usually at the bottom of meanness'. The authors further advised: 'As soon as the little boy can walk and talk he should be encouraged by his mother to play the man.'[48]

Children who were shielded from painful emotions would be incapable of responding appropriately to fearful events. The book *Faith or Fear in Child Training* (1934) terrorised parents with stories like the following:

> 'Jump!' called the fireman to the twelve-year-old girl trapped in a burning house, and they held their arms to catch her; but she couldn't jump; she had always been afraid to jump down, even a step or two. It led back to the fact that she was past two [years of age] before she was allowed to go up and down the stair [sic] alone.[49]

For this minority of counsellors the feminisation of childcare advice had gone too far, especially when it came to the emotional management of boys. This anxiety, however, had to wait until the Cold War before spreading more widely.

Meanwhile a major shift was occurring in the philosophy of the emotions: the behaviourist revolution. As we saw in the case of 'Albert B' earlier in this chapter, behaviourists placed great emphasis on fear in governing behaviour. In the words of John B. Watson, when the serpent tempted Eve he 'did not ask her to introspect, to look into her mind to see what was going on. No, he handed her the apple and she bit into it.'[50] Infants did not have instinctual emotional responses, but conditioned ones. Like other sets of habits, emotions had to be learned. So, fear was not an instinctive reaction to phylogenetically predetermined objects or events, but was a learned response occurring on 'signals' or conditioned stimuli that made infants (like 'Albert B') anticipate pain.

Consequently it came as no surprise to these psychologists that children shared their mother's fears.[51] This shared community of fear within the family was not due to inheritance or psychic mechanisms: it was learned. After all, the behaviourists pointed out, there was no direct relationship between fear and vulnerability. Indeed, the most defenceless of all human beings (the new-born child) was the least fearful of all God's creatures. Only loud noises and falling could puncture a baby's false sense of security. The infant's confidence began to collapse around the age of eight months but, even then, infants remained supremely unafraid of many threats. Only after the age of six, did anticipatory fears displace the immediate, tangible fears of the child's early life. Of these anticipatory fears, the most interesting was the fear of death. According to behaviourists, even children as old as five were rarely able to clearly distinguish themselves from the external world sufficiently to conceive of lifelessness. Until the age of nine, when death assumed a fearful presence, it was typically conceived of as a person. Thereafter the fear of death changed from a 'vague and evanescent' presence to an 'urgent, pervasive, and persistent' anxiety.[52]

In line with behaviourist ideology, the solution for such intense fears lay in indoctrination. In the words of the psychologist John Yerbury Dent in 1941, education should include 'the unemotional witnessing of a birth and of a death', in which the 'spectacle' should 'be one of interest and nothing more'.[53] It was a statement that could have come out of Aldous Huxley's *Brave New World*, published less than ten years earlier, in which positive conditioning enabled people to watch others die with no flicker of emotion. As Dr Gaffney explained to the Savage in the novel, 'Death conditioning begins at eighteen months. Every tot spends two mornings a week in a Hospital for the Dying. All the best toys are kept there, and they get chocolate cream on death days. They learn to take dying as a matter of course.' 'Like any other physiological process,' explained the Head Mistress.[54]

Behaviourists battled with recalcitrant parents who, by failing to competently disguise their emotions, were breeding apprehensive children. Once a child had been nurtured in fear, the only antidotes were reconditioning or social imitation. From the 1920s parents were encouraged to 'recondition' their child by associating the feared object (or situation) with something pleasant and, even better, to combine reconditioning with 'social imitation' in which the fearful child could observe other children amusing themselves with the feared object (or in the feared situation).[55] Mary Cover Jones, one of the leading proponents of such techniques in the 1920s, warned against too hasty application of conditioning. After all, associating the fearful object with, for instance, a favourite food might actually cause the child to attach a fear reaction to the food.[56] Because of such doubts, from the 1930s increasing emphasis was put on the importance of social imitation, despite the difficulty many parents experienced in maintaining a consistently 'courageous attitude'.[57] Nevertheless, in the hands of a sophisticated 'manipulator', conditioning combined with social suggestion was widely viewed as the most effective way of transforming the cowardly child into a confident one.[58]

Not everyone was convinced by the behaviourist story. For some, notions of maturation and evolution complicated the issue of emotional expression in childhood. According to one branch of child psychology, children's fears could only be understood in terms of the life of the species: children 'recapitulated' the life of the race. Children who trembled in the dark were 'recapitulating ancestral fear'. We will be looking in more depth at recapitulation theory in the next chapter, but for the purposes of children's fears, the theory led to the conclusion that there was no point in exhorting children to 'not be silly' since they would inevitably evolve beyond their fears in due course.[59]

In the 1930s the prolific authors Arthur Thomas Jersild and Mrs Frances Baker Holmes jointly published works stressing that infantile fears were not conditioned but changed naturally over time. In early infancy immediate stimuli such as noise, strange objects or persons, painful stimuli and the loss of support aroused children's fears. Between the ages of two and five these fears were replaced by fear of the dark and anticipatory fears, which, in turn, eventually gave way to anxiety about personal status, including the fear of failure and ridicule.

The authors' interpretative framework was heavily influenced by recapitulation theory: the problem was that modernity had stripped fear of its adaptive function. As they contended in 1935, human glands and muscles were geared for physical struggle against tangible dangers. Yet human physiology could 'avail but little against a great number of conditions feared by civilised human beings'. While humanity's ability to 'entertain fancies and conjectures has tremendously enlarged the scope of his fears, his glands have . . . remained in the jungle . . . Fleet limbs help but little when one is pursued by a shadow.' Modern anxieties were subverting physiological mechanisms designed to ensure the survival of the species.

At the same time Jersild and Holmes believed that certain fears were innate and these developed as children matured. One of these innate fears was racial. In a particularly revealing example they described a white-skinned infant who had been looked after since birth by a dark-skinned maid. At the age of six months, however, the child suddenly became extremely wary of the maid. In the authors' words: 'The emergence of fear of the maid corresponded in time to the first signs of fear in response to strangers, and the first clear signs that the child could distinguish between strangers and familiar persons.' So, even though the maid had nurtured the infant since birth, at a particular age an instinctive racial identification of who constituted a 'stranger' caused the infant to become fearful. Jersild and Holmes believed that most children would simply 'grow out of' their fears, retaining only those which were useful for the survival of the species and, although it is never stated explicitly, there is the implication that fear of the darker stranger was one of these fears they regarded as useful for the survival of the white race.[60]

Finally, the other theory that had an impact on childcare manuals before the Second World War was that associated with William James and Carl Georg Lange. Although there were differences between their accounts, what became known as the James–Lange theory of the emotions postulated that vasomotor disturbances and muscular movements were the *cause* of emotions, rather than the *result* of them. That is to say, rather than emotions producing organic states, the organic states produced the emotion. In James's words: 'The order in which the events occur is as follows: An exciting fact is perceived. This percept is followed by certain bodily changes. The feeling of these bodily changes as they occur is the emotion.'[61] Emotions had no existence apart from physiological changes; emotions were nothing more than a product of an individual's physiology.[62] The individual felt frightened because she was running away.[63]

This had implications in terms of childcare. The emotional and physical comportment of children needed to be tackled simultaneously. In the words of Henry Addington Bruce in *Your Growing Child* (1927), the child who was 'trained to sit and stand and walk erect, with chest raised, and his whole attitude one of confidence is far less likely to be emotionally uncontrolled than a child permitted to acquire a slouching posture'.[64] The author of *The Psychology of Youth. A Book for Parents* (1929) concurred, advising parents to adopt the insights offered by the James–Lange theory. Children should be encouraged to adopt a physical stance of fearlessness since this posture would induce the emotion of courage. 'Whistling in the dark' was efficacious in overthrowing timidity. Throwing the body 'into the posture of gaiety and care-free ease' would cause apprehensions to seep away. Leave talk of the emotions alone, the author advised, and focus only on 'motion or expression'.[65] Such beliefs had a long life. As late as the 1960s some childcare manuals argued that physical fear was the result of the 'lack of muscular tone'. The child had to be given ways to develop muscular strength.[66] Moral courage was thoroughly tied to one's guts.

In the immediate postwar world a change could be observed. Even more than before, childhood acquired a discrete status as the precious age of innocence. Children's fears and anxieties were a scandal to parents and civil society alike. Supporting the family in its quest for the emotional stability of its youngest members was increasingly portrayed as requiring the help of a range of professionals, dedicated to promoting more 'caring' child-raising practices. If that failed, bringing the fearful child under the wing of new experts within child-guidance programmes was imperative.

Part of the shift was a response to the work of Dr Benjamin McLane Spock. In the early 1940s Spock began writing his authoritative books on childcare. Having been raised by a mother who was (according to Spock) 'too controlling, too strict, too moralistic', he was determined to promote 'easier, pleasanter ways to bring up children'. He also directed his fire against the behaviourists' mechanical view of childcare, which placed a moratorium on consolation and presumed that if a mother wanted her children to become musicians, she should play music to them. Spock's sympathies were firmly with parents who were bombarded with childcare instructions that, in many cases, served simply to 'unsettle them and undermine their natural impulses and their self-confidence'. In a world characterised by fragmentation of the extended family and greater mobility among young families, parents were increasingly forced to rely on the 'cure-inspiring expert' as opposed to the 'reassuring grandmother'.

Spock set out to change the role of the expert. He swore never to 'scare parents, or boss them around, or talk down to them' and he resolved 'to give not the earliest or the average age for each step [of child development] but the slowest that was normal'. Parents were to be reassured at the same time as their infants. After all, Spock maintained, behavioural problems in children were not always the results of parents' mistakes. As a result, Spock's *Common Sense Book of Baby and Child Care* (1946) emphasised the need for infants and children to be encouraged at every point. Affection became parents' *raison d'être*. His book sold three-quarters of a million copies in its first year, despite no advertisement or promotions. It has been translated into nearly forty languages.[67]

A dozen years later, in the revised edition of his first classic, Spock admitted that his tone had changed:

> When I was writing the first edition, between 1943 and 1946, the attitude of a majority of people towards infant feeding, toilet training, and general child management was still fairly strict and

inflexible. However, the need for greater understanding of children
and for flexibility in their care had been made clear by educators,
psychoanalysts, and pediatricians, and I was trying to encourage
this. Since then a great change in attitude has occurred, and nowadays there seems to be more chance of a conscientious parent's
getting into trouble with permissiveness than with strictness. So I
have tried to give a more balanced view.

Nevertheless, as in his earlier work, Spock heaped on reassurance.
'Remember that you know a lot about your child and that I don't
know anything about him,' he modestly reminded parents. Parents
should balance trusting their instincts with following their doctor's
advice. Crucial to Spock's story was that children's fears changed
over time. For instance, he predicted that, at about five months of
age, infants typically became afraid of unfamiliar people, so mothers
should ensure that 'strangers keep at a little distance'. For one-
year-olds loud noises and sudden movements suddenly became
scary. Therefore, if the vacuum cleaner 'bothers him', the mother
should cease to use it for a few months, until the fear passed.
Equally, at the age of two, infants often developed fears of the dark.
Spock advised that:

> If your child has become terrified about going to bed, the safest
> advice, but the hardest to carry out, is to sit by his cot in a relaxed
> way until he goes to sleep. Don't be in a hurry to sneak away before
> he is asleep. It alarms him and makes him more wakeful. This cam-
> paign may take weeks, but it should work in the end.

Everything should be done to ensure that the child was not frightened. If the child became fearful when his mother went away, she
should avoid doing so. Spock acknowledged that it was sometimes
necessary for the mother to go to work but if she 'had to go away
each day to work', she should avoid the 'anguished, unsure-whether-
you're-doing-the-right-thing expression', since that would add to
the child's uneasiness.
    Although Spock's message was ostensibly one of reassurance, his
psychoanalytic framework led him to place a lot of weight on

parental upbringing. When discussing the fears of children aged three to five, he wrote that, although he did believe that 'some children are born more sensitive than others; and all children, no matter how carefully they are brought up, are frightened by something', nevertheless,

> Fears are commoner in children who have been made tense from battles over such matters as feeding and toilet training, children whose imaginations have been over-stimulated by frightening stories or too many warnings, children who haven't had enough chance to develop their independence and sociability, children whose parents are over-protective . . . The uneasiness that the child has accumulated before now seems to be crystallized by his new imagination into definite threats.

The frightened child had to be given 'comforting reminders that you love him very much and will always protect him'.[68] In the postwar world children were absolved of responsibility for their fears.

Reassuring the child became the dominant tenor of advice manuals. Books with titles such as *Enjoy Your Baby* (1944) pleaded against coercive means of teaching the frightened child to 'be a man'. The 'bogey of the nursery' could only be dispelled through patient and sensible investigation and consolation. 'Teddy', for instance, would always be a comforting presence for the child alone in the dark.[69] Childhood was a period for amusement. Games and other forms of play should be used to cure children of their fears. For instance, *The Gift of the Child* (1946) suggested that the frightened child should be encouraged to make an exaggerated drawing of the fearful object or situation, and then, in an atmosphere of jollity, be allowed to stick a pencil through the drawing, screw it up and throw it into the fire.[70] This perspective even allowed for scary stories. While such licence to scare had been universally condemned in an earlier period, it was increasingly observed that children flirted with fear in their play life.[71] This flirtation with fear could be beneficial. In 1968 John Newson and Elizabeth Newson, the authors of *Five Years Old in an Urban Community*, explained it thus:

We may look upon play not simply as a way of repeating life experiences in an attempt to master their emotional implications, nor
solely as a rehearsal, symbolic or direct, of roles or of desires: but as
a means by which the child *tries out his emotions in a protected context*,
in preparation for the time when he will be held responsible for his
actions and will be expected to exercise reasonable control over his
feelings.[72]

For Bruno Bettelheim, in *The Uses of Enchantment* (1977), fairy
tales introduced children to evil and terror and were important in
teaching children how to control such feelings through mastery.[73]
Stories as different as 'Jack and the Bean Stalk' and 'Hansel and
Gretel' introduced children to terror, while simultaneously teaching
them that such emotions could be managed. As Marina Warner put
it more recently in her classic *No Go the Bogeyman* (1998), frightening literature and film allow children to 'find their double in the
mirror that the fragments held up to them: they are made to stare at
the possibility of their non-being, at death itself, but they then discover that they are still alive, outside the tale'. Through repeating
the frightening imaging, children found relief from terrifying fears
in the 'real world'.[74]
As the Cold War heated up there was a swift backlash to the message counselling restraint and compassion in childcare. As we saw,
even Spock was affected by this shift to greater strictness in childcare
when he warned against 'permissiveness' in the 1958 edition of
Common Sense Book of Baby and Child Care. From the 1950s many psychiatrists and child-welfare specialists began alerting parents to
ensure that their indulgence did not spell laxity. Childcare manuals
encouraged parents to test their children's courage. It was no coincidence that many of these manuals explicitly addressed fathers
and sons. One of these books, *How To Bring Out the Best in Your Child*
(1950), was particularly forthright. It advised the male reader to
confront his son with the words 'I want to see how brave you are'.
The father's actions were then carefully choreographed:

Smile as you grasp his left forearm with your right hand and hold
your right hand as if to test him by striking the upper part of his arm.

Give him a fairly light tap and say, 'Does that hurt?' (Wait for an
answer.) 'Well, I must say you are pretty brave — I'll make it harder
yet — *now*, does *that* hurt?' When he says 'No' you may say, 'You are
getting to be more like a man every day! You can bear quite a lot of
pain without showing it at all. That's fine!'

The illustration accompanying this lesson depicted a father adminis-
tering the test to a boy of around eight years of age.[75]

As this example suggested, children (especially sons) had to suffer
occasionally if they were to grow into courageous adults. Nancy
Catty, author of *Social Training. From Childhood to Maturity* (1951),
recommended that children be left to discover danger by themselves rather than be warned of threats by their parents. This was
necessary if children were to grow up 'physically fearless, and emotionally courageous'. Occasionally, Catty admitted, there would be
accidents but these were not as bad as the child becoming a 'timid
adolescent'. She continued: 'I am not advocating putting children
into dangerous positions, unnecessarily, but I am advocating that
sheltering children . . . may do even more harm than the physical
results of ignorance and rashness.'[76] Note the insertion of that word
'unnecessarily'.

In a typical Cold War manual, entitled *A Plan for Growing Up. The
Blue Book for Building Better Lives* (1945, reprinted 1957), Marion
Quinlan Davis argued that there had 'never been a time in the
world's history when courageous leaders were more needed than
they are today. This courage could only be instilled in people
through their parents in childhood.' She continued, insisting that
'Overzealous and fearful parents, who forbid their children the
normal experiences of childhood because there is an element of
danger in them, may breed cowards.' She then gave an example of an
Englishwoman whose fourth and sole-surviving son was sent on a
'dangerous mission to Africa'. When asked whether she had not
given enough for her country and why she did not forbid her last
child to go, she replied: 'Better to lose a life than a character.'
Parents had a duty to ensure that they did not weaken the child's
'moral fibre', concluded Davis. Mothers in particular had to be prepared to sacrifice the bodies of their children for a higher goal.[77]

As in the last example, during the Cold War there was a shift in many childcare advice manuals from an emphasis on the *child*, who was supposed to be fearless, to the *mother*, who was exhorted to show courage in training her children to be fearless, even if it led to a pitiful sacrifice. It was not uncommon for childcare manuals to focus on the fears of mothers even while ostensibly addressing those of children. Not only were mothers responsible for causing children's fears, but they were the frightened ones, responsible for the physical and emotional sustenance of fewer and fewer children. In 1947 Elizabeth Bradford addressed her book *Let's Talk About Children* to fearful mothers. She admitted that raising children was never easy and was fraught with fears for the mother, saying:

> it is very hard to know just where to draw the line between caution and fear. Think of a baby just at the creeping age, for instance. We would never put him down on the sidewalk to creep because we know it is far too dirty. Would we put him down on the living room rug? Would we keep him in a playpen all the time or would we keep him in a sterile nursery? Life, especially with children, is full of choices like that and sometimes it is very hard to decide where caution ends and exaggerated fears begin.[78]

As science encroached into the nursery, along with big business selling new cleaning ('sterilising') products, the fears of mothers grew.

As in the earlier period, the frightened child became an object of shame to the parents, who were held responsible for any show of childish weakness. In the words of *A Primer for Parents* (1968), the parents of fearful children might wonder if it was a 'reflection of their poor parenthood and worry that others may see that there is something wrong'.[79] Charlotte Del Solar, an instructor in child development at the Teachers' College at Columbia University, admitted as much in her *Child Guidance* (1950) when she argued that adults were 'bound to be impatient with the fearful, frightened child. We desperately want him to become courageous and stalwart. We see that his fears are cutting him off from exciting experiences. We may even be forced to admit that we are ashamed of this anxious child.' Nevertheless, she admonished frightened parents never to forget that 'there are no short cuts to courage'.[80] Crucial to all these admonitions was fear about 'over-protective' mothers and their 'emasculated' sons. Mothers who 'babyied' their children were creating timid and lonely adults.[81]

But mothers were not allowed to have it the other way either. At the same time as the 'over-protective mother' was being lambasted, there was also concern over the insufficiently maternal mother. In the late 1940s to the 1960s there was a strong backlash against employed mothers. Abandonment by the mother was characterised as the child's greatest fear. The solution was to regard the mother and child as 'a unit' which could not be divided until the child was over five years of age.[82] This was common even in the late 1960s, when one adviser pointed out that:

> Some children in their first school years are fearful that mother 'won't be there' when they return from school. The obvious course of action now is *to be there* if this is humanly possible. If you are a working mother, please have a reliable and affectionate substitute awaiting the child's return from school. *Regularity* and *reliability* are keynotes here.[83]

But, of course, the problem was circular: poorer mothers depended upon their paid employment, yet these were precisely the families that were least likely to be able to afford to pay for a 'reliable and affectionate substitute'.

Even worse, mothers whose children avoided school were increasingly pathologised. Although the first major paper on the problem of school avoidance was published by Melanie Klein in 1924, from 1941 a distinction was made between school phobia and truancy.[84] Unlike simple truants, school-phobic children experienced terror about going to school that was accompanied by nausea in the morning, vomiting, diarrhoea, abdominal cramps and chronic sleepiness. In its acute form, school phobia could easily reveal itself in hysterical, hypochondriacal and compulsive symptoms.[85] However, the chief targets of the child-guidance professionals and the psychiatrists was not the child but the mother.

The real failure was maternal. While the father was castigated for being absent, the mother's blunder lay in being all too present.

All commentators agreed that the mothers of school phobes were dependent types, liberal in child-rearing practices, over-protective, over-indulgent, sexually confused and insecure about their abilities to be 'good mothers'.[86] They were also more likely to have had their children late in life (that is, they were 'selfish') and, even if this was not the case, they were women who 'appeared distinctly older than their actual age'. As a result, they were both ambivalent about the birth and possessive afterwards. Because of the mother's age and appearance, her children were more likely to be isolated from other children and therefore particularly attached to their mother.[87] Phobic children were said to have been 'prone' to this fear because they had been brought up in a period when their fathers would have been away doing war service, which led the mother–son relationship (mother–daughter relationships were rarely mentioned) to become excessively intense.[88] The mothers of school phobes were anxious about their children deserting their maternal embrace.[89] The children should not be called 'school phobes' but 'mother philes'.[90]

The debate about school phobia also highlights women's anxiety about their performance as mothers in a period when they were deluged with advice. This was evident in an article written by a physician in the early 1960s in which he described the mother of school phobes as being one who

> tries so hard intellectually to rear her child 'by the baby book'; the woman who intellectually wants to breast-feed but who fails because she 'hasn't enough milk', who found breast-feeding unpleasant and painful; who protests too loudly about her failure, and who feels guilty about her inability 'to be a woman'; the mother who gives too much of the self in the actual care of the baby, fussing over it, over-stimulating with too many feeds and who becomes terrified by the child's cry; the mother who worries that the baby will die in his sleep, be dropped while bathing, catch a cold from the draught, who does not permit the occasional substitute care, lest she be considered 'unloving'.[91]

Or, in the words of another paper in 1957, the mother of a school phobe might superficially possess a demeanour of 'grown-up sophistication', but in reality she was a 'frightened and frustrated little girl'.[92] The school-phobic child and mother were merely exaggerated versions of 'normally frightened' children and mothers.

As the senior psychologist for the North Wales Child Guidance Clinics observed in 1959, both the mother and child needed therapy within the school guidance clinics in order to 'wean them from one another by helping them to grapple with their anxiety and ambivalent feelings'.[93] Since the problem was the mother, cure could only take place if the mother was treated.[94] In the words of researchers at the Institute for Juvenile Research in Chicago in 1941, it 'cannot be over-emphasized that the mother needs and is given treatment as is the child, and by treatment we do not mean advice'.[95] There was little discussion about how to treat fathers. Indeed, the researchers at the Institute for Juvenile Research went on to argue that although the father's neuroses 'played into the mother's difficulties and led to greater disturbance and frustration in her, and thus indirectly to greater conflict in the child', treatment of the mother alone was 'a more direct route to a resolution of the conflicts of the child. Fortunately, from a practical point of view, the mother is freer to come for treatment than would be the average father.'[96] It was often sufficient to treat the mother, not the child at all.[97]

The manipulation of the child's fears was animated by debates about emotional discipline within society more generally: after all, strategies of change (authoritarian versus gentle, for instance) reflected different dreams and hopes for the future, when these children would be adults. As the emotional standards applied to children increasingly diverged from those applied to adults, parental anxieties became more pressing. Disciplinary disputes over the nature of the child's emotional life recreated the child as an enigma. Teachers, child psychologists and employees at Child Guidance Clinics rallied round to educate hapless young parents weary and frustrated by children who were afraid of the dark, distressed by nightmares and harbouring a multitude of irrational fears. But, whether it involved a medical, psychological or educational project, the fears of children rapidly seeped away to the peripheries: what was really under scrutiny was the fears and anxieties of their nervous parents. This was explicitly acknowledged by some child-advice books, as one title, *Don't Be Afraid of Your Child. A Guide to Perplexed Parents* (1952), attested.[98] As we shall see in Chapter Eleven, by the end of the twentieth century fears *of* the child took precedence over the child's fears.

CHAPTER FOUR

Nightmares

And his steps follow the stream
Past rusting apparatus
To its gloomy beginning, the original
Chasm where brambles block
The entrance to the underworld;
There the silence blesses his sorrow,
And holy to his dread is that dark
Which will neither promise nor explain.

AUDEN, 'THE AGE OF ANXIETY'

Educationalist Raymond Bellamy had not experienced a nightmare for several years when, at 3.40 a.m. on 9 August 1914, he was heard making a 'distressing sort of noise' in his sleep. When his roommate roused him, Bellamy felt 'weak, scared' and his heart was 'fluttering' wildly. Although he continued to feel frightened for some time, he had sufficient presence of mind to record his nightmare. In the dream, Bellamy had been driving a horse-drawn buggy up and down a hill and across a stream. Not being overly fond of horses, he was afraid about whether he would be able to unhitch the buggy. Suddenly he found himself in an oppressively crowded building where a couple drew him into an earnest discussion about a sinister woman hiding in the rabble. This couple planned to break this woman's power by slipping away and meeting at a spring further down the road. Bellamy fretted about whether he would be able to find the stream. Again the dream's geography shifted, depositing Bellamy outside a window through which he was peering into a room where the menacing woman was talking to his wife. The evil woman had heard of the scheme to weaken her powers and, in retaliation, had hypnotised Bellamy's wife into believing she was a big black cat. In Bellamy's words:

> Immediately, I was filled with a great fear for my wife and with a raging anger against the woman. I broke out into calling her all kinds of names, especially saying, 'You devil, you devil,' and trying to get through the window to her. I tore out the screen, but had a great difficulty in doing so. When I finally succeeded . . . I threw it at her head, but she did not dodge, but sat boldly upright and seemed to defy me.

In the midst of his curses he was woken up. One of his first thoughts was: what does it mean?

Bellamy's psychological explanation for his terrifying dream forged links between the content of the nightmare and events in his life. At the time of the nightmare he was teaching in the summer school at Emory and Henry College, a liberal-arts college in Virginia. His wife had gone to visit her family and 'in order to keep from getting too lonesome', he had invited one of the young men from the school to be his roommate. A number of events in the nightmare seemed to echo recent experiences. For instance, he remembered a conversation with a friend about horse-drawn buggies and this friend had given him instructions on how to drive to a nearby spring. Shortly before his nightmare he had read a book on the Salem witch trials. In another book he had read that an infamous Russian murderess had sat 'coolly and impudently' during her trial. Furthermore, the most recent letter from his wife had announced that she was about to visit a scary acquaintance later that day. It seemed appropriate to Bellamy that his wife might be punished by thinking she was a cat since he had once met a melancholic woman who believed she had been transformed into a cat. This woman's mental suffering was 'about the keenest that I have ever observed'.

In addition, Bellamy had attended a church service that day ('unwillingly and from a sense of duty') and had been irritated by the hocus-pocus being propagated. At the time he had joked that he wanted to swear and throw something at the pastor. The dream 'gave me the chance of my life to fulfil this desire, and I seized the opportunity by breaking into a stream of profanity (not very successful profanity, I fear, as I never use it when awake and therefore was not in very good practice)' and throwing the window screen at the pernicious witch.

Finally, however, Bellamy believed that his nightmare had exposed his guilty conscience. On the evening of his frightening dream he had been walking home with a group of students. A couple of the young women were going in a different direction, but when Bellamy gallantly offered to accompany them, his roommate had huffily objected. It 'occurred to me that he probably thought I was not within my bounds as a married man', and so he had 'vaguely wished' that he had some way of proving his love for his wife. According to Bellamy, he 'could not have asked for a better opportunity to serve and show my love for my wife than the dream gave me, and at the same time it assured me of my affection for her'.

Bellamy admitted that this interpretation of his nightmare was not as 'modern' as it might have been: after all, he had eschewed sexual interpretations and had made little use of the 'chaotic inferno' of psychoanalysis. In addition, he was happy to revert to older, non-psychological explanations for nightmares. Bellamy believed that his body was 'speaking' its own language. He had been sleeping on his back and, because it had been raining, he had closed the window, so restricting ventilation in his bedroom. In his words:

> I am strongly inclined to give the physical elements a large amount of the responsibility for the dream, and I have not found occasion to change my mind in this matter. I think that even the inability to jump through the window in my dream was caused by the weak and exhausted state of my body, due to the poor circulation and cramped position.[1]

As with many people at the turn of the century, somatic, psychological and psychoanalytical interpretations of dreams coexisted in uncertain fellowship.

Although nightmares bedevil a fifth of adults and two-fifths of young children, there is no uncontested explanation for their appearance and the terror they induce.[2] In earlier centuries terrifying midnight reveries were understood to involve some kind of communication with the 'other world'. For instance, dreams that induced anxiety or alarm were brought about by devils pressing upon the sleeper's chest. They might even be evidence of the workings of black magic or proof of possession. These views had been firmly rejected by all but the most superstitious commentators by the nineteenth century. Instead of possessing demonic significance, nightmares were blamed increasingly upon the capricious body. As with Bellamy, simple errors of judgement — taking a nap after a heavy meal or dozing on your back — was all that was required to prompt a terror dream. To avoid nightmares people needed to ensure that their stomach did not press upon abdominal blood vessels, generating excessive pressure on the diaphragm, lungs and heart, and interfering with the flow of blood to the brain.

As with many states of fear (see Chapter Three), children's bodies rendered them particularly susceptible to terror dreams, especially if they were the offspring of nervous or rheumatic parents.[3] 'Insanity, hysteria, neurasthenia, epilepsy, chorea [the 'dancing disease'], and nervous dyspepsia' were often present in the families of nightmare sufferers.[4] Even among people born to healthy families, 'injudicious feeding', constipation, worms and lack of fresh air could induce a nightmare, especially when aggravated by the 'forcing system in education'.[5] Concerned parents of child sufferers needed to take swift and effective managerial action. *Religion and Medicine. The Moral Control of Nervous Disorders* (1908), co-authored by a physician and two clergymen, advised parents of children who were afraid at night to avoid exciting them with stories before they went to sleep:

> All morbidity of imagination should be checked and the mind strengthened and developed by simple, practical, scientific reading.

With the growth and maturing of the body many of these childish fears gradually disappear. Hence the need for open-air exercise, nutritious food, and the avoidance of an over-stimulation of the brain by too much mental work. Finally, a few reassuring suggestions administered in a firm voice to the child when he is in a half-waking, half-sleeping state, will be found to be of the greatest value. Happily the child-mind is most amenable to suggestion.[6]

Above all, the child's diet and activities had to be monitored. The usefulness of giving a child some 'mild purgative medicine' was widely recommended by those who blamed disorders of digestion as a cause of nightmares.[7] The author of *The Management of Children* (1906) provided mothers and nurses with a list of things to guard against when dealing with children troubled by bad dreams:

> If the gums are swollen or pressed upon by an advancing tooth, ask the doctor if he thinks it proper for them to be lanced. The diet, mode of feeding, etc., must be reviewed . . . The sufficiency and proper character of the motions must be attended to. All sources of nervous excitement must be removed or avoided, and the child had better also be put in a warm bath every night before going to bed. A short course of a tonic like syrup of phosphate of iron or quinine also often does good.[8]

Physicians also endorsed hypnotics, such as chloral hydrate, bromide of sodium and hyoscyamus (or henbane), claiming that such remedies possessed an 'excellent reputation' for children and could be 'given in considerable doses with perfect safety and the best results'.[9] Above all, children should not be chastised for nightmares. The fact that they 'raised the house' in the middle of the night was not to be regarded as 'naughty', advised one commentator in 1906: nightmares were a protest of the body and the child had no control over them.[10] As G. Stanley Hall advised in 1897, 'hygiene and regimen' demanded that children as well as adults avoid placing any strain on their organs of digestion and circulation before crawling into bed.[11]

These somatic explanations for nightmares persisted throughout the twentieth century. For instance, A. J. J. Ratcliff's *A History of Dreams* (1923) observed that dreams were profoundly sensitive to 'states of the body'. According to him, this explained why the gothic-horror novelist Ann Radcliffe would resolutely feast on indigestible food before going to sleep: nightmares fed the plots of her novels.[12] Even William S. Walsh, a keen apostle of psychoanalysis and author of *The Psychology of Dreams* (1920), warned nightmare sufferers against sleeping on their backs (he advised them to tie a thickly knotted band of cloth around their abdomen so they would be unable to turn in their sleep). Walsh also had words of reprimand for the parents of nightmare sufferers. He observed that an 'injudicious act' on the part of a parent could result in nightmares for the child, as could 'improper story-telling' (especially 'cheap paper-back novels, ghost, Indian, detective and similar stories'). Walsh also criticised 'overzealous teachers' who threatened children with anecdotes about the devil and hell's torments. Although he counselled sympathy and reassurance, he also warned that some children would take advantage of the kindness shown to them. 'Should it become a matter of decision between the rod and direful threats in an effort to correct the child,' he advised, 'the former ought to be preferred.'[13]

For all these commentators nightmares were a serious issue because of the damage they inflicted on the body. Of the eight principal systems of the body, it was the respiratory, nervous, circulatory, and alimentary systems that were most profoundly affected. Late-nineteenth-century physicians were deeply concerned that nightmares might lead to a hysterical paralysis within the sleep state. This, in turn, might result in the more 'morbid drama' of death.[14] As late as the 1920s one author warned people of 'low vitality' that they risked stroke or haemorrhage during frightening dreams, since such dreams raised their blood pressure and, if their arterial walls had already been hardened, could cause these arteries to rupture.[15] People with heart disease, high blood pressure or respiratory problems (such as asthma) were also at risk. In the words of one article, 'Dreams as the Cause of Death and Disease' (1920), 'repeated tormenting dreams will cause even cortical injury in adults leading to cerebral lesions of a serious nature in later life'.[16] Even if spared such dire consequences, the nightmare sufferer might still be troubled by indigestion, constipation and a general feeling of nervousness the following day.[17] Nightmares were the result *of* physical debasement and, in turn, culminated *in* bodily harm.

Nevertheless, by the end of the nineteenth century psychological theories about nightmares overrode somatic ones. Evolutionary speculation fuelled much of the discussion. According to this view, all kinds of fear — including those inspired by nightfall and nightmares — were inherited from a primordial past. In the 1890s G. Stanley Hall was at the forefront of such arguments. As the president of Clark University (in Worcester, Massachusetts), editor of the *American Journal of Psychology* and founder of the American Psychological Association, which launched the discipline of psychology in America, he received great acclaim for his ideas. Hall was a leading proponent of 'recapitulation theory': the notion that the infant 'recapitulated' or 'repeated' the history of the race. He set out his ideas in a seminal study entitled 'A Study of Fears', published in his journal in 1897. In this essay he compiled the fears of 1701 people, most of whom were under the age of twenty-three. To these accounts he added 386 supplementary reports and other returns, making a work of four thousand pages. Hall's methodology was dubious: quantity triumphed over consistency, interviewers breezily prompted interviewees and no distinction was made between introspective description, reminiscence and hearsay. Even worse, he unabashedly admitted that he purposely selected what he regarded as salient items, 'dropping what was irrelevant'. As such, Hall's article is more useful for what it tells us about his influential propositions concerning the nature of fear within dreams than what it says about the content of actual nightmares in the late 1890s.

Hall regarded fear as the most important emotion in the evolution of the species, believing that it was impossible to comprehend the enormity of humanity's progress simply by reference to consciousness. He saw the conscious ego as 'a very inadequate and partial manifestation of the soul'; it was a 'feeble, flickering taper in a vast factory full of machinery and operative, each doing its work in unobserved silence'. Rather, the emotion of fear was the driving force in humanity's great and glorious assembly plant. As 'anticipatory pain',[18] fear was the emotion that enabled humanity's ancestors to

make that 'great step upward'. The 'first utilization of past experience' enabled humanity's ancestors to anticipate and therefore avoid
danger. Of course, Hall conceded, fear was a painful emotion, but
the degree of pain emanating from fear states was less than that
posed by the threat. As a consequence, there was 'economy in the
substitution'.

Hall's basic proposition was that 'function' survived 'structure'.
As a starting point he observed that most fears were simply irrational in modern contexts. People feared those same threats that had
plagued members of the early species. As he put it:

> Night is now the safest time, serpents are no longer among our
> most fatal foes, and most of the animal fears do not fit the present
> conditions of civilised life; strangers are not usually dangerous, nor
> are big eyes and teeth; celestial fears fit the heavens of ancient super-
> stition and not the heavens of modern science . . . the intensity of
> many fears, especially in youth, is out of all proportion to the excit-
> ing cause. The first experiences with water, the moderate noise of
> the wind, or distant thunder, etc., may excite faint fear, but why
> does it sometimes make children on the instant frantic with panic?

He concluded that human 'instinct-feeling' was 'incalculably more
ancient than the intellect'. Traces of the primordial past lingered —
in the individual's body, soul and emotional life. Since humanity's
ancestors floated and swam far longer than they had walked, it did
not surprise Hall that 'vestigial traces' (such as 'monstrous births')
or rudimentary organs ('gill slits under the skin of our necks', for
instance) of this inheritance were evident. Even more speculatively,
he believed that vestigial traces of the past affected human souls
(assuming, as Hall did, that souls could be observed). He accused
those who wished to deny this fact of making the soul 'more limited
in its backward range' than the body. 'I am too idealistic and cannot
think so meanly of the soul as to do this,' he sternly lectured. What
was true of body and soul was also true of the emotions.

While admitting that his theory could not be proved, Hall
declared himself strongly of the opinion that humanity's fears
encompassed 'some of the oldest elements of psyche life, some faint

reminiscent atavistic echo from the primeval sea'. Why did some people harbour a great fear of water? he asked. The answer was easy: at some time in the long distant past, life in the sea gave way to life on land. As a consequence, the 'higher animals swam less and less' and water became dangerous 'in proportion to this loss of power'. Those animals that adapted best to land flourished and became increasingly fearful of the sea. Their fear had to be 'very strong because it must control the old love'. On rare occasions this love of the sea erupted back into consciousness. Indeed, this explained why women (rather than men) were more likely to commit suicide by drowning: 'the female organization is more con-servative of archaic influences than the male', Hall mused.[19] The abstract past traced its path directly to modern fears. Fear of thun-der signalled that 'primitive consciousness' possessed a great reverence for the 'powers above'; fear of eyes dated from the time when human ancestors competed for survival with other large-eyed animals. Humanity's inheritance from that 'long war of all against all within his own species' was terror.

As a result of these reflections Hall reserved a special place for dreams and nightmares. After all, it was in sleep that the soul's 'old scars' were able to struggle to consciousness, convincing the organ-ism of its vulnerability. Despite the great lapse of time, the threat that night posed to humanity's ancestors 'still rules our nerves'. For Hall, this also explained why children's nightmares were crowded with exotic and extinct animals, monsters and ghosts. These images (or 'memories', as he wished them to be known) bore witness to the effect of the remote past upon the human soul.[20]

Recapitulation-based interpretations of dreams and nightmares had a long life. As late as the 1940s scholars such as Nandor Fodor published a range of supportive articles on nightmares in presti-gious academic journals, including the *Journal of Nervous and Mental Disease*, the *American Journal of Psychotherapy* and *The American Imago*. For instance, Fodor believed that nightmares involving water reca-pitulated the birth of the dreamer. In his words:

Life on this planet began in the tepid primeval sea of countless ages past . . . Many millions of years later, the most stupendous step in evolution was accomplished: the adaptation of aquatic life to existence on solid ground. Not since, has evolution taken a comparable stride. Yet, in our short lifetimes, we may witness often — each time a child is born — what is at least a symbolic re-enactment of this epochal event.

At birth, the child is 'thrown from the waters to the land, as its first land-ancestors were stranded on the shore by the ebb of the ocean's warm tide'. Not surprisingly, the child responded with fear and rage, as had the child's remotest ancestors. In nightmares involving water, the individual repeatedly relived this birth trauma or 'organismic memory'.

Since there is a great deal of repetition in Fodor's analysis (he applied identical reasoning to explain every type of nightmare), only one further example will suffice. Nightmares about being eaten alive could also be traced to humanity's primordial inheritance. Fodor reminded readers that, in the pre-natal state, the embryo

> epitomizes the physical evolution of man from the life spark stirring in the mind of the primeval ocean to the human stage. After birth, under the pressure of parental and social discipline, the child re-enacts the moral evolution of mankind. At birth, the child is a savage and compares with a cannibal. It tests reality by the mouth and destroys that which it assimilates. The behaviour is instinctual but in the child's dependent state it is fraught with far-reaching consequences. Family disapproval of the child's behaviour is bound to arise. Frightened or made conscious of guilt, the child expects destruction through being devoured by the powerful parents.

During nightmares about being devoured, the child retrieved this 'organismic memory' in terrifying vividness. In 'pain and terror', the infant was

> disgorged from a place of warmth and security when we were born. To be eaten or to be swallowed is a reversal of this process. Parental anger mobilizes the trauma of birth. The result is fear beyond control in the waking state and nightmares of terrifying intensity while we are asleep.

If nightmares were a product of humanity's ancient history, could sufferers ever find relief? Fodor was optimistic. All that was required was an emotional acceptance of the 'mental error' involved in dreaming, combined with an intellectual understanding of the process of displacement that took place in their sleep world. Proof of the effectiveness of his cure was (allegedly) to be found in the way Fodor treated servicemen suffering from nightmares after the trauma of the First World War. He accepted that disturbed servicemen had endured a 'personal misfortune': their experiences in the foxholes had dramatically increased their propensity to claustrophobia and nightmares involving suffocation. Nevertheless, to cure such men it was necessary to teach them to interpret their nightmares on a 'biological level'; that is, they needed to understand that their real fear was furtively cloistered in their unconscious. The source of their fear dated from the time of birth when the umbilical cord was cut, leaving the infant struggling for its first breath. This insight into the origin of their panic would relieve nightmare-prone servicemen of their 'burden of individual misfortune'.[21] Biology, not bombs, terrified servicemen.

Fodor's fusion of racial inheritance and birth trauma was popular in the 1950s, although many commentators minimised the recapitulation aspects of such theories while retaining this emphasis on that 'perilous journey through the vaginal passage'.[22] Nightmares were the soul's way of tapping into both primordial angst and birth trauma.

At the same time as Hall and his supporters were developing their theories on the east coast of America, a more profound strand of dream theory was being expounded in Vienna. By his early forties Sigmund Freud had become interested in dreams after observing that his patients often mentioned them spontaneously. His classic text *The Interpretation of Dreams* was published on 4 November 1899 (although it retained the printed date of 1900 because Freud wished it to be associated with the new century). Despite selling only 351 copies in its first six years, the book fundamentally changed the modern understanding of dreams and nightmares. Henceforth the interpretation of both became a two-way affair in which the dreamer was involved in a process of obscuring and concealing dream-meaning while the analyst responded by unravelling and revealing.

Freudian interpretations of dreams represented a fundamental break with earlier somatic and evolutionary readings. For Freud, a mental image (such as a dream) must have a mental cause. In *The Interpretation of Dreams* he argued that dreams provided the clearest reflection of the unconscious and wish fulfilment. In sleep the ego relaxed, allowing psychic conflicts and desires that were usually carefully repressed to blunder into consciousness. Because these conflicts and desires were by their nature profoundly disturbing, they could appear only in a distorted form. Consequently the parts of the dream that were remembered upon awakening (the 'manifest content') were a disguise for the 'latent content', which was too distressing to be recalled. Emotions were particularly intense in dreams and were often not related to the manifest content of the dream because the ego distorted dreams through a number of mechanisms, the most important being displacement, projection, symbolism and condensation.

In displacement, an urge was repressed and redirected to another person or object, while in projection it was projected upon somebody else. For instance, instead of the sleeper dreaming about killing her mother (which would be too disturbing and cause her to awaken), she might dream about her mother being eaten by a lion (displacement) or her sister killing their mother (projection). In symbolisation, the repressed urge reappeared as a symbol — and certain manifest symbols always possessed the same latent meaning. For example, the number three always referred to male sexual organs; balloons were erections; caves or boxes indicated female genitalia; running down stairs or inside a house alluded to sexual intercourse; and teeth falling out suggested castration anxiety as punishment for masturbation. Finally, in condensation, the repressed urge was condensed into a brief image. After one or more of these processes had taken place, 'secondary revision' occurred: that is, the dreamwork was given some superficial meaning or storyline. This became the dream's manifest content. Once the latent content of the dream was analysed, the disguised fulfilment of wishes would become obvious.[23]

Freud analysed one of his own childhood dreams to illustrate his thesis. When he was seven or eight he dreamed that two or three people with bird's beaks carried his beloved mother into the room. This dream was so terrifying that he immediately woke up and insisted that his mother come into his room to comfort him. He recalled that in the nightmare his mother had the same peaceful look on her face as had his grandfather when he was in a coma immediately before he died. Further, the bird's beaks resembled the deities on Egyptian tomb reliefs that he had seen in Philippson's Bible. He also recalled that a boy called Philip had recently taught him the vulgar word for 'coitus' — the first time Freud had heard this word. His anxiety, therefore, was not caused by his dreaming that his mother was dying, but by his repressed sexual craving.[24] Dreams were a form of wish-fulfilment.[25]

Disturbed sleep was a particular feature of nightmares or terror dreams. Such dreams allowed some of the repressed urges to seep into the conscious mind, causing the dreamer to awaken. According to Freud, anxiety dreams were those in which the 'content had undergone the least distortion'.[26] Nightmares were

> an expression of immoral, incestuous and perverse impulses or of murderous and sadistic lusts. The dreamer reacts to many of these dreams by waking up in a fright in which case the situation is no longer obscure to us. The censorship has neglected its task, this has been noticed too late, and the generation of anxiety is a substitution for the distortion that has been omitted.[27]

These ideas transformed perceptions of dreams and nightmares. Innumerable scholars, including Ernest Jones, Freud's disciple and translator, adopted and adapted the Freudian creed. Like Freud, Jones dismissed the somatic interpretation of nightmares. In 'On the Nightmare' (1910) he poured scorn on doctors who merely peddled 'irrelevant advice on matters of general hygiene, coupled perhaps with the administration of such potent remedies as silica and cinnabar or with a half-jocular remark concerning the assimilable [sic] capacity of the evening meal'. Jones pointed out that:

a patient whose stomach is half destroyed with cancer may commit all sorts of dietary indiscretions, including even indulgence in cucumber — the article of food that is most looked askance at in relation to Nightmare — he may even sleep on his back, and will still defy medical orthodoxy in not suffering from any trace of Nightmare.

On the other hand, a regular sufferer of nightmares

> may be scrupulously rigorous in regard to both the quality and quantity of all that he eats, may in fact develop a *maladie de scrupule* [scruples, or, in modern terminology, obsessive-compulsive disorder] in this direction, that he may martyr himself with elaborate precautions to avoid these and other 'causes' of the malady, and by means of a contrivance of spikes ensure against ever lying — let alone sleeping — on his back, but despite all his endeavours he will have to endure as many and as severe attacks as before.

According to Jones, both the explanation and solution to the problem of nightmares was psychoanalysis. He reminded his readers that Freud had proved that *Angst* (broadly translated as 'anxiety') was caused by 'various abnormalities in the function of the sexual activities of the individual', particularly sexual repression or the 'unsatisfactory functioning' of the individual's sexual life. Dreams, including terror dreams, were the 'fulfilment in the imagination' of a desire that had been repressed in the individual's waking state. For Jones, this helped explain why nightmares occurred most frequently in people who slept in any position other than the supine or prone position since these were the postures in which 'the love embrace' was 'normally consummated'. Overeating could also provoke those forbidden erotic desires that induced nightmares. According to Jones, the fact that a heavy meal was

> apt to be followed by an accession of erotic desire is an observation acted on by every roué; that it, like alcohol, tends to dull the activity of the conscious inhibitions of the waking state and so release suppressed mental trends is so well known as to make it comprehensible

that it may occasionally play some part in the evocation of Nightmare. A full stomach may also act by arousing the sensation of a heavy weight lying in, and therefore on, the abdomen.

To illustrate his point, Jones quoted the following example of a nightmare, told by a French writer:

> A young Lady, of a tender, lax habit, about fifteen, before the menses appear'd, was seiz'd with a fit of this Disease [Nightmare], and groan'd so miserably that she awoke her Father, who was sleeping in the next room. He arose, ran into her chamber, and found her lying on her Back and the Blood gushing plentifully out of her Mouth and Nose. When he shook her, she recover'd and told him, that she thought some great heavy Man came to her beside, and, without further ceremony, stretched himself upon her. She had been heard moaning in sleep several nights before; but, the next day after she imagin'd herself oppress'd by that Man, she had a copious eruption of the menses, which, for that time, remov'd all her complaints.

Jones interpreted the young lady's nightmare as exposing her struggle between two conflicting emotions: dread of and desire for sexual intercourse. Because both impulses were powerful, so too was her dreamtime distress. He also observed that her nightmare had started immediately before her first menstrual period, a time when 'erotic feeling is in most cases most ardent'.[28]

In *Nightmare, Witches, and Devils* (1931) Jones went further. He still accepted Freud's belief that nightmares were 'always an expression of intense mental conflict' centring around 'some form of "repressed" sexual desire', but, he observed, this was true of all fear dreams. What distinguished nightmares from other anxious dreams was the fact that the nightmare brought to the mind's surface that *most* repressed of sexual desires — in other words, nightmares expressed a mental conflict over an incestuous desire.[29]

In his exposition of Freud's views about dreams and nightmares, Jones merely placed special emphasis on incestuous wishes. Carl Gustav Jung went much further. In his early work he had accepted Freud's distinction between the latent and manifest dream content,[30] but he had changed his mind by the 1930s, arguing that the 'manifest dream-picture is the dream itself and contains the whole meaning of the dream'.[31] This dramatic split with Freud originated in a confrontation over their analysis of each other's dreams. According to Jung:

> Freud had a dream — I would not think it right to air the problem it involved. I interpreted it as best I could, but added that a great deal more could be said about it if he would supply me with some additional details from his private life. Freud's response to these words was a curious look — a look of the utmost suspicion. Then he said, 'But I cannot risk my authority!' At that moment, he lost it altogether. That sentence burned itself into my memory; and in it the end of our relationship was already fore-shadowed. Freud was placing personal authority above truth.[32]

Jung then embarked on what he described as 'a period of inner uncertainty' — could even be called a 'state of disorientation' – in which he resolved not to employ any specific theory when analysing his patients. Instead, he would simply listen to what they said of their own accord.[33] As Jung later advised, therapists should 'never apply any theory but always ask the patient how *he* feels about his dream images. For dreams are always about a particular problem of the individual about which he has a wrong conscious judgment.' Dreams were 'the natural reaction of the self-regulating psychic system'.[34] Or, as Jung wrote in 'On the Psychology of the Unconscious' (1953), 'Nature is often obscure or impenetrable, but she is not, like man, deceitful. We must therefore take it that the dream is just what it pretends to be, neither more nor less. If it shows something in a negative light, there is no reason for assuming that it is meant positively.'[35] In a later work, he continued this line of thought, arguing that

> What Freud calls the 'dream-façade' is the dream's obscurity, and this is really only a projection of our own lack of understanding. We say that the dream has a false front only because we fail to see into it. We would do better to say that we are dealing with something like

a text that is unintelligible not because it has a façade — a text has no façade — but simply because we cannot read it. We do not have to get behind such a text, but must first learn to read it.[36]

As a category of dreams, nightmares had a special position in Jung's philosophy. For him, below the unconscious mind of the individual was the collective unconscious, the universe of primitive humanity. Nightmares were an expression of this racial unconscious. All dreams and nightmares contain images and symbols shared by all humanity. Archetypes or primordial images arose out of the collective unconscious, which could be tapped into in sleep.

While Jones and Jung were chipping away at Freud's pristine dream edifice, a much more incisive critique of the Freudian emphases on wish-fulfilment and the sexual aetiology of nightmares occurred as a result of the First World War. From 1915 medical personnel were listening to the grisly and profoundly disturbing dreams recited by men returning from the field of battle. Terrifying nightmares of being unable to withdraw bayonets from their enemies' bodies persisted long after the slaughter.[37] It was not uncommon for combatants to dream about the horror of becoming separated from comrades or of receiving a 'sudden call to arms and the inability to find some indispensable article of attire or combat'.[38] The dreams might occur 'right in the middle of an ordinary conversation' when 'the face of a Boche that I have bayoneted, with its horrible gurgle and grimace, comes sharply into view', an infantry captain complained.[39]

Such nightmares did not always occur during the war itself. First World War soldiers like Rowland Luther did not suffer until after the armistice when, he admitted, he 'cracked-up' and found himself unable to eat or sleep properly, deliriously reliving his experiences of combat.[40] George W. Crile's *A Mechanistic View of War and Peace* (1915) was one of many books published during the war which described the unique nature of soldiers' dreams. Their dreams were

always the same, always of the enemy. It is never a pleasant pastoral dream, or a dream of home, but a dream of the charge, of the bursting shell, of the bayonet thrust! Again and again in camp and hospital

wards, in spite of the great desire to sleep, a desire so great that the
dressing of a compound fracture would not be felt, men sprang up
with a battle cry, and reached for their rifles, the dream outcry startling their comrades, whose thresholds were excessively low to the
stimuli of attack.[41]

How could Freud's notion of wish-fulfilment be applied to such
terrifying reveries?

The anthropologist and psychologist William H. R. Rivers led the
revisionist interpretation of nightmares. Rivers was a Fellow of St
John's College, Cambridge and during the war was posted to
Craiglockhart hospital, near Edinburgh, where he became renowned
for his innovative and sympathetic treatment of men suffering from
'shell shock'. 'The Repression of War Experience' (1918), *Instinct
and the Unconscious* (1920) and *Conflict and Dream* (published posthu-
mously in 1923), emerged from his wartime work. Fundamental to
Rivers's approach was his claim that terrifying war dreams were
due to the repression of terrifying episodes in combat. As one of his
patients, the famous war poet Siegfried Sassoon, wrote in a poem
about combat-inspired nightmares which shared its title with
Rivers's scientific papers, 'The Repression of War Experience'
(1917):

> Now light the candles; one; two; there's that moth;
> What silly beggars they are to blunder in
> And scorch their wings with glory, liquid flame —
> No, no, not that, — it's bad to think of war,
> When thoughts you've gagged all day come back to scare you . . .

In *Conflict and Dream* Rivers set out most clearly his views on
nightmares. He began by observing that the nightmares experienced by combatants in the First World War were generally a
'faithful reproduction' of harrowing events they had actually experienced. These nightmares were accompanied by such exceptionally
intense terror that dreamers would wake up screaming, sweating
profusely, shaking and suffering from violent heart palpitations.
Some would vomit repeatedly. Because these dreams could recur,

sometimes several times in one night, terrified dreamers would refuse to go to sleep for fear of a repetition of the agony. The most striking feature of these nightmares was that they did not include any of the displacements or symbolism that Freud regarded as paramount characteristics of dreaming. There was 'absolutely nothing of the grotesque or fantastic', Rivers observed: 'the dream follows the grim reality faithfully'. Indeed, any introduction of symbols or other transformations of the actual event were generally a sign of the waning of the nightmare's emotional force. This observation that the intensity of fear was in inverse proportion to the amount of transformation occurring within the dream was in harmony with Freud's view that 'one of the results of the transformation of the latent into the manifest content of the dream is to lessen or inhibit its affective character'.

Nevertheless, these nightmares could not be reconciled with Freud's assertion that dreams were a form of wish-fulfilment. 'It is difficult to see how such awful and terrifying experiences such as those of dreams of this kind can be the result of wishes of the dreamer,' Rivers argued. In place of wish-fulfilment, he maintained that the dream was 'the attempted solution of a conflict, an attempt to solve a conflict of the waking life by such means as still remain open when the higher levels of mental activity have been put out of action by the inhibition of sleep'. After all, his fearful patients had been actively engaged in keeping out of their consciousness the horrific experiences of war that were depicted so exhaustively in their dreams. In Rivers's words:

> So far as desire enters into causation, the dream is the direct negation of a wish, the wish not to be subjected to the repetition of a painful experience, the wish leading to a process of repression in the waking life which in turn produces the dream in sleep.

The nightmare was not wish-fulfilment but 'an expression of the complete negation of a wish' to forget trauma.[42]

Rivers presented this argument even more candidly in a paper delivered to the psychiatric section of the Royal Society of Medicine in December 1917, in which he said:

If a person voluntarily represses unpleasant thoughts during the day
it is natural that they should rise into activity when the control of the
waking state is removed by sleep . . . If the painful thoughts have
been kept from the attention throughout the day by means of occupation, it is again natural that they should come into activity when
the silence and isolation of the night make occupation no longer possible. It seems as if the thoughts repressed by day assume a painful
quality when they come to the surface at night, far more intense than
is even attained if they are allowed to occupy the attention during the
day. It is as if the process of repression keeps the painful memories
or thoughts under a kind of pressure during the day, accumulating
such energy by night that they race through the mind with abnormal
speed and violence when the patient is wakeful, or take the most
vivid and painful forms when expressed by the imagery of dreams.[43]

The only solution to nightmares was to encourage the sufferers to
gradually surrender memories of war trauma to consciousness. In
this way the nightmares would start being transformed and would
eventually stop altogether.

Psychological understandings of nightmares received a blunt rebuttal in the second half of the twentieth century. In particular, since the
1970s investigations into nightmares have substituted biological certitude for the interrogation of meaning. The biological foundation
for this transformation in the understanding of nightmares was laid
in 1953 when the Chicago physiologist Nathaniel Kleitman discovered that, during certain periods of sleep, the eyes began to move in
a particular fashion.[44] Biologically, sleep could be divided into five
stages. The first four stages were designated 'non-rapid eye movement' (NREM) while the fifth stage was appointed 'rapid eye
movement' (REM). An average person experienced four or five
REM periods during a sleep of six to eight hours. It was found that
individuals who were woken during an REM period would often be
able to recall a dream. In other words, REM was the site of dreams
and the most common kind of nightmares. In contrast, another, less
typical kind of frightening dream, generally called a 'terror dream'
or 'an incubus attack', occurred in Stages 3 and 4 of sleep, before

the REM period.[45] Terror dreams were different from ordinary nightmares. In *Sleep and Wakefulness As Alternating Phases in the Cycle of Existence* (1939) Kleitman had described night terror thus:

> Suddenly, while fully asleep, after a short period of agitation and one or two groans, the child sits up in his bed, eyes wide open and facial expression one of terror. Pale, covered with perspiration, he extends his trembling arms as if to protect himself against an approaching enemy.[46]

Sufferers often engaged in aggressive 'fight or flight' movements. They would awaken, but remained drowsy and disorientated and were unsure whether or not their 'terrifying hallucinatory experience' had been 'just a dream'. Most failed to recall their terror the following morning. While the normal heart rate for people in a sitting position is between sixty-eight and seventy-two beats per minute and people experiencing ordinary nightmares (in REM sleep) had an increased heart rate of ninety-two beats per minute, the heart-rate of people suffering night terrors during NREM sleep could be triple the normal rate. According to some physiologists, terror-dreams occurred when people were *not* dreaming, or not in a REM period.[47] They were not disorders of sleep but disorders of awakening.

After the discovery of REM and NREM sleep, the biological approach to nightmares had a profound impact. Fundamentally, dreams, nightmares and terror dreams were stripped of significant 'meaning'. For some neuroscientists dreams and nightmares were a way the brain rid itself of unimportant information. Dreams stopped the brain from becoming overloaded. We dream in order to forget.[48] Others regarded dream images as the result of random bursts from nerve cells in the brainstem during REM sleep: they were simply the brain's attempt to make sense of stray signals generated by the lower brain.

A representative example of these neurological approaches can be found in the work of the neuroscientists Mircea Steriade and Robert W. McCarley. In *Brainstem Control of Wakefulness and Sleep* (1990) they attacked the science behind Freud's theories of dreams,

claiming that 'the biological state of REM sleep and its psychological counterpart of dreaming' were a direct consequence of the
'rhythmic operation of a brain oscillator that internally and periodically activates brain [sic] in such a way as to produce the characteristic
features of REM sleep and the distinctive formal characteristics of
dreams'. In other words, 'many of the formal features of dreaming
correspond with the kind of brain activation during REM sleep'.
The fact that people forget their dreams was not due to the repression
of forbidden wishes, but simply to the biological fact that long-term
memory storage was halted during REM sleep. People only remembered their nightmares if they were woken up in the middle of them.
In sleep the brain was 'activated internally by neural activity origi-
nating in the brainstem oscillator'. This activation was not driven by
sexual or aggressive instincts, as Freud would argue, but was 'moti-
vationally neutral'. Sensory and motor systems were often intensely
animated during nightmares. While all dreams were visual, approximately 65 per cent of dreams and nightmares involved auditory
systems (such as screaming) and 8 per cent activated vestibular
system (such as the 'falling' sensation typical of many nightmares).[49]
Steriade and McCarley regarded the absence of reports of pain within
dreams (even among dreamers suffering constant pain in their waking
lives) as evidence that dreams represented 'a separate biological state'
from wakefulness and did not merely transform experiences in the
individual's waking life. The 'bizarre' elements of nightmares were
not a way in which the unconscious disguised forbidden wishes, but
were simply due to the biological nature of REM sleep. Steriade and
McCarley explained that, in REM sleep

> there is a different mode of brain activation — internal instead of
> external, as in waking — and there is a simultaneous activation of
> many brain sensory and motor systems not ordinarily activated
> together in waking . . . The synthesis of these brain events may pro-
> ceed as in waking, but bizarreness may result from the attempt to
> knit together the often contradictory and incongruent elements.

The brain 'synthesised' sensory and motor information in dreams
and nightmares in the same way that it did in the waking state. The

difference was simply that, in sleep, 'the sensory part of our brain may be activated to produce the image of a wall, while the muscle command area of the brain is sending out signals to produce walking, thus we dream of walking through a wall'.[50]

However, although dreams have no intrinsic meaning, neuroscientists did recognise that humans were enthusiastic in *ascribing* meaning to their night-time reveries. 'As in interpreting a Rorschach card', Steriade and McCarley admitted that:

> meaning may be *attributed* to a dream, since all stimuli, internally or externally generated, may be seen as meaningful in the context of individual experience. In the *attributed* meaning, motivational themes may arise. Starving men dream of food, but in an undisguised way. Similarly, sexual wishes are presented without disguise, although these and other dream elements are couched in the language of the dream, which is visual, plastic, sensory, action-rich, not verbal, obsessive, and abstract. In psychotherapy the dream is an ally, not because it disguises but because it expresses.[51]

It was essential to disabuse nightmare sufferers of the belief that nightmares actually 'meant anything'. The notion that they forecast a future tragedy or were indications of an underlying psychopathology had to be jettisoned, and the frightening images of sleep exposed as random nerve-cell activity.[52] Sensible treatment regimes involving systematic desensitisation (which will be discussed in the next chapter) might be useful, in conjunction with medication such as tricyclic antidepressants.[53]

Finally, however, this neurophysiological approach to dreams and nightmares had a further major implication. As the cognitive psychologist Harry T. Hunt asked: 'Is dreaming . . . a form of thinking — a symbolic imagination unique to man (older children or adults)? Or is it a species-specific constructed "life space" — contingent only on the cortical activation of the REM state?'[54] After all, EEG recordings of sleeping cats showed visual system activation during REM sleep.[55] In the REM state the eye movements of the lower animals were functionally similar to their eye movements in the waking state.[56] If dreaming was simply a form of perception, it had to be shared by any animal in the REM stage of sleep. Of course, if animals in REM sleep dream, their dreams

> would presumably reproduce their species-specific life world, but not creatively reorganize or recombine it. The squirrel's dream tree is then no more symbolic than its waking tree. It presumably dreams in the motorically organized, sequential 'stories' of its waking life, just as we do.

However, because the lower animals were capable of associative learning, but not capable of 'the sort of recombinatory novelty that is basic to human symbolism', their dreams would not represent the same 'meaningful symbolic expression' as they did for humans.[57]

Finally, even within the neuroscientific paradigm of dreaming, language and cognition were essential in the construction of the dream or nightmare. In this way it was not surprising to observe how dream theory fundamentally influenced the process of dreaming. Thus Jung's nightmares bore all the trademarks of Jungian theory. They featured 'strikingly "archetypal" and uncanny visualizations of mythical figures, fantastic settings, and psychedelic transformations of size, shape, and geometric structure'. In contrast, Freud's nightmares were replete with 'latent' meanings lurking beneath the 'manifest' dream structure. 'Unlikely visualizations' were drawn 'predominantly from his own recent past experience and only made sense through the related memories to which his free associations would lead him'.[58] We dream the nightmares we narrate.

Debates about nightmares were fundamentally concerned with questions of meaning. What did it mean 'to mean'? Humanity's genetic inheritance, obscure desires and chaotic brain waves became sites of struggle even within sleep. According to many, the physiology and psyche of the dreamer were bared in night-time reveries. Nightmares were part of humanity's stimulus-response mechanism or capacity for repressing disquieting needs. For others these theoretical debates about extreme states such as nightmares directed attention to more troubling questions about what it meant to be human. Was humanity at the mercy of capricious brainstems or was there a unique cognitive and imaginative realm possessed by humans but not shared by other animals? As we will see in the next chapter, many of these issues were also central to understanding other extreme fear states, such as phobias.

Nevertheless, it is easy to exaggerate the impact of these revolutions in evolutionary, psychological, psychoanalytical and neuroscientific thought. While these theories have preoccupied scientists, they failed to bury lingering traces of 'pre-modern' doctrines about dreams as some sort of communication with the 'other world'. Superstitious fears survived well into the modern period. Even in the twenty-first century, many people give credence to the view that dreams involve interaction with the supernatural. While in the Middle Ages nightmares were generally thought to be dispatched by demons, in the twentieth century they were more likely to be interpreted as prophecies sent by spirits or arising out of a 'collective unconscious'. The business of deciphering nightmares has reinvented that spiritual realm rejected by the main theorists of the nightmare.[59]

CHAPTER FIVE

Phobias

. . . this guilt the insoluble
Final fact, infusing his private
Nexus of needs, his noted aims with
Incomprehensible comprehensive dread
At not being what he knows that before
This world was he was willed to become.

AUDEN, 'THE AGE OF ANXIETY'

Sometimes nightmares were lived in daylight. The fright occa-sioned by phobias exceeded all others. Phobias were never 'normal' — after all, the objects or sites of terror were profoundly commonplace — but the panic they inspired, their persistence and their uncontrollability were immeasurable. In the early decades of the twentieth century, a man known simply as 'Vincent' was one such sufferer. Vincent was an educated, middle-class man who har-boured a fearful secret: from the age of twelve he had suffered from agoraphobia, or the fear of open spaces. His condition did not even have a name before the eighteenth century, and it was not until 1786 that the word 'phobia' was used on its own.[1] But the focus of Vincent's particular phobia was a most modern affliction. Agoraphobia was the first phobia to generate a detailed psycholog-ical analysis, when, in the early decades of the nineteenth century, François Leuret described a case. Even so, the term 'agoraphobia' was not coined until 1873. As with most agoraphobics, Vincent's affliction dominated his life. It had developed very gradually. At the age of twelve he was 'taken suddenly with "spells" which lasted about thirty minutes'. These took the form of a chill or 'coldness' that would possess his entire body. Believing that Vincent was suffering some kind of temporary stoppage of circulation, the family doctor prescribed hot baths followed by the vigorous rubbing of his body with rough towels and stimulants. Vincent's 'spells' only gradually metamorphosed into a phobia.

His first agoraphobic attack was triggered by a tragedy in his community. One day his eleven-year-old playmate disappeared. Initially it was believed that the boy had slipped into the river and drowned; then rumours spread that, 'being a venturesome lad', he had run away from home. However, one morning in late autumn the boy was found at the bank of the river with his throat cut. A local village woman was charged with murder. Thereafter Vincent was afraid to be alone, to enter a barn or climb a neighbouring hill. Decades later he was still incapable of looking at a hill or tall building without a feeling of dread. Crossing a wide street or bridge was a tribulation almost too great to bear. During the First World War his dread of a particular bridge was so overwhelming that he would have preferred to 'face a nest of Boche machine guns' than cross the river. His account of his life was peppered with words such as 'agony', 'dark dread', 'embarrassing', 'handicapped', 'victim' and 'endurance'. 'Is there any hope of a cure?' he cried:

> Can I ever take my place in the world unhandicapped as other men are, and enjoy a single day undepressed by dark dread? . . . I see a man hobbling past my house on crutches, a cripple for life, and I actually envy him. At times I would gladly exchange places with the humblest day-labourer who walks unafraid across the public square or saunters tranquilly over the viaduct on his way home after a day's work.[2]

Vincent kept his affliction a secret all his life, never even mentioning it to his physician and he used a pseudonym when writing of his phobia in the *American Journal of Psychology* in 1919. Despite his seemingly successful life, in his own mind he was ' a nervous wreck, weak, worthless'.

What Vincent may not have realised was that, according to conservative estimate, irrational terrors were shared by 77 out of every
thousand normal people. More than two people in every thousand
were *severely* disabled by their phobia yet only a quarter of these were
receiving treatment.[3] Only a small proportion of phobics was suffering from Vincent's particular affliction. Although agoraphobia
generated the most debate, its reputation was undeserved except in
the history of therapy. After all, although half of all people undergoing treatment for phobias were suffering from agoraphobia, less
than 1 per cent of the phobic population had to endure this particular phobia. In contrast, phobias of injury, illness and death were five
times more prevalent yet only a third of all phobics under treatment
came under these headings.[4] Furthermore, since phobias were culturally imagined, new phobias constantly developed (such as phobias
about spaceships).[5] Nevertheless, it was agoraphobia, with its
implicit threat to civil society, which seemed to characterise the
extremes of pathological fear.

In the previous chapter we looked at Sigmund Freud's theory of
dreams. He was to make an even bigger impact when he turned his
attention to phobias. In a series of articles written in the mid-1890s
Freud insisted upon the need to distinguish 'true obsessions' from
phobias. In obsessions 'an idea forces itself upon the patient'. This idea
was accompanied by an 'associated emotional state', such as anger,
remorse, doubt or anxiety. In contrast, in the case of phobias the
associated emotional state was *always* anxiety. In addition, while obsessions were varied and specialised, phobias were more predictable.[6]
Phobias either represented an exaggerated fear of things that frightened most people, such as death, illness, snakes and night (Freud
called these 'common phobias') or they were 'specific phobias', which
included being afraid of objects or situations that generally inspired no
fear (for instance, open spaces or writing). Both types of phobia were
caused by 'the accumulation of sexual tension, produced by abstinence or by frustrated sexual excitation', as occurred in coitus
interruptus, impotence, 'excitation without satisfaction' and enforced
abstinence.[7] For this reason Freud regarded phobias as 'extremely
frequent in modern society, especially among women.'[8]

Initially Freud linked phobias with hysteria, but in his more mature work phobias became an anxiety disorder. In his *New Introductory Lectures on Psychoanalysis* (1932) he argued that phobias were the expression of both the anxiety and the defence against it. Phobias were an attempt to contain 'intolerable anxiety created by situations and conflicts of which the person would rather be or remain unaware'. In Freud's words:

> In phobias it is very easy to observe the way in which this internal danger is transformed into an external one — that is to say, how a neurotic anxiety is changed into an apparently realistic one. In order to simplify what is often a very complicated business, let us suppose that the agoraphobic patient is invariably afraid of feelings of temptation that are aroused in him by meeting people in the street. In his phobia, he brings about a displacement and henceforth is afraid of an external situation. What he gains by this is obviously that he thinks he will be able to protect himself better in that way. One can save oneself from an external danger by flight; fleeing from an internal danger is a difficult enterprise.[9]

Freud's most famous analysis of phobia involved a young boy. In 1909 he published 'A Phobia in a Five-Year-Old Boy'. This painstaking analysis (140 pages in extent) was concluded even though Freud saw Hans only once and got most of his data second-hand, from Hans's father. Even Freud acknowledged that 'It is true that during the analysis Hans had to be told many things which he could not say himself . . . he had to be presented with thoughts which he had so far shown no signs of possessing and . . . his attention had to be turned in the direction from which his father was expecting something to come.' In current psychoanalytic practice Freud's analysis of 'Little Hans' is regarded as flawed. Nevertheless, the case became a classic in the history of psychoanalysis and is one of the most cited investigations of irrational, excessive fear.

Hans's phobia involved a terror of horses so severe that he refused to venture outside. Freud unearthed the fact that seeing a heavy tram horse falling down in the street precipitated Hans's fear. Hans began experiencing nightmares in which a horse would come into his room and bite him. His anxiety gradually extended to horse carts, furniture vans and buses. Freud concluded that the phobia was the result of repressed hostile emotions against his father (whom he wanted to 'fall down', like the horse) and ambivalent feelings against his mother (whom he wanted to possess after his father's demise: the box-like carts and other vehicles represented the womb). Being bitten by the horse represented Hans's fear of retaliation from his father. The fear of horses for Hans was less intolerable than fear of his father. Furthermore, for him, fear of the street involved avoiding going outside while the fear of the self offered no remedy. In other words, for the Oedipal Hans, anxiety was 'free-floating' and could have been projected on to any convenient object that could be avoided. The object (horses) was a convenient way to cope with for-bidden desires.[10] Freud held that, as in his analysis of nightmares, fearful emotions would seep away only once the real source of the anxiety was identified.

The impact of Freud's ideas cannot be exaggerated. Innumerable commentators were indebted to his analysis, even though many were willing to embrace only some of his conclusions. In particular, Freud encouraged the idea that phobias were linked to the sex and death drives. Sex took the paramount place. Agoraphobics were said to be frigid or impotent: their sexual urges either lacked 'goal-direction' or were repressed on the grounds that they were too strong. Ignoring the fact that many agoraphobic individuals were women, other psychoanalysts contended that agoraphobia was due to the individual's identification with his own penis. Because the streets between houses were equated with the 'vagina dentata' (vagina with teeth), an agoraphobic man was 'really' afraid lest his penis was bitten off when he ventured into the street.[11] Similarly, for Karl Abraham, a close associate of Freud, the fear of spiders was symbolic of the unconscious fear of bisexual genitalia or 'the penis embedded in the female genitals'.[12]

In 1941 the psychoanalytically inclined author of *Anxiety and its Treatment* argued that in men, and sometimes in women too, phobic anxiety was often caused by 'sexual constipation'. The book's author, John Yerbury Dent, cited the example of a scaffolding over-seer he had treated. Over the previous nine months this man had become progressively more afraid of heights, a phobia that was injuring his pride as well as his work. After all, 'the men under him had begun to notice what they called his "cowardice" and took a fiendish pleasure in making him take quite unnecessary walks along high and exposed planking.' So strong was his terror that he was reduced to crawling along the scaffolding. Dent believed that he understood the true cause of the phobia when he recalled that the overseer's wife was suffering from severe osteoarthritis and, as a consequence, had rejected her husband's sexual advances for the past nine months. According to Dent, sexual abstinence was the key to the overseer's phobia. After relieving his 'sexual congestion' by re-establishing sexual intercourse (presumably with his wife), the overseer became immune to giddiness, his manliness once again assured.[13]

Other psychoanalytically inclined commentators explicitly linked the sex and death drives in creating phobias. In his book *Phobia* (1931) John Vassos argued that many phobias arose from a puritanical conception of sex as sin. In a remarkable passage he explained that phagophobia, or phobia related to swallowing, was

> peculiar to homosexuals, and its causes need not here be elaborated at length as they are sufficiently obvious . . . Here, again, the conviction of sin causes havoc. The inner belief that his abnormal sex-life and its gratification are a sin, combined with the premonition that he may be led to a greater sin in the practice of certain refinements of perversion, are the original conflicts which produce this strange malady. Phagophobia is thus a self-induced punishment for the harboring of unnatural desires; it is closely akin to insanity and its victims are certainly among the most pathetic of all the phobics.

According to Vassos, homosexuals unconsciously yearned to escape from their disordered life. More generally in phobics, the 'normal' desire for death — the 'strong desire to let ourselves go, in utter weariness, and be carried on the bosom of the stream to the eternal nothingness that is death' — was exaggerated. For people with a phobia of running water, the desire for death was so strong

that their unconscious would react against its own longing for obliteration by developing a terror of water. Even water flowing from a
domestic tap was menacing. Vassos added that within this 'complex
of unbalanced imaginings' there might also exist a fear of the
'unknown, predatory creatures that lurk in ocean and river' which
posed a castration threat.

In another example Vassos argued that the fear of sharp and
pointed objects (aichmophobia) was due to the suppression of the
sexual urge that made a man wish for death or castration in order to
'release him from the fury of impulses he is unable to gratify'.
Consequently pointed objects held a special appeal and the individual did not trust his own power to resist them: 'He is fascinated and
terrified by sharp and pointed instruments that may release the
surging flow of blood — a symbol for an orgasm, in which the
entire body makes a last, convulsive sacrifice.'[14] Sex and death were
fatally fused at the conception of phobic terrors.

As is implied in some of these accounts, many psychoanalytical
interpretations of phobia stigmatised sufferers. For instance, one
branch of psychoanalysis claimed that the phobia was a form of
manipulation. Thus the female phobic exhibited her helplessness
and weakness to everyone in a display that was both abject and
aggressive. 'Everyone, look!' her anxiety proclaimed, 'my mother
let me come into the world in this helpless condition, without a
penis.'[15] Phobic fears were instrumental, contended the psychoanalyst Dr Edmund Bergler in 1935. Noting that agoraphobics could
only go outside in the presence of a trusted guide, he called them
'despots' or 'tormenting, subconsciously aggressive spirits' who
acted as 'martyrs with all the martyr's airs'. He expressed little
sympathy for 'the obstinacy and iron-willed persistence with which
they make their habitual announcement: "I cannot go out into the
street alone".'[16]

Other criticisms of agoraphobics were more insidious. For
instance, in 1952 an influential textbook maintained that agoraphobia was a response to the desire to be raped. The agoraphobic was
afraid to go outside, believing that she would faint and fall. But that
was exactly the position that the agoraphobic unconsciously desired,
being attracted to the idea of sexual molestation. By refusing to go

into the streets — 'street-walking, one might say' — the agora-phobic avoided temptation. As the author concluded: 'there is nary an old maid who — afriad [sic] there might be a burglar under the bed — doesn't hope there is one!'[17]

Psychoanalysis was not the only therapy for excessive fear states. The science of neurology, with its growing confidence in brain map-ping and brain surgery, promoted a blunter treatment for extremes of fear. With a single caress of a knife, what came to be known as lobotomy or psychosurgery seemed destined to cut through the cant associated with excessive fear states and free hapless patients from their debilitating handicap. Many types of patient were wheeled into the operating theatre to undergo this procedure, among them an attractive child known only as 'O.T.'. She was admitted to Boston Psychiatric Hospital on 2 February 1944, aged fourteen. Within a few months surgeons had deliberately cut away part of her brain. She had been lobotomised for being fearful.

O.T. had been a particularly timid adolescent. For a few years, when anyone entered the room O.T. would be found hiding under a bed or cringing in a corner. When forced to go out, she would conceal her face behind a piece of cloth. O.T.'s mother seemed inca-pable of dealing with her queerly shy adolescent. Indeed, the doctors observed that the girl's mother was 'odd', evasive and immoral (O.T. was illegitimate). When the doctors questioned O.T. about her behaviour, her explanation was disarmingly simple: she was ugly and was afraid that people would laugh at her. This fusion of 'bad blood' and fearful behaviour initially led the surgeons to dose O.T. with sodium amytal (the 'truth drug'), during which time she spoke about masturbating and her anxiety lest this shameful act gave her pimples. Not content with this admission, they subjected O.T. to nineteen electro-shock treatments, before trying psychotherapy. But nothing relieved O.T. of her fears. Finally, ten months after admission — and just four days before Christmas — this fourteen-year-old child was sedated, holes were drilled in her skull and a razor-sharp 'stiletto' was inserted, severing the fibres linking the thalamus and prefrontal areas of the brain.

O.T.'s lobotomy was not an immediate success. Indeed, if anything, she became *less* sociable afterwards. It took six weeks before the surgeons could report that she had begun smiling in the presence of other people. By February 1945 O.T. was able to admit that her former shyness was due to a belief that God had made her ugly as punishment for 'sexual promiscuity'. On 7 March she was discharged from the hospital with 'undiagnosed psychosis, complete recovery' stamped on her file. According to her physicians, O.T. experienced only one relapse. On 18 October she was readmitted to hospital in a state of severe agitation and depression, provoked by being caught fornicating with her mother's boyfriend. In hospital O.T. complained of being lonely and then publicly announced that she was in love with her doctor. For her doctor this was fortunately a short-lived crisis, and a much calmer O.T. was discharged ten days later. Three years after the operation O.T.'s mother was questioned about her daughter's progress. She grumbled that her seventeen-year-old lobotomised daughter 'no longer bothered about things', was irresponsible and had to be supervised when performing household chores. However, because her fears had disappeared, O.T. became one of thousands of American children and adults said to have been successfully cured of severe fear states by having healthy brain tissue removed during radical surgery.[18]

As in the case of O.T., lobotomy involved the destruction of normal brain tissue in order to alleviate some psychiatric disorder or psychological state. Although its history can be traced back forty thousand years, in the modern period the procedure was first deliberately performed in 1893, when G. Burckhardt, a Swiss psychiatrist in charge of a male mental institution, decided to apply to humans the technique that his German colleague Dr F. L. Goltz had carried out on animals. When Burckhardt published his findings in the early 1890s, the medical community generally dismissed them and the procedure was ignored until 1933, when John F. Fuller of Yale University published his research on the brains of chimpanzees. The Portuguese physician Dr Egas Moniz was impressed by Fuller's work and (in collaboration with his colleague Almeida Lima) decided to test the procedure on twenty patients at a mental hospital near Lisbon.[19] Initially Moniz had injected alcohol into the brain in order to destroy tissue. In time, however, he developed a spear-shaped device called a leucotome to cut cores from the white matter in the frontal area of the brain, thus severing the fibres linking the thalamus and the prefrontal areas. Holes would be drilled in the skull and the leucotome inserted into the frontal lobes. When this was in place, a cutting wire was extruded from near its end, forming a loop. By rotating the leucotome cones of brain tissue were destroyed. Moniz won the Nobel Prize for Medicine in 1949 for his work. Despite this honour, it was left to neurologists like Walter Jackson Freeman and his collaborator James W. Watts at George Washington University in Washington DC to adapt and popularise lobotomy as the most effective cure for psychological states such as phobia.

Lobotomy rapidly became part of mainstream medicine, despite the fact that when Freeman first began performing lobotomies he used an ice pick from his own kitchen (later he was to call it a 'stiletto'). Between 1936 and 1941 there were only a dozen publications a year dealing with psychosurgery. By 1951 this number had grown to around three hundred each year, gradually declining again to a dozen in the 1960s.[20] Unfortunately it is impossible to estimate the number of people who underwent lobotomy. According to one conservative estimate, between 1935 (when Moniz first began experimenting) and 1951, over twenty thousand people were lobotomised.[21] Another account concluded that there were thirty-five thousand operations in America between 1936 and 1978. The number dropped from a high of five thousand in 1949 to around five hundred each year since 1970.[22] At the peak of psychosurgery, 63 per cent of all state hospitals in America used it.[23] There was a revival in its use in the 1970s, although its proponents eschewed the name 'lobotomy', substituting terms like 'stereotaxic tractotomy', 'functional neurosurgery' and 'psychosurgery'. The International Congress of Psychosurgery, the first of which had been held in 1948, resumed meetings in 1970, 1972, 1975 and 1978. Only the introduction of stronger psychiatric drugs in the 1980s saw psychosurgery fall into abeyance again.

Between 1936 and 1955 and again in the 1970s, surgeons used lobotomy to cure innumerable mental illnesses, including one of the most intractable psychiatric disorders in America and Britain at the time: chronic fear. For healthcare professionals at this time, it was imperative that more effective ways were developed for relieving severe fear states. In the 1930s the number of first admissions to psychiatric hospitals was increasing at a rate of 80 per cent a year.[24] The result was severe congestion: in American state hospitals the ratio of patients to physicians exceeded 250:1.[25] Furthermore, the Second World War dramatically increased the pool of frightened people. Even before the war ended, a couple of influential psychosurgeons were predicting that:

> war and postwar conditions are sure to add tremendously to the mental strain imposed on the population of this and every other country. There will be many thousands of individuals who, because of bereavement, worry, over-work, individual dislocation, and actual losses and injuries, are going to be fear-ridden and anxiety-stricken to the point of social and mental despair. As far as the present evidence goes, these are precisely the types of individuals for whom psycho-surgery offers the most relief.[26]

According to neurosurgeons, other techniques — including the use of metrazol, insulin and electro-shock treatment, as well as psychotherapy — had been disappointing in treating severe phobic states.[27] Some of these treatments *caused* even more terror than they cured. In 1941, an article in the respected journal *Diseases of the Nervous System* described the 'storm' that occurred when patients were injected with metrazol, a camphor-like substance that caused an epileptic seizure. For patients undergoing metrazol treatment

> a fleeting but quite definite and almost animal-like expression of fear . . . appears just before the first tonic convulsive tightening of the body . . . It is almost haunting in character . . . Particularly it is noted in fine featured young patients, both male and female. Fanciful as it may seem and perhaps out of place in objective study, it seems as though one is carried back in time and sees in [patients] fear appearing at a lower biological level.[28]

Some physicians bragged that, before patients in a 'metrazol storm' suffered a major seizure, they could prolong the state of abject terror for up to three hours.[29] Convulsions were so severe that they caused spinal fractures in 42 per cent of cases.[30]

Electro-shock treatment (properly known as electroconvulsive therapy, or ECT) was also of disputed effectiveness. The only thing agreed upon was that it scared patients, often excessively. Although most patients were said to have 'much less dread of ECT than they would in the course of visiting the dentist', it was 'not uncommon' for patients to develop such a dread of it that they were unable to continue treatment. In particular, male patients associated ECT with dread of castration. As a physician at the Veterans Administration at Chillicote, Ohio, noted in 1950:

> Electroshock is almost always interpreted as a punishment . . . Many patients show marked panic reactions on entering the treatment room, and must be handled calmly and gently to avoid any appearance of threatening the patient's masculinity. Even placing the mouth gag in the patient's mouth can be interpreted as forcing him to perform fellatio, and must be handled very professionally . . . Many patients recovering from electroshock have been observed looking under the covers to see if their genitals were still intact.[31]

Not surprisingly, neuropsychiatrists reported cases of patients vowing (like Vincent, at the beginning of this chapter, who swore that he would prefer to 'face a nest of Boche machine guns' than confront his phobia) that they would 'rather go through Dunkirk all over again' than undergo another shock.[32] One such terrified patient was Stanley Law, who underwent ECT in a north Staffordshire hospital during the late 1940s and 1950s in an attempt to cure his phobia. 'I lay fully conscious on the table, full of trepidation,' he began,

> surrounded by male nurses, insulation was pasted to my temples, a rubber pad was stuck between my jaws, and the electrodes were placed in position; in much the same way pigs were prepared in the slaughterhouse. The low voltage electricity was switched on, I felt the early vibrations, and then I knew no more. Upon regaining consciousness, I found myself much as I was before. I was on a kind of

table. I didn't for a time know where I was or who I was. Gradually,
I saw the mass of equipment around me, vagueness was replaced by
a slight awareness. I had some sort of idea that I knew the lady by my
side, although I didn't for some time realise that she was my wife.
My memory was affected. Part of me wanted to panic now, but I
couldn't. All I felt was a benumbing, vegetative, timeless, motion-
less dimness, a lack of sensory perception, and a startling diminution
of the life force.

Law underwent this treatment seven times before being returned
home with his fears 'dulled' although not eradicated.[33] His experience was fairly common. As one leading report concluded in 1982,
although some patients felt 'temporarily relaxed and less tense' after
ECT, for most, anxiety was 'aggravated by the fear of the treatment
or by side effects', such as memory impairment and the feeling of
unreality.[34]

But psychosurgeons were also sceptical about the efficacy of the
'talking cure' in relieving severe fear states.[35] It was no coincidence
that Walter Jackson Freeman, the most vocal promoter of psychosurgery, was one of the early members of the Society for
Biological Psychiatry, an organisation extremely hostile to Freudian
ideas. In collaboration with Dr Mary Frances Robinson, Freeman
contended that psychosurgery was more effective than psychoanalysis. In their book *Psychosurgery and the Self* (1954) Freeman and
Robinson insisted that the purposes of both procedures were identical: that is, changing patients' personalities and making it possible
for sufferers to 'go back to their homes and to survive in the very
environment in which their disorders developed'. But psychosurgery performed this *volte-face* with 'dramatic speed',
rendering unnecessary the 'long, painful process of developing
insight in the patients'.[36] Accusations by psychoanalysts that lobotomy was simply medical sadism were disregarded.[37] As one
proponent of lobotomy drily commented, it was not surprising that
doctors influenced by psychoanalysis would have difficulty recon-
ciling 'the facts of frontal lobotomy' with the 'linguistic complexities
of psychoanalytic theorizing'.[38]

Finally, and rather bizarrely, some psychosurgeons argued that psychosurgery was a logical advance on psychoanalysis. A book titled *The Dark Side of the House* (1968) described psychosurgery as simply the 'next development' after psychoanalysis. The authors argued that while the 'mystical humanism of psychoanalysis unearths the past in order to let a patient enter the real present', the 'destructive attack of the psychosurgeon takes away tomorrow by stilling anxiety for the same reason'. Memory was at the centre of both procedures: psychotherapy, however, dealt with the present by analysing past memories, while psychosurgery dealt with the present by eradicating anticipation of the future.[39]

The question was whether or not lobotomy was more effective than psychoanalysis. At the start it must be noted that, although psychosurgery was at the heart of psychiatry at the time, it was always regarded as a 'last resort'. The problem remained: when was that point reached, and who was to decide? 'Heroic therapy' was not alien to physicians attracted by lobotomy. After all, they had employed metrazol, insulin and electro-shock treatment for decades. It was not such a great leap to turn to lobotomy. However, from one point of view, lobotomy did seem to 'work'. The statistics are highly contested, but the proportion of patients said to benefit from the operation was estimated to be around 50 per cent (with, perhaps, another 30 per cent improving in the longer term).[40] Although scar tissue caused convulsions in approximately 10 per cent of patients, mortality rates were low (less than 3 per cent).[41]

Furthermore, of all the mental illnesses eliciting a surgical approach, the highest rate of success was achieved with severe anxiety. Indeed, whatever the patient's ailment, the reduction of fear and anxiety was the most consistent result of surgery. A survey in 1951 concluded that fearfulness was reduced from excessive levels to normal levels in 87 per cent of patients.[42] According to a neurosurgeon at the second International Congress of Psychosurgery in 1972, lobotomy was an effective procedure for people suffering extreme obsessions, such as being too frightened to drive a car for fear of running over a pedestrian or too afraid to leave their homes because they might have inadvertently left the water tap on. After surgery such patients continued to 'exhibit a rigid and meticulous personality', but they were no longer 'overpowered' by their obsessions.[43] In most cases there was the 'almost immediate cessation of agitation and apprehension'.[44] The speed with which fearfulness disappeared could be startling. In 1939 Freeman and Watts described the reactions of a patient who suffered extreme anxiety during a lobotomy carried out under local anaesthetic:

> He was quite restless upon the table, asking that the covers be raised so that he could breathe, requesting sips of water, and grasping the hand of the nurse at every opportunity. He was unable to carry on a coherent conversation because of his intense anxiety. The pulse rose to 140 and the blood pressure to 145 during the cutting of the fibers on one side [of his brain]. With the first cut on the opposite side his anxiety left him, the pulse dropped to 80 and the blood pressure to 110, and although he was unable to carry on a conversation, he admitted that all fear and anxiety left him.

Generally, Freeman and Watts argued, anxiety and nervous tension disappeared when the first incision on the opposite side was made. They acknowledged that for a day or two after the operation patients would be incontinent, sluggish and disorientated, but thereafter they exhibited a degree of 'placidity and indifference that forms a striking contrast to their previous apprehensive state'. Fear and anxiety were banished for ever.[45]

Even in cases where the operation was not a complete success, surgeons observed that, whatever the other side effects, fear and anxiety states were alleviated. Freeman and Robinson described operating on a 'vigorous-looking woman with strong features and thick grey hair brushed straight back from face' who suffered from severe anxiety, irritability and sleeplessness. Four years after the operation they were disappointed to discover that the woman's conversation had become rambling and profuse. She told them:

> I never think about the past; it's too long ago. I keep house after a fashion; don't care how it looks. I smoke too much. Can't sit still long enough to listen to the radio, but I go to church regular — yes, ma'am! And to the movies whenever I can get the money out of my husband. My son asks me 'What will you do if Dad dies?' I said, 'I'll

go live with you!'. She threw her head back and laughed, uproari-
ously. 'I'll tell you one thing — I'll never get married again!' When
asked if she was unhappy with her husband, she laughed again and
shouted, 'No, I beat the devil out of him!'

However, although the operation had transformed this patient into
a 'euphoric, boisterous, and tactless' woman, she was no longer
anxious. The authors were keen to emphasise, however, that of the
fifty-one cases they re-examined years after the operation, this
woman was the only one who was clearly still disturbed. More typically, former patients were relaxed and quiescent, usually to an
exaggerated degree.[46]

As these examples suggest, lobotomy profoundly affected people's
emotional lives. 'Tension, agitation, obsessive brooding . . . self-
consciousness, shyness . . . and excessive reserve were reduced',
claimed one surgeon, adding that 'the individual is often less sensitive
to criticism, rebuke or scorn'. Yet even he admitted that lobotomised individuals possessed a 'more superficial or shallow affective
life'.[47] Indeed, the difference between people opposed to lobotomy
and proponents of the operation lay not in describing its effects but in
ascribing *meaning* to the effects. For psychosurgeons it was com-
mendable that lobotomised people were rendered passive and
anxiety-free. The way the operation helped to 'manage' people
described as disruptive was central to its popularity. As two defend-
ers of psychosurgery brazenly acknowledged, lobotomy was a very
popular procedure with *relatives* of fearful patients,[48] even if patients
were in 'a constant state of terror' about the operation and were 'so
terrified that [they] tried suicide with broken glass' rather than submit
to it.[49] With very few exceptions, docility was a guaranteed effect of
the operation.

Surgeons were uncertain about the precise *mechanism* that made
prefrontal lobotomy an effective way of reducing severe fear states,
but they understood its effects.[50] Psychosurgery reduced fear by
blunting any sense of self-identity. As Robinson and Freeman put
it in 1950: post-operative people lost their capacity to feel 'self-
continuity': they were 'very much interested in satisfying their
desires, but they seem to be entirely uninterested in themselves as

persons.'[51] In other words, lobotomy destroyed the patient's interest in 'the subjective experiences that were so absorbing to him
previous to the operation'.[52] Freeman and Watts had made a similar point back in 1939:

> The frontal lobes are concerned with the projection of the individ-
> ual-as-a-whole into the future, with the formation of an image of the
> individual-as-he-is-becoming . . . The frontal lobes are not centers
> of intelligence nor of emotion, nor are they directly concerned with
> the energy drive of the individual. They assemble the available data,
> synthesize them, plan a course of action with the ideal in mind,
> and, equipped with energy of response and with appropriate affec-
> tive tone, project the individual into the future, direct him toward
> his goal — and criticize his shortcomings.[53]

After the operation, lobotomised individuals often lacked an
image of themselves in relation to the outside world, because they
were unable to project themselves into the future. This explained
why they found consecutive thinking difficult and were listless, indif-
ferent to the opinions of others and lacking ambition.[54] Even the
ever-optimistic Freeman described the lobotomy as 'surgically-
induced childhood'.[55]

But there was a flood of criticisms of psychosurgery. Methodological
flaws plagued psychosurgeons. Psychosurgeons were reminded that
their lobotomised patients' recovery might have been due to the superior care and attention they received in hospital compared with the fate
of patients treated more conventionally in overcrowded 'mental
wards'. Psychosurgeons were accused of exaggerating their success
rates and attributing all beneficial changes to the operation, even when
improvement was delayed by a couple of years. It was highly conceivable that many lobotomised patients would have recovered without the
operation. Indeed, one survey in the 1970s showed that half of all psy-
chotics experienced significant improvement even without any form of
treatment. In the words of one critic:

> Psychiatric ailments tend to fluctuate in intensity. Psychosurgery is
> commonly performed when a patient is most desperate and usually

most impaired; therefore the probability of some improvement after the operation (particularly when periods up to two years are considered) is high, as improvement would be likely even without the operation.[56]

It was the cultural critique of psychosurgery that was the most hard-hitting. Initially many of the attacks on psychosurgery focused on its use in prisons to subdue belligerent felons.[57] This employment of surgery as a means of social control earned a great deal of denunciation. Critics sneered that surgeons might as well leave the brain alone and simply cut off a criminal's hands or penis since this would be even more efficacious in reducing his capacity for mischief.[58] Other critics were troubled about the dubious suggestion that lobotomy was most effective in curing the fears of Jews, African Americans and women.[59] Indeed, compared with men, women were twice as likely to be 'stilettoed'. Admittedly, higher proportions of women were diagnosed with those forms of insanity that were believed to benefit most from prefrontal lobotomy (psychoses and psychoneuroses, for instance), whereas males predominated in diagnoses of organic brain disorders, alcoholism and personality disorders.[60]

Nevertheless, opponents of lobotomy were also aware that gender-based differences in perceptions of post-lobotomy life also placed women at higher risk of being given the operation. After all, it was widely acknowledged that a lobotomised woman was profoundly suited to housewifery, whereas the employment of lobotomised men was regarded as much more problematic.[61] Psychosurgery aimed to restore individuals to 'productive citizenship' — something an emotionally passive woman was adapted for, unlike her male counterpart.[62]

As these critiques gained force, lobotomy increasingly fell into disrepute.[63] It is wrong, however, to place too much emphasis on social criticism. The decline in lobotomies between the mid-1950s and the 1970s was partly a matter of supply. The Second World War had bolstered the number of people suffering psychiatric disorders: by the mid-1950s most of these sufferers had been dealt with.[64] In addition, psychiatry was increasingly incorporated into the medical profession, where it was policed by medical doctors rather than neurologists or biologists. The psychiatric vocation increasingly needed the legitimacy of medicine in order to attract funds.[65] Psychiatrists were forced to adapt to the professionalisation of medicine.

In addition, alternatives to lobotomy — for instance, psychoactive drugs, such as chlorpromazine (Thorazine) — became available. In comparison with these shifts, the influence of bad publicity, including Tennessee Williams's *Suddenly Last Summer* (1958), Ken Kesey's *One Flew Over the Cuckoo's Nest* (1962) and Elliott Baker's *A Fine Madness* (1964), is easy to exaggerate. Most crucially, there was the therapeutic revolution of the end of the twentieth century: radical surgery became unnecessary, at the same time as the status of psychotherapy blossomed. Fear and anxiety remained central to the American psyche, but its solution was to be found on the couch or at the pharmacy rather than in the operating theatre.

Psychosurgery also had to cope with the hostility of behaviourists. As we saw in Chapter Three, in the 1920s the father of behaviourism, John B. Watson, showed how easy it was to create a phobia of white mice in an eleven-month-old boy named 'Albert B'.[66] Behaviourists saw fears as maladaptive conditioned responses. Since only the fear of loud noises and the fear of falling were regarded as innate, neurotic symptoms (such as phobic reactions) were evidence of 'faulty learning'.[67] There was 'no neurosis underlying the symptom, but merely the symptom itself. Once you get rid of the symptom, you eliminate the neurosis.'[68] According to these psychologists, this helped explain why, after puberty, women were said to experience more phobias than men.[69] In the words of Isaac M. Marks, one of the most influential contemporary psychiatrists treating phobics, this gender difference was due to 'greater masculine aggression due to androgens and social learning, differential exposure of the sexes to particular situations, and differences in their sexual obligations'.[70] But whether the patient was male or female, behaviourists emphasised the phobic's *conduct* as opposed to psychoanalysts' focus on emotions. In the exalted words of a committed adherent writing in 1968, because behavioural therapy emphasised the patient's conduct, the objective naturalistic language of research psychiatrists is thus recapturing some of the great insights of traditional morality which religionists seem to have lost. A psychological revolution in the making emphasizes creative humanism rather than traditional metaphysics. Clearly, there is but one temple in the world, and that is the body of man. Nothing is holier than this high form. We touch heaven when we lay our hands on a human body. And the hand that helps is holier than the lips that pray.[71]

The chief problem with the behaviourist account was its 'equipotentiality premise': its assumption that people could be 'conditioned' to fear any object or event. In Pavlov's famous phrase, 'any natural phenomenon chosen at will may be converted into a conditioned stimulus'. However, this was not the case. People were much more likely to fear some objects than others. Phobias relating to snakes were popular (even among people who had never seen a snake), whereas phobias relating to lambs were not. And it ignored the fact that many phobias were not the result of any specific frightening event linked with the phobic object or situation. A study conducted in 1950 of fifty people with a phobia of travel revealed that only five had experienced any frightening event linked with travel.[72] In other instances, as with school-phobic children, the lack of an alarming 'trigger' was even more common since overprotective parents ensured that their children were exposed to fewer frightening situations than non-school-phobic children.[73] In order to deal with the criticism that phobias were not caused by a frightening experience, behaviourists turned to 'vicarious responses' or the importance of imitation in conditioning behaviour.[74]

Given these interpretations of the behavioural nature of phobias, it is not surprising that the 'know thyself' dictum of Plato, Kierkegaard and Freud was jettisoned for a focus on modifying present habits.[75] One of the most influential behaviourists dealing with phobias from the 1950s was Joseph Wolpe, a medical psychologist. He had become disillusioned with psychotherapy in the 1950s and, musing on the idea that behaviour was learned, he proposed that it could also be unlearned. Wolpe's early experiments involved teaching cats to fear certain things by giving them electric shocks in the presence of certain sound and visual stimuli. He then reversed the procedure, teaching the cats to love these sounds and sights by associating them with food.

For humans, Wolpe proposed 'systematic desensitization treatment', during which phobics would be taught to relax their muscles and then asked to imagine increasingly frightening situations while in a state of calm relaxation. Relaxation was incompatible with fear, and countered the fear response. Patients would gradually be exposed to and taught to tolerate fearful things. Phobics had to be helped to *imagine* exposure to the phobic object or situation and, in the process, this would progressively hold less fear for them.[76] 'Live imitation' could be used, involving models who would enact ways of preventing or interrupting fear responses.[77] In all these instances, biofeedback, or the use of instruments to measure pulse rate, respiration rate and electrodermal responses, was used to ensure that the patient was completely relaxed before being exposed to fearful stimuli. In modern techniques, such procedures may be carried out with the patient wearing a virtual-reality helmet.[78] Admittedly, behaviourists accepted that their arch-enemies the psychotherapists might help some patients. After all, patients undergoing psychotherapy were encouraged to repeatedly discuss their conflicts, which acted as a form of desensitisation. But behaviourists accused psychoanalysts in particular of 'mistaking a mere correlational process for a causal one'. Insight did not *cause* the remission of phobic symptoms: rather, insight was a *result of* the remission of symptoms.[79] In contrast, they argued that it was possible for a person to be cured without understanding either their past or the cause of their profound fright.

Another form of behaviourist treatment took the opposite approach. Instead of gradually exposing phobics to the object or situation that terrorised them, behaviourists required patients to immerse themselves in anxiety and 'experience their fear as fully as possible'.[80] 'Reactive inhibition therapy', also known as 'direct therapeutic exposure' or 'flooding' was popularised by Isaac M. Marks and Stanley Rachman at the Maudsley Hospital, London, from the 1960s. There were many variations, but the basic treatment involved 'repeated or extended exposure, either in reality or fantasy, to objectively harmless, but feared, stimuli for the purpose of reducing negative affect'. This was 'non-graded' treatment, because exposure to the fearful situation or object was intense, immediate and recurrent.[81] Unlike forms of desensitisation that took place gradually and under relaxing conditions, 'flooding' often excited profound anxiety, which only faded after repeated exposure.

'Marsha' was one woman who underwent 'flooding'. In the late 1970s she was a twenty-eight-year-old housewife and interior decorator who suffered from a severe form of obsessive-compulsive disorder. Marsha was tormented by uncontrollable 'visual thoughts' that she would grievously injure her one-year-old daughter, Karen, by tipping a pot of boiling water or oil over her, thrusting a pencil or scissors in her eyes, throwing her in a blazing fire or driving over her in the car. On bad days these sadistic thoughts would dart into her mind every few minutes. Marsha probably had not read any Freud, but she had imbibed sufficient knowledge of psychoanalysis to believe that 'at some level' her unconscious must *want* to harm Karen, although consciously the idea was abhorrent to her. As a result Marsha suffered a guilty conscious on behalf of her unruly unconscious. To make matters worse, the only way she could find relief from obsessional thoughts was by 'checking behaviours', that is, by actually holding scissors close to Karen's eyes and then pulling them away at the last moment. Although Marsha never hurt her daughter, her sadistic fantasies dominated her waking life, making her scared to be alone with Karen and incapable of effectively disciplining her for fear of being unable 'to stop'.

Desensitisation treatment involved forcing Marsha to visualise in intense visual detail harming her daughter. The transcript of a typical scene went as follows:

Psychologist: Close your eyes. OK, now. Maybe we can go through a scene with Karen. Let's try to imagine yourself actually doing it. I want you to start thinking about taking a sharp object, putting it to her face. You walk in and see her face. You take the pencil and you put it up to her. You feel yourself getting more and more overwhelmed by the urge and you are holding back just as if somebody is almost forcing your arms to move. Can you see her now as you do this?

Marsha: Uh-huh.

Psychologist: Feel it now. You are looking at her and you see her eyes and your pencil. You start to push it in. Feel the urge become greater and greater. And you start to feel that sinking feeling like it is slipping away. It is like you can't control your hands now.

Marsha: Uh.

Psychologist: You lose control of your hands. Something snaps in your mind . . . Push it. Push it in.

Marsha: (Crying) . . .

Psychologist: Jab. Jab. See it. Over and over and over. Jabbing in and out. Jabbing in and out. Jab, jab, jab, jab, jab. It's like you've totally lost control. You have gone completely crazy. There's no control . . . You are horrified but your hand just keeps poking it further into her. Right into her face. Right into her flesh. Right into her eyes. See the eyes now. Poke. She is looking at you. Jab, jab.

Although Marsha was encouraged to imagine hurting her daughter, she was also reassured that it was not 'really' happening. As the psychologist told her, 'Do you think Karen is hurt by any of this? . . . Then how does it hurt her to imagine things? . . . Fantasies won't hurt you and they won't hurt her.' Marsha was encouraged to repeat such fantasies, so that they became 'routine'. Through fantasy she was also taught to express her anger against (among other people) her family doctor. She believed, without cause, that he thought she was a 'sicko'. The interview continued, with Marsha sobbing throughout:

Psychologist: Why don't you look at the doctor now and tell him he can just go to hell . . . You have every right to feel that way. It's true. Look at him. Pound him again and look at him. Come on and pound him. Reach down now and take his hands and put them around his throat. Go ahead. Feel his throat. You squeeze his throat.

Feel it. Squeeze. Look at it. Look at him. Squeeze on that neck for
what he did to you. You're going to fix it so he won't do it to you or
anyone else.

Marsha was encouraged to practise such scenes at home and,
when she admitted that during her 'good days' she preferred not to
think violent thoughts, the psychologist announced that he had to
sign a 'contract with the client' (Marsha) requiring her to practise
the scenes routinely.

The process of cure was a long one: as soon as Marsha became
desensitised to one obsessive thought (such as poking out Karen's
eyes), she would switch to another (for instance, pouring hot oil
over Karen). Each obsession had to be 'flooded' separately.
Nevertheless, after twenty-two sessions Marsha understood both
that thoughts did not hurt anyone and that it was legitimate to have
hostile feelings towards her daughter. Her obsessive-compulsive
behaviours gradually faded.[82] It was a radical and painful cure for an
equally radical and painful affliction.

Phobias and obsessive disorders were the most tenacious of fears.
Their irrationality both inspired and frustrated the medical community, and further confused notions of what it meant to be
human. After all, Vincent's agoraphobia and Little Hans's horse
phobia depicted the bewildering absence of any limit to what might
be terrifying: ergasiophobia, pnigophobia, ballistophobia, grapho-
phobia — respectively, fear of activity, of choking, of projectiles, of
writing — were all candidates for phobic fear. In contrast to a
belief in humanity's unlimited imagination, psychosurgery eradicated fears by destroying people's sense of self-consciousness: did
this make lobotomised individuals like O.T. less than human? And,
finally, Marsha's inability to distinguish between thoughts and action
rendered her incapable of translating the one thought that mattered (love for her young daughter) into action. Our madness
defined what it meant to be human. Despite belonging to a dazzling
community of frightened people, sufferers like Vincent, Hans,
O.T. and Marsha were the most lonely of victims. We don't even
know their true names. Instead of our hearing about the ways they

constructed their pain, phobias and other obsessional fears became the site where the great clash between different forms of 'truth' were played out.

Psychoanalytical, neurological and psychological truths faced up to one another in a bruising battle of wits, each claiming to possess a particular expertise in diagnosing and curing extremes of fear. The institutions immersed in this war were some of the most powerful, yet their diagnoses were often crudely stigmatising and the cure condemned excessively scared individuals to endless performances, in which the very mechanisms and rites that seemed to promise relief became the recurrent ordeal. Anguish was to be banished by the imposition of authority. The unanswerable question was: which?

Afterword to Part Two: Psychohistory

As we have seen in the last three chapters, the natural and social sciences were informed by extremely different, even contradictory theories about the nature of emotions such as fear. Whether examining the emotional lives of children and their parents, or the intensely individual terrors associated with nightmares and phobias, we are struck by the diversity of meaning proffered by competing sciences. Clearly the answer to the question: 'What is fear?' depends as much upon the psychological and philosophical theory of the commentator as it does on the situation in which the emotion emerges.

However, many historians are willing to employ one period-specific theory of fear to analyse people in the past. The most influential of these theories has been the psychoanalytical one. It would be difficult to overestimate the power of this discourse: even historians who would be horrified to be indicted for writing psychohistory can be heard glibly referring to repression, the unconscious or the ego. For instance, although Peter Stearns and Carol Z. Stearns firmly insist that historians cannot use 'contemporary psychology to elucidate past behavior',[1] in their book *Anger* (1986) they write about emotional experiences being 'conditioned' by the 'unremembered and unconscious legacy of infancy', as well as by the 'conscious and cognitive structures' of cultural rules about expressing emotions.[2]

This slippage is hardly surprising. As Peter Gay, the most eminent advocate of psychohistory, correctly reminds his readers, historians always employ psychological theories when they have to infer motives for the conduct of historical actors.[3] The psychoanalytical model has proved popular.[4] One of the most sophisticated examples is Gay's multi-volume *The Bourgeois Experience. From Victoria to Freud* (1984 to 1996).[5] His work is the finest illustration of non-reductionist psychoanalytic history. Conventional Freudian themes such as aggression, repression, defence mechanisms, the Oedipus complex, childhood sexuality, castration anxiety, penis envy and the superego all play an important part in Gay's history of nine-teenth-century life. According to Gay, the historian can interpret dreams and can 'read the sequence of themes in a private journal as though it were a stream of free associations; he can understand public documents as condensations of wishes and as exercises in denial; he can tease out underlying unconscious fantasies from pre-occupations pervading popular novels or admired works of arts'.[6] The task of the psychohistorian is to show how fear arises from indi-vidual psychic conflicts. Fear is lodged within the subterranean architecture of the soul and psychohistorians set themselves up as tourists on History's great pier, winkling out subconscious anxieties from the cockleshells of the past.

This is not the place to rehearse the forceful refutations of psy-chohistory in detail.[7] Briefly, however, there is no reason to assume that historical actors are psychologically 'packaged' in the same way as those patients analysed by Freud. Too often psychoanalytical explanations for emotional responses emerge out of the model itself. In 1997 the eminent historian of science Michael Hunter daringly convened a conference to psychoanalyse the seventeenth-century scientist Robert Boyle, according to Freudian, Jungian and Kleinian perspectives. The resulting publication, a special edition of the *British Journal for the History of Science*, is both an insightful study of Boyle and a disturbing reflection of the effect the choice of psycho-logical model has on historical interpretation. Even Hunter refers to 'the disconcerting variety of disparate schools in which contempo-rary psychoanalysts are ranged', making it difficult to see how the historian should choose between competing psychoanalytical expla-nations for emotional behaviour.[8] For instance, when Peter Gay argues that 'a youth proved his manliness by drinking, swearing, fighting and fornicating. Sexual triumphs were so many trophies the adolescent collected on the road to manhood; each of his perform-ances verified the virility by which he and his cohort set great stock', depending on the model applied, the young man's motives could include oral (the esteem of his friends), anal (rebellion against parental demands of 'cleanliness being next to godliness') or phallic (competing with his father) explanations.[9]

As Fred Weinstein put it in his thought-provoking article 'Psychohistory and the Crisis of the Social Sciences' (1995): 'if the notion of a collective unconscious means anything at all, why should there be such variation?' After all, 'these orientations depend for their explanatory force on problematic conceptions of unconscious motivations that do not permit us to discriminate among an ever increasing number of equally plausible interpretations'.[10]

The problem becomes even more acute when we study compet-ing sciences. For instance, in Chapter Five we investigated the way different psychological knowledges influenced phobic fear. The application of a psychoanalytical interpretation becomes just one of many ways to culturally understand phobic reactions. In other words, Freud's interpretation of anxiety neuroses is precisely what is being placed within an historical context. For this author, attempting to write a history of fear in the twentieth century, which of necessity involves reflecting on a number of psychological paradigms, there is no reason to privilege a turn-of-the-century psychoanalytical proto-type over (for instance) a mid-nineteenth-century evolutionary or late-twentieth-century neurological one.

PART THREE

Whorls of Irrationality

Introduction

In 1926 a radio play titled *Broadcasting from the Barricades* engendered alarm all over Britain. The text of that play seems innocuous to us today but, for many interwar Britons, images of a maundering, enraged mob of unemployed men and women was scary. A dozen years later an even bigger frenzy occurred in America when a radio broadcast called *The War of the Worlds* caused over a million Americans to panic, believing that Martians had landed on the East Coast. These two events have many things in common, most notably the way in which fear arises from uncertainties inherent in our relationships with other people. In both 1926 and 1938, heated debates between the political left and the political right, as well as between the rich and the poor, served to render radio audiences susceptible to alarm.

There was another factor, however. The mass media itself played a role. These two radio broadcasts were cast in a framework that many people found irresistibly 'real', and made them deaf to announcements at the beginning and during both broadcasts about the fictive nature of the story. Rather, listeners were predisposed to panic, having already concluded that the world was a frightening place. In the words of a young college student who had panicked after hearing the radio broadcast in 1938: 'I didn't have any idea exactly what I was fleeing from, and that made me all the more afraid.'

CHAPTER SIX

Social Hysteria

Misfortunes they fear; for they flinch in their
     dreams at the scratch
Of coarse pecuniary claws, at crying images,
Petulant, thin, reproachful,
Destitute shades of dear ones.

AUDEN, 'THE AGE OF ANXIETY'

Rational, scientific investigation into the emotions was a world apart from the day-to-day fragmented cultural anxieties that beset individuals in the interwar years. While psychoanalysts perched next to couches, corduroy-clad psychologists prodded mice and men in laboratories, and white-gowned surgeons peered into brains, popular literature warned that fear had become more important in the regulation of daily life than love.[1] Fear was 'never more active', insisted the author of a 'heal-yourself' book titled *Mastering Fear* (1935).[2] Scientific advances might have caused some forms of fear to subside but, as the Archdeacon of Westminster observed in the early 1930s, science also 'brought to light fresh terrors in their stead'. Superstitious terrors had been exposed as false magic but people faced 'legions of new alarms that beset life from the cradle to the grave.'[3] The speed of technological development seemed overwhelming. Political certainties crumbled. Once rearmament resumed and the European threat once again menaced people's security, fear's grip tightened. As the author of an article titled 'The Age of Fear', published in *The Listener* on 4 August 1937, put it, 'there could be no doubt about it', the modern world was 'badly scared — and showed it. Fear was the leading motive of its actions and the chief propelling power of its public.' Faith 'burned low', emotionally scorching its disillusioned disciples.[4]

Without question, in both Britain and America the 1920s and 1930s were years prone to panic. In Britain the most bizarre example of mass panic occurred as a result of an innocuous radio satire. The year was 1926. The man responsible for the broadcast that incited panic was thirty-eight-year-old Father Ronald Knox. He was an unlikely figure for scandal. Although he had forsaken the Anglican fellowship for Roman Catholicism in 1917, according to his biographers Knox was 'the least political of men', who was 'happiest in the traditional contexts of English life' at Eton and Oxford.[5] Yet, on 16 January 1926, without intending anything mischievous, Father Knox inadvertently relinquished his role as priestly intermediary between God and mere mortals to become interwar Britain's supreme intimidator.

Father Knox's play *Broadcasting from the Barricades* was transmitted at 7.40 on Saturday evening, 16 January, from the BBC's George Street Studios in Edinburgh, yet provoked hysteria throughout Britain. For us today, the play is unremarkable. After a prefatory statement informing listeners that it was a work of humour and imagination, the play took the form of a news broadcast in which Father Knox described an unemployed crowd that went wild. The play began with a lot of noise ('Bzz! Bang! Bzz!') followed by a lisping lecture on eighteenth-century literature given by Mr William Donkison.

The lecture finished and the news began. Items about a cricket match and an act of heroism in which a waterman saved a child from the Thames were immediately followed by a report on a demonstration of unemployed people in Trafalgar Square. The leader of the demonstration, Mr Popplebury, was identified as the secretary of the National Movement for Abolishing Theatre Queues, and was said to be inciting the crowd to sack the National Gallery. As was characteristic of the BBC in the 1920s, the newsreader paused at this point to inform listeners that the National Gallery had been erected in 1838 to house the famous Angerstein collection. He continued his lesson by adding: 'A new wing, designed by Mr E. M. Barry, RA, was added in 1876. It contains many well-known pictures by Raphael, Titian, Murillo, and other artists.' The radio audience was then informed that the crowd was obeying Popplebury's orders and sacking the gallery. At this point the news broadcast ended and listeners were 'connected' to a band at the Savoy Hotel. This dance music was interrupted by a weather report, more on the Test Match and an announcement that the unemployed had begun pouring through Admiralty Arch and, 'in a threatening manner', were approaching the back of the government buildings in Whitehall. A brief history of the Arch was given. The crowds were then described throwing empty bottles at ducks floating in the pond in St James's Park. Listeners were told that Sir Theophilus Gooch would next be lecturing them on the Housing of the Poor.

Once again, however, there was confusion, and the newsreader admitted that Gooch would not be addressing them because he was being roasted alive in Trafalgar Square. His date of birth and career were respectfully disclosed, along with the repeated statement that he was being roasted alive by the unemployed mob. The band at the Savoy Hotel once again filled in the break. A further news report occurred, announcing that a famous film actress had just arrived at Southampton. The unemployed crowd (still under orders from Mr Popplebury, Secretary of the National Movement for Abolishing Theatre Queues) were then reported to be demolishing the Houses of Parliament with trench mortars ('The building of the existing Houses of Parliament was begun in 1840. The designs were those of Sir Charles Barry. The structure roughly forms a parallelogram, 900 feet in length by 300 in width. The internal decorations, frescoes, and statues are deservedly admired. The building is made of magnesia limestone from Yorkshire . . .'). The destruction of this building culminated in the falling of the clock tower housing Big Ben. Henceforth, listeners were informed, Greenwich time that evening would be tolled by the repeating watch of Uncle Leslie, a popular children's storyteller from Edinburgh.

More violence was in hand, and it was announced that Mr

Wotherspoon, the Minister of Transport (a position of momentous importance, then as now) had been hung from a lamp-post in Vauxhall Bridge Road. A moment later there was a formal apology: Wotherspoon had not been hung from a lamp-post but from a tramway post. Listeners were once again serenaded by the Savoy Band but the music was suddenly interrupted by a report that the crowd had blown up the Savoy Hotel. Finally, the crowd moved towards the BBC's London headquarters itself. The final words were: 'One moment please, . . . [sic] Mr Popplebury, secretary of the National Movement for Abolishing Theatre Queues, with several other members of the crowd, is now in the waiting room. They are reading copies of the *Radio Times*. Good-night everybody; good-night.'[6]

Reading this satire today, it seems unbelievable that many radio listeners in 1926 would actually panic. But that is what happened. The twenty-minute programme was scarcely over before listeners all over the country became agitated, besieging local police stations, the BBC's regional centres, newspaper offices and the Savoy Hotel, demanding 'how soon the tide of civil war might be expected to sweep in [our] direction'.[7] The manager of the Savoy calculated that in addition to around two hundred local calls, the hotel answered hundreds of trunk calls from Manchester, Newcastle, Hull, Leeds, Scotland and even Ireland, asking if it was advisable to cancel room bookings. Other callers demanded reassurance about the safety of friends staying at the hotel.[8] In Newcastle the Sheriff was nervously uncertain about what precautions he should be taking to ensure that anarchy did not spread to his part of the country, while the wife of the Lord Mayor of that city was reported to have been 'greatly upset' at being unable to contact her husband (who was out at dinner) to inform him about the rising 'red tide of revolution'.[9] The *Irish Telegraph* could not refrain from reporting that numerous listeners rang its offices, breathlessly enquiring: 'Is it true that the House of Commons is blown up?'[10]

If listeners entertained any doubts about the veracity of the broadcast, these were dispelled remarkably quickly. Indeed, they proved particularly adept at interpreting coincidences in a way that confirmed pre-held fears. In some areas of the country the late arrival of the Sunday papers was interpreted as confirmation that something was seriously amiss in London. (This was to ignore the more sensible explanation that there had been heavy snow across southern England and London was experiencing its lowest temperatures in eight years.) As rumours circulated, women fainted and elderly listeners prayed for their nation's survival.[11] All over the country people feared for the preservation of the metropolis, torn apart, it seemed, by a civil war between a riotous mob of unemployed people and the forces of law and order.

Luckily it was a short-lived panic which dissipated within twenty-four hours but, because many embarrassed and angry BBC listeners complained, the Corporation's officials were forced to humbly doff their hats. They hoped that 'any listeners who did not realise it [was a fictional play] will accept our sincere apologies for any uneasiness caused. London is safe, Big Ben is still chiming and all is well.'

Clearly the broadcast sounded plausible. Unusually for the time, the play was enlivened by realistic 'sound effects' of explosions, falling buildings and terror-stricken crowds. J. C. S. MacGregor confessed that he was 'one of those who worked the simple sound-effects (an orange-box to be hacked, torn, and stamped to pieces, and a sack of broken glass to be dumped on the studio floor) which convinced listeners from Land's End to Berwick-on-Tweed that the Savoy Hotel was indeed falling in ruins'. It also fell to MacGregor to explain the hoax to listeners, after Knox and the producer had left the studio and gone out to dinner. In his words, Knox and the producer

had scarcely left the building, and the debris of the Savoy Hotel was still lying about in the studio, when the telephone rang. Was it really true, asked an agitated voice, that revolution had broken out in London? I gave reassurances . . . The next caller was more difficult. His wife had a weak heart, and had fainted at the news; and when he gathered from me that the whole thing was fictitious, he exploded. What, he asked with some vigour, did the BBC mean by it? Did we realise that we had grossly misled the country, and were playing into the hands of the Bolshevists? I was young in the service then, and it took all my tact to dispose of this gentleman, and of others who in quick succession telephoned to voice the same sentiments.[12]

Callers demanded that Father Knox, the director of the broadcasting studio in Edinburgh, and the BBC publicly apologise, which
they duly did. While they admitted that they regretted the misun-
derstanding, they could not resist pointing out that the

> rapidity with which the scenes are supposed to be enacted, the
> peculiar repetition of sentences in two or three different ways, and
> the unfamiliar words used — such as listeners being 'connected
> up' to the Savoy Bands, should have told people that they were not
> genuine announcements.

They could also have mentioned that listeners should have been
alerted to the absurdity of the broadcast simply by the fact that the
announcement that Uncle Leslie (a character who gave children's
talks from Edinburgh) would take over sounding the time after Big
Ben's demise was clearly ludicrous. In an exasperated but polite
tone, the BBC sighed: 'It is hardly credible that if we were giving out
news of such a national crisis we should intersperse snatches of
dance music.'[13] Nevertheless, the Corporation bowed to pressure to
'take no risks with its public's average standard of intelligence' in the
future[14] and Knox refused to speak on the radio again until 1930.

Why might such a satirical programme prove so frightening?
After all, an announcement at the start of the talk highlighted its fictional character, and there were numerous clues within the
broadcast pointing to satire. The answer to this question lies in the
economic, social and political tensions pervading 1920s Britain, in
addition to the peculiarly believable nature of radio. Economic and
political insecurity was ravaging the nation. Left-wing papers were
quick to identify class-based fears to be at the heart of the panic.
'Supposing the imaginary news announcer told his listeners that a
Tory mob had marched on Eccleston Square and blown up the offices
of the T. U. C.!' exclaimed the *Daily Herald*.[15] The *Leeds Weekly
Citizen* was also queasy about 'this kind of allusion to the unemployed, at a time when so many are suffering so badly from the
failure of our social system to provide them with work and sustenance'.[16] The previous decade had contained innumerable hints that
workers were no longer willing to tolerate persistently high levels of

scarcity: at grassroots level, socialist organisations were expanding and the trade union movement was becoming increasingly militant, its membership having soared from three million in 1911 to nearly seven million by 1921.

In addition, unemployment was high and rising. Although the middle classes actually experienced a dramatic *decline* in economic fears in the interwar years (their living standards increased, owing to stable wages and declining prices), nevertheless they were troubled by mounting guilt about the widening discrepancy in wealth between themselves and a growing unemployed underclass. In the winter of 1920 one and a half million insured workers in Britain were unemployed and many more uninsured workers were being laid off or offered only shortened hours of labour. Furthermore, only a few months before Knox's broadcast, miners had risen up with the cry 'enough is enough', striking against their bosses who threatened their already precarious livelihood.

This class-based discord exposed deep fears in many middle-class citizens about social and economic inequality. Particularly (although not exclusively, since working-class conservatives were a stubborn minority) for the upper and middle classes, the miners' strike was further evidence of the collapse of a culture of deference. Middle-class guilt about resistance to wide-ranging reforms aroused powerful emotions, while high inflation and the housing crisis caused further uneasiness among that sector of society.

Another development alarming the middle classes was the polarisation of politics in Britain, underlined by the establishment in 1920 of the Communist Party of Great Britain (CPGB). Although the CPGB was feared out of all proportion to its membership, 'Red internationalism' rendered the communists a threat to 'British values'. Political disquiet rumbled to the surface. The *Daily Herald* reported that the BBC's controversial broadcast incited the 'political passions' of listeners. The paper disclosed that, at one dinner party, the programme inflamed the 'violent anti-Labour convictions' of the host, at which point he began to angrily lecture his guests about the pernicious events allegedly taking place in London.[17] Might 'the left' have succeeded in mobilising disaffected workers? In 1918 the Labour Party's Clause Four, calling for the common ownership of 'the means of production, distribution and exchange', had been written into its constitution. Furthermore, Labour now had a chance of grasping power. Although the Conservatives were still the largest single party in the House of Commons in 1923, their feud with the Liberals meant that defeat in the January 1924 election was seen as inevitable. The *English Review* lamented this fact:

> We stand at the moment when the sun of England seems menaced with final eclipse. For the first time in her history the party of revolution approach their hands to the helm of State, not only, as in the seventeenth century, for the purpose of over-throwing the Crown, or of altering the Constitution, but with the design of destroying the very basis of civilised life.[18]

The 'helm of State' did pass into the hands of the Labour Party in 1924 and, ominously for the political right, Ramsay MacDonald, the first Labour Party Prime Minister, signed a General and Commercial Treaty with the Soviet Union. For many Conservatives this was proof that more was at stake than mild leftism — communism had insinuated itself into the highest level of government.

Such concerns were exacerbated when, in October 1924, MI5 intercepted a letter purporting to have been written by Grigori Zinoviev, chairman of the Soviet Union's Comintern. This letter urged British communists to encourage subversion within the British army and prepare for revolution. It was 'indispensable to stir up the masses of the British proletariat', the letter informed British communists, reminding them that 'armed warfare must be preceded by a struggle against the inclinations to compromise which are embedded among the majority of British workmen . . . Only then will it be possible to count upon complete success of an armed insurrection'. Zinoviev reflected optimistically that, even in England, 'events themselves may more rapidly revolutionise the working masses than propaganda', suggesting that a revived strike movement or harsh governmental repression might also be effective in stirring the masses to action. This was inflammatory stuff, so it was hardly surprising that the Prime Minister should attempt to ensure that the

'Zinoviev letter' remained secret. When details were leaked to the press just four days before the second General Election of 1924, there was pandemonium. While the Conservative press maintained that the letter was genuine, Labour supporters claimed it was a forgery aimed at bringing down the Labour government. The sales ratio of anti-Labour to Labour newspapers was almost ten to one, so the result of the propaganda war was a foregone conclusion.[19] Although the letter was later proved to be a forgery, written by White Russian émigrés, many Labour MPs lost their seats in the second election and the Conservatives were returned to power.

At the time of Father Knox's 1926 broadcast, memories of Zinoviev's threatening letter remained strong. Media coverage of *Broadcast from the Barricades* was quick to link the programme to an alleged communist threat. For instance, on the same page where the *Daily Mail* published its account of the panic, it printed 'Lying Propaganda', a column informing readers that around 250,000 broadsheets 'full of illiterate Communist violence and shameful perversions of truth' were being distributed weekly throughout the United Kingdom. 'Their only object is to create hatred and discontent and to bring about a state of affairs which may give the disgusting tyranny of Communism a chance to seize upon this country,' the *Mail* warned.[20] Other newspapers made a more direct link between the broadcast and communism, concerned that the panic would dilute 'warranted' concern about the Red Menace. 'Frankly,' the editor of the Catholic paper *The Tablet* pontificated,

> we wish that Father Knox had not done this. Few literary deeds are more facile and more tiresome than the shoving of serious things into a droll context. And a Red revolution is a very serious thing indeed. There are in England groups of hireling Communists who must have been enormously encouraged by the fact that many Britons were badly scared last Saturday.[21]

Although indispensable to understanding reactions to the broadcast, this social context was insufficient to incite fright in the hearts and minds of listeners. The medium was also the message: the fact that news of a riotous crowd terrorising London was broadcast on

the radio was crucial. Much of the hysteria was due to the fact that
BBC news was considered to be especially reliable. The BBC's
monopoly of the medium and its government-guaranteed political
neutrality rendered radio news profoundly authoritative. As one
panic-stricken person hoarsely maintained on the telephone to a
journalist for a Liberal Welsh paper immediately after being
informed that the broadcast was a hoax, 'No . . . there *must* be
something in it, we have heard it over the wireless.' When this call
was followed by many others, even the journalist answering the
telephone began to have his doubts, wondering if, after all, 'there
was not something in it'.[22] Similarly, the *Daily Mail* reported that
when people were told it was a hoax, they refused to believe it: 'We
have heard it on the wireless,' callers reminded the sceptical newspaper reporters, 'Why, we have even heard the explosions!'[23]

Predictably, during the nervous dissection of the panic in the days
following the broadcast, much attention centred on this ability of
radio to engage the emotions. The wireless proved 'incapable of
catching up with rumour', claimed the *Daily Express*.[24] Its power was
especially potent in remote areas of Britain and when newspaper
offices were closed, thus preventing people from attempting to
verify news reports.[25] The emotional vulnerability of isolated or
housebound listeners meant that radio had to act responsibly when
infusing 'satire with realism'.[26]

In response to the panic, papers took the opportunity to insist on
the superiority of the printed word over the spoken word. 'There
are scare newspapers,' admitted 'The Star Man' at the *Star*, 'but
their statements can be read, re-read, and rejected.' In contrast,
'the broadcast alarm is perhaps only half-heard, and, if misunderstood, cannot be corrected.' He could not resist adding, 'until the
newspapers come out'.[27] Others agreed, contending that the hoax
illustrated the 'rather terrifying possibilities for the new science of
"broadcasting"': 'Here is a means by which vast communities, susceptible to any sort of rumour, might be reached with swift and
calamitous results,' warned the *Irish Times*. It continued, imagining
what would happen if a 'red rising' really *had* erupted in London.
Radio headquarters would be a priority target for revolutionaries:
seizing control of the radio waves

would enable its leaders to circulate in a couple of hours such false news as would go far to demoralise public opinion. Think, too, how much trouble enemies of the [Irish] Free State could achieve through a very brief possession of the resources of [Irish radio].

The effects of 'malignant misuse' of radio was 'illimitable'. It predicted that 'in the next war' the 'hostile possibilities of "broadcasting" will be a serious problem for all the High Commands.'[28] A 'free' radio was the most formidable revolutionary medium.

'Subversives' were only a threat because some people were susceptible to their message. Just who were hoaxed by Knox's tale of violence on the streets of London? Generally the answer to this question appeared simple: every group claimed that *other* groups had been tricked, not themselves. *The Times* reported the incident only through its Dublin correspondent, implying that only the Irish had been fooled.[29] Father Knox claimed that Scotsmen saw the joke, unlike their English counterparts (pointedly adding that he would not have thought a child would have been deceived by the play).[30] The *Weekly Scotsman* agreed with Knox, brazenly reporting that even the BBC had conceded that the vast majority of people protesting against the broadcast resided in England. According to them, sturdy Scots had failed to be emotionally hoodwinked while Irish listeners were more likely to be 'interested' as opposed to 'concerned' by the broadcast.'[31]

Similarly, across the Atlantic, the *New York Times* was convinced that such a panic 'could not happen in this country'. It claimed that the infrastructure of American radio — with over six hundred broadcasting stations scattered over the country — simply would not be able to sustain a nationwide panic as happened with the centrally controlled airwaves in the United Kingdom. The paper could not have been more wrong. As we shall see next, only a dozen years later, in 1938, a similar panic occurred in America when radio audiences became panic-stricken after hearing a broadcast purporting to describe an invasion of Martians. In 1926 the Liberal MP and writer on economic matters Sir Leo Chiozza Money had berated the BBC for airing *Broadcasting from the Barricades*, claiming, 'I should not have made a worse joke if I had rung you up on the telephone and

announced that I had murdered my grandmother!'[32] Echoing these
comments in 1938, Senator Clyde Herring of Iowa fumed, 'Radio
has no more right to present programs like that than someone has in
knocking on your door and screaming.'[33] Both men recognised
radio's ability to spark intense panic in its hapless listeners.

The American panic was even more cataclysmic than that caused by
Father Knox's satire. On a Sunday evening, 30 October 1938, a play
broadcast on CBS Radio caused over a million Americans to flee their
homes in fright, believing that the vanguard of an invading army from
outer space had landed in the farmlands of New Jersey. The man
responsible was not a priest of the Roman Catholic persuasion, but
Orson Welles, a twenty-three-year-old high-priest-in-training within
the broader church of radio and film. His theatre company was called
the Mercury Theatre and the provocative play was a version of H. G.
Wells's classic novel *The War of the Worlds*, originally published in 1898
but adapted by Howard Koch for the radio performance. The night
they chose to broadcast it was the eve of Halloween, a night also
known as Mischief Night or Devil's Night.

Like Knox's *Broadcast from the Barricades*, Welles's play imitated
a news bulletin. It began with Welles's voice, notifying listeners
that, in the early years of the twentieth century, Americans knew
that 'this world was being watched closely by intelligence greater
than man's and yet as mortal as his own.' This alien intelligence
was 'cool and unsympathetic, regarding this earth with envious
eyes' and was 'slowly and surely' plotting against humanity.
Welles's statement was interrupted by the weather forecast, followed by an interlude in which listeners were regaled by the music
of Ramon Raquello and his orchestra, ostensibly broadcast live
from the Meridian Room in the Hotel Park Plaza in downtown
New York.

The music was briefly interrupted by a special news bulletin
reporting explosions of gas on Mars. Reporter Carl Phillips then
interviewed Professor Pierson of the Princeton Observatory about
the astronomic import of the activity on the planet. Professor
Pierson reassured listeners that the chance that there was life on
Mars was 'a thousand to one'. At this point the announcer informed

listeners that a huge flaming object had landed near Grovers Mill, New Jersey. Phillips and Pierson promptly set out to investigate. They found a scene of confusion as crowds of bewildered people milled around a large, unidentified capsule. Phillips was heard interviewing the people at the scene, including the tongue-tied owner of the farm on which the capsule had landed. Suddenly a 'curious humming' was heard and the cylinder began to open. In a high-pitched and distressed tone, Phillips provided live commentary on what he was witnessing:

> Good heavens, something is wriggling out of the shadow like a gray snake. Now it's another one, and another. They look like tentacles to me. There, I can see the thing's body. It's large, large as a bear and it glistens like wet leather. But that face, it . . . Ladies and gentlemen, it's indescribable. I can hardly force myself to keep looking at it. The eyes are black and gleam like a serpent. The mouth is V-shaped with saliva dripping from its rimless lips that seem to quiver and pulsate. The monster or whatever it is can hardly move. It seems weighed down by . . . possibly gravity or something. The thing's rising up . . .

The crowds at the scene could be heard panicking, especially when the captain and two policemen who were advancing towards the Martians waving a white handkerchief were incinerated by a mysterious death ray. The ray was then directed at the crowd and Phillips fell silent, presumably killed. After a slight hesitation the announcer broke the ominous silence with the words: 'Ladies and gentlemen, due to circumstances beyond our control, we are unable to continue the broadcast from Grovers Mill. Evidently there's some difficulty with our field transmission.' Brigadier General Montgomery Smith, commander of the state militia at Trenton, New Jersey, was introduced next, revealing that the region had been placed under martial law. While firemen and Red Cross workers worked to minimise damage, Professor Pierson could be heard whispering a number of plausible scientific explanations for the death ray. Listeners were informed that only 120 men survived of the seven-thousand-strong army sent in to defeat the invaders. All the others had been crushed beneath the monster's metal feet or burned to cinders by the ray.

The Secretary of the Interior, sounding remarkably like President Roosevelt, then came on air, pleading with Americans to remain calm and place their faith in God 'so that we may confront this destructive adversary with a nation united, courageous, and con-secrated to the preservation of human supremacy on earth.' Listeners were privy to desperate attempts made to defeat the enemy, but the artillery battery in the Watchung Mountains and bomber crews all were eventually silenced. America seemed doomed when the Martians effortlessly invaded New York City and wiped out the entire American army, artillery and air force. New York radio fell silent. The only sound that listeners could hear was Professor Pierson musing aloud if he was the last man on earth.

Pierson then encountered a stranger and in the resulting conver-sation the two men pondered whether the 'game is up' for the human race. The stranger imagined ways of surviving, but when he fantasised about hijacking one of the death rays and turning it on fellow humans as well as Martians, Pierson was disgusted and could be heard walking away. Pierson eventually discovered that the Martians had all died, 'slain, after all man's defenses had failed, by the humblest thing that God in His wisdom put upon this earth' — bacteria.

Well before this cutesy ending, people all over America had rushed out of their homes in fright. Out of six million listeners, 1.2 million believed that there really had been an invasion from Mars, home of the God of War. The panic was nationwide, although its intensity varied. Eighty per cent of southern listeners were terrified, compared with between 69 and 72 per cent of listeners in the Middle Atlantic states, East and North Central states and the Mountain and Pacific States. Only 40 per cent of listeners in New England were terrified, but this was probably due to the fact that these listeners would have had to deliberately tune in to the channel specifically to hear *The War of the Worlds*.

Hundreds of thousands of people threw bread, blankets and babies into their cars and sped westward. Friends and relatives were telephoned and warned of the impending calamity. In contrast, other listeners were too stunned to move. Alone or hugging their pets, they found themselves too petrified to budge from their position next to the wireless set. Some listeners closest to Grovers Mill and New York hallucinated, actually believing that they could see the flames or feel the heat of the fires consuming the city. Prayers, pleadings and promises besieged the heavens. Women and men fainted; children and dogs howled. Many found disquieting relief in hysteria.

When news of the fictive nature of the broadcast spread, listeners were angry. Accusing the radio station of causing 'grievous bodily or mental injury', they instituted a total of $750,000 in damage suits against the CBS.[34] Although none of the claims was eventually substantiated, there were furious complaints against the abuse of the radio waves. The Federal Communications Commission received 644 pieces of mail commenting on the broadcast, of which 60 per cent were unfavourable.[35] As with Father Knox's broadcast, apologies were demanded. The CBS promised not to 'use the technique of a simulated news broadcast within a dramatization when the circumstances of the broadcast could cause immediate alarm to numbers of listeners'. Welles was forced to apologise, but this failed to calm some particularly enraged listeners. For instance, A. G. Kennedy, a judge in South Carolina, was particularly acrimonious. He addressed Welles thus:

> Your radio performance Sunday evening was a clear demonstration of your inhuman instincts beastial [sic] sensuality and fendish [sic] joy in causing distress and suffering. Your savage ancestors, of which you are a degenerate offspring, exulted in torturing their enemies and war captives, and you doubtless revelled in feindish [sic] delight in causing death to some and great terror, anguish and suffering to thousands of helpless and unoffending victims of your hellish designs. Your contemptable [sic], cowardly, and cruel undertaking, conceived by a demon and executed by a cowardly cur is doubtless in keeping with your sense of humor . . . I would not insult a female dog by calling you a son of such an animal. Your conduct was beneath the social standing of and [sic] what would be unbecoming and below the moral perception of a bastard son of a fatherless whore.[36]

After the panic, the question on everyone's lips was, how could it have happened? The play had been an adaptation of a book written by the British novelist H.G. Wells and published in 1898, at a time when there was an undercurrent of fear about German militarism. The verisimilitude of Wells's novel had attracted attention from the start. In a review in *Nature* on 10 February 1898 the author warned readers that 'the possibility' of invasion was 'convincingly stated' in the novel, adding that 'it is to be hoped for the sake of peace of mind of terrestrial inhabitants, that Mr Wells does not possess prophetic insight'.[37] By the interwar years science fiction often dwelt on fears of invasion by extraterrestrial beings. Indeed, in 1926, the first pulp devoted exclusively to science fiction was issued, called *Amazing Stories*. In its first issue it published Edmond Hamilton's short story 'Monsters of Mars', a space opera involving a battle against threatening aliens from Mars.

The fact that *The War of the Worlds* was part of an old tradition of literature dealing with Martians should have been obvious to listeners. The fictive nature of the broadcast was mentioned at both the beginning and the end of the programme, as well as twice during commercial breaks. But many listeners claimed not to have heard these announcements. As Sarah Jacobs of Illinois insisted: 'They should have announced that it was a play. We listened to the whole thing and they never did. I was very much afraid.'[38] Over 40 per cent of the audience had tuned in late and missed the preliminary announcement. These listeners were already frightened beyond reason well before the commercial breaks.

As with *Broadcasting from the Barricades*, most listeners were too scared to check the authenticity of the broadcast and failed to verify the report by switching to a different radio station. Indeed, between a quarter and a third of the audience made no attempt whatsoever to check the veracity of the news report. Instead, they either sat transfixed by the programme or fled within minutes of hearing about the invasion. Of those who *did* attempt to confirm the facts about the invasion, between a tenth and a quarter did so with remarkable ineptitude, seeking confirmation rather than refutation of the crisis.

Even the most implausible pieces of evidence were interpreted as confirming a pre-existing belief in the invasion. Listeners looked outside and saw deserted streets, which they interpreted as evidence that their neighbours had been gassed. If, on the other hand, they saw crowds of people, they imagined that their neighbours were fleeing the pernicious invaders. A young man recalled:

> I was alone with my two younger brothers. My parents had gone to a party in Newark. When [the radio announcer] mentioned 'citizens of Newark, come to the open spaces', I got scared. I called my mother to find out what to do and there was no answer. I found out later that they had gone to an empty apartment so that they could dance. Nobody was left at the place I phoned. My only thought was that the flames had overcome my parents.[39]

This panic was contagious, infecting most profoundly those who had been informed of the broadcast by friends or relatives. As one listener put it, 'My sister called up and I immediately got scared. My knees were shaking.'[40] Family and friends fed on one another's terror.

There were broader explanations for why people panicked. As with the British panic, the *War of the Worlds* broadcast occurred in a country undergoing social dislocation and labour strife. Many Americans were frightened of unemployment. Seven months earlier, on 14 April 1938, President Roosevelt had announced on the radio that the programme of economic and social recovery that had been under way since 1933 had 'received a visible setback'. He warned his listeners against their 'fear of war abroad, fear of inflation, fear of nation-wide strikes' — the Presidency and the Congress were capable of providing the security that Americans craved, he claimed. 'There is no reason and no occasion for any American to allow his fears to be aroused or his energy and enterprise to be paralyzed by doubt or uncertainty,' Roosevelt announced. He outlined a programme of national recovery that would not only serve the economic needs of Americans but would also safeguard 'their personal liberties — the most precious possession of all Americans. I am thinking of our democracy. I am thinking of the recent trend in other parts of the world away from the democratic idea.' It was an astute analysis of the fears of the 1930s. As early as 1932 the social commentator Walter Lippmann commented:

> The anxiety which has gripped the American spirit is not pri-
> marily to the actual [financial] losses which almost everyone has
> suffered . . . The problem is one of fear of what is to come: the fear
> of the wage earner that his wages will be cut or even that he will lose
> his job entirely, the fear of the employer that he will not be able to
> meet his obligations, the fear of men that they will not be able to pay
> their taxes, or the interest and instalments on mortgages, the fear
> that savings will be lost, and so on and so forth. These individual
> fears spread like an hysteria in a crowd which is trapped in an inclo-
> sure [sic] and cannot find the exits, and the hysteria itself accelerates
> the very evils that men fear.[41]

It was with such worries in mind that Roosevelt coined his famous dictum that 'Nothing is so much to be feared as fear itself' in an attempt to convert very real anxieties about economic decline into a psychological mood.

Even more frightening was the fact that war was looming. Many listeners wondered whether the reported Martians were actually Germans or Japanese. In the words of one listener, 'I knew it was some Germans trying to gas all of us. When the announcer kept call-ing them people from Mars I just thought he was ignorant and didn't know yet that Hitler had sent them all.'[42] There were suspicions that the meteor would turn out to be a new type of Zeppelin. After all, military technology seemed to be advancing with unimaginable speed. It was impossible to keep up with all the changes. As a lis-tener said, 'I happened to tune in when the meteor had just fallen. I do not know how I finally found out. I never believed it was anyone from Mars. I thought it was some kind of new airship and a new method of attack.'[43] Life was confusing; Americans were feeling lost, disenfranchised and unable to make sense of the world around them. 'So many off things are happening in the world,' one listener admitted. 'Science has progressed so far that we don't know how far it might have gone on Mars. The way the world runs ahead anything is possible.'[44] This anxiety that 'anything is possible' left people fumbling around for an explanation. Mrs Ferguson, a housewife from New Jersey, recalled:

> I knew it was something terrible and I was frightened. But I didn't know just what it was. I couldn't make myself believe it was the end of the world. I've always heard that when the world would come to an end, it would come so fast nobody would know — so why should God get in touch with this announcer?[45]

Within the broadcast, the testimony of respected experts — an astronomer, a professor, a general, the vice-president of the Red Cross and the Secretary for the Interior, for instance — only exacerbated people's terror. These authority figures were supposed to clarify events, but their presence simply confirmed that 'things were bad'. 'I knew it was an awfully dangerous situation when all those military men were there and the Secretary of State spoke,' explained a listener.[46] It only increased the verisimilitude of their pronouncements that these experts also admitted to being confused and frightened. As the announcer stammered, 'Incredible as it may seem, both the observation of science and the evidence of our eyes lead to the inescapable assumption that those strange beings who landed in the Jersey farmlands tonight are the vanguard of an invading army from the planet Mars.'[47] Fear-speak was to be believed.

Again, as with *Broadcasting from the Barricades*, the medium of radio was crucial. Listeners expected the radio to be factual and authoritative. Radio was an exceptionally popular medium at this time. Twenty-seven and a half million American families (out of a total of thirty-two million) possessed radios — a higher proportion of families enjoyed the use of a radio than owned a telephone or car, or could boast of residing in a home with plumbing or electricity.[48] A much greater number of people depended upon the radio for news, rather than upon newspapers or magazines. As one listener explained, 'We have so much faith in broadcasting. In a crisis it has to reach all people. That's what radio is here for.'[49] Radio had been used to broadcast election returns and to disseminate important information. Less than a year earlier, at 7.25 on the evening of 6 May 1937, the German Zeppelin the *Hindenburg* burst into flames at

Lakehurst, New Jersey, where it was attempting to moor. Herbert Morrison was a radio reporter broadcasting live from the scene. His anguished cries of 'It's burst into flames . . . Get out of the way, please, oh my, this is terrible, oh my, get out of the way, please . . . Oh, the humanity and all the passengers!' became the first live radio coverage of a disaster. As a consequence, listeners were very attentive to and 'believing' of what they heard over the radio. Only weeks before the American broadcast, millions of Americans had waited by their radios to get the latest news about impending war. One listener admitted, 'I feel insecure because although we are not in the war, we are so near it. I feel that with new devices on airplanes, it is possible for foreign powers to invade us. I listened to every broadcast during the European crisis.'[50]

During this time broadcasts of all kinds had been interrupted to give news, as happened in *The War of the Worlds*. Radio news was believed more than newspaper reportage. A *Fortune* poll asked people: 'Which of the two — radio or newspapers — gives you news freer from prejudice?' Half of those questioned said that the radio was more reliable, while 17 per cent trusted newspapers more (the remainder were unsure or felt that there was 'no difference' between the trustworthiness of the two media). So, when bewildered news announcers in *The War of the Worlds* began using colloquial expressions, listeners were amazed. Even more so when they heard 'ordinary people' talking — a policeman warning, 'One side, there. Keep back, I tell you', for instance, or another voice shouting, 'the darn thing's unscrewing'.[51] Real geographical locations were mentioned by name — Grovers Mill, Princeton, Trenton, Plainsboro, Allentown, Morristown, the Watchung Mountains, Bayonne, the Hutchison River Parkway, Newark, the Palisades, Time Square, Fifth Avenue, the Pulaski Highway and the Holland Tunnel. Listeners could easily map the progress of the terrifying Martians.

Finally, the power of the radio as an anti-democratic medium fuelled concerns around this panic. The potential for radio to disrupt democratic political processes was widely discussed before 1938. Indeed, three years before Orson Welles's radio broadcast, Hadley Cantril, the man who conducted the first detailed analysis of the *War of the Worlds* frenzy, wrote *The Psychology of Radio* (1935) with the psychologist Gordon W. Allport. Although the authors generally adopted an optimistic tone, they were influenced by the crowd theory of men like Gustave Le Bon, Wilfred Trotter and William McDougall (as discussed in Chapter Two), and consequently warned that:

> The radio more than any other medium of communication, is capable of forming a crowd mind among individuals who are physically separated from one another . . . Heretofore 'crowds' meant . . . clusters of people sharing and giving expression to a common emotion. But now, as never before, crowd mentality may be created and sustained without the contagion of personal contact. Although such 'consociate' crowds are less violent, and less dangerous than congregate crowds — the radio can create racial hatred but not itself achieve a lynching — still to a degree the fostering of the mob spirit must be counted as one of the by-products of radio.

They warned that the radio was 'preëminent as a means of social control and epochal in its influence upon the mental horizons of men'.[52] After the Welles fiasco, Dorothy Thompson, a columnist for the *New York Tribune*, reflected in similar terms:

> No political body must ever, under any circumstances, obtain a monopoly of radio. The power of mass suggestion is the most potent force today . . . If people can be frightened out of their wits by mythical men from Mars, they can be frightened into fanaticism by the fear of Reds, or convinced that America is in the hands of sixty families, or aroused to revenge against any minority or terrorized into subservience to leadership because of any imaginable menace.[53]

As we saw at the beginning of this chapter, the radio had already inspired a minor Red scare in England in 1926: more serious would be its possibilities for panic during the Cold War.

A seam of political alarm underlay both British and American culture in the interwar years. In 1926 and again in 1938, the radio tapped into this diffuse sense of apprehension. On both occasions radio dramatists discovered the ease with which panic could be sparked in an edgy, alienated group of individuals, all huddled nervously around radio sets. 'Things have happened so thick and fast since my grandfather's day that we can't hope to know what might happen now,' confessed one man reflecting on the panic of 1938, adding, 'I am all balled up.'[54] Fears about economic and political events rapidly converted into outlandish dread of agitated mobs and menacing aliens from outer space. Threatened on all sides, men and women simply anticipated the worst, and failed to judge the broadcasts according to the usual criteria of plausibility, consistency and verifiability. Unidentified anxieties quickly became full-scale panic. As we shall see later, on 11 September 2001 the mass media also played a role in inciting fears of attack. Millions of Americans and Britons first heard of the terrorist attack on the Twin Towers in New York through the radio and television, and many initially believed that it was a hoax 'like *War of the Worlds*'. In 1926, 1938 and 2001, the most ordinary fears seemed to come extraordinarily alive. On the earlier two occasions, however, the novelty of the means of communicating the story of national disaster made it believable, while in 2001 audiences immediately disbelieved their eyes, having 'seen it all before'. In the context of the new millennium, 'it' was 'just another' Bruce Willis film. The icons given to us through film and electronic games provided the lens through which 11 September was designed, experienced and viewed. In 1926 and 1938 art imitated life, while in 2001 life imitated art.

Afterword to Part Three: Fear versus Anxiety

No one disagrees that fear and anxiety are agonising emotions. Like the people frightened by the two spoof radio broadcasts in 1926 and 1938, we feel attacked from without and from within, and our fear is both panoramic and indeterminate. In analysing responses to fear, a distinction is often made between 'fear' and 'anxiety'. In one case a frightening person or dangerous object can be identified: the flames searing patterns on the ceiling, the hydrogen bomb, the terrorist. More often, anxiety overwhelms us from some source 'within': there is an irrational panic about venturing outside, a dread of failure, a premonition of doom. Therefore, according to most commentators, the word 'fear' is used to refer to an immediate, objective threat, while anxiety refers to an anticipated, subjective threat. Anxiety is described as a more generalised state, while fear is more specific and immediate. The 'danger object' seems to be in front of us in fear states, while in anxiety states the individual is not consciously aware of what endangers him or her. As Freud, arguably the designer of the modern concept of anxiety, put it: '*Anxiety* relates to the condition and ignores the object, whereas in the word *Fear* attention is focussed on the object'.[1]

This demarcation between fear and anxiety may be useful for psychologists and psychoanalysts, but historians must be extremely wary about imposing such distinctions on emotional states in the past. For one thing, were the people who panicked in 1926 and 1938 afraid or anxious? They believed the threat was actual and imminent, yet they were clearly reacting to a morass of uncertainties about changes within their communities and nations.

More to the point, given the themes of this book, what is a fear for one individual or group may be an anxiety for another. The distinction between the two states is defined according to the stimulus, but what is an 'immediate and objective' threat for one group may simply be an 'anticipated and subjective' threat for another group. Indeed, because one common response to threat is scapegoating, it could be argued that the only difference between a fear and an anxiety is the ability of individuals or groups to *believe* themselves capable of assessing risk or identifying a (supposed) enemy. To put it another way, the difference lies in the ability to externalise threat, which provides a sense of personal invulnerability. The difference between fear and anxiety may reside solely in social, hierarchical responses. In fear states, individuals are consciously able to take measures to neutralise or flee from the dangerous object, while purposeful activity fails individuals whose subjective experience is anxiety. But the ability or inability to 'neutralise or flee' ('fight or flight') is a question of power relations within historical communities — not a fundamental difference between the object or state causing an emotional response.

Furthermore, as we see throughout this book, in the negotiation between the individual and the social group, the difference between fear and anxiety oscillates wildly. In historical time, anxiety is easily converted into fear, and vice versa. The uncertainty of anxiety can be whisked away by processes of naming an enemy (it may be a plausible or implausible enemy), converting anxiety into fear. The 'work' of fear is commercial work: converting anxieties into fears is the function of a range of new professionals and, in pharmaceutical terms, is big business. It also has a political function: scapegoating, for instance, enables a group to convert an anxiety into a fear, thus influencing (for instance) voting preferences against an 'outsider' group. In Chapter Eleven the fear of crime is depicted as an example of the process of converting anxiety into fear. In other words, debates about the fear of crime were a reflection of anxiety about change more generally and were used to legitimise control over subordinate groups.

If anxiety can be turned into fear, and thus provide an enemy to engage with, fear can, similarly, be converted into anxiety. For instance, again in Chapter Eleven, we will see an instance where there was an attempt to convert legitimate fears of nuclear accident into the irrational anxiety of 'radiophobia'. Indeed, there have been good historical reasons why certain groups might wish to convert fears into anxieties. Increasing uncertainty over the identity of a threat or the probability of a risk has implications for social affiliation. Anxiety states tend to make people withdraw from one another, unlike fear states, which are more liable to draw people together, either for comfort or to defend themselves more effectively against the danger.[2] When modern individuals become plagued by anxiety (rather than fear) states, they prove less dependent upon associative groups and more prepared to adopt individualistic solutions. The political implications of this are evident, with groups 'playing off' fear and anxiety, according to their aim. Between the 1950s and the 1970s governments tried to convince people that their fears of nuclear war were 'irrational' anxieties rather than 'rational' fears, thus discouraging the impulse to unite with other fearful persons against the common threat.

However, this is not to argue that historians must never use this distinction between fear and anxiety, but merely to warn against using the terms out of the context of the time in which they are being employed. After all, as we shall see again in the Afterword to Part Four, it is no coincidence that the word 'anxiety' became more popular as the twentieth century progressed — partly because of the decline in external threats to the individual's existence experienced by Britons and Americans in that period, but also because of the conversion of fear into anxiety through the therapeutic revolution. Whereas in the past the frightened individual might turn to the community or a religious institution for advice and comfort — a process that often involved the delineation of an evil 'other' — as the twentieth century progressed, the emotion became increasingly individualised, appropriated by the therapist or, in the most isolated fashion, the contemporary 'self-help' movement. The modern construction of the unique self as residing 'within' the body and accessible to psychotherapeutic confession prioritises the language of anxiety. As a consequence, anxiety may have been higher in late-twentieth-century America because of the greater cultural resonance of therapy in that country, but also because in Britain a much more entrenched class structure served to dilute some forms of status anxiety.

PART FOUR

Zones of Confrontation

Introduction

War domesticates terror. Whereas before the First World War fears of total destruction were largely focused on nervous anticipation of slow but corrosive degeneration, from 1914 military conflict was increasingly regarded as posing the greatest threat to humanity. In the hands of war-crazed politicians and other civil servants, the hardware for mass killing achieved an alarming ferocity, unlike anything seen before. The power to annihilate humanity was placed decisively in the hands of people who set out to extend the killing fields into everyday civilian environs. The front lines were still made up of young British and then American servicemen engaged in a bloody struggle to the death, but the civilians they were supposed to be defending were also being terrorised. In the next three chapters the stumbling words of Private Arthur Hubbard are heard ('it makes my head jump to think of it,' he writes after the Battle of the Somme in 1916), but so too are the hysterical stammerings of an unnamed insurance clerk who was buried alive when a bomb dropped on his London home in 1941 (he is heard promising his unconscious and half-buried wife that he will carry her to safety in the 'wilds of Scotland'). The Cold War merely served to prolong people's fright. As one small boy in Chicago begged his mother, 'Please, Mother, can't we go some place where there isn't any sky?' In the face of total war, no one felt safe. Ever.

CHAPTER SEVEN

Combat

. . . survivors play
Cards in kitchens while candles flicker
And in blood-splattered barns bandaged men,
Their poor hands in a panic of need
Groping weakly for a gun-butt or
A friendly fist, are fetched off darkling.
Many have perished; more will.

AUDEN, 'THE AGE OF ANXIETY'

William Manchester was a scared young American, flung down on the island of Okinawa during the Second World War and expected to act with bravado and bravery. One day, after hearing that a sniper was killing men in a neighbouring battalion, he noticed an inconspicuous fisherman's shack propped against a low hill. From the angle of fire he guessed the sniper's location. He also observed that the hut had windows facing his men, making them possible targets. Fleeing was not an option: Manchester knew that he had to go on the offensive. This was a scary thought. After all, he was not a particularly aggressive man — as a youth he had been unable to trade punches with his schoolmates — but the sniper posed a direct and immediate threat that could not be ignored. When menaced, Manchester told himself, humans reacted like caged animals: there should be a sign around their necks warning: 'This animal is vicious; when attacked it defends itself.' He recognised that he 'could be quick' or he 'could be dead'. His options were limited. With wiry humour he quickly concluded that it would be impossible to turn his back on the shack and run through the battalion squealing, 'A Jap's after me! A Jap's after me!' He also decided that it would discredit him in the eyes of his subordinates if he timidly ordered another soldier to kill the sniper. Worse: if he gave such an order, he feared that his subordinates might not even bother obeying. After all, he was a new NCO, a 'gangling, long-boned youth, wholly lacking in what the Marine Corps called "command presence".'

Finally, after procrastinating for a few minutes after discovering that no one in his battalion possessed any grenades, Manchester 'took a deep breath' and, 'sweating with the greatest fear I had known till then', began dashing towards the shack, zigzagging and dropping every dozen steps. It was not until he approached the door of the shack that he remembered that he had forgotten to don his steel helmet. His vulnerable skull rendered him 'utterly terrified'. 'I could feel a twitching in my jaw, coming and going like a winky light signaling some disorder,' he recalled, and 'various valves were opening and closing in my stomach. My mouth was dry, my legs quaking, and my eyes out of focus.' But there was no retreat so, taking another deep breath, he kicked down the door and raced inside, only to find an empty room leading into a bedroom. He dashed forward, firing widely to his right. Luckily the sniper's rifle was tangled in its harness and, realising he was trapped, he merely backed away into the corner 'with a curious, crablike motion'. This was the first Japanese soldier Manchester had ever seen at close quarters, and the first man he had ever fired at. His first shot missed, but

> the second [shot] caught him dead-on in the femoral artery. His left thigh blossomed, swiftly turning to mush. A wave of blood gushed from the wound; then another boiled out, sheeting across his legs, pooling on the earthen floor . . . he emitted a tremendous, raspy fart, slumped down, and died.

In panic, Manchester just kept firing, until disgust gagged him. 'Then I began to tremble,' he admitted, 'and next to shake, all over.

I sobbed, in a voice still grainy with fear: "I'm sorry".' He vomited and urinated in his skivvies, wondering 'Is this what they mean by "conspicuous gallantry"?'[1]

Manchester's distressing encounter with war's terror exposed the underlying glossolalia of combat — that hubble of sounds, screeches and stutterings that were the language of emotion. Time and again combatants stammered that they could not 'take it' any more. Like Manchester, their bodies reverted to a more primitive state. These were men whose starkly emotional sentences attested to how 'the sights cannot be explained in writing. Writing is not my line. No fighting either For them that wants to let them fight Because I will never like it no no never' or, as another terrorised private put it, 'I admit I am a coward. A bloody, bleeding coward, and I want to be a live Coward than [sic] a dead blasted Hero.'[2] There were many such accounts of the physical effects of unrestrained terror, including more poignant descriptions like the one a private sent to his mother after the Battle of the Somme, simply saying: 'It makes my head jump to think about it.'[3] The Second World War poet and combatant Shawn O'Leary summarised the aftermath of war's panic in a poem of 1941:

> And I —
> I mow and gibber like an ape.
> But what can I say, what do? —
> There is no saying and no doing.[4]

It is a truism, but of all the emotions in combat, fear was the most dominant. The combatant may strive for enjoyment in war[5], but if this was achieved it was due only to the remarkable resilience of the human imagination. Whatever a soldier's rank, fear was his persistent adversary. Its effects upon the body were particularly evident in wartime. During the Second World War a series of interviews of men in two combat infantry divisions found that only 7 per cent claimed that they never felt afraid. In contrast, three-quarters of the men complained of trembling hands, 85 per cent were troubled by sweating palms, and 89 per cent tossed sleeplessly in their beds at night.[6] Under the influence of fear, one Medical Officer explained, blood moved from the digestive tract in order to be 'utilized by the muscles and brain in mobilizing the whole organism for danger'. Frightened soldiers experienced epidemics of diarrhoea (as did American soldiers immediately prior to the landing on Iwo Jima), suffered chronic gastrointestinal problems, or escaped into 'dyspeptic invalidism'.[7] Fear disturbed the functioning of the nervous system. In the words of the author of an article in the *Edinburgh Medical Journal* in 1941:

> the normal peristaltic movement of the stomach ceases, food lies like a dead weight, the bowels are constipated, palpitation occurs, the blood pressure is raised . . . Such conditions may lead to organic bodily disorders which cannot be cured by the drugs of the physician or the knife of the surgeon, unless the emotional factors are also treated.[8]

It was not enough to merely repress the *inward consciousness* of fear because the body would betray itself through its respiration, circulation, digestion and excretion.[9] Frightened soldiers would be in poor physical condition, irrespective of their conscious desire to win through. More importantly, fear could jeopardise the military mission. It inhibited aggression, disrupted discipline and overrode more positive emotions such as loyalty to comrades.[10] Under the spell of fear, soldiers either shot their rifles wildly or found that their hands shook so much that they could not load ammunition.[11] Terror created psychiatric casualties. Indeed, it was argued that outbreaks of fear did the greatest damage to military morale. It was even more dangerous than mortal physical wounds, which at least might arouse the survivors to renewed acts of aggression against the enemy. In contrast, soldiers who witnessed their comrades give way to terror were often rendered 'ineffective' themselves.[12] For this reason fear was often described as a 'virus', insidious and infectious.[13]

Nevertheless, this 'virus' was not wholly without value. For some senior military spokesmen fear was beneficial, so long as it did not spill over into hysteria or anxiety neuroses. Indeed, fearlessness was proof of stupidity and was characteristic of men who possessed a 'callousness of mind' which made them put at risk not only

themselves but their comrades.[14] More importantly, fear was said to
have the physiological and psychological effect of preparing the body
for 'fight or flight' responses.[15] During both world wars there was
a widespread belief that fear could be converted into fury.[16] For
instance, in 1916 the eminent surgeon and psychologist George W.
Crile published *A Mechanistic View of War and Peace*, which described
the soldier about to go into battle as 'activated' to attack:

> He is under extreme emotion. His heart pounds loudly against his
> ribs, his hands tremble, his knees shake, his body is flushed with
> heat, he is drenched with sweat . . . His brain is activated by the
> approach of the enemy. The activated brain in turn stimulates the
> adrenals, the thyroid, [and] the liver. In consequence thyeoiodin,
> adrenalin, and glycogen are thrown into the blood in more than
> normal quantities. These activating substances are for the purpose of
> facilitating attack or escape.

The eventual assault was orgasmic. According to Crile, soldiers
'find relief in any muscular action; but the supreme bliss of forgetfulness is in an orgy of lustful satisfying killing in a hand-to-hand
bayonet action, when the grunted breath of the enemy is heard,
and his blood flows warm on the hand'. Combatants reverted to 'the
period when man had not controlled fire, had not fashioned
weapons; when in mad embrace he tore the flesh with angry teeth
and felt the warm blood flow over his thirsty face'. Deep within the
breast of 'the cultivated man of to-day' lurked 'the beast of the phy-
logenetic yesterday'.[17]

This link between physiological and emotional responses was
made more soberly by E. G. Boring and Marjorie Van de Water in
their classic study *Psychology for the Fighting Man* (1943). The book
made a huge impression, rapidly selling 380,000 copies (at the time,
the largest figure for any book by academic psychologists). One of
their main arguments was that:

> fear is the body's preparation for action. The heart pounds faster,
> pumping blood more rapidly to the arms and legs and brain, where
> the oxygen is needed. The lungs do their part by quickened

breathing. Blood pressure goes up. Adrenaline, which is nature's own 'shot in the arm', is poured liberally into the blood to act as fuel for the human fighting machine. Subtle changes in body chemistry, automatically effected by powerful emotion, serve to protect the soldier in action in ways he would never think of, if he had to plan for himself. His blood clots more readily. He loses temporarily the sense of fatigue even though he may have been dog tired.[18]

But Boring and Van de Water went much further than Crile. After all, they had a political mission: to promote psychology as an indispensable discipline within the military. As Boring admitted in a letter to his collaborator in May 1943: 'I think [*Psychology for the Fighting Man*] will leave the reader with the impression that man is a mechanism, that there are laws that govern his actions, that he ought to take that point of view toward human problems in the Army, that psychology is a great thing. That is all I thought the [book] was for.'[19] As part of their attempt to promote a particular vision of psychology as a 'science' which was useful for the military, the authors deliberately adopted metaphors based on 'man as machine' (for instance, in their assertion that fear was 'fuel for the human fighting machine'). Psychologists could be effectively employed as engineers catering to the human mechanism. *Psychology for the Fighting Man* was a bid to reassure both their clients (the military) and their patients that this relatively new profession of military psychology could 'repair' the scared combatant.

For military psychologists war provided a special challenge. After all, as they were forced to acknowledge, the scientifically constructed human subject in war was not the same as the human subject in peacetime. Medical Officers divulged that in battle '*normal*' was *always* pathological. In the words of the author of 'Psychiatric Observations in the Tunisian Campaign' (1943): 'A state of tension and anxiety is so prevalent in the front lines that it must be regarded as a normal reaction in this grossly abnormal situation. Where ordinary physiological signs of fear end, and where signs and symptoms of a clinical syndrome begin, is often difficult to decide.'[20]

It was a familiar dilemma. In a 1943 issue of the *Bulletin of the*

United States Army Medical Department, Lieutenant Colonel Stephen
W. Ranson (chief of the 7th Army Psychiatric Center) explained that
'the pathologic battle reaction can be understood only in terms of
the normal battle reaction'. He continued:

> The psychiatrist inexperienced in evaluating combat reactions is
> likely to judge manifestations of fear and anxiety by civilian stan-
> dards, in relation to which the combat normal is distinctly
> pathologic . . . The untried soldier has never experienced repeated
> fear-producing stimuli of such intensity as those he will endure in
> combat . . . Both he and the inexperienced medical officer whom he
> may ask to review his case are often quite unprepared to recognize
> his symptoms as lying within the range of the normal reaction to
> combat fear and fatigue.

Ranson went further, declaring that it was normal for combatants
to experience 'marked psychosomatic symptoms'. He gave the
example of a soldier who presented himself to the battalion surgeon
with the following complaints: 'I can't stand them shells. My stomach hurts. They tear my stomach to pieces.' In such a case the
military physician had to be aware that the symptoms 'merely
describe in emotional phraseology one of the normal psychosomatic
reaction patterns to battle stress'. They were the 'normal response
to combat' as experienced by practically all soldiers in the front
lines and should not be used to keep a man behind the lines.
But Ranson was not writing only about soldiers with mild stomach upsets. According to him, it was perfectly normal for
combatants to suffer muscular tension, freezing, shaking and tremor,
excessive perspiration, anorexia, nausea, abdominal distress, diarrhoea, urinary frequency, incontinence of urine or faeces, abnormal
heartbeat, breathlessness, a burning sense of weight oppressing the
chest, faintness and giddiness. He insisted that:

> Neither [the soldier] nor the physician should expect that he will be
> relieved of the symptoms, since they are merely the normal auto-
> nomic response to fear in this soldier. It is as irrational to expect
> psychotherapy to relieve or remove such symptoms as to expect it to

prevent dampness and chills during combat in inclement weather. The soldier must 'learn to live with it'.[21]

Not only did combat's terrors create a paradox — pathological reactions were evidence of a normal constitution — they were also regarded as modernity's most bitter legacy. Indeed, although we have seen that many senior military commentators recognised the beneficial effects of fear during military assaults, the technology of modernity militated against these favourable effects. Basically, the nature of modern warfare dramatically reduced those occasions on which the mobilisation of the body's resources to fight was of any use. On a simple level, this was due to that unequal competition between technology and corporeality. In the words of two prominent psychiatrists in the last year of the Second World War:

> the calamitous and horrifying situations produced by modern war machines penetrate deeper and more acutely sensitive levels. Destruction is on a larger scale. Scarcely anyone is immune. Speed makes suddenness and unpredictability the rule. The organism must be continuously mobilized and on the alert, which means more continuous stimulation and strain and consequent fatigue.[22]

In other words, mechanised terror, extreme mobility, vastly more efficient killing machines, omnipresent danger and unpredictability sparked intense and unruly panic.

But there was more to it than this. Commentators during both world wars recognised that the primitive, inherited, animalistic nature of fear in warfare was simply not compatible with modern conditions of combat. In the words of the author of *Shell Shock and Its Lessons* (1917):

> In natural fighting, face to face with his antagonist, and armed only with his hands or with some primitive weapon for close fighting, the uppermost instinct in a healthy man would naturally be that of pugnacity, with its accompanying emotion of anger. The effect of every blow would be visible, and the intense excitement aroused in the

relatively short contest would tend to obliterate the action of other instincts such as that of flight, with its emotion of fear.

In contrast, trench fighting and artillery barrages created a battlefield in which the foe was invisible, the weapons of war impersonal.[23] As a consequence, the fear response — honed through the centuries by 'flight or fight' instincts — was utterly frustrated. As the chief neurologist at Netley military hospital in Hampshire explained:

> the [physiological] changes which accompany fear and anger are entirely useless if the emotions are not followed by the associated instinctual activity. So fixed, however, is the primitive association of anger with fight and fear with flight, that when the natural sequels of these emotions are restrained, they continue to give rise to suprarenal and probably thyroid activity. Thus the ceaseless fear felt by the constitutionally timid when exposed to the horrors of war results in constant over-secretion of the suprarenal and thyroid glands, the physiological results of which are not followed by the muscular activity of flight for which they are the preparation. The unexpended energy may be so extreme that the soldier is incapacitated by it.[24]

The great theorists of the emotions concurred with this view. George W. Crile, in *The Origin and Nature of the Emotions* (1915), observed that 'the effect of the stimulus of fear upon the body when unaccompanied by physical activity is more injurious than is an actual physical contest which results in fatigue without gross physical injury'. He reminded his readers that the physiological effects of fear would injure the body if they were not accompanied by action.[25]

This blocking of elemental 'fight or flight' responses was believed to be a main cause of combat fatigue and anxiety neuroses. If soldiers could not fight or otherwise engage in 'manipulative activity', and were not permitted to flee, they responded by becoming profoundly anxious — an emotion which was crippling. The absence of any outlet for aggressive tendencies put soldiers at risk of psychological disorders, argued numerous military psychiatrists.[26] Medical Officers observed that non-combatants within the military suffered the highest level of psychological breakdown, presumably because the pacific nature of their jobs brought them little 'satisfaction'.[27] As one military psychiatrist noted: 'people accommodate themselves better to the more *natural* strain of hunting and being hunted than they do to the strain of heavy shelling and bombing.'[28] For these commentators, the technology of long-distance killing, with its emphasis on anonymous agency and random aggression, placed an unbearable strain on men's physiological inheritance.[29]

From the point of view of senior military advisers this physiological crisis was exacerbated by a cognitive problem: too many modern soldiers were educated, and thus resistant to rationalisations and primitive conversions (such as the psychological process of 'converting' fear into a physical symptom like mutism or paralysis).[30] Throughout the twentieth century military commentators looked back with nostalgia to the time when (they claimed) men went into battle with 'vacant minds', incapable of 'measur[ing] their chances of survival'.[31] The 'threshold of fear' had been falling.[32] Men of 'natural courage' — those men who simply responded to the dictates of their instincts — were regarded as rare beings indeed by the twentieth century. This was a theme in the main military journals as late as 1976, when the *Army Quarterly and Defence Journal* lamented the passing of the 'armies of the pre-1914 era'. According to this analysis, before the First World War men were of 'stronger fibre . . . less influenced by cultural and soft social conditions and often lacked the faculty for deep thought which drew no picture of danger or feeling of fear. It might be said that such men possessed a natural courage, which really was a courage of insensibility to danger.' The article deplored the greater value placed on life, claiming that while men's bodies had deteriorated, 'Trotskyism and pacifism' had grown.[33] Technological sophistication and ideological refinement had transformed modern men into cowards.

Whether because an outlet for primitive 'fight or flight' responses no longer existed given the nature of modern warfare, or because the cognitive faculties of modern men enabled them to 'outwit' their instinctual urges, the physiological impact of fear still remained. However, between the First and Second World Wars a shift took place: in military medicine, fear states such as hysteria underwent a steep decline, giving way to a proliferation of anxiety neuroses. Admittedly, there was a class dimension to this trend. Throughout the century officers were much less likely to be diagnosed as suffering from hysteria than were men in the Other Ranks. As a chapter in *War Wounds and Air Raid Casualties* noted in 1939, 'rather naïve, simple, not very intelligent' soldiers were prone to hysteria. A private might not be overtly fearful in the firing line and he often obeyed orders with animal-like dumbness, but would break down suddenly in response to a particular stressful event. In contrast, an officer

> with his training, his sense of responsibility, [and] his higher ego ideal [or ideas of courage instilled by training and example], could and did tolerate enormous amounts of anxiety before the final breakdown, but, because of his ego ideal, could not sanction the complete flight of conversion hysteria. The man in the ranks, with no ego ideal, no sense of responsibility to anyone but himself, had nothing to inhibit the mechanism of [psychological] conversion, whatever it is, which gave him so complete an escape.[34]

Rank was not the only factor which distinguished hysterics from anxious neurotics. There was a surprising gender element to hysteria. It was discovered that women in the Women's Auxiliary Air Force were reputedly *less* likely to suffer from hysterical conversion disorders than their male counterparts in the air force. An analysis of nearly a thousand air-force women suffering psychiatric problems found that emotionally traumatised women 'tended to show an overt emotional upset rather than one masked by physical symptoms'. The explanation was clear. According to the researchers

> the socially acknowledged and permitted emotionalism of women allows for a more direct expression of adaptive and emotional difficulties, and that this renders prolonged and inconvenient physical symptoms superfluous. Men, on the other hand, submit to a sterner social and emotional code. They have, therefore, a greater need to

preserve their self-esteem by the development of a more complex
disguise or escape mechanism.[35]

Women's ability to talk about being scared prevented them from
becoming hysterical.

Nevertheless, whether male or female, officer or private, the
fear engendered by modern warfare was less likely to be linked to
the multiple threats to survival than to the crippling anxiety arising
out of the stripping away of individual agency. Increasingly, coping
with fear on the battlefield was linked to the ability of combatants to
strike out and kill the enemy. Referring to combat on a tropical
island, Colonel Bleckwenn complained that there was 'no escape':

> The repeated mental insult of constant shelling finally dulls the
> normal sensorium, and men become automatons . . . Many admit of
> retrograde amnesia as though there were a mild concussion, fol-
> lowing the explosion of bombs and heavy shells. This was more
> common among the men who were unable to retaliate against the
> enemy attack. The men who manned the antiaircraft guns, the
> machine gunner, and even the rifle man, suffered less in these
> attacks. They could release and expend the pent-up emotions and
> burn up, through activity, the glycogen mobilized by excessive adre-
> nal activity. They were less tense when it was over. By comparison,
> the unarmed inactive soldier who sought shelter in a foxhole or slit
> trench showed a greater pallor and less facial expression, a greater
> paucity of free associated movement, some tremor and all the signs
> of excessive adrenalization, and a thalamic syndrome. It took him
> longer to regain his normal poise.[36]

Typically, a fighter pilot who had seen active service in light
bombers during the Battle of France described the devastating emotional effects of being unable to see his targets or witness the effects
of his bombs. He was so frightened that he could not sleep and
would burst into sweat even climbing into his aeroplane. All this
changed during the Battle of Britain, however. In his words: 'success
in the game is the great incentive to subdue fear. Once you've shot
down two or three the effect is terrific, and you'll go on till *you're*

killed. It's the love of the sport rather than sense of duty that makes you go on without minding how much you are shot up.'[37] In other words, the emotional response of excitement brought on by the 'intimate contest' inhibited exaggerated fear responses. The authors of the classic study *Men Under Stress* (1945) said, when explaining why airmen were terrified of flak yet found engaging with an enemy plane exhilarating:

> Enemy planes are objects that can be fought against. They can be shot down or outmanoeuvred. Flak is impersonal, inexorable and . . . deadly accurate. It is nothing that can be dealt with — [a] greasy black smudge in the sky until the burst is close. Then it is appreciated as the gaping holes in the fuselage, the fire in the engine, the blood flowing from a wound, or the lurch of the ship as it slips out of control.[38]

Similarly, as a survey of psychiatric casualties during the Second World War concluded: 'As long as the soldier feels that in some way he is able to control the dangers of the battle field by his own behavior, his sense of security is reasonably good.'[39]

This point was argued most forcefully by William H. R. Rivers in one of the most insightful books on the psychology of war to come out of the First World War. We were introduced in Chapter Four to Rivers, who used his experience in treating men like the poet Siegfried Sassoon to theorise about the nature of nightmares. However, in *Instinct and the Unconscious* (1922) he turned his attention to war neuroses. Rivers observed that many combatants succeeded in suppressing their fear 'even when the danger is so insistent and unavoidable that death or violent injury is inevitable'. Airmen involved in serious air accidents often felt no fear whatsoever as they fell to what seemed like a sure death. Instead, the rare survivors reported feeling a sense of 'interest such as might be taken by the mere witness to a spectacle'. This feeling of 'distance' changed under other circumstances. In Rivers's words: 'It is when some line of action is still possible, but this action is recognised to be fruitless and in vain, that fear, often in the acute form we call terror, is likely to supervene.'[40]

Thus it was the emotional response of impotence (or the 'blocking of the instinct of self-expression', as the chief of Britain's Morale Branch during the Second World War euphemistically described not being able to kill) that frightened combatants most of all.[41] It was not uncommon for Anti-Aircraft Artillery personnel (men and women) as well as machine-gunners and riflemen to be allowed to continue firing rounds even after their target had long fled because this enabled their fear to dissipate.[42] Furthermore, the stressful aspects of being placed in a passive role in wartime helped explain the disjuncture between risk and fear. Crew in medium bombers (which were forced to keep to course irrespective of danger) consistently displayed much higher levels of fear than fighter pilots, who at least could maintain the myth of control over their fate. This was despite the fact that it was well known that only a quarter of all medium-bomber crew would be killed compared with half of all fighter pilots.[43] If a combatant could not *act*, he was more susceptible to fear.[44]

The disjuncture between risk and fear was also revealed in the types of weapons that combatants found most terrifying. A report titled 'The Moral Effect of Weapons' (1943) investigated the reactions of three hundred wounded American and British servicemen in North Africa to various weapons. The researchers discovered that there was no correlation between the tendency of these men to fear a weapon and the likelihood of being wounded by it; nor, indeed, were they influenced by the fact that an individual *had* been wounded by it. These men's fears were not 'rational'. Dive-bombers and mortar fire, for instance, were feared out of proportion to their ability to inflict casualties, while the deadly machine gun was rarely mentioned as being at all frightening. Instead, weapons were feared most strongly if the combatant believed that the enemy had an advantage in the use of that weapon. It was the feeling of 'inequality' — often described as 'injustice' by the men — which was at the heart of fear. When they were asked why they were afraid of a particular weapon, the 'inability to retaliate', the 'feeling of vulnerability' and the 'speed and surprise of the attack' were all as important as 'effectiveness' or 'accuracy'.[45]

These debates about the extreme emotional responses to passivity when under attack had a major impact on training servicemen to

cope with combat. The importance of 'channelling' fear was relatively rare during the 1914–18 war but was central to discussions by
the Second World War. By that stage the most important thing men
should do in a fearful situation was to engage in 'purposeful or
manipulative activity'. Diversion was crucial.[46] As the author of
Psychology and the Soldier put it in 1942:

> When troops are being subjected to intensive dive-bombing or
> artillery fire, for instance, and have to wait for some time before
> they are called upon to repel the main attack, it is advisable to divert
> their minds from present dangers by ordering some form of activity.
> Messages can be passed up and down the line, rounds of ammunition
> can be polished and counted, there can be a little more digging in,
> rifles can be sighted at eight hundred yards, two hundred yards,
> five hundred yards — anything, indeed, that will help men to forget
> their fear. For even the bravest of men can feel afraid. The only dif-
> ference between a brave man and a coward is that the fear of the one
> is controlled whilst the fear of the other is uncontrolled.[47]

'Manipulative activity' was considered to be one of the best remedies for mortal terror.[48] Salvation could be found in action, insisted
Lord Moran in *The Anatomy of Courage* (1945): 'To dull emotion he
must do something; to remain immobile, to stagnate in mind or
body, is to surrender without terms.'[49]

By the Second World War the majority of senior military psychiatrists and psychologists endorsed an approach that emphasised
both the physiological imperative of the 'fighting instinct' and the
cognitive sway of 'reasoning'. Edward A. Strecker was one such
physician. He was consultant to the Bureau of Medicine and
Surgery for the American Navy, consultant to the Secretary of War
for the American Air Force and President of the American
Psychiatry Association. In 1944 he wrote at length about the need
to teach men that fear was 'a natural and to-be-expected phenomenon' and that rather than using up energy to suppress this normal
emotion, men should use it in 'controlling behavior stimulated by
fear and making such behavior effective in overcoming the enemy'.
He argued forcibly that fear created 'a tremendous reservoir of

potential fighting strength which when transformed into dynamic
fighting power [would] gain the determining victories on the bat-
tlefields of the global war'.[50]

In the same year an article in *War Medicine* by Major William G.
Barrett agreed. He was concerned with the fear reactions of airmen
and stressed that it was crucial to tell them that fear was normal. In
Major Barrett's words:

> Conscious recognition of fear can in itself help to relieve tension.
> This relief must be made available by the breaking down of inhibi-
> tions against such recognition. This will help remove that 'fear of
> fear' which so often adds an unnecessary burden. One can show, fur-
> thermore, the important role of fear in mobilizing the reserves of
> the mind and body for combat or escape. Thus it is presented as a
> normal and beneficial emotion, the physiological correlates of which
> work to the person's advantage.

He went further, however, arguing that this understanding of the
physiology of the emotions would be particularly important in maintaining the emotional well-being of those airmen who found
themselves in fearful situations but who had 'comparatively little
opportunity for the relief afforded by violent motor activity'.
Airmen who could not strike back against the enemy (bomber crew,
for instance) would be able to use their knowledge of the physiology
of fear to channel their 'cruder motor activities' towards positive,
energy-consuming skills.[51] This refrain that the energy expended by
fear reactions should be channelled into positive activity was unques-
tioned in the second half of the century.[52]

There were other ways in which the military attempted to discipline the emotions of combatants. Teaching men to respond
automatically to orders, to ignore rumours, to focus on their leaders and comrades and to become accustomed to the fog and noise of
battle were crucial.[53] Although unofficial hardening processes (as
when experienced servicemen would set out to deliberately frighten
green troops with horror tales of combat) were also important,[54]
military training itself placed a great deal of emphasis upon preparing men to be frightened. Realism training was one main form of

this.[55] An example was the 'lunk trainer', invented in 1943. This was an inexpensive installation designed to accustom men's senses to battle sensation. Servicemen were exposed to screams coming from a phonograph recording, wind and noise from an aeroplane motor and propeller and odours from decomposing meat. The device was called a 'lunk trainer' because it separated 'lunks' from effective servicemen.[56]

Another way of training men to be fearless was to teach them to act automatically, without thought, in an emergency. But there was a major problem with this response. There were, in fact, only a limited number of routine actions that could be taught. In the words of Samuel A. Stouffer in his formidable study of the attitudes of servicemen during the Second World War:

> Most types of danger situations in combat require varying responses, depending upon the particular mission the man was assigned to carry out, the protective resources which happen to be available in his immediate vicinity, and other highly specific characteristics of the particular situation in which the danger occurs.[57]

This was why automatic training was less important than training men to obey orders immediately and even, if necessary, make their own judgement. Realism training was crucial in this because it taught men to think under terrifying conditions and it developed their self-confidence. It enabled men to build up their own psychological defence mechanisms prior to combat.

Leadership was also emphasised. Any attempt to restrict men's fear depended upon ensuring that leadership was respected, particularly at platoon level.[58] This was not a new phenomenon, but had been popularised by Captain J. F. C. Fuller in *Hints of Training Territorial Infantry* (1913). According to Fuller, when under an 'unrelenting storm of lead', officers must 'swallow their fears, clench their fists, and strike out boldly, not only for themselves and their men, but for their General, their regiment, and their army'.[59] Because much panic arose out of 'loose talk' by officers in the presence of their men, it was important to ensure that the officer always exhibited confidence and calmness, so that his men could feel that their safety was in good and secure hands.[60] According to a military instructor in 1942, the spread of rumours led to panic:

> Loose talk overheard by enlisted men indicating lack of confidence in superiors spreads rapidly and is multiplied. The influence of an officer is powerful. His men realize that their safety rests in his hands. If he is confident, cheerful, determined, calm — these qualities are reflected in his command and prevent the spread of wild rumors. If, on the other hand, he is nervous, irritable, worried, uncertain, he is sowing the seeds of panic.[61]

Such arguments were based on the belief that people were innately imitative, so fear could be reduced through witnessing the fearlessness of superiors or comrades.[62] Some commentators went so far as to recommend that 'born heroes' should be sent to mingle with the men to provide a role model to emulate.[63]

Most commentators agreed that, for combatants, the fear of being killed came a long way behind the fear of being thought a coward ('fear of fear').[64] As one private put it just after landing at Suvla Bay: 'At heart I believe everybody had the same pre-occupation — would they show the white feather when it really came to it?'[65] In his *Psychology and the Soldier* (1942) Norman Copeland drew on his experiences as an eighteen-year-old stationed at a Casualty Clearing Station for the wounded during the First World War. He believed that the fear of being seen to be afraid was the *only* fear a man felt when going into battle. In a letter written during the First World War, Shaw described the numerous tactics combatants preparing for battle employed in an attempt to eradicate or shroud their fears:

> Some were joking, some silent, and most were smoking. A few hard jokes were heard and generally were intended as a stimulant to courage — that is the time to see patriotism . . . And yet, through all the talking and critical observations of the enemy's fire, every man seemed a little frightened. I once read in a book somewhere that the Fear a soldier experiences before going into action is the Fear that his comrades may think him afraid. I know myself that this

is the only Fear a man has, he is afraid to show his Fear, and that
makes him brave.[66]

This fear of showing fear was probably worse for officers than for
the Other Ranks. Indeed, it impelled some officers to request that
they be relieved of their rank 'since they did not feel that they
were fit to retain responsibility for the behavior and safety of
other persons'.[67] In both the American and British armies during
the Second World War, there was a concerted attempt to teach
soldiers that this was a normal fear, shared by all, and best alleviated by frank discussion with their comrades.[68] An influential
book mentioned earlier, *Psychology for the Fighting Man*, emphasized this fact time and again. Very few men were actually
ashamed of fear, but the vast majority were afraid of *showing*
fear.[69]

Nevertheless, a process of acclimatisation could be observed.
Many combatants admitted that the experience of mass death diminished their fear of dying. As Lieutenant A. G. May noted:

Somehow one gets used to seeing the dead, [sic] I remember the first
of our dead I saw and all I could think of was that he looked peaceful
and feel sorry for his folks . . . After a while I think one becomes
thick skinned or case hardened to seeing our own men dead, maybe
this is not unreasonable but it would be bad to be emotional about
this.[70]

Major Vere E. Cotton had a similar experience. In a letter to his
mother on 15 October 1915 he described his emotions when he first
saw a dead body:

One was struck by the indifference of the other men who probably
knew him well, but when later on one found oneself following the
body on a stretcher down a communication trench one found one's
own feelings were precisely similar . . . I was interested to find how
'natural' it seemed . . . Somehow war is war and mercifully one's
feelings adapt themselves to circumstances which otherwise would
be unbearable.[71]

W. Clarke put it most clearly, arguing that men became 'hard-ened'. 'You got fed up with being frightened and hungry, cold, wet and miserable and often you just didn't care whether you survived,' he recalled, adding, 'Seeing so many corpses became just another sight.'[72] The omnipresence sense of 'fate' created a kind of indiffer-ence that made men less afraid. As Kenneth Cousland put it, after noting that neither himself nor his comrades thought much about being killed: 'The general outlook was fatalistic, "If your number is on the bullet, there's nothing you can do about it", so you carried on with your job.'[73] Even when wielding the bayonet, soldiers expressed feelings not of fear but exaltation or a detachment.[74]

The process of psychic numbing took longer for some combat-ants. Lieutenant A. B. Scott, for instance, described the process as incremental rather than instantaneous. In his diary for 17 July 1918 he admitted that he was 'going all to pieces'. He confessed that:

> my imagination is killing me. Last night I was alone inspecting the wire when for some Hellish reason I saw a picture of myself disabled by a bullet and lying for hours until I bled to death — days it would have been for my vitality is tremendous. For several minutes I couldn't move, covered with a clammy sweat and paralysed with fear.[75]

It only took a month in the front lines for him to change his tune. He had just experienced some extremely heavy fighting when, on 18 August 1918, he wrote:

> Slowly and surely I am breaking up, and now I am so far gone that it is too much trouble to go sick. I am just carrying on like an automa-ton, mechanically putting up wire and digging trenches while I wait, wait, wait for something to happen — relief, death, wounds, any-thing, anything in earth or hell to put an end to this, but preferably death — I am becoming hypnotised with the idea of Nirvana — sweet, eternal nothingness.[76]

Fear had killed off his imagination, transforming him into just another automaton of war.

Factors such as habituation and overwhelming weariness were

clearly crucial in explaining why a person might feel mortally afraid on one occasion and resigned on another. But not everyone was believed to be equally susceptible to fear in combat situations in the first place.[77] During the First World War, for instance, big-game hunters, miners, lumberjacks, and explorers were consistently described as less likely to succumb to fear in war because they had already learned to discipline their emotions.[78] In contrast, clerks and men with an 'artistic temperament' were more likely to 'catch the "jumps"'.[79] In wartime, when courage was at a premium and national identity was promoted particularly dogmatically, accusations of cowardice were more likely to be thrown at racial groups. For instance, as we shall see in the next chapter, during the air raids on London, Jews were singled out for expressing excessive terror. They were said to lack the 'British' tradition of conquering adversities, of bulldog endurance.[80] In contrast, it was widely argued that the famous 'British Phlegm', or reluctance to express emotion, was one reason for the higher level of 'war shock' among British troops, compared with their Spanish or French comrades.[81]

Of course, within the 'British race' there were distinctions: the 'quantity of Celtic blood' in their veins made Scottish Highlanders, Welshmen and Irishmen much more emotional than their comrades from the Lowlands of Scotland or the English midlands.[82] In America, black Americans were commonly regarded as more easily terrified.[83] Black Americans 'will fight as courageously and recklessly as the most pugnacious white man', noted one commentator, before adding that it was unfortunate that anything that was 'unusual or startling touches off his hair-trigger nerves. He has many traits which are childish.' As a consequence, it was widely believed that black troops needed particularly secure leadership.[84] John Richards, who commanded a black unit during the First World War, made a similar comment, claiming that the black soldier had

an extraordinary nervousness, does not like the dark, lacks will and initiative. This last appears most clearly in the case of non-commissioned officers. Many will handle their men very credibly behind the lines. In hard conditions, however, the best of them, though showing no apparent fear, seem to be struck dumb. They do what they are told, but move as if bewildered. I think they lack the free, independent spirit that stirs in the breast of the white; that rises within him when the shells are falling thick and says, 'I am a better man than any —— Boche, and I am coming through.'

Richards reminded his readers that 'races develop slowly' and since these men were slaves only a few years earlier and 'a few years before that they were children in the jungles', the military had to be patient.[85] They were particularly susceptible to mass suggestion.

The problem was what to do with those service personnel who succumbed to a severe fear reaction. They had to be dealt with swiftly. Treatment had its counterpart in civilian contexts, but there were aspects peculiar to the military situation that made it unique. These exceptional features included the fact that the fear of just one individual could severely risk the lives of many others; Medical Officers often had to deal with large numbers of emotionally fearful men within a relatively small geographical space; and the long-term financial burden for the state was potentially immense.

By the Second World War curing service personnel who were suffering from serious fear and anxiety states was said to be dependent upon three rules: decentralisation, expectancy and simplified methods. First, it was imperative that fearful men were treated as near as possible to the scene of their trauma. Psychological processes of 'suggestion' (or confidently assuring the patient of a swift recovery) became less effective the further away the traumatised person was taken from the site of mental injury. Decentralisation also meant that the fearful person remained aware of the needs of his comrades. Secondly, the frightened man had to be constantly reassured that cure was not only inevitable, but also imminent. This expectation of rapid cure was all-important. The term 'combat fatigue' was regarded as immeasurably superior to terms such as 'shell shock', 'concussion' and 'psychoneurosis' because it indicated a transient condition that would not leave any long-term defects. The man only needed a bit of sleep.

Finally, all methods of cure should be kept simple. Rest, food, warmth, shelter and a compassionate interview were effective cures.

In the words of a major in the Medical Corps during the Second World War: 'These immature, poorly endowed patients are suggestible; they adopt easily the emotional climate of the ward, hence the nurses and ward men by creating an atmosphere of poise, reassurance and security can allay much fear.' He added that 'punitive rigid personnel' would probably only augment the men's fears and that 'wardmen of the same cultural background' were best placed to allay the fears, particularly the fears of patients from rural areas.[86]

These military spokesmen represented the benign side to the military. There was a much more unforgiving way of dealing with frightened combatants. Men who showed their fright were severely castigated. They were described as 'dull and backward', 'psychologically inadequate individuals' and 'ineffectives' who required 'salvaging'.[87] If they broke under the strain they were 'childish', 'narcissistic' and 'feminine'.[88] Other responses were harsher still. After the Second World War one colonel, writing in the *Military Surgeon*, insisted that men who had panicked in combat should be sterilised — only such a measure would prevent men from showing fear and then passing on to another generation their mental weaknesses. Fear could be inherited. 'Is it not time that our country stopped being soft,' he argued, 'and abandoned its program of mollycoddling no-goods?'[89] Men had to be prepared to give not only their limbs or life for their country, but their 'guts' and 'nerves' as well.[90] Human sympathy took second place to the rational disciplining of fear.

Of course, particularly in battle, the emotions had to be controlled, and fear was treated more harshly than any other emotion. Coercion was often used in the front lines to get a man or group of men to fight. Rather unconvincingly, 'panic may be checked by officers firing on their own men', opined an article in 1914 published in the *American Review of Reviews*.[91] Or, as the lecture notes of Major Harvey Llewellyn Jones of the 104th Ammunition Train bluntly put it in 1918, 'of all animals, man is the most cowardly'. His recommendation? Punishment. 'There would be nothing to say on this subject if we had to lead only brave and honest men. Unfortunately there is a certain percentage of cowards in all armies. These men start panics. They must be punished.'[92]

During the First World War one private described what happened when soldiers were too scared to go 'over the top' when ordered: 'If they didn't go, they was shot. They used to count down (to zero) and the "Over the top" and then the Military Police would come along and see that they had all gone over. Some was coughing, some was spewing, some was singing, some was shouting — ah, it was terrible.'[93] Men who exhibited signs of fear were typically punished, not to steel *their* nerves but to provide an example to others.[94]

Among combatants, however, attitudes to those who exhibited cowardly actions varied widely. In a detailed survey of three hundred Second World War combatants, 70 per cent thought that the 'chronic deserter' should be shot, while only 8 per cent wished a similar fate on the 'green man who [was] afraid' and just 3 per cent considered the same treatment to be appropriate for the 'veteran who cracks'. The preferred treatment for such a soldier was to remove him from the lines — something that was recommended by only 16 per cent of respondents for the 'green man who was afraid', who was much more likely to have his 'squad talk to him' or to be made to 'stay and face it'.[95] Combatants in the front lines were more sympathetic towards their frightened comrades. They were hesitant about condemning the men they served alongside: 'who was I to reprove them?' one asked.[96]

It was the power and volatility of such emotions — the giddy swinging from panic to resignation, and back again to panic — that posed the greatest challenge to the military. Nothing disturbed senior military personnel more than witnessing their 'man-machine units' cowering in terror.[97] In combat, the emotions of individuals had to be subordinated to those of the group. By the Second World War the effects of fear were thought to be controllable through military training, fatherly leadership, support of the group and 'manipulative activity'. In the new civilian armies the officers had to remodel themselves as fatherly figures, dispensing reassurance more often than retribution.

Naturally, for those servicemen who failed to 'respond' to this new, benign way of disciplining the emotions, the threat of punishment remained potent. The basic fact was still, as senior officers frequently lamented, that human beings were not robots, and no science was capable of 'measur[ing] [man's] strength, plot[ting] their course, and predict[ing] accurately the outcome of battle'. Instead, 'Men who have been shy and timid developed into "tigers", and men who have all their lives bullied and dominated others about them cowered in fear and panic.'[98] Physiological reactions and psychological conflicts produced a tumbling confusion of emotions in the confrontation between the individual and technology. The murderous strength and rigidity of the machine was effortlessly subverted by the fluidity of the emotions: fear and anger, exhilaration and resignation — these were the everyday lot of the individual at war.

CHAPTER EIGHT

Civilians Under Attack

Houses flame in
Shuddering streets

AUDEN, 'THE AGE OF ANXIETY'

In the previous chapter service personnel trembled in the sights of diabolical weaponry, but they were not alone in their fearfulness. By the end of the Second World War new techniques of mass destruction had reached unprecedented levels, resolutely extinguishing the already tenuous distinction between civilians and combatants. By September 1942 the death rate of British civilians had exceeded that of British soldiers and this remained the case until D-Day, in mid-1944. Nevertheless, when we examine the emotional lives of British civilians in the line of fire during the Second World War, these mortal terrors often pale beside the grim dread of separation from loved ones or even the startling exhilaration of engagement in a life-and-death struggle.

Take the example of an unnamed 'Young Girl', one of thousands of Britons who found themselves under aerial bombardment in the autumn of 1940. Sitting in her kitchen listening to the roar of ack-ack fire, she described her fear as a 'nasty nervous feeling' or 'bloated' sensation that made her restless. Desperate to escape the confines of her home, she took her brother ('E') for a walk. It was a beautiful summer night, and the burning docks made the scenery

even more picturesque, so she felt her fear seep away. The two children sat on the grass and calmly watched bombs falling: 'Being in the
open, you feel more in control when you can see what's happening,'
she decided. Then, abruptly, there was 'the weirdest scratching
sound just above the roofs', followed by 'the most God-awful crash'
that made the earth 'judder'. Forty years later this Young Girl recalled what happened next:

> 'Hey, it's not too healthy here!' E dragged me up from the grass. I
> didn't seem to be doing *anything* — just cowering. I don't know
> what I meant to do, or what I was feeling . . . a funny blank.
>
> I remember racing towards the house, E pulling me and yelling.
> The oddest feeling in the air all around, as if the whole air was
> falling apart, quiet silently. And then suddenly I was on my face, just
> inside the kitchen door. There seemed to be waves buffeting me, one
> after another, like bathing in a rough sea. I remember clutching at
> the floor, the carpet, to prevent myself being swept away. This smell
> of carpet in my nose and trying not to be swept away, and I could
> hear Mrs R screaming. E was nowhere, the lights were gone, it was
> all dust. I didn't even wonder if she was all right . . . Didn't give him
> a thought . . . I just didn't *think* of answering or doing anything
> about anything. Almost a tranquil feeling.

She heard the normally amiable Mr R screaming, 'Down, everybody, get *down*. Do what I tell you, get your heads down!', giving
contradictory orders, and then noisily scolding his wife. It was only
when she crawled back outside that it dawned on her that 'I *might*
have been hurt — I had been in *actual danger*. Up to that minute I
had taken everything for granted, in a queer brainless sort of way, as
if it were all perfectly ordinary.' It was a dazzling thought. Later that
night a neighbouring woman piled seven blankets and a hot water
bottle on the Young Girl's bed and referred darkly to '*delayed* shock',
implying 'this dread phenomenon would hit me before the night was
out'. But there was no such trauma awaiting her in the dark:

> 'I've been *bombed*,' I kept saying to myself, over and over — trying
> the phrase on like a new dress, to see how it fitted. 'I've been

bombed — me'. It seems a terrible thing to say, when so many must have been killed, but never in my life have I experienced such *pure and flawless happiness*.[1]

The Young Girl's elation at being alive while others died was a solitary and transient emotion. In Britain the spread of war to civilian populations aroused a new set of anxieties for both potential victims and their political masters. Even in America, which was only slightly scathed by war on its own soil, the necessity of maintaining high morale was paramount. After all, if the fears aroused by 'total warfare' were not controlled, they could sabotage the war effort. For this reason self-styled scientific specialists on the emotions warned that the state could not afford to ignore 'the knowledge which psychoanalysts and psychiatrists have about anxiety, panic, aggression, submission, death, fears, etc.'. Failure to exploit psychological insights would be as fatal for 'world civilization' as was the reckless failure of states to invest in military hardware.[2] The governance of emotion was essential to a war that saw the science-fiction horror of H. G. Wells's *The War in the Air* (1908) dropped on everyone's doorsteps.

Despite the dramatic escalation of violence against civilian populations during the Second World War, British civilians had been threatened before in wartime. During the First World War Zeppelins rained bombs on London in 1915 and Gotha-Giant bombers followed in 1917. In total they dropped around 225 tons of bombs, killing 1300 people.[3] Anticipating these bombing sprees, public officials, politicians and psychologists predicted that Britons would panic. In April 1914 readers of the *Journal of the Royal United Services Institute* were alerted to the possibility that if an enemy power attempted an aerial 'knock-out blow' on Britain, the resultant 'panic and riot' might 'force the home government to accept an unfavourable peace'.[4] Such fears were fuelled by observations on human behaviour in disaster. As we saw in Chapter Two, crowd theorists warned about the dangers of emotional 'contagion' within groups under attack. Wilfred Trotter's *Instincts of the Herd in Peace and War* (1910) and Gustave Le Bon's *The Psychology of the Great War* (translated into English in 1916) insisted that the 'collective mind' was inherently inferior, and this was particularly true in wartime.[5] Even a mild panic would have 'an immediate effect in weakening rational judgement', warned Trotter.[6]

Fears that aerial attack would result in 'civil conflict and passionate disorder' were even foreshadowed in pre-war novels such as H. G. Wells's *The War in the Air* in which he described New York City being bombarded by German 'flying machines'. In this prophetic novel the destruction of New York was made all the more poignant because it was 'the supreme type of the City of the Scientific Commercial Age' and had 'long ousted London from her pride of place as the modern Babylon'. But mercantile greatness could never compensate for the effects of terror upon the human organism. In Wells's novel, when the German airships passed over New York the crowds gathered in Madison Square hastily scattered and in the 'panic rush from Brooklyn Bridge' many people were crushed to death.

The anxieties of these social commentators seemed to be borne out by the events during the First World War. Londoners *did* panic when Zeppelins appeared over their city. The hopelessness engendered by the awareness that there was 'no adequate system of defence' and 'our homes lay at the mercy of the enemy, of whose murderous intentions no doubt remained' was pronounced, according to the author of *The Defence of London 1915–1918* (1923).[7] Some people found themselves temporarily trapped, like the woman who was travelling on a train during a raid by Zeppelins. She admitted to being 'dreadfully frightened' and felt that, despite her prayers, one of the Zeppelins 'must see our train, whatever else it didn't see, and drop a bomb on the very carriage in which I was. But nothing happened . . . I could never get used to raids, they frightened me terribly.'[8] Others were able to act — although not always wisely. On the streets people fought to gain admission to Underground stations, where they could find some shelter, and drastic measures had to be taken to control them.[9] For instance, one Special Police sub-inspector reported the measures taken in the South Kensington shelter:

At this station there was a spare platform, and this we made into a nursery. We would not permit any crying or shrieking. Those who could not control themselves were not allowed in the nursery. The children were laid out in two rows with a passageway between. They slept quietly on their rugs and pillows until the 'All Clear' enabled their parents to take them home again. Parents and other shelterers were made to sit or lie on the platforms in two rows. We found that if allowed to walk about they were inclined to make a rush if there was any unusual sound, and as the platforms were usually packed it was impossible to control the more nervous members of our congregation. By forbidding any chairs or boxes to be brought below and by keeping everybody lying or sitting down, we put an end to any likelihood of a stampede.

When any emotional displays of fear occurred, two 'specially hefty' men abruptly imposed order.[10] More often, frightened individuals were cajoled into restraining their emotions, as in a poem entitled 'Zeppelins' (1920):

> From a blur of female faces
> Distraught eyes stand out,
> And a woman's voice cries:
> 'The Zeppelins — they are attacking us;
> Kingsland Road is alight,
> Stoke Newington is burning.
> Do you not hear the guns?
> Oh, what shall we do?'
> We make jokes to reassure them.
> I shiver: chill? excitement? fear?[11]

Such an explosive array of emotions was ominous. After the First World War the great military theorist J. F. C. Fuller anticipated that the increased sophistication of wars in the future would make panic even more likely. In tones reminiscent of H. G. Wells's prophetic musings, he wrote:

in future wars, great cities, such as London, will be attacked from the air, and that a fleet of 500 aeroplanes each carrying 500 ten-pound bombs of, let us suppose, mustard gas, might cause 200,000 minor casualties and throw the whole city into panic within half an hour of their arrival. Picture, if you can, what the result will be: London for several days will be one vast raving Bedlam, the hospitals will be stormed, traffic will cease, the homeless will shriek for help, the city will be in pandemonium. What of the government at Westminster? It will be swept away by an avalanche of terror. Then will the enemy dictate his terms, which will be grasped at like a straw by a drowning man.[12]

Both Wells and Fuller were wrong. Despite the fact that many more tons of explosives were dropped in a single raid during the Second World War than during all of the bombing of Britain in the 1914–18 war, the cities under attack did not descend into pandemonium. Without question, people might have had good grounds to panic. The bombing of Britain began in September 1940 when the Luftwaffe added the terrorisation of civilians to its mission of destroying aircraft, obliterating armament factories and disrupting communications and supply routes. From August to mid-November two hundred raiders bombed London each night except one. Thereafter people in Birmingham, Bristol, Coventry, Southampton, Liverpool, Plymouth, Cardiff, Portsmouth, Avonmouth, Swansea, Merseyside, Belfast, Clydeside, Hull, Sunderland, Newcastle and Nottingham were hit. In all, forty-three thousand people were killed and another 139,000 injured.

Relying to some degree on the experience of the First World War bombardment of the British mainland, governmental advisers predicted that if Britain were bombed again there would be widespread panic. Ominously, while local authorities were told in July 1938 to expect thirty thousand civilian casualties each day of the forthcoming war, psychiatric casualties were expected to outnumber these physical casualties by three to one.[13] According to Trotter, even before war was declared, Londoners could be seen 'openly running away'. 'People of whose nerves better might have been expected confessed to an uncontrollable alarm' as they 'feverishly scratched open' trenches within which to crouch in the event of attack. Trotter observed that 'stoical endurance' had been replaced by something 'which the thoughtful mind could not refuse the ominous name of panic.'[14] Others concurred, warning that, in the event of attack, scared civilians would become 'completely oblivious of everything but the immediate necessity for self-preservation. A terrified human being loses all; humanitarian qualities and interests, becoming more nearly bestial in behaviour than in any other circumstances'.[15] Nearly a quarter of Londoners questioned by Mass Observation in 1941 expected there to be mass panic if Britain was invaded.[16]

Thankfully, these predictions were spectacularly overstated. Throughout Britain people observed how their family and friends 'stood up' to air raids in this conflict better than they had during the First World War, when they were in less danger.[17] The ability to show a degree of bravado was highly esteemed, as were fatalism and a resigned state of mind.[18] In the words of one young woman in 1942:

> I have often thought, since this war started, that dying might be quite pleasant, because one would meet so many people one knew . . . I am a fatalist. This feeling has intensified since the war. I have felt pretty near disaster during raids, but it has never worried me. I have a simple faith in God which leaves everything in His hands, and if I am to die young, well there is nothing I can do to stop it.[19]

But, as combatants found, the process of acclimatisation was gradual. People were 'really frightened' at the start of the war when the sirens began screeching, but, by the end of 1940, they were 'taking little notice of sirens' unless these were accompanied by the noise of planes, gunfire or bombs.[20] In the end 95 per cent of people who were able to find refuge in one of the large communal shelters reported getting adequate sleep.[21] Indeed, during bombardments the main problem for the police and air-raid wardens was not restraining panic reactions, but getting people to act with sufficient decisiveness and speed. This caused the Chief Constable on the Isle of Wight to complain that the condition of the public is becoming more callous and in spite of all possible action by both police and wardens, including the use of the loud speaker on the police car, we cannot get the public to take cover. They will stand about in doorways and gossip at corners and the youth of this Island . . . have been impertinent to a degree. Industrialists going about their work or keeping their shift going, I would admire, but I cannot admire these foolish people who set this extremely bad example and who lounge about in a sort of absurd bravado.[22]

His concerns were echoed throughout the country, with service-men on leave being the chief offenders, followed closely by drunken revellers.[23]

This is not to imply that war on the home front did not cause alarm, but merely that, for many Britons, bombs were less fright-ening than a host of other things. Claustrophobia led some to put on a show of bravery by remaining at home during the raids rather than risk a phobic attack in the shelters.[24] Blackouts were particu-larly feared.[25] In the words of one Mass Observation report: 'Poor puzzled people. No one in the village seems to know what to make of this mysterious war. Unanimity is obtained only when the Black Out is mentioned. Everyone loathes it and their nerves are on edge because of it.'[26] To quell the fear of crime during blackouts, judges increased their sentences — instead of receiving twelve months' imprisonment, a thief who had carried out his trade during a black-out might find himself locked up for eighteen months.[27] But whether or not such policies deterred criminals, they certainly did little to calm the nerves of men, women and children on the streets after dark.

More importantly, it was usual for people to find the anticipation of danger much more frightening than actual disaster. This was a common experience for civilians in wartime Britain, where people reported that their terrifying nightmares of future military conflict vanished with the declaration of war in 1939.[28] During the air raids it was the surprise elements of the attacks that proved the most frightening. This was why people coped better with the conven-tional raids of the early years of the war than with the later attacks by V-bombs, which did not provide any warning.[29] Undeniably, *waiting* for air raids was emotionally wearing. When they came there was almost a sense of relief. In the words of a report prepared by Mass Observation in 1940: 'One is relieved to find how little bombs can do as compared with the mental picture one had . . . Soon raids became a part of the routine of life, an unpleasant part like walking home from work in the snow or having mild indigestion.'[30]

The authorities were surprised by these reactions, proudly claiming that it proved that 'civilisation does not of necessity sap our courage'.[31] Indeed, when Mass Observation conducted a survey on people's subjective feelings of happiness in wartime in 1941, they made a remarkable discovery. Although the majority of people were either not emotionally affected at all by the war (slightly less than a third of respondents) or were made less happy by the war (just over a third of respondents), 12 per cent of men and 20 per cent of women said that the war had actually made them happier.[32]

A similar resilience could be seen among British children, like the Young Girl at the beginning of this chapter.[33] Separation from their parents turned out to be much more terrifying than being bombed out of their homes.[34] Whatever fears children possessed were rapidly dissipated in the playing of war games.[35] As we saw in Chapter Three, when the child was afraid it was said to be 'really' the fault of their parents, especially the mother. After all, it was widely reported that children only became frightened if they had fearful mothers.[36] It was crucial that mothers did not 'wobble' when faced with frightened children.[37] To help them, advice manuals proliferated, recommending that they 'try to conceal [their] own feelings' about the death of loved ones from the child and encouraging them to treat air raids in a matter-of-fact fashion.[38] Preventing a child's fears depended upon mothers keeping a 'rigid control' on their 'emotions, expressions and actions'.[39]

It seemed as if exerting a 'rigid control' over fear reactions was widely successful. Remarkably, there were relatively few psychiatric casualties, of whatever age group.[40] By December 1940 only twenty-five people in London and three people elsewhere in England had been admitted to psychiatric hospitals as a result of neuroses arising out of the raids.[41] A Home Intelligence report in

February 1941 noted that only 5 per cent of people who had been 'incapacitated by air-raids' showed symptoms of 'nervous shock'. This surprised commentators. Psychologists had expected untrained, undisciplined and relatively passive civilians to suffer much higher levels of decapitating fear. After all, why should the civilian rate of emotional breakdown be so low compared with levels of collapse in the military services? The differences were particularly pronounced since, before D-Day, British civilians had been much more in the firing line than British servicemen. The best answer to this riddle was produced by the psychologist P. E. Vernon. Unlike servicemen, Vernon observed, civilians

> have greater freedom and initiative in moving about and controlling their own actions. They can often express their fears outwardly with less shame, indeed they are encouraged to take shelter from danger, instead of always having to be ready for duty. But above all there is not the same hysterical conflict situation in the civilian between the present danger and the imagined security of the hospital or of the home country, as there was in the army in the last war. The civilian is never tempted to think that it would be an advantage to be sick or wounded, and he is already in, or close to, his own home.[42]

Those civilians who did suffer extreme fear reactions in wartime were regarded as being 'predisposed' to emotional instability in the first place.[43]

At least that was the view at first. By the middle of the conflict the opposite effect was being observed: people with pre-existing neuroses actually experienced a *reduction* in their levels of anxiety during the war. Those people who had been concerned about their own 'deviations from normality' before the war were reassured to discover that 'normal' people now shared their fears. According to the famous psychiatrist Irving J. Janus, war provided 'the opportunity for gratifying unconscious self-punitive needs'. Masochistic patients improved since they had been provided with 'objective opportunities for undergoing inconveniences and for risking their lives'.[44] Neurotics turned out to be remarkably calm about being threatened from the skies. As one man confessed: 'Oh, I'm not worried about the bombs — it's this queer tickly feeling in the back of my head [that bothers me].' Similarly, a woman who had harboured obsessional fears of infidelity and murder before the war admitted: 'I'm afraid I can't get very concerned about bombs; I wish I could, it would be more normal.' She was living quite happily in a heavily bombed area.[45]

Indeed, neurotics generally adapted very well to bombardment. An inner-London psychiatrist observed the effect of war on an unmarried man whom he had treated for an 'obstinate' neurotic depression for six years before the war. This man had failed to 'emancipate himself from his mother' and had 'numerous sex-guilt factors, some of which date back to his earliest childhood'. Nevertheless, once bombs began dropping on London, his symptoms vanished and, having joined the Air Raid Protection service, he behaved calmly and heroically. Admittedly, this psychiatrist believed that part of the 'extraordinary toughness of some well-established psychoneurotics to aerial bombardment' might be explained by the fact that their emotional lives were so preoccupied with their own, internal anxieties ('usually relating to sexual difficulties') that they had no emotion left for 'simple bodily fear'. But, he noted, psychiatrists should not ignore the pride neurotics experienced about being able to contribute to the business of their communities and the sense of reassurance they received by seeing other people 'as worried as they have felt over the years'.[46]

Then tragedy struck in 1943. On 3 March complacent observations about the unruffled demeanour of Londoners under attack was shattered. Bethnal Green Underground Station had been used by hundreds of predominantly working-class people seeking shelter from the bombs. On that fateful Wednesday evening, between five and six hundred people were already in the shelter when the alert sounded at 8.17. Those who had not already sought refuge began hurrying towards the shelter. In the ten minutes after the alert had sounded, 1500 more people had entered the shelter. Gunfire could be heard, although it seemed to be coming from a distance. Then, at 8.27, an Anti-Aircraft Artillery battery about a third of a mile from the station fired a salvo of rockets. People who had not yet reached safety panicked. Many threw themselves on the ground, waited for a lull in the noise and then continued their race towards the refuge. Some were screaming, 'They are starting to drop them!' or, 'It's a landmine!'

Tragically, terrified people reached the steps of the underground shelter at the same time. A woman and her baby stumbled on the steps. Within a few seconds hundreds of panic-stricken people had fallen on top of one another. The roar of gunfire and rockets smothered the screams and moans of the men, women and children jammed at the bottom of the crush. To make matters worse, some of the people trying to enter the shelter believed that they were being deliberately held back, so they pushed all the harder against those in front. The confusion lasted less than a quarter of an hour, but when the police finally restored order, few of those at the bottom of the pile were alive.

Disentangling the bodies was a slow and arduous job — indeed, it took until midnight for the police, Civil Defence Services, Home Guard and Women's Volunteer Service to complete the job. In the end the bodies of 173 men, women and children were retrieved. Twenty-seven men, eighty-four women and sixty-two children under the age of sixteen had perished. Most showed signs of 'intense compression', according to the official report into the tragedy.[47] The strong as well as the weak proved vulnerable: Dick Corbett, former British bantamweight boxing champion, was among those crushed to death. A further fourteen men, thirty-three women , and fifteen children were injured, many so seriously that as late as 11 March only seven men, fifteen women and eight children had been discharged from hospital. Remarkably, among the survivors was the mother who had stumbled first. But her baby died. Ironically, no bombs had been dropped. The nearest bomb fell more than two miles away: as nineteenth-century crowd psychology had predicted, the panicking crowd was homicidal.

Lawrence Rivers Dunne, a Metropolitan Police magistrate, led the governmental commission which looked into the cause of the tragedy. He was hampered from the start by the secret nature of the inquiry. Rumours proliferated. On the streets relatives and dependants of the dead lobbied passionately (although 'with no sign of hysteria', according to one report) for a public inquiry and, when they were refused, 'deep resentment affected local morale.'[48] But the Home Secretary, Herbert Morrison, defended the decision to keep the calamity hushed up. He admitted to being apprehensive lest the Germans realise how easily they could spark panic simply by dis-organising the life of Londoners (and, indeed, Lord Haw Haw, that 'renegade traitor from Germany', did use the panic at Bethnal Green in his broadcast propaganda).[49] Morrison insisted that, firstly, there were matters of security to worry about: 'anything bearing on British psychology under strain is of value to the enemy'. It was 'impossible to make a fair summary of the report, or even of the conclusions, without conveying information valuable to the enemy'. Secondly, it would be bad for morale if news of a panic got out. Thirdly, 'irresponsible or disaffected local interests and personages' might use the public inquiry as propaganda. Finally, he reminded doubters 'We are at war.' The nerves of Britons were to remain classified.[50]

What caused the nerves of these Londoners to suddenly shatter? In part, fear had been aroused by guilt. Londoners had already undergone sustained bombing in the winter of 1940–1, and (as we have seen) proved remarkably resilient. But 1943 was different. Immediately before the Bethnal Green panic Britons had become aware of the devastating raids carried out by British and American bombers on Germany. As a consequence, since 16 January, when they had heard of the raid on Berlin, many people in London were awaiting German retaliation. The day before the Bethnal Green panic Londoners had been informed of another heavy raid on Berlin. Reprisals were expected. As Dunne observed, people

> take a most intelligent interest in the accounts of our bombing of the enemy, particularly remembering what they themselves experi-enced. They did not miss the optimistic accounts in our press of the results achieved on this occasion, and had noted the changed nature of bombing tactics and the accounts of the results of the ultra-heavy bombs coming into use. The result was that people had made up their minds that in case of an alert it was necessary, or, at any rate, wise to get into deep shelter with as little delay as possible.

He described their attitude as 'a little nervous and apprehensive', although no more than they ought to be.[51] People were very much aware that the 'new bombing tactics' which the British had used in Berlin gave people less time to seek shelter once alerted of danger. Indeed, the bombing might coincide with an alert.[52] Given these apprehensions, it was easier to understand why people would have panicked on 3 March 1943 when they heard the noise of battle. For frightened men, women and children, a dreadful attack was not only expected; it was their 'comeuppance'.

As with explanations for panic in the early decades of the century, structural engineers and architectural designers were initially lambasted for the tragedy. The Bethnal Green air-raid shelter had been open since October 1940 and was one of the largest in London. Sixty per cent of the public shelter accommodation in the borough was housed in this single shelter — a far higher proportion than in neighbouring boroughs. The shelter could hold five thousand people in bunks and the same number again if refuge alone was required. However, since 1941 only a few hundred people were regularly sleeping in the shelter, so, on the night of the panic, many people were unfamiliar with what were later described as its design foibles. These defects were numerous. For one thing, there was only one entrance and it came directly off the main pavement. The entrance and passageways were only dimly lit. Nineteen uneven steps led people from the street to a large hall but, once in the hall, they had to walk down an escalator of seventy steps into the main part of the shelter. Furthermore, not only were there no handrails down the centre of the stairwell, there was also no crash barrier, thus 'allowing a straight line of pressure from the crowd seeking entrance to the people on the stairs'.[53] Looked at after the event, a crush seemed almost inevitable.

Indeed, many people who heard the rumours about the tragedy wondered why a similar tragedy had not happened before.[54] The government was bombarded with letters alerting them of other 'criminally unsafe' air-raid shelters, including the tube stations at Kennington, Piccadilly, Marble Arch, Warwick Avenue, Knightsbridge, Liverpool Street, Trafalgar Square, Waterloo and Victoria, as well as Aldgate Metropolitan Railway station and Romford

LNER station. Some of these concerned citizens described situations which could have easily resulted in a deathly panic. Mrs Cecil Hatchwell of West Kilburn, for instance, complained about the steep steps leading into her local tube station shelter from Warwick Avenue. She described a recent occasion when a 'terrible crowd' of people

> all fighting to get through the tiny opening (as the gates were half shut). The guns were going which all helped to terrify them, they were screaming out 'save my baby'. I was torn away from my little girl, & fighting against the crowd was pushed through towards the steps. Of course it was pitch black & one could see nothing. If one person had lost their footing, exactly the same accident would have happened, but thank God, we were saved this.[55]

Other letter writers observed that security at many shelters had become exceedingly lax in recent years. Manpower shortages within the military had led to the conscription of policemen, further reducing the number of police patrolling shelter entrances. In fact, from the summer of 1941 there had no longer been a policeman permanently posted at the entrance to the Bethnal Green shelter. This was why, on 3 March 1943, it took ten minutes after the disaster for the first constable to arrive at the station.[56]

While the official inquiry emphasised structural and procedural flaws, ordinary British citizens were more anxious to identify the 'real' culprits. Scapegoating was one of the main responses to the Bethnal Green panic. As the psychiatrist Joost Meerloo observed about war in general:

> Other people are identified with that part of ourselves of which we disapprove, and thus hatred for the object of our identification grows within us; in fact, it becomes the personification of our fear even though it may be only a symbolic scapegoat like the *Jew* or the *Negro*. Much hatred and persecution of minorities can be traced to unanalyzed, unexplained fear.[57]

Foreigners, Jews, criminals and irresponsible young people became the symbolic scapegoats for all that went wrong at the Bethnal Green shelter. Of these four 'enemies within', foreigners were regarded as being the most blameworthy. This was the view of a spinster named Lilian Edith Gerwood, from Epping. In shocking turquoise ink and large capitals she informed the Home Secretary on 10 March 1943 that the culprit for the tragedy at Bethnal Green may have been 'foreign shoes'. In her words:

> Was the disaster due to shoes soled with a slippery composition such as has been used in the repair of shoes owned by me? These shoes have caused me to fall. I have also witnessed another fall although I have no authority to attribute it to the same cause. Has this abominable substance been imported or are we as a nation guilty of the atrocity.

She signed off with the words: 'Yours in the service of our King and Country'.[58]

Lilian Gerwood's suspicions about the dangers of foreign imports were comparatively subtle. Many others blundered in and identified the culprits as Jews. Despite the fact that the Bethnal Green shelter was not located in a Jewish area (indeed, before the war this part of Bethnal Green had been an active fascist centre and only five of the 178 people who died were Jewish)[59], rumours blaming Jews spread throughout the country.[60] As one anonymous writer put it in a letter dated 11 March 1943:

> Being on the spot at the time of the trouble I was able to observe the cowardly display of fear by the foreign born Jews they [sic] simply lost their heads in their desire to get under shelter causing one solid mass resulting in suffocation I [sic] remember quite well the trouble in the East End in the last war — Fear in the Jews.

The author concluded his letter by insisting on the 'truth' of his accusation, 'although the Jewish influence might cause this information to be suppressed'. He refused to sign his correct name on the grounds that it would cause him to lose his job.[61]

Another person, signing himself 'Bethnal Green', blamed the fact that the Air Raid Patrols were 'run by the wrong people' — that is, Jews. In addition, he claimed that these Jewish officials were '100 per cent Communist'. He called for the borough's patrols to be 'cleaned up of such people'.[62] A postcard sent to the Tube Shelter Disaster committee by J.W. Skelton of Ilford, on 10 March 1943, went straight to the point: 'What we hear here about The Tube Disaster is that the Jews did all the nasty work by their fright and *pushing behind*. Turn the dirty dogs out of the Country.'[63] Another letter writer went further. One letter, addressed 'The Retreat . . . Southgate N13', declared that:

> there is a considerable amount of disquietude in the minds of many Londoners when they realize that the worldwide reputation they have earned for valour and morale in the heavy air raids on the Capital should now be besmirched by the recent happenings in a East London Tube. Whatever the result of the Enquiry one thing is absolutely necessary that the world should know that the cowardly panicky and stampeding victims of their own death trap, were not Britishers but a pack of foreign and English Shirks. I have spoken to many of my fellow Londoners and they all express the same desire that the true facts should become known.

It was signed 'Perisha Judean'.[64]

Jews were not the only group scapegoated. Other witnesses blamed local criminals. An anonymous writer pointed his finger at the 'yobbos' who hung around the entrance of the shelter smoking, only rushing down the stairs when they heard a bomb fall.[65] Some identified the criminals as part of the 'Woods or West gang' or as members of a 'gang' run by Dick Corbett, Razor Newman (otherwise known as Slasher Newman) and 'Fascist hooligans' who had been 'out on the "buzz"' that evening.[66] Hooligans would steal the valuables that women brought with them into the shelters. 'Round up the Fascist hooligans,' one person demanded.[67] Such letter writers insisted on remaining anonymous, since they were terrified of reprisals. As one of them drily put it: 'This letter must be anonymous as a razor slash on a dark night can be rather a nuisance.'[68] Henry N. Bloomfield, who owned an insurance brokerage in Cricklewood, argued that the entrance to the shelter 'no doubt helped the pickpockets and Fascists in that area to forment [sic] a panic, and my hope is that most of the latter paid the penalty of their inhuman beastliness'.[69] These commentators urged the inquiry to find out 'if there was a crush on any previous occasion which may have given the alleged gang the idea to make use of a future occurrence for conducting their activities'.[70]

Finally, there were those who simply blamed the panic on immoral and selfish young people. A person signing himself 'Bethnal Green Resident' claimed that the shelter was used to hide deserters and was a 'secret meeting place, causing homes to be broken up'.[71] Albert E. G. Saunders, from East London, argued that 'quite a lot of people of both sexes and of all ages' were 'only concerned with themselves and their own thought; and it is their own selfish action that is the primary cause of disaster in crowds'.[72] For others, local mothers were partially responsible for the panic because they were bringing their children back into the city instead of keeping them evacuated in safer areas. This was the line taken by Councillor Percival James Bridges, the Chief Shelter Warden, and thus someone who was accused of being partly culpable for the tragedy. He claimed that part of the problem had been the rapid increase of children in the area. In his words:

> It is impossible for women with very small children to travel into the Shelter quickly enough to allow for the mad rush of people from half-a-dozen public houses, a large number of people caught in the streets, and others who still continually congregate on all corners of the road junction where this Shelter is situated.

He recommended that they establish a separate entrance for mothers and children and other 'slow going traffic'.[73] The report of the inquiry agreed with this, stating that in recent months a large number of children who had been evacuated had returned to the area and parents were naturally anxious to get them to safety as soon as possible.[74] One particularly vicious letter was written by G. E. Stevens of Portsmouth. It read:

> The city I am writing from has had its fair share of warnings and I know the conduct which is carried inside and around the shelters.

Did some of those people have them selves [sic] to blame . . . Have you any details of the people that was killed and injured as to whether they came up from the shelter to smoke and by doing so making the doorway and passage crowed [sic], which is a general habit carried on outside of most shelters. Now the conduct of these people are as follows, as soon as the guns open out fire they think of one thing that is self and the result is terrific rush and by doing this they put fear into the public entering the shelter also the women and children who are already in the shelter and make them think there is something very serious happening. When these people are spoken too [sic] about the glow of their cigarette by an ordinary person they take no notice has [sic] it one think self first [sic] and in the shelter. Then there are the people who lay in bed until the Guns open and there is another terrific rush, which is a serious thing for a large shelter.[75]

These views were shared by others. Phyllis Violet Kay of Maida Vale was sufficiently worried to write a letter to the inquiry. She recalled how she had recently arrived in London from Brighton and had been allotted three bunks in the Warwick Avenue shelter. She described her first experience of a raid:

When we got to the Tube entrance, I was very amazed to find the staircase all the way down crowded with people — men and women — blocking the way — anxious to see the gun-fire and yet feel near enough to safety to make a dash for it if a bomb fell around. I had to force a way through this crowd for myself & 2 boys, by now very frightened, & the staircase being half in the open was naturally very dark & similar things might have happened.[76]

People were afraid of their neighbours: German bombs were only one of many threats.

In response to these emotional reactions, all the inquiry was able to do was to reassure people that the culprits were not some vile stranger or irresponsible nonconformist, but that panic could seize anyone, even good, ordinary citizens like those who died at Bethnal Green. The inquiry's report noted that fascists and criminals were as little responsible for the tragedy as were the Jews. 'There were some deaths among men with criminal records,' Dunne concluded, but 'their relatives are as much entitled to sympathy as any of the other victims.'[77] Besides structural adjustments, the best solution was to ensure that a strong 'leader' was present to provide guidance for frightened people. If a leader was not able to be present in the flesh, his voice could be recorded, giving instructions and reassurance audibly. A car engineer who styled himself Geo Ramsey wrote to the Home Secretary advising him that lives would have been saved if 'a calm and powerful voice [had] been able to direct and control those unfortunate people'. He noted that police and civil-defence personnel were trained to remain calm in emergencies, and so recommended that they be routinely fitted with a collapsible or telescopic megaphone in order to control crowds. He offered to design one that would resemble a collapsible metal drinking cup.[78]

William Medlicott of Hampstead Gardens proposed a similar solution. He had been caught up in a rush once inside Piccadilly Circus station. This experience led him to note that people slowed down when they entered the security of the station, causing problems for those still attempting to enter. The solution, he believed, was to employ someone to shout, 'Move along quickly please' or to install a loudspeaker saying the same thing.[79] Dunne cautiously endorsed this approach in his report. While admitting that it was unlikely that the police could have done much even if they had been present, he added that:

> At the same time it would be folly not to recognise that even a single tactful and determined man may often by timely action avert what a number could not subsequently prevent. While I have in the past noticed that the appreciation of certain sections of the population of London for the Metropolitan police is occasionally tempered with a certain reserve, more than one witness before me shewed a touching confidence in the sedative effect that even one policeman would have had in the turmoil of that night.[80]

In the end, however, this panic could have occurred in any number of shelters, even those regarded as 'ideal' by the inquiry. Terror was 'irrational', but this made it more rather than less potent. It was spurred on by feelings of guilt and afterwards was interpreted in the light of communal hatreds. Furthermore, it was a panic that people strove to forget as soon as possible, preferring to wallow in fanciful notions of 'British bulldog courage'. This process of forgetfulness was completed at the end of the war when, in a booklet celebrating the residents of Bethnal Green, readers were blatantly informed that 'the attitude and behaviour of the population as a whole during raiding was admirable . . . Throughout the war not a single case of panic was witnessed . . . East End humour was the great antidote to fear — of that there was no lack and some of it was of rare quality.'[81] The great terror of 1943 had been erased from history.

As the tragedy at Bethnal Green illustrated, some Britons were suffering from debilitating fear as a result of the air raids. Fred Bennett Julian's *Psychological Casualties in Air Raids and Their First-Aid Treatment* (1940) was one of the earliest attempts to provide air-raid wardens, clergymen and social workers with a guide for dealing with such casualties. According to Julian, it was normal for people to be terrified when under bombardment: after all, the 'instinct of self-preservation' was the strongest of all human instincts. This was why it was important not to confuse a frightened person with a coward. The 'really brave man' might be terrified but remained willing to 'serve his group', unlike the coward who gave 'unrestricted outlet' to his instinct of self-preservation. Most men, Julian believed, had a sufficiently strong ego-ideal (or ideas of courage instilled by training and example) to be brave. But, he acknowledged, the civilian under bombardment was in a much more difficult position emotionally than the combatant. Soldiers were 'accustomed to command or be commanded' and were imbued with 'soldierly conceptions and loyalty to regiment and king'. Julian asked:

> What of the civilian? His loyalty to group, his country, his conception of what is expected of him as a man or a gentleman, may be operative; but there must be many who are controlled by neither external nor internal discipline, truly a dangerous situation, and one of those disadvantages of democracy which Socrates painted in

lurid colours. The fact is that there is a real need for authority in times of emergency, and that authority must not be remote but familiar.

This was a restatement of Le Bon's view that only the imposition of a higher authority could control the 'suggestible mob'. Just as psychotherapists recognised that 'it is not what they do or say to their patients which helps the latter, but what they are. A psychotherapist must himself have got rid of his conflicts and complexes, and attained an inner harmony, before he can really help his patients', so too air-raid wardens, clergymen and social workers had to conquer their own fears when under bombardment in order to lead the crowd in the paths of emotional righteousness.[82]

As in the catastrophe at Bethnal Green, certain groups were castigated for acting in a particularly scared fashion during the war. As observed throughout the century, gender and class were major categories distinguishing the fearful. Women were assumed to be less capable of calculating the 'mathematical probability' of escaping harm[83] and their bodies were said to be frailer, making them particularly susceptible to panic if bombs dropped when they were menstruating, lactating or experiencing a menopausal crisis.[84]

Class also mattered. In July 1941 the Mass Observation guru Tom Harrisson told the British Psychological Society that because working-class housewives lacked a 'country line of retreat' or any spare cash to spend on a hotel or railway journey, they were particularly in need of emotional succour. According to Harrisson, these housewives were profoundly shocked by the 'disappearance of the fifty-one landmarks of daily life' which they had accepted 'with almost as little question as primitive man accepted the force of gravity'.[85] Even men from the 'humbler classes' were believed to be generally inadequate during onslaughts. Air-raid wardens from the working classes were simply unaccustomed to 'controlling people'. 'How they'll react in a street full of panic-struck people I don't know,' lamented one warden in Bolton.[86] Ironically, this alleged emotional inadequacy of working-class people was partly a result of their communality. After all, as we saw in Chapter Two, there was no clear correlation between panic and non-adaptive responses. During the Second World War psychologists and sociologists analysing responses of people under bombardment observed that, while poorer citizens were more timid and panicky, they often acted in extremely effective ways in the air-raid shelters.

In contrast, a Mass Observation report in 1940 noted that 'among middle-class people there is sometimes a striking lack of co-opera-tion and even courtesy in air-raid shelters'.[87] Intellectuals and Labour Party supporters were 'more resistant to the traditions and social attitudes of the majority' (such as 'the belief that the British improve with misfortunes'), which made them less capable of with-standing the emotional demands of war.[88] So, according to these commentators, when humble citizens occupying East End shelters exhibited 'bull-dog fearlessness', it was only because they lacked the capacity for higher thought.

More surprisingly, though, ex-servicemen were accused of not acting with sufficient heroism. In 1941 the *Lancet* reported that male cases of emotional breakdown outnumbered female cases by a ratio of thirty to eighteen. This was not ascribed to the higher levels of fear-ful stimuli that men were exposed to, but to the fact that servicemen had something to gain by invalidism. Respite from further danger and the prospect of a pension were fantastic temptations.[89] But, in addi-tion to these factors, it was recognised that being bombed during the Second World War 'reactivated' memories of combat from the 1914–18 conflict. A railway guard who had served honourably in France during the First World War found himself unusually petrified during the bombing of London. On one occasion he refused to leave the shelter after the 'all clear' siren had sounded. Under the influence of narco-analysis (the use of barbiturates to facilitate the recovery of repressed memories), he was heard responding to his wife's taunts of cowardice: 'Why didn't they do me [kill me] in the last war? . . . What a coward . . . I'm sorry, girl, I can't 'elp it . . . I'm not going out . . . All right, call me a coward.' When this man had served in France during the Great War he had found that opportunities for retaliating against the enemy in France were a release for his aggres-sion: in contrast, during the Second World War, when unable to retaliate, he rapidly developed hysterical reactions.

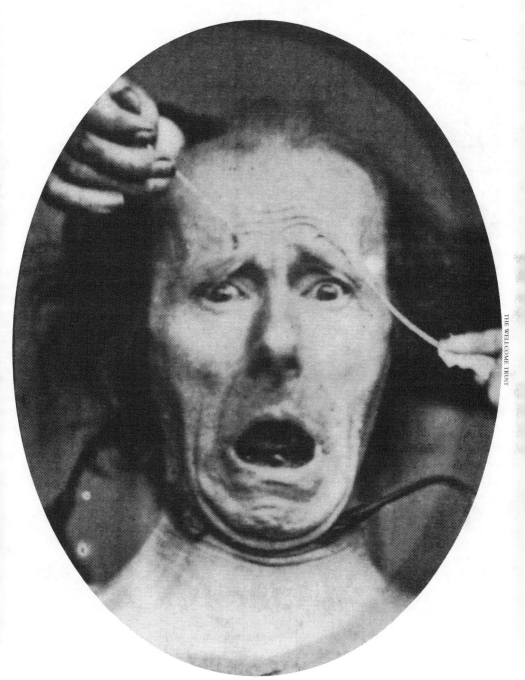

Duchenne de Boulogne applying electrodes to 'An Old Man's' face, contorting the muscles to resemble fear (1860s)

'A Child's Nightmare'

Frank Vester's 'security coffin' guarding against premature burial

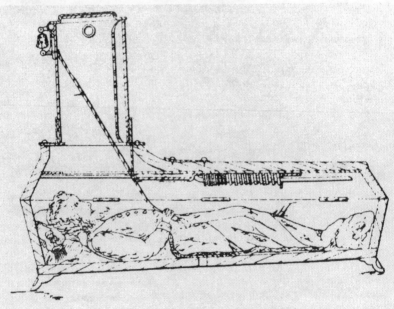

Fig. 1. Burial case with square tube attached to lid and extending above grave. The ladder is fixed to right side, cord and bell to the left.

Panic on the Titanic: 'Major Archibald Butt, in a crisply pressed uniform, prevents shabbily dressed steerage passengers from taking women's places in the boats'

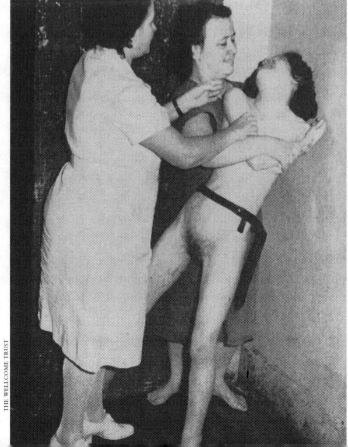

Walter Freeman and James Watts' photograph of a woman being dragged to her lobotomy (1950). The original caption read: 'Other patients have to be held'. A Fischer family photograph, c. 1917

Combat photograph during the Second World War

'God of Vectorey'. Drawing by Harry Turner, 7¹/₂ years. Second World War

A still from the film on the nuclear war, *The War Game* (1966)

The monument to *The War of the Worlds* at Grovers Mill, New Jersey, where the Martians supposedly landed in 1938

SEPTEMBER 23, 1985 • $1.50

People weekly

AMERICA'S HOTTEST MAGAZINE IS NOW £1.20

FEAR & AIDS
IN HOLLYWOOD

It is a town near hysteria. Since Rock Hudson's confession, actresses have been shunning love scenes with gay co-stars. Two actors are starting private blood banks. In a world known for easy sexuality, even a social kiss is suspect. 'This is the last stop, honey, right in your own home,' says Cher, who has lost three friends to AIDS and wonders every day who will be next . . .

(Continued on page 28)

VINTAGE MAGAZINE

Fear and Aids in Hollywood

NATIONAL GALLERY OF AUSTRALIA

Keith Haring's colour screenprint for ACT UP

'Evil Video. Did Chucky Inspire Jamie's Murder?'

Still from *Godzilla* (2000)

Children's drawing in 'War on Terrorism', *The Independent*, 29 September 2001

Still from Alfred Hitchcock's *North by Northwest* (1959)

'Passive endurance' was exceptionally difficult for these 'old soldiers'.[90] Whether stung with guilt for being responsible for the death of a comrade in the First World War ('a long-deferred punishment was about to be carried out', explained one commentator in the *British Journal of Medical Psychology* in 1944)[91] or worried that they were being punished for having failed to decisively crush the enemy sufficiently during the First World War, thus laying the way for a new generation of comrades to be slaughtered, 'old soldiers' were particularly susceptible to the 'wind-up'.[92]

The emotional conflicts of many ex-servicemen can be illustrated by examining the responses of one unnamed insurance clerk, aged forty-four, who was admitted to Guy's Hospital in London with hysterical paralysis of his left arm. In his words: 'I think this arm is crushed. I cannot use my shoulder, my arm burns horribly.' Five days before he was admitted to hospital he had been in a shelter that had been hit. He described how

> there was a thud, a shower of stuff on my head, I kicked myself free, the shelter had split open. I felt my left shoulder was jammed. I saw my wife's feet sticking out of the muck, I tried to pull her out but my left arm had no strength . . . Everything happened in such a mist of pain and blackness I don't remember it properly.

Both he and his wife, Dolly, were eventually rescued, but his hysterical paralysis persisted, despite undergoing psychological suggestion. Then, one day, his physician took him to a quiet room and gave him an injection of the anaesthetic Evipan, popular in narco-analysis. Under this drug this clerk began to speak 'with emotion which had been lacking in his previous account'. With his eyes tightly closed he rambled hysterically:

> I'll get you out, Dolly — I can't use my left arm. Say something. I'll pull you out. Someone will come soon. Let me catch hold of your feet. Dolly, I want you so. Oh, if I had a spade. I can't shift this concrete. Don't show a light or they'll see you. I don't want to go in no car. I must get the others out or I'll die. My back hurts. Oh my shoulder. Oh my knee! Come on, old girl.

At this point he began to wave his right arm about, calling out:

> If my left arm was right I could do it. Damn old Hitler, if only I
> could get at the swine. Why can't I fit wings on my car? I'll teach
> them to bomb the girls and the kids. House, car, all the damn lot's
> gone. Never mind we can sleep in the tent. Thank God, I've got my
> Dolly. Poor little Betty, she's covered with blood. I don't want no
> doctor. Never mind about me, I can take it. Blimey, if they gave me
> a plane. Oh, Dolly, I thought you was a gonner. Damn the house, let
> it blow to hell as long as you're safe. I'll be late for the office, but
> they'll have to wait. Never mind, old girl, we'll take you up to the
> wilds of Scotland and we'll fish for some trout, never mind the
> [sign saying] trespassers will be prosecuted.

His right arm suddenly stopped waving and he began talking about
his experiences in Mesopotamia during the First World War, when
he was the sole survivor of an expedition in the desert:

> I'll join up with the natives and go up country, shoving the boat
> down. We'll shove around Alexandria if we have to. Six of us of
> the whole squadron. I'll shoot the first blasted Arab that pinches
> my grub. Think they can scare me with their tom-toms? What
> does the sheik [sic] give me his damn daughter for? Think I want
> to be a princess's gigolo? Where the hell can I get a boat? This
> sand is never ending. I'm damn thirsty. Anyway, old boy, pull
> your belt in, stick it, we'll find an oasis soon. What's that? Can I
> drive a motor-boat? I can drive anything. When I say full speed
> ahead we'll run through the swine. I'm going to beat it to England
> as soon as I can.

He then described catching a cargo boat to England:

> What's this Newport, home at last. Don't tell 'em anything, tell 'em
> you've been abroad and let them find out the rest. A pass to London,
> please. I'm sorry, Sir, I've lost all etiquette. I've come off the desert.
> No-one knows I've made it. I've come off alone. What have I got a
> pith hat for? Hello, mother, I've just come back to England. I've had

a jolly time, no danger. I've been travelling about a lot. What did I do? Oh, odds and ends. Oh well, I'm all right now.

He concluded his monologue by reassuring his wife that they would 'be all right'. At that point his physician 'vigorously reassured him that he would be well'. When the clerk woke up his hysterical symptoms had vanished and his arm was normal. He returned to work after a short period of rest in the countryside (although not in the 'wilds of Scotland').[93]

Psychiatry and psychology were not only sciences for the clinic. By the Second World War they were being employed by the state as a 'weapon of war'. The War Office discovered that they required psychological advice on key questions of civilian morale. In 1939 alone the War Office commissioned two substantial reports on what sparked mass panics, and how they could be avoided. The first report originated out of a meeting between the Operations Branch and leading physicians, psychiatrists and psychologists. Participants included Professor J. B. S. Haldane (the geneticist), Dr John T. MacCurdy (a leading expert on shell shock during the First World War) and Dr Pryns Hopkins (a psychoanalyst). Their recommendations became part of everyday psychological practice throughout the war. According to them, trust was essential: people were to be repeatedly told that 'this is a civilian's war, or a People's War, and therefore they are to be taken into the Government's confidence as never before'. Citizens active in the Labour movement were to be recruited into the state apparatus in larger numbers: after all, these people possessed a particularly virulent suspicion of the media and their confidence in the wise governance of the Cabinet was important in converting the wider public. Because women who were not engaged in war work were assumed to be particularly susceptible to panic, their morale had to be enhanced by insisting on the value of their labour. Laundresses, for instance, were to be reminded that they were vanguard troops in the war against epidemics of typhus. Although Haldane was rebuked when he suggested that people might be encouraged by stories about the fortitude of Spaniards and Chinese civilians under aerial bombardment (he was informed that Britons might resent being told to 'Behave like a Chink'), it was agreed that fear of aerial attack had to be converted into rage against the enemy's criminal conduct. Above all, people should be encouraged to share their fears with their fellow sufferers.[94]

The second report, dated 20 September 1939, had a narrower remit. In this circular the Director of Home Publicity reiterated the need to control information. This made the job of Chief Regional Information Officer particularly important. Rumours had to be stifled as quickly as possible. Air-raid wardens were advised to use fantastic examples from the First World War as evidence for the pernicious effect of gossip. The rumours in 1914 about Russian troops tramping throughout the British Isles were agreed to be a good instance. The 'science and mechanism of war' would distract fearful citizens from the fearful aspects of conflict. Citizens should also be educated about the level of risk they faced through the science of probabilities. In the words of the Director of Home Publicity: '100 dead in the town sounds a lot, but 1 death for every 80,000 inhabitants is a less terrifying and, incidentally, a truer description of the facts.'[95]

Other psychological reports emphasised the need to 'condition' people to the roar of disaster. This had long been recommended in military training, but it was now applied to civilian populations. Air-raid drills were instigated in order to desensitise people through repetition while at the same time reassuring them that there was something they could *do* in the event of an attack.[96] As Alexander Reid Martin put it: 'There is something fundamental about regularity — about rhythm — that promotes a sense of security.'[97]

Air-raid wardens, in particular, needed to be conditioned to the noise of bombardment. Dr A. E. Carver even conducted an experiment in which wardens were made to attend 'blitz-concerts', recorded and played to them on gramophones in the cellars of Caldecote Hall, Warwickshire. The doctors found that repeated exposure to this noise led to a gradual reduction in the levels to which blood pressure soared initially.[98] The much-hated air-raid sirens were defended on the grounds that they psychologically prepared people for fear, giving them time to construct defences against it.[99] People had to be reminded that 'noise is not dangerous', even though it was one of the primary causes of fear.[100] Self-treatments were recommended as well, including rational advice on reducing intake of sedatives and alcohol[101] and less rational measures such as exercises involving 'straining tummy muscles as if he were on the seat of the W.C. and constipated — to strain and thus push the blood up into his head'.[102]

Psychoanalytical approaches to panic also became important for the first time in British history. This enabled physicians to shift the aetiology of trauma away from the obvious threat of death raining down from the skies towards an event that happened much earlier, in infancy. For these spokesmen, deprivation of parental love and care in infancy predisposed people to anxiety states in wartime.[103] In other words, fear originated *within* the individual, not from without. According to Alexander Reid Martin, in a paper presented at the Symposium on Panic held by the Association for the Advancement of Psychoanalysis in New York in 1942:

> those who follow defensive patterns of living are more likely to panic. Their very passivity and defensive living are related to their deep conviction that the outside world is fundamentally and entirely hostile. Much of the hostility from which they recoil is a reflection of their own inner hostility.[104]

Martha Wolfenstein also wrote from within the psychoanalytical tradition. In *Disaster. A Psychological Essay* (1957) she observed that during air-raid drills some children were frightened, while others took it calmly. She said this was because the individual's

> own impulses or fantasies of punishing agencies are projected on the external world . . . These were individuals who in their family relations experienced extreme hostility together with great fear of retaliation if they expressed it. They felt that they would be precipitated into great danger if the hostility which they inhibited precariously and with great effort were to break through. This, then, was the explosion which they dreaded, the image of which became projected on the outer world.[105]

A woman who had been untroubled by anxiety in previous raids might suddenly become profoundly anxious during another raid, primarily because she had written a disagreeable letter to her mother and identified the raid with the 'punishing mother of her childhood'.[106] In another case R. J. Bartlett (of King's College London) described a man who was terrified after his house was demolished just after he and his family had left it to go to the public shelter. Bartlett explained his terror in terms of three interacting causes: dental sepsis, gross ill-treatment in childhood and an unfaithful marriage charged with guilt and fear.[107] Their fears were merely a 'new rationalization' or 'displaced content' for pre-existing anxieties.[108] The solution was clear: if medical personnel adopted a protective, parental attitude, anxious people would be promptly pacified.[109] As the author of an article on 'The Mental Aspects of A.R.P. [Air Raid Protection]' put it in 1939: the scared person had to be treated like a child who simply wanted the assistance of a strong adult capable of making the horror 'go away'. That adult 'must appear in the patient's fantasy as a steady and kindly parental figure, a reassuring representative of a good or respected authority'.[110]

Not everyone was convinced. For instance, air-raid wardens were generally unimpressed with psychoanalytical approaches. In Leeds wardens were sent on psychology courses. In a report on the lectures the *Yorkshire Post* sneered at the notion that abnormal fear might arise from a 'severe shock of some years ago'. 'Does this mean that the air raid warden, encountering a person suffering from panic after the bombs have begun to fall, is to take him aside to some quiet corner and proceed to psycho-analyse him on the spot?' the paper jeered, adding that 'a thorough course of psycho-analysis may last for a year or more — rather a long time for the air raid warden and his patient to spend together in a dugout'. Instead, they recommended dealing with victims of hysteria by reducing them 'as humanly as possible to a state of temporary insensibility'.[111] Taking the view that panic was a virus that could spread, practically minded psychologists instructed air-raid wardens (and others) faced with a panic-stricken individual to act 'immediately and drastically'. An hysterical individual who did not respond to an order to 'shut up' should be kicked in the shins or punched on the nose. As a concession, it was accepted that if a woman was hysterical, someone of her own sex should administer the punch.[112] As air-raid wardens, social workers and clergymen were advised in 1940: 'Those who create scenes should be dealt with drastically — a bucket of water or a severe box on the ears may be quite sufficient. We may need a corps of sanctified knockers-out.'[113]

Luckily the average person did not need to be beaten into submission. Most dealt with their fears through 'magic thinking'. This took innumerable forms. Typical was the reaction of a twelve-year-old boy from Tyneside when Wilkinson's Lemonade Factory was bombed and hundreds of people sheltering in its basement were killed. He recalled that:

> Terrible rumours started going round. People so crushed they couldn't be recognized; people sitting down there without a mark on them, just dead. Mothers with babies still in their arms. A man still holding his accordion . . . Everybody was just stunned. I couldn't cope. Why had God let it happen? Then the stories changed. Wicked things had gone on in that shelter. People had taken drink down there; held parties. Music and dancing every night. Immorality, and they didn't care who saw it . . . People said it was a Judgement. God is not mocked! It was like Sodom and Gomorrah. Everybody felt much better after that.[114]

Panicky terror was stilled by conjuring up a God who punished, but also rewarded His own. It was a popular fantasy. The playwright Bernard Kops, for instance, recalled a terrifying experience of being caught in a crush outside Liverpool Street Station during an air raid. The police were refusing to let more people into the air-raid shelter. In his words:

> I stood there in the thick of the crowd, thinking there would be a panic and we would all be crushed to death. It was the worst experience I had up till then and I wanted to rush out of that crowd, but I was jammed tight. I would have preferred to take my chances in the street with the bombs. Anything was preferable to that crush. I shouted my head off, went limp and was carried along by the surging

masses, trying to hold on to my separate identity. The people would not give up and would not disperse, would not take no for an answer. A great yell went up and the gates were opened and my mother threw her hands together and clutched them towards the sky. 'Thank God, he heard me.' As if she had a special line to Him and he had intervened with the Government on behalf of the Kops family.[115]

Others quietly refused to 'tempt Providence' by saying things like 'There has not been a warning tonight' or 'we will be fine'.[116] Even secular signs of hope were embraced. Countless Londoners claimed to be comforted by the fact that the monarchy remained in London during the Blitz. In the words of one mother: 'Of course London's safe enough or the King and Queen would not be here, or the refugees — as long as they're here you can feel sure things are alright.'[117]

Superstitious beliefs flourished, particularly among women. A survey in 1941 revealed that 86 per cent of women and half of men admitted to observing superstitions. Furthermore, women observed more than eight times as many superstitions as men.[118] Advertisement columns of newspapers and popular weeklies were full of advertisements for products such as: 'S sung Sin, the Chinese Faith Charm. Wear one and fear nothing. Direct from the Mystic East' (price 1s 6d); 'The famous Rothschild Talisman on which the fortune of that family depends' (2s); 'The Special Talisman of Rabbi Solomon for all good' (2s); 'The lovely Amulet containing Nine Drops guaranteed and certified to be from England's most famous Wishing Well. It entitles you to Nine Wishes' (2s 6d).[119]

Astrology also promised a safer world. There was a large and expanding market in specialist astrology publications such as editions of *Old Moore's Almanack* during the war. Indeed, Foulsham's edition claimed to sell three million copies on average each year during the war.[120] Two-thirds of adults during the war read the astrology columns in newspapers.[121] In 1941 not only did 40 per cent of Britons entertain some degree of belief in astrology, but 10 per cent of people made astrology a 'major interest in their lives and allow it to play some part in forming their conduct'.[122] According to reports during the war, Britons liked the way astrology appeared to interpret confusing events and trends. The boom in astrology was a 'symptom of the loss of Christian strength among working people [and] the absence of any satisfactory external standard against which to measure these times'.[123]

Being primarily optimistic, astrology became a way people could convince themselves that they were born under a lucky star and that, even in dangerous times, 'less harm would come' to them. Another advantage was that astrology 'did not involve any external procedure, any tiresome ritual, any subscriptions to a church's funds, any new social code, and unselfishness or moral effort'. It was 'a purely personal, almost wholely [sic] self-interested affair; and from it there was nothing to lose'.[124] It provided daily reassurance so that even if the predictions turned out to be false, they would still have given temporary relief from stress.[125] Astrology also provided a way to allay fears about the ability of the British military forces to 'win': after all, Hitler would be defeated by his own horoscope.[126]

Fear was war's birthright. British civilians were deliberately terrorised during the Second World War and although the numerous ways they coped with the terror of being attacked from the skies were remarkable, periods of panic were not infrequent. On many occasions fear was palpably present — witness the screams of people racing towards the shelters. The presence of danger was obviously a reason for their terror, but it was exacerbated by other factors such as guilt. In 1943, residents of Bethnal Green were expecting to be bombed into oblivion because they somehow 'deserved it', British bombers having terrorised Berliners a few days before. This link between guilt and panic is one that some twenty-first-century scientists recognise. For instance, scientific investigations into ways to eradicate fear, carried out at the University of California at Irvine, New York University, Columbia University and the Ponce School of Medicine in Puerto Rico have found that fear travels the same neural pathways as guilt: 'so a prophylactic against one could guard against the other'.[127] Medicate fright out of existence, and guilt will vanish as well.

At other times, shock came after the danger was over — the

'delayed shock' that the Young Girl's neighbour darkly referred to at the start of this chapter. This emphasis on *post*-traumatic emotional responses was not cemented into cultural understandings of trauma until the cataclysm of the Vietnam War. Like the term 'combat fatigue', which, as we saw in the previous chapter, implied that the sufferer just needed a 'long nap', the term 'post-traumatic stress disorder' (PTSD) insinuated the idea of a 'post' to trauma. However, it was a 'post' that was increasingly psychologised, to the extent that nowadays victims of a bewildering range of normal (albeit unpleasant) life events are routinely offered counselling. In contrast, the Young Girl just 'got on with life'.

CHAPTER NINE

Nuclear Threats

How, above all, will they end? By any natural
fascination of frost or flood or from the artful
Obliterating bang whereby God's rebellious image
After thousands of thankless years spent in thinking about it,
Finally finds a solid
Proof of its independence

AUDEN, 'THE AGE OF ANXIETY'

At 10.45 on the morning of 8 February 1951 enemy planes dropped nuclear-primed bombs over New York City. Mrs Bertha Smith, a sixth-grade teacher in Public School 75 at 735 West End Avenue, responded promptly to the 'sudden white flash', ordering her young charges to 'take cover'. Children threw themselves to the ground, curling into tight balls with their backs to the window. Within less than a minute the attack was over: it had been the first 'no signal' drill in America.

Children, teachers and parents were all duly terrorised. Despite evidence to the contrary, the principal of Public School 75 insisted that the drills had been carried out in a way that did not excessively 'alarm' the children. According to him, parents supported the drills, believing that 'even if their children were alarmed . . . it is still more important to have them ready for any eventuality'.[1] Yet in many schools fear had been brutally instilled. For instance, the principal of an elementary school in Queens, New York, walked into a classroom during a drill and yelled at a little boy who had not covered himself properly: 'Your right arm is burned off! Your right leg is gone! And half your face is burned away!' The child became hysterical. Other teachers used the threat of forcing disruptive children to sit next to a window (and thus at risk of being savaged by glass shards during any enemy attack) as a way of enforcing good behaviour.[2] Children were raised to fear.

In what was reputedly a typical case, Andy Hanover, a seven-year-old in Boston, was so disquieted by the bomb that he was unable to concentrate on the routines of daily life and his sleep was ravaged by nightmares. Nevertheless, he boasted that: 'If the enemy comes, I'll mow 'em down. It's awful the things that can happen. Babies are killed, children's homes are burned. All we can do is pray.'[3] A seven-year-old girl tearfully explained that she had to wear an identification tag 'so that people will know who I am if my face is burned away', while other children refused to ever remove their 'dog-tags', even in bath or bed, in the belief that they were a talisman which would miraculously save their lives in the event of an atomic-bomb attack.[4] Tensions were raised even further during the Cuban missile crisis of 1962. Deborah, who turned eleven that year, recalled:

> You can imagine what I thought when my normally reassuring mother went up to the corner market . . . and came home, and right in front of me, proceeded to unload box after box of canned goods for the basement . . . I honestly believed, with no denial present, that the end was, quite possibly, near. I was a nervous wreck. I usually rode my bike from one end of Allentown to the other, day in and day out, pretending and practicing — I thought — driving a car. That week I went only up the block and to the corner and came back . . . I remember every chunk of sidewalk on my side of Union Street between 24th and 25th St. I wanted to be able to hear my mother yell if the 'button' got pushed. Come to think of it, my dad didn't go to the office that week. They were both around, which was a novelty. God, I was scared.[5]

When one teacher in the Midwest asked her class of nine-year-olds, 'What are you most afraid of?', thirty of the thirty-two pupils answered 'bombs' and they unanimously included 'no more wars' in a list of their three biggest wishes.[6] In another survey carried out in the early 1960s, 350 youngsters were asked to 'think about the world as it may be about ten years from now: what are some of the ways in which it may be different from what it is today?' Without any prompting, 70 per cent of the children spontaneously mentioned the bomb — either by envisaging a gruesome existence underground or describing wholesale destruction.[7] As one small boy in Chicago begged his mother: 'Please, Mother, can't we go some place where there isn't any sky?'[8]

The responses of American parents to the drills were confused, at best. In the June 1951 issue of *Today's Woman* André Fontaine addressed the question of 'how should parents respond to the threat of nuclear holocaust?' At no point did he mention the possibility of a political response. For Fontaine the problem of nuclear weapons was one of psychology, not politics. The issue was not the proliferation of nuclear warheads, but panic. Fontaine argued that the only curb to panic was the stable family. He reminded parents that, during the blitz on London during the Second World War, children were frightened only to the extent that their parents showed themselves to be cowed (a belief that was widespread, as we saw in the previous chapter). In his recommendations Fontaine expressed faith in the increasingly powerful discipline of child psychology. 'In our own home,' he wrote,

> we dreamed up an idea that seemed appropriate and the psychologist I asked agreed it was good. We took our kids down into the cellar one day. One section of our cellar has three and a half walls of bricks. This, we said, would be a good shelter and the whole family could work together to fix it . . . Then, if we ever did get bombed — which was highly unlikely, I said — we'd have a safe and warm place to go.

As an afterthought he added that he was 'no expert on bomb shelters, but that isn't the point'.[9]

Fontaine was right: in the event of a nuclear attack individual survival was not going to be the point. In 1951 many Americans were only just beginning to recognise the destructive power of nuclear warheads. Only the day before the first 'no signal' atomic drill in New York City, an atomic bomb was exploded in Nevada. The blast was felt in Los Angeles, 250 miles away. Captain Edward Boyce, pilot of a Transworld Airlines plane bound from New York to Los Angeles, saw the explosion from his plane. He recalled:

> It was just like the sun exploding. All of Nevada looked like it was on fire. The sky was absolutely clear over the Southwest. I saw the light reflected off the mountains further east, then turned to see this huge thing growing, and getting redder until it finally died out. I think it hung there in the sky for more than ten seconds. It was a frightening thing, really terrifying, far worse looking than anything I had imagined.[10]

This blast was caused by a conventional nuclear bomb, similar to the one used to end the Second World War. The following year the first hydrogen bomb was tested. While the bombs dropped on Hiroshima and Nagasaki were equivalent to fifteen thousand tons of TNT, the hydrogen bomb was equivalent to twenty-five million tons of TNT, and as much as fifty-six million tons in some tests.[11] People had good reason to be terrified.

The postwar world was consumed with fears and anxieties that had arisen out of those terrible six war years. Economic fears may have abated, albeit slowly, as the British and American economies flourished, but a 'cold war' introduced the possibility of total annihilation. For many people the Cold War was more frightening than the Second World War — after all, America had been spared the worst ravages of battle and even the assaults on Britain were of a much smaller magnitude than those experienced elsewhere in Europe. Indeed, as we saw in the previous chapter, while British citizens had good reason to be much more fearful than their American counterparts during the Second World War, their fortunes were reversed during the Cold War. Scientific modernity had taken on a distinctly menacing dimension with the dropping of the uranium and plutonium bombs on Hiroshima and Nagasaki in August 1945. The following year John Hersey's immensely popular book *Hiroshima* (1946), forced readers to recognise that 'It could happen to us!'

But the real spark to nuclear terror came on 24 September 1949, when it was announced that the Soviet Union had tested an atomic bomb. Then, in November 1952, the first trial of the hydrogen bomb took place. The North Atlantic Treaty Organization's war games of 1955, in which the release of 335 nuclear bombs over Germany was simulated, brought the extent of expected destruction to everyone's attention, as did the first passage high over America of the Soviet Union's *Sputnik* satellite two years later. Finally, in September and October 1962, Americans became aware of a dramatic extension in the probability of a Third World War when Soviet missiles were spotted just ninety miles from Florida. America's monstrous nuclear advantage had failed to deter Khrushchev from installing missiles in Cuba.[12] As the influential sociologist Anthony Giddens reminded his readers: 'We can never be sure that deterrence "works", short of the actual occurrence of a nuclear combat — which shows that it does not.'[13]

There was a brief lull in nuclear fears between 1964 and the mid-1970s, in part because tests went underground, making them less visible and diminishing the danger. In addition, official propaganda focused increasingly on the 'good atom' (atomic power), while activists were preoccupied with protesting against the Vietnam War. The Outer Space Treaty (1967) and the Non-Proliferation Treaty (1968) also contributed to an easing of tensions. However, from 1979 fears once again grew, with major accidents at nuclear reactors in Three Mile Island in that year and at Chernobyl in 1986, and the increasing bellicosity of Ronald Reagan's presidency, which insisted on developing a space-based nuclear weapons defence system (the Strategic Defense Initiative or 'Star Wars') in 1983. In that year over half of all teenagers in the United Kingdom believed that a nuclear war would occur in their lifetime, and nearly three-quarters believed it was inevitable at some time in the future.[14] As we shall see in the final chapter, with the onset of 'new war', concerns about the nuclear (and biological) capabilities of terrorists and 'rogue states' have re-emerged. Late modernity could not escape the threat of nuclear apocalypse.

From the early 1950s nuclear physics threw 'a large parenthesis around all our little securities'. If people were more fearful it was because there was 'more to be afraid of', one observer rightly noted in 1953.[15] Those who did not fear were simply 'blind and obtuse'.[16] These fears did not flare up in response to vague apocalyptic imaginings. Before the fifties fears about the end of the world were occasionally stirred up. For instance, in 1910, Halley's comet's close call to the earth resulted in fears of mass poisoning by the gases inside its tail. On 18 May 1910 the *New York Times* reported that the 'terror occasioned by the near approach of Halley's comet' had 'seized hold of a large part of the population of Chicago'. In New York, it was reported, 'some of the more superstitious [people living] in the sections largely inhabited by foreigners were on the verge of panic . . . Many prayed on bended knees in the streets and parks, and several religious processions took place in different parts of the city.'[17]

Other panics about the end of the world were even more fantastical, involving Martians, for instance, as during the *War of the Worlds* fiasco of 1938 (described in Chapter Six). But by the mid-1950s a single, man-made bomb could achieve unimaginable catastrophe. In 1955 an Atomic Energy Commissioner admitted to American citizens that the explosion of a hydrogen bomb would 'render the earth uninhabitable to man'.[18] With the means of world devastation available to the elite of a few nations, fear became widespread. No longer were humanity's primary enemies hidden in the crevices of individual unconsciousness, capable of being lured out by a reassuring confidant. Instead, the fate of humankind seemed to rest with people no one trusted: soldiers, scientists and statesmen.

Nuclear holocaust was the greatest threat of the twentieth century. In the nuclear age it was no longer possible to mute the fear of death with a belief either in the afterlife or the lasting value of family or even civilisation. The individual, community and nation: all would be destroyed. It was widely predicted that future historians ('if there are any') would call the 1950s and 1960s the 'Age of Fear'.[19] Dread was the most rational emotion in the world in these decades. Confidence in American superiority in the world, coupled with the unusual threat of war on their own territory, made Americans particularly susceptible to such fears. With only one

exception, from the late nineteenth century to the Cold War
Americans had become accustomed to their citizens' blood staining
only foreign soil in war. Even during the Second World War, when
the threat from Japan was real, anxiety about an invasion was muted
and comfort was taken in the expanse of ocean separating America
from its enemies. Long-range aeroplanes and nuclear warheads
destroyed this sense of security.

Both sides in the nuclear debate harnessed fear to their cause. For
those who defended the building up of a nuclear arsenal, stimulating
fear about the communists was intended to guarantee 'freedom
from fear' in the 'free world'. Deterrence — the main strategic
response to the development of nuclear weapons — had fear as its
main mechanism. In the words of Sir Winston Churchill, addressing
the House of Commons on 1 March 1955, Britons must reach the
stage 'where safety will be the sturdy child of terror, and survival the
twin brother of annihilation'.[20]

Those opposing nuclear deterrence also employed the language of
nuclear terror. A public-affairs programme in 1946 for the
University of Denver used characteristic language when it warned
people that a 'time bomb is under your home. It is ticking slowly
away. Even while I talk, even while you listen, time is running out.
America must act, if we are to choose the road of atomic peace
rather than atomic war.'[21] Anti-nuclear protesters insisted that the
question was not 'would' but '*when* shall I be blown up?'[22] At the
same time, they argued, fear was a tool, manipulated by politicians
who preferred citizens to be passive and unable to contemplate
other ways of resolving ideological conflicts. But fear would never
cast out fear, they warned.[23] The prevailing mood of passivity in the
face of the nuclear threat was particularly invidious within scientific
communities, subjected to 'loyalty committees' and often funded by
the military. American physicists were hardest hit, with 90 per cent
of funding of some schools coming from military sources[24]. As
Albert Einstein warned:

> Most people go on living their everyday life: half frightened, half
> indifferent, they behold the ghastly tragi-comedy that is being per-
> formed on the international stage before the eyes and ears of the

world . . . It would be different if the problem were not one of things made by Man himself, such as the atomic bomb . . . It would be different, for instance, if an epidemic of bubonic plague were threatening the entire world. In such a case, conscientious and expert persons would be brought together and they would work out an intelligent plan to combat the plague. After having reached agreement upon the right ways and means, they would submit their plan to the governments. These would hardly raise serious objections but rather agree speedily on the measures to be taken . . . They certainly would never think of trying to handle the matter in such a way that their own nation would be spared whereas the next one would be decimated. But could not our situation be compared to one of a menacing epidemic?[25]

Einstein was not only drawing attention to the threat of the annihilation of entire populations. The effects of radiation scared people too. The fact that radiation could cause genetic mutations that were passed through the generations had been widely known since 1927, thanks to the research of the geneticist Hermann Joseph Muller.[26] But it was not until the 1950s that Americans began to feel the effect of nuclear testing. Between 1951 and 1963, when the nuclear tests moved underground, around 100 tests were carried out in the Nevada desert, causing severe problems with radioactive fallout. Then, on 1 March 1954, the Bravo test produced lethal levels of fallout over 7000 square miles and poisoned Japanese fishermen aboard the *Fukuryu Maru* (*Lucky Dragon*) in the Bikini Atoll. As a consequence, by the late 1950s around half of all Americans believed that fallout from nuclear tests was dangerous and that continued testing jeopardised the health of future generations.[27]

The polluting aspects of the nuclear threat became a common theme in fiction and films depicting the future, most famously in the case of Godzilla, a prehistoric monster resurrected as a result of H-bomb experiments. Godzilla first appeared in 1956 in the movies *Godzilla: King of the Monsters* and *Rodan*, and he returned in at least sixteen feature films thereafter. Novels like Margot Bennett's *The Long Way Back* (1954) included plants rendered carnivorous by nuclear poisoning, while Tyrone C. Barr's *The Last Fourteen* (1959) had one of the fourteen survivors of a nuclear war being killed by a giant featherless duck. Radiation was portrayed as the invisible enemy, silently infecting everything in its path. In *Them!* (1954), the biggest-grossing film of that year, the pollution brought about by radiation was explicitly linked to Cold War communist threats. When the military eventually took action against the killer ants, a journalist asked, 'Has the Cold War gotten hot?' The film ended ominously after the destruction of the giant ants, with the following exchange:

> **Graham:** If these monsters got started as a result of the *first* atom bomb in 1945, what about all the other ones that have been exploded since then?
>
> **Medford:** When man entered the atomic age he opened a door to a new world. What we'll eventually find in that new world nobody can predict.

Fears about generals[28], scientists[29], super-computers[30] and terrorists[31] were a staple in this genre, as was the argument that nuclear war was simply an inevitable consequence of paranoid Cold War animosities.[32] The socio-political destructiveness of nuclear war was also portrayed in these fantasies. For instance, as a result of nuclear war, societies reverted either to savagery, as in Harlan Ellison's *A Boy and His Dog* (1969), or dictatorships, as in Jim Harman's story 'The Place Where Chicago Was' (1962).[33] Finally, probably the most striking imaginative images of nuclear holocaust were contained in the novels and non-fiction of Philip Wylie. His *Tomorrow!* (1954) did not flinch from describing a woman sitting on some stairs after the nuclear attack, vainly attempting to shove her unborn baby back inside her split belly.[34] In 1956 *Tomorrow!* was dramatised on the radio by Orson Welles, the director of *The War of the Worlds*. But this time it was not a hoax.

Despite widespread anxieties about the future, most people responded in inconsistent ways to the nuclear threat. For instance, in the late 1940s around 60 per cent of Americans surveyed believed that they would be killed in the event of an atomic attack.[35] Nevertheless, as another major survey in 1946 revealed, only a quarter of Americans confessed to being worried about the atomic bomb. The 'non-worriers' were not unaware of their parlous state, but they could not see the point in fretting about a threat over which they were powerless, nor did they believe it was worthwhile worrying incessantly about a danger that would kill them so quickly anyway.[36]

A similar survey carried out by the American Institute of Public Opinion in the early 1950s found that half of people living in the largest American cities believed that there was a 'distinct likelihood of an atom bomb attack on their cities in the event of another war'. A further quarter thought there was a fair chance that their cities would be bombed. Only 17 per cent thought it unlikely. However, their fears did not translate into political action. When asked whether they were involved in a civil-defence programme, 93 per cent responded 'no'.[37] This suggested that high levels of fear about nuclear war did not result in widespread political action to reduce the likelihood of war.

In both Britain and America peace activists were a beleaguered minority. Although the former's Campaign for Nuclear Disarmament (CND) was formed in 1958 and engineered some successful protests (such as the Aldermaston marches), it was virtually moribund between 1963 and 1979. Even in the late 1980s total membership of peace movements was only two hundred thousand and was drawn mainly from the middle classes.[38] The eminent psychiatrist Robert Jay Lifton coined the term 'nuclearism' to describe the 'personal invulnerability' people felt. Even watching frightening films of nuclear holocaust could encourage apathy. The ABC television film *The Day After* (1983) showed what would happen if a Soviet nuclear-primed bomb hit a missile site close to Kansas City. Over two hundred million people watched the film all over the world. Yet many viewers found the film oddly reassuring since, despite the horrific scenes, there were survivors who began the task of rebuilding civilisation. As two researchers observed after studying the impact of such films on audiences:

> Intense public debate before the showing of controversial films tends to diffuse their impact and supplies viewers with the arguments

they need to cope with the experience. Some people, for example, found *The Day After* less horrific than they had expected and it may have raised their optimism about the chances of surviving a nuclear war. Other images came from folk memories of World War II: there is the tendency to reduce the unknown into a series of familiar (and ultimately reassuring) scenes.[39]

Even those rare novels and films that showed the utter destruction of the world, such as *On the Beach* (novel: 1957; film: 1959), still contained a romantic plot and other distractions, potentially trivialising the threat. Indeed, after the 1980s, nuclear war was celebrated in musical videos and games. One of the most popular video war games was *Nuclear Strike*, released in 1997. A fan of this game explained its attraction thus: 'The interactive environments is what made me play the game over and over. At times, I usually spend hours just blowing up anything in my way, whether it makes me fail the mission or not, I really admire the explosion effects and the scene of destruction.'[40] Nuclear fears were also among its pleasures.

Denial and avoidance were more common responses to nuclear terror.[41] Even the media backed away from the topic. For instance, in 1966 the BBC commissioned a forty-seven-minute long documentary on nuclear war. The resulting film by Peter Watkins, *The War Game*, depicted what would happen if a thermonuclear missile hit the county of Kent. The panic, the extent of devastation and the inability of the civil-defence authorities to alleviate the effects of the explosion and firestorm were depicted with brutal realism. However, although the film won an Oscar for Best Feature Documentary, BBC Television declined to show it on the grounds that it was 'too horrifying'. When the producer of documentaries for the BBC was asked whether she approved of this decision, she answered in the affirmative:

Having lived in the South-east of England throughout the [Second World] war, having seen how people behave in circumstances of war and bombing, it was an absolute slander on humanity. [Watkins's] observations were profoundly wrong . . . This is not the way people behave toward each other in times of stress . . . I think it was a *stinking* film. We don't need these emotional left-wing intellectuals to tell us that we can destroy the world.[42]

It was 'better' that people did not think about such matters.

Indeed, the greater the fear, the greater the denial. In an experiment in 1958, 139 people in New York and Philadelphia were shown drawings related to nuclear war and asked to make up stories about the drawings. It was discovered that the more explicit the drawings, the more reluctant people were to allow the idea of war to creep into their stories.[43] Psychologists such as Joost Meerloo argued that the immense weight of fear in the postwar world paradoxically increased the likelihood that people would 'surrender passively' to the fearful situation.[44] Nuclear-inspired fears were regarded as socially damaging not because they elicited flight, but because they could lead to 'a paralysis of judgment and action that tends to prevent the maximum use of available resources and thereby prevents preserving the maximum number of lives'.[45] As commentators during wartime and the Cold War warned, frightened people tended to simply 'surrender passively to the feared situation' instead of mobilising to fight against the evil.[46] Fear of the bomb could

> operate in us in the same manner as the fear of magic power operated in primitive societies. Such fear paralyzes the human mind, hypnotizes it, makes it passive. In this paralyzed stupor, man conjures up the evil he fears; it leads him to surrender passively to fate. Inwardly he is already prepared to accept death and destruction.[47]

The 'ostrich' position was popular, even among religious spokesmen. For instance, in 1958, the Archbishop of Canterbury went so far as to counsel people against being anxious about the possibility of destruction. After all, he asserted, it might be within the providence of God that humans should blow themselves up.[48] In an address to scientific clubs at Boston College, the Most Reverend Richard J. Cushing, Archbishop of Boston, also believed that the 'spiritual man' should not be frightened. Nuclear fear was part of the material world but, he reminded his listeners, the spiritual realm was immeasurably more powerful. Indeed, Cushing regarded the threat of nuclear holocaust as a positive force:

> It may be that the atomic bomb, in all its perversity and horror, is the 'good news of damnation' for our society, that it may frighten us into those righteous, intelligent actions necessary for the organization of human society — not a thousand years hence — but now — lest we be destroyed by this infernal instrument which the refusal of our forebears to organize society made somehow necessary in the minds of the militarists.[49]

But the time for a spiritual renewal was long over. Fear paralysed the nation.

For authorities at both local and national level, the fear generated by the threat of nuclear attack was fuelled by the recognition that such an attack would provoke widespread havoc and panic. This would take many forms, including epidemics of 'pseudo-radiation sickness' and other neurotic disturbances among health fanatics.[50] Certain groups were believed to be especially prone to panic at the prospect of imminent attack. Many commentators speculated that illiterate people and poor immigrant groups would be the first to flee and since 'such groups make up a substantial proportion of urban populations living in closest proximity to presumed "designated ground zero"', this was agreed to be an exceptionally serious state of affairs.[51]

More seriously, 'ordinary people' were already jumpy. Indeed, an article by American novelist Philip Wylie pointed out that 'a huge fraction of the public, perhaps the majority, *already* display clinical symptoms indicative of hysteria and predisposing to panic'. McCarthyism was proof of this. Wylie pointed out that even if America managed to rid itself of every single communist, this

> would not slow down a single Soviet reactor or alter by a jot the master schemes of the Kremlin. To feel that the whole 'fight' against communism is the *relatively minor* and *wholly local* problem of 'spies' is to be very hysterical indeed. But the emotion does serve to drain away a gigantic amount of hysterical energy in a seemingly effective effort — which actually merely *deludes* millions.

In the event of an attack, full-blown panic was inevitable, he warned.[52] As early as 1948 a colonel in the Army Medical Corps notified army doctors that 'Mr and Mrs America have been so frightened by the information they have received to date, that if a bomb were dropped on one of our cities tomorrow, mass hysteria would probably cause the unnecessary loss of many lives'.[53] In 1966, when Hadley Cantril, the psychologist who investigated the *War of the Worlds* panic, was asked whether people would *still* panic in response to a radio broadcast such as Orson Welles's in 1938, he replied in the affirmative. Since 1938, he noted:

> We have seen the development and use of atomic weapons; we know about the existence of Intercontinental Ballistic Missiles (ICBM) and their immense destructive power. And we hear talk of satellites spinning about our tiny globe carrying atomic warheads that could be quickly guided to any target on earth. Such destructive forces against which there appears to be so little protection can only enhance the possibility of delusions that would be even more plausible than the invasion of Martians — and that would not require the combined talents of H. G. Wells and Orson Welles to set off.[54]

It was no coincidence that sightings of UFOs began immediately after the Second World War, a tangible reflection of nuclear and Cold War fears. In the words of Jung in his book *Flying Saucers* (1959), the basis for rumours about flying saucers was 'an *emotional tension* having its course in a situation of collective distress or danger, or in a vital psychic need. This condition undoubtedly exists today, in so far as the whole world is suffering under the strain of Russian policies and their still unpredictable consequences'. In their threatened state, people projected their fears into interstellar space, 'where the rulers of human fate, the gods, once had their abode in the planets'. [55]

Because of this emphasis on the arousal of emotional extremes in disasters, it was widely believed that a nuclear enemy might set out primarily to provoke panic, as opposed to simply obliterating persons and property.[56] As we saw in the previous chapter, an attack on morale was feared even during the Second World War, such an attack relying on conventional weapons of terror. By the Cold War it was possible that 'panic and not the hydrogen bomb may be the ultimate weapon'.[57] Indeed, it was widely noted that the greatest danger of nuclear attack would not be the 'invisible particles floating in the air', but 'the hysteria caused by propaganda which could grow to such a peak that whole populaces could grow out of control of their governments'.[58] According to a Federal Civil Defense Administrator serving under President Eisenhower, 90 per cent of emergency measures developed in response to the nuclear threat were designed to prevent panic.[59]

Despite all the evidence from the two world wars about how people reacted in disaster or while under attack, it was widely feared that anxieties about the effects of a nuclear explosion were so strong that even the threat of a strike alone would lead to mass panic.[60] Even more than conventional warfare, atomic warfare was liable to contain those features that increased the risk of panic: restricted and narrowing escape routes, brief forewarning, a prolific traffic in rumour and prevailing awareness that time was limited.[61] Furthermore, for survivors, fear would not begin or end with the explosion. Instead, they would be confined in claustrophobic fallout shelters, anxious of the danger of contamination, uncertain about long-term possibilities of survival and fearful about whether family and friends had managed to find refuge in time.[62] Survivors would fear not so much death, but 'death in life'.[63] In the words of the author of *Management of Human Behaviour in Disaster* (1967):

> Survivors of a nuclear explosion are likely to exhibit exaggerated reactions of shock, fear, apprehension, despair. These may persist for much longer due to the extent of the destruction and losses, the bleakness of the future and continuing fear of radioactive effects. Under these conditions it may be much more difficult to evoke adaptive behaviour.

Survivalist literature created a Hobbesian world in which every individual or small group competed against every other individual or group. In the event of atomic attack, the survivors would be largely cut off from one another, engaged in furious struggle for resources.

Civil-defence workers were rightly concerned about the impact this would have upon democratic institutions. In the words of 'Dangers of Shelter Psychology' (1962):

> To burrow beneath the ground for weeks, even longer, means for human beings a denial of most of the values which have been acquired slowly and painfully in the process of creating a democratic society. Instead of community, there is a splintering into isolated individuals or tiny groups. Instead of cooperation, there is violent competition for available space. Instead of mutual aid, there is a selfish struggle for individual survival. [64]

Effective familial role behaviour might be activated, but emergency community and other organisational roles were predicted to fail.[65]

As a consequence, many of the proposed remedies for the turmoil that would inevitably be created by nuclear attack turned out to be merely palliatives. In 'Psychological Problems of A-Bomb Defense' (1950), the leading war psychologist Irving L. Janis drew comparisons with front-line combat experiences. He noted that, at the front, combatants were encouraged to dig foxholes as shelter, despite the fact that these would be of no use in a direct hit. Similarly, faced with nuclear danger, people should be encouraged to 'provide themselves with something equivalent to a foxhole', such as lining the walls of their basements with concrete or bricks despite the fact that this would provide little shelter in the event of a nearby explosion.[66]

Other counsel was knowingly wrong. Three leading physicians argued in the *US Armed Forces Medical Journal* (1951) that, in order to prevent panic in the event of an atomic-bomb attack, it 'should be made clear that danger from residual radiation is nil, and that the danger of a repeated attack is also nil. Persons who have escaped gross injury should be informed that the attacked city is now a relatively safe spot.'[67] Civil-defence literature consistently minimised 'the consequences of a nuclear attack' while simultaneously 'exaggerating the potential of civil defence measures'.[68]

Finally, some recommendations were simply ludicrous. For instance, the California Office of Civil Defense's *Panic Control and*

Prevention. Instructor's Manual and Teaching Outline (1951) prescribed
the regular and copious feeding of survivors. This portrayed shelters
as places where people would sit around engaging in community
singing (which was believed to alleviate the 'inclination to vocalize
which may result in screaming'), community dancing and playing
cards.[69] Such advice was satirised in novels like Gina Berriault's *The
Descent* (1960), in which the military promoted a diversionary publicity campaign featuring 'Miss Massive Retaliation' songs such as:

> Blow my heart to little bits
> Never, never call it quits
> Mister, send your missile my way . . .
> Conflagrate me, oh please do,
> The man on top's got to be you.
> Mister, send your missile my way.
> That mushroom cloud is me,
> It's only me in ecstasy.
> Mister, send your missile my way![70]

In more sober accounts, personal liberty and civil rights were of
no consequence. Countless literary and cinematic representations of
nuclear disaster placed security before freedom. For instance, the
film *Them!* featured killer ants, fantastic mutants produced by radiation from an atomic-bomb test. Individual liberties were sacrificed
in the interests of secrecy and the 'general good'. A man who saw
one of these ants was locked up so that the story did not leak. A scientist warned the military committee that the ants 'must be kept a
secret to avoid a nationwide panic . . . absolute secrecy is essential;
there isn't a police force in the world who could handle the panic'.

Cinematic fantasies aside, security's priority over freedom was a
main theme in advice manuals at the time. Civil-defence literature
repeatedly emphasised the need to militarise society in the event of
a nuclear attack. Conformity was of paramount importance.
'Destructive persons' (otherwise called 'primary reactors') were
to be identified and neutralised before they became 'obtrusive',
'behind-the-scenes' operators, wreaking havoc among 'secondary
reactors' (that is, other people).[71] According to the California Office

of Civil Defense, people had to adhere strictly to evacuation plans: 'nonconformity is socially irresponsible behavior', they insisted, warning that 'special sanctions' would be 'applied against nonconformists in the event of an evacuation crisis'.[72] Familiarity with air-raid drills would ensure that people would passively fall into a familiar drill procedure, thus keeping their minds busy and reducing the likelihood of panic.[73]

Above all, freedom of speech was demonised and conflated with the spreading of rumours. According to many disaster commentators, censorship would be acceptable so long as people could be led to believe that they were not being fed deliberate lies. News had to present as many 'facts' as possible, so that people would not feel the need to have recourse to rumour. Individual rumours had to be discredited as enemy propaganda.[74] People needed to be taught to place their own death in context: they were 'not to lose a sense of proportion about it', as the California Office of Civil Defense bizarrely advised.[75]

As this literature implied, nuclear disaster was to be treated as a matter of human psychology, rather than politics or economics. Civil Aid Workers were informed that although they had not been formally trained in psychology, a significant component of their work concerned 'human factors'. Some aid workers resisted this definition of their duty, arguing that 'All that may be true, but the state of mind is dependent upon the existing situation. Repair the utilities, reopen communications, restore government, and confusion will disappear.' To this the California Office of Civil Defense responded:

> True enough, but to accomplish these reforms requires the cooperation of the devastated community. However excellent the engineering and formal planning may be, it is still necessary for you to deal directly with the people, including their emotional states of confusion, misunderstanding, prejudice, shock, hatred, suspicion, and bitterness.[76]

Confusion foreshadowed panic. Irrespective of the veracity of the message, a 'calm, authoritative voice' broadcast on an 'intact public address system' was crucial.[77] As the *Bulletin of the Atomic Scientists* put it in 1953: 'The human being whose normal picture of the world around him is suddenly torn to pieces struggles to replace it with another picture so that he can steer his activity.' Loudspeakers and radios in public shelters would reorientate people, preparing them for a transformed world.[78] Since many people would not have access to radios in the event of a nuclear attack, and since rubble and fires would prevent ground vehicles from getting information to them, disaster agencies recommended the use of light planes, preferably helicopters, which would broadcast information and 'counteract panics'. All information had to be given in a factual, calm and easily understood manner so that 'depressed, fearful, and resentful victims of the disaster' would be able to understand it.[79]

Disaster experts and civil-defence personnel set out to predict the responses of people in the event of a nuclear attack. In *The Social Psychology of Civil Defense* (1982) Ronald W. Perry justified analysing non-nuclear disasters in order to be able to predict human responses during nuclear ones. He admitted that because people expected a nuclear disaster to pose 'a particularly threatening hazard with the potential for extraordinarily long-term negative effects', they might respond in a unique fashion. Nevertheless, he insisted that 'natural hazards differ as much among themselves as they are different from nuclear attack'. It was legitimate to 'examine nuclear attack within the same conceptual and analytic framework as any other disaster, whether natural or man-made', since all disasters shared certain features.[80]

For social psychologists like Perry, nuclear terror stimulated interest in panic reactions more generally, the assumption being that detailed analysis of human reactions in other disasters would help predict future responses to nuclear calamity.[81] In 1952 America's National Research Council established a Committee on Disaster Studies, responsible for investigating civil disasters. By 1957 this had become a permanent body, the Disaster Research Group, which was influential in shaping domestic policy concerning the minimisation of damage in the event of nuclear attack. This group conceded that non-nuclear disasters were significantly less deadly than what would be expected in the event of nuclear catas-trophe, but claimed that data acquired by probing these 'ordinary'

disasters would 'produce definite patterns of behavior that can indi-
cate how most men, women, and children would be apt to act in
time of H-bomb horror'. After all, as the Technical Director of the
Disaster Research Group coolly remarked: 'A man buried alive in a
burning house is a man buried alive in a burning house regardless of
whether it was a gas-main explosion or a hydrogen bomb that set the
house afire.'[82]

With these assumptions in mind, the group began reviewing the
existing literature on disasters, while also commissioning reports on
catastrophes as they occurred. But, from the outset, its research was
plagued by difficulties involved in defining two concepts: panic and
adaptability. First, what did it mean to say that an individual or a
group panicked? In Chapter Two we examined panic in public spaces
at the end of the nineteenth century. For the disaster experts at that
time, the term 'panic' was not problematic. It was assumed that
everyone knew what a panic was when they observed it. By the
mid-twentieth century, however, the meaning of the word was disputed and no one agreed on its exact definition and legitimate
application.

According to one definition, panic referred to 'a condition of
fear or anxiety together with a disorganization of behaviour'. Others
merely defined it as 'sudden overpowering fear'. The word could
include everything from the mass hysteria witnessed as the *Titanic*
sank in 1912 to the overly hasty surgery carried out by doctors after
the tornado in Worchester, Massachusetts, in 1952.[83] The definition
of 'panic' was complicated even further by the insistence of some
commentators that panic always involved flight behaviour.[84] In contrast, the definition of panic as devised by the Federal Civil Defense
Administration in 1955 defined it as 'highly emotional behavior
which is excited by the presence of an immediate severe threat, and
*which results in increasing the danger for the self and for others rather than
reducing it*'. In other words, panic was more than simply 'excited
behavior' and flight was 'not necessarily panic, for flight may result
in *reducing* the danger'.[85]

These definitions of panic led directly to the second problematic
concept: adaptability. Numerous empirical studies showed that many
people in disaster areas panicked because they were frightened not

for themselves but for their family and friends. Furthermore, such people actually adopted extremely effective ways to help their loved ones. A major study of the reactions of people in Beecher, Illinois, after a large tornado in 1953 illustrated this form of adaptation. A fifth of the residents interviewed after the tornado described themselves as acting in a dysfunctional way. However, the study found that those who claimed to have panicked were not only consistently *more* active during the disaster, but were also the people who acted extremely effectively. According to these researchers, panicky behaviour was better defined as consisting of responses which rendered individuals incapable of playing a 'socially approved role'. They defended the adoption of a definition of panic that was linked to *group* adaptation.[86]

Nevertheless, other disasters revealed opposite behaviour which culminated in a 'panic-crush', as in the Iroquois Theatre fire discussed in Chapter Two. Obviously, researchers had to discriminate between 'adaptive for the individual' and 'adaptive for the group'. Disaster theorists frequently pointed out that selfish behaviour — such as trampling over other people in flight from a burning theatre — could be adaptive behaviour for the individual involved. The social psychologist Alexander Mintz, for instance, drew attention to the individual's perceptions of the 'reward structure'. When a theatre was on fire, orderly evacuation might save everyone, so individuals were not required to consider sacrificing their own interests. However, if only one person in that orderly evacuation decided not to co-operate, those who waited their turn were faced with the option of following suit or being burned to death. Behaviour that was non-adaptive for the group might be adaptive for the individual.[87] It was no coincidence that, in a period of deterrence and grim individualism, the ruthless sacrifice of others for the sake of one's own survival could be defined as rational.[88]

What did research on non-nuclear crises suggest about how people might act in the case of a nuclear war? What the disaster literature rarely mentioned was that fact that many people were not afraid in the face of a cataclysm. Indeed, there could be something strangely exciting about it. Like Pan (the son of Zeus, who gave us the word 'panic' after causing the mortals who startled him from his sleep to flee in intense fear), disasters inspired excitement as well as fear. Films, novels and poetry often fed off this desire to be frightened by disaster. Living through a disaster, or viewing it from a distance, provoked a vicarious pleasure: responses such as 'I have escaped!' or 'I am alive!' The fact of survival bestowed an exhilarating sense of invulnerability upon individuals.[89] This was the emotional response to catastrophe that the Young Girl in the previous chapter experienced after being bombed during the Blitz.

As already mentioned, more prosaic responses to disasters included resignation and denial. When warned of forthcoming disaster, many people simply refused to accept that it would happen or they insisted that they would not be personally injured. Many disaster experts were concerned that the most common problem in 'managing' people in disasters was not preventing hysterical flight but getting them to move at all. In areas periodically subjected to natural disasters a 'disaster culture' often developed, in which people took immense pride in their indefatigable stoicism. In such situations the sense of awe when faced with violent nature often overrode fear and deterred people from fleeing.[90] Even more typically, familial ties triumphed over fear states. In 1961 more than half a million people were evacuated from the coastal areas of Texas and Louisiana in order to flee from Hurricane Carla. However, over a third of residents refused to leave their homes, despite acknowledging danger. The people who fled tended to be tourists and other transients — those people with no familial or community links to the area.[91]

Such considerations caused problems for local authorities, who were uncertain about just when and how people should be warned about impending disaster. It was fairly typical for officials responsible for alerting people to threats to fret about giving out 'too much' information. It was better, claimed one Chief of Police in Indiana in response to a tornado warning in the 1960s, to restrict information to personnel in First Aid Centres and the civil-defence forces in order to avoid public panic.[92] Indeed, fear of alarming the public was so great that information of impending disaster was often withheld completely. In 1953 the Boston Weather Bureau did not issue a tornado warning until it was too late on the grounds that the forecasters were scared of the frenzy that might occur if people heard the word 'tornado'.[93] In such circumstances decision-makers were caught in a difficult position: if an official 'decided against issuing a warning, and death and destruction occur, will he not be blamed? May he not even be blamed unreasonably?' Yet 'if he decides to issue a warning and the danger does not materialize, may he not be criticized for getting people upset?'[94] It was an irreconcilable dilemma.

In order to provide guidance, disaster experts identified four situations that predisposed people to panic when faced with danger. Firstly, partial entrapment was liable to make people panic. If there was the *possibility* of escape, people were much more likely to take fright than they would be if all routes were closed to them.[95] Secondly, when the threat was seen as imminent, leaving little time to devise ways to respond, people were likely to 'freeze'. Emotional extremes would be exacerbated if, thirdly, a blocked or jammed escape faced them. Fourth, confusion and uncertainty about the nature and intensity of the threat was particularly distressing.[96] Fear of the unknown contributed greatly to panic states. When people did not know what was happening either within or without the disaster area, they responded by panicking.[97] In other words, panic was not the normal response to disasters, but was only present in certain, limited circumstances.

In contrast, the normal response of individuals in disaster zones was to immediately set about rescuing those around them and clearing up the mess, often with 'unbelievable calmness and efficiency'.[98] As two eminent American disaster sociologists, E. L. Quarantelli and Russell R. Dynes, writing in 1970, concluded:

> Disaster victims act positively, not irrationally or passively. Mutual help and self-help are frequent. Psychological disturbances do not render the impacted population helpless. Much of the initial rescue work is done by the victims themselves who do not wait to be told what to do. Contrary to the public image, movement toward the impact area is more significant than movement away.[99]

Other researchers noted that in disasters people reacted according to a 'script'. Those who possessed a script to cope with disaster were less likely to suffer from crippling fear. In many instances it was because they had skills that could be used in disaster situations. According to one survey in the 1960s, almost half of all men possessed skills that they could use to good effect in disasters. The fact that only a sixth of women possessed such skills was said to be one reason for higher rates of non-adaptive behaviour among women compared with men.[100] For these researchers disasters were a form of theatre in which participants responded according to specific social cues. Some were 'better at it' than others, but most satisfied at least their family and friends that they had acted appropriately.

After the acute period of the disaster was over, it was even easier to act according to group expectations. These expectations were largely determined by the stability of familial or communal ties. One crucial factor in adapting to trauma was the ability of survivors to rapidly resume myths of community. In most instances this applied only to the immediate familial group. Conservative political rhetoric of the 1960s to 1980s encouraged the belief that reunion with family members was crucial in adapting successfully to disasters. As the formidable psychiatrist William C. Menninger observed after the flooding of the Kansas River at Topeka in 1966, which left ten thousand people homeless, acute anxiety was more likely to be experienced by distant friends and relatives of the victims than by those directly affected.[101] During this tornado relatives helped over 40 per cent of victim families. Furthermore, in no case had these victims requested help: it had been given spontaneously.[102] In contrast, people without dependants were much more likely to exhibit flight behaviour. In one study in the early 1960s only 6 per cent of male heads of households with dependants fled a disaster zone, compared with 15 per cent of male heads of households who lacked dependants.[103] In the words of two Swedish observers in 1977:

> The family is not only one of the primary groups. It is the most common primary group and one of the most long-lasting and stable ones. This statement holds in spite of the often mentioned and much exaggerated statement of the family as an institution changing to a short-living and unstable phenomenon. Being together with one's family and kin will not only reduce anxiety, but will have adaptive value: i.e. enhance the chances for the individual to survive.[104]

The sociologist C. E. Fritz called this the creation of a 'therapeutic community' after disasters, which provided a 'buffer against severe psychological damage' by setting in motion certain 'auto-therapeutic processes'. Thus severe mental health problems were probably fewer after a disaster than before it.[105]

There was a negative side to this process, however: the saving of the family often became the dominant goal, leading to the abandonment of strangers. It is no wonder that transient populations were more likely to panic in disasters: not only did they lack anyone willing to make the effort to rescue them, but in large-scale disasters they were more likely to be afraid for the safety of their more-distant families and were painfully aware that they were regarded as expendable or, at the very least, 'consumers' of the scarce resources devoted to rescue. To put it another way, as we saw in the previous chapter, hatred flourished in disasters. The process of scapegoating was crucial to human reaction to adversity. The Cocoanut Grove Night Club fire in 1942, in which 488 people were killed, illustrated the power of this tendency. The sixteen-year-old bus boy who sparked off the fire when he lit a match in order to change a light bulb provided a convenient scapegoat. His 'foreign-sounding name' (Stanley Tomaszewski) encouraged the view that he was a dangerous outsider. Survivors did not want to acknowledge that they had regressed to an 'uncivilised' state of panic, preferring to insist that a 'foreigner' had caused the tragedy.[106]

Although predicting how people responded in the event of attack was regarded as a crucial first step in learning how to make them act 'correctly', not all disaster researchers were happy about using such research in a nuclear context. There were dangers in extrapolating from non-nuclear disasters to nuclear catastrophe. After all, the devastation that could be wrought by a nuclear attack was simply not comparable to other types of disaster. This concerned men like Major G. I. Wilkes. He was horrified when Brigadier Sir Otho Prior-Palmer, the Member of Parliament for Worthing, argued that being fried in a tank was not much worse than being fried by an H-bomb. Wilkes reminded Prior-Palmer that, during the Second World War, he had seen men 'frying' to death in a tank. It was a 'hideous and terrifying experience'. However, he did not believe that it would be 'as dreadful as dying from the effects of a nuclear explosion'. He continued:

> That it is an academic question may well be true in its arithmetical context, in that groups of three, four or five men dying in Army tanks is a proposition of vastly different proportions to the annihilation of the human race. The only thing that has kept man fighting in the past has been the promise and the hope for the life of the future. The H-bomb . . . threatened to destroy both promise and hope.[107]

This point was also made by the novelist Philip Wylie, who had been a consultant on the psychological effect of weapons to the Federal Civil Defense Administration. In 1954 he attacked his former employers in an article in the *Bulletin of the Atomic Scientists*, reminding them that nuclear holocaust would be totally different from other disasters. How would Americans cope with the 'sticky human gobs around them'? Would they be capable of dealing with the burns, mass nudity and hysteria? 'Nearly all,' he feared, 'will try to get out of town before it is too late.' He added: 'What we *have* done is to accumulate a mass of costly, official data to show that, since we Americans do not panic when poisoned by potato salad at a church social, we shall not panic if nuclear holocaust obliterates our city-cores'.[108]

There were other reasons to question the idea that a study of human reactions to 'ordinary' disasters would give some clue as to reactions in the event of nuclear detonation. After all, in a nuclear assault, people in the targeted areas would never have the security of nearby shelters, nor would they be assured that they would have time to flee. Only a minority of people believed that they would survive such an attack. The warning time in a nuclear attack could be non-existent, or as little as six hours. People would lack time to either flee or otherwise adapt to the prospect of death.[109] Although a nuclear attack would begin and end rapidly, the enormous number of casualties and the nature of their injuries would prove petrifying. Faith in the ability of society to resume its normal functions would be low; fear of long-term radiation high. It was likely that emergency agencies would be completely crushed. People who survived

in shelters would find themselves isolated, desperately defending
their territory against all possible intruders, plagued by fears for
loved ones who were not in the shelter, and fearful about levels of
radioactivity outside the shelter.[110] The cumulative effect of a
nuclear disaster — its geographical spread, duration and scope —
was incomprehensible.[111]

Realistic commentators, such as the prolific war commentator
Irving J. Janis, pointed out that it was fantasy to hope that preparation for a nuclear attack would eliminate intense feelings of fear. No
matter how well prepared, he argued, people would become
'extremely apprehensive as soon as they learn that the first A-bomb
attack [has] occurred in this country'. He was not arguing that
people should be left unprepared, however. After all, adaptive plans
would not eliminate fear but they might enable people to channel
their reactions in more appropriate ways.[112]

Others simply pointed out that the unrealistic instructions being
propagated would not prevent intense fear reactions from taking
place. A report published in the *Bulletin of the Atomic Scientists* in 1955
stated that:

> For those living in a potential area of total destruction, there will
> never be the security of nearby shelters nor, for the populations of
> many cities, will there ever be the comforting and stabilizing belief
> that they will assuredly have time to reach safety outside of the city.
> Neither are they likely to have assurances from appropriate author-
> ities that atomic attacks can be effectively deflated.[113]

Robert Jay Lifton, Eric Markusen and Dorothy Austin put it most
poignantly in 'The Second Death: Psychological Survival After
Nuclear War' (1984):

> Because of the singular capacity to destroy both the human and nat-
> ural environments, nuclear war constitutes a disaster very different
> from those previously experienced . . . Students of normal psy-
> chology, observing how normal human beings derive a sense of
> self-definition and stability in the world, have found consistently
> that there is no self without attachment. Human beings attain

definition by interacting with other people and the natural environment. We apprehend ourselves only as situated in the world . . . The
landscape of our mind reflects the geography of the world. Nuclear
war, in the totality of its effects, can be seen as destroying the matrix
of relationships that make us human: our families, our communities,
our urban, rural, and wilderness environments.

In other words, although psychological responses such as flight
might enable short-term survival, in the longer term nuclear war
would not enable individuals to retain the essence of 'humanness':
'wrenched from the matrix that creates meaning, people may well
cease to function as caring and conscious beings . . . nuclear war
may tear apart . . . the contextual relationships that confer our sense
of ourselves'.[114]

The authors also noted that:

increasing the time the survivors must spend in disaster limbo decreases
their chances of healthy psychological recovery. It is clear that in the
event of a nuclear war, there will be no outside therapeutic community
with which a survivor can process his experience and reintegrate.
There will be no unaffected healers . . . Psychological recovery is
impaired if survivors perceive the disaster at hand as 'manmade'. In settings where human agency is seen to be at fault, observers have found
that survivors harbor widespread feelings of betrayal by those whom
they trusted. The spiral of resulting recrimination substantially under-
mines whatever community spirit remained.[115]

Finally, there were concerns about the political message involved
in using data on civil disasters to understand nuclear war. Because
disaster specialists claimed that the only thing differentiating people's
reactions to nuclear disasters from their reactions to non-nuclear
disasters was their perception that nuclear attack was more horrifying, governments were encouraged to lessen their citizens' dread of
nuclear war. The mantra 'the only thing we have to fear is fear
itself' could make people less apprehensive about nuclear proliferation.[116] Politically, disaster research was suspect, some pacifistic
commentators warned. Helping people cope with nuclear horror

might become yet another step towards war. In the words of the editor of the 1954 special issue of the *Journal of Social Issues* devoted to the study of disasters: 'We live in the shadow of the sword. There will be those who feel that committing scientific resources to disaster research involves moral complicity with evil', although he went on to argue that 'the healthy exercise of rationality involved in submitting the inconceivably terrible to scientific scrutiny' was justification enough.[117]

The historian Guy Oakes was perceptive about the function of civil defence in his book *The Imaginary War* (1994). He observed that:

> Emotional management would channel public anxieties about nuclear war into civil defense activities, convincing Americans that their fears of annihilation were groundless. The representation of a nuclear attack on the United States as a limited and manageable disaster, not fundamentally different from a flood or a hurricane and amenable to the strategies and tactics of crisis management, would persuade Americans that they could protect themselves in such an attack by learning the requisite civil defense procedures and techniques.

Oakes argued persuasively that Americans would pay the price of deterrence only 'if they could be assured that a nuclear attack on their own cities would not be too costly'. They had to be convinced that, at the very least, survival was possible. Both optimists and cynics accepted this claim. Whether or not it was 'true', national security depended upon people believing it. Even for cynics, civil defence would convince Americans that they could protect themselves and

> this conviction, in turn, would provide the necessary support for deterrence, which would protect the American people by preventing nuclear war. The real objective of civil defense, then, was not to protect the public in a nuclear attack. This was impossible. Rather, civil defense would forestall such an attack by creating a popular tolerance for deterrence. But Americans would tolerate deterrence only if they believed that in the event of its failure, they would still

survive. This meant that it was necessary to promote civil defense not primarily as a means of legitimating deterrence, but as a means of ensuring survival.[118]

Disaster research enabled people to pretend that a nuclear disaster *was* somehow comparable to other disasters with a more limited range — a hurricane, for instance. The civil-defence publication *Survival Under Atomic Attack* (published by the FCDA and distributed to twenty million people in 1950 and 1951) told readers that atomic bombs were 'only' one type of bomb. The main difference was radioactivity, but this could be avoided through simple techniques of household management. Radioactivity was like a household germ that could be destroyed. The Geiger counter was marketed as just another household appliance. The ethos of civil defence emphasised the 'house-proud ethic of the postwar middle class' and appealed to the 'putatively traditional and small-town virtues of self-help, mutual assistance, and community spirit, which would continue to stand Americans in good stead even in the extremes of nuclear war.' Through middle-class emotional management, survival was proffered.[119]

Nightmares about the end of the world have always plagued humanity, but the nuclear-inspired fears of the 1950s period onward were a powerful rebuttal to the optimism of commentators as varied as political liberals, technocrats and scientists. The philosopher Michel Foucault expressed the issue succinctly when he wrote that 'what might be called a society's "threshold of modernity" has been reached when the life of the species is wagered on its own political strategies'. He continued: 'For millennia, man remained what he was for Aristotle: a living animal with the additional capacity for a political existence.' In contrast, 'modern man is an animal whose politics places his existence as a living being in question'.[120]

The Cold War introduced new elements into the 'fear of war' paradigm of earlier decades: courage, honour and hope had no place in the new warfare of the twentieth century. Everything was uncertain. Who was responsible for 'pushing the button'? Could people 'trust' machines and supercomputers not to malfunction? How real was the Soviet threat? Were entire populations being manipulated? Would a nuclear war be as bad as 'they' say — and who exactly were 'they'? But, more fundamentally, the nuclear debate of the mid-century was frightening precisely because it represented a shift in the claim of absolute force: humanity secured the powers previously the exclusive reserve of God. Indeed, humanity's powers were ultimately more conclusive than those of God, in being able to annihilate irredeemably and without possibility of redemption. The election of man (and it was primarily regarded as a masculine prerogative) into a position of omnipotence included an element of guilty pride which, in turn, evoked fear of punishment. As we shall see in Chapter Eleven, it was not until the 1980s that these apocalyptic fears were exchanged for more insidious ones, such as global warming and pollution. Nevertheless, in the twenty-first century, when the nuclear armament of India and Pakistan has become a reality, the fear of nuclear holocaust has once again shifted to 'them', an evil and corrupt 'other'. Today newly terrified Americans and Britons demand nuclear disarmament for every nation, save our own.

Afterword to Part Four: Narrativity

Throughout this book a great deal of attention has been paid to shifts in the way fear is narrated by historical actors. As we discussed earlier, it is important to look at shifts in the *languages* of fear. Emotionologists remind us to ask: 'How is the word "fear" used in cultural contexts?' However, fear does not only follow its uses in language; it also possesses its own narrative. To be understood, individuals communicating their fears need to conform to certain narrative structures, including genre, syntax, form, order and vocabulary. Furthermore, the act of speaking (or writing) one's fear changes the *sensation* of fear. In the words of the historical anthropologist William Reddy, emotional utterances or acts have a 'unique capacity to alter what they "refer" to or what they "represent"'.[1] In other words, shifts in the way people narrate fear alter their subjective experience.

For instance, before the Second World War combat accounts used the language of instincts to describe their emotions in war. Fear and panic in combat involved the feeling of being 'taken over' by 'primitive blood-lust', only returning to their 'real selves' afterwards. This language was drawn from evolutionary notions about emotions arising out of universal instincts such as self-preservation, curiosity, pugnacity, self-assertion, self-abasement, parental love and revulsion.[2] As William James put it in *Principles of Psychology* (1905), 'every stimulus that excites an instinct excites an emotion as well'.[3] These instincts were inherited 'from the brutes' and could not be avoided.[4] In a typical account from the First World War,

Charles Stewart Alexander described his emotions in combat as a heady mixture of 'fiendish joy' and terror, arising out of being suddenly overwhelmed by 'primitive instincts'.[5] In the terror of combat men reverted to their animalistic inheritance. This language began changing after 1939 and was dramatically different by the 1960s, when the fashionably self-conscious, psychoanalytical style of war memoirs encouraged a more detailed, more individual and more confessional rendering of reminiscences and battle stories. In other words, by the Vietnam War popular Freudianism resulted in an increase in sexual metaphors to describe the fear engendered by combat — most typically the description of fear in combat as inciting an 'ache as profound as the ache of orgasm'.[6] During the earlier period the language of instincts was the language of fear. By the 1960s the language employed was that of psychoanalysis, the language of anxiety.

The problem of causation cannot be avoided. Did the shift in the nature of war (factors such as greater distance between enemies, and the killing of civilians) lead to increased anxiety, or did changes in the labels with which men could 'make sense' of what was going on around them change the way they 'actually experienced' combat? The answer is 'both', but historians have proved better at analysing the former than the latter. In historical time many things actually do (or do not) 'happen', but the very act of narrating changes and formulates the 'experience'. After all, from the moment of action (in this case, combat), the event entered into imagination and language, to be interpreted, elaborated, structured and restructured. As the Vietnam story-teller Tim O'Brien wrote in *The Things They Carried* (1990):

> it's difficult to separate what happened from what seemed to happen. What seems to happen becomes its own happening and has to be told that way. The angles of vision are skewed . . . And then afterwards, when you go to tell about it, there's always that surreal seemingness, which makes the story seem untrue, but which in fact represents the hard and exact truth as it seemed.[7]

The act of narrating emotions — to oneself as much as to others — is dependent upon the ordering mechanisms of grammar, plot and genre. To the extent that these mechanisms are historical, the way emotions are experienced have a history.

The narrativity approach implies that there is no body to the emotions at all: everything is reduced to discourse. One of the problems with this approach is that it imposes an absolute plasticity to the individual, always in thrall to disciplining discourses and institutions. Even biology is portrayed as constructed by cultural regimes of power.[8] Indisputably, though, fear has a physiology, as do all emotions. This aspect has always been difficult for historians. On the one hand, a strong tendency within the social sciences has disembodied the emotions, portraying them as trivial by-products of rational, class-based responses to material interests. The disciplinarian separation of the social and biological sciences and the 'privileged theoretical position given to concepts such as reason' ensured that allegedly irrational and visceral forces in human history were sidelined.[9] The emphasis on rationality followed the belief that arguments about change over time can be constructed only through the analysis of ideology or economic structures. Furthermore, focusing on human rationality seemed a more respectful way of interpreting people's behaviour in the past.

Even when historians were faced with clear examples of terror or panic, they were keen to impose a sober, dispassionate logic (often of an economic nature) to human behaviour.[10] George Rudé wrote that the crowd during the French Revolution consisted of 'ordinary men and women with varying social needs, who responded to a variety of impulses, in which economic crisis, political upheaval, and the urge to satisfy immediate and particular grievances all played their part'.[11] Historians have been more comfortable analysing 'utilities' or 'moral economies' than studying the ebb and flow of anger, hatred and fear. Individuals and groups in terrifying situations are portrayed as economic subjects in trousers and skirts, calmly calculating personal and social risk in the nuclear bunkers in Washington DC.

Nevertheless, the argument that historians can only analyse the emotions discursively does not deny that emotions have a physiology. As I argued in the Introduction to this book, although there is no *consistent* visceral response to fear, the emotional body rapidly gives forth a multitude of signs: the heart pounds faster or seems to freeze, breathing quickens or stops, blood pressure soars or falls and sometimes adrenalin floods into the bloodstream. Although there is a theatre to the physiology of fear — with executives acting out anxiety neuroses while postal workers revel in the drama of hysteria — it is not always choreographed according to any pre-determined schema of class, gender or ethnicity.

PART FIVE

Realms of Anxiety

Introduction

Instead of the tangible threats to corporeal existence that are occasioned by war, the last few decades of the twentieth century are characterised by more nebulous anxiety states, focusing on fatigued environments of flesh and fellowship. Cancer and crime, pain and pollution: these fears isolate us. The acceleration of rates of change and the fact that threats seem to be everywhere — in the earth, air and sun — is bewildering. The fact that many of these risks are invisible and global also makes them more frightening because they are impossible to manage or avoid. Notions of 'trust' become old-fashioned as each individual or small community struggles to make some kind of sense of their fearful surroundings.

In earlier chapters we saw how one of the most popular responses to fear is scapegoating or externalising fears on to 'others'. In the late twentieth century this mechanism continues to be employed, but identifying a harmful 'other' becomes more difficult. There seems to be no way of calculating risk or apportioning blame. Even clear distinctions — for instance, between sick and healthy people — are no longer certain. The cancer tumour grows unseen until it is too late; the AIDS virus loiters in the body until it strikes. With advances in genetics, people are aware that death is always present, programmed in our very identity, yet curiously difficult to define. When physicians working in terminal wards of hospitals can boast about having to 'go water the vegetables', we are right to fear our dehumanisation.

CHAPTER TEN

The Body

Lies and lethargies police the world
In its periods of peace. What pain taught
Is soon forgotten; we celebrate
What ought to happen as if it were done,
Are blinded by our boasts. Then back they come,
The fears that we fear.

AUDEN, 'THE AGE OF ANXIETY'

One day in 1946, in Denver, Colorado, Edna Kaehele made a discovery 'so monstrous that it would set off a chain reaction which, before I had done with it, was to give me irrefutable proof of the eternal triumph of life over death'. She had been feeling slight discomfort and nausea for many months before she had the courage to book an appointment with her physician. Rather than being diagnosed with a mild gall bladder problem or 'touch of liver', or told that she was entering the menopause, Kaehele was given a 'death sentence'. She was told that she had cancer and was expected to die within six months. Terrified by the mention of that 'unclean word', Kaehele reacted with 'horror beyond which there is no reasoning'. The 'dark, brackish' taste of death filled her mouth. Her new foe — a 'deadly, loathsome enemy' — seemed invincible. In her words:

Cancer! The word filled the universe. I could feel it start from some place too deep for conscious thought, whirring to slow life, swelling to immense proportions, bursting at last with the force of an atomic explosion somewhere in the top of my head. *Cancer!* Cancer! CANCER!

Cancer! From that day on it was to repeat itself with varying degrees of intensity until it became the dominant theme of my troubled existence. Truly cancer has been well named. It is a crab-like scavenger reaching its greedy tentacles into the life of the soul as well as the body. It destroys the will as it gnaws away the flesh.

She chose a lonely confrontation with cancer: only her immediate family and two close friends were informed of her poisonous secret. Despite undergoing treatment with radiation (the machine was yet another 'frightening monster from which there was no escape'), radium, liver injections, blood transfusions and heavy doses of vitamins, her weight fell from 145 pounds to ninety and she was often too weak to get out of bed. To her face, Kaehele's physicians proffered cure but, behind her back, relatives were told that treatment would only provide a 'breathing space' and they should consider whether her life was worth the expense of such procedures. This duplicity on the part of her physicians did not anger Kaehele as much as the cruelty of constantly waiting for 'cancer pain' that never came. Kaehele castigated her doctors for failing to tell her that:

Cancer pain is not necessarily the most frightful of all pains. Many other things are more excruciatingly painful . . . My greatest agony was in waiting expectantly twenty-four hours a day for the unbearable pain that I confidently expected to begin at any minute. The mental anguish was worse than any physical suffering I ever experienced. And that, at least, was unnecessary . . . It is the unknown that terrifies.

Instead, Kaehele learned the hard way to deal with pain in the same way as women do in 'natural childbirth'. She also ardently embraced psychosomatic medicine. 'Letting blind panic over cancer go unchecked until it poisons our lives,' Kaehele insisted, was 'as stupid as ignoring the approach of an obviously rabid dog — and as fatal.' As a matter of dogma, she claimed that the cure for cancer was a high-protein diet, positive thinking and unwavering faith in the ability to conquer the 'foreigner' within. A cancer diagnosis was not a 'death sentence'. Indeed, because 'fully as many people die of the fear of [cancer] as are killed by the cancer itself', confidence in being able to 'live with cancer' was imperative. In her words: 'if in some fashion the patient can only keep going until nature takes over, the natural functioning of the body will oust or wall off this appalling offender.' Although she vowed that she was not a 'cancer-convert', her religious beliefs also helped her survive. She remembered the exact moment when 'all fear of cancer, utter and absolute, left me'. One September afternoon she had retired to her bedroom to lie down when, with her

> mind idly flitting from one thing to another, a sudden sense of inef-fable well-being seemed to pervade me and to lift me up for a breathless interval completely outside my mortal body. I felt no fright at all, merely surprise, and in my mind there burst the exul-tant thought: 'This is dying!' No thought of panic, of unfinished work, or loved ones left behind; just sheer and utter joy in the simple fact of death. Only it wasn't death — it was life. In that moment I lost all fear of cancer because I had faced death not with resignation but with eagerness.[1]

Thereafter Kaehele was no longer tormented: she could 'live with' her cancer. We don't know when she actually had to face her death, but in 1959, a dozen years after she had been diagnosed as having half a dozen months to live, she published an inspirational self-help book called *Sealed Orders*. Her story, however, provided one example of the resilience of the human imagination in con-structing defences against the fear of dying.

Kaehele's personal drama had started in 1946, a year after wartime threats had abruptly ended. It was a period in which the threat of direct attack receded, only to be replaced with more free-floating anxieties. 'Modern individuals' were plagued by 'obtrusive and less transitory' emotional states, observed the Professor of Social Medicine at Oxford University in 1948.[2] That same year a major British survey revealed the intensity of people's 'personal and irrational' forms of anxiety. Although only one in nine Britons expressed any financial fears, a quarter harboured generalised fears about society or the world. An additional quarter were afraid of animals, a fifth could not stand heights, space, water or caves, a tenth were apprehensive in the dark and one in twenty trembled at any allusion to supernatural phenomena.[3]

As the self-help text *Antidote to Fear* (1962) put it, 'fear is the greatest curse in our world today — and its greatest danger'. Fear 'enters into and bedevils virtually every relationship and it might even be true to suggest that there exists hardly one individual in a million who is not the victim of some form of it'. For the courageous man who claimed not to be conscious of being afraid, fear and anxiety were probably 'affecting him from below the conscious levels, subtly poisoning many of his reactions to life'.[4] Militarist threats to corporeal existence had ceased but the Freudian revolution now permeated popular consciousness, ensuring that fear and anxiety reigned supreme in all aspects of life. As Kaehele discovered, the most terrifying of these pervasive anxieties were related to bodily decay.

The emotional lives of men and women underwent dramatic shifts in the 1950s. For the majority of Britons and Americans, improved welfare provisions and rising life expectancy alleviated fears of abject privation and the risk of meeting an early or, as it came to be known, a 'premature' death. Nevertheless, affluence did not eradicate bodily anxieties altogether. Infectious hazards such as plague, cholera, leprosy, tuberculosis, smallpox and typhoid fever lost their ability to command terror, only to be replaced by a pervasive sense of dread about chronic ailments. For three decades after the Second World War no disease was feared more than cancer, the great symbol of doom. This was not the case at the end of the previous century. In 1896 the *American Journal of Psychology* reported that when people were asked which diseases they feared, only 5 per cent named cancer, while between a quarter and a third drew attention to the scary nature of each of the following ailments: smallpox, lockjaw, consumption and hydrophobia. In the fear-stakes, being crushed in a rail accident or during an earthquake, drowning, being burned alive, hit by lightning, or contracting diphtheria, leprosy or pneumonia all ranked higher than cancer.[5]

In contrast, it came as no surprise to researchers half a century later that 70 per cent of women interviewed in Manchester and Salford immediately identified cancer as their greatest fear when asked to point out the 'most alarming' disease from a list that included tuberculosis, heart trouble, asthma and rheumatism.[6] These women were justified in fearing the C-word: after all, cancer was a leading cause of death. While in 1900 tuberculosis killed three times the number of people ravaged by cancer, within a couple of decades only heart ailments surpassed cancer as the most common cause of death.[7] Between the Second World War and the 1970s it was also a disease increasingly likely to elicit radical surgical responses; that is, women with breast cancer were increasingly subjected to extensive removal of breast tissue.

Even the language of surgery became more combative. In the words of a physician writing in *Surgeon* in 1946, the failure to perform sufficiently extensive surgery on women with breast cancer (a 'formidable enemy') was 'nothing less than surgical cowardice'.[8] Aggressive surgical responses to breast cancer did not decline in popularity until the late 1970s, beset by doubts about their effectiveness, the increased politicisation of women, who were now demanding explanations for their treatment regimes, and (particularly in America) legislation which insisted that patients be apprised of all treatment options in order to be able to give informed consent.[9]

Nevertheless, the risk of mutilation and death was not sufficient reason for cancer panic. Until the AIDS epidemic of the 1980s cancer was the most stigmatised disease of the twentieth century. It posed a threat not only to life but also to an individual's sexuality and identity. Even cancer organisations portrayed cancer as 'an insidious, dreadful, relentless invader'. In 1957, the physician and cancer educationalist George W. Crile blamed these cancer organisations for having 'fashioned a devil out of cancer'. Crile lamented that they 'have bred in a sensitive public a fear that is approaching hysteria. They have created a new disease, cancerophobia, a contagious

disease that spreads from mouth to ear. It is possible that to-day cancerophobia causes more suffering than cancer itself.'[10]

The stigmatisation of cancer was evident everywhere. The father of
a boy who died of a brain tumour adopted the language of monstrosity to describe his son's affliction: cancer was a 'vicious invader', a
'gangster', a 'monster of productivity'.[11] Breast cancer was even more
contemptible. The failure of women, as protectors of their family's
health, to detect and eradicate the 'germ' within their own bodies
made them culpable of gross neglect. In the words of the public health
magazine *Hygeia* in 1945, the breast cancer patient had 'no one to
blame for the consequences but herself'.[12] It was even worse for
cancer patients who could not actually *see* their cancer. People with
internal, invisible malignancies felt that they had less mastery over the
situation and were consequently more frightened.[13] A cancer diagnosis threatened to define the individual's entire identity.

Ignorance about the cause of the disease exacerbated its stigmatisation. Cancer was portrayed as having been 'contracted' by people
exhibiting certain nasty psychological traits.[14] Even Sigmund Freud
could not escape this process. The psychoanalyst Wilhelm Reich
explained Freud's cancer of the jaw in terms of his 'bio-energetic
shrinking, a giving up of hope'. He asked: 'Why did [Freud] develop
cancer just at that time?' The answer?

> He was very unhappily married . . . He was very much dissatisfied
> genitally. Both his resignation and his cancer were evidence of that.
> Freud had to give up, as a person. He had to give up his personal
> pleasures, his personal delights, in his middle years . . . If my view
> of cancer is correct, you just give up, you resign — and, then, you
> shrink. It is quite understandable why he developed his epulis [the
> term Reich used to refer to Freud's cancer of the jaw]. He smoked
> very much, very much. I always had the feeling he smoked — not
> nervousness, not nervousness — but because he wanted to say
> something which never came over his lips. Do you get the
> point? . . . As if he had to 'bite something down'.[15]

Cancer sufferers were said to be masochists, chronic worriers or
unable to 'deal with' anger or sexuality. These behavioural or

psychological characteristics were responsible for the 'cellular chaos' which resulted in tumours. These theories were deeply flawed: they were based primarily on interviews with patients and took no account of the possibility that anxiety was the *result*, rather than the cause, of cancer. Furthermore, they failed to establish 'control groups' (after all, although many stressful people developed cancer, no account was taken of how many stressful people remained free of the disease) and they ignored other possible causes for the cancer, such as smoking.

Nevertheless, for non-cancer sufferers, speculation about the defective psychology of cancer patients provided some comfort. As we have seen, part of the pervasive anxiety about cancer was related to the invisibility of a 'cause'. Cancer's symptoms constituted the everyday pangs of existence and, thanks to the periodic eruption of environmental panics, its causes were feared to be omnipresent: they were the result of society's wanton abuse of Nature in the form of agricultural and industrial pollution, nuclear radiation and food adulteration (on which there will be more in the next chapter).[16] Attributing cancer to the character flaws of the sufferers was one attempt to deny the terrifyingly random nature of disease. Somehow the sufferer 'deserved' the disease. By abiding by certain moral tenets, healthy people could avoid the disease. As in all wars, the myth of the 'war against cancer' was that there was a clearly identified enemy that could be decisively defeated if the public and private 'will' to do so remained high.

The stigma attached to cancer had an adverse impact on attempts to diminish cancer's fury. Terrorised by exaggerated fears of the disease, people responded to its signs by acts of furious denial.[17] Studies in the 1950s and 1960s suggested that attempts to persuade people to report early symptoms of cancer by scaring them with the consequences of not doing so were counterproductive. Fear-arousing communications made people act defensively: they ignored warnings or acted aggressively by doing precisely the opposite of what was advised.[18]

The extent of the problem was suggested by an exhaustive study of cancer patients attending the Christie Hospital and Holt Radium Institute in Manchester in 1955. Although it was relatively easy to

detect the early signs of cancer of the breast, cervix, uterus, skin and
mouth, 45 per cent of 2700 patients attending the hospital had
delayed consulting their doctor for three months or more after the
appearance of obvious symptoms. Seventeen per cent delayed medical advice for more than a year. These patients recognised that early
diagnosis was crucial for curing the disease, but still failed to take
speedy action. When asked to explain their tardiness, fears of stigmatisation predominated. One fifty-nine-year-old woman admitted
delaying seeing a doctor for an entire year after detecting a lump in
her breast. She 'didn't tell a soul', including her husband, fearful that
he would force her to seek medical advice. Even when the lesion
began discharging pus and blood she admitted that she simply
dressed the abscess without actually looking at it, explaining that 'I
was terrified of it being something serious'. Fear of the very word
'cancer', combined with guilt at deceiving her husband and shame
about the way she was neglecting her health, terrified this woman
into a state of inertia. Only after her husband finally noticed the
lesion did she reluctantly go to the hospital, a full year after the
symptoms became apparent. Another woman, a 'retired ladies'
companion', delayed three years before seeking help, claiming that
she 'always tended to put anything unpleasant away'. She believed
that cancer was a 'dirty disease that people got who were dirty or
who had done something wrong'.

Other people with cancer-like symptoms found that their suspicions developed into free-floating anxiety that enveloped everything
from a horror of 'doctoring' to trepidation about the antiseptic
smell of hospitals. Many female patients were worried that they
might be banished from their homes because of the shameful nature
of their illness. Although many had never been admitted to hospital
before, they were capable of reciting an enormous number of alarming rumours of blunders within the wards. 'Going under the knife'
was a possibility that alarmed over a quarter of patients. Operations
were dreaded as 'just the beginning of a lot of trouble', in which
mutilation was inevitable. Furthermore, there was a widespread
misconception that surgery would cause the 'germ' of cancer to
spread. In the words of one patient: 'I always feel that if your're [sic]
cut there it just goes on and you have to have more done — the

beginning of a long process leading to the end.' As a result of these multiple fears, the researchers at the Christie Hospital and Holt Radium Institute found that people who suspected that their symptoms indicated a cancerous growth were actually *less* likely to seek treatment than people who simply observed the symptoms but did not suspect cancer. Fear of cancer prevented people from soliciting the most effective cure.[19]

Given this situation, it is not surprising to find that the widespread fear of cancer made it difficult for physicians to treat cancer patients.[20] A study in the 1960s showed that, when first diagnosed with cancer, around a third of patients simply repressed all knowledge of their diagnosis. Another quarter blamed their doctor for their illness and exhibited paranoid tendencies, fifteen per cent transformed their fear into a state of exhilaration, while the remaining patients responded in diverse ways, such as refusing to believe the diagnosis, becoming hypomanic or sublimating their fears into other activities.[21] These responses could seriously complicate effective treatment of the cancer. Patients' anxieties made them expand their catalogue of symptoms.[22] More seriously, delays in seeking treatment, coupled with fear of imminent death engendered immediately after the diagnosis, meant that patients frequently deteriorated quickly. As two psychiatrists lamented in 1952, 'the tumour plus the fear or illusion that the diagnosis means a fatal verdict, brings the patient to a state of melancholy and compulsive preoccupation with his symptoms, setting off a vicious circle that brings him sooner to the end of his resistance'.[23] Consequently, cancer patients were particularly difficult to treat 'simply because of the fact that fear may well have been exerting its distorting and damaging effect long before the patient seeks or obtains medical assistance'.[24]

It was an attempt to dissolve the myths associated with cancer that motivated Susan Sontag to write *Illness as Metaphor* (1990). 'The metaphors and myths . . . kill,' she insisted. She

> wanted to offer other people who were ill and those who care for
> them an instrument to dissolve these metaphors, these inhibitions.
> I hoped to persuade terrified people who were ill to consult doctors,
> or to change their incompetent doctors for competent ones, who

would give them proper care. To regard cancer as if it were just a disease — a very serious one, but just a disease. Not a curse, not a punishment, not an embarrassment. Without 'meaning'. And not necessarily a death sentence.[25]

The book has, rightly, become a classic.

As Sontag implied, the 'problem' of cancer-phobia was not confined to the patient. The doctor–patient relationship was compromised by cancer fears. Reluctance to mention the C-word meant that only those cancers terminating in death were given the dreaded diagnosis. Those cancers that were successfully treated tended to be placed in a number of miscellaneous categories, further contributing to the cycle of fear that implied that a cancer diagnosis was a death sentence.[26] To their astonishment, physicians discovered that patients who suspected that they had cancer frequently failed to even ask for the name of their affliction. In the words of Sir Stanford Cade of Westminster Hospital in 1963, the cancer patient often accepted 'amputation of breast or arm or leg, colostomy, tracheostomy, etc., without asking the diagnosis.'[27]

This was a little *too* convenient for doctors who shared their patients' fears about cancer.[28] As two commentators conceded in 1959: 'Medical men are not endowed with special courage, and they have not themselves been insulated from the accumulation of human experience on which the fear of cancer is based.'[29] As a consequence, even patients who wanted information about their illness often encountered reticent doctors. In 1930 a London radiologist addressed the British Institute of Radiology about the question of giving patients accurate diagnoses. He recalled that some years earlier it was customary *not* to tell a woman that she had cancer. Men were given their diagnosis straightforwardly, whereas the truth was hidden from the 'weaker sex'. However, he noted, this was no longer the case: 'women have taken their place beside men in almost all the business of life, and there would seem to be no further justification for withholding disturbing knowledge simply because of the patient's sex.' He noted that some men also 'went to pieces' when they received the informa-tion, so each case had to be judged on its merits. Nevertheless, he went on,

It is, fortunately, not necessary that the word cancer should even be mentioned. It is possible to establish a perfect understanding between doctor and patient without any definite statement. When a complete removal of the breast is recommended, most women know, or at least strongly suspect, what this means. It is a mistake to give any patient an opening to ask forthwith, 'Is it cancer?' The advice as to operative removal should be coupled with a statement that it will be necessary for some time afterwards to employ X rays at intervals, in order to avoid any risk of return [of the tumour]. This suggestion of the possibility of recurrence is in nine times out of ten sufficient to stop the patient from asking a direct question; at the same time, she is comforted by the thought that something will be done to forestall what she dreads.[30]

In the late 1950s 90 per cent of physicians admitted that they preferred not to give cancer patients an honest and straightforward diagnosis.[31] In 1956, a physician published an article entitled 'The Care of Cancer in Practice' in the *Practitioner*, in which he confessed that he had rarely told patients that they had cancer. 'I have seldom encountered a mind sufficiently prepared or with deep enough religious convictions to accept such news,' he argued, 'and even then, the views of the relations must be respected because they must live with the patient.' The author observed that patients rarely asked whether they had cancer, although many must have 'an inner consciousness of the truth'. When the patient began deteriorating 'we anticipate the question which must surely come', but at precisely that time 'the patient's mind becomes cloudy, conversation becomes more and more irrational, and finally unconsciousness supervenes'. Most died 'without ever suspecting the real nature of their disease'. Those who believed in telling the patient the diagnosis were warned by this physician that the truth merely made 'management' more troublesome and added to the 'sum of human misery and despair'. Relatives could be told since this would 'make them less susceptible to ill-informed gossip and tales of drugs with magic properties', but the patient should be kept in the dark or, if in pain, lobotomised.[32]

Even physicians who agreed that it was 'morally wrong' to withhold a truthful diagnosis from patients who 'persistently' asked for one, sanctioned denying information to patients hailing 'from areas, still to be found here and there in the British Isles, where the mere mention of cancer . . . engenders a dread which deters them even from investigation in hospital'.[33] Arguments favouring giving patients accurate diagnoses were almost entirely based on the pragmatic grounds that the information might render the patient more obedient to medical dicta.[34] Within less than a couple of decades, however, these debates were to sound distinctly old-fashioned, as physicians came face to face with another highly stigmatised illness — but one which elicited very different responses from the sufferers.

The 1980s brought a new threat to people's consciousness. This time it was not a disease of longevity, but of youth: AIDS. The syndrome was first officially recognised on 5 June 1981, when the weekly report of the Centers for Disease Control published an article titled 'Pneumocystis Carinii Pneumonia [PCP] in Los Angeles' about the sudden increase in sales of a drug used to treat the rare disease PCP. Since all the patients were homosexual, it was initially called Gay Related Immune Deficiency (GRID), but within a year the Centers for Disease Control had adopted the name Acquired Immune Deficiency Syndrome, or AIDS. In 1983 the virus responsible was identified and in 1986 the virus was labelled the Human Immunodeficiency Virus (HIV).

Well before its scientific classification, contracting AIDS had become one of the major fears of the late twentieth century. The fear about sexually transmitted diseases, which had declined after 1910, suddenly exploded again in the 1980s with AIDS. Awareness of the disease had affected the gay community for many years, but it developed into a panic in the mid-1980s, spurred by Rock Hudson's rapid demise in 1985.[35] The actor's tragic death was prominently exhibited on the front pages of newspapers, along with 'before and after' photographs. His status as a virile heterosexual icon who had cavorted on the screen with Doris Day, Elizabeth Taylor and Linda Evans only served to heighten anxiety that even this embodiment of American manhood could have been 'contaminated', even 'feminised', by an extraordinary and obscure virus. In the words of one man, interviewed by USA Today in October 1985: 'I thought AIDS was a gay disease, but if Rock Hudson's dead it can kill anyone.'[36]

A fear of fluid sexuality created a panic of vulnerability. A *New York Times* poll on 12 September 1985 found that over half of the Americans polled believed that AIDS was the most serious disease menacing humanity.[37] AIDS replaced cancer as the terrifying illness of the century: henceforth obituary notices for people who died of 'ordinary' cancers no longer contained the euphemistic words 'died of a long illness', fearing that readers might assume that the death was AIDS-related.

As with cancer scares, AIDS sufferers were stigmatised. As we saw earlier in the chapter, in the case of 'ordinary cancers' it was convenient to speculate that certain psychological traits had 'caused' the illness. This psychologising tendency increasingly broke down with AIDS. After all, why point to psychological traits such as anal retentiveness when buggery was an easy target? But this stigmatised AIDS even more. It was a disease of perversion. Unlike cancer, where the diagnosis was often hidden from patients, AIDS patients were confronted with their ailment and they, in turn, tried to conceal their diagnosis from family and friends.[38] To homosexuals, heroin users, Haitians and haemophiliacs (the groups believed to be most vulnerable to the disease) such anxieties were wholly rational. After all, commentators habitually confused the terms 'communicable' and 'contagious'. The person who was HIV-positive was often called a 'carrier', as though they hauled an evil 'something' within their bodies. Some physicians refused to treat members of these groups: surgeons were reluctant to operate, dentists to treat.[39]

There were cases of gay men being charged with assault on the grounds that they might have exposed other people to infection. Police at the International Conference on AIDS in Washington DC in 1987 wore rubber gloves when they arrested demonstrators. People who tested positive for HIV were quarantined by their colleagues.[40] Hostile commentators proposed that the disease be called WOGS, or Wrath of God Syndrome. The evangelist Jerry Falwell designated AIDS a 'Gay plague'. Hatred even applied to child sufferers. For instance, in 1987, three haemophiliac sons (aged between eight and ten) of the Ray family of Arcadia, Florida, tested positive for HIV. They were barred from school and when a court order readmitted them the local community boycotted the school. On 28 August 1987 members of the community even burned down the family house. The rhetoric of disease was used to legitimise the surveillance and stigmatisation of outside groups.

Uncertainty about the cause of this new killer exacerbated fears. As we will see in the next chapter, the disease struck at a time when there was widespread fear about environmental threats, such as pesticides. The whole of society seemed polluted. The boundaries between 'clean' and 'dirty' were uncertain. Wild stories proliferated. Had right-wing groups deliberately spread the disease? Could infection be transmitted by contaminated batches of 'poppers' (amyl or butyl nitrate)? Was it possible to spread the virus through casual contact — a handshake, for instance? Was 'leakage' already taking place? This fear was exacerbated by a much-publicised article in the *Journal of the American Medical Association* in 1983 that suggested that AIDS could be spread through casual contact within families. In the words of these scientists, 'children living in high-risk households are susceptible to AIDs and that sexual contact, drug abuse, or exposure to blood products is not necessary for disease transmission'.[41] Would the disease seep across boundaries, eroding differences between 'respectable' and 'disreputable' members of society? Fear of the 'gay plague' encouraged homophobic views, such as those expressed by Chaim Bermant in the *Daily Telegraph* on 3 September 1991:

> When I first heard of them they were known as bum-boys. Then it was nancy-boys, and pansies and fairies, and fruits and fags, and faggots and poofs and poofters, and queers and gays. Gay was the name they eventually chose. Now they are reverting to queers, but given their disposition should they not be calling themselves kamikazes? I ask the question in all seriousness, for they not only seem to have a death-wish themselves, but an apparent readiness to inflict death on others.[42]

Anti-homosexual propaganda even promoted the idea that the infective agent was sperm itself. 'Killer sperm' did not harm women because their 'rugged' vaginas were the 'natural' receptacles for sperm. Vaginas had 'evolved over the millennia so that their bodies can deal with these foreign invaders; men, not thus blessed by nature, become vulnerable to the "killer sperm" of other men'. In other words, when sperm entered a man's body through homosexual intercourse, he had no resistance to infection.[43] Racial profiling was also rampant. For instance, when a British white heterosexual male was asked how HIV spread, he replied:

> Monkeys in Africa. I think that was what I heard and that was passed through God-knows-what to get through [to Britain]. I've heard some extreme stories about how it reached our shore [much laughter]. Which I care not to utter . . . It was just meant to be bestiality, I suppose . . . I could probably imagine it would be something like in their tribe in Africa would probably be more prone to that sort of thing . . . If a man caught it and he had sex with his wife and someone came along, I don't know how these tribes work so I don't know the moral judgement you place on them. Someone could come along and pay some money and have sex with his wife and then he could take it back to his country and give it to his wife.[44]

This response may have been particularly crude, but it was not aberrant. It was not surprising, then, that the widespread persecution of those groups within society who were at highest risk of HIV infection increased their resistance to the scientists claiming to understand the syndrome. As one gay physician in San Francisco admitted, when he first became aware of the disease he simply could not accept the explanations being given by public health figures. 'A disease that killed only gay white men?' he queried. 'It seemed unbelievable. I used to teach epidemiology, and I had never heard of a disease that selective. I thought, They are making this up. It can't be true. Or if there is such a disease it must be the work of some government agency — the F.B.I. or the C.I.A. — trying to kill us all.'[45] This fear of science spread widely.

A British black heterosexual male also believed that the disease was 'an experiment':

> It could be used as a weapon. I suppose, it could be used as a weapon, I don't know. The Americans get up to a lot of things, you

know? People think they're the most innocent people but they're not, there's a lot of things that goes on behind shut doors. I reckon they could have sort of formed it as a weapon or just a daily experiment, one of the experiments they do there, in laboratories . . . yeah, there are the chances that it could have been an experiment of like maybe an animal had this unknown disease or whatever, and they probably took samples of its blood or whatever, could have been a monkey, a chimpanzee, anything you know, and it could have leaked out, it's one of those possibilities, and you know, bit like Chernobyl type of thing.[46]

Others observed that this scenario was not without precedent. After all, between 1932 and 1972 the Tuskegee study in Alabama involved six hundred black men with syphilis who were not treated in order to study the progress of the disease. In the words of another British black heterosexual male:

I reckon America has got a lot to do with it, a lot more to do with it than we think. I've read about it . . . in the 1940s where a group of black GI prisoners of war were contaminated with hepatitis or syphilis or what's the name. They were let back into the community just to see. So they gave it to their wives and their children and it seems they used them like guinea pigs really, they didn't tell them that they had it, you see. Now if something like that could of happened, it doesn't surprise me that something like that could happen [with AIDS] as well.[47]

Within the gay community there was widespread alarm. Promiscuity became menacing. Perhaps only cybersex was safe. Certainly human contact was fraught with danger. When Randy Shilt's *And the Band Played On. Politics, People and the AIDS Epidemic* (1987) was published, the villain was personified in Gaetan Dugas, 'Patient Zero'. Dugas was a promiscuous gay flight attendant who was linked epidemiologically to forty of the first 241 men with AIDS.[48] One English professor claimed that after reading Shilt's book:

I still shudder — whether with voyeuristic pleasure or zero-at-the-bone fright I can't tell — whenever I recall the lurid bathhouse scene where Patient Zero exchanges bodily fluids with a Castro Street clone and then cackles vampirically as he reveals his fulminant lesions: 'I've got gay cancer . . . I'm going to die and so are you.'[49]

Such images of the 'gay killer' placed a heavy burden on the homosexual community. Many were too afraid to test for HIV status, fearing stigmatisation whatever the result of the test. They also feared the response of the legal system to any revelation that they were infected: could they be liable to prosecution if they engaged in sexual acts? Would they be quarantined, lose their jobs or have to pay exorbitant insurance fees?

As with cancer, the language of war was mobilised. In January 1987 the cover of *Scientific American* had the virus looking like a grenade, primed for detonation. Like the Greeks hidden inside the Trojan horse in ancient Greek myth, the virus was portrayed as hiding away inside a helper T-cell. In the words of an article in *Time* entitled 'Returning Fire Against AIDS', in June 1991, the virus was compared to Stealth fighter planes, possessing 'hidden parts that do not show up on the immune system's radar screen'.[50] Depicted in language that had been abandoned during the Cold War, the virus was a terrorist: a stealthy enemy, concealing itself in the body until ready to strike. Even worse, it was described as 'a terrorist's terrorist, an Abu Nidal of Viruses'.[51] The virus activated 'suicide programs' like suicide bombers.[52] Randy Shilt's *And the Band Played On*, 'gay cities' such as San Francisco were portrayed as battling 'against an encroaching viral invader' which 'bred international death', like a revolutionary enemy, and monstrous imagery abounded. Films such as *Alien* drew on fears of 'irregular sex' (the extraterrestrial monster entered the body of the astronaut by insemination through the mouth) and the disruption of gender norms (a monster was expelled from the astronaut's belly in a hideous parody of birth). Shilt described the virus thus: 'At any time, without any coherent reason, the virus could emerge from its victims' blood and violently seize their lives' — like an alien, violently bursting forth out of the flesh of its victim.[53]

As with cancer, fear of AIDS hindered prevention and treatment regimes. From the start the disease was politicised. After all, Ronald Reagan's conservative Republican administration was devoted to reducing the role of federal spending and had the support of the religious Right. The gay community was split between those seeking increased funding and those concerned with the more traditional goal of reducing government intervention in their lives. Funding of medical research was focused on chronic illnesses of the middle classes such as cancer, rather than acute diseases of marginalised groups. As with cancer in the 1950s, AIDS education was driven by fear. In 1988 the Health Education Authority's advert simply consisted of large white letters against a black background: 'What is the Difference between HIV and AIDS? Time', thus reminding HIV-positive individuals of their ultimate end. Morality tales dominated the scene. One American television advertisement included the story of an unfaithful husband who said, 'I was cheating [on my wife] . . . It's not worth it.' In Britain, the slogan 'AIDS: how big does it have to be before you take notice?' was shown among the frightening symbols of coffins, tombstones, icebergs, pneumatic drills and volcanoes. Culturally powerful images of blood and semen flowed to the graveyard.

However, there was something new about this fear: the so-called victims mobilised against it. AIDS activism was powerful, notably after the founding of ACT UP (AIDS Coalition to Unleash Power) in New York in 1987. They refused to act like Edna Kaehele, the cancer sufferer discussed at the beginning of this chapter, who suffered and fought her disease in secret. In contrast, AIDS activists explicitly substituted anger for fear — anger against stigmatisation, discrimination and the government's stingy funding initiatives. Their actions caused a revolution in the relationship between health professionals and patients. A more co-operative model became common, with patients claiming an interest in research.[54] The mysterious withholding of information about illnesses by physicians still occurred, but was increasingly condemned. And even cancer sufferers benefited. Cancer organisations run by cancer patients and their supporters learned from AIDS activism how better to fight in their own interest, and defy the fear of death by combining with their fellows.[55]

As Edna Kaehele and many HIV-positive individuals understood, the fear of pain was the most terrifying aspect of illness. According to a Mass Observation poll in 1942, the vast majority of people expressed no fear of death, but nearly a quarter of men and half of women were frightened of the act of dying and in particular the physical pain associated with dying. It was the point of 'transition from death to another state which is *the* unknown, the thing about which no-one seems to have formed any ideas at all'.[56] How much pain would be associated with this ripping from one life to the next? For seriously ill individuals, pain was the forbidden encounter.

From the 1930s this embargo on physical distress was one result of the shift of the act of dying from the private sphere of the home to the medical realm of hospital or hospice. While in the mid-nineteenth century fewer than one in ten deaths took place in hospitals, public lunatic asylums or workhouses, by the late 1960s over half of deaths occurred in hospitals. Within two decades this figure had reached 70 per cent of deaths.[57] This shift occurred in part because smaller families, an ageing population, the greater propensity of women to work outside the home and increased mobility of familial members reduced the resources necessary for the efficient management of a domestic death.[58]

However, one of the consequences of this shift was the more intensive use of effective painkillers for the dying patient. The establishment of the hospice movement vastly expanded this process of ensuring that the dying experienced no discomfort. In 1967 Dame Cicely Saunders had opened St Christopher's Hospice, the first hospice in London, dedicated to 'total care' of the terminally ill. From this date the hospice movement set out purposefully to improve the quality of life for the dying. The management of pain was its chief rationale. The fear and experience of pain among the terminally ill was regarded as a sign of medical incompetence.

This new outlook represented a major shift in the management of dying. As we saw in an earlier chapter, in the nineteenth century consciousness during the process of dying was regarded as having definite benefits. For instance, the book *Christian Care of the Dying and the Dead* (1878) berated 'men of the world' who were unable to look steadily at death and, when dying, required drugs so potent that they were 'launched into another life in a state of stupor or utter unconsciousness'. The Christian should be able to bear the torments of dying, secure in the knowledge that 'in the day of his decease he shall be blessed'.[59]

In contrast, by the mid-twentieth century fear of pain loomed larger than the fear of death's aftermath. As one prominent physician observed in the 1930s, some of his patients were 'continually crying out for relief by death'. Their pain was more terrorising than death. In his words, there were 'worse things than death, and one of those things is for a human being to be reduced below even animal existence by a vegetative state, just existing.'[60] Even in death, the 'quality of life' was more important than any advantages that might be achieved by purging the soul. Echoing these sentiments in 1941, a writer in *Nature* drew attention to people's fears of being 'tied for the rest of one's life to a broken and pain-engendering body.' He argued that people's 'increased sensibility to pain and disablement' was a peculiarly 'civilised' fear. It was

> a symptom of our demand for life at a higher level than which sufficed our ancestors, a level which is incompatible with disablement or prolonged pain. It is not life *tout court* that we want, but life which can be lived out to the full scope and limit of our faculties. If we cannot have life at this freedom and of this intensity — and we cannot if we are in continual and recurrent pain — many of us would sooner be without it altogether.[61]

The fact that the suffering patient often could not distinguish between fear and pain also made the management of both imperative. As Robert A. Senescu argued in 'The Development of Emotional Complications in the Patient with Cancer' (1963), it was more correct to talk about a 'pain and fear response', since the two were intimately associated:

> Pain is defined basically as a reaction to damage. Fear is the anticipation of pain and damage. The individual in pain may be regarded as always fearful in the sense that he anticipates more pain. It has

long been noted that complaints of pain vary greatly with the emotion or mood of the patient and further that there is no simple direct relation between pain and the extent of the damage or wound.[62]

Rather than sudden death, people were fearful about the excessive prolongation of life once all delight had been removed. From the mid-twentieth century it was the physician's duty to ensure that consciousness of dying was 'mercifully clouded' by chemical and other biological processes.[63] While past generations were more likely to fear death for its aftermath, in more recent times people were more likely to fret about the actual physical process of dying. The fear of death was no longer fear of judgement but 'fear of the infringement taking place upon our right to life, liberty, and the pursuit of happiness'.[64]

As a result, pain and the fear of pain in patients became evidence of shoddy management. Medical students at Harvard University in the 1930s were taught that if morphine did not give comfort, it meant either that it had not been administered in a way which would enable it to be circulated or too small a dose had been supplied. 'There is no limit to the amount that may be properly given,' their lecturer insisted.[65] Or, as a physician at St Joseph's Hospice in London with experience at over nine hundred deathbeds advised in the 1960s, between 30 and 40 per cent of patients at the hospice knew that they were dying and wanted to talk about it. The questions they invariably asked were: 'Shall I be in pain?' 'Will it be very long?' 'Will it be in my sleep?' Consequently, it was imperative that staff administered 'sufficient' doses of sedative, otherwise dying patients might lose confidence in the expertise of their attendants and suffer a terror all the more horrible for their sense of being abandoned.[66] In its twentieth-century medical guise, pain was to be avoided at all costs, irrespective of what happens after death. Emotion had to be stripped from the process of dying, leaving only physiological 'signs'. For the observers, death's sting was also removed as the terminally ill simply 'slipped away'.

Nevertheless, despite all the concern over achieving the 'easy death', physicians constantly observed that the fear of death faded as people grew older. A Mass Observation survey in 1942 asked fifty men and fifty women whether they feared death. Eighty-four per cent of the men and 72 per cent of the women said, 'Not at all.' Fearlessness rose with age.[67] For the very elderly who believed in an afterlife, death was merely an uncomfortable step from one life to another, while, irrespective of piety, death could be a welcome release for patients plagued with ill health.[68] In another survey, carried out in 1961 at the Whittington Hospital in London, 220 geriatric patients, with an average age of eighty, were interviewed and closely monitored by senior nursing staff. In a subsequent report on the findings in the *Lancet*, Dr A. N. Exton-Smith stated that the vast majority of these patients accepted death with resignation but without fear. Only 3 per cent felt anxious. Furthermore, in most cases, death was quick and easy: 40 per cent of patients were unconscious for three hours or more before they died and a further 15 per cent died suddenly. Exton-Smith annotated his research with comments on the naturalness of death at old age. Pain was rarely a problem. Defining pain as any kind of suffering that did not respond to aspirin, he found 'the poverty of constitutional reactions to infection and injury' to be 'remarkable'. In other words, as patients approached physiological death, pain became blunted. Their bodies' 'need for the warning normally conveyed by symptoms' was 'no longer needed', so they were able to bear afflictions which would have caused agonising pain in younger people.[69] If there was one emotion that prevailed at death, it was sadness rather than fear.[70] If spared pain and the fear of pain, people slipped into death easefully.[71]

However, innovations in scientific procedures complicated debates about how to improve the dying person's 'quality of life'. The debates examined in Chapter One about identifying death by observing failures of the circulatory, respiratory and nervous systems suddenly seemed archaic. Organ transplant, life-support systems, intravenous nutrition, dialysis, and resuscitation techniques not only prolonged the act of dying, but also introduced uncertainty about its completion.

Although it took a decade to gain widespread approval, the description of 'brain death' was a dramatic event in the diagnosis of death when it was first applied in 1959. In America political sanction for the brain death diagnosis came in 1968 with the publication of the report of the Ad Hoc Committee of the Harvard Medical School to Examine the Definition of Brain Death, which proposed making whole brain death the criterion for pronouncing a person dead.[72] According to this definition, an individual was declared dead if they lacked spontaneous muscular movements, respiration and reflexes. In addition, an isoelectric EEG had to show a flat response and the individual had to be unreceptive to externally applied stimuli. The President's Commission for the Study of Ethical Problems in Medicine and Biomedical and Behavioral Research in 1981 further refined the American definition of brain death by including states of deep coma combined with an absence of brainstem reflexes.

In Britain the Conference of Medical Royal Colleges and their Faculties in the United Kingdom (1976) also coupled brain death with the death of the person. In its words: 'permanent functional death of the brain stem constitutes brain death and . . . once this has occurred further artificial support is fruitless and should be withdrawn. It is good medical practice to recognise when brain death has occurred and to act accordingly, sparing relatives from the further emotional trauma of sterile hope.'[73] This shift in the definition of death was not a response to conceptual uncertainties. Instead, changing technologies, in particular the development of transplant surgery, had created an immense demand for 'fresh' donor organs that could only be met by the invention of 'brain death'. In addition, once the first human heart transplant had been successfully performed, in early December 1967, the heart was no longer identical to the 'person' — since it could be 'bypassed'. The only organ that was essential to life was the brain.

Henceforth surgeons could legitimise the removal of organs from bodies when the heart was still beating. The idea of 'beating-heart cadavers' or 'ventilated corpses' brought to the fore earlier anxieties regarding death. In other words, in the late twentieth century the fear of being wrongly assumed to be alive (denied the opportunity to 'die with dignity') was augmented by the possibility of being wrongly declared dead (resulting in premature burial).[74] As one concerned commentator observed in 1969, 'many souls who were consigned to the graveyard *properly* in the past 'may have been only in the state of clinical death by the most advanced standards today. Viewed in this way, it is not inconceivable that the reported numbers of premature burials was an *underestimation* (and perhaps still is).'[75] As we saw in Chapter One, late-nineteenth-century scares about premature burial and dissection had been dampened by the assurances of newly professionalised physicians. From the 1960s confidence in that profession was crumbling fast. In part this was a result of the more diffuse distrust of authority which characterised these years. The environmentalism and anti-militarism of the Vietnam War era spawned doubts about authorities in general.

In particular, physicians were accused of possessing a fragmented, unsympathetic approach to their patients. Were they at risk of regarding their patients' bodies as 'containers of biologically useful material'? The commercial demand for human organs, driven by the success of transplant surgery, caused concerns about whether the brain death definition was paving the way to euthanasia, vivisection and even manslaughter.[76] There was a revival of nineteenth-century suspicions of 'body snatchers'. In the words of an unnamed public health official, quoted in *Newsweek* in 1967: 'I have a horrible vision of ghouls hovering over an accident victim with long knives unsheathed, waiting to take out his organs.'[77] Indeed, one study warned that America's Uniform Anatomical Gift Act and related statutes enabled relatives and even municipalities to 'harvest' an individual's organs after 'death' as long as there was not clear evidence of refusal before the individual's supposed demise.[78]

In no group was the fear of organ snatching more pronounced than in America's black community. An editorial in *Ebony* in March 1968 openly referred to alarm in these circles that white doctors were experimenting on black patients. Organ transplantation was deeply unpopular among many black Americans because they feared that any such gift from a black American would encourage physicians to 'hurry the death in order to complete a transplant', especially if the recipient was white.[79] Scientists and physicians were increasingly reviled in popular culture. For instance, in the 1960s, eleven feature films were released portraying the illegal harvesting of human organs, while other films blurred the line between the dead and the living, leading to a cinematic epidemic of Frankenstein's monsters, mummies and zombies.[80]

Even within medical circles there were anxieties about the new definitions of death. Physicians and surgeons remained divided, with some calling for a return to a 'systems orientated view of death', based on the failure of circulatory, respiratory and nervous systems, while others urged the profession to adopt a more radical definition of death. 'Cognitive death', or the loss of personal identity or 'higher brain' facilities, begged the question of which higher functions had to be 'lost' before a person with a beating heart was considered dead. Whatever the approach, it was frequently observed that medical professionals involved in transplants used language which suggested that they did not really believe that potential 'organ donors' were dead. For instance, when health professionals asked families for permission to harvest the organs of a brain-dead person, they often used phrases such as: 'There is nothing more that we can do — we're just keeping him alive so you can consider organ donation.'[81] It was also observed that sometimes when a brain-dead individual was cut open in order to remove organs, the heartbeat quickened and the blood pressure soared, casting doubt on the belief that the brain was really 'dead'.[82] Perhaps nowhere was the spectre of the 'mad doctor' more explicit than in Jack Kevorkian's Prescription: Medicide (1991), in which he argued the case for voluntary euthanasia while simultaneously launching a bitter attack on organ transplants. He castigated physicians for 'arbitrarily' deciding when to 'harvest' organs. They 'compound the infringement by neglecting to use anesthesia during the removal of organs from brain-dead patients, thereby subjecting them to the unknown and unknowable risk of potentially excruciating and absolutely undetectable pain'.[83] According to Kevorkian, people had the right to choose the time, means and nature of their own death, but organ harvesting by physicians was 'medicide'.

Finally, another aspect of death anxiety was linked with fears about the dehumanisation of the dying process. In the words of the author of The Gods of Life (1994):

The classic deathbed scene, with its loving partings and solemn last words, is now part of history. In its place is a drugged, unconscious patient full of tubes for breathing, eating, and elimination, a sub-human object for manipulation by the medical technicians. Who can remain unhorrified hearing a doctor on a terminal ward remark that he must 'go water the vegetables'?[84]

Except for the 10 per cent of deaths which were unexpected (through accidents, suicide or murder), death was prolonged in a way not experienced in earlier decades. Deathly fears had gone a full circle. In the nineteenth century people fretted over the accuracy of medical definitions of the 'signs of life' and were frightened of being cleaved and quartered after death on the dissection table. In the late twentieth century people found themselves equally denied access to the deathbed, but when they turned to physicians to depict and decipher acts of dying, they confronted uncertainty and callousness, and suspected sadism. Not only was the soul absent from deathbed considerations, the body itself was hooked to a machine that took precedence over the free will of the dying person. Whether the patient was suffering from cancer, AIDS or any of the many ailments of modernity, the technologically prolonged death was a frightful proposition.

In Chapter One we saw that fears associated with death were primarily concerned with uncertainties surrounding the individual's societal and everlasting status. By the end of the twentieth century death anxieties were firmly located in bodily experiences. The explosion in anti-ageing creams, exercise regimes and cosmetic surgery was a response to the fear of dying. Once at death's portal, pain was the dreaded encounter that had to be avoided through the application of increasingly powerful analgesics. The question of 'how many' painkillers were needed to eradicate physical suffering slid into panicky debates about the death-dealing powers of physicians such as Dr Harold Shipman, who 'played God' with such poise. Death might have been noisily embedded in films, newspapers and PlayStation games, yet was strangely silent when it came to addressing individual vulnerability. The issue became: have *they* removed pain; have *I* been respectable?

Fears of the body's vulnerability were exacerbated by the fact that repeated and often contradictory scientific reports increasingly made the threats to individual vigour seem free-floating. Cancer lurked everywhere in the environment. Taking responsibility for modern forms of sin (such as smoking or drinking excessively) became increasingly confusing, making it difficult for people to evaluate their risk. The medicalisation of death finally stripped the Beyond of both heaven and hell, leaving dying people with little to ward off their fears of annihilation. Even their death took place in 'bits': death was no longer a unitary, transcendent phenomenon but a 'syndrome' that could be measured, weighed and packaged in what seemed like innumerable ways.

The media's obsession with death only intensified uncertainties. Despite a vast expansion in communication networks, which enabled people to watch and hear the death throes of vastly more people than ever before, reactions to death were remarkably cool. War, famine, pestilence and violence figured routinely in the mass media, but responses to this suffering elicited emotions such as horror, pity, indifference, but rarely fear. The only exception was when death threatened ourselves — thus fear might have prevented a tourist from visiting Haiti, but this was not fear *for* the dying masses in Haiti but fear *of* them. Greater exposure to mass dying made us less afraid of the death of others and more able to view that death 'objectively', without grief or other emotion.

CHAPTER ELEVEN

Strangers

Too soon we embrace that
Impermanent appetitive flux,
Humorous and hard, which adults fear
Is real and right, the irreverent place,
The clown's cosmos.

AUDEN, 'THE AGE OF ANXIETY'

In Boston, Massachusetts, on 11 October 1985, Nancy Venables Raine was raped. In the minute that it took to deposit her rubbish in the outside bins, a violent stranger crept into her home. A few minutes later he had her blindfolded and 'trussed like a chicken' on the bed. She never saw her assailant. In her words, henceforth she 'lived with sudden fear the way others live with cancer. The fear was always there, in warrens just below the surface, waiting.' There seemed to be no meaning to the rape. Why was she chosen? Why didn't the rapist kill her as he threatened to do? Who was he and would he return? What rite or public ceremony could she utilise to defy the trauma? Her struggle to find some language to contain the terror of those few hours culminated in her memoir *After Silence* (1999).

Raine's rape was harrowing. Realising that her rapist was 'feasting on' her fear, she forced a 'strange calmness' to envelop her terror. 'In the initial moments of the attack, when my terror was uncontrollable,' she observed, the rapist 'gained strength.' Raine likened her emotional detachment during her ordeal to that described by the explorer David Livingstone when he was seized by a lion in Africa. Livingstone had described how the lion growled 'horribly close to my ear'. It

> shook me as a terrier dog does a rat. The shock produced a stupor similar to that which seems to be felt by a mouse after the first shake of a cat. It caused a sort of dreaminess, in which there was no sense of pain nor feeling of terror, though [I was] quite conscious of all that was happening . . . This singular condition was not the result of any mental process. The shake annihilated fear, and allowed no sense of horror in looking round at the beast. This peculiar state is probably produced in all animals killed by the carnivora [sic]; and, if so, is a merciful provision by our benevolent Creator for lessening the pain of death.[1]

But, as Raine admitted, the benevolent Creator was nowhere to be found on 11 October. The moment her rapist departed, terror overwhelmed her. Although she had the presence of mind to call the police, and coped with the subsequent examinations and interrogations, her world seemed to have turned into a nightmare, dominated by an 'incubus who attacked in the light of day'. Solitude became a torment.

In distress, she turned to the psychological and psychiatric sciences for guidance. Her responses were contradictory, however. At one stage in her memoir she correctly observed that:

> The human response to overwhelming life experience is viewed by modern medicine as an anxiety disorder, an illness of the mind. Because I do not like to think that the man who raped me infected me with a mental illness, I resist calling the effects of overwhelming terror an illness. I claim my sanity, and view my response as human, even appropriate and dignified.

Yet Raine *did* turn to a smorgasbord of psychological theory. She embraced psychotherapy and psychiatric constructions of her emotional pain as post-traumatic stress disorder (PTSD), as defined in the third edition of the American Psychiatric Association's *Diagnostic and Statistical Manual of Mental Disorders* (1980). She even undertook Francine Shapiro's Eye Movement Desensitisation and Reprocessing (EMDR) therapy. This was a form of desensitisation to extreme fear states, involving repetitive eye movements resembling those found in the REM stage of sleep, which, as we saw in Chapter Four, is the stage when dreams and nightmares occur. Raine also approved of scientific studies which claimed that terror ('even a single instance of it') physically altered the brain ('forever'). There was 'a terrorist inside my brain', she wrote, and 'the terrorist in my head was probably biological'. In observing her inability to sit with her back to any door, Raine endorsed Daniel Goleman's argument in *Emotional Intelligence* (1995) that, after severe emotional trauma, the locus ceruleus (a structure located in the brainstem) would begin secreting copious quantities of adrenalin and noradrenalin whenever it perceived situations resembling the original trauma. There was no escaping it: Raine became 'obsessed with the possibility that he might strike again, and at any moment' — and, of course 'he' did strike, 'again and again', in her feverish imagination.

It was two and a half years after the rape before Raine regained 'emotional health'. Symbolically, however, the decisive moment of healing occurred in 1993 when she showed a painting entitled *Raped and Trussed* at an exhibition in Santa Cruz, California. The work depicted a chicken carcass lying on a bed, with a green monster's head protruding from beneath. At the side of the painting she had scribbled the 'terrible words' spoken by her rapist. At the exhibition she mused about how

> It's so strange . . . to see people looking at my worst nightmare, but it's even stranger to realize that I'm standing here looking at other people looking at my worst nightmare. It changes the nightmare . . . It doesn't frighten me anymore.

The stranger had been banished from her life, along with the 'self' who had been trussed like a chicken and raped on 11 October 1985.[2]

Nancy Raine's ordeal did not end when the rapist crept out of her home. As for millions of women in Britain and America, fear of rape was woven into the everyday fabric of her life. It was an ambient fear, a low-level but constant unease, present in public spaces (especially at night) even though, as Raine discovered, women might be vulnerable to attack in daylight and within their own homes. The author of *The Demon Lover. The Sexuality of Terrorism* (1989) grasped the terror of many women, hearing footsteps behind them when walking along dark, deserted streets. They were 'a Man's footsteps. She knows this immediately, just as she knows she must not look round. She quickens her pace in time to the quickening of her pulse. She is afraid. He could be a rapist. He could be a soldier, a harasser, a robber, a killer.' But he also 'could be none of those. He could be a man in a hurry. He could be a man walking at his normal pace. But she fears him. She fears him because he is a man. She has reason to fear.'[3] In many periods of history women have been frightened of public streets (witness the dread experienced by working-class women during the Jack the Ripper murders), but it was a discourse of fear that proliferated in the late twentieth century. After all, although women have been raped and murdered throughout previous centuries, the *fear* of rape did not generate a discourse of terror among feminists of earlier periods. Child prostitution and the threat of venereal disease animated debate, but not the threat of rape or adult sexual assault.[4] It was only from the 1970s that feminist activists identified women's dread of sexual assault as *the* central fear of women. They were driven by a political agenda involving a passionate critique of Western patriarchal society.

At the Rape Conference of the New York Radical Feminists in 1971, Florence Rush argued that sexual anxieties were pervasive among girls and women 'because it is an unspoken but prominent factor in socializing and preparing the female to accept a subordinate role: to feel guilty, ashamed, and to tolerate through fear, the power exerted over her by men'.[5] Or, in the words of Susan Brownmiller in her influential polemic *Against Our Will* (1975), early man's

> discovery that his genitalia could serve as a weapon to generate fear must rank as one of the most important discoveries of prehistoric

times, along with the use of fire and the first crude stone axe. From prehistoric times to the present, I believe rape has played a critical function. It is nothing more or less than a conscious process of intimidation by which *all* men keep *all* women in a state of fear.[6]

This was clearly nonsense. Brownmiller's ahistorical, essentialist account emphasising the biological nature of 'all men' and 'all women' ignored the complexity of culture and ideology. As we have seen throughout this book, fear 'bunched' people in ways different to those predicted by gender relations according to feminists (or, for that matter, class relations according to Marxists).

Women were not the only group for whom a panic evolved concerning their risk of sexual violation: the endangered purity of children also generated a moral panic. Fears associated with child mortality might have been in free fall since the late nineteenth century, but anxiety about sexual harm multiplied. In the nineteenth century, for instance, there were numerous panics about the abuse of children, most notably concerning the ruinous effects of corporal punishment and the scares that followed W. T. Stead's exposé of juvenile prostitution in the *Pall Mall Gazette* in 1885.[7] But a century later the emphasis on prostitution and corporal punishment gave way to more pervasive fears about the 'everyday' sexual abuse of the young.[8]

Some indication of the panic over child sexual abuse can be seen in the wildly divergent statistics concerning the extent of the problem. For instance, in England and Wales at the start of the twenty-first century, statistics on the number of victims ranged from 3500 annually to 72,600, fuelling fears that the crime was out of control.[9] The American Humane Association claimed that in the USA there were between 2000 and 4300 cases of child sexual abuse in 1976 and 1977, while another survey alleged that (in 1979) the figure was an incredible 44,700.[10] Still other reports inflated the numbers to 210,000 new cases each year — implying that 10 per cent of American women and 2 per cent of American men had been sexually abused.[11] In 1977 the topic even merited its own specialist journal, entitled *Child Abuse and Neglect*, and in the 1980s popular films and television programmes joined the frenzy. The Emmy-nominated *Fallen Angel* (1981), as well as *Something About Amelia* (1984), *Nightmare on Elm Street* (1984), *When a Bough Breaks* (1986) and *A Child's Cry* (1986) brought anxieties about child abuse to a wider public.

In 1990 the *New York Times* reported that a panel of childcare experts appointed by the government had concluded that 'child abuse and neglect in the United States now represents a national emergency'.[12] Feminists, religious groups, social workers, psychiatrists, lawyers and journalists all had an interest in propagating frightening tales of paedophilia. This was especially the case in periods when it was politically expedient to portray 'the family' as threatened. In the 1920s and again in the 1960s, when there was a relatively high tolerance of sexual experimentation, fear about sexual abuse was low. In contrast, when the sexual revolution was 'in retreat' during the 1980s, fears surged.[13] It is no wonder that the mass media designated child abuse an 'epidemic'.[14]

Technological innovations stoked these fears by 'unveiling' ever more cases of child abuse. For instance, from the 1940s paediatric radiology led to the 'rediscovery' of child abuse as physicians increasingly attributed physical malformations in infants to physical abuse as opposed to somatic afflictions such as rickets.[15] Similarly, sexual child abuse received a major boost after 1986 when the *Lancet* published research suggesting that anal rape could be detected through reflex anal dilatation (RAD). Using this technique (which involved parting the buttocks and observing the anus for half a minute to see whether or not it dilated), in conjunction with other signs, in July 1987 Dr Marietta Higgs and Dr Geoffrey Wyatt of Middlesbrough General Hospital in Cleveland, England, diagnosed 121 children as victims of sexual abuse. They had the children and their siblings, who were feared to be 'at risk', forcibly removed into 'care'. The hysteria over the accusations sparked a major panic which made parents afraid of taking their children to a hospital or clinic in case the children were taken away. Although much scientific evidence refuted the significance of RAD in indicating abuse (noting that constipated children with faeces sitting high in the bowel might show such signs, as well as the fact that anal fissures could be seen in non-abused children),[16] and the Cleveland Inquiry into the incident found that most of the allegations were unfounded, the panic over abuse was perpetuated by authors unwilling to accept that Cleveland in the 1980s had not been a hotbed of sexual child abuse.[17]

Whether represented as a pathetic specimen of a man (1950s), sex fiend (1970s) or serial paedophile (1980s), the shadowy figure of the child abuser was portrayed as unstoppable, incapable of treatment and worthy only of prison. Even worse, from the 1980s the paedophile-murderer was less likely to be regarded as a monster outside of society — he was now the father, neighbour, teacher or politician. In other words, the fear became diffuse, focusing on the child's intimate caretakers. The very 'ordinariness' of the child abuse, coupled with anxiety about possible complicity in abuse as reflected in the worship of youth in popular culture, rendered the fear even more intense. As Marina Warner has put it, the desires of paedophiles enacted

> some ghastly masquerade of the way so much of the rest of society also 'loves children': by stimulating their desires, by exploiting their vulnerability and suggestibility, by finding them irresistibly cute, by staging, in any number of advertisements, films and infant beauty pageants, the performance of their seduction.[18]

The last bastion of purity in a 'world of overtly sexualised consumer products' had been corrupted.[19] In the words of Georges Vigarello in *A History of Rape* (2001):

> The consequence of the crime is no longer immortality but psychic death; it is no longer a question of debauchery but of the shattering of identity, an incurable wound to which the victim seems doomed. This gives a quite new importance to child rape. Sexual violence becomes the worst violence of all, a crime all the more atrocious in that its victim is a creature projected as an ideal of purity, a potentiality all the more absolute in that the traditional image of fathers and of authority has lost its potency.[20]

As a result of this moral panic children were increasingly constrained and policed. In 1971 80 per cent of children aged between
seven and eight went to school on their own, whereas by 1990 only
9 per cent did so. Increased car ownership was clearly part of the
explanation for this shift, but it was also strongly influenced by new
fears about risks facing children in the modern world.[21] The threat
was not limited to the public arena: restrictions on children's exploration even occurred in the home. As children rapidly became more
computer-literate than their parents, cyberspace was increasingly
feared to be the paedophile's first port of call. Neither children nor
parents had a way of visually testing the identity of the sender, who
was suspected of posing as a child. Even the words 'net' and 'web'
sparked fears of the entrapment of young children.[22] 'Blocking' programmes and even secret programmes allowing parents to spy on
their children's emails were effectively marketed alongside other
'Children Safety Products and Services', including hidden video cam-
eras, personal alarm systems that could be attached to children to
register movements, 'Know Your Nanny' surveillance systems and
transmitters 'to monitor child to help prevent child abduction'.[23]

Fears for children's safety were only part of the story. After all,
there was also a proliferation of discourses concerning the fear *of*
children. Again, this was not a modern invention. During earlier
scares associated with child abuse, the child could also be
demonised. During the 1885 scare in England over child prostitution, a lawyer defending his client against accusations of having sex
with a 'precocious' girl maintained that 'there would soon have to be
a society for the protection of men and boys, and not of women and
girls'.[24] In the later twentieth century children were demonised to
a much greater degree; they were potentially murderous. Horror
films such as *The Exorcist* (1973), *The Omen* (1976) and *Carrie* (1976)
portrayed demonic children. 'Real-life' reportage warned about
more everyday manifestations of danger. For instance, in 1993 the
New York Times reported the results of a survey of children in grades
six to twelve, revealing that 9 per cent had fired a shot at someone
at some time. Eleven per cent had been shot.[25] The same year
British parents experienced a crisis when two ten-year-old children,
Jon Venables and Robert Thompson, killed the toddler James

Bulger. Sections of the media suggested that the two boys had been influenced by the horror movie *Child's Play 3* (1992), which Jon Venables's father had recently rented. However, Jon had not been living with him at the time and denied having seen the film, 'claiming that he did not like horror films'. Nevertheless, the case stimulated a moral panic over violent videos and films.

The title of *Child's Play 3* was scary in itself — drawing attention, as it did, to the ambivalence of children's play that led to Bulger's murder. The face of the demonic doll Chucky, the star of the film, was plastered on the cover of the *Daily Mirror* and *Sun* newspapers. On 26 November 1993 *The Times* warned that:

a whole generation of children are growing up in a culture saturated by images of gratuitous cruelty and bestial violence . . . There is now a widespread addiction to viewing monstrous horror — often misogynistic and sexually degrading — which is presented so naturalistically that, to the impressionable, it has become part of the furniture of reality.

Interestingly, though, this editorial singled out children from 'corners of Britain remote from the drawing rooms where "freedom of expression" is so uncritically defended'.[26] In other words, the children to fear were from deprived backgrounds. Two days later, however, the *Sunday Times* was more democratic about it: we will 'never be able to look at our children in the same way again . . . All over the country, parents are viewing their sons in a new and disturbing light,' it announced despairingly.[27]

These fears relating to violence and abuse have often been called 'moral panics', as originally conceived by Stanley Cohen in his *Folk Devils and Moral Panics* (1972).[28] In a moral panic a substantial group of people become frightened and hostile; their mood is volatile and there is a severe disproportion between the nature of the threat and the degree of fear that 'sober empirical evaluation' would warrant. 'Expert opinion' and media copy often emphasise the novelty of the threat and the dramatic speed with which it develops.[29]

Whether linked to children (in the form of child abuse and child abusers) or to adults (in the form of anxieties about violent crime), fear of violence was, from the late 1960s, a classic example of a moral panic. There had been similar moral panics before this time. In the middle decades of the nineteenth century, for instance, there were periodic flurries of fear relating to street violence, culminating most notably in Britain's garrotting panic of 1862. Although the crime rate was low by the standards of the late twentieth century (in 1862, the robbery rate was three per 100,000 in England and Wales, compared with forty-six in the 1980s),[30] it was a very real moral panic, spurred on by memories of the French Revolution as well as 'home-grown' violence related to Chartism, the development of 'yellow journalism' from the 1850s and the mass-membership trade unions of the late nineteenth century.

However, moral panics over crime were very different in the nineteenth century from those of the late twentieth century. From the late-1960s the pervert, mugger and hooligan replaced the robber or 'garrotter'.[31] In 1968, when a Gallup poll asked Americans to identify 'the most important problem facing the country today', 'crime and lawlessness' was given second place.[32] Anxieties increased in the 1980s and 1990s. A national sample of Americans in 1989 placed crime as the most serious problem facing their neighbourhoods (it was listed above unemployment and problems with childcare or education) and within five years crime had replaced the economy as Americans' foremost concern.[33] It was also a rising panic. Between 1989 and 1994 the percentage of Americans who said they were 'truly desperate' about crime almost doubled, from 34 per cent to 62 per cent.[34]

Most worryingly, the panic over crime was particularly high among the elderly, many of whom believed that their neighbours would not even bother to call the police if they witnessed the respondent's home being burgled.[35] A couple of local studies in the late 1970s revealed that 85 per cent of elderly people were afraid to go out at night or to use public transport,[36] while even in daytime 90 per cent would change their direction of travel or cross the street just to avoid teenagers.[37] These fears, combined with declining visual and auditory acuity, meant that many elderly people became profoundly suspicious, often becoming virtual prisoners in their own homes, where viewing violent television dramas intensified their alarm.

In Britain as well, crime incited profound anxieties. The 1983 British Crime Survey found that one in three respondents felt 'fairly unsafe' or 'very unsafe'. What was particularly striking about this survey was the gender difference in fear: nearly half of the women questioned admitted that they felt unsafe, compared with only 13 per cent of men.[38] Rape was singled out as a particularly virulent threat. Nearly a third of all women, and 41 per cent of women under the age of thirty, claimed to be *most* afraid of rape, and half of all women said they avoided going out unaccompanied at night.[39] Rape was not only feared for its physical pain, but also because it was polluting. Rape victims like Nancy Raine, discussed at the beginning of this chapter, were apprehensive about the reactions of other people to their rape. Collecting evidence of the rape was humiliating; being questioned about their sexual history embarrassing. Would the police find evidence of *sufficient* resistance? If the signs of consent or lack of consent were presumed to be written on the body, when was 'enough'? And would the rapist have to be faced in court?

For raped women, these anxieties were legitimate, but the moral panic over fear of violence (whether defined sexually or more broadly) was not in proportion with actual risk. An America survey in the late 1970s found that over half of women were afraid of being raped, a proportion nine hundred times higher than the percentage of women raped. Seventeen per cent of respondents were afraid of being murdered, yet only one in ten thousand persons would suffer this end.[40] Fear of crime did not reflect the risk of becoming a victim. After all, women and the elderly were most fearful, yet the risk of being attacked was higher for males and younger persons.[41] Trepidation about likely attackers was also skewed. Strangers, for instance, were regarded as posing the greatest threat, even though only 12 per cent of murders and a third of rape cases involved people who were strangers to each other.[42] This was what terrified a junior college student known simply as Sandra. In the 1990s she described her 'biggest fear' as being 'randomly taken away', and her

body to be found in a forest or in a ditch, you know, and have my family saying: 'I thought she just went to the store, but she never returned'. You know . . . That is really scary. I mean, the very thought that any time I am walking anywhere, and some lunatic can take control of you and kill you and end your life like that. And, many times they rape and torture you before killing you . . . that is the worst.

When asked 'How likely do you think that an incident like that can happen to you?' Sandra replied, 'I really do not know, but *it seems very real to me*.'[43] Her sense of powerlessness was stoked by media report-ing which consistently portrayed women as vulnerable in public places. As the authors of *The Female Fear* (1989) discovered, victim-isation surveys revealed that for every four sexual attacks on women, three women got away while only one rape was completed, yet in newspapers, for every fourteen reports about rape, thirteen were about completed rapes while only one woman was reported to have foiled the attack. Such reporting conveyed the impression that it was inevitable that an attempted rapist would prevail over his victim.[44]

The chief casualty of the moral panic over criminal violence was trust. Fear of sexual attack dramatically altered women's everyday relationships with male acquaintances and strangers. A survey in the early 1990s found that nearly 70 per cent of women believed that 'all kinds of men, many of them normal and respectable in other ways, are rapists'.[45] In the words of one Londoner in 1985:

You never know whether to trust people or not. I was at a CND meeting a few weeks ago and this man offered me a lift home. It was pouring with rain, and he gave me a lift home and behaved perfectly properly. That's the trouble — all the time you're dependent on their willingness not to do anything to you. It's like when you're walking home alone. I go to a lot of meetings, and you're coming home about tenish or later, and you're walking along a fairly quiet road and you see this man walking towards you . . . you're depend-ent on their good will not to do anything to you . . . It's this thing of trusting, you've either got to trust everybody or trust nobody, because how can you tell? They don't walk around with 'sex offender' written on their forehead. They're just like ordinary people.[46]

This Londoner did not let her fear of sexual predators unnerve her about protesting against her greater fear of nuclear holocaust. For other women, fear of rape was more debilitating. In the words of a seventeen-year-old Latina speaking in the late 1990s:

> I don't do many things that I would like to do. OK. That's true. But I know that when my boyfriend does not let me out after dark it is because he cares about me and he wants to protect me. He is a man and he knows the streets better than I. There is a shitty world out there! Women are molested all the time. I am not going to go out at night just to show how tough I am.[47]

These were not unusual responses to perceptions of danger in the streets. In 1965 and 1972 Gallup polls found that between 50 and 60 per cent of women were afraid to walk alone at night on streets near their own home. Less than a fifth of men admitted to such timidity.[48] A survey of crime in selected American cities in the late 1990s revealed that over half of women changed their behaviour because of fear of crime, compared with less than a third of men.[49] Fear constrained people's lives. The important factor about these constraining behaviours, however, is that instead of reducing fear of crime, they constantly reminded people of their vulnerability. Constraining and cautious behaviour actually increased fear.[50]

It also provided an excuse to communicate less easily expressed fears. Fear of crime often emerged out of uneasiness about 'change' in general. For instance, in the 1930s, in post-reconstruction America, fear of black male rapists arose out of white American insecurities about national unity, black emancipation, shifting gender roles and labour unrest. In the words of one historian:

> As Southern whites grappled with the reality that they were no longer masters, while their Northern counterparts watched fearfully a steady migration of newly freed blacks to cities above the Mason-Dixon line, many white Americans perceived themselves as a race patently under siege.

The result was moral panics about black rapists, which led to the lynching of between three thousand and ten thousand black men in Louisiana, Mississippi, North Carolina, New Orleans, Atlanta, East St Louis, and Chicago.[51] Decades later, in the 1960s and 1970s, fear of crime arising out of the race riots also masked fears of racial integration, which were much more difficult to discuss publicly.[52] It was not surprising to find that a study of residents in Baltimore in the early 1970s revealed that fear of crime was highest among whites most antagonistic to racial reform (42 per cent of whom were afraid of crime in their neighbourhood) and lowest among the strongest supporters of racial equality (only 13 per cent were afraid of crime in their area).[53]

Racially orientated fears were not only held by white Americans. For instance, an investigation of fear of crime among women in New York in the 1990s found that the strongly racialised image of criminals was shared by nearly all respondents, regardless of ethnic or socio-economic background. A typical response was that of Gladys, a dark-skinned Latina who admitted that she was 'afraid of Black and Hispanic people and they are my people'. Or, as Meredith, an African American woman, whispered nervously, 'I feel ashamed by saying this, but the image that comes to my mind when I think about criminals is that of a brother.'[54] Moral panics over crime were not merely (indeed, rarely) a fear of victimisation, but masked other fears about inner-city degeneration and anxiety about change more generally.

Throughout the century fear of crime was used to legitimise increased surveillance over subordinate groups — a response suggested by the joke: 'A liberal is someone who has not yet been mugged.' But in the late twentieth century there was a change in the nature of this surveillance: modern panics over crime expressed doubt about the ability of the government and justice systems to regulate behaviour. 'New prudentialism' represented a different way of distributing risks, with individuals, households and communities taking responsibility for uncertainty within their own lives.[55]

By 1985 the term 'surveillance society' had punctured the earlier optimism of the 'information society'. Crime was made part of everyday routine. In the words of the criminologist David Garland:

In contrast to earlier criminologies, which began from the premise that crime was a deviation from normal civilized conduct, and was explicable in terms of individual pathology or else faulty socialization, the new criminologies of everyday life see crime as continuous with normal social interaction and explicable by reference to standard motivational patterns. Crime becomes a risk to be calculated (both by the offender and by the potential victim) or an accident to be avoided . . . rather than a moral aberration which needs to be specially explained.[56]

From the policing of potential criminals, the emphasis shifted to considerations about the responsibilities of victims. According to this view, it was difficult to avoid the conclusion that certain victims of crime 'deserved it'. Now victims were expected to change their habits in order to reduce their exposure to crimes. 'Gated communities' and street surveillance became popular. Property-marking devices, safes, security glass, credit cards, patrols, supervised parking areas, closed-circuit television and more effective car locking systems became essential to modern life. As a consequence, since the 1970s, Category 6A of the Standard Occupational Classification — that is, 'protective service occupations' — has become one of the fastest-growing sectors of the American economy and the use of private security increased from a $3.3-billion business in 1969 to one worth $52 billion in 1991.[57] The market in CCTV doubled between 1983 and 1987, and in the 1990s was expanding at 40 per cent per annum.[58]

In Britain, Neighbourhood Watch, a neighbourhood-based surveillance organisation established in 1982, involved over eighty thousand schemes by the end of the 1980s.[59] According to the International Professional Security Association, in the late 1980s there were twenty thousand security firms in Britain. In the late 1950s the industry's sales were worth less than £5 million per annum: by the 1970s the figure was £55 million. The British Security Industries Association (which accounted for 90 per cent of the industry's business) claimed that, among its non-manufacturing members, turnover had increased to around £120 million in 1976. By 1987 it was over £800 million.[60] 'Victimisation prevention', in contrast to crime prevention, stigmatised the victims of crime, who had to take precautions to ensure that they could not be accused of 'deserving it' through having not taken adequate precautions.

Nevertheless, the ability of individuals or groups to adopt such technologies of safety were highly stratified, and depended on perceptions of powerfulness and powerlessness. In working-class neighbourhoods fear of crime did not generally lead residents to group together since there was little (if any) sense that they could protect themselves by changing either local or national crime policy, let alone effect a redistribution of resources. 'New prudentialism' was a class-based response to fears facing modern individuals.

The fear of crime was not the most potent fear dogging late-twentieth-century societies. There was another category of danger that frightened many Britons and Americans as the century staggered to its conclusion: ecological degradation. In 1991 a Gallup poll revealed that more than 80 per cent of American adults were anxious about the effects of air and water pollution, as well as the loss of wildlife habitat. Acid rain, nuclear waste, global warming and the loss of tropical rain forests disturbed more than 60 per cent of respondents.[61] Video surveillance and electronic tagging could not control these hazards. In the words of Murray Bookchin in *Remaking Society* (1990):

> We live under the constant threat that the world of life will be irrevocably undermined by a society gone mad in its need to grow — replacing the organic by the inorganic, soil by concrete, forest by barren earth, and the diversity of life-forms by simplified ecosystems; in short a turning back of the evolutionary clock to an earlier, more inorganic, mineralized world that was incapable of supporting complex life-forms of any kind, including the human species.[62]

Bookchin's apocalyptic comments were made in the last decade of the twentieth century, but ecological fears really burgeoned from the middle of that century, when widespread and indiscriminate spraying of pesticides began to generate concern. The fact that no one quite knew what effect insecticides would have on the ecology led many people to advise caution. As an article in *Reader's Digest* put it in 1959, if pest-eradication programmes continued to be carried out 'we shall have been witnesses, within a single decade, to a greater extermination of animal life than in all the previous years of man's history on earth . . . This may be a wildly pessimistic view. Nobody knows. But why risk it?'[63] Popular publications with no obvious environmentalist agenda also expressed a sense of disquiet. Even *Sport Illustrated* titled an article 'The Deadly Spray' (1960) and claimed that 'Man's chemical warfare against his insect enemies has at last reached the point where it threatens the well-being of man himself.'[64] Fears about the effect of pesticides also appeared in films of the period. Alfred Hitchcock's *North by Northwest* (1959), for instance, included one of the most evocative scenes about the threats posed by crop-dusting planes. The film's hero, Roger Thornhill (played by Cary Grant), was attacked by a small crop-duster that sprayed bullets and a thick cloud of poisonous dust over the idyllic countryside. Famously, Bob Dylan sang about these anxieties in 'A Hard Rain's A-Gonna Fall' (1963) in which rivers and forests are poisoned, and the faces of those responsible are shrouded.

Dylan's song had followed the publication of a remarkable book by the biologist Rachel Carson. *Silent Spring* (1962) initiated the 'Age of Environmentalism'. Not everyone embraced its uncompromising message. *Time* attacked Carson for using 'emotion-fanning words' and 'frightening and arousing her readers'.[65] A reader of the *New Yorker* exclaimed: 'As for insects, isn't it just like a woman to be scared to death of a few little bugs! As long as we have the H-bomb, everything will be O.K.'[66] But many more readers were entranced by *Silent Spring*, which rapidly topped the best-selling non-fiction lists and remained there thirty-one weeks. By the beginning of 1963 more than half a million copies were in print.[67]

Carson's message was blunt: a neo-Malthusian catastrophe was looming. Chemicals such as agricultural insecticides had poisoned the environment. For Carson the danger of poisoning was equal to that posed by nuclear weapons. *Silent Spring* began by portraying an idyllic world that had been destroyed after a 'strange blight crept over the area'. Livestock and vegetation had been destroyed and people were falling sick. 'No witchcraft, no enemy action had silenced the rebirth of new life in this stricken world,' Carson reminded her readers: 'The people had done it themselves.' The 'grim spectre' had 'crept upon us almost unnoticed'. It was a war like other wars, but one which was 'never won'. All life was 'caught in its violent crossfire'. This threat ranked alongside nuclear holocaust:

> Along with the possibility of the extinction of mankind by nuclear war, the central problem of our age has therefore become the contamination of man's total environment with such substances of incredible potential for harm — substances that accumulate in the tissues of plants and animals and even penetrate the germ cells to shatter or alter the very material of heredity upon which the shape of the future depends.

'Big business' and the 'ruthless power' of science were also castigated. According to Carson, agribusiness had forged an unholy pact with science and had chosen short-term goals (such as increased agricultural production) over the long-term well-being of the species. She did not call for a complete ban on chemical insecticides: she simply warned her readers that agribusiness and science did not have their interests in mind. It was an argument premised on notions of individual rights and freedoms: 'We have subjected enormous numbers of people to contact with these poisons, without their consent and often without their knowledge,' she insisted.[68]

By the 1970s the language of ecological catastrophe popularised by Carson was changing.[69] For instance, in *The Closing Circle* (1972) Barry Commoner warned that synthetic products such as detergents and plastics were wreaking havoc on the environment, but instead of drawing on Cold War rhetoric of environmental holocaust he adopted the language of accountancy:

> The present system of production is self-destructive; the present course of human circulation is suicidal. The environmental crisis is sober evidence of an insidious fraud hidden in the vaunted productivity and wealth of modern technology-based society. This wealth has been gained by rapid short-term exploitation of the

environment system, but it has blindly accumulated a debt to nature (in the form of environmental destruction in developed countries and of population pressure in developing ones) — a debt so large and so pervasive that in the next generation it may, if unpaid, wipe out most of the wealth it has gained for us. In effect, the account books of modern society are drastically out of balance, so that, largely unconsciously, a huge fraud has been perpetrated on the people of the world. The rapidly worsening course of environmental pollution is a warning that the bubble is about to burst, that the demand to pay the global debt may find the world bankrupt.[70]

For the rest of the twentieth century, this language of risk dominated discussions about global warming, pollution and environmental disaster. As social theorist Krishan Kumar put it in 1995:

Secular apocalypses tend to be statistical — the extrapolation of long-term trends, or the calculation of 'statistical risk parameters' threatening human existence. The end will come as the result of a steady increase in population, or a slow poisoning of the planet. Catastrophe will be expressed in lines on a graph rather than in the imagery of the Book of Revelation.[71]

Insecticides and synthetic products were only two of innumerable threats. Risks proliferated: there was salmonella in eggs, listeria in soft cheese, alar in apples and botulism in hazelnut yoghurt. In America, after milk was found to be infected with BST and Strontium 90, one SANE (Committee for a Sane Nuclear Policy) advertisement warned that even 'Dr Spock is Worried'. With the advent of bovine spongiform encephalopathy (BSE) in Britain in 1990, Nature was portrayed as 'threatening to pollute culture, as culture had earlier polluted nature by rupturing the boundaries between herbivore and carnivore'.[72] In the face of such threats, however, even the government could not be trusted to advise and protect. In September 2001 the *Guardian Weekly* published an article entitled 'Epidemic in waiting' which described BSE as probably the most cynical act of biological warfare ever waged against a civilian population by a western government. The British government put the narrow business interests of its farming and meat industries before the health of its population and that of other countries.[73]

Sites of safety became profoundly dangerous: the superbug, *Staphylococcus aureus*, surfaced in hospital wards. Enthusiastic use of miracle drugs such as antibiotics was found to have dangerous consequences. As the editor of *Consuming Fears. The Politics of Product Risks* (1986) put it:

> there is hardly an item on the supermarket shelf that is not thought to pose a danger of some sort. The dangers are not trivial. Frequently used products have been linked to a multitude of diseases that kill or disable. Coffee may cause pancreatic cancer, eggs atherosclerosis, and aluminium pots can contain aflatoxin, a powerful carcinogen; some hair dryers may release asbestos fibers that, if inhaled, can produce asbestosis, a deadly lung ailment. This morning's corn flakes may contain hazardous amounts of the pesticide EDB. Tonight's aspirin promises relief, but also the possibility of an ulcer in the not-too-distant future.[74]

The consumerist dream of corporeal satisfaction turned into a nightmare.

Fears were exacerbated by the incalculable nature of the risk. What was the 'threshold' at which a 'good outcome' (such as increased living standards) became a 'bad outcome' (pollution). Exactly *who* was a polluter: every eighteen-year-old purchasing his or her first car or just the colossal guzzlers of energy? There seemed to be no way of evaluating risk or even knowing when it might be approaching calamitous levels. Even science could not be guaranteed to provide answers. According to one survey of 990 English-language horror films produced between 1931 and 1984, a quarter of films portrayed science as the primary source of danger.[75] It is no surprise that parliamentary debates about the legality of new reproductive technologies and using human embryos for research frequently appealed to two doctors: Dr Frankenstein and Dr Mengele, the notorious medical experimenter in the Nazi concentration camps.[76] The scientist portrayed in the film *The Vampire Bat* (1933) personified many people's anxieties when he defended his experiments in creating life with the words:

> Mad? Is one who has solved the secret of life to be considered mad? Life, created in the laboratory. No mere crystalline growth, but tissue, living, growing tissue that moves, pulsates, and demands food . . . What are a few lives when weighed in the balance against the achievements of biological science? Think of it. I have lifted the veil. I have created life. Wrestled the secret of life from life.

The scientifically constructed nature of risk was most obvious in the debates during the 1970s about the safety of the two popular pesticides Aldrin and Dieldrin. Despite using identical data, scientists in America concluded that they were an 'unacceptable carcinogenic hazard', whereas British scientists declared them 'safe'. These divergent conclusions were largely a product of the different scientific communities evaluating the evidence. The British Medical Research Council's Toxicology Unit had close ties to the chemical industry, while in America many of the scientists had links to the National Cancer Institute (NCI). Umberto Saffiotti, head of the NCI's Chemical Carcinogenesis Program and principal adviser to the US Environmental Protection Agency, argued:

> That we take a position of caution and prudence in the matter of exposing the entire population to the potential hazards of chemical carcinogens is dictated by the tragic knowledge that . . . out of 200 million Americans now living, 50 million will develop cancer and 34 million will die of it, yet most cancers appear to be caused by environmental factors and therefore could be preventable.[77]

In contrast, J. M. Barnes, head of the Toxicology Unit and principal adviser to Britain's Pesticide Safety Precautions Scheme, used identical data to argue that:

The safety of man from hazards presented by pesticide residues will not necessarily be increased by crying 'wolf' on every conceivable occasion that some direct or indirect carcinogenic activity can be detected in a substance filling a valuable role as a pesticide. Without pesticides, many people would die for other reasons long before they reached the age at which they might develop cancer. Cancer was widespread long before modern pesticides were synthesized. If chemical carcinogens are responsible for any significant fraction of human cancer of unknown origin it is probable that such carcinogens will be of natural origin. With aflatoxin, cyasin, and the pyrrolidizing alkaloids before us as examples of carcinogens found widespread in nature, it would be unwise if not irrational to try to create undue alarm about carcinogenic hazards from pesticides that display no carcinogenic activity even faintly comparable with that of the compounds listed above.[78]

These two scientists were operating from completely different scientific notions of risk. Saffiotti's prudent strategy was based on the belief that a single 'trigger' was sufficient to incite cellular chaos while Barnes's more permissive (and more traditional) strategy required prolonged contact between the cell and the chemical. In both cases the links of the experts with powerful political organisations influenced the outcome of their scientific deliberations.[79] It was hardly surprising, therefore, that many people simply did not trust scientists to act in their interests.

Scientific ignorance made matters worse. After all, in 1985 only 5 per cent of American adults met a minimum measure of scientific literacy (for instance, 40 per cent of those surveyed believed in lucky numbers).[80] How were such people to evaluate the respective merits of scientific advice? Many people were much more likely to be influenced by exaggerated accounts of environmental apocalypse. In the words of the author of *How to Stay Young and Healthy in a Toxic World* (1999):

I hope that these frightening examples [of the poisoned environment] will help convince you that environmental degradation — and

the health threats involved — is underway at a pace unimaginable a
few decades ago . . . One great difference is that present-day environmental health threats are unlikely to be as straightforward and
visible as smoke belching from a factory chimney, though there are
still plenty of these around. As our technology becomes more complex in leaps and bounds, nature's responses are growing harder
even for experts to read. But it is clear that we don't fully understand all the health consequences when we make tradeoffs of
large-scale destruction of natural resources for immediate, industrial
rewards. We severely underestimate Mother Nature. She probably
has many more unpredictable responses in store for us.[81]

For all we know, 'Mother Nature' might be a capricious, hysterical
woman, setting out to destroy humanity.

Nuclear energy stimulated the most potent of all environmental
fears. While the Cold War portrayed nuclear terror as a fear of
total destruction, by the 1980s this had been converted to a much
more insidious anxiety about the slow pollution of the environment
by nuclear energy plants. Throughout the 1980s between 82 and 90
per cent of Britons agreed with the statement that 'waste from
nuclear electricity stations has a very or quite serious effect on the
environment', while between 45 and 58 per cent agreed that 'a
serious accident at a British nuclear power station is very or quite
likely in the next ten years'.[82] Two other polls in the mid-1980s
found that around 60 per cent of Britons were 'pessimistic' about
the 'ability to dispose of waste from nuclear power plants in an
acceptable way', while between 41 and 45 per cent were 'pessimistic' about the 'ability to run nuclear generating plants without
serious accidents'.[83] Uncertainty about how people should respond
to these threats was prevalent. For instance, common responses
among people living close to plants where there were clusters of
leukaemia was 'Where do you move to?' 'How do you know it's
safe?' and 'There's no safe place anywhere, and every day it gets
worse.'[84]

Even scientists were divided about what constituted a safe level of
radiation. As Ulrich Beck noted in 'The Reinvention of Politics'
(1994): 'Insurance experts (involuntarily) contradict safety engineers.

While the latter diagnose zero risk, the former decide: uninsurable. Experts are undercut or deposed by opposing experts.'[85] So, while US Federal guidelines stated that 'if the predicted peak of contamination for milk reaches 15,000 picocuries per liter from I-131 [iodine 131]', responsible officials should remove the cattle from pasture and milk from the shops,[86] other responsible scientists argued that it was dangerous to expose developing foetuses and small infants to 500 picocuries.[87] Either way instances of the arbitrary raising of limits on 'acceptable dose' have been increasing since the 1960s, further inciting fears.[88]

The legitimacy of feeling anxious about safety guidelines was made bitterly clear to many East-Coast Americans in March 1979, after one of the two generator units at the Three Mile Island nuclear power plant released radioactive steam, forcing 200,000 residents to flee the area. Nevertheless, Metropolitan Edison (which owned the nuclear reactor) attempted to cover up the extent of radiation that had been released. The nuclear energy trade's blatant adherence to profits over human well-being was truly frightening. When a 'siting specialist' from the Department of Energy spoke to groups of residents in Conway, New Hampshire, about a proposal to situate a nuclear waste dump in nearby Hillsboro, a ten-year-old boy asked, 'What if it leaks? There'll be no more me.' The siting specialist answered by saying, 'That wouldn't happen for hundreds of years', to which the boy replied, 'Oh, don't you care about the future?' This forced the official to admit that 'personal sacrifices must be made'.[89] As even children recognised, nuclear fears were not only a response to anxiety about any individual's existence, but trepidation about the survival of future generations and humanity itself. The threat was 'low probability', but 'high consequence'.

The difficulty with risks such as those posed by nuclear power plants was related to uncertainty about the nature of the danger. As with environmental dangers in general, a troubling aspect of nuclear fears was the inability of people to assess risk. Radiation was invisible. It 'leaked' silently into the environment. The Presidential report on the 1979 nuclear accident at Three Mile Island stated that:

Never before have people been asked to live with such ambiguity. The Three Mile Island accident — an accident we cannot see or taste or smell . . . is an accident that is invisible. I think the fact that it is invisible creates a sense of uncertainty and fright on the part of people that may well go beyond the reality of the accident itself.[90]

In Britain one of the most notorious scares involving 'silent leakage' occurred at the Sellafield (formerly Windscale) nuclear energy plant in Cumbria, which was infamous for accidents.[91] In November 1983 three million people watched the Yorkshire Television documentary *Windscale: The Nuclear Laundry*, which made a link between radioactive discharges at Sellafield and the fact that levels of leukaemia and other cancers among children under fifteen years of age were ten times higher in areas near to the plant than further afield. The combination of cancer-phobia, wildly exaggerated media attention to 'human-monsters' and the fact that most of the victims were children generated a considerable scare. The *Daily Express* dubbed the documentary the 'chiller of the week', claiming it was an 'horrific picture of evil cancer radiation getting into the sea, the air, the cattle, the vegetables and eventually the people'. The *Sun* headlined its discussion 'Village of the Damned' and claimed that 'the spiders are big and strangely coloured, some geese are deformed. And cattle can suffer from abnormalities'. For the *Observer* it was 'a corner of Cumbria where calves are born deformed and ramblers walk at their peril'.[92]

The resulting inquiry, chaired by a former president of the Royal College of Physicians, Sir Douglas Black, concluded that there was an increased incidence of leukaemia among young people in the vicinity of Sellafield, but alleged that the increased levels could not be attributed 'with certainty' to radioactive discharges. Black told the local television channel that 'to live in the neighbourhood of Sellafield confers no greater risk than many which we normally accept in our daily living. Now I'm not saying there is no risk, I'm merely trying to put it in some form of perspective.'[93]

Black's emphasis on probabilities did little to allay alarm. In the words of an undated Greenpeace pamphlet titled *The Windscale File. A Lay-Guide to Living (and Dying) with a Nuclear Neighbour*, people distrusted the nuclear apologists, believing that they were quite willing to play 'nuclear roulette' with innocent lives.[94] Even Harold Bolter, the longest-serving director of British Nuclear Fuels (Sellafield's owners), expressed doubts about the efficiency of the establishment and criticised the 'culture of secrecy' which made the public so anxious about nuclear fuels.[95]

The response of the nuclear industry was to label such fears 'irrational'. After the Three Mile Island accident in 1979, the Secretary of Health who urged the immediate evacuation of pregnant women and small children from the contaminated area was later fired for being an 'alarmist'.[96] As in the nuclear scares of the 1950s, people who were apprehensive about nuclear energy plants in their areas were suffering from 'radiophobia'. In the words of a nuclear physicist, anxious to defend his profession:

> The public has been driven insane over the fear of radiation. I use the word 'insane' purposefully since one of its definitions is loss of contact with reality. The public's understanding of radiation dangers has virtually lost all contact with the actual dangers as understood by scientists.[97]

In America during the late 1990s the Department of Energy even employed a prominent psychiatrist to help 'counter the public's "irrational fear" about nuclear power'. A critic described this appointment as 'an attempt to demonstrate that opponents of nuclear power are mentally ill'.[98] And there *was* a 'madness' associated with these fears. In the words of one woman who had fled from the Three Mile Island disaster:

> I felt sure at the time that we had gotten quite a bit of radiation and at that point you don't know if you're going to die next week. But because of this, was our life going to be cut short? Just exactly what was going to happen? We still don't know. Are the kids going to get it? Is my husband going to get it? It's nothing you dwell on, I can tell you, because if you dwelled on it every day, you'd be crazy.[99]

This woman recognised the danger. In Anthony Giddens's words: 'Chernobyl is everywhere.'[100]

There were other characteristics of nuclear accidents that made them terrifying. As the anthropologists Mary Douglas and Aaron Wildavsky asked in *Risk and Culture* (1982): 'why is asbestos poisoning seen to be more fearsome than fire?'[101] One answer to this question drew a distinction between scientific and social rationality. In the words of Kai Erickson, scientists

> will dismiss this fear [of toxic poisoning] as irrational if, like most experts, we assess the danger by calculating the odds of an accident and then estimating the number of casualties likely to result from it. But there are other reasonings and other reckonings at work in the world. Maybe we should understand radioactive and other toxic substances as naturally loathsome — horrors, like poison gas, that draws on something deeper in the human mind.

What makes these toxic threats so scary is their unbounded, insidious nature. By literally 'creeping under the skin', silently, without giving notice, they 'taint'. Toxins violated 'all the rules of plot':

> Some of them have clearly defined beginnings, such as the explosion . . . Others begin years before anyone senses that anything is wrong . . . [And] toxic accidents never end. Invisible contaminants remain a part of the surroundings — absorbed into the grain of the landscape, the tissues of the body, and, worse of all, into the genetic material of the survivors.[102]

The problem was deciding how to respond. The political responses of groups such as Greenpeace generated extensive mistrust and alarm about big business and science, but failed to muster a vast band of people willing to actively support their activities. More commonly, individuals responded in similar ways to how they responded to their fear of crime: 'new prudentialism' had its counterpart in 'new puritanism'. Fear of the polluting aspects of modern society led many people to respond in individualistic ways. With only a few exceptions (the anti-globalisation movement being the most prominent), people turned not to the body politic but the body corporeal for a solution. The keyword was detoxification. As the first sentence in *How to Stay Young and Healthy in a Toxic World* (1999) insisted, 'A healthy body is a clean body.'[103] Toxins had to be 'flushed' from the 'system'. The fear of premature ageing took the place previously reserved for fears of premature burial. By 1987 American health clubs grossed $5 billion while diet foods and vitamin products grossed nearly $77 billion.[104] Health clubs began offering computerised 'risk analysis' to predict what the individual might suffer and even die from in the future.

Advice books such as *How to Live 100 Years* (1978) and *Superyoung. The Proven Way to Stay Young Forever* (1998) belied their spectacular titles by offering sensible advice about the benefits of a sensible diet and regular exercise.[105] The self-help book *Why Die Young?* promised 'life extension and rejuvenation the natural way' through dietary changes. In particular, the author singled out refined and manufactured foods as particularly pernicious, discouraging his readers from eating processed breakfast foods, 'papier-maché [sic] mushy foods' (meaning puddings and pies), tinned foods, 'embalmed, highly seasoned artificially preserved concoctions which seduce the eye in the delicatessen shops' (pernicious foods included sausages and pickled onions), sugar, flour, tea and coffee.[106]

Stop Ageing Now! The Ultimate Plan for Staying Young and Reversing the Ageing Process (1996) placed its belief in the consumption of a cocktail of vitamins (A, C, and D), beta carotene, chromium, zinc, calcium, magnesium, selenium, glutathiane, coenzyme Q-10, ginkgo, garlic and soybeans.[107] *Resetting the Clock* (1996) and *The Anti-Ageing Zone* (1999) prescribed Human Growth Hormone, DHEA, melatonin, oestrogen, progesterone and testosterone.[108] The ageing process could be obscured, if not delayed, by cosmetic surgery. As the 'baby-boomers' aged they faced chronic degenerative diseases as opposed to the infections of the past. They also faced a business world that prioritised youth and flexibility over experience.

Late-twentieth-century Britain and America were characterised by nebulous and confusing fears. The child was not only sexual (as Freud warned[109]) but murderous; the very groups dedicated to empowering women ended up frightening them with lurid claims about innate male depravity; technological promises of a wealthier future polluted the world and resulted in declining standard of living; people attempted to stave off death with agonising routines in front of the exercise video in which 'the real' strove to become a 'copy of the image'. The psychologisation of society drew fears inwards: crime was no longer an event that 'happened', but something that was always 'happening', a constant presence in the negotiations between psyche and body.

To be raped, for instance, meant becoming a 'rape victim' — a permanent facet of identity. There was now a 'rape trauma syndrome'[110] that went through stages, unlike in earlier periods, when rape occurred within a defined geographical and temporal space. Nancy Raine, at the beginning of this chapter, initially rejected the idea that a rapist had 'infected [her] with a mental illness' called post-traumatic stress disorder, but in the end her endless adoption of a stream of psychological treatments signalled her acceptance of herself as permanently altered by her status as a 'rape survivor'. In the past the fear of rape was linked to fear of its social effects; by the end of the twentieth century it was the fear of suffering an internal or psychic trauma.

Of course, social anxieties still existed. Indeed, they may have grown as the nature of the 'audience' expanded immeasurably and became even more anonymous. No longer was the individual primarily concerned about his or her standing within an identifiable and intimate community. Instead, the individual was painfully aware of being exposed to a mass of unidentifiable, unknowable people, from anonymous financiers dealing with credit to any scanner of the Internet. With the vast expansion in the mass media during the twentieth century, dangers were publicised to an unprecedented degree, making them seem almost boundless.

This proliferation of 'risk-speak' was not accompanied by any more effective ways of comprehending and countering threats. The perceived efficacy of religious knowledge declined while scientific and other knowledge systems failed to wholly replace them. The same experts who pontificated over dangers (radiation, for instance) were the ones who created them in the first place (in the form of nuclear weapons and energy). No one could be trusted — even

these self-designated experts disagreed violently between themselves about what humanity should truly fear. The science that
revealed the splendour of the universe was incapable of being
grasped: instead, the emptiness of space was crushing.

Afterword to Part Five: Aesthesiology

The important question becomes: what is the relationship between individual emotions and society? Historians always need to ask: what is fear *doing*? The history of the emotions cannot ignore power relations. Too often the psychoanalytical assumption that fear resides in the individual psyche leads to the individualising of historical change, as in the early work of Eric Erikson.[1] This approach individualises categories of oppression by reducing them to psychological states. Such a use of 'fear' turns social inequality into a psychological mood — for instance, the emotions resulting from being unable to defend oneself against a threat become a psychological disposition. In contrast, fear is not simply spawned within individual psyches, before stretching out towards other subjects or objects. Dynamic psychology is simply not 'dynamic' enough when applied to the past.

Equally, the 'feeling-rules' of the emotionologists and social constructivists often portray emotion-work (negotiating relationships between individual psychology and social institutions) as a one-way process, in which emotional expression is constrained within a set of societal norms. But emotion-work is not only about the 'struggle for emotional control' (as the Stearns entitled one of their books) — a process generally conceptualised as suppressing emotional expression. It is also about evoking the emotion of fear. Even more importantly, it is not necessary to adopt a pre-determined category of power to explain the relationship between the individual and societal fears. Much work within emotionology starts with categories such as class or gender and seeks to attribute emotions to those groups. For instance, work on sentimentality in nineteenth-century America assigns a gender to emotions — they are either feminine or masculine, rarely both.[2] Methodologically, however, it is wrong to assume that any particular emotion belongs to social groups. It is not the case that members of the working classes feared the same thing, or that women or members of an ethnic community shared emotional experiences. Fear 'bunches' individuals in different ways. Finally, this emphasis on what fear is *doing* avoids the constructivists' dilemma that the fear-speak or fear-act *is* the fear, inviting the conclusion that if men neither acted frightened nor said they were frightened, then they were not frightened. In the words of the anthropologist William Reddy:

> emotives do things to the world. Emotives are themselves instruments for directly changing, building, hiding, intensifying emotions. There is an 'inner' dimension to emotion, but it is never merely 'represented' by statements or actions. It is the necessary (relative) failure of all efforts to represent feeling that makes for (and sets limits to) our plasticity.[3]

Emotions are not simply reports of inner states.

Crucially, emotions such as fear do not belong only to individuals or social groups: they mediate between the individual and the social. They are about power relations. Emotions lead to a negotiation of the boundaries between Self and Other or One Community and Another. They align individuals with communities. In the words of Sara Ahmed in reference to hate, emotions mediate the boundaries between 'bodily space' and 'social space'. In other words, fear is a form of 'emotional labour' that endows 'objects and others with meaning and power'.[4] The feminist slogan 'the personal is political', takes on new meaning in the history of emotional expression.

In the process of 'emotion-work', fear sorts people into positions of social hierarchy. An illustration of the way fear places people into various hierarchical groups may be seen by examining the phenomenon that came to be termed 'school phobia'. As we saw in Chapter Five, from 1941 a new category was applied to children who were afraid of school. Instead of being defined as truants, a certain group of these children were renamed 'school phobes'. Skipping school remained truancy for working-class children, but it was medicalised for middle-class children through the invention of a psychological illness, tended by psychiatrists in the rapidly growing number of school guidance clinics. The way these children and parents experience school avoidance is, as a consequence, emotionally different. By distinguishing truants from school phobes, managers of the emotions assigned children (and their parents) to their appropriate social and economic classes.

Although certain types of fear have tended to present themselves within subordinated groups, reinforcing their subordination, it is not the case that the historian can 'read' these different groups according to a schema devised by other theorists, whether they be sociologists, psychologists or economic historians. As we have seen throughout this book, fear 'bunched' people in ways different from those prescribed by gender relations according to feminists (or, for that matter, class relations according to Marxists). In other words, it is possible to fear sexual violence without being a servant or a woman, even if many of these fearful people may be legitimately grouped in those positions within power relations. This approach draws attention to the fact that fear is not simply an emotional response belonging to underprivileged groups. After all, fear is a most democratic emotion, afflicting everyone who contemplates their risk of dying.

The holy trinity of class, gender and ethnicity cannot be jettisoned, but historians of the emotions must be wary of identifying certain emotions with certain classes through a definitional approach. Instead, emotions align people with others within social groups, subjecting them to power relations. Without emotional exchange, no amount of shared characteristics will create either the group (such as class) or social action (such as class conflict). Emotional history enables historians to jettison notions of 'false consciousness'. This approach draws attention to the fact that groupings are diverse (most of the people who panicked while listening to Welles' 'War of the Worlds' broadcast in 1938 were uneducated, but not all) and transient (the terror of being mugged might rapidly transform itself into fury against the criminal).

Emotions may create or reproduce subordination but can also unravel it. It is not that different classes have different fears but, through the articulation of individual psychology and social groups, types of subordination are reproduced socially and historically. Fear animates relationships between the individual and social group. In other words, it is not simply the case that social structures shape fear (a physician might expect a woman to become hysterical when diagnosed as suffering from an incurable cancer, while he would expect a man in a similar circumstance to exhibit signs of resilience); fear also shapes social structures (a panicking AIDS sufferer might be perceived to be gay or a haemophiliac, and the response to the individual differed accordingly). In both cases, fear is a social enaction: it is about the distribution of power.

Conclusion: Terror

He began the day as a clerk
working for the Dean Witter brokerage
on the 74th floor of the World Trade Center
and ended it as an
extra in a real-life sequel to *Towering Inferno*.

SUNDAY TIMES, 1993[1]

As the twentieth century shuddered to an end this sentence from the *Sunday Times* characterised humanity's fears more accurately than Auden's long poem of 1946 'The Age of Anxiety'. Unalloyed terror rendered obsolete Auden's pervasive uneasiness. For the clerk on the seventy-fourth floor of the World Trade Center (WTC) when it was bombed in 1993 by a group of Egyptian, Pakistani and Palestinian terrorists, life imitated art — the art of disaster movies such as *The Towering Inferno* (1974). Immediately after this terrorist attack an editorial in the *New York Times* cautioned that, 'If the attack against the World Trade Center proves anything, it is that our offices, factories, transportation and communication networks and infrastructures are relatively vulnerable to skilled terrorists.'[2] Even more starkly, *Time* reported that:

> Americans were not accustomed to what so much of the world had already grown weary of: the sudden, deafening explosion of a car bomb, a hail of glass and debris, the screams of innocent victims followed by the wailing sirens of ambulances. Terrorism seemed like something that happened elsewhere — and somewhere else a safe distance over the horizon. And then, last week, in an instant, the World Trade Center in New York City became Ground Zero . . . If the explosion . . . turns out to be the work of terrorists, it will be a sharp reminder that the world is still a dangerous place. And that the dangers can come home.[3]

In 1993 six people had been killed, more than a thousand injured and at least 2300 men and women plunged into the Hades of post-traumatic stress disorder.[4] Eight years later, however, this apocalyptic warning was realised thousands of times over. On 11 September 2001 four commercial airplanes were hijacked over the eastern USA. At 8.45 a.m. the first plane smashed into the North Tower of the WTC. It was followed eighteen minutes later by another plane crashing into the South Tower. Within the hour a third plane had rammed into the Pentagon Building in Washington DC, while the final plane ploughed into a field near Shanksville, Pennsylvania. In total, around three thousand people were killed. At the beginning of the twenty-first century terrorists had demonstrated the ease with which the previous century's great symbol of technological prowess — the aeroplane — could kill, maim, and terrify millions of people throughout the world. The 'new warfare' that had for many decades provoked terror in the Middle East, Africa and the former Soviet republics now threatened Americans and Britons, fuelling a sense of fright that no one could avoid.

Scared observers struggled to find a language to express what they were witnessing. As we saw in Chapter Six, during the illusory threats to national survival in 1926 in Britain and in 1938 in the USA, people were terrorised by media-inspired reports of revolutionary uprisings and assaults by hostile Martians. But in 1993 and

2001, when the terrorist attacks were all too real, instead of arousing fear the mass media enabled people to cope with their terror by shrouding it in familiar fictive modes. On the one hand, 'real-time' television coverage of the attacks on the WTC and the Pentagon in 2001 provided many viewers with an illusion that they understood what was happening. In the words of a reporter for the *New York Times*:

> the images were terrifying to watch, yet the coverage was strangely reassuring because it existed with such immediacy, even when detailed information was scarce. Imagine how much worse the nightmare would have been if broadcasting had been destroyed. On a day of death, television was a lifeline to what was happening.[5]

Twenty-four-hour television coverage made the event 'real' for millions of Americans sitting in their homes, offices and bars desperately trying to dampen down their rising panic.

On the other hand, the languages and images drawn from disaster literature and horror movies were appropriated by dismayed observers as the most democratic discourse on fear. Because the image of two aeroplanes crashing into the WTC was surreal — 'art' more than 'life' — the language of artifice seemed fitting. As we shall see later, many observers felt that what they were witnessing was simply unbelievable, a fiction. Was it a stunt, like Welles's radio broadcast of *The War of the Worlds*?[6] On that earlier occasion the novelty of the means of communicating the story of national disaster made it believable, while in 2001 listeners immediately disbelieved their ears, having 'heard it all before'. Even the visual images on television were initially doubted: the footage was 'just another' Bruce Willis film. Iconic images presented through film and electronic games provided the lens through which 11 September was designed, executed and experienced. In 1926 and 1938 art imitated life; in 2001 life imitated art. As Jonathan Rosenblum reflected in 'The Day the World Changed' (2001), people 'would have to go back to Orson Welles' 'War of the Worlds', his realistic radio broadcast of a Martian invasion, to capture the panic this morning on the streets of Manhattan'. According to him, 'The kamikaze bombings on Washington DC in an old Tom Clancy novel and the attack on Manhattan from the sky a la [the film] *Independence Day*' were 'no longer in the realm of fiction'.[7]

Fictive attacks had crossed over into the lived experience of millions of people in New York City that day. The genre the attack most closely resembled was that of horror and disaster films. Kristin Peri, a thirty-one-year-old woman who had been employed by the Deutsche Bank, next door to the WTC, summarised the attitude of many when she said that it was 'like watching a movie, the way the building exploded and people just running'.[8] The panicking crowds on the streets of New York resembled 'a horror film running in overdrive, jumping frames and cutting in and out'.[9] For some the scenes were reminiscent of *Godzilla* (1989) in which a giant lizard — the creation of a nuclear test explosion off the coast of French Polynesia twenty years earlier — was unleashed on unsuspecting people in Manhattan.

America was receiving its 'payback' — not as a consequence of its experiments in nuclear annihilation, but for its imperialist ambitions. As one New Yorker described it: 'everyone was running as if Godzilla was chasing us. I was knocked over and then someone else ran right over me.'[10] Another eyewitness stammered: 'People started to stampede, like a Godzilla movie running uptown. It was like "Night of the Living Dead", zombies walking uptown all in shock.'[11] As we saw in Chapter Two in the discussion on disasters, extreme fear made people panic: people in wheelchairs were toppled over and, at the piers, boats nearly capsized as scared people mobbed them in an effort to get as far away from the disaster as possible. America was under attack, and no one knew when the horror of the day would end.

The over-representation of media-infused images shook people's grasp of reality. For Ashleigh Banfield of MSNBC, moving down New York's streets that day was 'like driving through a movie set'.[12] Tom Shanks, television writer for the *Washington Post*, exclaimed that after the attacks New York resembled 'scenes from such movies as *The Towering Inferno* and *Independence Day*'. He had to remind himself that 'this wasn't special effects. It was actually happening, and viewers sat powerless and traumatized as they saw it happen.'[13]

Howard Rosenberg, his counterpart at the *Los Angeles Times*, concurred:

> Pictures of suffering were almost surreal, at some points capturing
> bodies being blown from exploding towers along with debris, and
> tiny specks of humanity tragically leaping to their deaths just ahead
> of the flames. It was a case of life seeming to imitate the special
> effects of bad movies, whether the grisly deaths of Towering Inferno
> or the aliens of Independence Day hovering above the U.S. with
> plans to attack the president.[14]

The reality of death was captured through the phantasm of celluloid. Distinguishing between the real and the imaginary could be perplexing. In the words of Walter Metz:

> I tried to tearfully explain to my three year old son, Alex, that the
> televised images of planes crashing into the World Trade Center
> were not scenes from a movie. He didn't believe me, and still
> doesn't. I'm not sure I can blame him: the alien destruction of the
> Empire State Building in Independence Day . . . looks awfully
> similar to what's been on CNN this past two weeks.[15]

Even those who witnessed people jumping out of buildings or burning alive found the sights oddly recognisable. As Trent Eglin put it in an article in the *Santa Cruz Sentinel* on 12 October 2001: 'In a way, that added to our distress and dismay, many of us found both our role as viewer and the scene itself eerily familiar. Only this time, there was nothing even remotely satisfying about it.'[16] The confused account by Michael Derby, who escaped from the WTC on 11 September, accurately characterised 'reality' for many survivors. He admitted that he 'was watching people die for the first time in my life. But I knew what that looked like, because I'd grown up seeing those things. Everything looked like what I'd seen before.'[17] The effect was uncanny, in Freud's sense. In *The 'Uncanny'* (1985), he argued that an uncanny effect was

> often and easily produced when the distinction between imagination
> and reality is effaced, as when something that we have hitherto

regarded as imaginary appears before us in reality, or when a symbol takes over the full functions of the thing it symbolizes, and so on.[18]

On 11 September 2001 an uncanny thing happened: scary films came extraordinarily alive.

The uncanny effect was consistent with the trajectory of film history. Ever since the 1970s craze for disaster movies, film barons in Hollywood had dedicated their talents to producing more and more spectacular scenes of catastrophe. Explosive extravaganzas set in scrupulously realistic urban settings dominated the genre. On 11 September, however, producers and audiences alike confronted a terrorist coup, an event so terrifying that artistic replication was unthinkable. In the most direct way possible, this was the dilemma facing the producers of an updated, twenty-first-century version of *The War of the Worlds*. Pendragon Pictures had planned to release the film on Halloween, 2002, in imitation of Orson Welles's famous radio broadcast of the story on Halloween sixty-four years earlier. In a press release early in 2001, director Timothy Hines boasted that 'the approach to our [film] production has a great deal in common with the approach Orson Welles took [on the radio] . . . and we will make history on Halloween night, 2002.'[19] The terrorist attack on the WTC shattered his plans. Reflecting on the events of 11 September, and the fact that a Pendragon principal and investor in the *War of the Worlds* movie had been killed that day, Hines admitted that it had been

> a very difficult time for everyone. The whole world was touched by the WTC experience. For us personally those planes slammed directly into our lives. We lost a very close friend and have been in mourning. We also watched portions of our fictional screenplay being played out on September 11th. I knew immediately we couldn't do War of the Worlds as conceived. It was a strange time.[20]

The entire script had to be rewritten, with the twenty-first-century setting relocated to a period regarded as 'safe' for a contemporary audience — that is, to H. G. Wells's original milieu at the turn of the nineteenth century. The film was rescheduled to be released in the spring of 2005. Hines bravely noted that he was 'now convinced that the only way to make WAR OF THE WORLDS is to be one hundred percent true to the book. In the light of current world events, Wells' vision is more timely than ever and it needs to be translated to the big screen intact.'[21] When accused of 'giving in to terrorists' by rewriting the script, producer Susan Goforth replied:

> What they didn't know is that our [pre-11 September] updated version had scenes with people jumping from burning buildings and planes falling out of the sky. Portions of the script were so close to the WTC attack, I don't think the world would ever have accepted that version.[22]

The more explicit fantasies of horror film had predicted 'real life'. As with the clerk whose words opened this section, who felt as if he had become an 'extra in a real-life sequel to *Towering Inferno*', there was an alarming uncanniness about the boundaries between life and art, whether it was people flinging themselves from skyscrapers in *The Towering Inferno* in 1974, the White House being vaporised by aliens in *Independence Day* in 1995 or the monster in *Godzilla* ravishing New York City in 1998. In real life, as in the movies, humanity was being warned against arrogant expansion of the city upwards, ever-expanding imperialism and the wanton abuse of the environment through nuclear testing. The terrifying dangers facing individuals, communities and even nation states were the product of our own destructive urges. Although 11 September was no great turning point (after all, throughout the 'long twentieth century' most Britons and Americans regarded themselves as fearful), it did intensify the feeling that now, as in the past, we live in an Age of Anxiety in which fears are ubiquitous. No one is exempt.

The Age of Terrorism was heralded by the explosions of 'Little Boy' and 'Fat Man' over the cities of Hiroshima and Nagasaki in 1945 and thrived during the Cold War. For the millions of children cowering beneath their school desks during the 'no signal' atomic drills of the 1950s (see Chapter Nine), it must have seemed wholly unfair that their governments were unable to make peace with another world power. As we have seen throughout this book, when it came to terror the most vulnerable endured the most. Even after the collapse of the Berlin Wall in 1989, there was no respite. The Red Menace was followed by the Terrorist Monster. Of course, terrorist fears were not new. After all, the Cold War spurred its own hordes of 'freedom fighters' and 'revolutionaries' willing and able to cause panic on a large scale. Furthermore, there had been terrorists throughout modern history. In *Reflections on the Revolution in France* (1790) Edmund Burke castigated 'thousands of those hell hounds called terrorists' — referring to the democrats thronging the streets of Paris in his time. In the second half of the nineteenth century Ireland and Europe had more than their share of violent militants. The lament of a British policeman in 1898 sounds familiar to modern ears. He regretted that 'murderous organizations' had escalated since 1858 when Felice Orsini attempted to assassinate the French emperor, Napoleon III. Terrorists at the end of the nineteenth century, he said,

> are more daring, they are served by the more terrible weapons offered by modern science, and the world is nowadays threatened by new forces which, if recklessly unchained, may some day wreak universal destruction. The Orsini bombs were children's toys compared with the later developments of infernal machines . . . the dastardly science of destruction has made rapid and alarming strides.[23]

Since that policeman made this observation, the 'dastardly science of destruction' has grown exponentially. As we saw in Chapters Seven and Eight, the most terrifying offences against British and American civilians were created with defence in mind: shrapnel, fighter aircraft, biological weapons and the nuclear bomb were devised in our laboratories. During the Second World War terror rained down from the skies on civilians throughout Britain. Military-directed terror had come home.

By the 1970s terrorists were showing that they had learned the lesson of modern warfare, and American as well as British civilians became targets of first choice. For Americans terrorism was the 'new Vietnam'[24] and in Britain 'the Muslim' gradually replaced 'the Irish' as the new terrorist threat of the century. In the West, Islamic fundamentalism was equated with Nazism and communism. As during the Cold War, fears of extremists were infused with anxiety about the place of America in the world. It was a fear infused with guilt. As Ivan Korshunov, the leader of the Russian dissidents, shouted at the First Lady in the film *Air Force One* (1997): 'You murdered 100,000 Iraqis to save a nickel a gallon on gas. Don't lecture me on the articles of war!' Muslims were a majority of the population in forty-five countries in the world: there were one billion of 'them'. A headline in the *National Review* warned that 'The Muslims are Coming! The Muslims are Coming!'[25] Another commentator warned that 'Fear of the Green Menace (green being the colour of Islam) may well replace that of the Red Menace of World Communism'.[26] The second Cold War was announced.

It proved remarkably easy to disseminate fears of this supposed threat. In 1977 and 1978 85–90 per cent of the population of the USA and Britain regarded terrorism as a very serious problem.[27] Indeed, in 1977 and 1978 for 55 per cent of Americans and 71 per cent of Britons the threat was sufficiently grave for them to advocate the introduction of the death penalty for captured terrorists.[28] In 1986 even the unpromising state of the economy, rising unemployment and poverty, escalating drug abuse, environmental pollution and the possibility of a new international conflict failed to topple terrorism from its lead in the fear polls. Terrorism remained the 'number-one issue of concern'.[29]

The fear of terrorism was incited in the usual ways. As with the moral panic over child abuse, terrorism received disproportionate attention in the mass media. High-flown rhetoric about the escalation of danger was common. Despite the fact that only seventeen people were killed by terrorists in America between 1980 and 1985, the *New York Times* published an average of four stories about terrorism each issue.[30] Between 1989 and 1992 only thirty-four Americans were killed by terrorists throughout the world, but over 1300 books were catalogued under the rubric 'terrorists' or 'terrorism' in American libraries.[31] Respected political figures stirred up anxieties. For instance, in the early 1980s many Americans became particularly fearful when President Reagan announced that terrorism had increased by three or four times since 1968 and that over half of terrorist incidents had been 'aimed at' Americans.[32] Portraying the violence as targeting all Americans ignored major issues about terrorist objectives, and elided problems of defining 'terrorist'. After all, in 1980 the CIA dramatically raised its estimate of the number of terrorist incidents affecting Americans between 1968 and 1979 from 3336 to 6719.[33] Quietly, they had decided to include hoaxes and threats in their definition of 'terrorist incidents'. People were right to be anxious about the question: what is terrorism? (and whether or not Iraq, Iran, Syria and North Korea counted as 'terrorist states'). In 1990 President George Bush claimed that Americans were living in 'the age of the terrorist': it was a fear that his son, President George W. Bush, was to reiterate a dozen years later.[34]

Scary metaphors punctuated debates about terrorism. As we saw in Chapter Ten, until the AIDS epidemic of the 1980s the most stigmatised of all diseases was cancer. Whether referring to the 'vicious invasion of cancer' within the body, the 'vile cancer of criminality' or the 'cancer of population growth', cancer-talk was inherently frightening. As a metaphor, cancer was easily applied to terrorism. Even cancer organisations linked terrorism with the disease. For instance, an article posted on the website of Lymphomation, an organisation for people suffering from Non-Hodgkin's Lymphoma, was entitled 'Fighting Cancer and Terrorism'. The author drew strong parallels between the two 'wars'. He began by arguing that 'normal life' was now habitually threatened by terrorists, making life a 'constant fight for survival', as it was for cancer patients. The

> sickness and unreality we feel at diagnosis [of cancer] is very much like the experience of Americans on September 11 and its aftermath. The enemy is also similar. It comes from ourselves and is somehow twisted (mutated) [sic] to become something that betrays us — that seeks our death. Just as every siren post 9-11 evokes renewed fear of assault and senseless violence; every new feeling and symptom carried with it a fear that the cancer is back or growing.

The survival of the human race depended on 'cooperation and rules of conduct', but both cancer and terrorist cells had 'lost this connection'. Furthermore, the author continued, the

> remedies for cancer and terrorism have much in common. We can bomb the terrorists and the people who live there and thereby apply a kind of chemotherapy. We may or may not provide nutrition and protection to the residents of cities who are in harm's way. We have 'smart' bombs that are not always so smart that resemble radio-labeled antibodies — that carry radiation to specific cells. We might try to cut off the supply of funds to terrorists just as antiangiogenic treatments can sometimes stop the blood supply to tumors.

'Cancer and terrorist cells' needed 'vigorous and coordinated' action if they were to be killed off once and for all time.[35]

His sentiments were echoed elsewhere on the Internet in an article titled 'Fighting the Cancer of Terrorism'. Readers were informed that the author 'know[s] more about cancer than I would like'. Cancer was

> a systematic disease with local manifestations. I find it useful to think of terrorism as a form of systematic cancer. We can treat the local manifestations, but that is not good enough. We have to address the entire system if we want a cure. And as with cancer, there are no silver bullets just lots of hard work, difficult medicine, luck, hope, and time.[36]

Yet another Internet article made the same point in the terse words: 'It's time for us to declare a holy war on terrorism, a cancer that's so far proved impossible to excise. We must be thorough and we must act quickly; otherwise, we're dead.' The writer concluded by stating: 'Humanity aside, it's self-preservation; the world is too small for this cancer to exist without spreading.'[37]

Although cancer was one of the most popular metaphors used to talk about terrorism, it was not the only one. Even when not branded a cancer, terrorism was portrayed as an unspecified, but insidious mental or physical affliction. In 1984 the US Secretary of

State, George Shultz, claimed that 'depraved' and 'psycho-pathic' terrorists were spreading a 'contagious disease' and had to be 'treated'[38] while an editorial in the *New York Times* after the 1993 bombing of the WTC described the perpetrators as 'unimagined terrorists and other socio-paths determined to settle scores with us'.[39] Metaphors invoking calamitous afflictions were common in moral panics and served to both stigmatise terrorist acts as particularly evil (and thus different from ordinary crimes) and reduce resistance to extreme measures to 'kill off the virus' of terrorism. The terrorist became a superhuman menace who was difficult to combat and was 'above and beyond' ordinary social and political constraints.

Furthermore, from 11 September 2001 such fears were exacerbated because danger suddenly seemed to be everywhere. In Chapter Eleven we looked at the late twentieth century's emphasis on risk, where many individuals felt that they no longer had any realistic way of calculating the seriousness of threats posed by nuclear energy or environmental pollution. For large numbers of people fear of terrorism bordered on a phobia. In an article entitled 'The Cost of Complacency' and published in *Fortune* on 1 October 2001, the author queried why Americans had not done more to protect themselves from terrorism. His answer was simple:

> Perhaps part of the answer — only part — is that we are peppered with alarming threats every day. In a society in which attention and funding are the resources everyone competes for, sounding an alarm is a powerful strategy. On any given day during which we were warned about terrorism, we were also warned about the enormous looming dangers of asteroids, earthquakes, greenhouse gases, biological warfare, and mad cow disease . . . Travellers arriving at Los Angeles airport are told they must stand at least 5 feet outside the terminal to light up a cigarette, so great does California consider the danger of second-hand smoke. It isn't easy for us to evaluate all these threats, though in fact they range from minuscule to serious. Instead we tend to merge them into a mildly menacing cloud that always surrounds us. We learn to live with it, since we feel generally helpless to do much about its shifting, confusing elements.[40]

For the frightened, the disjuncture between risk and degree of fear widens. This was noted earlier in the twentieth century, when soldiers during the Second World War were much more afraid of dive-bombers than machine guns, despite the fact that machine guns claimed many more lives (see Chapter Ten). After 11 September people were stunned when they realised that two domestic airlines could topple all 110 floors of the WTC, the architectural symbol of America's corporate greatness. Watching the Twin Towers crumble was a strong reminder of the failure of modern humanity to control its environment. No elite could safeguard mere underlings. Just after 11 September, Gregory Gargiso, a New York City fireman, put it succinctly in the *Architectural Record*. He drew attention to *The Towering Inferno*, a film that was prefaced by the words: 'To those who give their lives so that others may live — to the firefighters of the world — this picture is gratefully dedicated.' In the film the fire chief meets the architect of the blazing building and says, 'Maybe now they [the financiers, architects, and bureaucrats] will listen to what we [the fire service] have to say.' But in the face of the new threat, guarantees of safety were ludicrous. In Gargiso's words:

> I will say that because of money and politics (those being the biggest two) that fire concerns — or, better yet, how fire treats the elements of the building — are relegated to a low position on the laundry list of concerns when a 'super' or a 'jumbo' gets erected. I know the flak is coming: I can hear people screaming already: 'We do, we do, we always pay attention to the fire code and the building code.' Maybe that's where the problem lies: the code. No code written is sufficient for two jumbo jets flying into buildings.[41]

In other words, the architectural, engineering and fire protection services would *never* be able to promise invulnerability. Bosses and workers alike were right to fear the multi-storey buildings of modernity. Ironically, the World Trade Center was the tallest building in the world until the Sears Building was opened in 1974, the same year as *The Towering Inferno* was released.[42]

The danger of the collapse of buildings was not merely a local problem — one that had confronted engineers, architects and insurers throughout the century. As we saw in the last chapter, risk had become globalised. Idyllic resorts in Bali and Africa were vulnerable. Could New Zealand be next? An obscure airliner or trendy pub could be on the terrorists' hit list. This was a threat conducted on a 'human scale': the victims were familiar and widely perceived as innocent, underscoring human fragility.

No one could predict when terrorists might strike and few understood why they might be targeted. The striking disproportion between the power of the victimiser and that of the victim was particularly terrifying. Compact pistols and the ease of hiding weapons (when Black September hijacked Sabena Airlines Flight 517 in May 1972, the two female terrorists hid detonators in their bras and hand grenades in their cosmetic boxes) greatly aided the early terrorists. But even the slimmest of box-cutters and most discreet quantities of gunpowder concealed in the heel of a shoe could bring ruin.

Even worse, what would happen if terrorists adopted the most modern weapons of mass destruction? Millions could die if the smallpox virus was released in a city. New pathogens and toxins were constantly being invented. In the words of the author of 'The Nightmare of Bioterrorism' (2001), 'biology in the last decade has been what physics was in the 1940s and 1950s: a field of exponential discovery. What seemed impossible in 1980 was accomplished by 1990 and, by 2000, had become ho hum fodder for high school biology classes.'[43] Dread of nuclear terrorism was just as great as that associated with bioterrorism. In the words of Charles B. Strozier, speaking at a conference on human hazards in January 2002:

> Nuclear weapons totalize politics, religion, indeed the self. One might say that apocalypse is the totalism of death. They open up new possibilities for violence, new opportunities that in the past required God to carry out. The agency shifts. Humans can control their own destiny, which in the hands of the responsible is wonderfully empowering. In the hands of the paranoid, that power is terrifying.[44]

At the end of the twentieth century this fear was not primarily concerned with terrorist ownership of nuclear technologies and materials (after all, terrorists had long attempted to acquire fissile materials), but was influenced by anxieties that terrorists had become more willing to *use* this class of weapon. In 1996 the Director of Central Intelligence could confidentially state that 'terrorist groups with established sponsors probably will remain hesitant to use a nuclear weapon, for fear of provoking a world wide crackdown or alienating their sponsors'.[45] Within a few years, however, such hopes were shattered. A more ruthless breed of terrorist had emerged who did not feel constrained to minimise carnage. If terrorists were prepared to die in the course of the attack, there was very little either officials or bystanders could do to prevent a bloodbath. No longer was anyone capable of echoing the words of a Federal Aviation Administration official, speaking in 1989: 'Terrorists are not very common in the U.S. We do not have Abu Nidal running around the streets of New York or Detroit.'[46] The threat seemed ubiquitous; the enemy only dimly identified. The threat was 'objective' and 'immediate', but purposeful activity against the danger was uncertain.

In such a cultural climate, simply employing the word 'terrorist' stimulated fear. When the eminent critic Susan Sontag argued that 'metaphors and myths . . . kill' she was referring to the way the stigmatised word 'cancer' incited fears that discouraged sufferers from seeking medical help and thus hastened their death.[47] Similarly, the label 'terrorism' was used by governments and other official agencies to incite fears that could then be used to justify speedy and potentially counterproductive military operations. In other words, the word 'terrorist' was so frightening in itself that it deflected attention from the serious consideration of foreign policy and incursions into civil liberties at home. As Bethami A. Dobkin expressed it in *Tales of Terror* (1992), the term 'terrorist' was 'more than a descriptor of political violence'. It was also 'a functional term that warrants certain strategic responses and precludes others'. The panic that resulted from terrorist fears diverted attention from the 'causes of political violence and [has] united public support for reactionary policies.' In other words, the public hysteria over terrorism increased 'support for direct military action in foreign conflicts' which directly contributed to the growing terrorist risk.[48] Edward

Said adopted a similar position in 'The Essential Terrorist' (1988).
According to him, the invidious use made of the word 'terrorist'

> has spawned uses of language, rhetoric and argument that are fright-
> ening in their capacity for mobilizing opinion, gaining legitimacy and
> provoking various sorts of murderous action. And it has imported
> and canonized an ideology with origins in a distant conflict, which
> serves the purpose here of institutionalizing the denial and avoidance
> of history. In short, the elevation of terrorism to the status of a
> national security threat (though more Americans drown in their
> bathtubs, are struck by lightning or die in traffic accidents) has
> deflected careful scrutiny of the government's domestic and for-
> eign policies.

Increased surveillance of public places, expansion of the powers of
the military and law-enforcement agencies, tightening of border
controls, 'stomping down' on recent immigrants, campaigns to justify torture in police interrogations and assassinations abroad, and
the launching of 'pre-emptive strikes' on other nation states were
some of the reactions to that fearful word 'terrorist'.

There were other responses to fears of terrorism. Terror of swift
annihilation made people react in ways typical of frightened people
throughout the century. For instance, immediately after the attack of
11 September there was a renewal of 'the American community' in
response to danger: church attendance soared, prayer vigils sprang
up at the corner of suburban enclaves and people rushed to embrace
their loved ones. But at the same time as the words 'I love you'
seemed to echo around the world, an evil 'Other' was being identified and preparations made to defeat it. As we have seen throughout
this book, when frightened people stop fleeing from the feared
object or situation, they seek to fight, even if a scapegoat has to be
invented. With the 9/11 attack there was a relief that — finally —
the enemy could be defined as an 'outsider'. It was no longer the
CIA (as in the Kennedy conspiracy in 1963) or a crazed American
(as in the 1995 bombing of the Murrah Federal Building in
Oklahoma City), but foreign Islamic 'fundamentalists'. Although
there was considerable unease with the adroit way these terrorists

were able to assimilate into Middle America, the relief of their otherness was clear. The enemy could be identified: he was 'the Muslim'.

The supposed threat posed by 'the Arab' — a synonym, albeit inaccurate, for 'Muslim' — was a virulent one. After the attack on the Twin Towers a thousand people thought to be 'Arab' were assaulted and at least six murdered.[49] Virulent hatreds erupted. For instance, Mr Phil Beckwith, a former chief petty officer in the navy and retired truck driver, typified the response of many Americans after 11 September when he insisted that he knew 'just what to do with these Arab people. We have to find them, kill them, wrap them in pigskin and bury them. That way they will never go to heaven.' Forty-five-year-old Bruce Cristina, a worker at Ogden Metalworking in Ogden, Utah, advised his government to 'level the country that's harboring them. The whole country. Let the world know that we're not going to put up with terrorism of any magnitude. Go in there and do the job. Hit them with whatever we're got.'[50] The interwar fantasy of the Arab as propagated by Lawrence of Arabia — the Arab as Bedouin on a camel in the desert — was supplanted by the figure of the sinister, bearded fundamentalist who did not allow nine-year-old girls to go to school or boys to fly kites. Instead of recognising that Western imperialism and support for oppressive regimes in the Shah's Iran, Nimeri's Sudan, Lebanon and Palestine had alienated millions of people all over the Muslim world, America and its allies depicted this 'enemy' as an irrational, monolithic beast, epitomised by the names of the 'popes of Islam' — Gaddafi, Ayatollah Khomeini, Saddam Hussein and Osama bin Laden. Islam *was* extremism.

Although fear and hatred of the Arab certainly intensified after 2001, it had been a lingering presence for decades. Popular films such as the television documentary *Jihad in America*, screened in December 1994 and portraying a hostile Islam threatening the nation, aggravated uneasiness. Fictional representations of the evil Arab or Muslim were more insidious. Of the 900-plus English-language feature films that featured Arabs, analysed by Jack G. Shaheen's *Reel Bad Arabs* (2001), only a handful portrayed them favourably. In Shaheen's words:

> From 1896 until today, filmmakers have collectively indicted all
> Arabs as Public Enemy #1 — brutal, heartless, uncivilized, religious
> fanatics and money-mad cultural 'others' bent on terrorizing civi-
> lized westerners, especially Christians and Jews.[51]

The Western media portrayed Muslim leaders as backward-
looking figures from another age. In the words of David Balkin in
his article 'Time to Excise this Cancer of Terrorism': 'Every psycho
malcontent in the Arab world wants a piece of us . . . . They are
schizophrenic cavemen, with 21st century capacities.'[52] Even educated Muslims were regarded as radicalised, marginalised and often
violent revolutionaries, at war with modernity.[53] Of course, this
portrayal of the enemy was illusory. On 19 April 1995, when the
Murrah Federal Building was bombed, killing 168 workers and
children and wounding four hundred others, major American television networks were quick to draw attention to a man of 'Islamic
appearance' seen in the area. Arab Americans endured over three
hundred hate crimes in the aftermath of the bombing and there
were public calls for a pre-emptive strike on Middle Eastern
states.[54] Many Americans found it extremely disconcerting when
Timothy J. McVeigh, a clean-shaven former GI, was arrested, con-
victed and executed for the crime. Foreigners were also blamed
during the anthrax scare at the end of 2001. President Bush called
anthrax the 'second wave of terrorism' and, even after reports
began circulating that the spores were most likely to have been
spread by right-wing American political extremists or fanatical
anti-abortionists, Bush insisted that 'anyone that evil cannot be
American'.[55] Fear-provoking agents had to come from 'without'.

Throughout the century the reactions of people who have experienced major traumatic events, recent examples being the 1995
Oklahoma City bombing and the attack on the WTC in 2001, have
been the subject of much speculation and analysis. In the last quarter of the century there was a move to a 'trauma society'. According
to this view, every fearful event has a psychological backlash.
Twentieth-century individuals were much more aware of psychological thought and were therefore less able to employ the
conversions and rationalisations used in the past to cushion the

impact of reality. Furthermore, as we saw in Chapter Eleven, attention was just as likely to be focused upon the psychological threat posed by criminals as upon their threat to material security. In the context of terrorism, the invention of the 'trauma society' was also prevalent. In Northern Ireland the period 1969–98 (designated 'The Troubles') witnessed an orgy of bombs and assassinations, which killed over 3600 people.[56] However, the psychological effect was regarded as particularly grim. Between a fifth and half of survivors of terrorist explosions were described as suffering 'serious affective disturbance' such as agoraphobia, exaggerated startle reactions and post-traumatic stress disorder.[57]

Similarly, a great amount of attention was focused on the discovery that, two years after the Oklahoma City bombing, a fifth of children living 100 miles from the bombing were diagnosed as suffering from 'bomb-related difficulty functioning', or PTSD. These were children who had no *direct* contact with the bombing. The psychologists who conducted this survey stressed its 'important clinical implications. Parents, teachers, counselors, and others working with children must be alert to the potential for syndrome development in children with indirect exposure to traumatic events'.[58]

The psychological legacy of disasters — particularly man-made ones — outweighed the seriousness of any physical devastation. Death remained the ultimate terror, but psychological injury became more frightening than physical mutilation or ruin of a society's infrastructure. Earlier we looked at the way religious languages were gradually subsumed by psychological ones in terror management. Rather than tragedy being interpreted as a moral event, it became the site of a 'psychic wound'. The relevance of psychology was no longer questioned: disaster discourse simply focused on the *type* of psychological model most applicable to understanding an individual's fears or a group's panic.

It should come as no surprise, therefore, that after the terrorist attacks on 11 September, American attention concentrated on one group of people whose emotional needs were regarded as especially sacred — the young. It was widely estimated that around 75,000 children in the five boroughs of New York City suffered multiple symptoms of PTSD as a result of the attack on the WTC, while another

190,000 suffered from at least one of seven other mental health disorders.[59] In another survey of schools in Manhattan, a quarter of children were diagnosed as showing 'significant symptoms' of psychiatric disorders traceable to the terrorist attack. This proportion doubled among children in schools close to the WTC, many of whom had actually watched the aeroplanes flying into the towers from their school windows.[60] In such schools adjustment to what they had witnessed was exacerbated by the panic that followed the attacks, with parents besieging the schools in search of their children. There was 'chaos, confusion, panic — some kids were crying, parents screaming', according to one of the psychologists who carried out the survey.[61]

Whatever psychological model was adopted, these scenes of panic were said to destroy the children's sense of security. The children of America became the symbol for the trauma experienced by American society more broadly: innocence had been destroyed. In the words of Senator Hillary Clinton at a hearing held to 'address unmet mental health needs of children post 9-11', on that fateful day in September 'America's children lost a childhood filled with innocence and freedom'. Senator John Corzine went further, claiming that the terrorists had deliberately targeted children. 'One of the main goals of terrorism is to create fear among the general public and specifically against our most vulnerable citizens — our children,' he said, and continued:

> To fully fight terrorism, we must be prepared to fight the psychological war that terrorism inflicts and the victims it creates in its wake. It is critical that we hear the plea of Scarlet Taveras, a high school student who says, 'Please don't forget about the survivors who struggle each time a plane flies by' or the plea of Mary Ellen Salamone, a widow and mother of three, who tells that our children 'need it to finally be September 12.'[62]

The problem facing parents and psychologists was how to cope with children's fears. The Internet was saturated with requests for advice, asking the same sorts of questions that had been posed at the end of the twentieth century: 'Should we shield [children] from such horrors or talk openly about them?'[63]

Certain types of children were regarded as being more 'at risk' of suffering from prolonged fear and anxiety reactions. The saturation of the mass media with images of terrorist attack rendered children who watched a large amount of television footage of the attack particularly susceptible. This was observed after the Oklahoma City bombing when psychologists studying PTSD symptoms among children insisted that 'the potential for media coverage to serve as a traumatic reminder . . . cannot be overemphasised'.[64] It was no coincidence that the fourth edition of the *Diagnostic and Statistical Manual of Mental Disorders* (1994) included indirect as well as direct exposure to trauma in establishing the diagnosis of PTSD.

The experience of 11 September merely confirmed these fears. In the words of a Professor of Clinical Child Psychology at the University of Kansas:

The news media may inadvertently amplify and increase traumatic exposure . . . by showing graphic and emotionally laden images of terrorist acts and the aftermath; in previous eras, the public could only imagine such a scene of violence, whereas today we can experience it over and over again in Technicolor.[65]

More generally, though, the type of people regarded as especially likely to suffer extreme panic were those identified throughout this book — girls, who were regarded as more susceptible than boys, and children who had to cope with 'parental psychopathology'. Echoing the experience of severe fear reactions during the bombing of British cities during the Second World War, children with a history of prior trauma and those who were exposed to a 'poor parental response' also risked longer-term psychological damage.[66] Evidence from the Blitz of Britain during that war was frequently cited, especially the view that 'children will often take on the anxiety of adults around them'.[67]

Indeed, references to military conflict and the 'lessons learned' in that context were common. Psychologically, nearly all psychologists agreed the 'war on terrorism' was similar to other wars. All modern wars targeted civilians, making emotional management of entire populations central to 'winning the war', as we saw in the discussion of the two world wars in Chapter Eight. According to the commonplace rhetoric of trauma specialists, the 'mental scars' left by extremes of fear during war or terrorist attacks might be buried temporarily, but would eventually erupt. In the words of Christina Hoven, a psychiatrist who had studied the emotional responses of around 8300 children in New York City to the attack in 2001:

> We're talking about a very large population at risk. We know enough about the effects of the ravages of war. They [people traumatised by war] keep it a secret, they don't tell their children what they experienced. It's something you don't even want to repeat, but then suddenly there's a car accident and you relive it.[68]

As we saw in Chapter Seven, which focused on combat, most extreme fear reactions were conceptualised as 'normal battle reactions', with only exceptional instances of insanity excluded. Psychologists dealing with the aftermath of 11 September were equally concerned to differentiate 'normal' from 'pathological' fear reactions. As one social worker who had counselled teachers and parents at schools close to the WTC put it:

> How do we respond to parents when parents ask us, 'What should I do when my child is having nightmares?' How do we identify the normal process of trauma and grief? How do we differentiate that from something that is pathological? And if we do, what do we do about it?[69]

During terrorist attacks as well as during combat, the chief problem was that 'fight or flight' responses were often impossible: except in the immediate aftermath of an attack (when flight was desirable), the enemy was invisible — he could be neither fought nor fled. Even the weapons of war were impersonal. All that was certain was that it was a very uneven contest between technology and corporeality.

Unsurprisingly, after 11 September psychologists and psychiatrists throughout America lamented the fact that their services had not been sufficiently exploited. For instance, Eric M. Vernberg,

Professor of Clinical Child Psychology at the University of Kansas, believed that:

> Despite all the attention, sympathy and money donated to help people in Manhattan and surrounding areas, only one-third of the children with pronounced psychiatric symptoms had any contact with a counselor, psychiatrist, or other mental health provider in the six months after the attack. As a nation, we have invested in deterrence, surveillance, and revenge rather than addressing the profound psychological cost of terrorism.

Even the psychological counselling offered by organisations such as the Federal Emergency Management Agency and the American Red Cross was limited to the acute phase of the disaster, leaving long-term care to the limited resources of local mental health centres, schools, churches and private practitioners. Vernberg insisted that 'we find ourselves at a strange juncture: we have a relatively sophisticated science based knowledge of psychology, but we have not successfully put it into practice'.[70]

In other words, in contrast with what we saw in Chapter Two, which looked at disasters, by 2001 there was an expectation that 'mental health professionals' were imperative if people were to recover from their panic states. This represented a major shift from the situation earlier in the century, when individual will power was more likely to be emphasised. In the words of Johannes Müller, writing on *Hindrances of Life* (1909):

> The best method . . . by which to cultivate fearlessness is to employ it persistently as a test in any anxiety. Every victory strengthens our confidence, and the oftener we come scathless out of great difficulties and disasters, the more impregnable shall we become. Such experiences tend, naturally, to strengthen in us our feeling of superiority. It is for this reason that a life beset with dangers is always the best school for acquiring a brave spirit.[71]

By the twenty-first century danger did not strengthen but weakened the individual, who needed to enlist the help of a set of professionals to cope with the trials and tribulations of life. In the words of Helene Jackson of Columbia University's School of Social Work, parents worried about the way their children were coping with the terrorist attack had 'no idea where to go or who to speak to' yet they 'expressly ask' for psychological advice. She argued for the need for education in trauma counselling for all teachers. This was even more imperative because, Jackson believed, children who had previous experience of traumas such as child sexual abuse were particularly likely to suffer extreme anxiety after 11 September. In her words, 'We've learned that it's more than just the events at the World Trade Center that have created a crisis, particularly when you see those statistics of how many children suffered trauma prior to 9/11.' The solution was training in managing psychological trauma for all teachers in schools 'all over the country, and all over the world'. The mantra was 'mental health is the stepchild of all health'.[72] By the end of the twentieth century psychology framed, created and managed extremes of anxiety.

Nevertheless, despite the pathologising of children and adults in the aftermath of a terrifying situation, what is striking is the extent to which many people coped well in extremely frightening (and even lethal) situations. The resilience of the human imagination remains the most remarkable feature of humanity. As we have seen throughout this book, people often act in fearless ways, even when faced with terrible threats to themselves, loved ones and the wider society. Even among people suffering from severe phobic states, the creativity and courage with which they nursed day-to-day terrors was remarkable.

This book has focused on fear and its effects. But it must be remembered that many seemingly dangerous situations were not feared — indeed, certain groups of people even embraced some of the most widely held fears. For instance, as we have seen throughout the century, fears relating to science's ever-expanding knowledges have been pervasive. In particular, these fears have been likened to anxieties surrounding the question: 'What does it mean to be human?' The mad scientist was not always portrayed in fear-provoking ways, even in horror films. *The Fly* (1958) starred an obsessed scientist, Andre Delambre, who tests a matter-transfer machine on himself but inadvertently allows a fly to fly into the machine. He emerges with a fly's head and arm, while his own head and arm have been implanted on the fly. In one scene he tries to persuade his wife, Helene, that matter-transfer should not be feared:

> **Helene:** It's frightening. It's like playing God.
> **Andre:** God gives us intelligence to uncover the wonders of nature. Without that gift nothing is possible.
> **Helene:** Oh Andre, I get so scared sometimes. The suddenness of our age: electronics, rockets, earth satellites, supersonic flight. And now this. It's not so much who invents them. It's the fact that they exist.
> **Andre:** But you're not frightened of TV or radio or X-rays or electricity or that the earth is round.
> **Helene:** No, but everything's going so fast. I'm just not ready to take it all in. It's all so quick.
> **Andre:** Just do like Philippe [their son] does: accept them as part of normal life. They're facts, wonderful facts.

Andre was right: although science phobia persisted throughout the century, people often exhibited a strong ability to accommodate and assimilate its fearful aspects. For this reason the commentator in the 1930s who predicted that 'Future airplane travel is not likely to rival automobile travel due to the instinctive aversion to leaving terra firma' could not have been more wrong.[73] As we saw in Chapter Eleven, only certain aspects of science were feared — advances in genetics, for instance, rather than advances in Information Technology; or radiation (such as that emanating from nuclear power plants) rather than X-rays. A similar observation could be made about ill health and death. Although physical incapacity was a frightening prospect for most people, physically ill people often responded fearlessly to their ailments. Instead of being afraid, they might have simply been resigned. Instead of panic, they were proud. Illness — even if life-threatening — sometimes gave patients an intense feeling of freedom from the burdens of their lives and a licence to wallow in the overdue attention of their loved ones.[74] For many terminally ill people death promised a rest from discomfort; others regarded it merely as a 'fact of life' that gave meaning to every gasping breath.[75]

In other words, even the fear of death was not universal. As we saw in Chapter Ten, the disgrace of having cancer might have over-whelmed any feelings of fear about dying. Once miners trapped in serious mining disasters realised that rescue was unlikely, they reported that they lost their fear, simply persuading themselves that dying was 'going to sleep', 'more like a dream than anything' and 'we would never know what happened'. Their only anxieties were about how their families and friends would react.[76] There were other instances when shame could overwhelm fear. Responses to the financial panics of 1893, 1907 and 1929, for instance, included waves of suicide among people who preferred the certitude of death to the insecurity of the future. More courageously, some people willingly faced death for noble reasons. Firemen, lifeguards and air-raid wardens, for instance, often risked their lives to help others. Indeed, as argued early in this book, mutilation and pain might have frightened such individuals much more than death. There were greater things to fear than one's own death.

Finally, throughout this book, we have seen people who have been transformed in positive ways by their emotional experiences of danger. During the First World War John M. Conner told his diary that 'seeing your pals blown into bits, it makes a new man fellow in spirit, moral & character', while forty-year-old Mr Parrino's response to surviving the attack on the WTC was 'I'm not going to be the same guy. And I'm not going to pretend that life isn't going to be different. I'm saying hello to everyone I see in the street.'[77] The issue is not whether we are traumatised, but how we are transformed.

However, as Marina Warner observed in her classic book *No Go the Bogeyman* (1998), there was a 'contradiction at the heart of human responses to fear'. In attempting to 'undo enemy power', we 'make it visible'. In Warner's words:

> By making visible the predator, the intruder, the stranger whom we fear lurks beyond vision . . . by dragging the object of terror into shape in the common light of day, by imitating its imagined assaults and power, it can be controlled, or so it is hoped . . . In other

words, the drive to define and delimit 'home', to name and circumscribe the abode and the milieu to which one belongs and where one feels safe, leads to naming and defining things — and people — out there beyond the fence, on the other side of the perimeter wire.[78]

This process of identifying an outsider — someone 'on the other side of the perimeter wire' — has nasty consequences. The person or group blamed for the threat could be reviled and even attacked in turn. In the twentieth century there was a plethora of bogeymen, primarily different kinds of 'strangers'; the list could go on and on. This psychological process was noted with particular concern during the Second World War by commentators such as the psychiatrist Joost Meerloo. As we saw in Chapter Eight, he described the scape-goating process whereby we identify others with that part of ourselves of which we disapprove and there grows within us a hatred of the object of our identification.[79]

Meerloo's fundamental focus was on explaining how so many Germans could countenance the mass murder of the Jews, but Britain's responses to 'natives' in its empire could also be referred to. For instance, a number of times in this book men and women have described how the courage of the explorer and missionary David Livingstone enabled them to cope in extremes of danger. Nancy Venables Raine, for instance, who described her terrifying rape in Chapter Eleven, recalled Livingstone's emotional responses when he was attacked by a wounded lion.[80] Livingstone's courage while being flung side to side in the lion's jaw ('like a mouse') proved to be a role model that enabled her to 'go on'. Nevertheless, this same story of moral courage in the face of death was used in many children's stories to assert the superiority of the 'white man'. Take two children's books, both published in 1913 — Mary Entwistle's *The Child's Livingstone* and J. A. Staunton Batty's *Livingstone. The Empire Builder or 'Set Under the Cross'*. Entwistle described Livingstone's arrival in an African village that was being terrorised by 'big lions'. Indeed, 'so frightened were the black men and women that they dared not go outside the village gates. The boys and girls had to play near home. At night the lions roared so loudly

that the black babies woke up and cried', young readers were told.
According to Entwistle:

> The black men started out with their spears to hunt the lions. 'We
> will kill them all', they said, and they looked very fierce. But when
> the lions roared at them, how quickly they ran home again!
>
> Then David Livingstone helped them. He took his big gun, and
> the black men took their spears. They kept very close to Dr
> Livingstone, for he made them feel very strong. He shot one of the
> lions and it sprang upon him. It knocked him down and bit his arm
> very badly. It was such a strong, fierce lion that the Doctor felt like
> a mouse. The black men then thought that he was killed, and all but
> two of them ran away. But the two who stayed behind were brave,
> and helped Dr Livingstone to kill the fierce, growling lion. Then the
> poor frightened ones came back, when they saw the lion was dead.[81]

The racial lesson was clear: the imperial race possessed a superior
quota of courage in adversity. The African men were even incapable
of defending their 'black babies'.

Batty's children's book, based on this same incident, added gender
differentials to the analysis of fear. A schoolteacher called Miss Letty
is pictured telling the story of Livingstone's progression towards
the lion's mouth to a group of young children. After Miss Letty
described the ferocity of the lions, a child put up his hand, asking,
'Please, Miss . . . I've read that lions are rather cowardly, and don't
come near men unless they are obliged to.' Miss Letty replied:

> I believe that is so generally . . . but these lions are different. There
> were a great many of them, and they had found out how frightened
> the Bakatlas were. You see, these poor people, when they saw how
> fierce and cunning the lions were getting, began to think that there
> was some magic at work. They thought that one of the tribes had
> bewitched them, and had given them into the power of the lions.

In contrast to the cowardly, superstitious Africans, Livingstone
'was ready for any adventure'. While the villagers 'made a circle
around the hill', Livingstone and an African schoolmaster bravely

opted to confront the lions in the plain. According to Miss Letty, the schoolmaster 'fired at a lion but did not hit him, and the natives let [the lion] break through their ring, for they were too frightened to spear him. Livingstone began to feel that it was no good to go to kill lions with people who were so frightened.'

Suddenly Livingstone saw a lion and shot him, but the lion simply became enraged and bit Livingstone and the schoolmaster before dropping dead. The children were suitably impressed. For Miss Letty, however, the story did not end there. She concluded the chapter by reporting a conversation she overheard. As the children were leaving the room, they were talking to one another about the scary story of Livingstone in the lion's jaw. One child was reported as saying, 'Look here, Lizzie, and any of you girls . . . If you're frightened you just get in the middle, and George and I — we're the two biggest — we'll just go on the outsides.' In this account not only are the Africans cowardly, but girls are portrayed as needing the protection of boys.[82] The communal spirit rapidly converted itself into an ugly, chauvinistic one.

This was not the only contradiction at the heart of fear. In the process of coping with frightening threats by defining who is 'within' and who 'without', frightened people increased the risk of being threatened further. Frightened responses to terrorist attacks were clear examples: closing borders, withdrawing aid and engaging in pre-emptive strikes antagonised increasing numbers of people in hostile states. Many other examples could be mentioned. In wartime, for instance, servicemen were more likely to commit atrocities when they were terrified, but this, in turn, led their frightened enemy to respond with equal or even greater violence. Similarly, as we saw in Chapter Eleven, fear of crime encouraged people to shut themselves up in their homes at night. They ended up watching television dramas depicting lawless urban spaces, and this served to increase their fear of criminals outside their door.

And yet again there was a further contradiction in the nature of fear. As we have seen repeatedly in this book, fear is manipulated by numerous organisations with a stake in creating fear while promising to eradicate it. Fear circulates within a wealthy economy of powerful interest groups dependent upon ensuring that we remain scared. Theologians, politicians, the media, physicians and the psychological services depend on our fright. Despite the proliferation of discourses about fear, its eradication has never been seriously countenanced: substitution of fear-inspiring discourses, rather than obliteration, has been the goal.

The final contradiction is this: the pain at the heart of fear could simultaneously constitute part of the pleasure of this emotion. This contradiction was recognised by one of the great nineteenth-century theorists of the emotions, Alexander Bain. In his *The Emotions and the Will* (1859) he observed that:

> A genuine fright is undoubtedly an experience of pure misery; but a slight fear, with speedy relief occurring in times of dulness [sic] and stolid composure, acts like a stimulant on the nervous system. In the flush of high bodily vigour, danger only heightens the interest of action and pursuit . . . In proportion as the reality of evil is removed far from ourselves, we are at liberty to join in the excitement produced by the expression of fear.[83]

Although this aspect of fear has been broached only occasionally in this book, throughout the twentieth century people revelled in reading about gruesome rapes and murders in 'penny dreadfuls' and the 'yellow press', flocked to hear scaremongering sermons at Pentecostal gatherings and paid money to ride in dizzily swooping roller-coasters or watch horror films. For these people fear was a sensual release from everyday tedium. Fear — in particular those extremes of fear which involved the group rather than the lone individual — could bring pleasure, a 'shivering exaltation' that released the individual from the tiresomeness of the banal.[84] The glorious gothic fiction of Stephen King and Anne Rice — modern writers following in the tradition of the early gothic author Ann Radcliffe, about whom we heard in Chapter Four in connection with nightmares — turned fear into a pleasurable commodity, a 'Baudrillardian spectacle'.

These (and other) cultural productions could also lance people's fears. In *Beyond the Pleasure Principle* Freud showed how children created games about situations and objects they most feared in order to gain control.[85] For adults, cultural production involving threats, dangers, risks and fears enabled them to retreat to the state of childhood and play with what they found most scary. Just as alien invaders in *The Thing* (1951) and *Creature from the Black Lagoon* (1954) easily 'stood in' for Cold War fears of Russian invasion, so too people experimented with their fears through symbols and narratives. Terror became part of culture. Language transformed private terrors into a social event, providing decisive proof that the individual was no longer alone.

Throughout the century fear was employed in creative ways. Confrontation with danger and disasters produced a sense of the sacred that many people otherwise lacked. In this book there have been many instances of religious narratives seeking to expand and exploit people's fears in order to enforce particular patterns of behaviour. This should not blind us to the creative uses made of the spiritual. After all, it is important to recognise that, although the psychological sciences won the battle to dictate over humanity's fear and anxieties, religious succour still captured the hearts of people in fearful situations. In wartime, for instance, a sense of awe and metaphysical transcendence was reintroduced, although in a new form. Combatants, caught in a landscape of unrelenting terrorisation, turned not to religion for comfort, but to the superstitious sway of armulets, mascots and guardian angels. The existence of a benevolent God was remote in this fiendish man-made hell. For a minority, a belief in a loving God was important in allaying the fear of death. As one serviceman during the First World War recalled:

> I never really discovered the power of God within my own life until one day in France, when I was brought face to face with what seemed certain death. It was then that I prayed to God with my whole soul to bring me out alive and to give me another chance to work for Him. By a miracle I was spared, and since then my life has been changed. I understood what it meant to be born again.[86]

A similar sense of the spiritual existed during the Second World War. The popular 'London Journalist' reminded his readers during the air raids hitting British cities that feelings of panic came from being excessively 'body-conscious'. He exhorted his readers to remember that the 'real man that lives and survives' resides in the soul: 'If Hitler attacks us, he cannot touch the soul. If bombs fall they cannot kill "you".'[87] 'We all possess a bomb-proof life,' he declared, and God was the best 'nerve tonic'.[88] It was a common response in natural disasters as well. As one woman attested after a tornado hit Topeka, Kansas, on 8 June 1966:

> I didn't have any fear; I didn't really think I was going to be blown away. I know I was disturbed but there was really no hysteria. My thirteen year old daughter was quite scared. When it began to blow pretty hard she crawled under some screens that were leaning in the corner of the basement. She stuck her hand out to me and started crying hysterically. And I said, 'Now just calm down. If the Lord wants us now, we are probably just as ready as we'll ever be.' And I said, 'If you ask Him, He'll save us.' And she quieted down then.[89]

During all disasters examined in this book, a proportion of fearful victims turned to rituals and incantations such as prayer as a bridge to sanity.

Religion was only one cultural response to fear. Other narrative forms were also effective. Like dreaming (discussed in Chapter Seven), watching disaster films or reading horror literature could be 'a safe, routinized way of playing with death'.[90] Whether we accept a psychoanalytic line that people watching horror films were responding to 'atavistic terrors nearly as old as the reptilian brain',[91] or a behaviourist interpretation that the audience was undergoing a process of desensitisation, it is clear that these were all responses to that most prosaic and universal of fears: impending death. In the words of Martin Tropp in *Images of Fear* (1990):

> Horror stories, when they work, construct a fictional edifice of fear and deconstruct it simultaneously, dissipating terror in the act of creating it. And real horrors are filtered through the expectations of readers trained in responding to popular fiction, familiar with a set of images, a language, and patterns of behaviour. Horror fiction

gives the reader the tools to 'read' experiences that would otherwise, like nightmares, be incommunicable.

Horror stories and films were 'not nightmares transcribed, but fears recast into safe and communicable forms'.[92]

Similarly, writing or talking about fears of breast cancer or a resurgence of terrorist aggression could be a way of rehearsing death. As Nancy Venables Raine insisted, rearranging the furniture in her home and workplace to ensure that her back was never turned to the door provided a sense of autonomy in the face of imagined threats. By creatively constructing her physical environment, she developed a sense of cognitive and physical control. In other words, cultural production was humanity's buffer against the terror of threatened corporeality and imminent mortality. It provided a sense of transcendence, or a fantasy of another world. Rephrased using the language of the anthropologist Mary Douglas it soothed the consciousness of unclear borders — borders of the body (what was inside and outside), of nature (illness and death) and society (belonging and not belonging). Most important, as we have seen throughout this book, it enabled people to explore the question: 'What makes us human?'

What this reminds us is that there is nothing inherently wrong about fear. In many circumstances fear is an appropriate emotion to incite. Obviously parents are acting correctly when they evoke fears in their children: crossing roads, playing with fire and touching electrical sockets are rightly taught to be scary. In times of disaster or when faced with a serious threat, the 'flight' response of fear might also be beneficial — at least for those who survived.[93] Similarly, when patients were seriously ill, a certain amount of fear helped them to psychologically cope successfully with, for instance, major surgery. Patients who were too cheerful or apathetic before the operation fared less well than those patients who 'had time to assimilate the situation and to develop an appropriate anxiety'.[94] Finally, as we saw in the chapters dealing with warfare, fear could stimulate attention, sharpen judgement and energise combatants.[95] Fear kept men alert and more 'combat effective'.

Furthermore, fear could be beneficial not only for the way it encouraged people to act in safer ways: it could also promote more 'civilised' behaviour. For instance, drink-driving and anti-smoking campaigns used the fear of death to discourage anti-social or self-destructive behaviours. Indeed, fear was widely regarded as part of the civilising process. Much of the human urge to creativity depended upon fear — fear of death, rejection and loneliness. In the past this was a key idea for evolutionarily minded commentators. According to them, fear was the great adaptive emotion: it was the emotion that forged civilisation. As Grace Adams wrote in *Don't Be Afraid* (1935):

> If primitive man had never felt afraid there would be no human race today . . . if man had never had the capacity to fear, he would not now have the power to talk, to read, to imagine and to reason. Fear . . . must have been the first and for a long while the most powerful of all the traits of human mentality, the one from which the higher faculties had to evolve.[96]

But we do not have to embrace an evolutionary theory to note that fear could be a civilising emotion, forcing people to act in law-abiding and co-operative ways in order to gain the approbation of other people.[97] It was 'an integrator of social conduct whereby control was gained over the egoistic impulses', such as the fear of punishment or of public rebuff.[98] Only fear of the consequences restrained some people from doing evil.[99] In the words of H. E. Bryant in 1939, in fear of incurring public condemnation 'many a potentially dishonest man is kept honest; many a would-be criminal, law-abiding'. Furthermore, he insisted, fear of being rejected by others led people to act in ways that were often heroic. He concluded that fear tended 'to civilize and energize'.[100]

This idea can be expressed more positively in the sense that fear is a great and glorious stimulant that works in direct opposition to attempts to rigidly control our environment. We are right to fear. A world without fear would be a dull world indeed. It is sobering to contemplate a world where parents did not fear for their children or where death was as insignificant as eating a meal. In the words of a woman living in Britain during the First World War when under attack by Zeppelins: 'I was dreadfully frightened and said my prayers . . . I could never get used to raids, they frightened me terribly, as much for my two boys who were fighting in France as for myself. "If it is like this here, what must it be there?" I used to ask myself.'[101] A world without fear would be a world without love. Fear has been one of the most significant driving forces in history, encouraging individuals to reflect more deeply and prompting them to action. Indeed, much of the human urge to creativity depends upon fear — fear of being 'struck down in our prime', of being rejected, of not understanding how one's lover will respond and of self-consciousness. Anxiety is 'the dizziness of freedom', according to the philosopher Kierkegaard.[102] Finally, it is right to fear the pain suffered by others. 'How shall I face the fear which threatens you?', the lover asks his loved one.[103]

Notes

INTRODUCTION: FEAR

1 'A Former Sufferer', *How to Make a Speech Without Fear and Trembling* (London, 1921), 21–2.

2 Flora Bigelow Guest, *Casting Out Fear* (New York, 1918), 55.

3 This argument was given by Adolph Kielblock, *Stage Fright or How to Face an Audience* (Boston, 1891), 9–10, although he tended to think that the balance of sufferers was more evenly divided between the sexes. Also see Harry Campbell, 'Morbid Shyness', *British Medical Journal*, 26 September 1896, 806.

4 *Bashfulness Cured. Ease and Elegance of Manners Quickly Gained* (New York, 1872), 7, 9–11.

5 Elliott Webster, *Bashfulness* (Chicago, 1906), 91–2.

6 Dr E. L. Keyes, *The Fear of Death* (n.p., 1910), 3.

7 Dr Robert W. Mackenna, *The Adventure of Death* (London, 1916), 29.

8 John Jefferson, *An Antidote to Sudden Fear: Or, the Calmness in which Christians May Contemplate the Threatened Pestilence* (London, 1832), 3.

9 William Tebb and Colonel Edward Perry Vollum, *Premature Burial and How it May be Prevented with Special Reference to Trance, Catalepsy, and Other Forms of Suspended Animation* (London, 1896), 96.

10 Archdeacon R. H. Charles, *Courage, Truth, Purity* (Oxford, 1931), 34.

11 C. Whitaker-Wilson, *Nothing to Fear. A Bedside Book of Simple Philosophy* (London, 1952), 13–14.

12 Frederick William Faber, 1868, quoted in Joseph J. Mullen, *Psychological Factors in the Pastoral Treatment of Scruples* (Baltimore, 1927), vii.

13 William S. Walsh, *The Psychology of Dreams* (London, 1920), 204, 209–12. Also see Children's Welfare Federation of New York City, *Child Care Questions and Answers. Over 400 Questions Most Often Asked by Parents* (New York, 1948), 104, and Nathaniel Kleitman, *Sleep and Wakefulness as Alternating Phases in the Cycle of Existence* (Chicago, 1939), 388.

14 Herbert Signey Langfeld, 'The Judgment of Emotions from Facial Expressions', *Journal of Abnormal Psychology*, xiii (1918), 83, and Leo Kanner, *Judging Emotions from Facial Expressions* (Princeton, New Jersey, 1931), 17–18.

15 Paul Broks et al., 'Face Processing Impairments After Encephalitis: Amygdala Damage and Recognition of Fear', *Neuropsychologia*, 36 (1998), 59–70; Ruth Campbell et al., 'The Classification of "Fear" from Faces is Associated with Face Recognition Skill in Women', *Neuropsychologia*, 40 (2002), 575–84; M. L. Phillips et al., 'Time Courses of Left and Right Amygdalar Responses to Fearful Facial Expressions', *Human Brain Mapping*, 12 (2001), 193–202.

16 See Albert F. Ax, 'The Physiological Differentiation Between Fear and Anger in Humans', *Psychosomatic Medicine*, 15 (1953), 433–42; William M. Reddy, *The Navigation of Feeling. A Framework for the History of Emotions* (Cambridge, 2001), 12; S. Schachter and J. Singer, 'Cognitive, Social, and Physiological Determinants of Emotional State', *Psychological Review*, 69 (1962), 379–99. Note that this is still a highly debated area. For different opinions see Theodore D. Kemper, 'Sociology, Physiology, and Emotions: Comment on Shott', *American Journal of Sociology*, 85 (May 1980), 1418–23; Susan Shott, 'Emotion and Social Life: A Symbolic Interactionist Analysis', *Sociology*, 84 (May 1979), 1317–34; Susan Shott, 'Reply to Kemper', *American Journal of Sociology*, 85 (May 1980), 1423–6.

17 Clifford Geertz, *The Interpretation of Cultures* (London, 1975), 80–1. The phrase 'life of feeling' is Geertz quoting from S. Langer's *Feeling and Form* (New York, 1953), 372.

18 Major Libby Pulsifer, 'Psychiatric Aspects of Gastrointestinal Complaints of the Soldier in Training', *Military Surgeon*, 95.6 (December 1944), 482.

19 Quoted in Albert Barbaste, 'Scrupulosity and the Present Data of Psychiatry', *Theology Digest*, 1.3 (Autumn 1953), 182.

20 Simon Williams, *Emotion and Social Theory. Corporeal Reflections on the (Ir)Rational* (London, 2001), 63.

21 See the discussion by Calvin Thomas, *Male Matters. Masculinity, Anxiety and the Male Body on the Line* (Urbana, 1996), 16.

AFTERWORD TO THE INTRODUCTION: THE FACE OF FEAR

1 For example, see the sketches of Duchenne by his English translators: Emanuel B. Kaplan, in Dr G. B. Duchenne, *Physiology of Motion Demonstrated by Means of Electrical Stimulation and Clinical Observation and Applied to the Study of Paralysis and Deformities*, trans. and ed. Emanuel B. Kaplan (Philadelphia, 1949), ix–x, and G. V. Poore, in Dr Duchenne, *Selections from the Clinical Works of Dr. Duchenne (De Boulogne)*, trans. and ed. and condensed G. V. Poore (London, 1883), ix.

2 Emanuel B. Kaplan, in Dr G. B. Duchenne, *Physiology of Motion Demonstrated by Means of Electrical Stimulation and Clinical Observation and Applied to the Study of Paralysis and Deformities*, trans., ed. Emanuel B. Kaplan (Philadelphia, 1949), ix.

3 Ibid., xiii.

4 G. B. Duchenne de Boulogne, *The Mechanism of Human Facial Expression*, ed. and trans. R. Andrew Cuthbertson (Cambridge, 1990), 1, 9–12, 19–20, 31, 35–44, 48, 110–12, and *Selections from the Clinical Works of Dr. Duchenne (De Boulogne)*, trans., ed. and condensed G. V. Poore (London, 1883), 437–9, 448–50. Prior to this research, Duchenne had worked on the muscles more generally, propagating the view that electricity was more effective in curing

problems of the motor system than hydropathy ('water treatment') or drugs. Duchenne's experiments had a profound impact. His wider work on the electrical stimulation of paralysed limbs led to the cruel electric-shock treatments performed on 'shell-shocked' men during the First World War (Jean-Martin Charcot was Duchenne's pupil) and even today electrical stimulation of muscles and nerves, à la Duchenne, is widely used during cosmetic surgery. See John T. Hueston, 'Duchenne Today: Facial Expression and Facial Surgery', in G. B. Duchenne de Boulogne, *The Mechanism of Human Facial Expression*, ed. and trans. by R. Andrew Cuthbertson (Cambridge, 1990), 257. Ironically, this great physiologist of the emotions died as a result of paralysis.

5 Paul Ekman, 'Duchenne and Facial Expression of Emotion', in G. B. Duchenne de Boulogne, *The Mechanism of Human Facial Expression*, ed. and trans. R. Andrew Cuthbertson (Cambridge, 1990), 271.

6 R. Andrew Cuthbertson, 'The Highly Original Dr Duchenne', in G. B. Duchenne de Boulogne, *The Mechanism of Human Facial Expression*, ed. and trans. R. Andrew Cuthbertson (Cambridge, 1990), 230.

7 Charles Darwin, *The Expression of Emotions in Man and Animals*, 3rd edn., first published 1872, ed. Paul Ekman (London, 1998), 8, 17–25, 43, 69, 79, 99–105, 278–309, 356.

8 Carney Landis, 'Studies of Emotional Reactions. II. General Behavior and Facial Expression', *Journal of Comparative Psychology*, 4 (1924), 447–501, and Carney Landis, 'The Interpretation of Facial Expression in Emotion', *Journal of General Psychology*, II (1929), 59–72. Landis's conclusions were confirmed by M. Sherman, in *Journal of Contemporary Psychology*, 7 (1927), 265, 335. Also see Carroll E. Izard, 'Emotions and Facial Expressions: A Perspective from Differential Emotions Theory', in James A. Russell and José Miguel Fernández-Dols (eds.), *The Psychology of Facial Expression* (Cambridge, 1997); S. J. Rachman, *Fear and Courage* (San Francisco, 1978), 96.

9 Paul Ekman, Wallace V. Friesen and Silvan S. Tomkins, 'Facial Affect Scoring Technique: A First Validity Study', *Semiotica*, 3.1 (1971), 37–58; Paul Ekman, 'Duchenne and Facial Expression of Emotion', in G. B. Duchenne de Boulogne, *The Mechanism of Human Facial Expression*, ed. and trans. R. Andrew Cuthbertson (Cambridge, 1990), 282; Paul Ekman and Wallace V. Friesen, 'Constants Across Cultures in the Face and Emotion', in Henry Clay Lindgren (ed.), *Contemporary Research in Social Psychology. A Book of Readings*, 2nd edn. (New York, 1973), 336–47.

10 Peter Stearns, 'Emotion', in Rom Harré and Peter Stearns (eds.), *Discursive Psychology in Practice* (London, 1995), 40. Stearns used the example of 'anger' but I have substituted 'fear'.

CHAPTER ONE: DEATH

1 Spike [Cedric Wesley] Mays, *Reuben's Corner* (London, 1969), 13, 22, 26–9. Mays was born in 1907.

2 Cited in Linus Kline and C. J. France, 'The Psychology of Ownership', *The Pedagogical Seminary*, vi.4 (December 1898), 468.

3 Ibid.

4 *The Times*, 21 April 1877, 13.

5 Ruth Richardson, *Death, Dissection and the Destitute* (London, 1988), 271.

6 Public Record Office (London) (PRO) MH74/16.

7 For an insightful book on dissection and related fears in nineteenth-century America, see Michael Sappol, *A Traffic of Dead Bodies. Anatomy and Embodied Social Identity in Nineteenth-Century America* (Princeton, 2002).

8 'Horrors of the Dissecting Room', *Pall Mall Gazette*, 19 January 1888, in PRO HO45/10062/B2694.

9 Cited in 'Disposal of Deceased Paupers', *Echo*, 23 December 1887, PRO HO45/10062/B2694. Also see *The Weekly Times and Echo*, 25 December 1887.

10 Thomas Laqueur, 'Bodies, Death and Pauper Funerals', *Representations*, 1.1 (February 1983), 110.

11 Sir Arnold Wilson and Professor Hermann Levy, *Industrial Assurance. A Historical and Critical Study* (Oxford, 1937), 175. Also see 'A Fieldman', *The Industrial Assurance Agents' Companion* (1935), 30; Chris Christian, *Selling Life Assurance* (London, 1970), 147; William G. Fern, *Overcoming Fear. A Lecture Given to the London 'Sell More' Club*, 2nd edn. (London, 1932), 5.

12 Sir Benjamin Collins Brodie, *The Works of Sir Benjamin Collins Brodie*, vol. I (London, 1865), 185; Rev. William Nevins, 'Why So Loth to Die?' in Nevins et al., *Light in the Valley of Death; Or, Considerations Fitted to Strengthen the Faith, and Sustain the Mind, of the Dying* (Edinburgh, 1857), 7; William S. Savory, *On Life and Death: Four Lectures Delivered at the Royal Institution of Great Britain* (London, 1863), 177.

13 This is the work of Colin Scott, 'Old Age and Death', *American Journal of Psychology*, viii (1896), 67–122.

14 William Osler, *Science and Immortality* (London, 1904), 36–7. Also see Dr E. L. Keyes, *The Fear of Death* (n.p., 1910), 7.

15 William S. Savory, *On Life and Death: Four Lectures Delivered at the Royal Institution of Great Britain* (London, 1863), 175–6.

16 Oswald Browne, *On The Care of the Dying. A Lecture to Nurses* (London, 1894), 16–17.

17 William Eassie, *Cremation of the Dead: Its History and Bearings upon Public Health* (London, 1875), 53.

18 Henry E. Spencer, *Burial and Cremation: A Lecture* (London, 1881), 6–8.

19 G. Stanley Hall, 'A Study of Fears', *American Journal of Psychology*, viii.2 (January 1897), 152–3.

20 Cited in William Tebb and Colonel Edward Perry Vollum, *Premature Burial and How it May be Prevented with Special Reference to Trance, Catalepsy, and Other Forms of Suspended Animation*, 2nd edn., first published 1896 (London, 1905), 26.

21 Dr Alexander Wilder, *Perils of Premature Burial. A Public Address Delivered Before the Members of the Legislature, at the Capitol, Albany, New York, January 25th, 1871* (London, 1895), 10.

22 'Premature Burial', *Embalmers' Monthly*, xxi (1908), 72. Estimate by Dr John Dixwell, of Harvard University, in 1908.

23 Dr Stenson Hooker and the late Colonel E. P. Vollum, *Premature Burial and Its*

Prevention, 2nd edn. (London, 1910), 3.

24 Max Levy, *Why Modern Cremation Should Replace Earth-Burial* (San Francisco, 1885), 39

25 *Sheffield Daily Telegraph*, 25 September 1895, quoted in Dr Alexander Wilder, *Perils of Premature Burial. A Public Address Delivered Before the Members of the Legislature, at the Capitol, Albany, New York, January 25th, 1871* (London, 1895), 26; Edwin Chadwick, *Report on the Sanitary Conditions of the Labouring Population of Great Britain. A Supplementary Report on the Results of a Special Inquiry into the Practice of Interment in Towns. Made at the Request of Her Majesty's Principal Secretary of State for the Home Department* (London, 1843), 89; Max Levy, *Why Modern Cremation Should Replace Earth-Burial* (San Francisco, 1885), 39. Also see *To-Day*, 28 September 1895, and *Christian World*, 26 September 1895.

26 David Walsh, *Premature Burial: Fact or Fiction?* (London, 1897), 18–19.

27 Dr Alexander Wilder, *Perils of Premature Burial. A Public Address Delivered Before the Members of the Legislature, at the Capitol, Albany, New York, January 25th, 1871* (London, 1895), 17.

28 *Ziemssen's Cyclopedia of the Practice of Medicine*, vol. xix, 451–2, cited in Augustus G. Cobb, *Earth-Burial and Cremation. The History of Earth-Burial with its Attendant Evils, and the Advantages Offered by Cremation* (New York, 1892), 93.

29 The story was made into a film in 1962. The director was Roger Corman and the assistant director the future director of *The Godfather*, Francis Ford Coppola.

30 Edgar Allan Poe, 'The Premature Burial', in Poe, *The Premature Burial and Other Tales of Horror* (London, 1966), 15.

31 *Spectator*, 14 September 1895, quoted in Dr Alexander Wilder, *Perils of Premature Burial. A Public Address Delivered Before the Members of the Legislature, at the Capitol, Albany, New York, January 25th, 1871* (London, 1895), 24.

32 Dr Alexander Wilder, *Perils of Premature Burial. A Public Address Delivered Before the Members of the Legislature, at the Capitol, Albany, New York, January 25th, 1871* (London, 1895), 9.

33 *Jewish World*, 13 September 1895, cited in Dr Alexander Wilder, *Perils of Premature Burial. A Public Address Delivered Before the Members of the Legislature, at the Capitol, Albany, New York, January 25th, 1871* (London, 1895), 23.

34 Dr Stenson Hooker and the late Colonel E. P. Vollum, *Premature Burial and Its Prevention*, 2nd edn., (London, 1910), 6.

35 William A. Guy and David Ferrier, *Principles of Forensic Medicine*, 6th edn., rev. (London, 1888), 214, and Professor D. Ferrier, 'Death', in *Quain's Dictionary of Medicine*, cited in Dr Alexander Wilder, *Perils of Premature Burial. A Public Address Delivered Before the Members of the Legislature, at the Capitol, Albany, New York, January 25th, 1871* (London, 1895), 7.

36 Dr Henry M. Lyman, *Insomnia; and Other Disorders of Sleep* (Chicago, 1885), 35.

37 William Tebb and Colonel Edward Perry Vollum, *Premature Burial and How it May be Prevented with Special Reference to Trance, Catalepsy, and Other Forms of Suspended Animation*, 2nd edn., first published 1896 (London, 1905), 149.

38 Dr Alexander Wilder, *Perils of Premature Burial. A Public Address Delivered Before the Members of the Legislature, at the Capitol, Albany, New York, January 25th, 1871*

(London, 1895), 19–20. Also see Moore Russell Fletcher, *One Thousand Persons Buried Alive by Their Best Friends. A Treatise on Suspended Animation with Directions for Restoration* (Boston, 1883), 5.

39 Edward P. Vollum, 'Tests for Death', *American Undertaker*, 2.10 (October 1901), 37, and 'Premature Burial', *Embalmers' Monthly*, xxi (1908), 14.

40 *Sussex Daily News*, 23 September 1895, quoted in Dr Alexander Wilder, *Perils of Premature Burial. A Public Address Delivered Before the Members of the Legislature, at the Capitol, Albany, New York, January 25th, 1871* (London, 1895), 26.

41 'Premature Burial', *Embalmers' Monthly*, xxi (1908), 14.

42 It never vanished entirely. For later examples see Thomas J. Bonniwell, *We Have to Die*, 2nd printing (New York, 1940), 169; Huw Thomas, 'Psychological Approach to Cremation', *Pharos*, 33.4 (November 1967) 1967, 88; Dr William S. Walsh, *The Mastery of Fear* (New York, 1924), 208–9; Alfred Worcester, *The Care of the Aged, the Dying, and the Dead* (Springfield, Ill., 1935), 42 (lectures to medical students at Harvard University).

43 Captain Ralph Smith, diary entry for 15 September 1916, in Liddell Hart Centre for Military Archives.

44 Felix Brown, 'Civilian Psychiatric Air-Raid Casualties', *Lancet*, 31 May 1941, 688.

45 William Tebb and Colonel Edward Perry Vollum, *Premature Burial and How it May be Prevented with Special Reference to Trance, Catalepsy, and Other Forms of Suspended Animation* (London, 1896), 96.

46 Dr Alexander Wilder, *Perils of Premature Burial. A Public Address Delivered Before the Members of the Legislature, at the Capitol, Albany, New York, January 25th, 1871* (London, 1895), 17.

47 *Manchester Courier*, 24 September 1895, cited in Dr Alexander Wilder, *Perils of Premature Burial. A Public Address Delivered Before the Members of the Legislature, at the Capitol, Albany, New York, January 25th, 1871* (London, 1895), 26.

48 Edgar Allan Poe, 'The Premature Burial', in Poe, *The Premature Burial and Other Tales of Horror* (London, 1966), 9. Also see William Tebb and Colonel Edward Perry Vollum, *Premature Burial and How it May be Prevented with Special Reference to Trance, Catalepsy, and Other Forms of Suspended Animation*, 2nd edn., first published 1896 (London, 1905), 11.

49 Dr William S. Walsh, *The Mastery of Fear* (New York, 1924), 208–9.

50 H. S. Eckels, 'The Danger of Burial Alive', *American Undertaker*, v.2 (March 1904), 6–7.

51 'A New Death Test', *Embalmers' Monthly*, xviii (1905), 163.

52 *Spectator*, 14 September 1895, quoted in Dr Alexander Wilder, *Perils of Premature Burial. A Public Address Delivered Before the Members of the Legislature, at the Capitol, Albany, New York, January 25th, 1871* (London, 1895), 24.

53 E. E. Carpmael (of the Medical Department, Berkeley University), in the *Morning Post*, cited in Dr Alexander Wilder, *Perils of Premature Burial. A Public Address Delivered Before the Members of the Legislature, at the Capitol, Albany, New York, January 25th, 1871* (London, 1895), 14.

54 John Page Hopps, *The Etherealisation of the Body* (London, 1894), 2.

55 Maeterlinck quoted in George Alfred Noble, *Cremation: Its History and Practice* (London, 1914), 14.

56 Augustus G. Cobb, *Earth-Burial and Cremation. The History of Earth-Burial with its Attendant Evils, and the Advantages Offered by Cremation* (New York, 1892), 90–1.

57 William Holder, *Cremation Versus Burial: An Appeal to Reason Against Prejudice* (Hull, 1891), 40.

58 For example, see Augustus G. Cobb, *Earth-Burial and Cremation. The History of Earth-Burial with its Attendant Evils, and the Advantages Offered by Cremation* (New York, 1892), 93, and Ronald Sutherland Gower, *Cleanliness Versus Corruption* (London, 1910), 3.

59 Max Levy, *Why Modern Cremation Should Replace Earth-Burial* (San Francisco, 1885), 39–40. Also see Dr Alexander Wilder, *Perils of Premature Burial. A Public Address Delivered Before the Members of the Legislature, at the Capitol, Albany, New York, January 25th, 1871* (London, 1895), 16.

60 Max Levy, *Why Modern Cremation Should Replace Earth-Burial* (San Francisco, 1885), 40.

61 *Sussex Daily News*, 23 September 1895, quoted in Dr Alexander Wilder, *Perils of Premature Burial. A Public Address Delivered Before the Members of the Legislature, at the Capitol, Albany, New York, January 25th, 1871* (London, 1895), 26.

62 Molly Weir, *Best Foot Forward* (Bath, 1979), 71.

63 For example, see Moore Russell Fletcher, *One Thousand Persons Buried Alive by Their Best Friends. A Treatise on Suspended Animation with Directions for Restoration* (Boston, 1883), 63, and *Surrey Comet*, 25 October 1924, in PRO MH74/30.

64 All from Howard Dittrick, 'Devices to Prevent Premature Burial', *Journal of the History of Medicine and Allied Sciences*, iii (1948), 161–71.

65 Cited in William Tebb and Colonel Edward Perry Vollum, *Premature Burial and How it May be Prevented with Special Reference to Trance, Catalepsy, and Other Forms of Suspended Animation*, 2nd edn., first published 1896 (London, 1905), 8. Also see 'Death Certification', *Medical Times and Hospital Gazette*, 31 (8 April 1903), 245, and Rev. J. Ingham Brooke, *A Lecture on Burial Reform* (London, 1879), 3.

66 See Dr Stenson Hooker and the late Colonel E. P. Vollum, *Premature Burial and Its Prevention*, 2nd edn., (London, 1910), 3.

67 William Tebb and Colonel Edward Perry Vollum, *Premature Burial and How it May be Prevented with Special Reference to Trance, Catalepsy, and Other Forms of Suspended Animation*, 2nd edn., first published 1896 (London, 1905), 369–70.

68 Edward P. Vollum, 'Tests for Death', *American Undertaker*, 2.10 (October 1901), 38–9. The training of physicians also worried the British Association: see William Tebb and Colonel Edward Perry Vollum, *Premature Burial and How it May be Prevented with Special Reference to Trance, Catalepsy, and Other Forms of Suspended Animation*, 2nd edn., first published 1896 (London, 1905), 369.

69 'Premature Burials', *American Undertaker*, 1.8 (August 1900), 14.

70 'Buried Alive', *Catholic World*, 1866, 808; William A. Guy and David Ferrier, *Principles of Forensic Medicine*, 6th edn., rev. (London, 1888), 213; Moore Russell Fletcher, *One Thousand Persons Buried Alive by Their Best Friends. A Treatise on Suspended Animation with Directions for Restoration* (Boston, 1883), 62; William Tebb and Colonel Edward Perry Vollum, *Premature Burial and How it May be Prevented with Special Reference to Trance, Catalepsy, and Other Forms of Suspended Animation*, 2nd edn., first published 1896 (London, 1905), 149.

71 *The Hospital*, 21 September 1895, cited in Dr Alexander Wilder, *Perils of Premature Burial. A Public Address Delivered Before the Members of the Legislature, at the Capitol, Albany, New York, January 25th, 1871* (London, 1895), 24–5.

72 Rev. J. Ingham Brooke, *A Lecture on Burial Reform* (London, 1879), 3; 'Death Certification', *Medical Times and Hospital Gazette*, 31 (8 April 1903), 245; Edward P. Vollum, 'Tests for Death', *American Undertaker*, 2.10 (October 1901), 38–9.

73 Harold Begbie, *Life of William Booth. The Founder of the Salvation Army*, vol. 1 (London, 1920), 228, quoting from one of General Booth's letters.

74 Arthur Brinckman, *Notes on the Care of the Sick and Practical Advice to Those in Charge of the Dying and the Dead* (London, 1879), 265.

75 Rev. Walter James Wyon, 'Sermon IV. The Christian Man's Fear', in *Six Addresses to Men, Delivered in the Church of SS. Philip & James, Oxford* (London, 1878), 102–3, 105–10.

76 Rev. James Murdoch, *Everlasting Punishment. A Sermon Preached Before the Free Synod of Aberdeen, and Published at Their Request* (Aberdeen, 1864), 28–9.

77 *The End of the World. A Plain Sermon Preached in a Village Church at a Harvest Home Festival* (London, 1866), 10.

78 Christopher Newman Hall, *The Antidote to Fear, with Illustrations from the Prophet Isaiah* (London, 1866), 15–16, 189.

79 E. L. Youmans and W. J. Youmans, 'Concerning the Belief in Hell', *Popular Science Monthly*, xii (March 1878), 629–30.

80 'Hell and Science', in *Catholic World. A Monthly Magazine of General Literature and Science*, xxvii.159 (June 1878), 321–36.

81 All in *That Unknown Country, Or What Living Men Believe Concerning Punishment After Death* (London, 1889), 285–322, 693–710, 867–79.

82 The Rev. George Wolfe Shinn, 'What Has Become of Hell?', *North American Review*, clxx (June 1900), 837–49.

83 *The Doctrines and Discipline of the Methodist Episcopal Church* 1836, 1884 and 1916; from James J. Farrell, *Inventing the American Way of Death* (Philadelphia, 1980) 94–5.

84 Kurt Riezles, 'The Social Psychology of Fear', *American Journal of Sociology*, xlix.6 (May 1944), 492.

85 Preston Bradley, *Mastering Fear* (Indianapolis, 1935), 165.

86 Peter Jupp, *From Dust to Ashes: The Replacement of Burial by Cremation in England 1840-1967* (London, n.d.), 1.

87 Dr Peter Fenwick and Elizabeth Fenwick, *The Truth in the Light. An Investigation of Over 300 Near-Death Experiences* (New York, 1997), 228, and Marget Grey, *Return from Death. An Exploration of the Near-Death Experience* (London, 1985), 102.

88 Edward Conlon, 'To the Potter's Field', *New Yorker*, 19 July 1993, 42–54.

89 George Gallup with William Proctor, *Adventures in Immortality* (New York, 1982), 3.

90 Carroll E. Simcox, *Is Death the End? The Christian Answer* (London, 1960), 6, 8.

CHAPTER TWO: DISASTERS

1 *Iroquois Theatre Souvenir Programme* (Chicago, 1903), 20.

2 Louis Guenzel, *Retrospects. The Iroquois Theatre Fire* (Chicago, 1945).

3 L. S. Penrose, *On the Objective Study of Crowd Behaviour* (London, 1952), 28.

4 J. Q. Dixon, 'Iroquois Theatre Fire, Chicago, 1903', in J. Qallan Dixon, *Wreck of the Steamship Titanic 1912 . . . And Including the Iroquois Theatre Fire, Chicago 1903* (Buffalo, New York, 1912), unpaginated (pp.8–9), written in 1903.

5 Anon, *Disasters on Sea and Land* (Manchester, 1881).

6 'Disaster at the Victoria Hall, Sunderland, 16–6–1883', in PRO HO205/227.

7 The horse is in the Sunderland Museum and Art Gallery: http://sunderland today.co.uk/Custom_pasges/CustomPage.asp?Page=1080.

8 Jesus's words are quoted in Matthew 9:14, Mark 10:14 and Luke 18:16.

9 Von Duprin, 'About Us', http://www.vanduprin.com/about_us.asp.

10 Wm. Paul Gerhard, *The Safety of Theatre Audiences and the Stage Personnel Against Danger from Fire and Panic* (London, 1899). This book was published by the British Fire Prevention Committee.

11 John R. Freeman, *On the Safeguarding of Life in Theatre. Being a Study from the Standpoint of an Engineer* (New York, 1906).

12 'The Tragedy at Paisley', *The Times*, 1 January 1930, 13.

13 Quoted in 'The Psychology of Panic in War', *American Review of Reviews*, 50 (October 1914), 628.

14 Dr M. Roth, *A Few Notes on Fear and Flight, and the Diseases they Cause and Cure; Also on the Means of Preventing and Curing the Effects of These Emotions* (London, 1871), 7–8.

15 James H. Geer, 'The Development of a Scale to Measure Fear', *Behaviour Research and Therapy. An International Multi-Disciplinary Journal*, 3 (1965), 52; Isaac M. Marks, *Fears and Phobias* (London, 1967), 78.

16 W. G. Slade, 'Earthquake Psychology', *Australasian Journal of Psychology and Philosophy*, x.1 (March 1932), 61–2.

17 *New York Times*, 16 January 1854.

18 Donald Hyslop, Alastair Forsyth and Sheila Jemima (eds.), *Titanic Voices. Memories from the Fateful Voyage* (Southampton, 1994), 135–8, 142.

19 *New York Times*, 20 April 1912, 14.

20 Josiah Morse, *The Psychology and Neurology of Fear* (Worcester, Mass., 1907), 70–1.

21 William Charles Loosmore, *Ourselves and Our Emotions. A Practical Study of the Behaviour of the Primitive Element of the Mind* (London, 1928), 78.

22 Abraham Mauritis Meerloo, *Aftermath of Peace. Psychological Essays* (New York, 1946), 69.

23 Ernst Huber, *Evolution of Facial Musculature and Facial Expression* (Baltimore, 1931), 99–101, 152–60

24 For the best discussion of Le Bon's work and influence see Susanna Barrows, *Distorting Mirrors. Visions of the Crowd in Late Nineteenth Century France* (New Haven, 1981).

25 Wilfred Trotter, *Instincts of the Herd in Peace and War*, first published 1910 (London, 1916), 115.

26 William McDougall, *Psychology. The Study of Behaviour* (London, 1912), 238.

27 William McDougall, *The Group Mind. A Sketch of the Principles of Collective Psychology with Some Attempt to Apply them to the Interpretation of National Life and*

Character (Cambridge, 1921), 24.

28 Ibid., 21–5, 40–1.

29 Quoted in Samuel Henry Prince, 'Catastrophe and Social Change. Based Upon a Sociological Study of the Halifax Disaster', PhD, Faculty of Political Science, Columbia University, 1920, 27.

30 Ibid., 36.

31 W. B. Cannon. 'The Emergency Function of the Adrenol Medulla in Pain and the Major Emotions', *American Journal of Physiology*, xxxiii.2 (2 February 1914), 358–72.

32 Samuel Henry Prince, 'Catastrophe and Social Change. Based Upon a Sociological Study of the Halifax Disaster', PhD, Faculty of Political Science, Columbia University, 1920, 49.

33 Ibid., 31.

34 Ibid., 36–40.

35 Charles S. Gardner, 'Assemblies', *American Journal of Sociology*, 19 (1914), 546.

36 *The Mastery of Fear. How to Attain It* (London, 1931), 7–8.

AFTERWORD TO PART ONE: EMOTIONOLOGY

1 Knight Dunlap, 'Are Emotions Teleological Constructs?', *American Journal of Psychology*, xliv (1932), 572–6.

2 Jan Lewis and Peter N. Stearns, Introduction, in Lewis and Stearns (eds.), *An Emotional History of the United States* (New York, 1998), 7.

3 Peter N. Stearns and Carol Z. Stearns, 'Emotionology: Clarifying the History of Emotions and Emotional Standards', *American Historical Review*, 90.4 (October 1985), 824.

4 Carol Z. Stearns and Peter N. Stearns, *Anger. The Struggle for Emotional Control in America's History* (Chicago, 1986), 219. 'Labelled' has been changed to English spelling. I have omitted the phrase 'there may be such an entity as basic anger' because I am not convinced of this.

5 Ludwig Wittgenstein, *Philosophical Investigations*, trans. G. E. M. Anscombe (Oxford, 1953), 188.

6 W. H. Sewell, *Christian Care of the Dying and the Dead; A Few Hints on Burial Reform, for Friendly Readers* (London, 1878), 6–7.

7 Carol Z. Stearns and Peter N. Stearns, *Anger. The Struggle for Emotional Control in America's History* (Chicago, 1986), 14.

8 Catherine A. Lutz, *Unnatural Emotions. Everyday Sentiments on a Micronesian Atoll and Their Challenge to Western Theory* (Chicago, 1988) and Catherine Lutz, 'The Domain of Emotion Words on Ifaluk', in Rom Harré (ed.), *The Social Construction of Emotion* (Oxford, 1998). Other examples include Howard Grabois, 'The Convergence of Sociocultural Theory and Cognitive Linguistics', in Gard B. Palmer and Debra J. Occhi (eds.), *Languages of Sentiment. Cultural Constructions of Emotional Substrates* (Amsterdam, 1999), 225; Hildred Geertz, 'The Vocabulary of Emotion: A Study of Javanese Socialization Processes', *Psychiatry*, 22 (1959), 225–36; Cliff Goddard, 'Anger in the Western Desert: A Case Study in the Cross-Cultural Semantics of Emotion', *Man*, new series,

26.2 (June 1991), 265–79; G. Howell, 'Rules Not Words', in Paul Heelas and A. Locke (eds.), *Indigenous Psychologies: The Anthropology of the Self* (London, 1981); Paul Heelas, 'Emotion Talk Across Cultures', in Rom Harré (ed.), *The Social Construction of Emotion* (Oxford, 1998), 234–66; Shinobu Kitayama and Hazel Rose Markus (eds.), *Emotion and Culture. Empirical Studies of Mutual Influence* (Washington, DC, 1994); James A. Russell, José Miguel Fernández-Dols, Antony S. R. Manstead and J. C. Wellenkamp (eds.), *Everyday Conceptions of Emotion* (Dordrecht, 1995); Anna Wierzbicka, *Emotions Across Languages and Cultures: Diversity and Universals* (Cambridge, 1999).

CHAPTER THREE: THE CHILD

1 Harriet Lane Hospital was connected to Johns Hopkins University.

2 John B. Watson, *Behaviourism* (London, 1925), 125–9.

3 Henry C. Wright, *The Empire of the Mother Over the Character and Destiny of the Race* (Boston, 1863), 4, 94, 104.

4 Dr M. Roth, *A Few Notes on Fear and Fright, and the Diseases They Cause and Cure; Also on the Means of Preventing and Curing the Effects of These Emotions* (London, 1871), 7, 18–20. Roth was responding to criticism of the theory by some physiologists who pointed out that there was no direct communication between the mother and the foetus.

5 Georgiana B. Kirby, *Transmission; or, Variation of Character Through the Mother* (New York, 1877), 8–10, 21.

6 Woodbury M. Fernald, *A View at the Foundations: Or, First Causes of Character As Operative Before Birth, From Hereditary and Spiritual Sources* (Boston, 1865), 131, 134–5.

7 For example, see Flora Bigelow Guest, *Casting Out Fear* (New York, 1918), 21; Edward L. Munson, *The Management of Men. A Handbook on the Systematic Development of Morale and the Control of Human Behaviour* (London, 1920), 112; William S. Walsh, *The Mastery of Fear* (New York, 1924), 272–3 and 285–7; 'A Doctor', *The Conquest of Fear* (London, 1941), 1; Marvin Earl Cox, *Child Life. A Scientific and Practical Treatise on the Study of Life and the Care, Education and Development of Children from Conception to Maturity* (Fargo, 1902), 21.

8 'A Medical Psychologist', *Fear and Depression. Their Causes and Self-Treatment* (Birmingham, 1939), 14.

9 Dr David Abrahamsen, *The Emotional Care of Your Child* (New York, 1969), 71.

10 Nandor Fodor, *The Search for the Beloved* (Utica, 1946), 12.

11 There were always powerful opponents of the theory of maternal impressions. Physiologists pointed out that there was no direct communication between mother and foetus. Others drew attention to observable facts, such as the physical well-being of infants born to women who had suffered appalling mishaps during earthquakes and the sensible children born to maniacal lunatics: see William S. Walsh, *The Mastery of Fear* (New York, 1924), 272–3.

12 For an illuminating historical account of children's fears see Peter N. Stearns, 'Girls, Boys, and Emotions: Redefinitions and Historical Change', *Journal of American History*, 80 (June 1993).

13 For example, see William B. Atkinson, 'Note on Night Terrors', *Alienist and Neurologist*, iii.4 (October 1882), 586, and Mary Elizabeth Buchanan, *Your Child's First Years and What You Can Do to Make them Healthy, Happy Ones* (n.p., 1935), 12.

14 Jacob Abbott, *Gentle Measures in the Management and Training of the Young; or, The Principles on Which a Firm Parental Authority May be Established and Maintained, Without Violence or Anger, and the Right Development of the Moral and Mental Capacities be Promoted by Methods in Harmony with the Structure and Characteristics of the Juvenile Mind* (New York, 1899), 18.

15 Ibid.

16 Mrs C. A. Hopkinson, *Hints for the Nursery* (Boston, 1863), 154. Also see John Stevens Cabot Abbott, *The Mother at Home; or, The Principles of Maternal Duty Familiarly Illustrated* (London, 1834), 109–10; Dr Harriet Bailey Clark, *Mothers' Problems. A Text-Book for Parents' Classes, Mothers' Associations, and Teachers of Children* (Philadelphia, 1922), 81.

17 Dr Harry Roberts, *The Mother's Advice Book. A Guide for Mothers on the Rearing, Feeding, Management, Clothing, Etc., of Children, With Recipes and Advice in Regard to All Troubles, Complaints, and Diseases of Childhood* (London, 1911), 72.

18 Clara Louise Burnham, 'How to Keep Your Child From Fear', *Appleton's Magazine*, xi.4 (April 1908), 426–7.

19 Mrs Pedley, *Infant Nursing and the Management of Young Children* (London, 1866), 113.

20 Elizabeth M. Sloan Chesser, *Child Health and Character* (London, 1927), 37. Also see *The Mastery of Fear. How to Attain It* (London, 1931), 29.

21 The University Society, *The Child's Welfare Manual. A Handbook of Child Nature and Nurture for Parents and Teachers* (New York, 1915), 138–9.

22 Tom A. Williams, *Dreads and Besetting Fears. Including States of Anxiety, Their Causes and Cure* (Boston, 1923), vi-vii and 9–10.

23 Dr Nathan Raw, 'Royal Medico-Psychological Association Annual Meeting: Fear', *Lancet*, 3 August 1929, 254.

24 Peter Fletcher, *Life Without Fear. Ten Talks on the Psychology of Christian Living* (London, 1936), 93.

25 Bert Ira Beverly, *In Defense of Children* (New York, 1941), 142; Marion Quinlan Davis, *A Plan for Growing Up. The Blue Book for Building Better Lives*, first published 1945 (New York, 1957), 179; Mrs Margaret White Eggleston, *Faith or Fear in Child Training* (New York, 1934), 3–4.

26 Grace Kincle Adams, *Your Child is Normal. The Psychology of Young Childhood* (New York, 1934), 92–3.

27 Bert Ira Beverly, *In Defense of Children* (New York, 1941), 139–41.

28 Mrs Margaret White Eggleston, *Faith or Fear in Child Training* (New York, 1934), 5. For another example involving a policeman see Marion Quinlan Davis, *A Plan for Growing Up. The Blue Book for Building Better Lives*, first published 1945 (New York, 1957), 180–1. Also see Winifred De Kok, *Guiding Your Child Through the Formative Years From Birth to the Age of Five* (New York, 1935), 77, and Peter Fletcher, *Life Without Fear. Ten Talks on the Psychology of Christian Living* (London, 1936), 25–6.

29 Charles Bray, *How to Educate the Feelings or Affections, and Bring the Dispositions, Aspirations, and Passions into Harmony with Sound Intelligence and Mortality*, 3rd edn. (New York, 1880), 62.

30 Ernest Rutherford Graves and Gladys Hoagland Graves, *Parents and Children* (Philadelphia, 1928), 85.

31 Samuel H. Preston and Michael R. Haines, *Fatal Years. Child Mortality in Late Nineteenth Century America* (Princeton, 1991), 208.

32 Geoffrey Rowell, *Hell and the Victorians* (Oxford, 1974), 12.

33 Mary Wade, *To a Miner Born* (Bedlington, 1984), 24.

34 Elizabeth K. Blackburn, *In and Out of Windows: A Story of the Changes in Working-Class Life 1902–1977 in a Small East Lancashire Community* (Burnley, 1980), 21.

35 Molly Weir, *Best Foot Forward* (Bath, 1979), 70–1.

36 Kathlyn Davenport, *My Preston Yesterdays* (Manchester, 1984), 21–2.

37 *The Fears of a Child. A Book for Children and Their Parents* (Stirling, 1906), 32–5.

38 Tom A. Williams, *Dreads and Besetting Fears. Including States of Anxiety, Their Causes and Cure* (Boston, 1923), 95.

39 Preston Bradley, *Courage for To-Day* (Indianapolis, 1934), 69.

40 Ernest Rutherford Graves and Gladys Hoagland Graves, *Parents and Children* (Philadelphia, 1928), 78.

41 Henry Addington Bruce, *Your Growing Child. A Book of Talks to Parents on Life's Needs* (New York, 1927), 24–5.

42 Professor Blumer's survey of 237 schoolchildren, quoted in Henry James Forman, *Our Movies Made Children* (New York, 1935), 107.

43 Henry James Forman, *Our Movies Made Children* (New York, 1935), 108, 111.

44 Henry Addington Bruce, *Your Growing Child. A Book of Talks to Parents on Life's Needs* (New York, 1927), 22, 24; Mary D. Chambers, *Care and Training of Boys and Girls from Birth to Adolescence* (Boston, 1925), 79; G. Hardy Clark, *A System for the Care and Training of Children*, 8th edn., rev. (Long Beach, California, 1927), 13–14; W. J. McBride, *The Conquest of Fear through Psychology* (London, 1936), 10–11; Bert Ira Beverly, *In Defense of Children* (New York, 1941), 138.

45 Henry Addington Bruce, *Your Growing Child. A Book of Talks to Parents on Life's Needs* (New York, 1927), 27–8, and Dr Harriet Bailey Clark, *Mothers' Problems. A Text-Book for Parents' Classes, Mothers' Associations, and Teachers of Children* (Philadelphia, 1922), 80–1.

46 Henry Addington Bruce, *Your Growing Child. A Book of Talks to Parents on Life's Needs* (New York, 1927), 18–19.

47 Cynthia Asquith, *The Child at Home* (New York, 1923), 118–19. Also see Ada Hart Arlitt, *The Child From One to Six. Psychology for Parents* (New York, 1930), 104, and Edna Dea Baker, *Parenthood and Child Nurture* (New York, 1922), 50.

48 Mrs Caroline Benedict Burrell and William Byron Forbush (eds.), *The Manual for Character Training. A Guide-Book for Teachers and Parents Based on the Young Folks Treasury* (New York, 1925), 23, 42, 79.

49 Mrs Margaret White Eggleston, *Faith or Fear in Child Training* (New York, 1934), 6. Also see John F. Williams, 'The Mischief of Fear', in *The Young Child. A Series of Five Lectures on Child Management Given Under the Auspices of the*

Victorian [Australia] Council for Mental Hygiene, November, 1930 (Melbourne, 1931), 15.

50 John B. Watson, 'Behaviorism – The Modern Note in Psychology' (1929), in 'Classics in the History of Psychology' in http://psychclassics.yorku.ca.Watson/ Bottle/Watson.htm, 8.

51 Harold Homer Anderson, *Children in the Family* (New York, 1937), 97.

52 Howard Becker and David K. Bruner, 'Attitude Toward Death and the Dead and Some Possible Causes of Ghost Fear', *Mental Hygiene*, xv (1931), 829; Maria Nagy, 'The Child's Theories Concerning Death', *Journal of Genetic Psychology*, 73.3 (1948); Joseph M. Natterson and Alfred G. Knudson, 'Observations Concerning Fear of Death in Fatally Ill Children and Their Mothers', *Psychosomatic Medicine*, xxii (1960), 460; Paul Schilder and David Wechsler, 'The Attitudes of Children Toward Death', *Journal of Genetic Psychology*, xlv (1934), 422.

53 John Yerbury Dent, *Anxiety and Its Treatment with Special Reference to Alcoholism* (London, 1941), 36.

54 Aldous Huxley, *Brave New World*.

55 Ada Hart Arlitt, *The Child from One to Six. Psychology for Parents* (New York, 1930), 115; Gertrude Emma Chittenden, *Living with Children* (New York, 1944), 99; Mary Cover Jones, 'A Study of the Emotions of Pre-School Children', *School and Society*, xxi.545 (6 June 1925), 758; Mark A. May, 'What Science Offers on Character Education', in Chicago Association for Child Study and Parent Education (ed.), *Building Character. Proceedings of the Mid-West Conference on Parent Education, February, 1928* (Chicago, 1928), 43.

56 Mary Cover Jones, 'A Study of the Emotions of Pre-School Children', *School and Society*, xxi.545 (6 June 1925), 757–8.

57 John Edward Anderson, *Happy Childhood. The Development and Guidance of Children and Youth* (New York, 1933), 71–3.

58 Mary Cover Jones, 'The Elimination of Children's Fears', *Journal of Experimental Psychology*, vii.5 (October 1924), 388.

59 Dr E. Graham Howe, 'Motives and Mechanisms of the Mind. IX. Defence Mechanisms: Fear', *Lancet*, 28 February 1931, 488.

60 Arthur Thomas Jersild and Mrs Frances Baker Holmes, *Children's Fears* (New York, 1935), 323–34.

61 William James, 'What is an Emotion?', *Mind*, 9 (1884), 189–90.

62 Ibid., 189–97.

63 Ibid., 189. It was only later, in 1890, that James conceded to some of his critics that the 'subtler' emotions might be non-organically based, in contrast to the 'coarser' emotions such as fear and anger.

64 Henry Addington Bruce, *Your Growing Child. A Book of Talks to Parents on Life's Needs* (New York, 1927), 38–9. Also see William Sune (William Henry Schoenau, Jr.), *Charm, Enthusiasm and Originality. Their Acquisition and Use* (Los Angeles, 1929), 86.

65 Jessica Garretson Cosgrave, *The Psychology of Youth. A Book for Parents* (New York, 1929), 62–6.

66 Mae Carden, *Let's Bring Them Up Sensibly* (Glen Rock, New Jersey, 1967), 65.

67 Benjamin Spock and Mary Morgan, *Spock on Spock* (New York, 1989), 17–18 and 133–5.

68 Benjamin Spock, *Baby and Child Care*, new, enlarged edn. (London, 1958), 11–12, 15, 237, 271, 354, 368–9.

69 Eileen Elias, *Enjoy Your Baby. Child Management in the First Five Years* (London, 1944), 56–61. Also see Ada Hart Arlitt, *The Child From One to Six. Psychology for Parents* (New York, 1930), 112–13.

70 John Dalley, *The Gift of a Child. A Handbook for Parents on the Training of Young Children* (London, 1946), 43.

71 See the discussion in C. W. Valentine, 'The Innate Bases of Fear', *Journal of Genetic Psychology*, xxxvii (1930), 418.

72 John and Elizabeth Newson, *Four Years Old in an Urban Community* (London, 1968), 203–4.

73 Bruno Bettelheim, *The Uses of Enchantment* (New York, 1977).

74 Marina Warner, *No Go the Bogeyman. Scaring, Lulling, and Making Mock* (London, 1998), 6.

75 Ray Coppock Beery, *How to Bring Out the Best in Your Child. Part Six* (Pleasant Hill, Ohio, 1950), 7–9.

76 Nancy Catty, *Social Training. From Childhood to Maturity* (London, 1951), 23–4.

77 Marion Quinlan Davis, *A Plan for Growing Up. The Blue Book for Building Better Lives*, first published 1945 (New York, 1957), 189.

78 Elizabeth Bradford, *Let's Talk About Children* (New York, 1947), 70.

79 Jerome S. Fass, *A Primer for Parents* (New York, 1968), 105.

80 Charlotte Del Solar, *Child Guidance* (n.p., 1950), 40.

81 Ray Coppock Beery, *How to Bring Out the Best in Your Child. Part Six* (Pleasant Hill, Ohio, 1950), 7, and Lyn Barrow, *Tantrums, Jealousy and the Fears of Children* (Sydney, 1968), 39–40.

82 Marian Grant, *Home and Children* (London, 1952), 60. Also see Ruth Thomas, *Children's Fears* (London, 1946), 2.

83 Lyn Barrow, *Tantrums, Jealousy and the Fears of Children* (Sydney, 1968), 32–3.

84 Melanie Klein, 'The Rôle of the School in the Libidinal Development of the Child', *International Journal of Psycho-Analysis*, 5 (1924), 312–31, and Adelaide M. Johnson, Eugene I. Falstein, S. A. Szurek and Margaret Svendsen, 'School Phobia', *American Journal of Orthopsychiatry*, 11 (1941), 702–11.

85 Adelaide M. Johnson, Eugene I. Falstein, S. A. Szurek, and Margaret Svendsen, 'School Phobia', *American Journal of Orthopsychiatry*, 11 (1941), 703.

86 Maurice Chazan, 'School Phobia', *British Journal of Educational Psychology*, 32.3 (November 1962), 215; L. A. Hersov, 'Refusal to Go to School', *Journal of Child Psychology and Psychiatry*, 1 (1960), 144; Adelaide M. Johnson, Eugene I. Falstein, S. A. Szurek and Margaret Svendsen, 'School Phobia', *American Journal of Orthopsychiatry*, 11 (1941), 703; J. H. Kahn, 'School Refusal. Some Clinical and Cultural Aspects', *Medical Officer*, c.22 (28 November 1958), 339; Jack H. Kahn and Jean P. Nursten, *Unwillingly to School. The Place of the Child Guidance Clinic in the Treatment of School Phobia* (Oxford, 1965), 26; Alfred Model and Elizabeth Shepheard, 'The Child Who Refuses to Go to School', *Medical Officer*, c.2 (11 July 1958), 41; G. A. V. Morgan, 'Children Who Refuse to Go to

School. Observations in "School Anxiety"', *Medical Officer*, cii.18 (30 October 1959), 223; Professor Milton J. E. Senn, 'School Phobias: The Role of the Paediatrician in their Prevention and Management', *Proceedings of the Royal Society of Medicine*, 55 (1962), 976–7; Mira Talbot, 'Panic in School Phobia', *American Journal of Orthopsychiatry*, xxvii (1957), 287.

87 G. A. V. Morgan, 'Children Who Refuse to Go to School. Observations in "School Anxiety"', *Medical Officer*, cii.18 (30 October 1959), 223.

88 Editorial, *The Times*, 24 November 1959, 13; J. L. Green, 'Truancy – or School Phobia', in National Association for Mental Health, *'Truancy – or School Phobia?' Being the Proceedings of the 15th Inter-Clinic Conference* (London, 1959), 15; Jack H. Kahn and Jean P. Nursten, *Unwillingly to School. The Place of the Child Guidance Clinic in the Treatment of School Phobia* (Oxford, 1965), 11; Jean P. Nursten, 'The Background of Children with School Phobia. A Study of Twenty-Five Cases', *Medical Officer*, c.22 (28 November 1958), 342.

89 J. H. Kahn, 'School Refusal. Some Clinical and Cultural Aspects', *Medical Officer*, c.22 (28 November 1958), 338; Adelaide M. Johnson, 'School Phobia', *American Journal of Orthopsychiatry*, 27 (1957), 307; Jack H. Kahn and Jean P. Nursten, *Unwillingly to School. The Place of the Child Guidance Clinic in the Treatment of School Phobia* (Oxford, 1965), 12–13; Samuel Waldfogel, John C. Collidge and Pauline B. Hann, 'The Development, Meaning and Management of School Phobia', *American Journal of Orthopsychiatry*, 27 (1957), 756.

90 J. L. Green, 'Truancy – or School Phobia', in National Association for Mental Health, *'Truancy – or School Phobia?' Being the Proceedings of the 15th Inter-Clinic Conference* (London, 1959), 11, and 'School Phobia', *Lancet*, 30 January 1960, 270.

91 Professor Milton J. E. Senn, 'School Phobias: The Role of the Paediatrician in their Prevention and Management', *Proceedings of the Royal Society of Medicine*, 55 (1962), 976–7.

92 Samuel Waldfogel, John C. Collidge and Pauline B. Hann, 'The Development, Meaning and Management of School Phobia', *American Journal of Orthopsychiatry*, 27 (1957), 761.

93 G. A. V. Morgan, 'Children Who Refuse to Go to School. Observations in "School Anxiety"', *Medical Officer*, cii.18 (30 October 1959), 221.

94 Ibid., 224. Also see 'School Phobia', *Lancet*, 30 January 1960, 270.

95 Adelaide M. Johnson, Eugene I. Falstein, S. A. Szurek and Margaret Svendsen, 'School Phobia', *American Journal of Orthopsychiatry*, 11 (1941), 707.

96 Ibid., 707–8.

97 Adelaide M. Johnson, 'School Phobia', *American Journal of Orthopsychiatry*, 27 (1957), 308.

98 For example, see Hilde Bruch, *Don't Be Afraid of Your Child. A Guide for Perplexed Parents* (New York, 1952).

CHAPTER FOUR: NIGHTMARES

1 Raymond Bellamy, 'The Analysis of a Nightmare', *Journal of Abnormal and Social Psychology*, 10 (1915), 11–18.

2 For example, see Husley Cason, 'The Nightmare Dream', *Psychological*

Monographs, xlvi.5 (1935), 37; Josephine C. Foster and John E. Anderson, 'Unpleasant Dreams in Childhood', *Child Development*, 7.2 (June 1936), 78; Charles Williams Kimmins, *Children's Dreams* (London, 1920), 38; M. J. Feldman and M. Hersen, 'Attitudes Towards Death in Nightmare Subjects', *Journal of Abnormal Psychology*, 72 (1967), 421–5.

3 Howard Barrett, *The Management of Children. A Book for Mothers and Nurses* (London, 1906), 477.

4 Henry M. Lyman, *Insomnia; and Other Disorders of Sleep* (Chicago, 1885), 179.

5 William B. Atkinson, 'Note on Night Terrors', *Alienist and Neurologist*, iii.4 (October 1882), 587.

6 Elwood Worcester, Samuel McComb and Isador H. Coriat, *Religion and Medicine. The Moral Control of Nervous Disorders* (London, 1908), 271.

7 Albert Westland, *The Child: A Medical Guide to its Care and Management* (London, 1910), 121.

8 Howard Barrett, *The Management of Children. A Book for Mothers and Nurses* (London, 1906), 478.

9 Henry M. Lyman, *Insomnia; and Other Disorders of Sleep* (Chicago, 1885), 112. Also see William B. Atkinson, 'Note on Night Terrors', *Alienist and Neurologist*, iii.4 (October 1882), 587.

10 Howard Barrett, *The Management of Children. A Book for Mothers and Nurses* (London, 1906), 478.

11 G. Stanley Hall, 'A Study of Fears', *American Journal of Psychology*, viii.2 (January 1897), 192–3. Also see Sanger Brown, 'The Disorders of Sleep', in Thomas L. Stedman (ed.), *Twentieth Century Practice. An International Encyclopedia of Modern Medical Science* (London, 1897), 828.

12 A. J. J. Ratcliff, *A History of Dreams. A Brief Account of the Evolution of Dream Theories, With a Chapter on the Dream in Literature* (London, 1923), 92, 94.

13 William S. Walsh, *The Psychology of Dreams* (London, 1920), 204, 209–12. Also see Children's Welfare Federation of New York City, *Child Care Questions and Answers. Over 400 Questions Most Often Asked by Parents* (New York, 1948), 104, and Nathaniel Kleitman, *Sleep and Wakefulness as Alternating Phases in the Cycle of Existence* (Chicago, 1939), 388.

14 Ch. Féré, 'A Contribution to the Pathology of Dreams and of Hysterical Paralysis', *Brain* 9 (1887), 488–93.

15 William S. Walsh, *The Psychology of Dreams* (London, 1920), 197. Also see Ernest Jones, 'On the Nightmare', *American Journal of Insanity*, lxvi (January 1910), 385.

16 Maurice Chideckel, 'Dreams as the Cause of Death and Disease', *Medical Record*, 98 (1920), 182–3. Also see W. S. Taylor, *Readings in Abnormal Psychology and Mental Hygiene* (New York, 1926), 591–4.

17 William S. Walsh, *The Psychology of Dreams* (London, 1920), 197.

18 This is also the view of H. M. Stanley (whom Hall mentions), in *Studies in the Evolutionary Psychology of Feeling* (London, 1895), chapters 7–8.

19 G. Stanley Hall, 'A Study of Fears', *American Journal of Psychology*, viii.2 (January 1897), 147–249.

20 Ibid., 188–9. For another account see Josiah Morse, *The Psychology and Neurology of Fear* (Worchester, Mass., 1907), 18, 51–9. These ideas were

adopted in many childcare manuals: for example, see G. Martin Bennett and Margaret Bennett, *The First Five Years of a Child's Life* (London, 1920), 33, and W. J. McBride, *The Conquest of Fear Through Psychology* (London, 1936), 12.

21 Nandor Fodor, 'Nightmares of Cannibalism', *American Journal of Orthopsychiatry*, v.2 (April 1951), 226–35; Nandor Fodor, 'Nightmares of Suffocation', *Journal of Nervous and Mental Disease*, 101.6 (June 1945), 557–65; Nandor Fodor, 'Nightmares of Water', *The American Imago. A Psychoanalytical Journal for the Arts and Sciences*, 5.2 (July 1948), 140–51.

22 J. A. Hadfield, *Dreams and Nightmares* (London, 1954), 183.

23 Sigmund Freud, *The Interpretation of Dreams*, in Freud's *The Standard Edition of the Complete Psychological Works of Sigmund Freud*, trans. James Strachey (London, 1953) 277–389, chapter 6, part 4, 94.

24 Ibid.

25 Later Freud revised this view about dreams as wish-fulfilment, arguing instead that nightmares represented a repetition compulsion, or the primitive tendency of the mind to repeat what had been experienced: Sigmund Freud, *Beyond the Pleasure Principle*, editions published in Leipzig and London, 1920 and 1955.

26 Sigmund Freud, *An Outline of Psychoanalysis* (London, 1940), 170–1.

27 Sigmund Freud, 'Some Additional Notes on Dream-Interpretation as a Whole', in Freud's *The Standard Edition of the Complete Psychological Works of Sigmund Freud*, trans. James Strachey (London, 1961) 132.

28 Ernest Jones, 'On the Nightmare', *American Journal of Insanity*, lxvi (January 1910), 383, 405–10, 414–15.

29 Ernest Jones, *Nightmare, Witches, and Devils* (New York, 1931), 40.

30 Carl G. Jung, 'Analysis of Dreams', in Jung, *Freud and Psychoanalysis*, trans. R. F. C. Hull (London, 1961), 25.

31 Carl G. Jung, 'The Practical Use of Dream Analysis', 1934, in Jung's *The Practice of Psychotherapy*, trans. R. F. C. Hull (London, 1954), 149.

32 C. G. Jung, *Memories, Dreams, Reflections* (London, 1963), 181.

33 Ibid., 194.

34 Carl G. Jung, *Analytical Psychology: Its Theory and Practice: the Tavistock Lectures* (London, 1968), 123.

35 Carl G. Jung, 'On the Psychology of the Unconscious', in Jung's *Two Essays on Analytical Psychology*, trans. R. F. C. Hull (London, 1953), 162.

36 Ibid., 97.

37 'Soldier's Dreams', *Lancet*, 23 January 1915, 210.

38 Ibid.

39 Quoted by Harvey Cushing, *From a Surgeon's Journal 1915-1918* (London, 1936), 489. Also see the Vietnam war poem by John McAfee, 'Open Season', in J. Topham (ed.), *Vietnam Literature Anthology*, rev. and enlarged edn. (Philadelphia, 1990), 80.

40 Rowland Myrddyn Luther, 'The Poppies are Blood Red', 37, Imperial War Museum (IWM) 87/8/1.

41 George W. Crile, *A Mechanistic View of War and Peace* (New York, 1915), 27.

42 W. H. R. Rivers, *Conflict and Dream* (London, 1923), 66–9.

43 W. H. R. Rivers, 'The Repression of War Experience', *Lancet*, 2 February 1918, 176. These ideas were adopted by notable Medical Officers and authors such as the neurologist Arthur F. Hurst, *Medical Diseases of the War*, 2nd edn. (London, 1918), 19.

44 E. Aserinsky and N. Kleitman, 'Regularly Occurring Periods of Eye Motility and Concomitant Phenomena During Sleep', *Science*, 118 (1953), 273–4, and W. Dement and N. Kleitman, 'The Relation of Eye Movements During Sleep to Dream Activity: An Objective Method for the Study of Dreaming', *Journal of Experimental Psychology*, 53 (1955), 339–46.

45 For example, see A. M. Arkin, J. S. Antrobus and S. J. Ellman, *The Mind in Sleep: Psychology and Parapsychology* (New Jersey, 1978); Arthur M. Arkin, 'Night-Terrors as Anomalous REM Sleep Component Manifestation in Slow-Wave Sleep', *Waking and Sleeping*, 2 (1978); C. Fisher, 'A Psychophysiological Study of Nightmares and Night Terrors. II. Mental Content and Recall of Stage 4', *Journal of Nervous and Mental Disease*, 158 (1974), 174–88.

46 Nathaniel Kleitman, *Sleep and Wakefulness as Alternating Phases in the Cycle of Existence* (Chicago, 1939), 388.

47 H. Gastaut and R. T. Broughton, in T. Wortis (ed.), *Recent Advances in Biological Psychiatry* (New York, 1965), and R. T. Broughton, 'Sleep Disorders: Disorders of Arousal?', in *Science*, 159 (1968), 1070.

48 F. Crick and G. Mitchinson, 'The Function of Dream Sleep', *Nature*, 30 (1983), 111–14.

49 Smaller proportions activated temperature, tactile, olfactory and gustatory systems.

50 The clearest description of McCarley's work can be found in William H. Moorcroft, *Sleep, Dreaming and Sleep Disorders* (Lanham, 1993), 260–1.

51 Mircea Steriade and Robert W. McCarley, *Brainstem Control of Wakefulness and Sleep* (New York, 1990), 417–33.

52 Kathryn Belicki and Marion A. Cuddy, 'Nightmares: Facts, Fictions and Future Directions', in Jayne Gackenbach and Anees A. Sheikh (eds.), *Dream Images: A Call to Mental Arms* (Amityville, 1991), 108.

53 Ibid., 109.

54 Harry T. Hunt, 'Toward a Cognitive Psychology of Dreams', in Jayne Gackenbach (ed.), *Sleep and Dreams. A Sourcebook* (New York, 1986), 253.

55 Mircea Steriade and Robert W. McCarley, *Brainstem Control of Wakefulness and Sleep* (New York, 1990), 428.

56 J. Herman, D. Barker and H. Roffwarg, 'Similarity of Eye Movement Characteristic in REM Sleep and the Awake State', *Psychophysiology*, 20 (1983), 537–43, and H. Roffwarg, S. Herman and C. Bowe-Anders, 'The Effects of Sustained Alterations of Waking Visual Input on Dream Content', in A. Arkin, S. Antrobus and S. Ellman (eds.), *The Mind in Sleep: Psychology and Psychophysiology* (Hillsdale, 1978), 295–349.

57 Harry T. Hunt, 'Toward a Cognitive Psychology of Dreams', in Jayne Gackenbach (ed.), *Sleep and Dreams. A Sourcebook* (New York, 1986), 252, 259.

58 Ibid., 266.

59 For example, see Nerys Dee, *Discover Dreams* (Wellingborough, 1989); G.

William Domhoff, *Finding Meaning in Dreams* (New York, 1996); Ifeoma R. Fiirter, *Interpreting Your Dreams and Visions* (Manchester, 2000); Lucy Goodison, *The Dreams of Women* (London, 1995); Craig Hamilton-Parker, *The Hidden Meaning of Dreams* (New York, 1999); David F. Melbourne and Keith Hearne, *The Meaning of Your Dreams* (London, 1999); Sally Morningstar, *Divining the Future* (London, 2000); Leon Nacson, *Interpreting Dreams A–Z* (Carlsbad, 1999); Julia and Derek Parker, *Dreaming* (London, 1993); Stearn Robinson and Tom Corbett, *The Dreamer's Dictionary. A Complete Guide to Interpreting Your Dreams* (London, 1984); Philippa Waring, *Omens from Your Dreams* (London, 1991).

CHAPTER FIVE: PHOBIAS

1 According to the OED.

2 'Vincent', 'Confessions of an Agoraphobic Victim', *American Journal of Psychology*, xxx (1919), 295–9. I strongly suspect that the author is G. Stanley Hall, the famous psychologist discussed in the previous chapter, but have been unable to prove it.

3 Unpublished study by Stewart Agras, D. Sylvester and D. Oliveau, quoted in Isaac M. Marks, *Fears and Phobias* (London, 1969), 76. Estimate based on a representative study of people in Greater Burlington in the 1960s. Other accounts rate the level of phobia as much greater. According to W. J. McBride, *The Conquest of Fear Through Psychology* (London, 1936), 35, and H. Addington Bruce introducing Tom A. Williams, *Dreads and Besetting Fears. Including States of Anxiety, Their Causes and Cure* (Boston, 1923), v, it could affect one in ten Britons.

4 Isaac M. Marks, *Fears and Phobias* (London, 1969), 76.

5 R. J. Kerry, 'Phobias of Outer Space', *Journal of Mental Science*, 106.445 (October 1960), 1386.

6 Sigmund Freud, 'Obsessions and Phobias. Their Psychical Mechanism and Their Aetiology', in *The Standard Edition of the Complete Psychological Works of Sigmund Freud*, iii (London, 1962), 74, 80–1. First published 1895.

7 Sigmund Freud, 'A Reply to Criticisms on the Anxiety Neurosis', in *The Standard Edition of the Psychological Collective Works of Sigmund Freud*, trans. James Strachey (London, 1953), 135–9.

8 Sigmund Freud, 'Obsessions and Phobias. Their Psychical Mechanism and Their Aetiology', in *The Standard Edition of the Complete Psychological Works of Sigmund Freud*, iii (London, 1962), 74, 80–1. First published 1895.

9 Sigmund Freud, *New Introductory Lectures on Psychoanalysis*, first published 1932 (London, 1974), 84.

10 Sigmund Freud, 'Analysis of a Phobia in a Five-Year-Old Boy', first published 1909, *The Standard Edition of the Complete Psychological Works of Sigmund Freud*, trans. James Strachey (London, 1955), 3–149.

11 Bertram Lewin, 'Phobic Symptoms and Dream Interpretation', *Psychoanalytic Quarterly*, 21, 1952, 304–5.

12 S. Rachman, *Phobias. Their Nature and Control* (Springfield, Ill., 1968), 215.

13 John Yerbury Dent, *Anxiety and its Treatment. With Special Reference to Alcoholism* (London, 1941), 32.

14 John Vassos, *Phobia* (New York, 1931), 11–12, 30, 57, 93–4.

15 Otto Fenichel, *Psychoanalytic Theory of the Neurosis* (New York, 1945), 200.

16 Dr Edmund Bergler, 'Psychoanalysis of a case of Agoraphobia', *Psychoanalytical Review*, xxii (1935), 392–3.

17 Ernst Hammerschlag, 'Psychiatry Applied to Internal Medicine', in Leopold Bellak (ed.), *Psychology of Physical Illness. Psychiatry Applied to Medicine, Surgery and the Specialties* (London, 1952), 35.

18 Milton Greenblatt and John S. Bockovem, 'Illustrative Cases of Lobotomy', in Milton Greenblatt, Robert Arnot and Harry C. Solomon (eds.), *Studies in Lobotomy* (London, 1951), 278–9.

19 Moniz was born Antonio Caetano de Abrere Freire in 1874 in Portugal. He adopted the name Egas Moniz (after a twelfth-century Portuguese patriot) early in his life.

20 Elliot S. Valenstein, 'Historical Perspective', in Valenstein (ed.), *The Psychosurgery Debate. Scientific, Legal and Ethical Perspectives* (San Francisco, 1980), 27.

21 John Farquhar Fulton, *Frontal Lobotomy and Affect Behavior. A Neurophysiological Analysis* (New York, 1951), 12.

22 John Kleinig, *Ethical Issues in Psychosurgery* (London, 1985), 7.

23 Jack D. Pressman, *Last Resort. Psychosurgery and the Limits of Medicine* (Cambridge, 1998), 147.

24 David Shutts, *Lobotomy. Resort to the Knife* (New York, 1982), ix.

25 Jack D. Pressman, *Last Resort. Psychosurgery and the Limits of Medicine* (Cambridge, 1998), 151.

26 Stanley David Porteus and Richard DeMonbrun Kepner, 'Mental Changes After Bilateral Prefrontal Lobotomy', *Genetic Psychology Monographs*, 29 (February 1944), 114.

27 Lauren H. Smith, Donald W. Hastings and Joseph Hughes, 'Immediate Follow Up Results of Electroshock Therapy', *American Journal of Psychiatry*, 100.3 (November 1943), 353.

28 S. Clark and Frank Norburry, 'A Possible Role of the Element of Fear in Metrazol Therapy', in *Diseases of the Nervous System*, 2 (1941), 196–8.

29 David Shutts, *Lobotomy. Resort to the Knife* (New York, 1982), 44.

30 http://www.epub.org.br/cm/n04/historia/shock_i.htm#meduna.

31 Henry Tanner, 'Physiological and Psychological Factors in Electro-Shock as Criteria of Therapy', *Journal of Nervous and Mental Disease*, iii (1950), 234–5.

32 W. Russell Brain and E. B. Strauss, *Recent Advances in Neurology and Neuropsychiatry*, 5th edn. (London, 1947), 146.

33 Stanley Noel Law, *Inspired Freedom* (London, 1975), 56–7.

34 Lothar B. Kalinowsky, Hanns Hippius and Helmfried E. Klein, *Biological Treatments in Psychiatry* (New York, 1982), 266. Also see William Beecher Scoville, 'The Effect of Surgical Lesions of the Brain on Psyche and Behavior in Man', in Arthur Winter (ed.), *The Surgical Control of Behavior. A Symposium* (Springfield, Ill., 1971), 54–5.

35 Stanley David Porteus and Richard DeMonbrun Kepner, 'Mental Changes After Bilateral Prefrontal Lobotomy', *Genetic Psychology Monographs*, 29 (February 1944), 114.

36 Mary Frances Robinson and Walter Freeman, *Psychosurgery and the Self* (New York, 1954), 15.

37 Gregory Zilboorge, *A History of Medical Psychology* (New York, 1941).

38 George W. Kisker, 'Remarks on the Problem of Psychosurgery', *American Journal of Psychiatry*, 100.2 (September 1943), 180.

39 Yale David Koskoff and Richard Goldhurst, *The Dark Side of the House* (New York, 1968), xxi.

40 John Farquhar Fulton, *Frontal Lobotomy and Affect Behavior. A Neurophysiological Analysis* (New York, 1951), 103, and George W. Kisker, 'Remarks on the Problem of Psychosurgery', *American Journal of Psychiatry*, 100.2 (September 1943), 181, and Stanley David Porteus, *A Psychologist of Sorts. The Autobiography and Publications of the Inventor of the Porteus Maze Test* (Palo Alto, 1969), 187.

41 Jack D. Pressman, *Last Resort. Psychosurgery and the Limits of Medicine* (Cambridge, 1998), 205.

42 Robert Arnot, Beatrice Talbot and Milton Greenblatt, 'One to Four Year Follow-Up of 205 Cases of Bilateral Prefrontal Lobotomy', in Milton Greenblatt, Robert Arnot and Harry C. Solomon (eds.), *Studies in Lobotomy* (London, 1951), 106.

43 William Beecher Scoville, 'Psychosurgery and Other Lesions of the Brain Affecting Human Behavior', in Edward Hitchcock, Lauri Laitinen and Kjeld Vaernet (eds.), *Psychosurgery* (Springfield, Ill., 1972), 6–7.

44 Walter Freeman and James W. Watts, 'Prefrontal Lobotomy in the Treatment of Mental Disorders', *Southern Medical Journal*, 30.1 (January 1937), 31.

45 Walter Freeman and James W. Watts, 'An Interpretation of the Functions of the Frontal Lobe. Based on Observations in Forty-Eight Cases of Prefrontal Lobotomy', *Yale Journal of Biology and Medicine*, 11.5 (May 1939), 529–30, 535.

46 Mary Frances Robinson and Walter Freeman, *Psychosurgery and the Self* (New York, 1954), 16–17.

47 Milton Greenblatt, 'Psychosurgery: A Review of Recent Literature', in Greenblatt, Robert Arnot and Harry C. Solomon (eds.), *Studies in Lobotomy* (London, 1951), 38.

48 Stanley David Porteus and Richard DeMonbrun Kepner, 'Mental Changes After Bilateral Prefrontal Lobotomy', *Genetic Psychology Monographs*, 29 (February 1944), 114.

49 Robert Arnot, Beatrice Talbot and Milton Greenblatt, 'One to Four Year Follow-Up of 205 Cases of Bilateral Prefrontal Lobotomy', in Milton Greenblatt, Robert Arnot and Harry C. Solomon (eds.), *Studies in Lobotomy* (London, 1951), 106.

50 For discussion about the precise causal relationship see Ira C. Nichols and J. McVicker Hunt, 'A Case of Partial Bilateral Frontal Lobectomy. A Psychopathological Study', *American Journal of Psychiatry*, 96.5 (March 1940), 1065; Stanley David Porteus and Richard DeMonbrun Kepner, 'Mental Changes After Bilateral Prefrontal Lobotomy', *Genetic Psychology Monographs*, 29 (February 1944), 10; Lloyd H. Ziegler, 'Bilateral Prefrontal Lobotomy. A Survey', *American Journal of Psychiatry*, 100.2 (September 1943), 178.

51 Mary Frances Robinson and Walter Freeman, *Psychosurgery and the Self* (New York, 1954), 15, 18.

52 Walter Jackson Freeman and James W. Watts, *Psychosurgery in the Treatment of Mental Disorders and Intractable Pain*, first published 1942, 2nd edn. (Springfield, Ill., 1950), 237.

53 Walter Freeman and James W. Watts, 'An Interpretation of the Functions of the Frontal Lobe. Based on Observations in Forty-Eight Cases of Prefrontal Lobotomy', *Yale Journal of Biology and Medicine*, 11.5 (May 1939), 538.

54 Ibid., 537.

55 David Shutts, *Lobotomy. Resort to the Knife* (New York, 1982), 94.

56 Elliot S. Valenstein, 'Historical Perspective', in Valenstein (ed.), *The Psychosurgery Debate. Scientific, Legal and Ethical Perspectives* (San Francisco, 1980), 33–4.

57 For example, see Samuel Chaukin, *The Mind Stealers. Psychosurgery and Mind Control* (Boston, 1978).

58 Stanley David Porteus, *A Psychologist of Sorts. The Autobiography and Publications of the Inventor of the Porteus Maze Test* (Palo Alto, 1969), 196.

59 Milton Greenblatt, 'Psychosurgery: A Review of Recent Literature', in Greenblatt, Robert Arnot and Harry C. Solomon (eds.), *Studies in Lobotomy* (London, 1951), 21.

60 David Shutts, *Lobotomy. Resort to the Knife* (New York, 1982), 257.

61 Jack D. Pressman, *Last Resort. Psychosurgery and the Limits of Medicine* (Cambridge, 1998), 303–4.

62 Ibid., 198.

63 The revival of psychosurgery in the 1970s was a much more limited phenomenon. After all, although over seventy American neurosurgeons in 1971 had carried out lobotomies (there were three hundred operations that year), the vast majority were performed by only six neurosurgeons: Elliott S. Valenstein, *Great and Desperate Cures. The Rise and Fall of Psychosurgery and Other Radical Treatments for Mental Illness* (New York, 1986), 284.

64 John Kleinig, *Ethical Issues in Psychosurgery* (London, 1985), 8.

65 Jack D. Pressman, *Last Resort. Psychosurgery and the Limits of Medicine* (Cambridge, 1998), 12.

66 John B. Watson, *Behaviorism* (London, 1925), 125–9.

67 Tom Kraft and Ihsan Al-Issa, 'Behaviour Therapy and the Recall of Traumatic Experience – A Case Study', *Behaviour Research and Therapy. An International Multi-Disciplinary Journal*, 3 (1965), 55.

68 Foreword by I. Newton Kugelman to S. Rachman, *Phobias. Their Nature and Control* (Springfield, Illinois, 1968), viii.

69 As claimed by (among others) A. Stanley Webster, 'The Development of Phobias in Married Women', *Psychological Monographs. General and Applied*, 67.17 (1953), 2.

70 Isaac M. Marks, *Fears and Phobias* (London, 1969), 75–6.

71 Foreword by I. Newton Kugelman to S. Rachman, *Phobias. Their Nature and Control* (Springfield, Ill., 1968), ix.

72 J. H. Friedman, 'Short Term Psychotherapy of "Phobia of Travel"', *American*

Journal of Psychotherapy, 4 (1950), 259–78.

73 Samuel Waldfogel, John Coolidge and Pauline B. Hahn, 'The Development, Meaning, and Management of School Phobia', *American Journal of Orthopsychiatry*, 27 (1957), 757.

74 S. Rachman, *Phobias. Their Nature and Control* (Springfield, Ill., 1968), 38.

75 An almost identical phrase was used by Joseph H. Cautela, 'Desensitisation and Insight', in *Behaviour Research and Therapy. An International Multi-Disciplinary Journal*, 3 (1965), 59–60; Tom Kraft and Ihsan Al-Issa, 'Behaviour Therapy and the Recall of Traumatic Experience – A Case Study', in *Behaviour Research and Therapy. An International Multi-Disciplinary Journal*, 3 (1965), 55.

76 Joseph Wolpe, *Psychotherapy by Reciprocal Inhibition* (Stanford, 1958) and 'Behaviour Therapy in Complex Neurotic States', *British Journal of Psychiatry*, 110 (1964), 28–34.

77 See S. Rachman, *Phobias. Their Nature and Control* (Springfield, Ill., 1968), 164–7.

78 Barbara Olasov Rothbaum, Larry F. Hodges, Rob Kooper, Dan Opdyke, James S. Williford and Max North, 'Effectiveness of Computer-Generated (Virtual Reality) Graded Exposure in the Treatment of Acrophobia', *American Journal of Psychiatry*, 152.4 (April 1995), 626–8.

79 Joseph H. Cautela, 'Desensitisation and Insight', in *Behaviour Research and Therapy. An International Multi-Disciplinary Journal*, 3 (1965), 59–60. Also see N. Hobbs, 'Sources of Gain in Psychotherapy', *American Psychology*, 17 (1962), 741–7.

80 Nicolas Malleson, 'Panic and Phobia. A Possible Method of Treatment', *Lancet*, 31 January 1959, 225, 227.

81 Patrick A. Boudewyns and Robert H. Shipley, *Flooding and Implosive Therapy. Direct Therapeutic Exposure in Clinical Practice* (New York, 1983), 5.

82 Ibid., 181–96.

AFTERWORD TO PART TWO: PSYCHOHISTORY

1 Peter N. Stearns and Carol Z. Stearns, 'Emotionology: Clarifying the History of Emotions and Emotional Standards', *American Historical Review*, 90.4 (October 1985), 820.

2 Carol Zisowitz Stearns and Peter N. Stearns, *Anger. The Struggle for Emotional Control in America's History* (Chicago, 1986), 219. Also see Carol Z. Stearns, 'Lord Help Me Walk Humbly: Anger and Sadness in England and America, 1570–1750', in Carol Z. Stevens and Peter Stearns (eds.), *Emotional and Social Change: Towards a New Psychohistory* (New York, 1988), 68.

3 Peter Gay, *Freud for Historians* (New York, 1985).

4 For other sophisticated uses of psychoanalysis in history see Norbert Elias, *The Civilizing Process: Sociogenetic and Psychogenetic Investigations*, trans. Edmund Jephcott, 2 vols (Oxford, 1978); Sander L. Gilman, *Freud, Race, and Gender* (Princeton, 1993); Dominick LaCapra, *Representing the Holocaust: History, Theory, Trauma* (Ithaca, 1994); Lynn Hunt, *The Family Romance of the French Revolution* (Berkeley, 1992); Michael Hunter (guest ed.), 'Psychoanalysing Robert Boyle', *British Journal for the History of Science*, 32 (September 1999);

Lyndal Roper, *Oedipus and the Devil: Witchcraft, Sexuality, and Religion in Early Modern Europe* (London, 1994).

5 Peter Gay, *The Bourgeois Experience. From Victoria to Freud*, 4 vols (Oxford, 1984–96).

6 Peter Gay, *The Bourgeois Experience: From Victoria to Freud. Volume 1: Education of the Senses* (Oxford, 1984), 8.

7 For example, see Fred Weinstein, 'Psychohistory and the Crisis of the Social Sciences', *History and Theory*, 34.4 (December 1995).

8 Michael Hunter, 'Introduction', in Hunter (guest ed.), 'Psychoanalysing Robert Boyle', *British Journal for the History of Science*, 32 (September 1999), 259.

9 I am grateful to Fred Weinstein, 'Psychohistory and the Crisis of the Social Sciences', *History and Theory*, 34.4 (December 1995), 310.

10 Ibid., 311–12.

CHAPTER SIX: SOCIAL HYSTERIA

1 R. Kingman, 'Fears and Phobias', *Welfare Magazine*, 19 (1928), 149–54. Also see D. K. Henderson, 'The Significance of Fear', *Edinburgh Medical Journal*, xlviii (October 1941), 660, and Mark A. May, *Education in a World of Fear* (Cambridge, Mass., 1941), 1.

2 Preston Bradley, *Mastering Fear* (Indianapolis, 1935), x. Also see p.17. For other examples of this self-help industry see William Lee Howard, *Sex Problems Solved (Those of Worry and Work)* (London, 1927) and John Kennedy, *Worry. Its Cause and Cure* (London, 1946); T. Gilbert Oakley, *How to Conquer Your Nervous Fears* (London, 1939).

3 Archdeacon R. H. Charles, *Courage, Truth, Purity* (Oxford, 1931), 34.

4 Philip Guedalla, 'The Age of Fear', *Listener*, 4 August 1937, 221.

5 Robert Speaight, *Ronald Knox. The Writer* (London, 1958), 7, and Evelyn Waugh, *The Life of the Right Reverend Ronald Knox* (London, 1954), 190.

6 Text given in Ronald A. Knox, *Essays in Satire* (London, 1928), 279–87.

7 'The Misunderstood Satirist', *Manchester Guardian*, 18 January 1926, 6.

8 'Beyond a Joke!', *Daily Chronicle*, 18 January 1926, 3.

9 'A Lord Mayor Protests to the BBC', *Daily Express*, 19 January 1926, 1.

10 'Radio Silliness', *Irish Telegraph*, 18 January 1926, 1.

11 'Revolution Hoax by Wireless', *Daily Express*, 18 January 1926, 1. Also see 'The Simple Listener-In', *Manchester Guardian*, 18 January 1926, 6; 'Britain is Alarmed by Burlesque Radio "News" of Revolt in London and Bombing of Commons', *New York Times*, 18 January 1926, 3; 'A Skit Scare', *Edinburgh Evening News*, 18 January 1926, 8.

12 J. C. S. MacGregor, *Ariel*, 5 (June 1937), 28–9.

13 'Father Knox's Realism', *Star*, 18 January 1926, 9.

14 'Rumour and Humour', *Irish Times*, 18 January 1926, 4.

15 'Radio Politics', *Daily Herald*, 19 January 1926, 4. Also see 'A Discreditable Joke', *Daily Express*, 18 January 1926, 8.

16 'Harmful Humour', *Leeds Weekly Citizen*, 22 January 1926, 2.

17 'Night Shocks by Father Knox', *Daily Herald*, 18 January 1926, 1.

18 *English Review*, quoted in Lester Chester, Stephen Fry and Hugo Young, *The*

Zinoviev Letter (London, 1967), 18.

19 Lester Chester, Stephen Fry and Hugo Young, *The Zinoviev Letter* (London, 1967), 123.

20 'A Broadcast Skit', *Daily Mail*, 18 January 1926, 7.

21 Cited in Evelyn Waugh, *The Life of the Right Reverend Ronald Knox* (London, 1954), 192.

22 'A Wireless Scare', *Cardiff Times and South Wales Weekly News*, 18 January 1926, 11.

23 'A Broadcast Scare', *Daily Mail*, 18 January 1926, 7.

24 'A Discreditable Joke', *Daily Express*, 18 January 1926, 8.

25 'A Discreditable Joke', *Daily Express*, 18 January 1926, 8.

26 'The Misunderstood Satirist', *Manchester Guardian*, 18 January 1926, 6.

27 'The Star Man', 'The Joke that Failed', *Star*, 18 January 1926, 5.

28 'Rumour and Humour', *Irish Times*, 18 January 1926, 4.

29 'Father Knox's Wireless Talk', *The Times*, 18 January 1926, 6.

30 'Father Knox Interviewed', *Cardiff Times and South Wales Weekly News*, 23 January 1926, 9.

31 'Sacking of London', *Weekly Scotsman*, 23 January 1926, 1. Also see the similar comments of two Unionist papers, 'The Joke that Failed', *Weekly Scotsman*, 23 January 1926, 6 and 'Wireless "Revolution"', *Birmingham Mail*, 18 January 1926, 4.

32 'Britain is Alarmed by Burlesque Radio "News" of Revolt in London and Bombing of Commons', *New York Times*, 18 January 1926, 3.

33 Cited in J. P. Chaplin, *Rumor, Fear and the Madness of Crowds* (New York, 1959), 97–8.

34 Ibid., 98. None of these claims were substantiated.

35 Brian Holmstein and Alex Lubertozzi (eds.), *The Complete War of the Worlds. Mars' Invasion of Earth from H. G. Wells to Orson Welles* (Naperville, 2001), 20.

36 Ibid.

37 R. A. Gregory's review of *The War of the Worlds*, *Nature*, 10 February 1898, reproduced in Patrick Parrinder, *H. G. Wells. The Critical Heritage* (London, 1972), 75–6.

38 Hadley Cantril, *The Invasion from Mars. A Study in the Psychology of Panic with the Complete Script of the Famous Orson Welles Broadcast* (Princeton, 1940), 55.

39 Ibid., 93.

40 Ibid., 140.

41 Walter Lippmann, *Interpretations*, ed. Allan Nevins (New York, 1932), 12.

42 Hadley Cantril, *The Invasion from Mars. A Study in the Psychology of Panic with the Complete Script of the Famous Orson Welles Broadcast* (Princeton, 1940), 100.

43 Ibid., 99.

44 Ibid., 158.

45 Ibid., 47.

46 Ibid., 71.

47 Ibid., 74.

48 Ibid., x.

49 Ibid., 70.

50 Ibid., 160.

51 Ibid., 72.

52 Hadley Cantril and Gordon W. Allport, *The Psychology of Radio* (New York, 1935), vii, 212.

53 Cited in Brian Holmstein and Alex Lubertozzi (eds.), *The Complete War of the Worlds. Mars' Invasion of Earth from H. G. Wells to Orson Welles* (Naperville, 2001), 20.

54 Hadley Cantril, *The Invasion from Mars. A Study in the Psychology of Panic with the Complete Script of the Famous Orson Welles Broadcast* (Princeton, 1940), 158.

AFTERWORD TO PART THREE: FEAR VERSUS ANXIETY

1 Sigmund Freud, *A General Introduction to Psychoanalysis* (New York, 1952), 103.

2 This is only a tendency. After all, in political terrorisation within dictatorial regimes, fear may also separate people from one another, as in Chile during the Pinochet regime and Argentina during the 1976–83 dictatorship of Galtieri.

CHAPTER SEVEN: COMBAT

1 William Manchester, *Goodbye Darkness. A Memoir of the Pacific War* (London, 1981), 3–7.

2 Unnamed soldier in convalescent hospital, in Miss Dorothy Scholes, 'Papers of Miss Dorothy Scholes', unpaginated, Wigan Archives Service D/DZ.EHC, and Joanna Bourke (ed.), *The Misfit Soldier* (Cork, 1999), 32. In both, punctuation and capitalisation are as in original.

3 Private Arthur H. Hubbard, 'Letters Written May–November 1916', in IWM.

4 Shawn O'Leary, 'Shell Shock', in *Spikenard and Bayonet. Verse of the Front Line* (Melbourne, 1941), 20.

5 See my *An Intimate History of Killing: Face to Face Killing in Twentieth Century Warfare* (London, 1999).

6 M. Ralph Kaufman, "Ill Health" as an Expression of Anxiety in a Combat Unit', *Psychosomatic Medicine*, 9 (March 1947), 108.

7 Major Libby Pulsifer, 'Psychiatric Aspects of Gastrointestinal Complaints of the Soldier in Training', *Military Surgeon*, 95.6 (December 1944), 482. Also see Joost A. M. Meerloo, *Patterns of Panic* (Westport, Connecticut, 1950), 63.

8 D. K. Henderson, 'The Significance of Fear', *Edinburgh Medical Journal*, xlviii.10 (October 1941), 652. For other comments about the physiological effects of fear see Sir Arthur F. Hurst, 'The Etiology and Treatment of War Neuroses', in Thomas Hunt (ed.), *Selected Writings of Sir Arthur Hurst (1879–1944)* (London, 1969), 179–80. First published in the *British Medical Journal* 2 (1917).

9 G. Elliott Smith and T. H. Pear, *Shell Shock and its Lessons* (Manchester, 1917), 8.

10 See my *An Intimate History of Killing: Face to Face Killing in Twentieth Century Warfare* (London, 1999)

11 G. Stanley Hall, *Morale. The Supreme Standard of Life and Conduct* (New York, 1920), 36.

12 Edward A. Strecker, 'War Neuroses', *Military Surgeon*, 94.4 (April 1944), 196.

13 E. G. Boring and M. Van de Water, *Psychology for the Fighting Man. What You Should Know About Yourself and Others* (Washington, DC, 1943), 300–4; Lucio E. Gatto, 'Understanding the "Fear of Flying" Syndrome. I. Psychic Aspects of the Problem', *United States Armed Forces Medical Journal*, v.8 (August 1954), 1094;

Albert J. Glass, 'Preventive Psychiatry in the Combat Zone', *United States Armed Forces Medical Journal*, iv.5 (May 1953), 685; Richard J. Healy, *Emergency and Disaster Planning* (New York, 1969), 284; William McDougall, *Psychology. The Study of Behaviour* (London, 1912), 237–8; L. S. Penrose, *On the Objective Study of Crowd Behaviour* (London, 1952), 28; Duane P. Schultz, *Panic Behavior. Discussion and Readings* (New York, 1964), 13–14.

14 E. G. Boring and M. Van de Water, *Psychology for the Fighting Man* (Washington, DC, 1943), 304–5. Also see Edward L. Munson, *The Management of Men. A Handbook on the Systematic Development of Morale and the Control of Human Behaviour* (London, 1920), 108, and C. P. Symonds, 'The Human Response to Flying Stress', *British Medical Journal*, 11 December 1943, 740.

15 Air Ministry, *Psychological Disorders in Flying Personnel of the Royal Air Force Investigated During the War 1939–1945* (London, 1947), 65, and Albert J. Glass, 'Combat Exhaustion', *United States Armed Forces Medical Journal*, 11.10 (October 1951), 1472.

16 'Psychiatric Casualties. Hints to Medical Officers in the Middle East Forces', pamphlet published by the General HQ Middle East, September 1942, in the papers of Lieutenant Colonel William Hamilton Scriven, RAMC 1652/3 in the Contemporary Medical Archives Centre (London).

17 George W. Crile, *A Mechanistic View of War and Peace* (New York, 1915), 19–22.

18 E. G. Boring and M. Van de Water, *Psychology for the Fighting Man* (Washington, DC, 1943), 298–9.

19 Letter from E. G. Boring to Marjorie Van de Water on 19 May 1943, in his Private Papers, quoted in James Herbert Capshew, 'Psychology on the March: American Psychologists and World War II', PhD thesis, University of Pennsylvania, 1986, 220–1.

20 H. X. Speigel, 'Psychiatric Observations in the Tunisian Campaign', *American Journal of Orthopsychiatry*, 14 (1943), 381–5.

21 Lieutenant Colonel Stephen W. Ranson, 'The Normal Battle Reaction: Its Relation to the Pathologic Battle Reaction', *Bulletin of the United States Army Medical Department*, ix, supplementary number (November 1949), 3–6.

22 Edward A. Strecker and Kenneth E. Appel, *Psychiatry in Modern Warfare* (New York, 1945), 27. Also see Edward A. Strecker, 'War Neuroses', *Military Surgeon*, 94.4 (April 1944), 197.

23 G. Elliott Smith, *Shell Shock and its Lessons* (Manchester, 1917), 9–10. This argument that impersonal forms of fighting were the most frightening was also made by A. Hyatt Williams, 'A Psychiatric Study of Indian Soldiers in Arakan', *British Journal of Medical Psychology*, xxiii.3 (1950), 169.

24 Arthur F. Hurst, *Medical Diseases of the War*, 2nd edn. (London, 1940) 36; 1st edn. 1916.

25 George W. Crile, *The Origin and Nature of the Emotions. Miscellaneous Papers* (London, 1915), 64.

26 Lieutenant Commander R. A. Cohen and Lieutenant J. G. Delano, 'Subacute Emotional Disturbances Induced by Combat', *War Medicine*, 7.5 (May 1945), 285; Eli Ginzberg, John L. Herma and Sol W. Ginsberg, *Psychiatry and Military Manpower Policy. A Reappraisal of the Experience in World War II* (New York, 1953),

27; Maurice Silverman, 'Causes of Neurotic Breakdown in British Service Personnel Stationed in the Far East in Peacetime', *Journal of Mental Science*, xcvi.403 (April 1950), 497; 'The Third Meeting of Command Specialists is Psychological Medicine', 21 September 1940, 3, PRO WO222/1584; Major Edwin A. Weinstein and Lieutenant Colonel Calvin S. Drayer, 'A Dynamic Approach to the Problem of Combat-Induced Anxiety', *Bulletin of the United States Army Medical Department*, ix, supplementary number (November 1949), 1949, 15–16; Lieutenant Commander Meyer A. Zeligs, 'War Neurosis. Psychiatric Experiences and Management on a Pacific Island', *War Medicine*, 6.3 (September 1944), 168.

27 Major Marvin F. Greiber, 'Narcosynthesis in the Treatment of the Noncombatant Psychiatric Casualty Overseas', *War Medicine*, 8.2 (August 1945), 85.

28 'Psychiatry – Arakan Campaigns', undated, 6, in PRO WO222/1571.

29 John T. MacCurdy, *War Neuroses* (Cambridge, 1918), 14, 111. Similar arguments were made by G. Elliott Smith and T. H. Pear, *Shell Shock and its Lessons* (Manchester, 1919), 9–10.

30 Edward A. Strecker and Kenneth E. Appel, *Psychiatry in Modern Warfare* (New York, 1945), passim.

31 Lord Moran, 'Wear and Tear', *Lancet*, 17 June 1950, 1100.

32 Ibid.

33 Lt. Colonel A. T. A. Browne, 'A Study of the Anatomy of Fear and Courage in War', *Army Quarterly and Defence Journal*, 106.3 (July 1976), 299, 302. Based on a study of self-inflicted wounds in Normandy, June–August 1944.

34 Maurice B. Wright, 'Psychological Emergencies in War Time', in *War Wounds and Air Raid Casualties* (London, 1939), 178. For this division between officers as suffering from anxiety states and the other ranks' hysteria, see Surgeon Captain D. Curran, 'Functional Nervous States in Relation to Service in the Royal Navy', in Major General Sir Henry Letheby Tidy (ed.), *Inter-Allied Conferences on War Medicine 1942–1945* (London, 1947), 219–24; A. Hyatt Williams, 'A Psychiatric Study of Indian Soldiers in the Arakan', *British Journal of Medical Psychology*, xxviii.3 (1950), 133.

35 S. I. Ballard and H. G. Miller, 'Psychiatric Casualties in a Women's Service', *British Medical Journal*, 3 March 1945, 193–4.

36 Colonel William J. Bleckwenn, 'Neuroses in the Combat Zone', *Annals of Internal Medicine*, 23.2 (August 1945), 179–80.

37 C. P. Symonds, 'The Human Response to Flying Stress', *British Medical Journal*, 11 December 1943, 744.

38 Roy R. Grinker and John P. Spiegel, *Men Under Stress* (London, 1945), 34.

39 Major H. H. Garner, 'Psychiatric Casualties in Combat', *War Medicine*, 8.5 (November–December 1945), 350.

40 W. H. R. Rivers, *Instinct and the Unconscious. A Contribution to a Biological Theory of the Psycho-Neuroses*, 2nd edn. (Cambridge, 1922), 242.

41 Edward L. Munson, *The Management of Men. A Handbook on the Systematic Development of Morale and the Control of Human Behaviour* (London, 1920), 111.

42 Comments by Brigadier Stebbings and Captain J. A. G. Wilson in Major E. T. C. Spooner, 'Psychological Questions Relating to A. A. Personnel', 1942,

6–7, PRO WO222/66, and Francis Edwin Gillette, 'Methods of Psychological Warfare. A Lecture' (instructor's manual), 1942, 19.

43 S. J. Rachman, *Fear and Courage* (San Francisco, 1978), 71–2. For similar comments see Captain David G. Wright, 'Anxiety in Aerial Combat', in *Military Neuropsychiatry. Proceedings of the Association [for Research in Nervous and Mental Diseases], December 15 and 16, 1944, New York* (Baltimore, 1946), 118.

44 Sir Arthur F. Hurst, 'The Etiology and Treatment of War Neuroses', in Thomas Hunt (ed.), *Selected Writings of Sir Arthur Hurst (1879–1944)*, first published 1917 (London, 1969), 184–5.

45 'The Moral Effect of Weapons. Investigation into Reactions of Group of 300 Wounded Men in North Africa –1943', 1943, PRO WO222/124. Three hundred wounded men were asked for their reactions to a variety of weapons. Half of the men interviewed were American and the other half were British; nearly all had been wounded in North Africa. Just over half were infantrymen, a quarter were tank or artillery personnel and the rest were sappers, transport and services, and a small number were airmen.

46 Ladislas Farago, *German Psychological Warfare* (New York, 1942), 117, and Edward L. Munson, *The Management of Men. A Handbook on the Systematic Development of Morale and the Control of Human Behaviour* (London, 1920), 114.

47 Norman Copeland, *Psychology and the Soldier* (London, 1942), 75.

48 John Rickman, *War Wounds* (London, 1939), 169.

49 Lord Moran, *The Anatomy of Courage* (London, 1945).

50 Edward A. Strecker, 'War Neuroses', *Military Surgeon*, 94.4 (April 1944), 198.

51 Major William G. Barrett, 'Psychologic Armoring for the Air Force', *War Medicine*, 5.3 (March 1944), 143.

52 There are numerous examples, but also see the influential work of Albert J. Glass, 'Preventive Psychiatry in the Combat Zone', *United States Armed Forces Medical Journal*, iv.5 (May 1953), 685.

53 These are discussed in depth in my *An Intimate History of Killing. Face to Face Killing in Twentieth Century Warfare* (London, 1999).

54 Major Merrill Moore, 'Recurrent Nightmares: A Simple Procedure for Psychotherapy', *Military Surgeon*, 97.4 (October 1945), 283.

55 For much greater detail about 'realism training' see my *An Intimate History of Killing: Face to Face Killing in Twentieth Century Warfare* (London, 1999).

56 J. W. Bellah and A. F. Clark, 'The Lunk Trainer', *Infantry Journal*, 52.3 (1943), 72–5.

57 Samuel A. Stouffer et al., *The American Soldier: Combat and its Aftermath. Volume II* (Princeton, 1949), 222.

58 Edward L. Munson, *The Management of Men. A Handbook on the Systematic Development of Morale and the Control of Human Behaviour* (London, 1920), 116.

59 Captain J. F. C. Fuller, *Hints of Training Territorial Infantry. From Recruit to Trained Soldier* (London, 1913), 120–1.

60 Captain C. T. Lanham, 'Panic', *The Infantry Reader*, selected and ed. Colonel Joseph I. Greene, first published 1937 (New York, 1943), 288.

61 Francis Edwin Gillette, 'Methods of Psychological Warfare. A Lecture' (instructor's manual), 1942, 23.

62 Edward L. Munson, *The Management of Men. A Handbook on the Systematic Development of Morale and the Control of Human Behaviour* (London, 1920), 114. Conversely, the contagious nature of fear could make it spread as men imitated the frightened men of their team: Captain M. K. Wardle, 'Notes on Fear in War', *Army Quarterly*, iv (April 1922), 266.

63 George Sava, *War Without Guns. The Psychological Front* (London, 1943), 107.

64 John Dollard, *Fear in Battle* (Washington, DC, 1944), 19, 23.

65 Major W. Graham Wallace, 'Memoir of Service', 1935, 28–9, Liddell Hart Centre for Military Archives.

66 Norman Shaw, 'Papers', in a letter dated 14 July 1916, in IWM.

67 Major Benjamin Cohen and Major Roy L. Swank, 'Chronic Symptomatology of Combat Neuroses', *War Medicine*, 8.3 (1945), 143.

68 William C. Menninger, *Psychiatry in a Troubled World. Yesterday's War and Today's Challenge* (New York, 1948), 73.

69 W. A. S. Falla, 'Fear Factors in Flying Personnel', *Journal of Mental Science*, xcii.390 (January 1947), 47. Based on interviews of three hundred flying men.

70 Lieutenant A. G. May, 'Personal Experiences of the War Years 1915–1917', 18, IWM 88/46/1. Also see Dixon Scott, 'Letters', letter from Scott to A. N. Monkhouse, May 1915, in Manchester County Council archives.

71 Major Vere E. Cotton, 'Letters from the French & Italian Fronts. 1915–1919', letter to his mother on 15 October 1915, in IWM 93/25/1.

72 William Clarke, 'Random recollections of 14/18', 6, IWM 87/18/1. Clarke admitted that his feelings were different when a 'special mate' was killed, but this emotion was probably not fear but grief and he said it quickly vanished.

73 Lieutenant Colonel Kenneth H. Cousland, 'The Great War. A Former Gunner Looks Back', 61, Liddell Hart Centre for Military Archives.

74 For further discussion see my *An Intimate History of Killing. Face to Face Killing in Twentieth Century Warfare* (London, 1999).

75 Diary entry for 17 July 1918, in Lieutenant A. B. Scott, 'The Diary', in *32nd Division, Artillery & Trench Mortar Memories* (London, 1923), 66.

76 Ibid., 96.

77 For more on theories about susceptibility see my *An Intimate History of Killing: Face to Face Killing in Twentieth Century Warfare* (London, 1999).

78 Captain Charles K. McKerrow, 'Diaries and Letters', letter dated 11 November 1915, IWM; Edward L. Munson, *The Management of Men. A Handbook on the Systematic Development of Morale and the Control of Human Behaviour* (London, 1920), 106.

79 Arthur F. Hurst, *Medical Diseases of the War*, first published in 1916, 2nd edn. (London, 1940), 2, and Captain Charles K. McKerrow, 'Diaries and Letters', letter dated 11 November 1915, IWM.

80 Lord Horder, 'The Modern Troglodyte', *Lancet*, 19 April 1941, 501, and P. E. Vernon, 'Psychological Effects of Air Raids', *Journal of Abnormal and Social Psychology*, 36 (1941), 474.

81 See Edward Glover, *The Psychology of Fear and Courage* (Harmondsworth, 1940), 12–13.

82 Dr Robert W. MacKenna, *The Adventure of Death* (London, 1916), 31.

83 J. P. Chaplin, *Rumor, Fear and the Madness of Crowds* (New York, 1959), 92.

84 Jerome Dowd, *The Negro in American Life* (New York, 1926), 235–6.

85 John Richards, 'Some Experiences With Colored Soldiers', *Atlantic Monthly*, August 1919.

86 Henry W. Brosin, 'Panic States and their Treatment', *American Journal of Psychiatry*, 100 (1943), 59.

87 Major J. O. Langley, 'Tactical Implications of the Human Factors in Warfare', *Australian Army Journal*, 107 (April 1958), 14; Major H. A. Palmer, 'The Problem of the P & N Casualty — A Study of 12,000 Cases', 1944, 3, in Contemporary Medical Archives Centre, RAMC 466/49; 'Report of a Conference on Psychiatry in Forward Areas', 8–10 August 1944, 13, PRO WO32/11550.

88 Sir Andrew MacPhail, *Official History of the Canadian Forces in the Great War 1914–19. The Medical Services* (Ottowa, 1925), 278, and Philip S. Wagner, 'Psychiatric Activities During the Normandy Offensive, June 20–August 20, 1944', *Psychiatry*, 9.4 (November 1946), 356.

89 Colonel Amos R. Koontz, 'Psychiatry in the Next War: Shall We Again Waste Manpower?', *Military Surgeon*, 103.3 (September 1948), 200.

90 Major H. A. Palmer, 'The Problem of the P & N Casualty — A Study of 12,000 Cases', 1944, 11, in Contemporary Medical Archives Centre, RAMC 466/49.

91 'The Psychology of Panic in War', *American Review of Reviews*, 50 (October 1914), 629.

92 Captain LeRoy Eltinge, *Notes on Lectures on Psychology of War. Prepared by Major Harvey Llewellyn Jones, Commanding Horsed Section, 104th Ammunition Train* (Camp McClellan, Alabama, 1918), 4, 7.

93 Bert Rudge, 'Interview', 19–20, IWM.

94 Brigadier-General J. L. Jack, *General Jack's Diary 1914–1918* (London, 1964), 111, diary entry for 19 September 1915.

95 John Dollard, *Fear in Battle* (Washington, DC, 1944), 37.

96 Charles H. Mapp, 'Memoirs of Charles H. Mapp, M.B.E.', 29–30, in Liddell Hart Centre for Military Archives.

97 The phrase is Water S. Hunter's, in 'Psychology in the War', *American Psychologist*, 1 (1946), 479.

98 Captain Blair W. Sparkes and Brigadier General Oliver K. Niess, 'Psychiatric Screening of Combat Pilots', *United States Armed Forces Medical Journal*, vii.6 (June 1956), 811–12.

CHAPTER EIGHT: CIVILIANS UNDER ATTACK

1 'Young Girl, London', quoted in Robert Westall (compiler), *Children of the Blitz. Memories of Wartime Childhood* (Harmondsworth, 1985), 115–20. Emphasis in the original.

2 Leonard R. Sillman, 'Morale', *War Medicine*, 3.5 (May 1943), 502.

3 George H. Quester, 'The Psychological Effects of Bombing on Civilian Populations: Wars of the Past', in Betty Glad (ed.), *Psychological Dimensions of War* (London, 1990), 203.

4 Colonel Louis Jackson, 'The Defence of Localities Against Aerial Attack', *Journal of the Royal United Services Institute*, 58.436 (June 1914), 713.

5 Gustave Le Bon, *The Psychology of the Great War*, trans. E. Andrews (London, 1916), 31–3, and Wilfred Trotter, *Instincts of the Herd in Peace and War* (London, 1910).

6 Wilfred Trotter, 'Panic and its Consequences', in *The Collected Papers of Wilfred Trotter* (London, 1941), 191–2; first published in the *British Medical Journal*, 17 February 1940, 270.

7 Colonel A. Rawlinson, *The Defence of London, 1915–1918* (London, 1923), 4–5.

8 Dorothy Constance Peel, *How We Lived Then, 1914–1918* (London, 1929), 146.

9 George H. Quester, 'The Psychological Effects of Bombing on Civilian Populations: Wars of the Past', in Betty Glad (ed.), *Psychological Dimensions of War* (London, 1990), 203.

10 Dorothy Constance Peel, *How We Lived Then, 1914–1918* (London, 1929), 155.

11 'Zeppelins', in F. S. Flint, *Otherworld Cadences* (London, 1920), 54.

12 J. F. C. Fuller, *The Reformation of War* (New York, 1923), 150.

13 Ministry of Health, 'Report by the Advisory Committee', 20 July 1938, PRO MH76/128, and Richard Titmuss, *Problems of Social Policy* (London, 1950), 19–21.

14 Wilfred Trotter, 'Panic and its Consequences', in *The Collected Papers of Wilfred Trotter* (London, 1941), 191–2, first published in the *British Medical Journal*, 17 February 1940, 270. Trotter was referring to September and October 1938.

15 Thomas Stanley Rippon and Peter Fletcher, *Reassurance and Relaxation. A Short Textbook of Practical Psycho-Therapy* (London, 1940), 35.

16 Mass Observation Archives (Sussex) (MO), 'Invasion', 1941, 2, MO FR 576.

17 H. J. Bennett, *I Was a Walworth Boy* (London, 1980), 44, 46. For an excellent comparison of the differences between people's reactions to raids during the two world wars, see George H. Quester, 'The Psychological Effects of Bombing on Civilian Populations: Wars of the Past', in Betty Glad (ed.), *Psychological Dimensions of War* (London, 1990), 201–14.

18 For example, see MO, 'Shelter Psychology', 2 January 1941, 1, M-OA Topic Collection 'Air Raids', Box 6, 23/6/H.

19 An unnamed young woman quoted in MO, 'Report on Death', 1942, 12, MO FR1315.

20 'Conditioning to Bangs', *Lancet*, 14 March 1942, 330–1; P. E. Vernon, 'Psychological Effects of Air Raids', *Journal of Abnormal and Social Psychology*, 36 (1941), 459.

21 Dr Robert H. Thouless, 'Psychological Effects of Air Raids', *Nature*, 16 August 1941, 183. This was in contrast to those who sought refuge in the isolated Anderson shelters.

22 'Morale of Public During and After Air Raids. Extract from Chief Constable's Reports', report of the Chief Constable of the Isle of Wight, 14 September 1940, in PRO HO199/376. Also see the report by the Chief Constable of Warwickshire on 14 September 1940.

23 Letter from H. J. Dams, P.S. 4 of Petersborough, to the Chief Constable, 26 August 1940, about the reaction to an air-raid alarm on 25 August 1940, in PRO HO199/50.

24 Henry Wilson, 'Mental Reactions to Air-Raids', *Lancet*, 7 March 1942, 285.

25 MO, 'Reactions to the Blackout, September–November 1939', MO Archives, M-OA Topic Collection 'Air Raids', Box 1, 23/1/D, unnamed woman interviewed about the fear of rape during a blackout.

26 Ibid., unnamed woman interviewed on the underground.

27 'Crime in Black-Out', *Daily Telegraph*, 22 November 1939.

28 MO, 'Bad Dreams and Nightmares', July 1939, 3, MO FR A20.

29 *London Under Attack. The Report of the Greater London Area War Risk Study Commission* (Oxford, 1986), 178.

30 Tom Harrisson, 'Civilians in Air-Raids', 1 August 1940, 1, MO FR313.

31 'Air Raids, Discipline and Panic', *Lancet*, 7 May 1938, 1061.

32 Mass-Observation, 'Happiness in Wartime'. MO FR1947 and FR 1870.

33 For example, in the collection of letters and essays by children on the topic of air raids, there was very little sense of fear: see MO, 'Children's Attitudes to War 1940–42', MO TC59, Box 3, 59/3/F. Also see P. E. Vernon, 'Questionnaire on Psychological War-Work and on Air-Raids', 4 May 1941, 6, MO PR739.

34 Frank Bodman, 'Child Psychiatry in War-Time Britain', *Journal of Educational Psychology*, xxxv.5 (May 1944), 293–4.

35 'What Children Think of War', 30 April 1940, 7–8, an article for the *Picture Post*, in MO Report 87. Also see Dr W. Mary Burbury, 'Extract from the Belfast Telegraph, 22 June 1940. Managing Your Child in an Air Raid', in PRO HO199/389.

36 Grace McLean Abbate, 'Group Procedures Found Effective in the Prevention and Handling of Emotional Disorders', *Mental Hygiene*, xxvi (1942), 406; 'A Doctor', *The Conquest of Fear* (London, 1941), 1; Enid M. John, 'A Study of the Effects of Evacuation and Air Raids on Children of Pre-School Age', *British Journal of Educational Psychology*, xi.iii (November 1941), 179; Emanuel Klein, 'The Influence of Teachers' and Parents' Attitudes and Behavior Upon Children in War Time', *Mental Hygiene*, xxvi (1942), 436; Joost A. M. Meerloo, *Patterns of Panic* (Westport, Connecticut, 1950), 19.

37 The phrase is Martin's: Alexander Reid Martin, 'The Prevention of Panic', *Mental Hygiene*, xxvi (1942), 551.

38 Harold Homer Anderson, *Children and the Family* (New York, 1937), 105; Alice Cara Brill and Mrs May Pardee Youtz, *Your Child and Its Parents. A Textbook for Child Study Groups* (New York, 1932), 163; Dr W. Mary Burbury, 'Extract from the Belfast Telegraph, 22 June 1940. Managing Your Child in an Air Raid', in PRO HO199/389; Patricia Edge, *Training the Toddler* (London, 1944), 61.

39 Patricia Edge, *Training the Toddler* (London, 1944), 54, 56.

40 Alexander Reid Martin, 'The Prevention of Panic', *Mental Hygiene*, xxvi (1942), 546–47.

41 *Home Intelligence Weekly Report*, 12–19 February 1941, PRO INF 1/292.

42 P. E. Vernon, 'Psychological Effects of Air Raids', *Journal of Abnormal and Social*

Psychology, 36 (1941), 475.

43 Henry Stalker, 'Panic States in Civilians', *British Medical Journal*, 1 June 1940, 887.

44 Irving L. Janis, *Air War and Emotional Stress. Psychological Studies of Bombing and Civilian Defense* (New York, 1951), 80–1.

45 Felix Brown, 'Civilian Psychiatric Air-Raid Casualties', *Lancet*, 31 May 1941, 689.

46 Ibid.

47 Dunne, 'Tube Shelter Inquiry Report', 23 March 1943, 14, in PRO HO205/233.

48 Letter from Rt Hon. Sir Percy Harris MP to Morrison, dated 8 March 1943, in PRO HO205/227, and 'Letter to Ask the Secretary of State for the Home Department Whether He Has Any Statements to Make Regarding the Shelter Inquiry Conducted by Mr Dunne', 7 April 1943, oral answer to the Parliament department, in PRO HO205/28.

49 For example, see 'Extract from Daily Digest. World Broadcasts. Pt. 1', 8 March 1943 and 'Broadcast from Rome Radio on 5th March, 1943', both in PRO HO199/114. For Lord Haw Haw see Dunne, 'Tube Shelter Inquiry Report', 23 March 1943, 21, in PRO HO205/233.

50 Report dated 8 March 1943, in PRO HO205/227.

51 Dunne, 'Tube Shelter Inquiry Report', 23 March 1943, 4–5, in PRO HO205/233.

52 Dunne, 'Tube Shelter Inquiry Report', 23 March 1943, 22, in PRO HO205/233.

53 Dunne, 'Tube Shelter Inquiry Report', 23 March 1943, 23, in PRO HO205/233.

54 Dunne, 'Tube Shelter Inquiry Report', 23 March 1943, 24, in PRO HO205/233.

55 Letter from Mrs Celia Hatchwell of 87 Shirland Rd, London W9, dated 5 March 1943, in PRO HO205/29.

56 Dunne, 'Tube Shelter Inquiry Report', 23 March 1943, 18, in PRO HO205/233.

57 Joost Abraham Mauritis Meerloo, *Aftermath of Peace. Psychological Essays* (New York, 1946), 94–5.

58 Letter to Morrison by Miss Lilian Edith Garwood, of Inglewood, Theydon Park Road, Theydon Bois, Epping, dated 10 March 1943, in PRO HO205/29.

59 Letters from M. Gordon Liverman, J.P. and Chairman of the Board of Deputies of British Jews, to Dunne, on 11 March 1943 and from Rev. W. W. Simpson of the Council of Christians and Jews, dated 13 March 1943, in PRO HO205/231.

60 Herbert Morrison, 'Tube Shelter Inquiry. Draft. Confidential', in PRO HO205/28. Note that suspicions about the Jews were long-standing. See 'Fire Panic at School', *The Times*, 24 June 1913, 10, which draws attention to the fact that a group of school children who panicked at the cry of 'Fire!' were 'mainly Jewish'.

61 Letter from 'E.P.', dated 11 March 1943, in PRO HO205/236.

62 Letter signed 'Bethnal Green', undated, in PRO HO205/236.

63 Postcard from J. W. Skelton of Ilford, dated 10 March 1943, in PRO HO205/231.

64 Unsigned letter, addressed 'The Retreat . . . Southgate N13', dated 10 March 1943, signed 'Perisha Judean', in PRO HO205/29.

65 Anonymous letter, undated, in PRO HO205/236.

66 Three anonymous letters, one dated 11 March 1943 and the other two undated, in PRO HO205/236.

67 Anonymous letter, dated 11 March 1943.

68 Anonymous letter, undated, in PRO HO205/236.

69 Letter from Henry N. Bloomfield, of H. N. and R. Bloomfield Insurance Brokers and Assessors, Cricklewood, London NW2, dated 13 March 1943, in HO205/236.

70 Letter from L. Fabian, of 24 Park Place, Bayswater, London W2, on 11 March 1943, in PRO HO205/231.

71 Letter signed 'Bethnal Green Resident', dated 11 March 1943.

72 Letter from Albert E. G. Saunders, of 75 Roche House, Limehouse, London E1, dated 9 March 1943, in HO205/236.

73 Letter from Councillor Percival James Bridges to Dunne, dated 17 March 1943, in PRO HO205/228.

74 Dunne, 'Tube Shelter Inquiry Report', 23 March 1943, 22, in PRO HO205/233.

75 Letter from G. E. Stevens of 132 Arundel Street, Portsmouth, dated 5 March 1943, in PRO HO205/29.

76 Letter from Phyllis Violet Kay of 138A Elgin Avenue, Maida Vale, W9, dated 6 March 1943, in PRO HO205/29.

77 Dunne, 'Tube Shelter Inquiry Report', 23 March 1943, 21, in PRO HO205/233.

78 Letter to Morrison from Geo Ramsey (MFME) of Winlinton Garage, Automobile Engineers, of Irvine, dated 10 March 1943, in PRO HO205/29.

79 Letter from William Medlicott of 8 Hampstead Gardens, London NW11, in PRO HO205/29.

80 Dunne, 'Tube Shelter Inquiry Report', 23 March 1943, 18, in PRO HO205/233.

81 George F. Vale, *Bethnal Green's Ordeal 1939–45* (London, 1945), 13.

82 Fred Bennett Julian, *Psychological Casualties in Air Raids and Their First-Aid Treatment* (London, 1940), 1, 5, 8, 17.

83 P. E. Vernon, 'Psychological Effects of Air Raids', *Journal of Abnormal and Social Psychology*, 36 (1941), 470.

84 R. J. Bartlett, 'The Civilian Population Under Bombardment', *Nature*, 7 June 1941, 701, and H. Crichton-Miller, 'Somatic Factors Conditioning Air-Raid Reactions', *Lancet*, 12 July 1941, 32. If this is not direct plagiarism, then 'Bartlett' is Crichton-Miller's pseudonym.

85 Tom Harrisson, 'Summary of Talk to the British Psychological Society (July 1941)', 20 October 1941, 2–3, MO PR926.

86 Interview on 12 January 1939 quoted in MO, 'Investigation into A. R. P.',

1939, M-OA Topic Collection 'Air Raids', Box 1, 23/1/A.

87 MO, 'Interim Report on Metropolitan Air-Raids', 23 August 1940, 2, MO FR364.

88 P. E. Vernon, 'Questionnaire on Psychological War-Work and on Air-Raids', 4 May 1941, 6, MO PR739.

89 Felix Brown, 'Civilian Psychiatric Air-Raid Casualties', Lancet, 31 May 1941, 691.

90 H. Crichton-Miller, 'Somatic Factors Conditioning Air-Raid Reactions', Lancet, 12 July 1941, 33–4.

91 E. Stengel, 'Air-Raid Phobia', British Journal of Medical Psychology, 20 (1944), 135–43.

92 'Air-Raid Fear. A Report from Mass-Observation', 21 May 1940, 2, MO FR150.

93 Felix Brown, 'Civilian Psychiatric Air-Raid Casualties', Lancet, 31 May 1941, 688.

94 'Air Raids Memorandum on the Preservation of Civilian Morale', 1939, 1–8, in PRO HO199/434. Other participants included J. Swire and G. R. Barnes.

95 John Hilton (Director of Home Publicity), 'Ministry of Information. Home Publicity Division. Regional Circular No. 12. Hints for Preventing or Allaying Panic in Air-Raids', to the Chief Regional Information Officer, 20 September 1939, 1–3.

96 Grace McLean Abbate, 'Group Procedures Found Effective in the Prevention and Handling of Emotional Disorders', Mental Hygiene, xxvi (1942), 403.

97 Alexander Reid Martin, 'The Prevention of Panic', Mental Hygiene, xxvi (1942), 552.

98 For a description of the experiment see 'Conditioning to Bangs', Lancet, 14 March 1942, 330–1.

99 MO, 'Interim Report on Metropolitan Air-Raids', 23 August 1940, 2, MO FR364.

100 'Air Raids', a card entitled 'Nine Points. A Useful Reminder of Precautions', in MO Archives, M-OA Topic Collection 'Air Raids', Box 4, 23/4/A.

101 John Yerbury Dent, Anxiety and its Treatment with Special Reference to Alcoholism (London, 1941), 117.

102 Ibid., 114.

103 Fred Bennett Julian, Psychological Casualties in Air Raids and Their First-Aid Treatment (London, 1940), 9.

104 Alexander Reid Martin, 'The Prevention of Panic', Mental Hygiene, xxvi (1942), 549–50.

105 Martha Wolfenstein, Disaster. A Psychological Essay (London, 1957), 7.

106 Melitta Schmideberg, 'Some Observations on Individual Reactions to Air Raids', International Journal of Psychoanalysis, 23 (1942), 146–76.

107 R. J. Bartlett, 'The Civilian Population Under Bombardment', Nature, 7 June 1941, 701. For an identical discussion see H. Crichton-Miller, 'Somatic Factors Conditioning Air-Raid Reactions', Lancet, 12 July 1941, 31–2. If this is not direct plagiarism, then 'Bartlett' is Crichton-Miller's pseudonym.

108 Irving L. Janis, Air War and Emotional Stress. Psychological Studies of Bombing and Civilian Defense (New York, 1951), 81.

109 Fred Bennett Julian, *Psychological Casualties in Air Raids and Their First-Aid Treatment* (London, 1940), 10, and Alexander Reid Martin, 'The Prevention of Panic', *Mental Hygiene*, xxvi (1942), 551–2.

110 John Rickman, 'The Mental Aspects of A.R.P.', in *War Wounds and Air Raid Casualties* (London, 1939), 171.

111 'Air Raid Nerves', *Yorkshire Post*, 8 December 1939.

112 John Yerbury Dent, *Anxiety and its Treatment with Special Reference to Alcoholism* (London, 1941), 118–19.

113 Fred Bennett Julian, *Psychological Casualties in Air Raids and Their First-Aid Treatment* (London, 1940), 14. This remained an important way of treating hysterical people until the 1960s: see Richard J. Healy, *Emergency and Disaster Planning* (New York, 1969), 285; Robert F. Mahoney, *Emergency and Disaster Nursing*, 2nd edn. (London, 1969), 205–6.

114 Robert Westall (compiler), *Children of the Blitz. Memories of Wartime Childhood* (Harmondsworth, 1985), 126.

115 Bernard Kops, cited ibid., 107.

116 P. E. Vernon, 'Psychological Effects of Air Raids', *Journal of Abnormal and Social Psychology*, 36 (1941), 470.

117 'Air Raid Fear', 21 May 1940, 2, MO File Report 150.

118 MO, 'Report on Superstition. Part B. Observing and Feelings About Superstition', 26 November 1941, 1, MO PR 975.

119 Rev. G. R. Balleine, *What is Superstition? A Trail of Unhappiness* (London, 1939), 7.

120 MO, 'Mass Astrology, 1941', 1 July 1941, 7–8, MO FR 769.

121 MO, 'Mass Astrology, 1941', 1 July 1941, 1, MO FR 769.

122 'War Cabinet Civil Defence Executive Sub-Committee. The Effect of Journalistic Astrology on the Public Mind', July 1941, PRO HO199/454.

123 MO, 'Mass Astrology, 1941', 1 July 1941, 3, MO FR 769.

124 MO, 'Mass Astrology, 1941', 1 July 1941, 35, MO FR 769. Also see 'War Cabinet Civil Defence Executive Sub-Committee. The Effect of Journalistic Astrology on the Public Mind', July 1941, PRO HO199/454.

125 MO, 'Mass Astrology, 1941', 1 July 1941, 34, MO FR 769.

126 MO, 'Mass Astrology, 1941', 1 July 1941, 36, MO FR 769.

127 See the report in *The Village Voice*, reproduced in 'A Pill to Help you Kill Without Guilt', in *The Editor* (supplement in *Guardian* newspaper), 8 February 2003, 14.

CHAPTER NINE: NUCLEAR THREATS

1 'First "No Signal" Atom Bomb Drills are Staged in the City's Schools', *New York Times*, 8 February 1951, 35.

2 Albert Eugene Kahn, *The Game of Death. Effects of the Cold War on our Children* (New York, 1953), 14–15.

3 André Fontaine, 'Are Bomb Drills Scaring Our Kids?', *Today's Woman* (June 1951), 66.

4 Albert Eugene Kahn, *The Game of Death. Effects of the Cold War on our Children* (New York, 1953), 14, 23.

5 Quoted in Chris O'Brien, 'Mama, Are We Going to Die? America's Children

Confront the Cuban Missile Crisis', in James Marten (ed.), *Children and War. A Historical Anthology* (New York, 2002), 75.

6 André Fontaine, 'Are Bomb Drills Scaring Our Kids?', *Today's Woman* (June 1951), 66.

7 Sibylle K. Escalona, 'Growing Up with the Threat of Nuclear War: Some Indirect Effects on Personality Development', *American Journal of Orthopsychiatry*, 52.4 (October 1982), 602.

8 Albert Eugene Kahn, *The Game of Death. Effects of the Cold War on our Children* (New York, 1953), 23.

9 André Fontaine, 'Are Bomb Drills Scaring Our Kids?', *Today's Woman* (June 1951), 68.

10 'Great Blast Ends Atomic Test Series', *New York Times*, 7 February 1951, 16.

11 Lawrence Freedman, 'Nuclear Weapons Today', in Royal United Services Institute for Defence Studies (ed.), *Nuclear Attack: Civil Defence. Aspects of Civil Defence in the Nuclear Age. A Symposium* (Oxford, 1982), 42.

12 Foreword by Joseph S. Nye, Jr., in James G. Blight, *The Shattered Crystal Ball: Fear and Learning in the Cuban Missile Crisis* (Savage, 1990), xiv.

13 Anthony Giddens, *The Consequences of Modernity* (Cambridge, 1990), 128.

14 Survey conducted for *TV Times* in 1983 and quoted in *London Under Attack. The Report of the Greater London Area War Risk Study Commission* (Oxford, 1986), 177.

15 James A. Pike, *Beyond Anxiety. The Christian Answer to Fear, Frustration, Guilt, Indecision, Inhibition, Loneliness, Despair* (New York, 1953), 1. Also see Rev. Walter Sullivan, *Disturbers of Your Peace of Mind. Worry! Fear! Loneliness!* (New York, 1950), 16.

16 Philip Toynbee, 'A Reply', in Toynbee (ed.), *The Fearful Choice. A Debate on Nuclear Policy* (London, 1958), 92.

17 *New York Times*, 18 May 1910.

18 Spencer R. Weart, *Nuclear Fear. A History of Images* (Cambridge, Mass., 1988), 215–16.

19 For example, see CND, 'The Age of Fear' (London, 1962), 4, a statement of their policy.

20 Sir Winston Churchill addressing the House of Commons on 1 March 1955, cited in Ford Charles Ikle, *The Social Impact of Bomb Destruction* (Norman, 1958), 178.

21 Joyce A. Evans, *Celluloid Mushroom Clouds. Hollywood and the Atomic Bomb* (Boulder, 1998), 23.

22 Kenneth Heuer, *The End of the World. A Scientific Enquiry* (London, 1953), 13.

23 Professor Herbert Butterfield, *Human Nature and the Dominion of Fear* (London, 1968), 3.

24 http://www.ratical.org/radiation/KillingOurOwn/KOOintro.html.gz, 5.

25 Albert Einstein, 'The Menace of Mass Destruction', in Einstein, *Out of My Later Years*, first published 1947 (London, 1950) 204–5.

26 Hermann Muller, 'Artificial Transmutation of the Gene', in *Science*, lxvi.1699 (1927), 84–7.

27 Joyce A. Evans, *Celluloid Mushroom Clouds. Hollywood and the Atomic Bomb*

(Boulder, 1998), 106.

28 See the novel by Peter Bryant (Peter Byran George) *Two Hours to Doom* (London, 1958).

29 For example, the film *Dr Strangelove* (1963).

30 See the novel by Dennis Feltham Jones *Colossus* (London, 1966).

31 See the novel by Nicolas Freeling *The Gadget* (London, 1977)

32 See the novels by John Brunner *The Brink* (London, 1959) and Eugene Burdick and Harvey Wheeler *Fail-Safe* (New York, 1962).

33 Margot Bennett, *The Long Way Back* (London, 1954); Harlan Ellison, *A Boy and His Dog* (London, 1969); Jim Harman, 'The Place Where Chicago Was', in *Galaxy* (February 1962).

34 Philip Wylie, *Tomorrow!* (New York, 1954), 243. Also see his *Triumph* (New York, 1963).

35 *International Journal of Opinion and Attitude Research*, 1951, quoted by Donald N. Michael, 'Civilian Behavior Under Atomic Bombardment', *Bulletin of the Atomic Scientists*, xi.5 (May 1955), 173.

36 Mrs Sylvia Eberhart, 'How the American People Feel About the Atomic Bomb', *Bulletin of the Atomic Scientists*, 3.6 (June 1947), 148.

37 Eugene J. Sleevi, 'Civil Defense News', *Bulletin of the Atomic Scientists*, ix.8 (October 1953), 315.

38 Paul Byrne, *The Campaign for Nuclear Disarmament* (London, 1988), 1.

39 Sarah Lloyd and Mike Hally, *War and Civil Defence in North West England. Human Responses to War* (Manchester, 1989), 8.

40 Al, writing in http://www.videogamereview.com/reviews/Sony_Playstation/Action/Action-469.asp.

41 *London Under Attack. The Report of the Greater London Area War Risk Study Commission* (Oxford, 1986), 177.

42 Interviewed by Jack G. Shaheen, 'The War Game', in Shaheen (ed.), *Nuclear War Films* (Carbondale, 1978), 113.

43 William Abbott Scott, 'The Avoidance of Threatening Material in Imaginative Behavior', in John W. Atkinson (ed.), *Motives in Fantasy, Action and Society* (Princeton, 1958), 572–85.

44 Joost A. M. Meerloo, *Patterns of Panic* (Westport, Connecticut, 1950), 112–13.

45 Tom Stonier, *Nuclear Disaster* (Harmondsworth, 1963), 55.

46 Joost A. M. Meerloo, *Patterns of Panic* (Westport, Connecticut, 1950), 112–13. Also see H. Cantril, 'Causes and Control of Riot and Panic', *Public Opinion Quarterly*, 7 (1943), 669.

47 Joost A. M. Meerloo, *Patterns of Panic* (Westport, Connecticut, 1950), 98–9.

48 The Archbishop of Canterbury responding to Toynbee in Philip Toynbee, 'Thoughts on Nuclear Warfare and a Policy to Avoid It', in Toynbee (ed.), *The Fearful Choice. A Debate on Nuclear Policy* (London, 1958), 43.

49 Most Rev. Richard J. Cushing, 'A Spiritual Approach to the Atomic Age', *Bulletin of the Atomic Scientists*, 4.7 (July 1948), 222–3.

50 Donald N. Michael, 'Civilian Behavior Under Atomic Bombardment', *Bulletin of the Atomic Scientists*, xi.5 (May 1955), 176.

51 Ibid., 174.

52 Philip Wylie, 'Panic, Psychology and the Bomb', *Bulletin of the Atomic Scientists*, x.1 (January 1954), 37–40.

53 Colonel James P. Cooney of the Army Medical Corps, talking to army doctors at the Pennsylvania University Hospital, in *Army Doctors*, June 1948, 501.

54 Hadley Cantril, *The Invasion from Mars. A Study in the Psychology of Panic* (Princeton, 1982), vi–vii, preface from 1966 edn.

55 Carl G. Jung, *Flying Saucers. A Modern Myth of Things Seen in the Skies*, trans. R. F. C. Hull (London, 1959), 8–10.

56 William M. Lamers, *Disaster Protection Handbook for School Administrators* (Washington, DC, 1959), 26; Duane P. Schultz, *Panic Behavior. Discussion and Readings* (New York, 1964), 115–17; Eugene J. Sleevi, 'Civil Defense News', *Bulletin of the Atomic Scientists*, ix.8 (October 1953), 315.

57 William M. Lamers, *Disaster Protection Handbook for School Administrators* (Washington, DC, 1959), 26. Also see Duane P. Schultz, *Panic Behavior. Discussion and Readings* (New York, 1964), 115; Philip Wylie, 'Panic, Psychology and the Bomb', *Bulletin of the Atomic Scientists*, x.1 (January 1954), 37–40, 63.

58 *The Industrial Civil Defence Review*, 5.5 (May 1957), 101, quoting from *Manchester Guardian*, 15 April 1957.

59 Val Peterson in *Collier's*, 1953, quoted in Duane P. Schultz, *Panic Behavior. Discussion and Readings* (New York, 1964), 115.

60 Colonel James P. Cooney, speaking at the Pennsylvania University Hospital in Philadelphia, in *Army Doctors*, June 1948, 501; Ford Charles Ikle, *The Social Impact of Bomb Destruction* (Norman, 1958); Duane P. Schultz, *Panic Behavior. Discussion and Readings* (New York, 1964), 3–4.

61 H. D. Beach, *Management of Human Behaviour in Disaster* (Ottowa, 1967), 24.

62 Ibid., 95.

63 Ruth M. Fawell, *The Relevance of Courage* (London, 1965), 4.

64 Otto Kleinberg, 'Dangers of Shelter Psychology', in Seymour Melman (ed.), *No Place to Hide. Fact and Fiction About Fallout Shelters* (New York, 1962), 165. This is also seen in survivalist manuals.

65 H. D. Beach, *Management of Human Behaviour in Disaster* (Ottowa, 1967), 38.

66 Irving L. Janis, 'Psychological Problems of A-Bomb Defense', *Bulletin of the Atomic Scientists*, vi.9 (September 1950), 262.

67 John M. Caldwell, Stephen W. Ranson and Jerome G. Sacks, 'Group Panic and Other Mass Disruptive Reactions', *United States Armed Forces Medical Journal*, ii.4 (April 1951), 560.

68 Sarah Lloyd and Mike Hally, *War and Civil Defence in North West England. Human Responses to War* (Manchester, 1989), 8.

69 State of California, Office of Civil Defense, *Panic Control and Prevention. Instructor's Manual and Teaching Outline* (Sacramento, 1951), 41, 55.

70 Gina Berriault, *The Descent* (London, 1960), 58–9.

71 John M. Caldwell, Stephen W. Ranson and Jerome G. Sacks, 'Group Panic and Other Mass Disruptive Reactions', *United States Armed Forces Medical Journal*, ii.4 (April 1951), 556.

72 State of California, Office of Civil Defense, *Panic Control and Prevention*.

Instructor's Manual and Teaching Outline (Sacramento, 1951), 31–2.

73 Ibid., 36–7.

74 Ibid., 29–30.

75 Ibid., 61–2.

76 Ibid., 21.

77 Irving L. Janis, 'Psychological Problems of A-Bomb Defense', *Bulletin of the Atomic Scientists*, vi.9 (September 1950), 257.

78 Dwight W. Chapman, 'Some Psychological Problems in Civil Defense', *Bulletin of the Atomic Scientists*, ix.7 (1953), 281.

79 State of California, Office of Civil Defense, *Panic Control and Prevention. Instructor's Manual and Teaching Outline* (Sacramento, 1951), 24–5.

80 Ronald W. Perry, *The Social Psychology of Civil Defense* (Lexington, 1982), 32, 34.

81 Dwight W. Chapman, 'Some Psychological Problems in Civil Defense', *Bulletin of the Atomic Scientists*, ix.7 (1953), 280, and Otto N. Larsen, 'Rumors in a Disaster', *Journal of Communication*, 4 (1954), 111.

82 Dr Harry B. Williams, cited in Donald Robinson, *The Face of Disaster* (New York, 1959), 10.

83 For a report of this latter 'panic' see Edward D. Churchill, 'Panic and Disaster', *Annals of Surgery*, 138 (1953), 135–6.

84 In the psychological and sociological literature there is disagreement about whether or not panic behaviour *must* involve flight behaviour. According to E. Quarantelli, 'The Nature and Conditions of Panic', *American Journal of Sociology*, 60 (1954), 267–75, and Duane P. Schultz, *Panic Behavior. Discussion and Readings* (New York, 1964), 6–7, panic must include flight, while for writers like H. Cantril, 'Causes and Control of Riot and Panic', *Public Opinion Quarterly*, 7 (1943), 669–79, and Irving L. Janis, *Air War and Emotional Stress* (New York, 1951), panic is an emotional state which may or may not involve flight.

85 Federal Civil Defense Administration, 'The Problem of Panic', Civil Defense Technical Bulletin, TB-19-2 (June 1955), reprinted in Ralph Turner and Lewis M. Killian (eds.), *Collective Behavior*, 2nd edn. (Englewood Cliffs, 1972), 83. Emphasis in original.

86 William H. Form and Sigmund Mosow, *Community in Disaster* (New York, 1958), 84–8.

87 Described in Roger W. Brown, 'Mass Phenomena', in Gerdner Lindzey (ed.), *Handbook of Social Psychology. Volume II. Special Fields and Applications* (Cambridge, Mass., 1954), 860–1.

88 For a good example, using 'Prisoners' Dilemma' model, see Roger Brown, *Social Psychology* (New York, 1965), 739–43.

89 Martha Wolfenstein, *Disaster. A Psychological Essay* (London, 1957), 53, 153–9.

90 Harry Estill Moore, *. . . And the Winds Blew* (Austin, 1964), 195–6.

91 E. L. Quarantelli and Russell R. Dynes, 'When Disaster Strikes (It Isn't Much Like What You've Heard and Read About)', *Psychology Today*, 5.9 (February 1972), 67–8.

92 An unnamed Chief of Police, commenting in John Brouillette, 'A Tornado Warning System: Its Functioning on Palm Sunday in Indiana', Research Report

No. 15 *OCD Review Notice* (1966), 22.

93 H. B. Williams, 'Human Factors in Warning-and-Response Systems', in G. H. Grosser, H. Wechsler and M. Greenblatt (eds.), *The Threat of Impending Disaster: Contributions to the Psychology of Stress* (Cambridge, Mass., 1964), 88. Also see E. L. Quarantelli and Russell R. Dynes, 'When Disaster Strikes (It Isn't Much Like What You've Heard and Read About)', *Psychology Today*, 5.9 (February 1972), 67.

94 H. B. Williams, 'Human Factors in Warning-and-Response Systems', in G. H. Grosser, H. Wechsler and M. Greenblatt (eds.), *The Threat of Impending Disaster: Contributions to the Psychology of Stress* (Cambridge, Mass., 1964), 89. Also see Charles E. Fritz and Harry B. Williams, 'The Human Being in Disasters: A Research Perspective', *Annals of the American Academy of Political and Social Science* (January 1957), 43.

95 Roger Brown, *Social Psychology* (New York, 1965), 737; Federal Civil Defense Administration, 'The Problem of Panic', Civil Defense Technical Bulletin, TB-19-2 (June 1955), reprinted in Ralph Turner and Lewis M. Killian (eds.), *Collective Behavior*, 2nd edn. (Englewood Cliffs, 1972), 84; Neil J. Smelser, *Theory of Collective Behavior* (London, 1963), 136; E. Quarantelli, 'The Nature and Conditions of Panic', *American Journal of Sociology*, 60 (1954), 273.

96 L. S. Penrose, *On the Objective Study of Crowd Behaviour* (London, 1952), 28.

97 John M. Caldwell, Stephen W. Ranson and Jerome G. Sacks, 'Group Panic and Other Mass Disruptive Reactions', *United States Armed Forces Medical Journal*, ii.4 (April 1951), 548. These four factors were discussed by Federal Civil Defense Administration, 'The Problem of Panic', Civil Defense Technical Bulletin, TB-19-2 (June 1955), reprinted in Ralph Turner and Lewis M. Killian (eds.), *Collective Behavior*, 2nd edn. (Englewood Cliffs, 1972), 84.

98 L. Logan, L. Killian and W. Marrs, 'A Study of the Effect of Catastrophe on Social Disorganization', OCO report No. 29, Johns Hopkins University, 1952, quoted in Donald N. Michael, 'Civilian Behavior Under Atomic Bombardment', *Bulletin of the Atomic Scientists*, xi.5 (May 1955), 174.

99 E. L. Quarantelli and Russell R. Dynes, 'Editors' Introduction', *American Behavioral Scientist*, 13.3 (January–February 1970), 326.

100 Allen H. Barton, *Communities in Disaster. A Sociological Analysis of Collective Stress Situations* (Washington, DC, 1969), 138–9.

101 William C. Menninger, 'Psychological Reactions in an Emergency (Flood)', *American Journal of Psychiatry*, 109.2 (August 1952), 129.

102 Thomas E. Drabeck, William H. Key, Patricia E. Erickson and Juanita L. Crowe, 'The Impact of Disaster on Kin Relationships', *Journal of Marriage and the Family*, 37 (1975), 481–94.

103 Allen H. Barton, *Social Organization Under Stress: A Sociological Review of Disaster Studies* (Washington, DC, 1963), 32–3.

104 Orjan E. Hultaker and Jan E. Trost, *The Family and the Shelters* (Uppsala, 1977), 6–7.

105 Charles E. Fritz, 'Disaster', in R. K. Merton and R. A. Nisbet (eds.), *Contemporary Social Problems* (New York, 1961), 651–94.

106 Helene Rank Veltfort and George E. Lee, 'The Cocoanut Grove Fire: A Study

in Scapegoating', *Journal of Abnormal and Social Psychology*, 38 (1943), 141–2.

107 'H-Bomb Threatens Promise and Hope', *Worthing Herald*, 15 April 1960, in Gollancz's Papers, Modern Record Centre, Coventry, MSS 157/10/ND.

108 Philip Wylie, 'Panic, Psychology and the Bomb', *Bulletin of the Atomic Scientists*, x.1 (January 1954), 40.

109 Donald N. Michael, 'Civilian Behavior Under Atomic Bombardment', *Bulletin of the Atomic Scientists*, xi.5 (May 1955), 173.

110 H. D. Beach, *Management of Human Behaviour in Disaster* (Ottowa, 1967), 38, 95; Albert J. Glass, 'Psychologic Considerations in Atomic Warfare', *United States Armed Forces Medical Journal*, vii.5 (May 1956), 628.

111 Robert Jay Lifton, Eric Markusen and Dorothy Austin, 'The Second Death: Psychological Survival After Nuclear War', in Jennifer Leaning and Langley Keyes (eds.), *The Counterfeit Ark: Crisis Relocation for Nuclear War* (Cambridge, Mass., 1984), 288.

112 Irving L. Janis, 'Psychological Problems of A-Bomb Defense', *Bulletin of the Atomic Scientists*, vi.9 (September 1950), 260.

113 Donald N. Michael, 'Civilian Behavior Under Atomic Bombardment', *Bulletin of the Atomic Scientists*, xi.5 (May 1955), 173.

114 Robert Jay Lifton, Eric Markusen and Dorothy Austin, 'The Second Death: Psychological Survival After Nuclear War', in Jennifer Leaning and Langley Keyes (eds.), *The Counterfeit Ark: Crisis Relocation for Nuclear War* (Cambridge, Mass., 1984), 287–8.

115 Ibid., 289.

116 Jennifer Leaning and Langley Keyes, 'The Singularity of Nuclear War: Paradigms of Disaster Planning', in Leaning and Keyes (eds.), *The Counterfeit Ark: Crisis Relocation for Nuclear War* (Cambridge, Mass., 1984), 7.

117 M. Brewster Smith, 'Preface', *Journal of Social Issues*, x.3 (1954), 1. Also see Otto N. Larsen, 'Rumors in a Disaster', *Journal of Communication*, 4 (1954), 111.

118 Guy Oakes, *The Imaginary War. Civil Defense and American Cold War Culture* (New York, 1994), 6–8.

119 Ibid., 5, 126.

120 Michel Foucault, *The History of Sexuality. Volume I: An Introduction* (London, 1978), 143.

AFTERWORD TO PART FOUR: NARRATIVITY

1 William M. Reddy, 'Against Constructionism. The Historical Ethnology of Emotions', *Current Anthropology*, 38 (June 1997), 327.

2 William McDougall, *An Introduction to Social Psychology*, first published 1908 (London, 1912), 45–89.

3 William James, *The Principles of Psychology*, vol. 1 (New York, 1890), 442.

4 Rev. Stopford A. Brooke, *A Discourse on War*, first published 1905 (London, 1916), 1.

5 Charles Stewart Alexander, 'Letters to his Cousin', November 1917, Auckland Institute and Museum Library MSS 92/70.

6 Philip Capulo, *A Rumor of War* (New York, 1978), 254.

7 Tim O'Brien, *The Things They Carried* (New York, 1990), 210.

8 For an interesting critique see William M. Reddy, 'Against Constructionism. The Historical Ethnology of Emotions', *Current Anthropology*, 38 (June 1997), 327–51.

9 Margot L. Lyon, 'Emotion and Embodiment: The Respiratory Mediation of Somatic and Social Processes', in Alexander Laban Hinton (ed.), *Biocultural Approaches to the Emotions* (Cambridge, 1999), 185.

10 For example, see George Rudé, *The Crowd in the French Revolution* (Oxford, 1959), 232–3.

11 Ibid.

CHAPTER TEN: THE BODY

1 Edna Kaehele, *Living with Cancer* (London, 1953).

2 Dr John A. Ryle, 'The Twenty-First Maudsley Lecture: Nosophobia', *Journal of Mental Science*, xciv. 394 (January 1948), 2–3.

3 Mass Observation, 'Fear', Bulletin No. 14, 1948, 3.

4 H. K. Challoner and Roland Northover, *Antidote to Fear* (London, 1962), 15.

5 Colin Scott, 'Old Age and Death', *American Journal of Psychology*, viii (1896), 100–1. Based on a survey of 129 people.

6 Ralston Paterson and Jean Aitken-Swan, 'Public Opinion on Cancer. A Survey Among Women in the Manchester Area', *Lancet*, 23 October 1954, 858. Two thousand four hundred and three women responded. A fifth of them found the prospect of contracting tuberculosis most terrifying: this was the only disease which was feared much more by underprivileged women than by their wealthier sisters. The percentages alarmed by heart trouble, asthma and rheumatism never exceeded 12 per cent. Also see Oliver Cope, Chiu-An Wang and Alvaro Caro, 'Emotional Problems Commonly Encountered in General Surgery', in Harry S. Abram (ed.), *Psychological Aspects of Surgery* (Boston, 1967), 5.

7 See James T. Patterson, *The Dread Disease. Cancer and Modern American Culture* (Cambridge, Mass., 1987), 23–3.

8 Cushman D. Haagensen, 'A Technique for Radical Mastectomy', *Surgeon*, 19 (1946), 100–31.

9 For a detailed discussion see Barron H. Lerner, *The Breast Cancer Wars. Hope, Fear and the Pursuit of Cure in Twentieth-Century America* (Oxford, 2001), 223.

10 George Crile, *Cancer and Common Sense* (London, 1957), 147.

11 John Gunther, *Death Be Not Proud. A Memoir* (London, 1949), 31, 87–8.

12 Ora Marshino, 'Breast Cancer', *Hygeia*, 23 (March 1945), 176–7, cited in Barron H. Lerner, *The Breast Cancer Wars. Hope, Fear and the Pursuit of Cure in Twentieth-Century America* (Oxford, 2001), 60.

13 Dr Samuel L. Feder, 'Attitudes of Patients with Advanced Malignancy', in Group for the Advancement of Psychiatry (eds.), *Death and Dying. Attitudes of Patient and Doctor* (New York, 1965), 617.

14 For example, see Jerome Cohen, Joseph W. Cullen and L. Robert Martin (eds), *Psychosocial Aspects of Cancer*, New York, 1982; Gotthard Booth, *The Cancer Epidemic* (New York, 1979), 134–5, 230; L. LeShan, *You Can Fight for*

Your Life Wellingborough (1977); 'Personality and Cancer', in *Scientific American*, 186 (June 1952), 34; Harold Simmons, *The Psychogenic Theory of Disease: A New Approach to Cancer Research* (Sacramento, 1966).

15 Wilhelm Reich, *Reich Speaks of Freud*, ed. Mary Higgins and Chester M. Raphael (London, 1972), 6, 21.

16 For an in-depth discussion see James T. Patterson, *The Dread Disease. Cancer and Modern American Culture* (Cambridge, Mass., 1987), 256–7.

17 Also see Thomas P. Hackett and Avery D. Weisiman, 'Reactions to the Imminence of Death', in George H. Grosser, Henry Wochsler and Milton Greenblatt (eds.), *The Threat of Impending Disaster. Contributions to the Psychology of Stress* (Cambridge, Mass., 1964), 300, 310.

18 Godwin C. Chu, 'Fear Arousing Efficacy and Imminency', *Journal of Personality and Social Psychology*, 4.5 (1966), 517–24; James M. Dabbs and Howard Leventhal, 'Effects of Varying the Recommendations on a Fear Arousing Communication', *Journal of Personality and Social Psychology*, 4.5 (1966), 525–31; Irving L. Janis and Seymour Feshbach, 'Effects of Fear-Arousing Communications', *Journal of Abnormal and Social Psychology*, 48.1 (1953), 78–9; Howard Leventhal, Jean C. Watts and Francia Pagano, 'Effect of Fear and Instructions on How to Cope with Danger', *Journal of Personality and Social Psychology*, 6.3 (1967), 313–21.

19 Jean Aitken-Swan and Ralston Paterson, 'The Cancer Patient and Delay in Seeking Advice', *British Medical Journal*, 1 (12 March 1955), 623–7. Also see Sir Stanford Cade, 'Cancer: The Patient's Viewpoint and the Clinician's Problem', *Proceedings of the Royal Society of Medicine*, 56.1 (January 1963), 2, and Douglas G. French, 'The Care of Cancer in Practice', *Practitioner*, 177 (1956), 78.

20 Oliver Cope, Chiu-An Wang and Alvaro Caro, 'Emotional Problems Commonly Encountered in General Surgery', in Harry S. Abram (ed.), *Psychological Aspects of Surgery* (Boston, 1967), 5.

21 Karl Aimo Achte and M.-L. Vauhkonen, 'Cancer and the Psyche', *Annales Medicinae Internae Fenniae*, supplement no. 49, 56 (1967), 17–18.

22 John A. Ryle, 'The Twenty-First Maudsley Lecture: Nosophobia', *Journal of Mental Science*, xciv.394 (January 1948), 9. Also see Dr Kenneth Walker, *The Circle of Life. A Search for an Attitude to Pain, Disease, Old Age and Death* (London, 1942), 34.

23 Joost A. M. Meerloo and Adolf Zeckel, 'Psychiatric Problems of Malignancy', in Leopold Bellak (ed.), *Psychology of Physical Illness. Psychiatry Applied to Medicine, Surgery and the Specialties* (London, 1952), 47.

24 Robert A. Senescu, 'The Development of Emotional Complications in the Patient with Cancer', *Journal of Chronic Diseases*, 16 (1963), 814.

25 Susan Sontag, *AIDS and its Metaphors* (Harmondsworth, 1990), 102.

26 Jean Aitken-Swan and E. C. Easson, 'Reactions of Cancer Patients in Being Told Their Diagnosis', *British Medical Journal* (21 March 1959), 782.

27 Sir Stanford Cade, 'Cancer: The Patient's Viewpoint and the Clinician's Problem', *Proceedings of the Royal Society of Medicine*, 56.1 (January 1963), 3.

28 Jean Aitken-Swan and E. C. Easson, 'Reactions of Cancer Patients in Being Told

Their Diagnosis', *British Medical Journal* (21 March 1959), 782.

29 Ibid.

30 Francis Hernaman-Johnson, *Excessive Menstrual Bleeding. Its Treatment by X Rays and the Management of Patients Suffering from Cancer of the Breast* (London, 1930), 20–1.

31 According to a poll: see James T. Patterson, *The Dread Disease. Cancer and Modern American Culture* (Cambridge, Mass., 1987), 167.

32 Douglas G. French, 'The Care of Cancer in Practice', *Practitioner*, 177 (1956), 83–4.

33 Dr C. J. Gavey, 'Discussion on Palliation in Cancer', *Proceedings of the Royal Society of Medicine*, 48 (1955), 704.

34 Sir Stanford Cade, 'Cancer: The Patient's Viewpoint and the Clinician's Problem', *Proceedings of the Royal Society of Medicine*, 56.1 (January 1963), 3.

35 Rock Hudson was hospitalised on 23 July 1985 and died on 2 October.

36 *USA Today* in October 1985.

37 *New York Times*, 12 September 1985.

38 Susan Sontag, *AIDS and its Metaphors* (Harmondsworth, 1990), 124.

39 'Heart Surgeon Won't Operate on Victims of AIDS', *New York Times*, 13 March 1987, Y11.

40 For example, see *New York Times*, 13 March 1989.

41 J. Oleske, A. Minnetor, T. K. Coopers, A. de la Cruz, H. Abdieh, I. Guerrero, V. Joshi and F. Desposito, 'Immune Deficiency Syndrome in Children', *Journal of the American Medical Association*, 249 (1983), 2345–9.

42 Chaim Bermant, 'Practising Some Lethal Preachings', *Daily Telegraph*, 3 September 1991.

43 Paula Treichler, 'AIDS, Homophobia and Biomedical Discourse: An Epidemic of Signification', in Douglas Crimp (ed.), *AIDS. Cultural Analysis, Cultural Activism* (Cambridge, Mass., 1988), 46–7.

44 Hélène Joffe, *Risk and 'The Other'* (Cambridge, 1999), 41.

45 Cited by Paula Treichler, 'AIDS, Homophobia and Biomedical Discourse: An Epidemic of Signification', in Douglas Crimp (ed.), *AIDS. Cultural Analysis, Cultural Activism* (Cambridge, Mass., 1988), 47.

46 Hélène Joffe, *Risk and 'The Other'* (Cambridge, 1999), 48.

47 Ibid., 49.

48 Randy Shilt, *And the Band Played On. Politics, People and the AIDS Epidemic* (London, 1987).

49 James Miller, 'AIDS in the Novel: Getting it Straight', in Miller (ed.), *Fluid Exchanges: Artists and Critics in the AIDS Crisis* (Toronto, 1992), 258. He is referring to a passage in Randy Shilt's *And the Band Played On. Politics, People and the AIDS Epidemic* (London, 1987), 165.

50 Christine Gorman, 'Returning Fire Against AIDS', *Time*, 24 June 1991, 44.

51 Paula Treichler, 'AIDS, Homophobia and Biomedical Discourse: An Epidemic of Signification', in Douglas Crimp (ed.), *AIDS. Cultural Analysis, Cultural Activism* (Cambridge, Mass., 1988), 60.

52 Gina Kolata, 'How AIDS Smoulders: Immune System Studies Follow the Track of H.I.V.', *New York Times*, 17 March 1992, BB5.

53 These themes can be found throughout Randy Shilt's *And the Band Played On. Politics, People and the AIDS Epidemic* (London, 1987).

54 For further discussion see Steven Epstein, *Impure Science. AIDS Activism and the Politics of Knowledge* (Berkeley, 1996), 346.

55 Steven Epstein, *Impure Science. AIDS Activism and the Politics of Knowledge* (Berkeley, 1996), 348, and Ulrike Boehmer, *The Personal and the Political. Women's Activism in Response to the Breast Cancer and AIDS Epidemic* (New York, 2000), 16.

56 MO, 'Report on Death', 1942, 2–3, 11, 18, 21b, 23, 28, MO FR 1315.

57 Ann Cartwright, Lisbeth Hockney and John L. Anderson, *Life Before Death* (London, 1973), 2.

58 Norman Autton, *The Pastoral Care of the Dying* (London, 1966), 25.

59 W. H. Sewell, *Christian Care of the Dying and the Dead; A Few Hints on Burial Reform, for Friendly Readers* (London, 1878), 6–7.

60 'Patients Who Ask for Death', *Morning Post*, 17 November 1936, newspaper clipping from PRO MH58/305.

61 C. E. M. Joad, 'A Philosophy of Pain and Fear', *Nature*, 148.3742 (19 July 1941), 65.

62 Robert A. Senescu, 'The Development of Emotional Complications in the Patient with Cancer', *Journal of Chronic Diseases*, 16 (1963), 817.

63 John A. Ryle, *Fears May Be Liars* (London, 1941), 24.

64 Herman Feifel, 'The Function of Attitudes Toward Death', in Group for the Advancement of Psychiatry (eds.), *Death and Dying: Attitudes of Patient and Doctor* (New York, 1965), 638.

65 Alfred Worcester, *The Care of the Aged, the Dying, and the Dead* (Springfield, Ill., 1935), 45. Also see Ian Grant, 'Care of the Dying', *British Medical Journal* (28 December 1957), 1539.

66 Cicely Saunders, 'The Treatment of Intractable Pain in Terminal Cancer', *Proceedings of the Royal Society of Medicine*, 56 (1963), 196–7.

67 MO, 'Report on Death', 1942, 2–3, 11, 18, 21b, 23, 28, MO FR 1315.

68 This was observed throughout the period. For example, see Alexander Bain, *The Emotions and the Will*, first published 1859, 4th edn. (London, 1899), 165–6; John Hinton, 'The Psychology of Dying', in Norman Autton (ed.), *From Fear to Faith. Studies of Suffering and Wholeness* (London, 1971), 42; Colin Scott, 'Old Age and Death', *American Journal of Psychology*, viii (1896), 67–122.

69 Dr A. N. Exton-Smith, 'Terminal Illness in the Aged', *Lancet*, 2 (1961), 305–7. The survey was based on eighty men and 140 women in a geriatric unit. Note that 8 per cent of patients with cardiovascular problems were anxious.

70 John Hinton, 'The Psychology of Dying', in Norman Autton (ed.), *From Fear to Faith. Studies of Suffering and Wholeness* (London, 1971), 43.

71 For a psychoanalytical explanation for this see Felix Deutsch, 'Euthanasia: A Clinical Study', *Psychoanalytic Quarterly*, 5 (1936), 250–1, 359–63 and 367–8.

72 'A Definition of Irreversible Coma', *Journal of the American Medical Association*, 205 (5 August 1968), 85–8.

73 Conference of Medical Royal Colleges and their Faculties in the United Kingdom, 1976, 'Diagnosis of Brain Death', *British Medical Journal*, 1 (13 November 1976), 1187.

74 For a hilarious horror film on this subject see *Re-Animator* (1985), about med-
    ical students who discover a serum that revives the dead. The themes developed
    in this film include the definition of death, fears about science and scientists, the
    notion of 'brain death' (one of the cadavers brought back to life has been
    decapitated and carries his head) and the cruelty of not allowing someone to
    'die in dignity'. The film is broadly based on H. P. Lovecraft's serial novella
    Herbert West, Re-Animator (1922).

75 Robert Kastenbaum, 'Psychological Death', in Leonard Pearson (ed.), *Death
    and Dying. Current Issues in the Treatment of the Dying Person* (Cleveland, 1969), 7.

76 Michael Potts, Paul A. Byrne and Richard G. Nilges, 'Introduction: Beyond
    Brain Death', in Potts, Byrne and Nilges (eds.), *Beyond Brain Death. The Case
    Against Brain Based Criteria for Human Death* (Dordrecht, 2000), 2.

77 Unnamed public health official in *Newsweek*, 18 December 1967, 98.

78 Paul A. Byrne, Sean O'Reilly, Paul M. Quay and Peter W. Salsich, 'Brain
    Death – The Patient, the Physician and Society', in Potts, Byrne and Nilges
    (eds.), *Beyond Brain Death. The Case Against Brain Based Criteria for Human Death*
    (Dordrecht, 2000), 25.

79 Editorial in *Ebony*, 23 (March 1968), 118.

80 Martin S. Pernick, 'Brain Death in a Cultural Context. The Reconstruction of
    Death, 1967–1981', in Stuart J. Younger, Robert M. Arnold and Renie
    Schapiro (eds.), *The Definition of Death. Contemporary Controversies* (Baltimore,
    1999), 16.

81 Peter Singer, *Rethinking Life and Death. The Collapse of Our Traditional Ethics*
    (Oxford, 1995), 33.

82 Ibid., 36.

83 Jack Kevorkian, *Prescription: Medicide. The Goodness of a Planned Death* (Buffalo,
    1991), 166, 202.

84 Neil Elliott, *The Gods of Life* (New York, 1994), 93.

CHAPTER ELEVEN: STRANGERS

1 The original quote is in David Livingstone, *Travels and Researches in South Africa*
    (Philadelphia, 1859), 15.

2 Nancy Venables Raine, *After Silence. Rape and My Journey Back* (New York,
    1999), 1–3, 6, 10–20, 29, 37, 41, 56, 59–60, 152, 163–4, 178, 228, 248–50,
    271–4.

3 Robin Morgan, *The Demon Lover. On the Sexuality of Terrorism* (London, 1989),
    23.

4 Roy Porter, 'Rape – Does it Have a Historical Meaning?', in Sylvana Tomaselli
    and Roy Porter (eds.), *Rape. An Historical and Cultural Enquiry* (Oxford, 1986),
    222.

5 Florence Rush, 'Sexual Abuse of Children', in Noreen Connell and Cassandra
    Wilson (eds.), *Rape: The First Source Book for Women* (New York, 1974), 65–75.

6 Susan Brownmiller, *Against Our Will: Men, Women and Rape* (Harmondsworth,
    1975), 14–15.

7 For example, see George K. Behlmer, *Child Abuse and Moral Reform in England
    1870–1908* (Palo Alto, 1982); C. Hooper, 'Child Sexual Abuse and the

Regulation of Women: Variations on a Theme', in C. Smart (ed.), *Regulating Womanhood* (London, 1992), 54–77; Louise A. Jackson, *Child Sexual Abuse in Victorian England* (London, 2000).

8 I. Hacking, 'The Making and Molding of Child Abuse', *Critical Inquiry*, 17 (1991), 258–88 and Stephen J. Pfohl, 'The "Discovery" of Child Abuse', *Social Problems*, 24.3 (February 1977), 310–23.

9 Jon Silverman and David Wilson, *Innocence Betrayed. Paedophilia, the Media and Society* (Cambridge, 2002), 21.

10 Cited in David Finkelhor, *Child Sexual Abuse. New Theory and Research* (New York, 1984), 1. According to the American Humane Association, there were nearly twenty-three thousand cases of child abuse in 1982.

11 David Finkelhor, *Child Sexual Abuse. New Theory and Research* (New York, 1984), 2.

12 Martin Tolchin, 'U.S. Panel Declares Child Abuse Represents "National Emergency"', *New York Times*, 28 June 1990.

13 For the best account see Philip Jenkins, *Moral Panic. Changing Conceptions of the Child Molester in Modern America* (New Haven, 1998), 221–9.

14 Jon Silverman and David Wilson, *Innocence Betrayed. Paedophilia, the Media and Society* (Cambridge, 2002), 22, analysed interest in child sexual abuse in six leading British newspapers. See Diana E. H. Russell and Rebecca M. Bolen's *The Epidemic of Rape and Child Abuse in the United States* (London, 2000).

15 LeRoy Ashby, *Endangered Children. Dependency, Neglect, and Abuse in American History* (New York, 1997), 133.

16 For example, see N. Freeman, 'Child Sexual Abuse', *Lancet*, 31 October 1987, 1017; H. Kean, 'Child Sexual Abuse', *Lancet*, 31 October 1987, 1018; Royal College of Physicians of London, *Physical Signs of Sexual Abuse in Children* (Salisbury, 1991); R. Sunderland, 'Child Sexual Abuse', *Lancet*, 31 October 1987, 1018.

17 For example, see B. Campbell, *Unofficial Secrets. Child Sexual Abuse: The Cleveland Case* (London, 1988) and J. La Fontaine, *Child Sexual Abuse* (London, 1990).

18 Marina Warner, *No Go the Bogeyman. Scaring, Lulling, and Making Mock* (London, 1998), 386.

19 Marilyn Ivy, 'Have You Seen Me? Recovering the Inner Child in Late Twentieth Century America', in Sharon Stephens (ed.), *Children and the Politics of Culture* (Princeton, 1995), 86.

20 Georges Vigarello, *A History of Rape. Sexual Violence in France from the 16th to the 20th Century*, trans. Jean Birrell (Cambridge, 2001), 244.

21 M. Hillman, J. Adams and J. Whitlegg, *One False Move: A Study of Children's Independent Mobility* (London, 1990), 43–5.

22 Philip Jenkins, *Moral Panic. Changing Conceptions of the Child Molester in Modern America* (New Haven, 1998), 206.

23 For example, see http://ch.dmoz.org/Shopping/Children/Safety_Products_ and_Services/Surveillance_and_Monitoring_Systems.

24 *The Times*, 21 November 1885, 2.

25 *New York Times*, 20 July 1993, A6, cited in Joseba Zulaika and William A. Douglass, *Terror and Taboo. The Follies, Fables, and Faces of Terrorism* (New York, 1996), 187.

26 Editorial in *The Times*, 26 November 1993.

27 *Sunday Times*, 28 November 1993.

28 For a discussion of this term see Stanley Cohen, *Folk Devils and Moral Panics: The Creation of the Mods and Rockers* (London, 1972), 9.

29 For further discussion see Stuart Hall, Chas Critcher, Tony Jefferson, John Clarke and Brian Roberts, *Policing the Crisis. Mugging, the State, and Law and Order* (London, 1978), 16.

30 Rob Sindall, *Street Violence in the Nineteenth Century: Media Panic or Real Danger?* (Leicester, 1990), 162.

31 For an analysis of the 1970s moral panic over mugging see Stuart Hall, Chas Critcher, Tony Jefferson, John Clarke and Brian Roberts, *Policing the Crisis. Mugging, the State, and Law and Order* (London, 1978).

32 Hazel Erskine, 'The Polls: Fear of Violence and Crime', *Public Opinion Quarterly* (Spring 1974), 131.

33 Esther I. Madriz, 'Images of Criminals and Victims: A Study on Women's Fear and Social Control', *Gender and Society*, 11.3 (June 1997), 3, and Richard Berke, 'Crime is Becoming Nation's Top Fear', *New York Times*, 23 January 1994, A21.

34 According to a poll by the *National Law Journal*, cited by Esther I. Madriz, 'Images of Criminals and Victims: A Study on Women's Fear and Social Control', *Gender and Society*, 11.3 (June 1997), 5–6.

35 Richard A. Sundeed, 'The Fear of Crime and Urban Elderly', in Marlene A. Young Rifai (ed.), *Justice and Older Americans* (Lexington, 1977), 19–21.

36 'Afraid to Go Out at Night', *Crime Control Digest*, 12 (1978), 6–7, cited in Ron H. Aday, *Crime and the Elderly. An Annotated Bibliography* (New York, 1988), 26. This referred to elderly people in Montgomery County, Maryland.

37 'Fear of Teenagers Greatly Affects Life for the Nation's Elderly', *Crime Control Digest*, 14 (1980), 9–10, cited in Ron H. Aday, *Crime and the Elderly. An Annotated Bibliography* (New York, 1988), 28. This referred to two thousand elderly people in Pennsylvania.

38 1983 British Crime Survey, cited in Barrie Gunter, *Television and the Fear of Crime* (London, 1987), 3–4.

39 Ibid. For even higher reports of fear of rape, see Ruth E. Hall, *Ask Any Woman. A London Inquiry into Rape and Sexual Assault* (Bristol, 1985).

40 H. E. Figgie, *The Figgie Report or Fear of Crime: America Afraid: Part I: The General Public* (Ohio, 1980)

41 James Garofalo and John Laub, 'The Fear of Crime: Broadening our Perspective', *Victimology: An International Journal*, 3.3 (1978), 243.

42 Yves Brillon, *Victimization and Fear of Crime Among the Elderly* (Toronto, 1987), 51.

43 Esther I. Madriz, 'Images of Criminals and Victims: A Study on Women's Fear and Social Control', *Gender and Society*, 11.3 (June 1997), 347.

44 Margaret T. Gordon and Stephanie Riger, *The Female Fear* (New York, 1989), 69–70.

45 Patricia Weiser Eastell, 'Beliefs about Rape: A National Survey', in Eastell (ed.), *Without Consent. Confronting Adult Sexual Violence* (Canberra, 1993), 23.

46 Ruth E. Hall, *Ask Any Woman. A London Inquiry into Rape and Sexual Assault* (Bristol, 1985), 35–6.

47 Quoted in Esther I. Madriz, 'Images of Criminals and Victims: A Study on Women's Fear and Social Control', *Gender and Society*, 11.3 (June 1997), 34.

48 Hazel Erskine, 'The Polls: Fear of Violence and Crime', *Public Opinion Quarterly* (Spring 1974), 131. The statistics for men were that 17–22 per cent were afraid to walk at night in 1965 and 1972.

49 Reported in Esther I. Madriz, 'Images of Criminals and Victims: A Study on Women's Fear and Social Control', *Gender and Society*, 11.3 (June 1997), 11.

50 For studies see Allen E. Linka, Andrew Sanchirico and Mark D. Reed, 'Fear of Crime and Constrained Behavior: Specifying and Estimating a Reciprocal Effects Model', *Social Forces*, 66 (1988), 827–37, and Kenneth F. Ferraro, 'Women's Fear of Victimization: Shadow of Sexual Assault?', *Social Forces*, 75 (1996), 667–90.

51 Sandra Gunning, *Race, Rape and Lynching: The Red Record of American Literature, 1890–1912* (Oxford, 1996), 5–6.

52 L. E. Ohlin, 'The Effects of Social Change on Law Enforcement', in (no ed.), *The Challenge of Crime in a Free Society* (New York, 1971), 32. A similar process of scapegoating can be seen with the Irish in Boston, the Italians in Chicago, the Chinese in New York and English oil workers in the Shetlands: see S. E. Merry, *Urban Danger* (Philadelphia, 1981) and Susan J. Smith, *Crime, Space and Society* (Cambridge, 1986), 131. For a fascinating account based on modern Greece see Alexandra Bakalaki, 'Locked into Security, Keyed into Modernity: The Selection of Burglaries as Source of Risk in Greece', *Ethnos* (2003).

53 Frank F. Fursteinberg, 'Public Reaction to Crime in the Streets', *American Scholar*, 40.4 (autumn 1971), 606. Also see Susan J. Smith, *Crime, Space and Society* (Cambridge, 1986), 112.

54 Esther I. Madriz, 'Images of Criminals and Victims: A Study on Women's Fear and Social Control', *Gender and Society*, 11.3 (June 1997), 345.

55 The term is P. O'Malley's: see P. O'Malley, 'Risk, Power and Crime Prevention', *Economy and Society*, 21.3 (1992), 252–75 and P. O'Malley in A. Barry, T. Osborne and N. Rose (eds.), *Foucault and Political Reason* (1996).

56 David Garland, 'The Limits of the Sovereign State. Strategies of Crime Control in Contemporary Society', *British Journal of Criminology*, 36.4 (Autumn 1996), 447.

57 Esther I. Madriz, 'Images of Criminals and Victims: A Study on Women's Fear and Social Control', *Gender and Society*, 11.3 (June 1997), 5–6.

58 Les Johnston, *The Rebirth of Private Policing* (London, 1992), 74.

59 Ibid., 147.

60 Ibid., 73.

61 1991 Gallup poll, reported in Charles T. Rubin, *The Green Crusade* (New York, 1994), 5.

62 Murray Bookchin, *Remaking Society: Pathways to a Green Future* (Boston, 1990), 20.

63 Robert S. Strother, 'Backfire in the War Against Insects', *Reader's Digest*, 74 (June 1959), 69.

64 '*Sports Illustrated* Joins Anti-Pesticide Publications', in *Agricultural Chemicals*,

15 (June 1960), 86.

65 'Pesticides: The Price for Progress', *Time*, 80.13 (28 September 1962), 45–8.

66 H. Davidson's letter to the editor, *New Yorker*, 20 and 29 February 1995, 18.

67 J. E. de Steiguer, *The Age of Environmentalism* (New York, 1997), 29.

68 Rachel Carson, *Silent Spring* (Harmondsworth, 1965), 21–9. It first appeared serialised in the *New Yorker* in June 1962. For another apocalyptic vision in the 1960s, see Paul R. Ehrlich, *The Population Bomb* (London, 1968).

69 This point was made by M. Jimmie Killingsworth and Jacqueline S. Palmer, 'Millennial Ecology. The Apocalyptic Narrative from *Silent Spring* to *Global Warming*', in Carl G. Herndl and Stuart C. Brown (eds.), *Green Culture. Environmental Rhetoric in Contemporary America* (Madison, 1996), 21–45.

70 Barry Commoner, *The Closing Circle. Confronting the Environmental Crisis* (London, 1972), 295.

71 Krishan Kumar, 'Apocalypse, Millennium and Utopia Today', in Malcolm Bull (ed.), *Apocalypse Theory and the Ends of the World* (Oxford, 1995), 211.

72 Allison James, 'Eating Green(s). Discourses of Organic Food', in Kay Milton (ed.), *Environmentalism. The View from Anthropology* (London, 1993), 214.

73 K. Toolis, 'Epidemic in Waiting', *Guardian Weekend*, 22 September 2001, 27.

74 Harvey M. Sapolsky, 'Introduction', in Sapolsky (ed.), *Consuming Fears. The Politics of Product Risks* (New York, 1986), 3.

75 Andrew Tudor, *Monsters and Mad Scientists. A Cultural History of the Horror Movie* (Oxford, 1989), 21.

76 Brian P. Bloomfield and Theo Vurdubakis, 'Disrupted Boundaries: New Reproductive Technologies and the Language of Anxiety and Expectation', *Social Studies of Science*, 25.3 (August 1995), 537.

77 Umberto Saffiotti, 'Comments on the Scientific Basis for the "Delaney Clause"', *Preventive Medicine*, 2 (1973), 128–9.

78 J. M. Barnes, 'Carcinogenic Hazards from Pesticide Residues', in *Residue Reviews*, 13 (1966), 79.

79 I am greatly indebted to Brenda Gillespie, Dave Eva and Ron Johnston, 'Carcinogenic Risk Assessment in the United States and Great Britain: The Case of Aldrin/Dieldrin', *Social Studies of Science*, 9.3 (August 1979), 265–301, for this analysis.

80 Alan P. Lightman and Jon D. Miller, 'Contemporary Cosmological Beliefs', *Social Studies of Science*, 19.1 (February 1989), 127.

81 Ann Louise Gittleman, *How to Stay Young and Healthy in a Toxic World* (Los Angeles, 1999), 10.

82 Ken Young, 'Living Under Threat', in Roger Jowell, Sharon Witherspoon and Lindsay Brook (eds.), *British Social Attitudes. The 7th Report* (Aldershot, 1990), 84.

83 Connie de Boer and Ineke Catsburg, 'A Report: The Impact of Nuclear Accidents on Attitudes Towards Nuclear Energy', *Public Opinion Quarterly*, 52.2 (Summer 1988), 257. These were SOC/BBC polls in 1985 and 1986.

84 Phil Brown and Edwin J. Mikkelsen, *No Safe Place. Toxic Waste, Leukemia, and Community Action* (Berkeley, 1990), 75–6.

85 Ulrich Beck, 'The Reinvention of Politics: Towards a Theory of Reflexive Modernization', in Ulrich Beck, A. Giddens and S. Lash (eds.), *Reflexive*

Modernization: Politics, Tradition and Aesthetics in the Modern Social Order (Cambridge, 1994), 11.

86 http://www.fda/gov/ora/compliance_ref/cpg/cpgfod/cpg560-750.hml.

87 Harvey Wasserman, 'Time to Dispel the Nuclear Cloud', *Nation*, 24 May 1986, 721.

88 Harvey Wasserman, 'Time to Dispel the Nuclear Cloud', *Nation*, 24 May 1986, 721.

89 'The Story of a Town', *New York Times Magazine*, 11 May 1986, 20, quoted in Phil Brown and Edwin J. Mikkelsen, *No Safe Place. Toxic Waste, Leukemia, and Community Action* (Berkeley, 1990), xvi.

90 *Report of The President's Commission on the Accident at Three Mile Island* (Washington, DC, 1979), 81.

91 For example, according to Greenpeace, *Nuclear Briefing. Sellafield and Reprocessing* (London, 1990), 3, a fire in one of the plutonium-producing reactors in 1957 led to the release of radioactivity, allegedly causing over a thousand deaths from cancer.

92 S. M. Macgill, *The Politics of Anxiety. Sellafield's Cancer-Link Controversy* (London, 1987), 10, 16–21.

93 Ibid., 32.

94 Greenpeace, *The Windscale File. A Lay-Guide to Living (and Dying) with a Nuclear Neighbour* (London, n.d.), 1, 7.

95 Harold Bolter, *Inside Sellafield* (London, 1996).

96 Harvey Wasserman, 'Time to Dispel the Nuclear Cloud', *The Nation*, 24 May 1986, 722.

97 B. L. Cohen, *Before it is Too Late: A Scientist's Case for Nuclear Energy* (New York, 1983), 31.

98 Cited in Kristin Sharader-Frechette, 'Scientific Method, Anti-Foundationalism and Public Decision Making', in Rognar E. Lofstedt and Lynn Frewer (eds.), *The Earthscan Reader in Risk and Modern Society* (London, 1998), 45.

99 Quoted in Kai Erikson, 'Toxic Reckoning. Business Faces a New Kind of Fear', *Harvard Business Review* (January 1990), 122.

100 Anthony Giddens, *The Consequences of Modernity* (Cambridge, 1990), 124–5.

101 Mary Douglas and Aaron Wildavsky, *Risk and Culture, An Essay on the Selection of Technical and Environmental Danger* (Berkeley, 1982), 7.

102 Kai Erikson, 'Toxic Reckoning. Business Faces a New Kind of Fear', *Harvard Business Review* (January 1990), 118–26.

103 Ann Louise Gittleman, *How to Stay Young and Healthy in a Toxic World* (Los Angeles, 1999), 1.

104 Barry Glassner, 'Fitness and the Postmodern Self', *Journal of Health and Social Behavior*, 30.2 (June 1989), 180.

105 For example, see Luigi Cornaro and Gertrude Phillipson, *How to Live 100 Years* (Bognor Regis, 1978), and David Weeks and Jamie James, *Superyoung. The Proven Way to Stay Young Forever* (London, 1998)

106 Peter John Hudson, *Why Die Young? Life Extension and Rejuvenation the Natural Way* (Whitstable, 1983).

107 Jean Carper, *Stop Ageing Now! The Ultimate Plan for Staying Young and Reversing the*

Ageing Process (London, 1996).

108 Elner Cranton and William Fryer, *Resetting the Clock. 5 Anti-Aging Hormones that Improve and Extend Life* (New York, 1996), and Barry Sears, *The Anti-Ageing Zone* (London, 1999).

109 Sigmund Freud, *Group Psychology and the Analysis of the Ego*, trans. James Strachey (New York, 1989), 89–90.

110 For example, see Ann Wolbert Burgess and Lynda Lytle Holmstrom, *Rape: Victims of Crisis* (Bowie, 1974).

AFTERWORD TO PART FIVE: AESTHESIOLOGY

1 Eric Erikson, *Young Man Luther: A Study in Psychoanalysis and History* (New York, 1958).

2 For an otherwise insightful example of sentiment as masculine see Mary Chapman and Glenn Hendler (eds.), *Sentimental Men, Masculinity and the Politics of Affect in American Culture* (Berkeley, 1999), 7.

3 William M. Reddy, 'Against Constructionism. The Historical Ethnology of Emotions', in *Current Anthropology*, 38 (June 1997), 331. Reddy coined the word 'emotive' to refer to statements whose 'referent changes by virtue of the statement'. In other words, the 'external referent' that the emotive points to 'emerges from the act of uttering in a changed state'. So, the act of actually saying or writing the phrase 'I am afraid' changes the state of fear.

4 Sara Admed, 'The Organisation of Hate', *Law and Critique*, 12.3 (2001), 349, 355–6.

CONCLUSION: TERROR

1 Cited in James Der Derian, '*In Terrorem*: Before and After 9/11', in Ken Booth and Tim Dunne (eds.), *Worlds in Collusion. Terror and the Future of Global Order* (Basingstoke, 2002), 104. The quotation was not set out as a poem in the *Sunday Times* or these two books.

2 Editorial in the *New York Times*, 2 March 1993, cited in James Der Derian, '*In Terrorem*: Before and After 9/11', in Ken Booth and Tim Dunne (eds.), *Worlds in Collusion. Terror and the Future of Global Order* (Basingstoke, 2002), 103.

3 *Time*, 8 March 1993.

4 Cited in Eric Darton, *Divided We Stand. A Biography of New York's World Trade Center* (New York, 1999).

5 C. James, 'Live Images Made Viewers Witnesses to Horror', *New York Times*, 12 September 2001, A25.

6 This was a common observation, but see Leon Hale, 'Recalling the Day the World Stopped', in http://www.chron.com/cs/CDA/story.hts/special/sept11/1565775; Michael Hall, 'In the Grand Scheme of Human Events, Life Must Continue', in http://www.criticdoctor.com/features/newyork3.html; 'President's Message' [President of the University of Toronto], http://www.magazine.utoronto.ca/02winter/prc2.htm; Armando Rios, 'Sept. 11: The Day America Changed', in http://www/baxterbulletin.com/ads/chronology2001/page2.html.

7 Jonathan Rosenblum, 'The Day the World Changed', in http://www.jewish

mediasources.com/article/211. Also published in the *Jerusalem Post*, 14 September 2001.

8　Cited in Philip Delves Broughton, 'Death in the Towering Inferno', in http://www.telegraph.co.uk/news/main.jhtml?xml=/news/2001/09/12/wtower12.xml.

9　Cited by Bernie Heidkamp, 'Ours is a Country that Has Not Been Damaged in Our Lifetime by War or Natural Catastrophe But We've All Seen Independence Day', in http://www.poppolitics.com/articles/printerfriendly/2001-09-12-wtc.shtml.

10　Richard Wajdo, 'Was On His way to Work in the World Financial Center', in http://news.bbc.co.uk/hi/english/static/in_depth/americas/2001/day_of_ter ror/eyewitness/default.stm. Also see http://www.courttv.com/talk/chat_ transcripts/2001/0911eyewitnesses.html.

11　Jonathan Judd, in http://www.cnn.com/SPECIALS/2002/america. remembers/subsection.tower.html.

12　Cited by Bernie Heidkamp, 'Ours is a Country that Has Not Been Damaged in Our Lifetime by War or Natural Catastrophe But We've All Seen Independence Day', in http://www.poppolitics.com/articles/printerfriendly/2001-09-12-wtc.shtml.

13　Ibid.

14　Ibid.

15　Walter Metz, 'On Terrorism and Contemporary American Cinema', in http://www.montana.edu/metz/filmreviews/terrorism.htm, first published in *The Tributary* (Bozeman), October 2001.

16　Trent Eglin, 'Film Commentary', in http://www.surfnetusa.com/celtic-folk/movies/trenteglin/FilmCommentary4.htm. First published in the *Santa Cruz Sentinel*, 12 October 2001.

17　Cited in Dru Sefton, 'Assault on America', in http://www.newhouse.com/archive/story1a091401.html.

18　Sigmund Freud, *The 'Uncanny'*, in Albert Dickson (ed) *The Penguin Freud Library, Volume 14. Art and Literature*. First published 1919. (Harmsondsworth, 1985) 367.

19　'War of the Worlds – Update since the events of 11 September', in http://www.dowse.com/movies/wotw-news.html.

20　Director Timothy Hines, quoted in 'War of the Worlds – Update since the events of 11 September', http://www.dowse.com/movies/wotw-news.html.

21　Director Timothy Hines, quoted in 'Pendragon Pictures. War of the Worlds. Production Information Announcement', in http://www.scifi2k.com/misc_html/warworlds/press_release6.html.

22　Producer Susan Goforth, quoted in 'Pendragon Pictures News. Martians to Invade Sooner', in http://www.horrormoviemania.com/waroftheworlds/press.html.

23　Major Arthur Griffith, *Mysteries of Police and Crime*, vol. II (London, 1898), 469, quoted in William Laqueur, *The Age of Terrorism* (Boston, 1987), 313. Also see Barbara Arnett Melchiori, *Terrorism in the Late Victorian Novel* (London, 1985).

24　Lee E. Dutter, 'Ethno-Political Activity and the Psychology of Terrorism',

Terrorism, 10 (1987), 145.

25 Daniel Pipes, 'The Muslims are Coming! The Muslims are Coming!', *National Review*, 19 November 1990, 28–31, cited in John L. Esposito, *The Islamic Threat. Myth or Reality?* (New York, 1992), 168.

26 John L. Esposito, *The Islamic Threat. Myth or Reality?* (New York, 1992), 5.

27 Connie de Boer, 'The Polls: Terrorism and Hijacking', *Public Opinion Quarterly*, 43.3 (Autumn 1979), 410.

28 Ibid.

29 Robin Morgan, *The Demon Lover. On the Sexuality of Terrorism* (London, 1989), 30.

30 Joseba Zulaika and William A. Douglass, *Terror and Taboo. The Follies, Fables, and Faces of Terrorism* (New York, 1996), 13.

31 Ibid., 31.

32 Ronald Reagan, 'Remarks Following Pentagon Report on the Security of U.S. Marines in Lebanon, December 27, 1983', *Weekly Compilation of Presidential Documents*, 19 (1983), 1747, cited in Bethami A. Dobkin, *Tales of Terror. Television News and the Construction of the Terrorist Threat* (New York, 1992), 90.

33 Joseba Zulaika and William A. Douglass, *Terror and Taboo. The Follies, Fables, and Faces of Terrorism* (New York, 1996), 23. The CIA decided to include threats and hoaxes as terrorism.

34 Cited in Bethami A. Dobkin, *Tales of Terror. Television News and the Construction of the Terrorist Threat* (New York, 1992), 83. President George Bush made this comment in July 1990.

35 Karl Schwartz, 'Fighting Cancer and Terrorism – Our Fight is Similar', in http://www.lymphomation.org/messageNHL.htm.

36 Jock Gill, 'Fighting the Cancer of Terrorism', in http://www.penfield-gill.com/presentations/fighting_the_cancer_of_terrorism.htm. The author identified himself as a Democrat. Also see Paul Johnson, 'The Cancer of Terrorism', in Benjamin Netanyahu (ed.), *Terrorism* (New York, 1986), 31.

37 David Balkin, 'Time to Excise this Cancer of Terrorism', in http://www.seacoastonline.com/2001news/9_16balkin.htm.

38 George Shultz [Secretary of State], 'Terrorism and the Modern World', *Department of State Bulletin*, December 1984, 14, cited in Bethami A. Dobkin, *Tales of Terror. Television News and the Construction of the Terrorist Threat* (New York, 1992), 85–6.

39 Editorial in the *New York Times*, 2 March 1993, cited in James Der Derian, '*In Terrorem*: Before and After 9/11', in Ken Booth and Tim Dunne (eds.), *Worlds in Collusion. Terror and the Future of Global Order* (Basingstoke, 2002), 103.

40 Geoffrey Colvin, 'The Cost of Complacency', *Fortune*, 1 October 2001, 50.

41 Gregory Gargiso, 'In the Cause of Architecture', in http://www.archrecord.com/InTheCause/0402FDNY/fdny.asp. Originally published in *Architectural Record*.

42 The Sears Building was the tallest building in the world from 1974 to 1996, when it was surpassed by the Petronas Towers in Kuala Lumpur, Malaysia.

43 Laurie Garrett, 'The Nightmare of Bioterrorism', in http://www.foreignaffairs.org/the-nightmare-of-bioterrorism.html. Originally published in

Foreign Affairs, January/February 2001.

44 Charles B. Strozier, 'The World Trade Center Disaster and its Global Aftermath. Reflections and Meditations', at the John Jay College and FEMA Conference on Urban Hazards on 22 January 2002, reported in http://www.nycop.com/Stories/Jan_02/The_World_Trade_Center_Disaster/body_the_world_trade_center_disaste.html.

45 John Deutch, Director of Central Intelligence, 'The Threat of Nuclear Diversion', at the Hearing on Global Proliferation of Weapons of Mass Destruction, Part 3, Senate Permanent Subcommittee on Investigations, Government Affairs Committee, US Senate 104th Congress, 2nd Session, 20 March 1996, cited in http://www.isis-online.org/publications/terrorism/nightmare.html.

46 Jin-Tai Choi, *Aviation Terrorism. Historical Survey, Perspectives and Responses* (Basingstoke, 1994), 35.

47 Susan Sontag, 'AIDS and Its Metaphors', in Sontag, *Illness as Metaphor and AIDS and its Metaphors* (New York, 1990), 102.

48 Bethami A. Dobkin, *Tales of Terror. Television News and the Construction of the Terrorist Threat* (New York, 1992), 38, 83.

49 Mike Davis, 'The Flames of New York', *New Left Review*, 12 (November/December 2001), 48.

50 *New York Times*, 14 September 2001, A25.

51 Jack G. Shaheen, *Reel Bad Arabs. How Hollywood Vilifies a People* (New York, 2001), 2.

52 David Balkin, 'Time to Excise this Cancer of Terrorism', in http://www.seacoastonline.com/2001news/9_16balkin.htm.

53 John L. Esposito, *The Islamic Threat. Myth or Reality?* (New York, 1992), 178.

54 Jack G. Shaheen, *Reel Bad Arabs. How Hollywood Vilifies a People* (New York, 2001), 7. Also see Edward T. Linenthal, *The Unfinished Bombing. Oklahoma City in American Memory* (Oxford, 2001), 18.

55 R. Simon, 'Anthrax Nation', *US News and World Report*, 5 November 2001, 17.

56 Marie-Therese Fay, Mike Morrissey and Maria Smyth, *Northern Ireland's Troubles. The Human Cost* (London, 1999), 130.

57 For a summary of the studies see Ed Cairns and Ronnie Wilson, 'Psychological Coping and Political Violence: Northern Ireland', in Yonah Alexander and Alan O'Day (eds.), *The Irish Terrorist Experience* (Aldershot, 1991), 125.

58 Betty Pfefferbaum et al., 'Posttraumatic Stress Two Years After the Oklahoma City Bombing in Youths Geographically Distant from the Explosion', *Psychiatry*, 63.4 (Winter 2000), 366–7.

59 Ezra Susser, Helene Jackson and Christina Hoven, '2001, or New York City Schoolchildren', in http://www.fathom.com/feature/190150.

60 Eric M. Vernberg, 'Psychological Science and Terrorism: Making Psychological Issues Part of Our Planning and Technology', in http://merrrill.ku.edu/publications/2002whitepaper/vernberg.html.

61 Ezra Susser, Helene Jackson and Christina Hoven, '2001, or New York City Schoolchildren', in http://www.fathom.com/feature/190150.

62 Cited in 'Clinton, Corzine Hold NYC Field Hearing to Address Unmet Mental Needs of Children Post 9-11', in http://clinton.senate.gov/news/2002/2002613B56.html.

63 Jessica Hamblen, 'Terrorist Attacks. Children. A National Center for PTSD Fact Sheet', in http://panicdisorder.about.com/gi/dynamic/offsite. htm?site=http% 3A%F%2F%2Fwww.ncptsd.org%2Ffacts%2Fdisasters%2Ffs_ children_disaster.html.

64 Betty Pfefferbaum et al., 'Posttraumatic Stress Two Years After the Oklahoma City Bombing in Youths Geographically Distant from the Explosion', *Psychiatry*, 63.4 (Winter 2000), 367.

65 Eric M. Vernberg, 'Psychological Science and Terrorism: Making Psychological Issues Part of Our Planning and Technology', in http://merrrill.ku.edu/pub lications/2002whitepaper/vernberg.html.

66 Jessica Hamblen, 'Terrorist Attacks. Children. A National Center for PTSD Fact Sheet', in http://panicdisorder.about.com/gi/dynamic/offsite.htm?site= http%3A%F%2F%2Fwww.ncptsd.org%2Ffacts%2Fdisasters%2Ffs_children_ disaster.html

67 Ibid.

68 Christina Hoven, quoted in 'N.Y. Kids May Carry 9/11 Mental Scars as Adults', in http://abcnews.go.com/sections/us/DailyNews/homefront020827.html.

69 Ezra Susser, Helene Jackson and Christina Hoven, '2001, or New York City Schoolchildren', in http://www.fathom.com/feature/190150.

70 Eric M. Vernberg, 'Psychological Science and Terrorism: Making Psychological Issues Part of Our Planning and Technology', in http://merrrill.ku.edu/ publications/2002whitepaper/vernberg.html.

71 Johannes Müller, *Hindrances of Life* (New York, 1909), 90.

72 Ezra Susser, Helene Jackson and Christina Hoven, '2001, or New York City Schoolchildren', in http://www.fathom.com/feature/190150.

73 E. G. Dexter, 'Air "Flivvers"', *Scientific Monthly*, 38 (1934), 361–6.

74 John A. Ryle, 'The Twenty-First Maudsley Lecture: Nosophobia', *Journal of Mental Science*, xciv.394 (January 1948), 3.

75 John Hinton, 'The Psychology of Dying', in Norman Autton (ed.), *From Fear to Faith. Studies of Suffering and Wholeness* (London, 1971), 42.

76 Rex A. Lucas, *Men in Crisis. A Study of a Mine Disaster* (New York, 1969), 248.

77 John M. Connor, 'Diary', 21 November 1914, IWM, 87/10/1, and Mr Parrino, quoted in *New York Times*, 14 September 2001, A9.

78 Marina Warner, *No Go the Bogeyman. Scaring, Lulling, and Making Mock* (London, 1998), 181, 328.

79 Joost Abraham Mauritis Meerloo, *Aftermath of Peace. Psychological Essays* (New York, 1946) 94–5.

80 For another example of a phobic who was inspired by this story of Livingstone, see 'David', *The Autobiography of David —*, ed. Ernest Raymond (London, 1946).

81 Mary Entwistle, *The Child's Livingstone* (London, 1913), 10–11.

82 J. A. Staunton Batty, *Livingstone. The Empire Builder or 'Set Under the Cross'* (London, 1913), 46–8.

83 Alexander Bain, *The Emotions and the Will* (London, 1859), 92.

84 Martha Wolfenstein, *Disaster. A Psychological Essay* (London, 1957), 88–9.

85 Sigmund Freud, *Beyond the Pleasure Principle*, trans. James Strachey (New York, 1959), 32–5.

86 An unnamed serviceman quoted by Alfred Clair Underwood, *Conversion: Christian and Non-Christian. A Comparative and Psychological Study* (New York, 1925), 136. The man was the John Clifford Professor and Tutor in the History of Religions at Rawdon College, Leeds.

87 'A London Journalist' (Newman Watts), *In Case of Invasion. Panic or Peace? A Message for the Moment* (Worthing, 1940), 6.

88 Ibid. 23, 26.

89 James B. Taylor, Louis A. Zurcher and William H. Key, *Tornado. A Community Responds to Disaster* (Seattle, 1970), 9.

90 Morris Dickstein, 'Aesthetics of Fright', *American Film*, 5.10 (September 1980).

91 Jonathan Lake Crane, *Terror and Everyday Life. Singular Moments in the History of Horror Film* (London, 1994), 25.

92 Martin Tropp, *Images of Fear. How Horror Stories Help Shape Modern Culture (1818–1918)* (Jefferson, North Carolina, 1990), 4–5.

93 The most frequently cited example is the fleeing of people from Hiroshima after the bomb was dropped: see Duane P. Schultz, *Panic Behavior. Discussion and Readings* (New York, 1964), 6–7. Also see Enrico L. Quarantelli, 'The Nature and Conditions of Panic', *American Journal of Sociology*, 60 (1954), 267–75.

94 Victor H. Rosen, 'Psychiatric Problems in General Surgery', in Leopold Bellak (ed.), *Psychology of Physical Illness. Psychiatry Applied to Medicine, Surgery and the Specialties* (London, 1952), 54. Rosen was the adjunct psychiatrist at Mount Sinai Hospital, New York. Also see Louis Breger, Ian Hunter and Ron W. Lane, 'The Effect of Stress on Dreams', *Psychological Issues*, vii.3 (New York, 1971), 96–101; H. Deutsch, 'Some Psychoanalytic Observations in Surgery', *Psychosomatic Medicine*, 4 (1942), 105–15, I. L. Janis, *Psychological Stress* (New York, 1958).

95 Air Ministry, *Psychological Disorders in Flying Personnel of the Royal Air Force Investigated During the War of 1939-1945* (London, HMSO, 1947), 65; Major William G. Barrett, 'Psychologic Armoring for the Air Force', *War Medicine*, 5.3 (March 1944), 143; Edward A. Strecker, 'War Neuroses', *Military Surgeon*, 94.4 (April 1944), 198; C. P. Symonds, 'The Human Response to Flying Stress', *British Medical Journal*, 4 December 1943, 705.

96 Grace Adams, *Don't Be Afraid* (New York, 1935), 33–4.

97 H. E. Bryant, *Deliverance from Fear* (London, 1939), 4.

98 D. K. Henderson, 'The Significance of Fear', *Edinburgh Medical Journal*, xlviii (October 1941), 651.

99 Frank Bufford, *Casting Out Fear* (London, 1936), 11–12.

100 H. E. Bryant, *Deliverance from Fear* (London, 1939), 4.

101 Dorothy Constance Peel, *How We Lived Then*, 1929, 146.

102 Rollo May, 'Historical Roots of Modern Anxiety Theories', in Paul H. Hock and Joseph Zubin (eds.), *Anxiety*, 12–13 (New York, 1964); S. Kierkegaard, *The Concept of Dread* (Oxford, 1944).

103 Ruth Bedford, *Fear* (n.p., c.1930), 16.

Bibliography

ARCHIVAL SOURCES

Auckland Institute and Museum Library
Alexander, Charles Stewart, 'Letters to his Cousin', November 1917

Contemporary Medical Archives Centre (London)
Palmer, Major H. A., 'The Problem of the P & N Casualty — A Study of 12,000 Cases', 1944
Scriven, Lieutenant Colonel William Hamilton, 'Papers'

Imperial War Museum Archive (London)
Clarke, William, 'Random Recollections of 14/18'
Connor, John M., 'Diary'
Cotton, Major Vere E., 'Letters from the French & Italian Fronts. 1915–1919'
Hubbard, Private Arthur H., 'Letters Written May–November 1916'
Luther, Rowland Myrddyn, 'The Poppies are Blood Red'
May, Lieutenant A. G., 'Personal Experiences of the War Years 1915–1917'
McKerrow, Captain Charles K., 'Diaries and Letters'
Rudge, Bert, 'Interview'
Shaw, Norman, 'Papers'

Liddell Hart Centre for Military Archives (Leeds)
Cousland, Lieutenant Colonel Kenneth H., 'The Great War. A Former Gunner Looks Back'
Mapp, Charles H., 'Memoirs of Charles H. Mapp, M.B.E.'
Smith, Captain Ralph, 'Diary'
Wallace, Major W. Graham, 'Memoir of Service', 1935

Manchester County Council Archive
Scott, Dixon, 'Letters'

Mass Observation Archives (Sussex) (MO)
'Fear', Bulletin No. 14, 1948
File Report 150
FR A20
FR 150
FR 313
FR 364
FR 576
FR 769
FR 1315
FR 1870
FR 1947
'Invasion', 1941
M-OA Topic Collection 'Air Raids'
PR 739
PR 975
PR 926
Report 87

Modern Record Centre
Victor Gollancz's Papers

Public Record Office (London) (PRO)
HO45/10062/B2694
HO199/50
HO199/376
HO199/389
HO199/434
HO199/454
HO205/28
HO205/29
HO205/227
HO205/228
HO205/231
HO205/233
HO205/236
INF 1/292
MH58/305
MH74/30
MH76/128
WO32/11550
WO222/66
WO222/124
WO222/1571
WO222/1584

Wigan Archive Service
Scholes, Miss Dorothy, 'Papers of Miss Dorothy Scholes'

NEWSPAPERS AND PERIODICALS

Agricultural Chemicals, June 1960
Ariel, 5, June 1937
Birmingham Mail, 18 January 1926
Cardiff Times and South Wales Weekly News, 18, 23 January 1926
Christian World, 26 September 1895
Daily Chronicle, 18 January 1926
Daily Express, 18, 19 January 1926
Daily Herald 18, 19 January 1926
Daily Mail, 18 January 1926
Daily Telegraph, 22 November 1939, 3 September 1991
Ebony, 23 March 1968
Echo, 23 December 1887
Edinburgh Evening News, 18 January 1926
Editor (part of *Guardian*), 8 February 2003, 14
Guardian Weekend, 22 September 2001
Irish Telegraph, 18 January 1926
Irish Times, 18 January 1926
Jerusalem Post, 14 September 2001
Leeds Weekly Citizen, 22 January 1926
Manchester Guardian, 18, 19 January 1926, 15 April 1957
Medical Times and Hospital Gazette, 31, 8 April 1903
Morning Post, 17 November 1936
Nation, 24 May 1986
New Yorker, 20, 29 February 1995
New York Times, 16 January 1854, 18 May 1910, 20 April 1912, 18 January 1926, 7,
    8 February 1951, 12 September 1985, 13 March 1987, 13 March 1989, 28
    June 1990, 17 March 1992, 2 March 1993, 20 July 1993, A6, 23 January
    1994, 12, 14 September 2001
New York Times Magazine, 11 May 1986
Pall Mall Gazette, 19 January 1888
Santa Cruz Sentinel, 12 October 2001
Star, 18 January 1926
Sunday Times, 28 November 1993
The Times, 21 November 1885, 24 June 1913, 18 January 1926, 1 January 1930, 24
    November 1959, 26 November 1993
Time, 28 September 1962, 8 March 1993
To-Day, 28 September 1895
USA Today, October 1985
Weekly Scotsman, 23 January 1926
Weekly Times and Echo, 25 December 1887
Yorkshire Post, 8 December 1939

Published Books

Abbott, Jacob, *Gentle Measures in the Management and Training of the Young; or, The Principles on Which a Firm Parental Authority May be Established and Maintained, Without Violence or Anger, and the Right Development of the Moral and Mental Capacities be Promoted by Methods in Harmony with the Structure and Characteristics of the Juvenile Mind*, Harper and Brothers, 1899

Abbott, John Stevens Cabot, *The Mother at Home; or, The Principles of Maternal Duty Familiarly Illustrated*, John Mason, 1834

Abrahamsen, Dr David, *The Emotional Care of Your Child*, Trident Press, 1969

Adams, Grace, *Don't Be Afraid*, Covici Friede Publishers, 1935

Adams, Grace Kincle, *Your Child is Normal. The Psychology of Young Childhood*, Covici Friede Publishers, 1934

Aday, Ron H., *Crime and the Elderly. An Annotated Bibliography*, Greenwood Press, 1988

Air Ministry, *Psychological Disorders in Flying Personnel of the Royal Air Force Investigated During the War of 1939–1945*, HMSO, 1947

Anderson, Harold Homer, *Children in the Family*, D. Appleton-Century Co., 1937

Anderson, John Edward, *Happy Childhood. The Development and Guidance of Children and Youth*, D. Appleton-Century Co., 1933

Arkin, Arthur M., J. S. Antrobus and S. J. Ellman, *The Mind in Sleep: Psychology and Parapsychology*, Lawrence Erlbaum Associates, 1978

Arlitt, Ada Hart, *The Child From One to Six. Psychology for Parents*, McGraw-Hill Book Co., 1930

Ashby, LeRoy, *Endangered Children. Dependency, Neglect, and Abuse in American History*, Twayne Publishers, 1997

Asquith, Cynthia, *The Child at Home*, Charles Scribner's Sons, 1923

Autton, Norman, *The Pastoral Care of the Dying*, SPCK, 1966

Bain, Alexander, *The Emotions and the Will*, first published 1859, Longmans, Green and Co., 1899

Baker, Edna Dea, *Parenthood and Child Nurture*, Macmillan Co., 1922

Balleine, Rev. G. R., *What is Superstition? A Trail of Unhappiness*, Press and Publications, Board of the Church Assembly, 1939

Barrett, Howard, *The Management of Children. A Book for Mothers and Nurses*, George Routledge and Sons Ltd, 1906

Barrow, Lyn, *Tantrums, Jealousy and the Fears of Children*, A. H. and A. Reed, 1968

Barry, A., T. Osborne and N. Rose (eds.), *Foucault and Political Reason*, UCL Press, 1996

Barton, Allen H., *Communities in Disaster. A Sociological Analysis of Collective Stress Situations*, Ward Lock Educational, 1969

Barton, Allen H., *Social Organization Under Stress: A Sociological Review of Disaster Studies*, National Academy of Sciences – National Research Council, 1963

Bashfulness Cured. Ease and Elegance of Manners, Seth Conly Publisher, 1872

Batty, J. A. Staunton, *Livingstone. The Empire Builder or 'Set Under the Cross'*, Society for Promoting Christian Knowledge, 1913

Beach, H. D., *Management of Human Behaviour in Disaster*, Department of National Health and Welfare, Canada, 1967

Bedford, Ruth, *Fear*, n.p., *c*.1930

Beery, Ray Coppock, *How to Bring Out the Best in Your Child. Part Six*, Parents Association, 1950

Begbie, Harold, *Life of William Booth. The Founder of the Salvation Army*, vol. 1, Macmillan and Co., 1920

Behlmer, George K., *Child Abuse and Moral Reform in England 1870–1908*, Stanford University Press, 1982

Bennett, G. Martin and Margaret Bennett, *The First Five Years of a Child's Life*, George G. Harrap and Co., 1920

Bennett, H. J., *I Was a Walworth Boy*, Peckham Publishing Project, 1980

Bennett, Margot, *The Long Way Back*, Bodley Head, 1954

Berriault, Gina, *The Descent*, Arthur Barker Ltd, 1960

Bettelheim, Bruno, *The Uses of Enchantment*, Penguin, 1978

Beverly, Bert Ira, *In Defense of Children*, John Day Co., 1941

Blackburn, Elizabeth K., *In and Out of Windows: A Story of the Changes in Working-Class Life 1902–1977 in a Small East Lancashire Community*, Burnley, 1980

Blight, James G., *The Shattered Crystal Ball: Fear and Learning in the Cuban Missile Crisis*, Rowman and Littlefield Publishers, 1990

Boehmer, Ulrike, *The Personal and the Political. Women's Activism in Response to the Breast Cancer and AIDS Epidemic*, State University of New York Press, 2000

Bolter, Harold, *Inside Sellafield*, Quartet, 1996

Bonniwell, Thomas J., *We Have to Die*, Worthington Press, 1940

Bookchin, Murray, *Remaking Society: Pathways to a Green Future*, South End Press, 1990

Booth, Gotthard, *The Cancer Epidemic*, Mellen Press, 1979

Boring, E. G. and M. Van de Water, *Psychology for the Fighting Man. What You Should Know About Yourself and Others*, Infantry Journal, 1943

Boudewyns, Patrick A. and Robert H. Shipley, *Flooding and Implosive Therapy. Direct Therapeutic Exposure in Clinical Practice*, Plenum Press, 1983

Bourke, Joanna, *Dismembering the Male*, Reaktion, 1997

Bourke, Joanna, *An Intimate History of Killing: Face to Face Killing in Twentieth Century Warfare*, Granta, 1999

Bourke, Joanna, *Working-Class Cultures. Gender, Class and Ethnicity*, Routledge, 1995

Bourke, Joanna (ed.), *The Misfit Soldier*, Cork University Press, 1999

Bradford, Elizabeth, *Let's Talk About Children*, Prentice-Hall, 1947

Bradley, Preston, *Courage for To-Day*, Bobbs-Merrill Co., 1934

Bradley, Preston, *Mastering Fear*, Bobbs-Merrill Co., 1935

Brain, W. Russell and E. B. Strauss, *Recent Advances in Neurology and Neuropsychiatry*, 5th edn., J. & A. Churchill, 1947

Bray, Charles, *How to Educate the Feelings or Affections, and Bring the Dispositions, Aspirations, and Passions into Harmony with Sound Intelligence and Mortality*, 3rd edn., S. R. Wells and Co., 1880

Brill, Alice Cara and May Pardee Youtz, *Your Child and Its Parents. A Textbook for Child Study Groups*, D. Appleton and Co., 1932

Brillon, Yves, *Victimization and Fear of Crime Among the Elderly*, Butterworth, 1987

Brinckman, Arthur, *Notes on the Care of the Sick and Practical Advice to Those in Charge of the Dying and the Dead*, G. J. Palmer, 1879

Brodie, Sir Benjamin Collins, *The Works of Sir Benjamin Collins Brodie*, vol. I, Longman, Green, Roberts and Green, 1865

Brooke, Rev. J. Ingham, *A Lecture on Burial Reform*, J. Masters and Co., 1879

Brooke, Rev. Stopford A., *A Discourse on War*, first published 1905, British and Foreign Unitarian Association, 1916

Brown, Phil and Edwin J. Mikkelsen, *No Safe Place. Toxic Waste, Leukemia, and Community Action*, University of California Press, 1990

Brown, Roger, *Social Psychology*, Macmillan Co., 1965

Browne, Oswald, *On The Care of the Dying. A Lecture to Nurses*, George Allen, 1894

Brownmiller, Susan, *Against Our Will: Men, Women and Rape*, Penguin, 1977

Bruce, Henry Addington, *Your Growing Child. A Book of Talks to Parents on Life's Needs*, Funk and Wagnalls Co., 1927

Bruch, Hilde, *Don't Be Afraid of Your Child. A Guide for Perplexed Parents*, Farrar, Straus and Young, 1952

Brunner, John, *The Brink*, Victor Gollancz Ltd, 1959

Bryant, H. E., *Deliverance from Fear*, Epworth Press, 1939

Bryant, Peter (Peter Byran George), *Two Hours to Doom*, Boardman and Co. 1958

Buchanan, Mary Elizabeth, *Your Child's First Years and What You Can Do to Make them Healthy, Happy Ones*, Home Institute Inc., 1935

Bufford, Frank, *Casting Out Fear*, Student Christian Movement Press, 1936

Burdick, Eugene and Harvey Wheeler, *Fail-Safe*, McGraw-Hill Book Co., 1962

Burgess, Ann Wolbert and Lynda Lytle Holmstrom, *Rape: Victims of Crisis*, R. J. Brady Co., 1974

Burrell, Mrs Caroline Benedict and William Byron Forbush (eds.), *The Manual for Character Training. A Guide-Book for Teachers and Parents Based on the Young Folks Treasury*, University Society, 1925

Butterfield, Herbert, *Human Nature and the Dominion of Fear*, CND, 1968

Byrne, Paul, *The Campaign for Nuclear Disarmament*, Croom Helm, 1988

Campbell, B., *Unofficial Secrets. Child Sexual Abuse: The Cleveland Case*, Virago, 1988

Cantril, Hadley, *The Invasion from Mars. A Study in the Psychology of Panic with the Complete Script of the Famous Orson Welles Broadcast*, Princeton University Press, 1940

Cantril, Hadley, *The Invasion from Mars. A Study in the Psychology of Panic*, Princeton University Press, 1982

Cantril, Hadley and Gordon W. Allport, *The Psychology of Radio*, Harper and Brothers Publishers, 1935

Capulo, Philip, *A Rumor of War*, Ballantine, 1978

Carden, Mae, *Let's Bring Them Up Sensibly*, Mae Carden Inc., 1967

Carper, Jean, *Stop Ageing Now! The Ultimate Plan for Staying Young and Reversing the Ageing Process*, Thorsons, 1996

Carson, Rachel, *Silent Spring*, Penguin Books, 1965

Cartwright, Ann, Lisbeth Hockney and John L. Anderson, *Life Before Death*, Routledge and Kegan Paul, 1973

Catty, Nancy, *Social Training. From Childhood to Maturity*, Methuen and Co., 1951

Chadwick, Edwin, *Report on the Sanitary Conditions of the Labouring Population of Great Britain. A Supplementary Report on the Results of a Special Inquiry into the Practice of*

Interment in Towns. Made at the Request of Her Majesty's Principal Secretary of State for the Home Department, HMSO, 1843

Challoner, H. K. and Roland Northover, *Antidote to Fear*, Robert Hale Ltd, 1962

Chambers, Mary D., *Care and Training of Boys and Girls from Birth to Adolescence*, The Boston Cooking-School Magazine, 1925

Chaplin, J. P., *Rumor, Fear and the Madness of Crowds*, Ballantine, 1959

Chapman, Mary and Glenn Hendler (eds.), *Sentimental Men, Masculinity and the Politics of Affect in American Culture*, University of California Press, 1999

Charles, Archdeacon R. H., *Courage, Truth, Purity*, Basil Blackwell, 1931

Chavkin, Samuel, *The Mind Stealers. Psychosurgery and Mind Control*, Houghton Mifflin, 1978

Chester, Lester, Stephen Fry and Hugo Young, *The Zinoviev Letter*, Heinemann, 1967

Children's Welfare Federation of New York City, *Child Care Questions and Answers. Over 400 Questions Most Often Asked by Parents*, Doubleday and Co., 1948

Chittenden, Gertrude Emma, *Living with Children*, Macmillan Co., 1944

Choi, Jin-Tai, *Aviation Terrorism. Historical Survey, Perspectives and Responses*, Macmillan Press, 1994

Christian, Chris, *Selling Life Assurance*, Industrial Executive Training Consultants, 1970

Clark, G. Hardy, *A System for the Care and Training of Children*, 8th edn., rev., Seaside Printing Co., 1927

Clark, Dr Harriet Bailey, *Mothers' Problems. A Text-Book for Parents' Classes, Mothers' Associations, and Teachers of Children*, Judson Press, 1922

CND, 'The Age of Fear', CND, 1962

Cobb, Augustus G., *Earth-Burial and Cremation. The History of Earth-Burial with its Attendant Evils, and the Advantages Offered by Cremation*, G. P. Putnam's Sons, 1892

Cohen, B. L., *Before it is Too Late: A Scientist's Case for Nuclear Energy*, Plenum Press, 1983

Cohen, Jerome, Joseph W. Cullen and L. Robert Martin (eds.), *Psychosocical Aspects of Cancer*, Raven Press, 1982

Cohen, Stanley, *Folk Devils and Moral Panics: The Creation of the Mods and Rockers*, MacGibbon and Kee, 1972

Commoner, Barry, *The Closing Circle. Confronting the Environmental Crisis*, Jonathan Cape, 1978

Copeland, Norman, *Psychology and the Soldier*, George Allen and Unwin, 1942

Cornaro, Luigi and Gertrude Phillipson, *How to Live 100 Years*, New Horizon, 1978

Cosgrave, Jessica Garretson, *The Psychology of Youth. A Book for Parents*, Doubleday, Doran and Co., 1929

Cox, Marvin Earl, *Child Life. A Scientific and Practical Treatise on the Study of Life and the Care, Education and Development of Children from Conception to Maturity*, World's College of Therapeutics, 1902

Crane, Jonathan Lake, *Terror and Everyday Life. Singular Moments in the History of Horror Film*, Sage Publishers, 1994

Cranton, Elner and William Fryer, *Resetting the Clock. 5 Anti-Aging Hormones that Improve and Extend Life*, M. Evans and Co., 1996

Crile, George W., *Cancer and Common Sense*, Robert Hale Ltd, 1957

Crile, George W., *The Origin and Nature of the Emotions. Miscellaneous Papers*, W. B. Saunders Co., 1915

Crile, George W., *A Mechanistic View of War and Peace*, Macmillan Co., 1915

Cushing, Harvey, *From a Surgeon's Journal 1915–1918*, Constable and Co., 1936

Dalley, John, *The Gift of a Child. A Handbook for Parents on the Training of Young Children*, J. M. Dent and Sons Ltd, 1946

Darton, Eric, *Divided We Stand. A Biography of New York's World Trade Center*, Basic Books, 1999

Darwin, Charles, *The Expression of Emotions in Man and Animals*, 3rd edn., first published 1872, ed. Paul Ekman, HarperCollins, 1998

Davenport, Kathlyn, *My Preston Yesterdays*, Neil Richardson, 1984

'David', *The Autobiography of David* ——, ed. Ernest Raymond, Victor Gollancz, 1946

Davis, Marion Quinlan, *A Plan for Growing Up. The Blue Book for Building Better Lives*, first published 1945, Richards Co., 1957

Dee, Nerys, *Discover Dreams*, Aquarian, 1989

De Kok, Winifred, *Guiding Your Child Through the Formative Years From Birth to the Age of Five*, Emerson Books, 1935

Dent, John Yerbury, *Anxiety and Its Treatment with Special Reference to Alcoholism*, John Murray, 1941

De Steiguer, J. E., *The Age of Environmentalism*, McGraw-Hill Companies, 1997

Disasters on Sea and Land, John Heywood, 1881

Dobkin, Bethami A., *Tales of Terror. Television News and the Construction of the Terrorist Threat*, Praeger, 1992

'Doctor, A', *The Conquest of Fear*, Society for Promoting Christian Knowledge, 1941

Dollard, John, *Fear in Battle*, Infantry Journal, 1944

Domhoff, G. William, *Finding Meaning in Dreams*, Plenum Press, 1996

Douglas, Mary and Aaron Wildavsky, *Risk and Culture, An Essay on the Selection of Technical and Environmental Danger*, University of California Press, 1982

Dowd, Jerome, *The Negro in American Life*, Century Co., 1926

Duchenne, G. B., *Physiology of Motion Demonstrated by Means of Electrical Stimulation and Clinical Observation and Applied to the Study of Paralysis and Deformities*, trans. and ed. Emanuel B. Kaplan, J. B. Lippincott Co., 1949

Duchenne, G. B., *Selections from the Clinical Works of Dr. Duchenne (De Boulogne)*, trans., ed. and condensed G. V. Poore, New Sydenham Society, 1883

Duchenne, G. B., *The Mechanism of Human Facial Expression*, ed. and trans. R. Andrew Cuthbertson, Cambridge University Press, 1990

Eassie, William, *Cremation of the Dead: Its History and Bearings upon Public Health*, Smith, Elder and Co., 1875

Edge, Patricia, *Training the Toddler*, Faber and Faber, 1944

Eggleston, Mrs Margaret White, *Faith or Fear in Child Training*, Round Table Press, 1934

Ehrlich, Paul R., *The Population Bomb*, Ballantine, 1968

Elias, Eileen, *Enjoy Your Baby. Child Management in the First Five Years*, Evans Brothers Ltd, 1944

Elias, Norbert, *The Civilizing Process: Sociogenetic and Psychogenetic Investigations*, trans. Edmund Jepthcott, 2 vols, Basil Blackwell, 1978

Elliott, Neil, *The Gods of Life*, Macmillan, 1994

Eltinge, Captain LeRoy, *Notes on Lectures on Psychology of War. Prepared by Major Harvey Llewellyn Jones, Commanding Horsed Section, 104th Ammunition Train*, n.p., 1918

Entwistle, Mary, *The Child's Livingstone*, Oxford University Press, 1913

Epstein, Steven, *Impure Science. AIDS Activism and the Politics of Knowledge*, University of California Press, 1996

Erikson, Eric, *Young Man Luther: A Study in Psychoanalysis and History*, Faber and Faber, 1958

Esposito, John L., *The Islamic Threat. Myth or Reality?*, Oxford University Press, 1992

Evans, Joyce A., *Celluloid Mushroom Clouds. Hollywood and the Atomic Bomb*, Westview Press, 1998

Farago, Ladislas, *German Psychological Warfare*, G. P. Putnam's Sons, 1942

Farrell, James J., *Inventing the American Way of Death, 1830–1920*, Temple University Press, 1980

Fass, Jerome S., *A Primer for Parents*, Trident Press, 1968

Fawell, Ruth M., *The Relevance of Courage*, Friends Home Service Committee, 1965

Fay, Marie-Therese, Mike Morrissey and Maria Smyth, *Northern Ireland's Troubles. The Human Cost*, Pluto Press, 1999

Fenichel, Otto, *Psychoanalytic Theory of the Neurosis*, W. W. Norton, 1945

Fenwick, Peter and Elizabeth Fenwick, *The Truth in the Light. An Investigation of Over 300 Near-Death Experiences*, Berkley Books, 1997

Fern, William G., *Overcoming Fear. A Lecture Given to the London 'Sell More' Club*, 2nd edn., Modern Salesmanship, 1932

Fernald, Woodbury M., *A View at the Foundations: Or, First Causes of Character As Operative Before Birth, From Hereditary and Spiritual Sources*, Wm. V. Spencer, 1865

'Fieldman, A', *The Industrial Assurance Agents' Companion*, Stone and Cox Ltd, 1935

Figgie, H. E., *The Figgie Report or Fear of Crime: America Afraid: Part I: The General Public*, the author, 1980

Fiiriter, Ifeoma R., *Interpreting Your Dreams and Visions*, Robe, 2000

Finkelhor, David, *Child Sexual Abuse. New Theory and Research*, Free Press, 1984

Fletcher, Moore Russell, *One Thousand Persons Buried Alive by Their Best Friends. A Treatise on Suspended Animation with Directions for Restoration*, the author, 1883

Fletcher, Peter, *Life Without Fear. Ten Talks on the Psychology of Christian Living*, Group Publications, 1936

Flint, F. S., *Otherworld Cadences*, Poetry Bookshop, 1920

Fodor, Nandor, *The Search for the Beloved*, States Hospital Press, 1946

Form, William H. and Sigmund Mosow, *Community in Disaster*, Harper and Brothers, 1958

Forman, Henry James, *Our Movies Made Children*, Arno Press, 1935

'Former Sufferer, A', *How to Make a Speech Without Fear and Trembling*, J. Bennett, 1921

Foucault, Michel, *The History of Sexuality. Volume I: An Introduction*, Penguin, 1978

Freeling, Nicolas, *The Gadget*, Heinemann, 1977

Freeman, John R., *On the Safeguarding of Life in Theatre. Being a Study from the Standpoint of an Engineer*, American Society of Mechanical Engineers, 1906

Freeman, Walter Jackson and James W. Watts, *Psychosurgery in the Treatment of Mental Disorders and Intractable Pain*, 2nd edn., first published 1942, Charles C. Thomas, 1950

Freud, Sigmund, *A General Introduction to Psychoanalysis*, Boni and Liveright, 1920

Freud, Sigmund, *An Outline of Psychoanalysis*, Penguin, 1940

Freud, Sigmund, *The Interpretation of Dreams*, Macmillan Co., 1950

Freud, Sigmund, *Beyond the Pleasure Principle*, trans. James Strachey, Bantam Books, 1959

Freud, Sigmund, *New Introductory Lectures on Psychoanalysis*, first published 1932, Hogarth Press, 1974

Freud, Sigmund, *Group Psychology and the Analysis of the Ego*, trans. James Strachey, Bantam Books, 1989

Freud, Sigmund, *The 'Uncanny'*, Penguin, 2003

Fuller, J. F. C., *Hints of Training Territorial Infantry. From Recruit to Trained Soldier*, Gale and Polden Ltd, 1913

Fuller, J. F. C., *The Reformation of War*, Hutchinson and Co., 1923

Fulton, John Farquhar, *Frontal Lobotomy and Affect Behavior. A Neurophysiological Analysis*, W. W. Norton and Co., 1951

Gallup, George with William Proctor, *Adventures in Immortality*, Souvenir Press, 1982

Gay, Peter, *Freud for Historians*, Oxford University Press, 1985

Gay, Peter, *The Bourgeois Experience. From Victoria to Freud*, 4 vols., Norton, 1984–96

Geertz, Clifford, *The Interpretation of Cultures*, Hutchinson, 1975

Gerhard, William Paul, *The Safety of Theatre Audiences and the Stage Personnel Against Danger from Fire and Panic*, British Fire Prevention Committee, 1899

Giddens, Anthony, *The Consequences of Modernity*, Polity Press, 1990

Gilman, Sander L., *Freud, Race, and Gender*, Princeton University Press, 1993

Ginzberg, Eli, John L. Herma and Sol W. Ginsberg, *Psychiatry and Military Manpower Policy. A Reappraisal of the Experience in World War II*, King's Crown Press, 1953

Gittleman, Ann Louise, *How to Stay Young and Healthy in a Toxic World*, Keats Publishing, 1999

Glover, Edward, *The Psychology of Fear and Courage*, Penguin Books, 1940

Goodison, Lucy, *The Dreams of Women*, Women's Press, 1995

Gordon, Margaret T. and Stephanie Riger, *The Female Fear*, Free Press, 1989

Grant, Marian, *Home and Children*, Carey Kingsgate Press Ltd, 1952

Graves, Ernest Rutherford and Gladys Hoagland Graves, *Parents and Children*, J. B. Lippincott, 1928

Greenpeace, *Nuclear Briefing. Sellafield and Reprocessing*, Greenpeace, 1990

Greenpeace, *The Windscale File. A Lay-Guide to Living (and Dying) with a Nuclear Neighbour*, Greenpeace, n.d.

Grey, Marget, *Return from Death. An Exploration of the Near-Death Experience*, Arkana, 1985

Grinker, Roy R. and John P. Spiegel, *Men Under Stress*, J. & A. Churchill Ltd, 1945

Guenzel, Louis, *Retrospects. The Iroquois Theatre Fire*, the author, 1945

Guest, Flora Bigelow, *Casting Out Fear*, John Lane Co., 1918

Gunning, Sandra, *Race, Rape and Lynching: The Red Record of American Literature, 1890–1912*, Oxford University Press, 1996

Gunter, Barrie, *Television and the Fear of Crime*, John Libbey, 1987

Gunther, John, *Death Be Not Proud. A Memoir*, Hamish Hamilton, 1949

Guy, William A. and David Ferrier, *Principles of Forensic Medicine*, 6th edn., rev., Henry Renshaw, 1888

Hadfield, J. A., *Dreams and Nightmares*, Penguin Books, 1954

Hall, Christopher Newman, *The Antidote to Fear, with Illustrations from the Prophet Isaiah*, J. Nisbet and Co., 1866

Hall, G. Stanley, *Morale. The Supreme Standard of Life and Conduct*, D. Appleton, 1920

Hall, Ruth E., *Ask Any Woman. A London Inquiry into Rape and Sexual Assault*, Falling Wall Press, 1985

Hall, Stuart, Chas Critcher, Tony Jefferson, John Clarke and Brian Roberts, *Policing the Crisis. Mugging, the State, and Law and Order*, Macmillan Press, 1978

Hamilton-Parker, Craig, *The Hidden Meaning of Dreams*, Sterling, 1999

Healy, Richard J., *Emergency and Disaster Planning*, John Wiley and Sons, 1969

Heuer, Kenneth, *The End of the World. A Scientific Enquiry*, Victor Gollancz Ltd, 1953

Hillman, M., J. Adams and J. Whitlegg, *One False Move: A Study of Children's Independent Mobility*, PSI, 1990

Holder, William, *Cremation Versus Burial: An Appeal to Reason Against Prejudice*, Brown and Sons, 1891

Holmstein, Brian and Alex Lubertozzi (eds.), *The Complete War of the Worlds. Mars' Invasion of Earth from H. G. Wells to Orson Welles*, Sourcebooks MediaFusion, 2001

Hopkinson, Mrs C. A., *Hints for the Nursery*, Little, Brown and Co., 1863

Hopps, John Page, *The Etherealisation of the Body*, Williams and Norgate, 1894

Hudson, Peter John, *Why Die Young? Life Extension and Rejuvenation the Natural Way*, Pryor Publications, 1983

Hultaker, Orjan E. and Jan E. Trost, *The Family and the Shelters*, Uppsala Press, 1977

Hunt, Lynn, *The Family Romance of the French Revolution*, University of California Press, 1992

Hurst, Arthur F., *Medical Diseases of the War*, First published 1916, 2nd edn. Edward Arnold and Co., 1940

Huxley, Aldous, *Brave New World*, Chatto and Windus, 1959

Ikle, Ford Charles, *The Social Impact of Bomb Destruction*, University of Oklahoma Press, 1958

Iroquois Theatre Souvenir Programme, Rand, McNally and Co., 1903

Jack, Brigadier-General J. L., *General Jack's Diary 1914–1918*, Eyre and Spottiswoode, 1964

Jackson, Louise A., *Child Sexual Abuse in Victorian England*, Routledge, 2000

James, William, *The Principles of Psychology*, vol. 1, Henry Holt and Co., 1890

Janis, Irving L., *Air War and Emotional Stress. Psychological Studies of Bombing and Civilian Defense*, McGraw-Hill Book Co., 1951

Jefferson, John, *An Antidote to Sudden Fear: Or, the Calmness in which Christians May Contemplate the Threatened Pestilence*, the author, 1832

Jenkins, Philip, *Moral Panic. Changing Conceptions of the Child Molester in Modern America*, Yale University Press, 1998

Jersild, Arthur Thomas and Mrs Frances Baker Holmes, *Children's Fears*, Teachers College, Columbia University, 1935

Joffe, Hélène, *Risk and 'The Other'*, Cambridge University Press, 1999

Johnston, Les, *The Rebirth of Private Policing*, Routledge, 1992

Jones, Dennis Feltham, *Colossus*, Hart-Davis, 1966

Jones, Ernest, *Nightmare, Witches, and Devils*, L. & V. Woolf, 1931

Julian, Fred Bennett, *Psychological Casualties in Air Raids and Their First-Aid Treatment*, Society for Promoting Christian Knowledge, 1940

Jung, Carl G., *Analytical Psychology: Its Theory and Practice: the Tavistock Lectures*, Kegan Paul and Co., 1928

Jung, Carl G., *Flying Saucers. A Modern Myth of Things Seen in the Skies*, trans. R. F. C. Hull, Routledge and Kegan Paul, 1959

Jung, Carl G., *Memories, Dreams, Reflections*, Fontana, 1963

Jupp, Peter, *From Dust to Ashes: The Replacement of Burial by Cremation in England 1840–1967*, Congregational Church, n.d.

Kaehele, Edna, *Living with Cancer*, Victor Gollancz Ltd, 1953

Kahn, Albert Eugene, *The Game of Death. Effects of the Cold War on our Children*, Cameron and Kahn, 1953

Kahn, Jack H. and Jean P. Nursten, *Unwillingly to School. The Place of the Child Guidance Clinic in the Treatment of School Phobia*, Pergamon Press, 1965

Kalinowsky, Lothar B., Hanns Hippius and Helmfried E. Klein, *Biological Treatments in Psychiatry*, Grune and Stratton, 1982

Kanner, Leo, *Judging Emotions from Facial Expressions*, Psychological Review Co., 1931

Kennedy, John, *Worry. Its Cause and Cure*, The Psychologist, 1946

Kevorkian, Jack, *Prescription: Medicide. The Goodness of a Planned Death*, Prometheus, 1991

Keyes, Dr E. L., *The Fear of Death*, the author, 1910

Kielblock, Adolph, *Stage Fright or How to Face an Audience*, Geo. H. Ellis, 1891

Kierkegaard, *The Concept of Dread*, Oxford University Press, 1944

Kimmins, Charles Williams, *Children's Dreams*, Longmans, Green and Co., 1920

Kirby, Georgiana B., *Transmission; or, Variation of Character Through the Mother*, S. R. Wells and Co., 1877

Kitayama, Shinobu and Hazel Rose Markus (eds.), *Emotion and Culture. Empirical Studies of Mutual Influence*, American Psychological Association, 1994

Kleinig, John, *Ethical Issues in Psychosurgery*, George Allen and Unwin Ltd, 1985

Kleitman, Nathaniel, *Sleep and Wakefulness as Alternating Phases in the Cycle of Existence*, University of Chicago Press, 1939

Knox, Ronald A., *Essays in Satire*, Shead and Ward, 1928

Koskoff, Yale David and Richard Goldhurst, *The Dark Side of the House*, Dial Press, 1968

LaCapra, Dominick, *Representing the Holocaust: History, Theory, Trauma*, Cornell University Press, 1994

La Fontaine, J., *Child Sexual Abuse*, Polity, 1990

Lamers, William M., *Disaster Protection Handbook for School Administrators*, The American Association of School Administrators, 1959

Laqueur, William, *The Age of Terrorism*, Weidenfeld and Nicolson, 1987

Law, Stanley Noel, *Inspired Freedom*, Regency Press, 1975

Le Bon, Gustave, *The Psychology of the Great War*, trans. E. Andrews, T. Fisher Unwin, 1916

Lerner, Barron H., *The Breast Cancer Wars. Hope, Fear and the Pursuit of Cure in Twentieth-Century America*, Oxford University Press, 2001

LeShan, L., *You Can Fight for Your Life*, Thorsons, 1977

Levy, Max, *Why Modern Cremation Should Replace Earth-Burial*, Bacon and Co., 1885

Livingstone, David, *Travels and Researches in South Africa*, J. W. Bradley, 1859

Lloyd, Sarah and Mike Hally, *War and Civil Defence in North West England. Human Responses to War*, North West Planning Assumption Study, 1989

'London Journalist, A' (Newman Watts), *How to Live Calmly in War Time*, Pickering and Inglis Ltd, 1939

'London Journalist, A' (Newman Watts), *In Case of Invasion. Panic or Peace? A Message for the Moment*, the author, 1940

London Under Attack. The Report of the Greater London Area War Risk Study Commission, Basil Blackwell, 1986

Lovecraft, H. P., *Herbert West, Re-Animator*, Necronomicon Press, 1922

Lucas, Rex A., *Men in Crisis. A Study of a Mine Disaster*, Basic Books Inc., 1969

Lutz, Catherine A., *Unnatural Emotions. Everyday Sentiments on a Micronesian Atoll and Their Challenge to Western Theory*, University of Chicago Press, 1998

Lyman, Henry M., *Insomnia; and Other Disorders of Sleep*, W. T. Keener, 1885

McBride, W. J., *The Conquest of Fear through Psychology*, The Psychologist, 1936

MacCurdy, John T., *War Neuroses*, Cambridge University Press, 1918

McDougall, William, *An Introduction to Social Psychology*, first published 1908, Methuen and Co., 1912

McDougall, William, *Psychology. The Study of Behaviour*, Williams and Norgate, 1912

McDougall, William, *The Group Mind. A Sketch of the Principles of Collective Psychology with Some Attempt to Apply them to the Interpretation of National Life and Character*, Cambridge University Press, 1921

Macgill, S. M., *The Politics of Anxiety. Sellafield's Cancer-Link Controversy*, Pion Ltd, 1987

Mackenna, Dr Robert W., *The Adventure of Death*, John Murray, 1916

MacPhail, Sir Andrew, *Official History of the Canadian Forces in the Great War 1914–19. The Medical Services*, F. A. Acland, 1925

Mahoney, Robert F., *Emergency and Disaster Nursing*, 2nd edn., Macmillan Co., 1969

Manchester, William, *Goodbye Darkness. A Memoir of the Pacific War*, Little, Brown, 1981

Marks, Isaac M., *Fears and Phobias*, William Heinemann, 1967

Mastery of Fear. How to Attain It, Regent Press, 1931

May, Mark A., *Education in a World of Fear*, Harvard University Press, 1941

Mays, Spike (Cedric Wesley), *Reuben's Corner*, Eyre and Spottiswoode, 1969

'Medical Psychologist, A', *Fear and Depression. Their Causes and Self-Treatment*, Cornish Brothers Ltd, 1939

Meerloo, Abraham Mauritis, *Aftermath of Peace. Psychological Essays*, International Universities Press, 1946

Meerloo, Joost A. M., *Patterns of Panic*, Greenwood Press, 1950

Melbourne, David F. and Keith Hearne, *The Meaning of Your Dreams*, Blandford, 1999

Melchiori, Barbara Arnett, *Terrorism in the Late Victorian Novel*, Croom Helm, 1985

Menninger, William C., *Psychiatry in a Troubled World. Yesterday's War and Today's Challenge*, Macmillan Co., 1948

Merry, S. E., *Urban Danger*, Temple University Press, 1981

Moorcroft, William H., *Sleep, Dreaming and Sleep Disorders*, University Press of America, 1993

Moore, Harry Estill, *. . . And the Winds Blew*, Hagg Foundation for Mental Health, 1964

Moran, Lord, *The Anatomy of Courage*, Constable, 1945

Morgan, Robin, *The Demon Lover. On the Sexuality of Terrorism*, Methuen, 1989

Morningstar, Sally, *Divining the Future*, Lorenz, 2000

Morse, Josiah, *The Psychology and Neurology of Fear*, Clark University Press, 1907

Mullen, Joseph J., *Psychological Factors in the Pastoral Treatment of Scruples*, Williams and Wilkins Co., 1927

Müller, Johannes, *Hindrances of Life*, Mitchell Kennerley, 1909

Munson, Edward L., *The Management of Men. A Handbook on the Systematic Development of Morale and the Control of Human Behaviour*, George G. Harrap and Co., 1920

Murdoch, Rev. James, *Everlasting Punishment. A Sermon Preached Before the Free Synod of Aberdeen, and Published at Their Request*, George Davidson, 1864

Nacson, Leon, *Interpreting Dreams A–Z*, Hay House, 1999

Newson, John and Elizabeth Newson, *Four Years Old in an Urban Community*, George Allen and Unwin Ltd, 1968

Noble, George Alfred, *Cremation: Its History and Practice*, n.p., 1914

Oakes, Guy, *The Imaginary War. Civil Defense and American Cold War Culture*, Oxford University Press, 1994

Oakley, T. Gilbert, *How to Conquer Your Nervous Fears*, Health for All Publishing Co., 1939

O'Brien, Tim, *The Things They Carried*, Collins, 1990

Osler, William, *Science and Immortality*, Archibald Constable and Co., 1904

Parker, Julia and Derek Parker, *Dreaming*, Chancellor, 1993

Parrinder, Patrick, *H. G. Wells. The Critical Heritage*, Routledge and Kegan Paul, 1972

Patterson, James T., *The Dread Disease. Cancer and Modern American Culture*, Harvard University Press, 1987

Peel, Dorothy Constance, *How We Lived Then, 1914–1918*, John Lane, 1929

Penrose, L. S., *On the Objective Study of Crowd Behaviour*, H. K. Lewis and Co., 1952

Perry, Ronald W., *The Social Psychology of Civil Defense*, Lexington Books, 1982

Pike, James A., *Beyond Anxiety. The Christian Answer to Fear, Frustration, Guilt, Indecision, Inhibition, Loneliness, Despair*, Charles Scribner's Sons, 1953

Porteus, Stanley David, *A Psychologist of Sorts. The Autobiography and Publications of the Inventor of the Porteus Maze Test*, Pacific Books, 1969

Pressman, Jack D., *Last Resort. Psychosurgery and the Limits of Medicine*, Cambridge University Press, 1998

Preston, Samuel H. and Michael R. Haines, *Fatal Years. Child Mortality in Late Nineteenth Century America*, Princeton University Press, 1991

Rachman, S., *Phobias. Their Nature and Control*, Charles Thomas, 1968

Rachman, S. J., *Fear and Courage*, W. H. Freeman and Co., 1978

Raine, Nancy Venables, *After Silence. Rape and My Journey Back*, Virago Press, 1999

Ratcliff, A. J. J., *A History of Dreams. A Brief Account of the Evolution of Dream Theories, With a Chapter on the Dream in Literature*, Grant Richards Ltd, 1923

Rawlinson, Colonel A., *The Defence of London, 1915–1918*, Andrew Melrose, 1923

Reddy, William M., *The Navigation of Feeling. A Framework for the History of Emotions*, Cambridge University Press, 2001

Reich, Wilhelm, *Reich Speaks of Freud*, ed. Mary Higgins and Chester M. Raphael, Souvenir Press, 1972

Report of The President's Commission on the Accident at Three Mile Island, Government Printing Office, 1979

Richardson, Ruth, *Death, Dissection and the Destitute*, Penguin, 1988

Rickman, John, *War Wounds*, H. K. Lewis, 1939

Rippon, Thomas Stanley and Peter Fletcher, *Reassurance and Relaxation. A Short Textbook of Practical Psycho-Therapy*, George Routledge and Sons, 1940

Rivers, W. H. R., *Instinct and the Unconscious. A Contribution to a Biological Theory of the Psycho-Neuroses*, 2nd edn., Cambridge University Press, 1922

Rivers, W. H. R., *Conflict and Dream*, Trench, Trubner and Co., 1923

Robinson, Donald, *The Face of Disaster*, Doubleday and Co., 1959

Robinson, Mary Frances and Walter Freeman, *Psychosurgery and the Self*, Grune and Stratton, 1954

Robinson, Stearn and Tom Corbett, *The Dreamer's Dictionary. A Complete Guide to Interpreting Your Dreams*, Panther,1984

Roper, Lyndal, *Oedipus and the Devil: Witchcraft, Sexuality, and Religion in Early Modern Europe*, Routledge, 1994

Roth, Dr M., *A Few Notes on Fear and Fright, and the Diseases they Cause and Cure; Also on the Means of Preventing and Curing the Effects of These Emotions*, Henry Turner and Co., 1871

Rowell, Geoffrey, *Hell and the Victorians. A Study of Nineteenth Century Theological Controversies Concerning Eternal Punishment and the Future Life*, Clarendon Press, 1974

Royal College of Physicians of London, *Physical Signs of Sexual Abuse in Children*, Royal College of Physicians, 1991

Rubin, Charles T., *The Green Crusade*, Free Press, 1994

Rudé, George, *The Crowd in the French Revolution*, Clarendon Press, 1959

Russell, Diana E. H. and Bebecca M. Bolen, *The Epidemic of Rape and Child Abuse in the United States*, Sage Publications, 2000

Russell, James A., José Miguel Fernández-Dols, Antony S. R. Manstead and J. C. Wellenkamp (eds.), *Everyday Conceptions of Emotion*, Kluwer Academic Publishers, 1995

Ryle, John A., *Fears May Be Liars*, George Allen and Unwin Ltd, 1941

Sappol, Michael, *A Traffic of Dead Bodies. Anatomy and Embodied Social Identity in Nineteenth-Century America*, Princeton University Press, 2002

Sava, George, *War Without Guns. The Psychological Front*, Faber and Faber, 1943

Savory, William S., *On Life and Death: Four Lectures Delivered at the Royal Institution of Great Britain*, Smith, Elder and Co., 1863

Schultz, Duane P., *Panic Behavior. Discussion and Readings*, Random House, 1964

Sears, Barry, *The Anti-Ageing Zone*, Thorsons, 1999

Sewell, W. H., *Christian Care of the Dying and the Dead; A Few Hints on Burial Reform, for Friendly Readers*, Simpkin, Marshall and Co., 1878

Shilt, Randy, *And the Band Played On. Politics, People and the AIDS Epidemic*, Penguin Books, 1987

Shutts, David, *Lobotomy. Resort to the Knife*, Van Nostrand Reinhold Co., 1982

Silverman, Jon and David Wilson, *Innocence Betrayed. Paedophilia, the Media and Society*, Polity, 2002

Simcox, Carroll E., *Is Death the End? The Christian Answer*, SPCK, 1960

Simmons, Harold, *The Psychogenic Theory of Disease: A New Approach to Cancer Research*, General Welfare Publications, 1966

Sindall, Rob, *Street Violence in the Nineteenth Century: Media Panic or Real Danger?*, Leicester University Press, 1990

Singer, Peter, *Rethinking Life and Death. The Collapse of Our Traditional Ethics*, Oxford University Press, 1995

Smelser, Neil J., *Theory of Collective Behavior*, Routledge and Kegan Paul, 1963

Smith, G. Elliott and T. H. Pear, *Shell Shock and its Lessons*, Manchester University Press, 1919

Smith, Susan J., *Crime, Space and Society*, Cambridge University Press, 1986

Solar, Charlotte Del, *Child Guidance*, American Corp., 1950

Sontag, Susan, *AIDS and its Metaphors*, Penguin, 1990

Speaight, Robert, *Ronald Knox. The Writer*, Streed and Ward, 1958

Spencer, Henry E., *Burial and Cremation: A Lecture*, Hamilton, Adams and Co., 1881

Spock, Benjamin, *Baby and Child Care*, new and enlarged edn., Bodley Head, 1958

Spock, Benjamin and Mary Morgan, *Spock on Spock*, Pantheon Books, 1989

State of California, Office of Civil Defense, *Panic Control and Prevention. Instructor's Manual and Teaching Outline*, Office of Civil Defense, 1951

Stearns, Carol Z. and Peter N. Stearns, *Anger. The Struggle for Emotional Control in America's History*, University of Chicago Press, 1986

Steriade, Mircea and Robert W. McCarley, *Brainstem Control of Wakefulness and Sleep*, Plenum Press, 1990

Stonier, Tom, *Nuclear Disaster*, Penguin Books, 1963

Stouffer, Samuel A., *The American Soldier: Combat and its Aftermath. Volume II*, Princeton University Press, 1949

Strecker, Edward A. and Kenneth E. Appel, *Psychiatry in Modern Warfare*, Macmillan Co., 1945

Sullivan, Rev. Walter, *Disturbers of Your Peace of Mind. Worry! Fear! Loneliness!*, Paulist Press, 1950

Sune, William (William Henry Schoenau, Jr.), *Charm, Enthusiasm and Originality. Their Acquisition and Use*, Elan Publishing Co., 1929

Taylor, James B., Louis A. Zurcher and William H. Key, *Tornado. A Community Responds to Disaster*, University of Washington Press, 1970

Taylor, W. S., *Readings in Abnormal Psychology and Mental Hygiene*, D. Appleton and Co., 1926

Tebb, William and Colonel Edward Perry Vollum, *Premature Burial and How it May be Prevented with Special Reference to Trance, Catalepsy and Other Forms of Suspended Animation*, 2nd edn., first published 1896, Swan Sonnenschein and Co., 1905

That Unknown Country, Or What Living Men Believe Concerning Punishment After Death, D. E. McConnel, 1889

The End of the World. A Plain Sermon Preached in a Village Church at a Harvest Home Festival, n.p., 1866

The Fears of a Child. A Book for Children and Their Parents, Green Fields Press, 1906

Thomas, Calvin, *Male Matters. Masculinity, Anxiety and the Male Body on the Line*, University of Illinois Press, 1996

Thomas, Ruth, *Children's Fears*, National Association for Mental Health, 1946

Titmuss, Richard, *Problems of Social Policy*, n.p., 1950

Tropp, Martin, *Images of Fear. How Horror Stories Help Shape Modern Culture (1818–1918)*, Mcfarland and Co., 1990

Trotter, Wilfred, *Instincts of the Herd in Peace and War*, first published 1910, Ernest Benn, 1916

Tudor, Andrew, *Monsters and Mad Scientists. A Cultural History of the Horror Movie*, Basil Blackwell, 1989

Turner, Ralph and Lewis M. Killian (eds.), *Collective Behavior*, 2nd edn., Prentice-Hall, 1972

Underwood, Alfred Clair, *Conversion: Christian and Non-Christian. A Comparative and Psychological Study*, Macmillan Co., 1925

University Society, *The Child's Welfare Manual. A Handbook of Child Nature and Nurture for Parents and Teachers*, University Society, 1915

Vale, George F., *Bethnal Green's Ordeal 1939–45*, Council of the Metropolitan Borough of Bethnal Green, 1945

Vassos, John, *Phobia*, Covici Friede Publishers, 1931

Vigarello, Georges, *A History of Rape. Sexual Violence in France from the 16th to the 20th Century*, trans. Jean Birrell, Polity Press, 2001

Wade, Mary, *To a Miner Born*, Oriel, 1984

Walker, Kenneth, *The Circle of Life. A Search for an Attitude to Pain, Disease, Old Age and Death*, Jonathan Cape, 1942

Walsh, David, *Premature Burial: Fact or Fiction?*, Bailliere Tindall and Co., 1897

Walsh, William S., *The Psychology of Dreams*, Kegan Paul, Trench, Trubner and Co., 1920

Walsh, William S., *The Mastery of Fear*, E. P. Dutton and Co., 1924

Waring, Philippa, *Omens from Your Dreams*, Souvenir, 1991

Warner, Marina, *No Go the Bogeyman. Scaring, Lulling, and Making Mock*, Chatto and Windus, 1998

Watson, John B., *Behaviourism*, Kegan Paul, Trench, Trubner and Co., 1925

Waugh, Evelyn, *The Life of the Right Reverend Ronald Knox*, Chapman and Hall, 1954

Weart, Spencer R., *Nuclear Fear. A History of Images*, Harvard University Press, 1988

Webster, Elliott, *Bashfulness*, Wm. T. C. Hyde and Co., 1906

Weeks, David and Jamie James, *Superyoung. The Proven Way to Stay Young Forever*, Hodder and Stoughton, 1998

Weir, Molly, *Best Foot Forward*, Cedric Chivers, 1979

Westall, Robert (compiler), *Children of the Blitz. Memories of Wartime Childhood*, Viking, 1985

Westland, Albert, *The Child: A Medical Guide to its Care and Management*, Charles Griffin and Co., 1910

Whitaker-Wilson, C., *Nothing to Fear. A Bedside Book of Simple Philosophy*, Thorsons Publishers Ltd, 1952

Wierzbicka, Anna, *Emotions Across Languages and Cultures: Diversity and Universals*, Cambridge University Press, 1999

Wilder, Dr Alexander, *Perils of Premature Burial. A Public Address Delivered Before the Members of the Legislature, at the Capitol, Albany, New York, January 25th, 1871*, E. W. Allen, 1895

Williams, Simon, *Emotion and Social Theory. Corporeal Reflections on the (Ir)Rational*, Sage Publishers, 2001

Williams, Tom A., *Dreads and Besetting Fears. Including States of Anxiety, Their Causes and Cure*, Little, Brown and Co., 1923

Wilson, Sir Arnold and Professor Hermann Levy, *Industrial Assurance. A Historical and Critical Study*, Oxford University Press, 1937

Wittgenstein, Ludwig, *Philosophical Investigations*, trans. G. E. M. Anscombe, Basil Blackwell, 1953

Wolfenstein, Martha, *Disaster. A Psychological Essay*, Routledge and Kegan Paul, 1957

Wolpe, Joseph, *Psychotherapy by Reciprocal Inhibition*, Stanford University Press, 1958

Worcester, Alfred, *The Care of the Aged, the Dying, and the Dead*, Charles C. Thomas, 1935

Worcester, Elwood, Samuel McComb and Isador H. Coriat, *Religion and Medicine. The Moral Control of Nervous Disorders*, Kegan Paul, Trench, Trubner and Co., 1908

Wortis, T. (ed.), *Recent Advances in Biological Psychiatry*, Plenum Press, 1965

Wright, Henry C., *The Empire of the Mother Over the Character and Destiny of the Race*, Bela Marsh, 1863

Wylie, Philip, *Tomorrow!*, Popular Library, 1954

Wylie, Philip, *Triumph*, Doubleday and Co., 1963

Zilboorge, Gregory, *A History of Medical Psychology*, W. W. Norton, 1941

Zulaika, Joseba and William A. Douglass, *Terror and Taboo. The Follies, Fables, and Faces of Terrorism*, Routledge, 1996

Articles and Chapters in Books

Abbate, Grace McLean, 'Group Procedures Found Effective in the Prevention and Handling of Emotional Disorders', *Mental Hygiene*, xxvi, 1942

Achte, Karl Aimo and M.-L. Vauhkonen, 'Cancer and the Psyche', *Annales Medicinae Internae Fenniae*, supplement no. 49, 1967

'A Definition of Irreversible Coma', *Journal of the American Medical Association*, 205, 5 August 1968

Admed, Sara, 'The Organisation of Hate', *Law and Critique*, 12.3, 2001

'Air Raids, Discipline and Panic', *Lancet*, 7 May 1938

Aitken-Swan, Jean and E. C. Easson, 'Reactions of Cancer Patients in Being Told Their Diagnosis', *British Medical Journal*, 21 March 1959

Aitken-Swan, Jean and Ralston Paterson, 'The Cancer Patient and Delay in Seeking Advice', *British Medical Journal*, 1, 12 March 1955

Albright, David, Kevin O'Neill and Corey Hinderstein, 'Nuclear Terrorism: The Unthinkable Nightmare', in http://www.isis-online.org/publications/terrorism/nightmare.html., 13 Sept 2001

'A New Death Test', *Embalmers' Monthly*, xviii, 1905

Arkin, Arthur M., 'Night-Terrors as Anomalous REM Sleep Component Manifestation in Slow-Wave Sleep', *Waking and Sleeping*, 2, 1978

Arnot, Robert, Beatrice Talbot and Milton Greenblatt, 'One to Four Year Follow-Up of 205 Cases of Bilateral Prefrontal Lobotomy', in Milton Greenblatt, Robert Arnot and Harry C. Solomon (eds.), *Studies in Lobotomy*, William Heinemann, 1951

Aserinsky, E. and N. Kleitman, 'Regularly Occurring Periods of Eye Motility and Concomitant Phenomena During Sleep', *Science*, 118, 1953

'Assault on America', http://www.courttv.com/talk/chattranscripts/2001/0911eyewitnesses.html., 11 Sept 2001

Atkinson, William B., 'Note on Night Terrors', *Alienist and Neurologist*, iii.4, October 1882

Ax, Albert F., 'The Physiological Differentiation Between Fear and Anger in Humans', *Psychosomatic Medicine*, 15, 1953

Bakalaki, Alexandra, 'Locked into Security, Keyed into Modernity: The Selection of Burglaries as Source of Risk in Greece', *Ethnos*, 2003

Balkin, David, 'Time to Excise this Cancer of Terrorism', in http://www.seacoastonline.com/2001news/9_16balkin.htm

Ballard, S. I. and H. G. Miller, 'Psychiatric Casualties in a Women's Service', *British Medical Journal*, 3 March 1945

Barbaste, Albert, 'Scrupulosity and the Present Data of Psychiatry', *Theology Digest*, 1.3, Autumn 1953

Barnes, J. M., 'Carcinogenic Hazards from Pesticide Residues', *Residue Reviews*, 13, 1966

Barrett, Major William G., 'Psychologic Armoring for the Air Force', *War Medicine*, 5.3, March 1944

Bartlett, R. J., 'The Civilian Population Under Bombardment', *Nature*, 7 June 1941

Beck, Ulrich, 'The Reinvention of Politics: Towards a Theory of Reflexive Modernization', in Ulrich Beck, A. Giddens and S. Lash (eds.), *Reflexive Modernization: Politics, Tradition and Aesthetics in the Modern Social Order*, Polity Press, 1994

Becker, Howard and David K. Bruner, 'Attitude Toward Death and the Dead and Some Possible Causes of Ghost Fear', *Mental Hygiene*, xv, 1931

Belicki, Kathryn and Marion A. Cuddy, 'Nightmares: Facts, Fictions and Future Directions' in Jayne Gackenbach and Anees A. Sheikh (eds.), *Dream Images: A Call to Mental Arms*, Baywood Publishing Co., 1991

Bellah, J. W. and A. F. Clark, 'The Lunk Trainer', *Infantry Journal*, 52.3, 1943

Bellamy, Raymond, 'The Analysis of a Nightmare', *Journal of Abnormal and Social Psychology*, 10, 1915

Bergler, Dr Edmund, 'Psychoanalysis of a Case of Agoraphobia', *Psychoanalytical Review*, xxii, 1935

Bleckwenn, Colonel William J., 'Neuroses in the Combat Zone', *Annals of Internal Medicine*, 23.2, August 1945

Bloomfield, Brian P. and Theo Vurdubakis, 'Disrupted Boundaries: New Reproductive Technologies and the Language of Anxiety and Expectation', *Social Studies of Science*, 25.3, August 1995

Bodman, Frank, 'Child Psychiatry in War-Time Britain', *Journal of Educational Psychology*, xxxv.5, May 1944

Brabeck, Thomas E., William H. Key, Patricia E. Erickson and Juanita L. Crowe, 'The Impact of Disaster on Kin Relationships', *Journal of Marriage and the Family*, 37, 1975

Breger, Louis, Ian Hunter and Ron W. Lane, 'The Effect of Stress on Dreams', *Psychological Issues*, vii.3, 1971

Broks, Paul, et al., 'Face Processing Impairments After Encephalitis: Amygdala Damage and Recognition of Fear', *Neuropsychologia*, 36, 1998

Brosin, Henry W., 'Panic States and their Treatment', *American Journal of Psychiatry*, 100, 1943

Broughton, Philip Delves, 'Death in the Towering Inferno', in http://www.telegraph.co.uk/news/main.jhtml?xml=/news/2001/09/12/wtower12.xml

Broughton, R. T., 'Sleep Disorders: Disorders of Arousal?', *Science*, 159, 1968

Brouillette, John, 'A Tornado Warning System: Its Functioning on Palm Sunday in Indiana', Research Report No. 15 *OCD Review Notice*, 1966

Brown, Felix, 'Civilian Psychiatric Air-Raid Casualties', *Lancet*, 31 May 1941

Brown, Roger W., 'Mass Phenomena', in Gerdner Lindzey (ed.), *Handbook of Social Psychology. Volume II. Special Fields and Applications*, Addison-Wesley Publishing Co., 1954

Brown, Sanger, 'The Disorders of Sleep', in Thomas L. Stedman (ed.), *Twentieth Century Practice. An International Encyclopedia of Modern Medical Science*, Sampson Low and Co., 1897

Browne, Lt. Colonel A. T. A., 'A Study of the Anatomy of Fear and Courage in War', *Army Quarterly and Defence Journal*, 106.3, July 1976

'Buried Alive', *Catholic World*, 1866

Burnham, Clara Louise, 'How to Keep Your Child From Fear', *Appleton's Magazine*, xi.4, April 1908

Byrne, Paul A., Sean O'Reilly, Paul M. Quay and Peter W. Salsich, 'Brain Death – The Patient, the Physician and Society', in Potts, Byrne and Nilges (eds.), *Beyond Brain Death. The Case Against Brain Based Criteria for Human Death*, Kluwer Academic Publishers, 2000

Cade, Sir Stanford, 'Cancer: The Patient's Viewpoint and the Clinician's Problem', *Proceedings of the Royal Society of Medicine*, 56.1, January 1963

Cairns, Ed and Ronnie Wilson, 'Psychological Coping and Political Violence: Northern Ireland', in Yonah Alexander and Alan O'Day (eds.), *The Irish Terrorist Experience*, Dartmouth, 1991

Caldwell, John M., Stephen W. Ranson and Jerome G. Sacks, 'Group Panic and Other Mass Disruptive Reactions', *United States Armed Forces Medical Journal*, ii.4, April 1951

Campbell, Harry, 'Morbid Shyness', *British Medical Journal*, 26 September 1896

Campbell, Ruth, et al., 'The Classification of "Fear" from Faces is Associated with Face Recognition Skill in Women', *Neuropsychologia*, 40, 2002

Cannon, W. B., 'The Emergency Function of the Adrenol Medulla in Pain and the Major Emotions', *American Journal of Physiology*, xxxiii.2, 2 February 1914

Cantril, H., 'Causes and Control of Riot and Panic', *Public Opinion Quarterly*, 7, 1943

Capshew, James Herbert, 'Psychology on the March: American Psychologists and World War II', PhD, University of Pennsylvania, 1986

Cason, Husley, 'The Nightmare Dream', *Psychological Monographs*, xlvi.5, 1935

Cautela, Joseph H., 'Desensitization and Insight' in *Behaviour Research and Therapy. An International Multi-Disciplinary Journal*, 3, 1965

Chazan, Maurice, 'School Phobia', *British Journal of Educational Psychology*, 32.3, November 1962

Chideckel, Maurice, 'Dreams as the Cause of Death and Disease', *Medical Record*, 98, 1920

Chu, Godwin C., 'Fear Arousing Efficacy and Imminency', *Journal of Personality and Social Psychology*, 4.5, 1966

Churchill, Edward D., 'Panic and Disaster', *Annals of Surgery*, 138, 1953

Clark, S. and Frank Norburry, 'A Possible Role of the Element of Fear in Metrazol Therapy', *Diseases of the Nervous System*, 2, 1941

'Clinton, Corzine Hold NYC Field Hearing to Address Unmet Mental Needs of Children Post 9-11', in http://clinton.senate.gov/news/2002/2002613B56.html

Cohen, Major Benjamin and Major Roy L. Swank, 'Chronic Symptomatology of Combat Neuroses', *War Medicine*, 8.3, 1945

Cohen, Lieutenant Commander R. A. and Lieutenant J. G. Delano, 'Subacute Emotional Disturbances Induced by Combat', *War Medicine*, 7.5, May 1945

Colvin, Geoffrey, 'The Cost of Complacency', *Fortune*, 1 October 2001

'Conditioning to Bangs', *Lancet*, 14 March 1942

Conference of Medical Royal Colleges and their Faculties in the United Kingdom, 1976, 'Diagnosis of Brain Death', *British Medical Journal*, 1, 13 November 1976

Conlon, Edward, 'To the Potter's Field', *New Yorker*, 19 July 1993

Cope, Oliver, Chiu-An Wang and Alvaro Caro, 'Emotional Problems Commonly Encountered in General Surgery', in Harry S. Abram (ed.), *Psychological Aspects of Surgery*, Little, Brown and Co., 1967

Crichton-Miller, H., 'Somatic Factors Conditioning Air-Raid Reactions', *Lancet*, 12 July 1941

Crick, F. and G. Mitchinson, 'The Function of Dream Sleep', *Nature*, 30, 1983

Curran, Surgeon Captain D., 'Functional Nervous States in Relation to Service in the Royal Navy', in Major General Sir Henry Letheby Tidy (ed.), *Inter-Allied Conferences on War Medicine 1942–1945*, Staples Press Ltd, 1947

Cushing, Rev. Richard J., 'A Spiritual Approach to the Atomic Age', *Bulletin of the Atomic Scientists*, 4.7, July 1948

Cuthbertson, R. Andrew, 'The Highly Original Dr Duchenne', in G. B. Duchenne de Boulogne, *The Mechanism of Human Facial Expression*, ed. and trans. R. Andrew Cuthbertson, Cambridge University Press, 1990

Dabbs, James M. and Howard Leventhal, 'Effects of Varying the Recommendations on a Fear Arousing Communication', *Journal of Personality and Social Psychology*, 4.5, 1966

Davis, Mike, 'The Flames of New York', *New Left Review*, 12, November/December 2001

De Boer, Connie and Ineke Catsburg, 'A Report: The Impact of Nuclear Accidents on

Attitudes Towards Nuclear Energy', *Public Opinion Quarterly*, 52.2, Summer 1988

Dement, W. and N. Kleitman, 'The Relation of Eye Movements During Sleep to Dream Activity: An Objective Method for the Study of Dreaming', *Journal of Experimental Psychology*, 53, 1955

Der Derian, James, '*In Terrorem*: Before and After 9/11', in Ken Booth and Tim Dunne (eds.), *Worlds in Collusion. Terror and the Future of Global Order*, Palgrave Macmillan, 2002

Deutsch, Felix, 'Euthanasia: A Clinical Study', *Psychoanalytic Quarterly*, 5, 1936

Deutsch, H., 'Some Psychoanalytic Observations in Surgery', *Psychosomatic Medicine*, 4, 1942

Dexter, E. G., '"Air Flivvers"', *Scientific Monthly*, 38, 1934

Dickstein, Morris, 'Aesthetics of Fright', *American Film*, 5.10, September 1980

Dittrick, Howard, 'Devices to Prevent Premature Burial', *Journal of the History of Medicine and Allied Sciences*, iii, 1948

Dixon, J. Q., 'Iroquois Theatre Fire, Chicago, 1903', in J. Qallan Dixon, *Wreck of the Steamship Titanic 1912... And Including the Iroquois Theatre Fire, Chicago 1903*, Sovereign Publishing Co., 1912

Dunlap, Knight, 'Are Emotions Teleological Constructs?', *American Journal of Psychology*, xliv, 1932

Dutter, Lee E., 'Ethno-Political Activity and the Psychology of Terrorism', *Terrorism*, 10, 1987

Eastell, Patricia Weiser, 'Beliefs about Rape: A National Survey', in Eastell (ed.), *Without Consent. Confronting Adult Sexual Violence*, Australian Institute of Criminology, 1993

Eberhart, Mrs Sylvia, 'How the American People Feel About the Atomic Bomb', *Bulletin of the Atomic Scientists*, 3.6, June 1947

Eckels, H. S., 'The Danger of Burial Alive', *The American Undertaker*, v.2, March 1904

Eglin, Trent, 'Film Commentary', in http://www.surfnetusa.com/celtic-folk/movies/trenteglin/FilmCommentary4.htm

Einstein, Albert, 'The Menace of Mass Destruction', in Einstein, *Out of My Later Years*, Thames and Hudson, 1950

Ekman, Paul, 'Duchenne and Facial Expression of Emotion', in G. B. Duchenne de Boulogne, *The Mechanism of Human Facial Expression*, ed. and trans. R. Andrew Cuthbertson, Cambridge University Press, 1990

Ekman, Paul and Wallace V. Friesen, 'Constants Across Cultures in the Face and Emotion', in Henry Clay Lindgren (ed.), *Contemporary Research in Social Psychology. A Book of Readings*, 2nd edn., Wiley, 1973

Ekman, Paul, Wallace V. Friesen and Silvan S. Tomkins, 'Facial Affect Scoring Technique: A First Validity Study', *Semiotica*, 3.1, 1971

Erikson, Kai, 'Toxic Reckoning. Business Faces a New Kind of Fear', *Harvard Business Review*, January 1990

Erskine, Hazel, 'The Polls: Fear of Violence and Crime', *Public Opinion Quarterly*, Spring 1974

Escalona, Sibylle K., 'Growing Up with the Threat of Nuclear War: Some Indirect Effects on Personality Development', in *American Journal of Orthopsychiatry*, 52.4, October 1982

Exton-Smith, Dr A. N., 'Terminal Illness in the Aged', *Lancet*, 2, 1961

Falla, W. A. S., 'Fear Factors in Flying Personnel', *Journal of Mental Science*, xcii.390, January 1947

Feder, Dr Samuel L., 'Attitudes of Patients with Advanced Malignancy', in Group for the Advancement of Psychiatry (eds.), *Death and Dying. Attitudes of Patient and Doctor*, Group for the Advancement of Psychiatry, 1965

Feifel, Herman, 'The Function of Attitudes Toward Death', in Group for the Advancement of Psychiatry (eds.), *Death and Dying: Attitudes of Patient and Doctor*, Group for the Advancement of Psychiatry, 1965

Feldman, M. J. and M. Hersen, 'Attitudes Towards Death in Nightmare Subjects', *Journal of Abnormal Psychology*, 72, 1967

Féré, Ch., 'A Contribution to the Pathology of Dreams and of Hysterical Paralysis', *Brain* 9, 1887

Ferraro, Kenneth F., 'Women's Fear of Victimization: Shadow of Sexual Assault?', *Social Forces*, 75, 1996

Fisher, C., 'A Psychophysiological Study of Nightmares and Night Terrors. II. Mental Content and Recall of Stage 4', *Journal of Nervous and Mental Disease*, 158, 1974

Fodor, Nandor, 'Nightmares of Suffocation', *Journal of Nervous and Mental Disease*, 101.6, June 1945

Fodor, Nandor, 'Nightmares of Water', *The American Imago. A Psychoanalytical Journal for the Arts and Sciences*, 5.2, July 1948

Fodor, Nandor, 'Nightmares of Cannibalism', *American Journal of Orthopsychiatry*, v.2, April 1951

Fontaine, André, 'Are Bomb Drills Scaring Our Kids?', *Today's Woman*, June 1951

Food and Drugs Administration, http://www.fda/gov/ora/compliance ref/cpg/cpgfod/cpg560–750.html

Foster, Josephine C. and John E. Anderson, 'Unpleasant Dreams in Childhood', *Child Development*, 7.2, June 1936

Freedman, Lawrence, 'Nuclear Weapons Today', in Royal United Services Institute for Defence Studies (ed.), *Nuclear Attack: Civil Defence. Aspects of Civil Defence in the Nuclear Age. A Symposium*, Brossey's Publishers Ltd, 1982

Freeman, N., 'Child Sexual Abuse', *Lancet*, 31 October 1987

Freeman, Walter and James W. Watts, 'Prefrontal Lobotomy in the Treatment of Mental Disorders', *Southern Medical Journal*, 30.1, January 1937

Freeman, Walter and James W. Watts, 'An Interpretation of the Functions of the Frontal Lobe. Based on Observations in Forty-Eight Cases of Prefrontal Lobotomy', *Yale Journal of Biology and Medicine*, 11.5, May 1939

French, Douglas G., 'The Care of Cancer in Practice', *Practitioner*, 177, 1956

Freud, Sigmund, 'A Reply to Criticisms on the Anxiety Neurosis', in Freud, *Collected Works*, I, 1895

Freud, Sigmund, 'Obsessions and Phobias. Their Psychical Mechanism and Their Aetiology', in *The Standard Edition of the Complete Psychological Works of Sigmund Freud*, iii, first published 1895, Hogarth Press, 1962

Freud, Sigmund, 'Analysis of a Phobia in a Five-Year-Old Boy', first published 1909, *The Standard Edition of the Complete Psychological Works of Sigmund Freud*, trans. James Strachey, 1955

Freud, Sigmund, *The 'Uncanny'*, in Albert Dickson (ed.), *The Penguin Freud Library Volume 14. Art and Literature*, first published 1919, Penguin, 1985

Freud, Sigmund, 'Some Additional Notes on Dream-Interpretation as a Whole' in Freud, *The Standard Edition of the Complete Psychological Works of Sigmund Freud*, trans. James Strachey, Hogarth Press, 1925

Friedman, J. H., 'Short Term Psychotherapy of "Phobia of Travel"', *American Journal of Psychotherapy*, 4, 1950

Fritz, Charles E., 'Disaster', in R. K. Merton and R. A. Nisbet (eds.), *Contemporary Social Problems*, Harcourt Brace Jovanovich, 1961

Fritz, Charles E. and Harry B. Williams, 'The Human Being in Disasters: A Research Perspective', *Annals of the American Academy of Political and Social Science*, January 1957

Fursteinberg, Frank F., 'Public Reaction to Crime in the Streets', *American Scholar*, 40.4, autumn 1971

Gardner, Charles S., 'Assemblies', *American Journal of Sociology*, 19, 1914

Gargiso, Gregory, 'In the Cause of Architecture', in http://www.archrecord.com/InTheCause/0402FDNY/fdny.asp

Garland, David, 'The Limits of the Sovereign State. Strategies of Crime Control in Contemporary Society', *British Journal of Criminology*, 36.4, Autumn 1996

Garner, Major H. H., 'Psychiatric Casualties in Combat', *War Medicine*, 8.5, November–December 1945

Garofalo, James and John Laub, 'The Fear of Crime: Broadening our Perspective', *Victimology: An International Journal*, 3.3, 1978

Garrett, Laurie, 'The Nightmare of Bioterrorism', in http://www.foreignaffairs.org/the-nightmare-of-bioterrorism.html

Gatto, Lucio E., 'Understanding the "Fear of Flying" Syndrome. I. Psychic Aspects of the Problem', *United States Armed Forces Medical Journal*, v.8, August 1954

Gavey, Dr C. J., 'Discussion on Palliation in Cancer', *Proceedings of the Royal Society of Medicine*, 48, 1955

Geer, James H., 'The Development of a Scale to Measure Fear', *Behaviour Research and Therapy. An International Multi-Disciplinary Journal*, 3, 1965

Geertz, Hildred, 'The Vocabulary of Emotion: A Study of Javanese Socialization Processes', *Psychiatry*, 22, 1959

Gill, Jock, 'Fighting the Cancer of Terrorism', in http://www.penfield-gill.com/presentations/fighting_the_cancer_of_terrorism.htm

Gillespie, Brenda, Dave Eva and Ron Johnston, 'Carcinogenic Risk Assessment in the United States and Great Britain: The Case of Aldrin/Dieldrin', *Social Studies of Science*, 9.3, August 1979

Gillette, Francis Edwin, 'Methods of Psychological Warfare. A Lecture', n.p., 1942

Glass, Albert J., 'Combat Exhaustion', *United States Armed Forces Medical Journal*, 11.10, October 1951

Glass, Albert J., 'Preventive Psychiatry in the Combat Zone', *United States Armed Forces Medical Journal*, iv.5, May 1953

Glassner, Barry, 'Fitness and the Postmodern Self', *Journal of Health and Social Behavior*, 30.2, June 1989

Goddard, Cliff, 'Anger in the Western Desert: A Case Study in the Cross-Cultural Semantics of Emotion', *Man*, new series, 26.2, June 1991

Gorman, Christine, 'Returning Fire Against AIDS', *Time*, 24 June 1991

Grabois, Howard, 'The Convergence of Sociocultural Theory and Cognitive Linguistics', in Gard B. Palmer and Debra J. Occhi (eds.), *Languages of Sentiment. Cultural Constructions of Emotional Substrates*, John Benjamins Publishing Co., 1999

Grant, Ian, 'Care of the Dying', *British Medical Journal*, 28 December 1957

Green, J. L., 'Truancy – or School Phobia', in National Association for Mental Health, *'Truancy – or School Phobia?' Being the Proceedings of the 15th Inter-Clinic Conference*, National Association for Mental Health, 1959

Greenblatt, Milton, 'Psychosurgery: A Review of Recent Literature', in Milton Greenblatt, Robert Arnot and Harry C. Solomon (eds.), *Studies in Lobotomy*, William Heinemann, 1951

Greenblatt, Milton and John S. Bockovem, 'Illustrative Cases of Lobotomy', in Milton Greenblatt, Robert Arnot and Harry C. Solomon (eds.), *Studies in Lobotomy*, William Heinemann, 1951

Greiber, Major Marvin F., 'Narcosynthesis in the Treatment of the Noncombatant Psychiatric Casualty Overseas', *War Medicine*, 8.2, August 1945

Guedalla, Philip, 'The Age of Fear', *Listener*, 4 August 1937

Haagensen, Cushman D., 'A Technique for Radical Mastectomy', *Surgeon*, 19, 1946

Hackett, Thomas P. and Avery D. Weisiman, 'Reactions to the Imminence of Death', in George H. Grosser, Henry Wochsler and Milton Greenblatt (eds.), *The Threat of Impending Disaster. Contributions to the Psychology of Stress*, MIT Press, 1964

Hacking, I., 'The Making and Molding of Child Abuse', *Critical Inquiry*, 17, 1991

Hale, Leon, 'Recalling the Day the World Stopped', in http://www.chron.com/cs/CDA/story.hts/special/sept11/1565775

Hall, G. Stanley, 'A Study of Fears', *American Journal of Psychology*, viii.2, January 1897

Hall, Michael, 'In the Grand Scheme of Human Events, Life Must Continue', in http://www.criticdoctor.com/features/newyork3.html

Hamblen, Jessica, 'Terrorist Attacks. Children. A National Center for PTSD Fact Sheet', in http://panicdisorder.about.com/gi/dynamic/offsite.htm?site =http%3A%F%2F%2Fwww.ncptsd.org%2Ffacts%2Fdisasters%2Ffs_children_disaster.html

Hammerschlag, Ernst, 'Psychiatry Applied to Internal Medicine', in Leopold Bellak (ed.), *Psychology of Physical Illness. Psychiatry Applied to Medicine, Surgery and the Specialties*, J. & A. Churchill, 1952

Harman, Jim, 'The Place Where Chicago Was', in *Galaxy*, February 1962

Heelas, Paul, 'Emotion Talk Across Cultures', in Rom Harré (ed.), *The Social Construction of Emotion*, Basil Blackwell, 1998

Heidkamp, Bernie, 'Ours is a Country that Has Not Been Damaged in Our Lifetime by War or Natural Catastrophe But We've All Seen Independence Day', in http://www.poppolitics.com/articles/printerfriendly/2001-09-12-wtc.shtml

'Hell and Science', in *Catholic World. A Monthly Magazine of General Literature and Science*, xxvii.159, June 1878

Henderson, K., 'The Significance of Fear', *Edinburgh Medical Journal*, xlviii, October 1941

Herman, J., D. Barker and H. Roffwarg, 'Similarity of Eye Movement Characteristic in REM Sleep and the Awake State', *Psychophysiology*, 20, 1983

Hersov, L. A., 'Refusal to Go to School', *Journal of Child Psychology and Psychiatry*, 1, 1960

Hinton, John, 'The Psychology of Dying', in Norman Autton (ed.), *From Fear to Faith. Studies of Suffering and Wholeness*, SPCK, 1971

Hobbs, N., 'Sources of Gain in Psychotherapy', *American Psychology*, 17, 1962

Hooper, C., 'Child Sexual Abuse and the Regulation of Women: Variations on a Theme', in C. Smart (ed.), *Regulating Womanhood*, Routledge, 1992

Horder, Lord, 'The Modern Troglodyte', *Lancet*, 19 April 1941

Howe, Dr E. Graham, 'Motives and Mechanisms of the Mind. IX. Defence Mechanisms: Fear', *Lancet*, 28 February 1931

Howell, G., 'Rules Not Words', in Paul Heelas and A. Locke (eds.), *Indigenous Psychologies: The Anthropology of the Self*, Academic Press, 1981

Hueston, John T., 'Duchenne Today: Facial Expression and Facial Surgery', in G. B. Duchenne de Boulogne, *The Mechanism of Human Facial Expression*, ed. and trans. R. Andrew Cuthbertson, Cambridge University Press, 1990

Hunt, Harry T., 'Toward a Cognitive Psychology of Dreams', in Jayne Gackenbach (ed.), *Sleep and Dreams. A Sourcebook*, Garland Publishing Inc., 1986

Hunter, Michael, 'Introduction', in Hunter (guest ed.) 'Psychoanalysing Robert Boyle', *British Journal for the History of Science*, 32, September 1999

Hunter, Walter S., 'Psychology in the War', *American Psychologist*, 1, 1946

Hurst, Sir Arthur F., 'The Etiology and Treatment of War Neuroses', in Thomas Hunt (ed.), *Selected Writings of Sir Arthur Hurst (1879–1944)*, Spottiswoode, Ballantyne and Co., 1969

Ivy, Marilyn, 'Have You Seen Me? Recovering the Inner Child in Late Twentieth Century America', in Sharon Stephens (ed.), *Children and the Politics of Culture*, Princeton University Press, 1995

Izard, Carroll E., 'Emotions and Facial Expressions: A Perspective from Differential Emotions Theory', in James A. Russell and José Miguel Fernández-Dols (eds.), *The Psychology of Facial Expression*, Cambridge University Press, 1997

Jackson, Colonel Louis, 'The Defence of Localities Against Aerial Attack', *Journal of the Royal United Services Institute*, 58.436, June 1914

James, Allison, 'Eating Green(s). Discourses of Organic Food', in Kay Milton (ed.), *Environmentalism. The View from Anthropology*, Routledge, 1993

James, William, 'What is an Emotion?', *Mind*, 9, 1884

Janis, Irving L., 'Psychological Problems of A-Bomb Defense', *Bulletin of the Atomic Scientists*, vi.9, September 1950

Janis, Irving L. and Seymour Feshbach, 'Effects of Fear-Arousing Communications', *Journal of Abnormal and Social Psychology*, 48.1, 1953

Joad, C. E. M., 'A Philosophy of Pain and Fear', *Nature*, 148.3742, 19 July 1941

John, Enid M., 'A Study of the Effects of Evacuation and Air Raids on Children of Pre-School Age', *British Journal of Educational Psychology*, xi.iii, November 1941

Johnson, Adelaide M., Eugene I. Falstein, S. A. Szurek and Margaret Svendsen,

'School Phobia', *American Journal of Orthopsychiatry*, 11, 1941

Johnson, Adelaide M., 'School Phobia', *American Journal of Orthopsychiatry*, 27, 1957

Johnston, Paul, 'The Cancer of Terrorism', in Benjamin Netanyahu (ed.), *Terrorism. How the West Can Win*, Weidenfeld and Nicolson, 1986

Jones, Ernest, 'On the Nightmare', *American Journal of Insanity*, lxv, January 1910

Jones, Mary Cover, 'The Elimination of Children's Fears', *Journal of Experimental Psychology*, vii.5, October 1924

Jones, Mary Cover, 'A Study of the Emotions of Pre-School Children', *School and Society*, xxi.545, 6 June 1925

Judd, Jonathan, in http://www.cnn.com/SPECIALS/2002/america.remembers /subsection.tower.html

Jung, Carl G., 'Analysis of Dreams', 1909, trans. Mairet.,

Jung, Carl G., 'The Practical Use of Dream Analysis', 1934, edn. published 1961, CW16, para. 319, p. 149, trans. C. F. Baynes and N. S. Dell.

Jung, Carl G., 'On the Psychology of the Unconscious', *Two Essays on Analytical Psychology*, Routledge and Kegan Paul, 1953

Kahn, Jack H., 'School Refusal. Some Clinical and Cultural Aspects', *Medical Officer*, c.22, 28 November 1958

Kastenbaum, Robert, 'Psychological Death', in Leonard Pearson (ed.), *Death and Dying. Current Issues in the Treatment of the Dying Person*, Press of the Case Western Reserve University, 1969

Kaufman, M. Ralph, '"Ill Health" as an Expression of Anxiety in a Combat Unit', *Psychosomatic Medicine*, 9, March 1947

Kean, H., 'Child Sexual Abuse', *Lancet*, 31 October 1987

Kemper, Theodore D., 'Sociology, Physiology and Emotions: Comment on Shott', *American Journal of Sociology*, 85, May 1980

Kerry, R. J., 'Phobias of Outer Space', *Journal of Mental Science*, 106.445, October 1960

Killingsworth, M. Jimmie and Jacqueline S. Palmer, 'Millennial Ecology. The Apocalyptic Narrative from *Silent Spring* to *Global Warming*', in Carl G. Herndl and Stuart C. Brown (eds.), *Green Culture. Environmental Rhetoric in Contemporary America*, University of Wisconsin Press, 1996

Kingman, R., 'Fears and Phobias', *Welfare Magazine*, 19, 1928

Kisker, George W., 'Remarks on the Problem of Psychosurgery', *American Journal of Psychiatry*, 100.2, September 1943

Klein, Emanuel, 'The Influence of Teachers' and Parents' Attitudes and Behavior Upon Children in War Time', *Mental Hygiene*, xxvi, 1942

Klein, Melanie, 'The Rôle of the School in the Libidinal Development of the Child', *International Journal of Psycho-Analysis*, 5, 1924

Kleinberg, Otto, 'Dangers of Shelter Psychology', in Seymour Melman (ed.), *No Place to Hide. Fact and Fiction About Fallout Shelters*, Grove Press, 1962

Kline, Linus and C. J. France, 'The Psychology of Ownership', *The Pedagogical Seminary*, vi.4, December 1898

Koontz, Colonel Amos R., 'Psychiatry in the Next War: Shall We Again Waste Manpower?', *Military Surgeon*, 103.3, September 1948

Kraft, Tom and Ihsan Al-Issa, 'Behaviour Therapy and the Recall of Traumatic

Experience – A Case Study', *Behaviour Research and Therapy. An International Multi-Disciplinary Journal*, 3, 1965

Kumar, Krishan, 'Apocalypse, Millennium and Utopia Today', in Malcolm Bull (ed.), *Apocalypse Theory and the Ends of the World*, Blackwell, 1995

Landis, Carney, 'Studies of Emotional Reactions. II. General Behavior and Facial Expression', *Journal of Comparative Psychology*, 4, 1924

Landis, Carney, 'The Interpretation of Facial Expression in Emotion', *Journal of General Psychology*, II, 1929

Langfeld, Herbert Signey, 'The Judgment of Emotions from Facial Expressions', *Journal of Abnormal Psychology*, xiii, 1918

Langley, Major J. O., 'Tactical Implications of the Human Factors in Warfare', *Australian Army Journal*, 107, April 1958

Lanham, Captain C. T., 'Panic', in Colonel Joseph Greene (ed.), *The Infantry Reader*, Doubleday, Doran and Co., 1943

Laqueur, Thomas, 'Bodies, Death and Pauper Funerals', *Representations*, 1.1, February 1983

Larsen, Otto N., 'Rumors in a Disaster', *Journal of Communication*, 4, 1954

Leaning, Jennifer and Langley Keyes, 'The Singularity of Nuclear War: Paradigms of Disaster Planning', in Leaning and Keyes (eds.), *The Counterfeit Ark: Crisis Relocation for Nuclear War*, Ballinger Publishing Co., 1984

Leventhal, Howard, Jean C. Watts and Francia Pagano, 'Effect of Fear and Instructions on How to Cope with Danger', *Journal of Personality and Social Psychology*, 6.3, 1967

Lewin, Bertram, 'Phobic Symptoms and Dream Interpretation', *Psychoanalytic Quarterly*, 21, 1952

Lifton, Robert Jay, Eric Markusen and Dorothy Austin, 'The Second Death: Psychological Survival After Nuclear War', in Jennifer Leaning and Langley Keyes (eds.), *The Counterfeit Ark: Crisis Relocation for Nuclear War*, Ballinger Publishing Co., 1984

Lightman, Alan P. and Jon D. Miller, 'Contemporary Cosmological Beliefs', *Social Studies of Science*, 19.1, February 1989

Linka, Allen E., Andrew Sanchirico and Mark D. Reed, 'Fear of Crime and Constrained Behavior: Specifying and Estimating a Reciprocal Effects Model', *Social Forces*, 66, 1988

Lutz, Catherine, 'The Domain of Emotion Words on Ifaluk', in Rom Harré (ed.), *The Social Construction of Emotion*, Basil Blackwell, 1998

Lyon, Margot L., 'Emotion and Embodiment: The Respiratory Mediation of Somatic and Social Processes', in Alexander Laban Hinton (ed.), *Biocultural Approaches to the Emotions*, Cambridge University Press, 1999

McAfee, John, 'Open Season', in J. Topham (ed.), *Vietnam Literature Anthology*, revised and enlarged edn., American Poetry and Literature Press, 1990

Madriz, Esther I., 'Images of Criminals and Victims: A Study on Women's Fear and Social Control', *Gender and Society*, 11.3, June 1997

Malleson, Nicolas, 'Panic and Phobia. A Possible Method of Treatment', *Lancet*, 31 January 1959

Marshino, Ora, 'Breast Cancer', *Hygeia*, 23, March 1945

Martin, Alexander Reid, 'The Prevention of Panic', *Mental Hygiene*, xxvi, 1942

May, Mark A., 'What Science Offers on Character Education', in Chicago Association for Child Study and Parent Education (ed.), *Building Character. Proceedings of the Mid-West Conference on Parent Education, February, 1928*, University of Chicago Press, 1928

May, Rollo, 'Historical Roots of Modern Anxiety Theories', in Paul H. Hock and Joseph Zubin (eds.), *Anxiety*, Hafner Publishing Co., 1964

Meerloo, Joost A. M. and Adolf Zeckel, 'Psychiatric Problems of Malignancy', in Leopold Bellak (ed.), *Psychology of Physical Illness. Psychiatry Applied to Medicine, Surgery and the Specialties*, J. & A. Churchill, 1952

Menninger, William C., 'Psychological Reactions in an Emergency (Flood)', *American Journal of Psychiatry*, 109.2, August 1952

Metz, Walter, 'On Terrorism and Contemporary American Cinema', in http://www.montana.edu/metz/filmreviews/terrorism.htm

Michael, Donald N., 'Civilian Behavior Under Atomic Bombardment', *Bulletin of the Atomic Scientists*, xi.5, May 1955

Miller, James, 'AIDS in the Novel: Getting it Straight', in Miller (ed.), *Fluid Exchanges: Artists and Critics in the AIDS Crisis*, University of Toronto Press, 1992

Model, Alfred and Elizabeth Shepheard, 'The Child Who Refuses to Go to School', *Medical Officer*, c.2, 1 July 1958

Monitoring Systems, http://ch.dmoz.org/Shopping/Children/Safety Products and Services/Surveillance and Monitoring Systems., 2004Moore, Major Merrill, 'Recurrent Nightmares: A Simple Procedure for Psychotherapy', *Military Surgeon*, 97.4, October 1945

Moran, Lord, 'Wear and Tear', *Lancet*, 17 June 1950

Morgan, G. A. V., 'Children Who Refuse to Go to School. Observations in "School Anxiety"', *Medical Officer*, cii.18, 30 October 1959

Muller, Hermann, 'Artificial Transmutation of the Gene', *Science*, lxvi. 1699, 1927

Nagy, Maria, 'The Child's Theories Concerning Death', *Journal of Genetic Psychology*, 73.3, 1948

Natterson, Joseph M. and Alfred G. Knudson, 'Observations Concerning Fear of Death in Fatally Ill Children and Their Mothers', *Psychosomatic Medicine*, xxii, 1960

Nevins, Rev. William, 'Why So Loth to Die?' in Nevins et al., *Light in the Valley of Death; Or, Considerations Fitted to Strengthen the Faith, and Sustain the Mind, of the Dying*, Grant and Taylor, 1857

Nichols, Ira C. and J. McVicker Hunt, 'A Case of Partial Bilateral Frontal Lobectomy. A Psychopathological Study', *American Journal of Psychiatry*, 96.5, March 1940

Nursten, Jean P., 'The Background of Children with School Phobia. A Study of Twenty-Five Cases', *Medical Officer*, c.22, 28 November 1958

'N.Y. Kids May Carry 9/11 Mental Scars as Adults', in http://abcnews.go.com/sections/us/DailyNews/homefront020827.html

O'Brien, Chris, 'Mama, Are We Going to Die? America's Children Confront the Cuban Missile Crisis', in James Marten (ed.), *Children and War. A Historical Anthology*, New York University Press, 2002

Ohlin, L. E., 'The Effects of Social Change on Law Enforcement', in [no ed.], *The*

Challenge of Crime in a Free Society, Notre Dame Law School, 1971

O'Leary, Shawn, 'Shell Shock', in *Spikenard and Bayonet. Verse of the Front Line*, Bread and Cheese Club, 1941

Oleske, J., A. Minnetor, T. K. Coopers, A. de la Cruz, H. Abdieh, I. Guerrero, V. Joshi and F. Desposito, 'Immune Deficiency Syndrome in Children', *Journal of the American Medical Association*, 249, 1983

O'Malley, P., 'Risk, Power and Crime Prevention', *Economy and Society*, 21.3, 1992

Paterson, Ralston and Jean Aitken-Swan, 'Public Opinion on Cancer. A Survey Among Women in the Manchester Area', *Lancet*, 23 October 1954

'Pendragon Pictures News. Martians to Invade Sooner', in http://www.horror moviemania.com/waroftheworlds/press.html

Pernick, Martin S., 'Brain Death in a Cultural Context. The Reconstruction of Death, 1967–1981', in Stuart J. Younger, Robert M. Arnold and Renie Schapiro (eds.), *The Definition of Death. Contemporary Controversies*, Johns Hopkins University Press, 1999

'Personality and Cancer', *Scientific American*, 186, June 1952

Pfefferbaum, Betty, et al., 'Posttraumatic Stress Two Years After the Oklahoma City Bombing in Youths Geographically Distant from the Explosion', *Psychiatry*, 63.4, Winter 2000

Pfohl, Stephen J., 'The "Discovery" of Child Abuse', *Social Problems*, 24.3, February 1977

Phillips, M. L., et al., 'Time Courses of Left and Right Amygdalar Responses to Fearful Facial Expressions', *Human Brain Mapping*, 12, 2001

Pipes, Daniel 'The Muslims are Coming! The Muslims are Coming!', *National Review*, 19 November 1990

Poe, Edgar Allan, 'The Premature Burial', in Poe, *The Premature Burial and Other Tales of Horror*, Corgi Books, 1966

Porter, Roy, 'Rape – Does it Have a Historical Meaning?', in Sylvana Tomaselli and Roy Porter (eds.), *Rape. An Historical and Cultural Enquiry*, Basil Blackwell, 1986

Porteus, Stanley David and Richard DeMonbrun Kepner, 'Mental Changes After Bilateral Prefrontal Lobotomy', *Genetic Psychology Monographs*, 29, February 1944

Potts, Michael, Paul A. Byrne and Richard G. Nilges, 'Introduction: Beyond Brain Death', in Potts, Byrne and Nilges (eds.), *Beyond Brain Death. The Case Against Brain Based Criteria for Human Death*, Kluwer Academic Publishers, 2000

'Premature Burial', *Embalmers' Monthly*, xxi, 1908

'Premature Burials', *American Undertaker*, 1.8, August 1900

'President's Message' [President of the University of Toronto], http://www. magazine.utoronto.ca/02winter/prc2.html

Prince, Samuel Henry, 'Catastrophe and Social Change. Based Upon a Sociological Study of the Halifax Disaster', PhD, Faculty of Political Science, Columbia University, 1920

Pulsifer, Major Libby, 'Psychiatric Aspects of Gastrointestinal Complaints of the Soldier in Training', *Military Surgeon*, 95.6, December 1944

Quarantelli, E., 'The Nature and Conditions of Panic', *American Journal of Sociology*, 60, 1954

Quarantelli, E. L. and Russell R. Dynes, 'Editors' Introduction', *American Behavioral Scientist*, 13.3, January–February 1970

Quarantelli, E. L. and Russell R. Dynes, 'When Disaster Strikes (It Isn't Much Like What You've Heard and Read About)', *Psychology Today*, 5.9, February 1972

Quester, George H., 'The Psychological Effects of Bombing on Civilian Populations: Wars of the Past', in Betty Glad (ed.), *Psychological Dimensions of War*, Sage Publishers, 1990

Ranson, Lieutenant Colonel Stephen W., 'The Normal Battle Reaction: Its Relation to the Pathologic Battle Reaction', *Bulletin of the United States Army Medical Department*, ix, supplementary number, November 1949

Raw, Dr Nathan, 'Royal Medico-Psychological Association Annual Meeting: Fear', *Lancet*, 3 August 1929

Reagan, Ronald, 'Remarks Following Pentagon Report on the Security of US Marines in Lebanon, December 27, 1983', *Weekly Compilation of Presidential Documents*, 19, 1983

Reddy, William M., 'Against Constructionism. The Historical Ethnology of Emotions', *Current Anthropology*, 38, June 1997

Richards, John, 'Some Experiences With Colored Soldiers', *Atlantic Monthly*, August 1919

Rickman, John, 'The Mental Aspects of A.R.P.', in Rickman (ed.), *War Wounds and Air Raid Casualties*, H. K. Lewis and Co., 1939

Riezles, Kurt, 'The Social Psychology of Fear', *American Journal of Sociology*, xlix.6, May 1944

Rios, Armando, 'Sept. 11: The Day America Changed', in http://www.baxterbulletin.com/ads/chronology2001/page2.html

Rivers, W. H. R., 'The Repression of War Experience', *Lancet*, 2 February 1918

Roffwarg, H., S. Herman and C. Bowe-Anders, 'The Effects of Sustained Alterations of Waking Visual Input on Dream Content', in A. Arkin, S. Antrobus and S. Ellman (eds.), *The Mind in Sleep: Psychology and Psychophysiology*, Lawrence Erlbaum Associates, 1978

Rosen, Victor H., 'Psychiatric Problems in General Surgery', in Leopold Bellak (ed.), *Psychology of Physical Illness. Psychiatry Applied to Medicine, Surgery and the Specialties*, J. & A. Churchill, 1952

Rosenblum, Jonathan, 'The Day the World Changed', in http://www.jewishmediasources.com/article/211.

Rothbaum, Barbara Olasov, Larry F. Hodges, Rob Kooper, Dan Opdyke, James S. Williford and Max North, 'Effectiveness of Computer-Generated (Virtual Reality) Graded Exposure in the Treatment of Acrophobia', *American Journal of Psychiatry*, 152.4, April 1995

Rush, Florence, 'Sexual Abuse of Children', in Noreen Connell and Cassandra Wilson (eds.), *Rape: The First Source Book for Women*, New American Library, 1974

Ryle, John A., 'The Twenty-First Maudsley Lecture: Nosophobia', *Journal of Mental Science*, xciv.394, January 1948

Saffiotti, Umberto, 'Comments on the Scientific Basis for the "Delaney Clause"', in *Preventive Medicine*, 2, 1973

Sapolsky, Harvey M., 'Introduction', in Sapolsky (ed.), *Consuming Fears. Politics of Product Risks*, Basic Books, 1986

Saunders, Cicely, 'The Treatment of Intractable Pain in Terminal Cancer', *Proceedings of the Royal Society of Medicine*, 56, 1963

Schachter, S. and J. Singer, 'Cognitive, Social and Physiological Determinants of Emotional State', *Psychological Review*, 69, 1962

Schilder, Paul and David Wechsler, 'The Attitudes of Children Toward Death', *Journal of Genetic Psychology*, xlv, 1934

Schmideberg, Melitta, 'Some Observations on Individual Reactions to Air Raids', *International Journal of Psychoanalysis*, 23, 1942

'School Phobia', *Lancet*, 30 January 1960

Schwartz, Karl, 'Fighting Cancer and Terrorism – Our Fight is Similar', in http://www.lymphomation.org/messageNHL.htm

Scott, Lieutenant A. B., 'The Diary', in *32nd Division, Artillery & Trench Mortar Memories*, Unwin Bros., 1923

Scott, Colin, 'Old Age and Death', *American Journal of Psychology*, viii, 1896

Scott, William Abbott, 'The Avoidance of Threatening Material in Imaginative Behavior', in John W. Atkinson (ed.), *Motives in Fantasy, Action and Society*, D. Van Nostrand Co., 1958

Scoville, William Beecher, 'The Effect of Surgical Lesions of the Brain on Psyche and Behavior in Man', in Arthur Winter (ed.), *The Surgical Control of Behavior. A Symposium*, Charles C. Thomas Publisher, 1971

Sefton, Dru, 'Assault on America', in http://www.newhouse.com/archive/story1a091401.html

Senescu, Robert A., 'The Development of Emotional Complications in the Patient with Cancer', *Journal of Chronic Diseases*, 16, 1963

Senn, Milton J. E., 'School Phobias: The Role of the Paediatrician in their Prevention and Management', *Proceedings of the Royal Society of Medicine*, 55, 1962

Shaheen, Jack G., 'The War Game', in Shaheen (ed.), *Nuclear War Films*, Southern Illinois University Press, 1978

Sharader-Frechette, Kristen, 'Scientific Method, Anti-Foundationalism and Public Decision Making', in Rognar E. Lofstedt and Lynn Frewer (eds.), *The Earthscan Reader in Risk and Modern Society*, Earthscan, 1998

Shinn, Rev. George Wolfe, 'What Has Become of Hell?', *North American Review*, clxx, June 1900

Shott, Susan, 'Emotion and Social Life: A Symbolic Interactionist Analysis', *American Journal of Sociology*, 84, May 1979

Shott, Susan, 'Reply to Kemper', *American Journal of Sociology*, 85, May 1980

Sillman, Leonard R., 'Morale', *War Medicine*, 3.5, May 1943

Silverman, Maurice, 'Causes of Neurotic Breakdown in British Service Personnel Stationed in the Far East in Peacetime', *Journal of Mental Science*, xcvi.403, April 1950

Simon, R., 'Anthrax Nation', *US News and World Report*, 5 November 2001

Slade, W. G., 'Earthquake Psychology', *Australasian Journal of Psychology and Philosophy*, x.1, March 1932

Sleevi, Eugene J., 'Civil Defense News', *Bulletin of the Atomic Scientists*, ix.8, October 1953

Smith, Lauren H., Donald W. Hastings and Joseph Hughes, 'Immediate Follow Up Results of Electroshock Therapy', *American Journal of Psychiatry*, 100.3, November 1943

Smith, M. Brewster, 'Preface', *Journal of Social Issues*, x.3, 1954

'Soldier's Dreams', *Lancet*, 23 January 1915

Sparkes, Captain Blair W. and Brigadier General Oliver K. Niess, 'Psychiatric Screening of Combat Pilots', *United States Armed Forces Medical Journal*, vii.6, June 1956

Speigel, H. X., 'Psychiatric Observations in the Tunisian Campaign', *American Journal of Orthopsychiatry*, 14, 1943

Stalker, Henry, 'Panic States in Civilians', *British Medical Journal*, 1 June 1940

Stearns, Carol Z., 'Lord Help Me Walk Humbly: Anger and Sadness in England and America, 1570–1750', in Carol Z. Stearns and Peter Stearns (eds.), *Emotion and Social Change: Towards a New Psychohistory*, Holmes and Meier, 1988

Stearns, Peter N., 'Girls, Boys, and Emotions: Redefinitions and Historical Change', *Journal of American History*, 80, June 1993

Stearns, Peter, 'Emotion', in Rom Harré and Peter Stearns (eds.), *Discursive Psychology in Practice*, Sage Publishers, 1995

Stearns, Peter N. and Carol Z. Stearns, 'Emotionology: Clarifying the History of Emotions and Emotional Standards', *American Historical Review*, 90.4, October 1985

Stengel, E., 'Air-Raid Phobia', *British Journal of Medical Psychology*, 20, 1944

Strecker, Edward A., 'War Neuroses', *Military Surgeon*, 94.4, April 1944

Strother, Robert S., 'Backfire in the War Against Insects', *Reader's Digest*, 74, June 1959

Strozier, Charles B., 'The World Trade Center Disaster and its Global Aftermath. Reflections and Meditative http://www.nycop.com/Stories/Jan_02/The_World_Trade_Center_Disaste/body_the_world_trade_center_disaste.html

Sundeed, Richard A., 'The Fear of Crime and Urban Elderly', in Marlene A. Young Rifai (ed.), *Justice and Older Americans*, Lexington Books, 1977

Sunderland, R., 'Child Sexual Abuse', *Lancet*, 31 October 1987

Susser, Ezra, Helene Jackson and Christina Hoven, '2001, or New York City Schoolchildren', in http://www.fathom.com/feature/190150

Symonds, C. P., 'The Human Response to Flying Stress', *British Medical Journal*, 11 December 1943

Talbot, Mira, 'Panic in School Phobia', *American Journal of Orthopsychiatry*, xxvii, 1957

Tanner, Henry, 'Physiological and Psychological Factors in Electro-Shock as Criteria of Therapy', *Journal of Nervous and Mental Disease*, iii, 1950

'The Psychology of Panic in War', *American Review of Reviews*, 50, October 1914

Thomas, Huw, 'Psychological Approach to Cremation', *Pharos*, 33.4, November 1967

Thouless, Dr Robert H., 'Psychological Effects of Air Raids', *Nature*, 16 August 1941

Toynbee, Philip, 'A Reply', in Toynbee (ed.), *The Fearful Choice. A Debate on Nuclear Policy*, Victor Gollancz Ltd, 1958

Treichler, Paula, 'AIDS, Homophobia and Biomedical Discourse: An Epidemic of Signification', in Douglas Crimp (ed.), *AIDS. Cultural Analysis, Cultural Activism*, MIT Press, 1988

Trotter, Wilfred, 'Panic and its Consequences', *The Collected Papers of Wilfred Trotter*, Oxford University Press, 1941

Valenstein, Elliot S., 'Historical Perspective', in Valenstein (ed.), *The Psychosurgery Debate. Scientific, Legal and Ethical Perspectives*, W. H. Freeman and Co., 1980

Valentine, C. W., 'The Innate Bases of Fear', *Journal of Genetic Psychology*, xxxvii, 1930

Veltfort, Helene Rank and George E. Lee, 'The Cocoanut Grove Fire: A Study in Scapegoating', *Journal of Abnormal and Social Psychology*, 38, 1943

Vernberg, Eric M., 'Psychological Science and Terrorism: Making Psychological Issues Part of Our Planning and Technology', in http://merrill.ku.edu/publications/2002whitepaper/vernberg.html

Vernon, P. E., 'Psychological Effects of Air Raids', *Journal of Abnormal and Social Psychology*, 36, 1941

'Vincent', 'Confessions of an Agoraphobic Victim', *American Journal of Psychology*, xxx, 1919

Vollum, Edward P., 'Tests for Death', *American Undertaker*, 2.10, October 1901

Von Duprin, 'About Us', http://www.vonduprin.com/about_us.asp

Wagner, Philip S., 'Psychiatric Activities During the Normandy Offensive, June 20–August 20, 1944', *Psychiatry*, 9.4, November 1946

Wajdo, Richard, 'Was On His way to Work in the World Financial Center', in http://news.bbc.co.uk/hi/english/static/in_depth/americas/2001/day_of_terror/eyewitness/default.stm

Waldfogel, Samuel, John C. Collidge and Pauline B. Hann, 'The Development, Meaning and Management of School Phobia', *American Journal of Orthopsychiatry*, 27, 1957

Wardle, Captain M. K., 'Notes on Fear in War', *Army Quarterly*, iv, April 1922

'War of the Worlds – Update', in http://www.dowse.com/movies/woftw-news.html

Wasserman, Harvey, 'Time to Dispel the Nuclear Cloud', *Nation*, 24 May 1986

Watson, John B., 'Behaviorism – The Modern Note in Psychology', in 'Classics in the History of Psychology', in http://psychclassics.yorku.ca/Watson/Bottle/Watson.htm

Webster, A. Stanley, 'The Development of Phobias in Married Women', *Psychological Monographs. General and Applied*, 67.17, 1953

Weinstein, Major Edwin A. and Lieutenant Colonel Calvin S. Drayer, 'A Dynamic Approach to the Problem of Combat-Induced Anxiety', *Bulletin of the United States Army Medical Department*, ix, supplementary number, November 1949

Weinstein, Fred, 'Psychohistory and the Crisis of the Social Sciences', *History and Theory*, 34.4, December 1995

Williams, A. Hyatt, 'A Psychiatric Study of Indian Soldiers in Arakan', *British Journal of Medical Psychology*, xxiii.3, 1950

Williams, Harry B., 'Human Factors in Warning-and-Response Systems', in G. H. Grosser, H. Wechsler and M. Greenblatt (eds.), *The Threat of Impending Disaster: Contributions to the Psychology of Stress*, MIT Press, 1964

Williams, John F., 'The Mischief of Fear', in *The Young Child. A Series of Five Lectures on Child Management Given Under the Auspices of the Victorian Council for Mental Hygiene, November, 1930*, Melbourne University Press, 1931

Wilson, Henry, 'Mental Reactions to Air-Raids', *Lancet*, 7 March 1942

Wolpe, Joseph, 'Behaviour Therapy in Complex Neurotic States', *British Journal of Psychiatry*, 110, 1964

Wright, Captain David G., 'Anxiety in Aerial Combat', in *Military Neuropsychiatry. Proceedings of the Association [for Research in Nervous and Mental Diseases], December 15 and 16, 1944, New York*, Williams and Wilkins Co., 1946

Wright, Maurice B., 'Psychological Emergencies in War Time', in *War Wounds and Air Raid Casualties*, H. K. Lewis and Co., 1939

Wylie, Philip, 'Panic, Psychology and the Bomb', *Bulletin of the Atomic Scientists*, x.1, January 1954

Wyon, Rev. Walter James, 'Sermon IV. The Christian Man's Fear', in *Six Addresses to Men, Delivered in the Church of SS. Philip & James, Oxford*, A. R. Mowbray and Co., 1878

Youmans, E. L. and W. J. Youmans, 'Concerning the Belief in Hell', *Popular Science Monthly*, xii, March 1878

Young, Ken, 'Living Under Threat', in Roger Jowell, Sharon Witherspoon and Lindsay Brook (eds.), *British Social Attitudes. The 7th Report*, Gower Publishing Co., 1990

Zeligs, Lieutenant Commander Meyer A., 'War Neurosis. Psychiatric Experiences and Management on a Pacific Island', *War Medicine*, 6.3, September 1944

Ziegler, Lloyd H., 'Bilateral Prefrontal Lobotomy. A Survey', *American Journal of Psychiatry*, 100.2, September 1943

Index

Printed in the United States
by Baker & Taylor Publisher Services